# Theories and Systems
## of Psychology

# Theories and Systems
# of Psychology

### Fifth Edition

## Robert W. Lundin
*University of the South*

D. C. Heath and Company
Lexington, Massachusetts   Toronto

*Address editorial correspondence to:*

D. C. Heath and Company
125 Spring Street
Lexington, MA 02173

Acquisitions Editor: James Miller
Designer: Judy Miller
Production Coordinator: Dick Tonachel
Permissions Editor: Margaret Roll

Cover: Stanton MacDonald-Wright, *Conception Synchromy,* 1914, oil on canvas. Hirshhorn Museum and Sculpture Garden, Smithsonian Institution, Gift of Joseph Hirshhorn, 1966. Photo by Lee Stalsworth.

International Standard Book Number: 0-669-35446-5

Library of Congress Catalog Card Number: 94-73550

6789-QF-08 07 06 05 04

To my wife, Margaret,
without whose help this
book could not have been written

# PREFACE

The fifth edition of *Theories and Systems of Psychology* is intended for undergraduate students entering their first history, systems, or theories of psychology class; it is designed to be used in a one-semester course. My primary reason for undertaking this project was my dissatisfaction with the psychology texts I had encountered in over twenty years of teaching in this subject area.

This book differs from other psychology texts in several ways:

- It emphasizes historical antecedents from both philosophy and natural science without being a mere chronology of names, dates, and events.

- Rather than presenting a list of ideas, the book tracks the various trends that led to the development of a particular system or theory. For example, we begin our discussion of the early behaviorism of John Watson by first looking at the trends that influenced his work: French materialism, animal psychology of the late nineteenth and early twentieth centuries, Pavlovian conditioning, and functionalism. Similarly, in dealing with Gestalt psychology, we begin with a discussion of the influences of Kant, von Ehrenfels, and Mach.

- This text examines fewer theories and systems than do other texts, but explores these systems in greater depth and detail. The student will thus gain a more thorough knowledge of the theories studied.

In this edition, I have expanded the glossary and references sections. I have also updated the Suggested Further Readings at the end of each chapter. For those books written in a language other than English, I have cited the most appropriate translation whenever possible.

Many of the later chapters have been expanded as a result of reviewers' suggestions to incorporate more on humanistic, existential, psychodynamic, and cognitive psychologies. To that end, Chapter 16 (Cognitive Psychology) now features an expanded discussion of Chomsky, the origins of cognitive psychology, the computer, and artificial intelligence; Chapter 17 (Psychoanalysis) has an expanded treatment of Freud's theory of dreams; Chapter 18 (Heirs to Freud) includes more about Jung's personality types; Chapter 19 (Humanistic Psychology) now includes Roger's "fully functioning person" and an expanded version of Maslow's "hierarchy of needs"; Chapter 20 (Existential Psychology) provides an historical context and includes Frankl's search for meaning, and Chapter 21 (Psychology Yesterday, Today, and Tomorrow) updates the current status of the profession by including such areas as neuropsychology.

As with earlier editions, each chapter ends with an evaluation of the system or theory. Although evaluating and interpreting theories is often a subjective matter, I have followed many of the suggestions of my colleagues who reviewed this material. Both contributions and criticisms of the system or theory are presented. Particularly with current movements, I have tried to present a balanced viewpoint, giving each theory a fair and equal appraisal.

I am grateful to many people for their helpful suggestions. In particular, I am indebted to MaryAnn F. Bush, Nazareth College; Robert R. Hoffman, Adelphi University; James Gotsick, Morehead State University; Julian Keith, University of North Carolina at Wilmington; Dennis L. Micham, Nazareth College of Rochester; Yozan Dirk Mosig, University of Nebraska at Kearney; Richard A. O'Connor, Worcester State College; and Robert Shaw, University of Connecticut.

In short, the fifth edition of *Theories and Systems of Psychology* is not merely a history book. It provides a logical and coherent examination of the development of the various movements in psychology today, while expanding on humanistic, existential, and cognitive psychologies, as suggested by users of the previous edition.

Robert W. Lundin

# CONTENTS

# Theories and Systems
## of Psychology

# CHAPTER

# 1

# *Theories and Systems*

Among the natural sciences, psychology is relatively young, having evolved out of philosophy and the sciences of physics and biology. As an independent discipline, psychology is about a hundred years old. However, even during that period many changes have taken place. A variety of people have conjectured and theorized about what psychology was, is, or should be. Diverse opinions have existed about what its subject matter should be and what methods of investigation ought to be used.

## Systems in Psychology

As psychology has evolved during the present century, different groups of people who called themselves psychologists have banded together to put forth communities of ideas and efforts designed to direct the way psychology should go. When a particular group shared similar ideas and opposed others, a "school" of psychology was formed. During this period many schools evolved. For about fifty years, until World War II, these schools constituted tightly knit groups which stated, often in a very orderly manner, just what they considered psychology to be. Each school tended to arise in opposition to another, producing a great diversity of viewpoints which still exist today. Such schools have usually been identified as *systems* of psychology.

McGeoch[1] defined a system in the following statement. "By the term psychological system is implied a coherent and inclusive, yet flexible, organization and interpretation of the facts and special theories of the subject."[2]

---

[1]J. A. McGeoch, "The Formal Criteria of a Systematic Psychology," *Psychological Review,* Vol. 40 (1933), pp. 1–11.
[2]*Ibid.,* p. 2.

In a more general sense, Lichtenstein has defined a system in science as "a framework or scaffolding which permits the scientist to arrange his data in an orderly and meaningful way."[3] Applied to psychology, then, a system establishes a framework or orientation within which psychologists can work in relating the events which they consider to be psychological. The term "systematic" means orderly, and it is this order that distinguishes a system in psychology from haphazard thinking and observation.

At the beginning of this century there were only a few hundred people who called themselves psychologists. Gradually, more and more people entered the field, made observations, did experiments, and developed theories. The growth of knowledge became explosive. Even before the beginning of World War II the older and very tightly organized systems were becoming too limited to deal with all the facts that were emerging. As a result, highly specific theories of learning, perception, motivation, and personality developed, producing more narrowly restricted areas of psychology that did not attempt to explain the entire field. Yet, even today, these theories often still operate within a broader and less tightly knit framework. One can still think or operate within a framework that can be called behavioristic, psychoanalytic, or Gestalt.

This does not mean that systems no longer exist. Rather, they are more generalized, and exist to the degree that groups of people share some basic tenets. One might call them movements. These systems today exist more as orientations to psychology. For example, attitudes of psychoanalytically inclined individuals are still very much opposed to those of behaviorists, and yet both remain dominant in psychological theorizing and research.

## Theories, Hypotheses, and Laws

Compared to a large system of psychology which attempts to handle all aspects of psychology within one framework, theories are of a more limited nature. They tend to involve some particular aspect of psychology, such as learning, thinking, emotions, and so on. Theories should be based on some empirical data or facts which are already known from observation. But the known facts do not tell the whole story, so theories are constructed to fill in the gaps. Theories thus involve some assumed relationships. They have been defined in a number of different ways. For example, a theory might be considered as a proposition from which a large number of empirical observations may be deduced. For our purposes, we would prefer to consider a theory as a statement of assumed relationships between events that are observable. A theory, then, consists of *formal* (theoretical) propositions and *empirical* propositions. The formal propositions consist of the words and symbols constituting the assumed

---

[3]P. E. Lichtenstein, "Psychological Systems: Their Nature and Function," *Psychological Record,* Vol. 17 (1967), pp. 221–40.

aspects of the theory. The empirical propositions are the observations, experimental or otherwise, that make up the facts upon which the theory is based.

In setting up a theory, one starts with observations and then makes certain assumptions, often no more than educated guesses about the relationship between the facts one knows. These remain as assumptions until they can be tested. Many theories in psychology remain as theories, and as yet are unproven. A theory that can never be tested for verification is considered by many to be a bad theory. Conversely, theories that are considered to be good are those that can be tested through experimentation or some other method of observation. Some theories can only be tested by inference. In this instance, a theory is stated, experiments are done, but the results only imply the validity of the theory and do not directly prove or disprove it. Therefore, a good theory should be *heuristic*—that is, it should generate research that will lead to its confirmation.

Because theories are of a rather general nature, one may not be able to test an entire theory at any one time. For example, a theory of learning may have many aspects. We must consider how or why learning occurs, the various conditions which facilitate or inhibit it, the problems of learning complex or simple material, whether the learning is verbal or nonverbal, and so on. Therefore, more specific *hypotheses* must be set up. Like theories, hypotheses are assumptions, but of a more restricted nature. One might consider a hypothesis to be a hunch of a more preliminary sort. With regard to our example of a learning theory, a specific hypothesis about relationships may be stated and then tested by a series of more particular experiments. For example, one aspect of Tolman's learning theory (see chap. 15) was that learning in rats could take place in the absence of reward—that is, that learning was *latent.* He compared rats that were rewarded after every trial with those that were never rewarded and with those to which reward was introduced halfway through the experiment. He found that some learning did take place in the group that received the reward only part of the time. (For a more detailed description of the experiment, see p. 277.)

Sometimes, at a particular period in our knowledge of psychological events, it is impossible to test all aspects of a theory. Later, when more sophisticated instrumentation has been developed, a particular aspect of a theory may then be investigated. A rather simple example may illustrate the point.

In John Watson's declaration of behaviorism as a system of psychology, he had reduced psychological events to simple stimulus-response relationships, all of which he believed should be observable. To Watson, responses constituted muscle movements and glandular secretions. With this general specification of what psychology was all about, Watson was faced with the problem of how to explain thinking, an activity which certainly was not always observable to the naked eye. Thus, Watson hypothesized that thinking was nothing more than "subvocal speech," or talking to oneself. He assumed that thinking was reduced to small muscle movements in the vocal apparatus. In Watson's time there was no way to measure these movements. But, in succeeding decades, a refined technique of recording, called electromyography, was developed, whereby these minute movements could be amplified and thus observed and measured. Later researchers[4] gave some support to Watson's hypothesis that muscle movements occur in the vocal apparatus as well as in other parts of the body during thinking.

When hypotheses are tested and found to be true, and the aspect of assumption has been eliminated, one may state that a basic principle or law has been established. A law is considered to be a well-established relationship between events. When laws are well-established, further testing is no longer needed. As a young science, psychology is only now beginning to develop well-established laws. Over many years, physics, chemistry, and astronomy have developed many lawful relationships, such as laws of motion, gravity, planetary movement, and thermodynamics. So far, psychology has not been quite so successful, partly because it is still so fragmented by a diversity of viewpoints. One example of a law was stated by Thorndike (see chap. 10) in what he proposed as the "law of effect." This law stated that responses which led to satisfying consequences were "stamped in." It was later reformulated by Skinner in what he called the *principle of positive reinforcement*. When a certain response was followed by stimuli (generally rewards) which increased the probability of that response occurring again, the response was strengthened and the stimuli were identified as positive reinforcers.

Laws, in themselves, still have some hypothetical character, unless one believes that certain things are absolute or constitute "eternal truth." It should be pointed out that most of modern science deals in probabilities rather than certainties.

## Summary of the Characteristics of Theories, Hypotheses, and Laws

1.  A theory takes a number of observations and integrates them into a meaningful statement of relationships.

2.  A theory is made up of formal and empirical propositions. The formal propositions consist of words or symbols that attempt to "fill in" and make sense out of what has been observed. Empirical propositions constitute the observations or facts from which the theory is derived.

3.  A theory is tested by setting up specific hypotheses that can be demonstrated to be correct or incorrect. If correct, the theory gains strength. If incorrect, the theory is weakened and must be revised or abandoned.

4.  A good theory should be heuristic—that is, it should generate research that will eventually demonstrate its validity or falsity.

5.  When theories have been adequately tested and demonstrated to be valid, there is no need for further assumption and the term *law* or *principle* can be applied.

---

[4]E. Jacobson, "The Electrophysiology of Mental Activities," *American Journal of Psychology*, Vol. 44 (1932), pp. 677–94.

## Postulates

Fundamental to most systems in science, and psychology in particular, are postulates. The term has two usages. The first, and probably the most frequent, refers to a basic accepted assumption or set of assumptions. These are given and accepted without further question or test. Many of the early systems postulated the existence of a *mind* as separate from the body. (For a further discussion of the mind-body problem, see the section on basic issues below.) On the other hand, the early behaviorists postulated that psychology studied simple stimulus-response units of behavior. The postulate, then, is accepted without further question, and the psychologist undertakes his or her studies from there.

Postulates can be rather broad in nature or restricted to a particular theory or system. Lichtenstein[5] has distinguished a *postulate* from a *presupposition*. The presupposition is broader and more basic. For example, we accept the fact that the world of nature operates in an orderly fashion, or that the world in which we live is a real one. Reality is a physical thing, and not merely experiences as presupposed by Hume. The postulates, then, are more limited in scope, and are usually related to a particular system or systems.

Postulates may be specifically stated in a given system, or merely implied. Freud proposed the concept of a "mental apparatus" consisting of the *id,* the *ego,* and the *superego,* but nowhere in his writings did he specifically state it as a postulate. He accepted it, however, without further question and developed his system around it. On the other hand, the structuralists were more specific in their postulate stating that consciousness was the subject matter of psychology or that the relationship between the mind and body was a parallel one.

The second use of the term postulate is as a theoretical proposition. In this sense, the postulates are stated and then tested directly or by inference. The best example of this latter usage is to be found in Hull's theory of learning (see chap. 13). In the final statement of this theory,[6] he concluded with eighteen postulates and twelve corollaries that were formally stated in such a way that they served as a basis for experimental investigation.

## Constructs

A *construct* is a scientific term. It may be verbal, mathematical, or pictorial. According to some psychologists, constructs should always relate directly to the things they are describing. If properly defined, they refer to observable relationships. If one speaks of a construct of "fear" or "anxiety" one should identify the kinds of stimuli which give rise to the fear, along with a description of what responses the fear consists of.

Some constructs are simply inferred. These are presumed to aid in the interpretation of particular events, but do not relate directly to the observable events. Therefore, they are called *hypothetical constructs*. For example, Tolman

---

[5]P. E. Lichtenstein, *op. cit.*
[6]Clark L. Hull, *A Behavior System: An Introduction to Behavior Theory Concerning the Individual Organism* (New Haven: Yale University Press, 1952).

(see chap. 15) explained how a rat learned, by assuming there was a "cognitive map" which is built up in the rat's brain during the learning process. The construct is hypothetical because one cannot directly observe the map; it is merely inferred. Freud (see chap. 17) made use of many hypothetical constructs. For example, he talked about a "cathexis," which means an investment of psychic energy in an object. Psychic energy is not directly observable. Lewin (see chap. 15) thought of a person as an "energy system." These are only a few of the numerous hypothetical constructs the reader will encounter when studying psychological theories. Hypothetical constructs often remain as assumptions that cannot be tested. Many psychologists believe that they are useful in explaining relationships. Others disagree. The usefulness of hypothetical constructs in psychology thus remains a matter of opinion.

## Variables: Independent, Dependent, and Intervening

Many theories and systems in psychology are concerned with predicting certain results when previous conditions are known. For example, given event A, one can predict B. Here, one may say that a functional relationship has been formed. This is not merely a matter of theory, but of actual fact based on previous observations. A very simple example of such a relationship might be a reflex. If one shines light into the eye, the pupil will contract. In this instance, the light (stimulus) is identified as an *independent variable*. The resulting contraction (response) is called the *dependent variable,* because the contraction *depends* on the light stimulus. Of course, most psychological events are not that simple. However, in a well-constructed experiment, most aspects of the situation are controlled or held constant, while only one is varied or manipulated. As a result of the manipulation of the *independent variable,* one can observe certain changes in the resulting behavior identified as the *dependent variable* or variables, if more than one response measure is taken. As a result of the manipulation or change in the independent variable, one can observe orderly changes in the dependent variable.

Since this is not a text on experimental psychology or methodology, a simple example of the relationship between independent and dependent variables will suffice. Ordinarily, the degree of food deprivation will affect the rate at which an animal will work at some task, such as pressing a lever to get food. For example, Skinner found that, up to a point, the hours of food deprivation in a rat (independent variable) had a direct effect on the rate of its bar pressing to get food (dependent variable). The greater the deprivation, the faster the rat would press the lever for food. In this example, the relationships between the independent and dependent variables are directly observed. A change occurs in the environment (stimulus), which is followed by a change in behavior.

Some years ago, Woodworth (see chap. 11) objected to this rather simple statement of relationship between stimuli in the environment and the responses an organism made. He believed that what went on *inside* the organism was also important, so instead of using the paradigm S-R (stimulus-response), he introduced *S-O-R*. Thus, what happened inside the *organism* (*O*) was also a necessary part of the whole situation.

Later, Tolman (see chap. 15) took Woodworth's notion, elaborated on it, and introduced into psychology what was called the *intervening variable*. One does not directly observe the intervening variable, it is merely inferred. In the instance of the rat working for food, we may infer an intervening variable of "hunger." So we may say that a rat eats not only because it has been deprived of food but also because of an internal condition of "hunger." When we discuss Tolman's system, we shall see how elaborately he used intervening variables as an explanatory principle. Another learning theorist, Clark Hull (see chap. 13), also made extensive use of intervening variables. Although Tolman named the concept *intervening variables,* other psychologists have made use of it, regardless of the terms applied to these inferred states. In terms of our earlier discussion of constructs, intervening variables constitute one form of hypothetical constructs.

Not all psychologists are in agreement about the usefulness of intervening variables. Skinner (see chap. 13) dismissed them as adding nothing to an explanation of functional relationships. Kantor (see chap. 13) opposed the use of intervening variables and suggested that it was "a technique for loading the organism with internal principles and powers."[7]

Generally speaking, in most modern experimental psychologies the independent variable or antecedent condition is considered to be a stimulus or combination of stimuli, and the dependent variable is considered to be the response or behavior. However, there are exceptions, which Skinner[8] called *state variables.* These refer to antecedent conditions which are not considered to be stimuli. When introduced, they alter the *state of the organism.* For example, depriving an animal of food, injecting a drug, removing part of the brain, or administering electroconvulsive shock would be state variables. There is nothing mysterious about these variables, for they refer to legitimate observable prior conditions, and as a result of one of these operations, one may observe the changes in the dependent variable, the observable behavior of that organism.

## Operationism

Operationism in psychology seeks to define its concepts in such a way that they may be stated in terms of concrete operations performed. The notion originated in physics, and did not appear in psychology until the late 1930s. Thus, the concept is not really relevant to the earlier systems. The concept is limited primarily to those systems which aim at great objectivity. According to the operational principle, only events that can be described in terms of observable operations are allowable. Therefore, operationism rejects unobservables. Inter-

[7]J. R. Kantor, *Interbehavioral Psychology* (Chicago: The Principia Press, 1958), p. 262.
[8]B. F. Skinner, *The Behavior of Organisms: An Experimental Analysis* (New York: D. Appleton-Century Co., 1938).

vening variables or hypothetical constructs, if they are to be considered legitimately, must be reduced to operations. For example, operationally speaking, "hunger" can be defined as so many hours of food deprivation.

Operationism, as such, is not accepted by all psychologists or those who theorize in psychology. On the other hand, those who accept the principle will not allow concepts in their system that cannot be operationally defined. Furthermore, there are those who misuse the concept and attempt to define some intervening variables operationally when, in fact, this is not possible.

## Pragmatism

Pragmatism, particularly as set forth in the work of William James, stated that the validation of any knowledge is in terms of its consequences, values, and utilities. Knowledge that is worthwhile is going to be related to survival, one of the fundamental goals of life. What is pragmatic is what is practical.

## Positivism and Logical Positivism

Positivism is a theoretical and general scientific position that emphasizes parsimony and operationism in data and language and disdains theorizing and inference—in short, any method that produces positive knowledge. Logical positivism attempts to reduce psychology to physics and thus, because physics is fundamental to all sciences, secure psychology's status as a science. This pertains particularly to behaviorism, which strips psychology of all unobservable events, considering it to be a natural science.

## Functions of Psychological Systems and Theories

Lichtenstein[9] has suggested that psychological systems and theories should have certain functions which help to characterize them as such. Some of these are listed below:

1. **Organization.** A system should be able to organize diverse facts and principles, relating them in a way that is meaningful. A haphazard accumulation of data will lead only to confusion, disorder and misunderstanding.

2. **Closure.** Systems do not have all of the necessary facts at hand, so the closure function enables the psychologist to fill in the gaps. Along with the observed data, theoretical propositions may be included so things fit together in a meaningful whole.

3. **Heuristic function.** A system or theory which leads to the discovery of new findings, experimental or otherwise is said to have a heuristic function.

---

[9]P. E. Lichtenstein, *op. cit.*

The theory's propositions allow for the generation of new research. If this is not possible, the system will be quite sterile.

4. **Morale function.** Ordinarily, systems and theories are developed by people either working alone or in a group. These people share basic convictions and profit from interaction with each other.

5. **Limiting function.** This refers to what is going to be included or left out. Some theories and systems are more limited than others. For example, structuralism limited itself to the study of consciousness and pretty much left out any reference to behavior. On the other hand, behaviorism studies only behavior and omits any reference to consciousness. Furthermore, some theories and systems deal only with human beings as subjects, while others base their findings strictly on the results of animal studies.

## Some Basic Issues

It should be clear from the earlier discussion that many divergent systems and theories exist and have existed in psychology from its beginning. Psychologists have disagreed about what psychology is, what methods it should use, how it should present its data, and so on.

There are a number of issues that have existed throughout the development of psychological theorizing which are still current today. These issues are obviously controversial and are still widely contested. As psychology has evolved, some of the language or vocabulary may have changed, but the basic issues have remained.

In this section, we shall discuss some of the most important issues and the various stands psychologists have taken on them. At the beginning of our discussion, the names of many people, as well as general theories, may be unfamiliar, but as we proceed through the chapters which follow, the names and theories should become very familiar.

The list is not exhaustive. Some controversial issues in the past are no longer relevant today. Others are of lesser importance. We shall confine ourselves to those questions that may have deep historical roots, but that are still current today. On these issues, readers may judge for themselves which side of the matter seems valid, or perhaps they may not wish to take either side. Nevertheless, the issues remain, and are hopefully part of what should make the study of psychological theories and systems fascinating and fun.

### Mind versus Body

This is the oldest, and still one of the most important, of all issues in psychology today. It is usually stated as the *mind-body problem.* It originated in philosophy, and various earlier attempts to handle it will be presented in chapter 4. It is one of the recurrent themes in this book. Basically the issue is this: If one considers that in both humans and animals there exist a body and a mind, several questions arise: How does one get from the body processes to the mental processes, presuming that they are separate entities? How are the mind and body related? Is there a connection, or are they completely separate? Is there a mind at all? In psychology today, any system or theory which presumes both body *and* mind as part of psychology is called *dualistic*. Structuralism, the first psychological system to evolve, considered that both body and mind existed, and that their relationship was parallel. That is, something happened physically, that was correlated with parallel mental events.

The coexistence of body and mind went unquestioned until John Watson (see chap. 12), in 1913, pronounced that there *was no* such entity as a mind. He simply threw out the concept of mind, leaving only the body. For Watson, then, psychology became the study of the responses the body made to stimuli in its environment. Watson started a movement in psychology known as behaviorism, which exists today in a variety of forms. The one tenet that all behaviorists share is that the subject matter of psychology does not include any concept of mind or whatever other term one may wish to call it. For the behaviorists, mind refers to unobservable events which do not exist within a framework of space or time.

In earlier philosophies, the concept of mind was often identified with the theological notion of the soul or spiritual side of human beings. Before and after Watson, many psychologists have maintained the dualistic tradition in one form or another. In more recent times, the earlier, simple terms of mind, consciousness, or mental life have taken on new terms such as ego (in Freudian psychology), cognitive maps, psychic energies, tension systems, psychic fields of force, stimulus trace, and so on. Although the more recent concepts are far more subtle, some kind of separation of the mental from the physical is allowed. The basic issue, then, is should such dualistic concepts be allowed as part of the study of psychology? For the behaviorists, the issue is a very important one, since they feel that any reference to the mental side of life should be excluded. For other theories, such as psychoanalysis which still flourishes today, the existence of mind and body is accepted. Freud (see chap. 17), the founder of the psychoanalytic movement, formulated a rather complicated "mental apparatus" as a basic explanatory principle, and it was a very necessary part of his system.

### Subjectivism versus Objectivism

As an issue, this is closely related to the mind-body problem. An objective approach to psychology considers its data to be whatever can be seen or measured directly and precisely. To be objective is not necessarily synonymous with being experimental, although most experimental psychologists at least attempt to be as objective as they can in dealing with their data. However, if one were particularly interested in animal psychology, one might go out and observe various species in their natural habitat. One would report the relationships one observed, for example, a dominance hierarchy in monkeys, or territorialism. The methods would be objective, but not experimental.

Subjectivism, on the other hand, refers to a consideration of the more private or inner experiences a person has. One reports what one feels, thinks, or experiences. Since these events are a private matter for each individual, they cannot be shared except through words. The systems of structuralism (see chap. 7), Gestalt psychology (see chap. 14), and existential psychology (see chap. 20) have depended strongly on a subjective approach. The method usually used is called *introspection,* a looking into oneself and describing the experiences one has. Historically, the method is very old, dating back to St. Augustine in the fourth century (see chap. 3).

Structuralism, as a systematic approach to psychology, no longer exists today, but the recent movements of existential and humanistic psychology depend largely on subjective reports of one's thoughts, ideas, feelings, desires, and so on. The advocates of subjectivism maintain that this is a very legitimate part of psychology, a part that those who maintain an objective approach completely ignore. Other psychologists like to maintain both attitudes. They consider psychology to be the study of behavior (objective), as well as experience (subjective).

In many cases, the side of the issue one cares to take depends on what one considers the study of psychology to be. If one considers the important matters of experiences and inner feelings, then the subjective approach would be allowed. On the other hand, if one limits oneself only to observable behavior, subjectivism must be denied. The behaviorists, who deny any subjectivism, often find it difficult to handle private experiences. When you study the chapters on behaviorism (see chaps. 12 and 13), you shall see how the behaviorists have attempted to handle the problem. For the subjectivists, the problem is less compelling. They accept private experiences, reflect upon them, and report what they experience. According to the objectivists, if psychology is to be a science, it must deal only with observable events. The subjectivists maintain, on the other hand, that there is a part of psychology which cannot be studied objectively, but which still cannot be ignored.

## Quantification versus Qualification

Psychologists presume to gather data about living organisms, whether they are humans or animals. The issue of quantification versus qualification is often related to the objective-subjective issue. Subjective data are usually qualitative and cannot necessarily be quantified. A description of one's feelings can hardly be put into numbers. On the other hand, to quantify means to report one's findings somehow in numbers—some form of measurement must be taken. The measurement may be in terms of how often a particular response takes place (rate), of the amount of the response (magnitude), or of how long it takes for the response to occur (latency). In the case of rate, an example may be how many times a rat presses a bar in a given unit of time; in latency, how quickly one presses a button when a light is flashed on; in magnitude, how much saliva Pavlov's dogs secreted when the bell was rung.

Qualitative data may not be reduced to precise numerical measurement. When one hears a tone one may describe it as loud or soft. Or, when one feels a pain it may be intense, nagging, excruciating, and so on. One may observe how a bird builds a nest or how a cat feeds its young. In the last two examples, one gives a perfectly objective observation, but it is qualitative. Generally, those who prefer an objective approach to psychology tend to prefer quantification, but not always, as the illustrations of the bird and the cat exemplify. A subjective approach, on the other hand, usually must be qualitative in giving a verbal report, which is difficult to quantify. Some psychological theories limit themselves only to quantitative data, others to qualitative, and still others accept both. Those who stress a qualitative approach simply state that much data in psychology, for example, observing an illusion of apparent movement, cannot be reduced to simple measurement. Those who stress the quantitative side feel that rigorous measurement is a necessary condition of science.

The issue can also take the form of richness versus precision in terms of the data gathered. The clinical, or case-history, method in psychology is certainly qualitative. It can be argued that this method is far richer in gathering facts and unearthing many crucial aspects about a person's life history. This method was typically used by Freud and the later analysts.

At the other extreme are the rigorous experimenters who perform their work in a precise manner yielding results in a quantitative form but whose findings are limited to a specific problem. In their precision, these psychologists are not able to handle the richness of data achieved by the clinical method.

## Reductionism versus Nonreductionism

This is a very different issue, and one may be subjective or objective, prefer the quantitative or qualitative approach, and still take either stand on the issue of reductionism. The basic issue involves whether or not the subject matter of psychology (however it may be defined) may stand on its own as independent of other sciences, or should be reduced to a more basic level of analysis. A most extreme example of reductionism was proposed by Weiss (see chap. 12), who suggested that all behavior should be reduced to the activity of electrons and protons. Other psychologists who still maintain a reductionist point of view feel that, in the final analysis, psychological events should be reduced to biological processes. These reductionists believe that psychology, which deals with living organisms, is merely a branch of biology. Those psychologists who stress the importance of internal drives as motivating stimuli, or the importance of the nervous system in memory, definitely take a reductionistic point of view.

On the other hand, a number of diverse theories are nonreductionistic. Such learning theorists as Guthrie and Skinner (see chap. 13) considered psychology to be the study of responses of an organism to stimuli in the environment. The responses might be described in some quantitative manner, but need not be reduced further to physiological components. Lewin proposed a field theory (see chap. 15) where a person existed in a life space or psychological environment. He did not speak of stimulus-response units, but did consider a person to be affected by all the psychological facts exerted upon him or her at any given moment. Lewin saw no need to reduce psychology any further. The reductionists argue that the nonreductionists are merely *describing* and not *explaining* the basic causes of the psychological event, which they (the reductionists) feel must be found in internal physiological functions. The nonreductionists argue, on the other hand, that psychology is an independent study with its own subject matter, which is just as legitimate as that of physiology, chemistry, or physics, and does not need to be reduced to a more basic level.

## Molar versus Molecular

This issue involves the kind of unit the psychologist ought to study. Should one study the whole (molar), or break it down into its separate component parts (molecular)? Speaking in terms of behavior, the question is whether one should study the reactions of the entire or *whole* organism (molar), or limit oneself to a description of simple discrete reflexes or responses (molecular). Kantor (see chap. 13) stressed that psychology studied an entire organism's behavior at any given time, and the unit of analysis was the whole organism as it interacted with objects in its environment. Watson (see chap. 12), referred to earlier, believed we should study discrete molecular responses. In fact, his opponents called him a "muscle twitch" psychologist.

Other later behaviorists, such as Guthrie and Skinner, have followed Watson's example and have been known as S-R (stimulus-response) psychologists. In particular, Skinner (see chap. 13) suggested that the most scientific way to discover the laws of psychology was to take a bit of behavior, such as bar pressing in the rat or pecking responses by a pigeon to a disc on the side of a cage, and then manipulate the independent variables carefully to see what happened to that bit of behavior. This selection of small molecular units for careful analysis has been criticized by the molar people who oppose it as being too limiting an operation. Those who stress the molecular approach feel that selecting small, discrete units for analysis can be quantified more easily, and basic relationships can be discovered.

The issue of molar versus molecular is not limited to those who stress an objective approach to psychology. If we are dealing with perceptions or sensory experiences, which are more subjective, the issue is also involved. Wundt, who developed the first psychological system (see chap. 6), considered the task of the psychologist to be the analysis of a particular experience into its most basic elements of sensations and feelings. The Gestalt psychologists, who also stressed perception, rose up against this molecular approach, stating that it was impossible to break experiences down into elementary units. Psychology must deal with perception as a whole, and to break it down would destroy part of what one wished to study. They felt that the whole was not equal to the sum of its parts. A melody, for example, was more than the particular notes which made it up, and therefore, must be perceived as a whole. Thus, as in other issues we have considered, the molar-molecular issue is a matter of opinion.

## Determinism versus Teleology
## and Determinism versus Free Will

In order to have a deterministic view, one must presume that any behavior at the present moment is the result of the events that have happened earlier in the past history of the organism. To take a deterministic position simply means that one believes that the causes in the past determine what is going on at the present. The proponents of teleology, on the other hand, believe that the future affects the present. At the moment, the reader might think that such an idea of the future determining the present is rather absurd, but if we look more carefully, it is not so ridiculous as it may sound. Alfred Adler (see chap. 18), who was associated with Freud before he developed his own system, took a very strong teleological view of human beings. He believed that present behavior was guided by the future goals one set for oneself. If one set no future goals toward which to strive, one would end up doing nothing. According to Adler, we all have general and specific goals in the future toward which we direct our efforts, and it is these goals which influence how we act at the present time.

The notion of teleology in psychology is frequently described as *purposivism*—that is, behavior is not random, but has a purpose. This purpose is going to involve a direction with respect to the future. Two theorists, McDougall (see chap. 11) and Tolman (see chap. 15), who differed in most other respects, shared the concept of purpose. They felt that behavior was purposive or goal directed, and this purposivism was a basic characteristic of behavior of both animals and humans.

On the other hand, Freud (see chap. 17) and Watson (see chap. 12), who could not have been further apart in their theories, shared the concept that behavior (or whatever term one wishes to apply) is completely determined from past experiences, even from the time of birth. Although we might not be able to identify all events separately from the past, they all combine to determine the present activity. From the completely deterministic view, a person was not the master of his or her own fate. If one were brought up in a band of pirates, one would be a pirate, too. There were no alternatives so far as the determined behavior was concerned.

Watson took an extremely environmental point of view in his determinism. He said that if he were given a group of healthy infants and the entire control of their environment, he could make them into anything he chose—doctors, lawyers, merchant-chiefs, or even beggars or thieves. The determinists claimed that if psychology were to develop into a lawful science, relationships would be discovered which related past or antecedent events to present activity.

There is another side issue with regard to determinism: the notion of free will. It is perhaps more of a philosophical issue, but according to those who accept free will, one's behavior is not completely determined by past events, since humans are capable of making their own decisions because they possess the free will to do so. This will may or may not be dependent on past events. Humanistic psychologists take this position, for they believe that one of the aspects of being human is a capacity to make one's own decisions, not necessarily with regard to what has gone before. The determinists, on the other hand, maintain that any choice is a determined choice. The decision that is made results from the weight of past circumstances in one direction or the other.

Carl Rogers (see chap. 19), the most prominent leader of the humanistic movement, and B. F. Skinner, the recognized leader of behaviorism, engaged in a series of debates over several years. Rogers maintained that although some of our behavior is determined, there is a unique aspect of humans that allows them a freedom of choice and that is a special aspect of being human. A person is thus free to choose his or her own destiny, which can result in becoming a self-actualized individual. On the other hand, Skinner believed that whatever choice we make is determined by the weight of factors in that direction.

## Utility versus Purity

This issue takes a number of forms and arises out of philosophical concepts, as have several of the other issues discussed so far. A utilitarian point of view stresses that which is pragmatic or practical. It supports the notion that principles and facts discovered by psychologists ought to be useful and applied. Wundt and Titchener (see chaps. 6 and 7) developed a psychology which involved the analysis of conscious experience. This analysis was their sole aim for they wished to make theirs a pure psychology, not one that would be contaminated with pragmatic issues. In opposition, the functionalists (see chap. 9) were very much in favor of developing a psychology which could be put to useful ends.

The same issue exists today in attitudes toward psychological research. There are experimental psychologists who contrive problems and set up experiments just to see what happens. Whether or not their findings can be put to any practical use is not their concern. They are the "pure researchers." It is a kind of psychology for psychology's sake. On the other hand, some researchers are more interested in doing work which hopefully can be put to practical use, where applications can be made from the principles discovered in the laboratory. Such applications might apply to modifying the behavior of children, to maximizing efficient industrial operations, or to advertising. Of course, it may develop that some research intended to be "pure," may find practical applications in the end.

## Nativism versus Empiricism or Heredity versus Environment

This issue has deep philosophical roots, and will be introduced in more detail in chapter 4. It can be stated in a number of ways. Among the earlier psychologies that stressed the study of experience and perception, the issue was how much of our experience came to us naturally in an inherent or unlearned fashion, as opposed to how much was the result of direct experience or observation. Descartes, in the seventeenth century (see chap. 4), had stated that some ideas were inborn. Shortly thereafter, Locke asserted that all knowledge came from experience. Similarly, Kant (see chap. 4), at about the same time, stressed the importance of native or inborn perceptions of our world. In more contemporary psychology this nativistic notion was adopted by the Gestalt psychologists (see chap. 14) who felt that certain ways in which we perceived our environment came to us quite naturally without the need for prior learning. For example, by the time human infants could crawl, they could naturally perceive depth and would not fall into a pit or over a cliff. The empirical tradition, in science and psychology in particular, has stressed the importance of gaining what we know from our direct observation of the facts and *learning* about them through our senses.

Also, in contemporary psychology, the issue takes another form, that of the nature-nurture or heredity-environment controversy. Here, the issue is stated in terms of learned versus unlearned behavior. How much of our behavior is dependent on hereditary factors such as native talents or capacities, as opposed to pure learning? As we have already seen, Watson (see chap. 12), the founder of behaviorism, and other later behaviorists, stressed an extremely environmental view. He felt that if a person were normal, environment was all important in determining that person's behavior. Others, such as McDougall (see chap. 11) and, to a lesser degree, Woodworth (see chap. 11), have laid greater stress on the importance of inherited dispositions or predetermined ways of behaving. For example, McDougall accounted for the fact that we humans tend to be gregarious, by presuming that we all have an instinctive tendency in that direction. Learning might play a role in helping determine directions, but a great deal of the behavior might be "built in." After McDougall, the doctrine of instincts tended to fall into disfavor, and even animal psychologists tended to stress the importance of learning instead.

Today, the pendulum is swinging slightly in the other direction, with greater emphasis on instinctive behavior, particularly by the animal ethologists. Some psychologists feel that intelligence at the human level is based primarily on native or inherent endowment, depending on how effective the environment may be. Others, however, stress that intelligence is primarily a matter of experience and learning, provided that the person is not biologically damaged in some way. Prior to 1954 it was not uncommon to hear some people stating that certain races were either basically superior or inferior. However, on a more individual basis, the controversy is still very active about how much of a part heredity or environment plays in the determination of our behavior.

### Theory versus Data

Earlier in this chapter in dealing with the nature of psychological theory, we stated that a good psychological theory should begin with empirical propositions—that is, data. Psychology should aim toward a good synthesis of theory and concrete observations. To clarify the issue, let us look at both extremes.

Many personality theories, including those of Freud and the later analysts, have been criticized as depending too much on theory and not enough on well-collected data. Freud did have a kind of data: his observations of what his patients told him as they lay on his couch. These included their free associations and reports of their dreams. On the basis of these data, Freud constructed a very elaborate theory. His opponents criticized him not only for the unreliability of his data but for formulating constructs that seemed impossible to demonstrate—for example, psychic energy, libido, cathexes, and so-called punishments and rewards of the superego. What is left is largely theory.

At the other extreme are to be found psychologists who claim that theory is not necessary. They assert that all we need are the data, the results of an experiment. There is thus no need for theoretical propositions; the principles of psychology can be formulated from the data. Such a position was set forth by B. F. Skinner in an article entitled, "Are theories of learning necessary?"[10] His conclusion was that they were not. He asserted that if an experiment is properly and precisely executed with all proper controls, the results stand for themselves and add to the principles of psychology.[11]

There are, of course, many other issues, but we have tried to limit ourselves to the most important ones. As one reads through the chapters of this book, these issues should be kept in mind. Often, a particular issue becomes the crux of a theory. At other times, the issue will be less important, and may be referred to only in passing. For the most part, the basic criticisms of a particular theory are levied by those who take the opposite side of the issue at hand. These are the issues which divide psychologists, but if there were no issues, such varied and diverse theories and systems of psychology would not have developed.

Having considered some of the basic concepts involved in psychological theorizing, as well as some of the issues, we shall next consider the more specific systems and theories. In fact, the major portion of this book will be devoted to a discussion of these different systems and theories. As we have indicated earlier, psychology emerged as an independent discipline late in the nineteenth century. However, because psychology is a relatively young science, part of the excitement in understanding psychological theorizing comes from a knowledge of its historical antecedents. Although this book is not intended to be merely a history of psychology, some attention should be given to historical background.

Psychology has deep roots, particularly in philosophy and biology. Therefore, the next four chapters will be devoted to some of the historical factors which have had strong influences on psychology today. Here, we shall be concerned with the discoveries, ideas, and issues which have had the greatest influence on twentieth-century psychology. We shall begin with the naturalism of the ancient Greeks, where science and philosophy began. We shall then trace the route of the mind, primarily through philosophy. This will be followed by the body route, primarily through biology.

With this background, we can then consider the main theories and systems of psychology which have been predominant in this century. We cannot consider every theory that has ever been proposed. We prefer to limit ourselves to those that we feel have been the most important, and to deal with them in enough detail so that the reader will have more than a sketchy idea of what the various proponents have said.

---

[10]B. F. Skinner, "Are Theories of Learning Necessary?," *Psychological Review,* Vol. 57 (1950), pp. 193–216.

[11]For an extended discussion of this issue, as well as others mentioned in this chapter, see Michael Wertheimer, *Fundamental Issues in Psychology* (New York: Holt, Rinehart and Winston, 1972).

## Suggested Further Readings

*General Nature of Theories and Systems*

Lichtenstein, P. E., "Psychological Systems: Their Nature and Function." *Psychological Record,* Vol. 17 (1967), pp. 221–40. This paper, directed primarily to students of theories and systems, discusses at some length the characteristics as well as several other aspects of theory construction not considered in this chapter. A good overview that might well be considered as required reading.

McGeoch, J. A., "The Formal Criteria of a Psychological System." *Psychological Review,* Vol. 40 (1933), pp. 1–11. This is a classic paper written when systems were at their height.

*Operationism*

Benjamin, A. C., *Operationism.* Springfield, Illinois: Charles C. Thomas, 1955. A full treatment of the principle. Might be tough going in spots, but worth the effort.

Stevens, S. S., "The Operational Basis of Psychology." *American Journal of Psychology,* Vol. 47 (1935), pp. 323–30. Another classic paper in which operationism is presented as it applies specifically to psychology.

*Basic Issues*

Kantor, J. R., "The Evolution of Mind." *Psychological Review,* Vol. 42 (1935), pp. 455–65. A full treatment of the mind-body problem as applied to psychology. The issue is just as alive today, and Kantor's remarks are just as pertinent as when the article was written.

Vanderplas, J. M., *Controversial Issues in Psychology.* Boston: Houghton Mifflin Co., 1966. A book of readings on what the author considers to be or to have been the most controversial issues in psychology's development. Some are of historical interest only, such as the discussions of reaction time, but others are still quite current.

Wertheimer, M., *Fundamental Issues in Psychology.* New York: Holt, Rinehart and Winston, 1972. An excellent discussion of many of the basic issues in psychology. Discusses the issues considered in this chapter, as well as others not mentioned here.

*Philosophy of Science*

Feigl, H., and Broadbeck, M., *Readings in the Philosophy of Science.* New York: Appleton-Century-Crofts, 1953.

Kuhn, T. S., *The Structure of Scientific Revolutions,* 2nd ed. Chicago: University of Chicago Press, 1970. Two good books for those who wish to pursue the whole matter of the philosophy of science.

# CHAPTER

# 2

# *The Birth of Psychology in Ancient Greece*

Since psychology as an independent discipline, separate from philosophy and a variety of the sciences, did not develop until the late nineteenth century, the reader might well ask, why begin our study with the Greeks? Except for Aristotle, none of the Greeks formulated any very systematic position with regard to psychology. However, some of the other ancient scholars did discuss matters which we would consider to be psychological.

There is an even more important reason why we begin our study with the Greeks, which is relative at least to some positions in modern psychology today. Many persons believe that psychology is a natural and objective science of behavior based on experimentation and observation. Scientific psychology, as it has evolved in the twentieth century, has concerned itself with the real activity of living organisms. All psychologies today, of course, do not necessarily think in this way. We shall encounter many of these nonobjective approaches in later chapters. But, at least one important position, called, in the broadest sense, behaviorism (see chaps. 12 and 13), with its variations takes a strong stand as a naturalistic approach. By this we mean that we are dealing with events occurring in a real world of space and time. We share such a naturalistic position with many of the ancient Greek writers. It has been said that Aristotle was the first behaviorist.

The early Greeks, from the Hellenic period to the time of Aristotle, believed in a world they could observe. This is obvious from their emphasis on science, including mathematics and astronomy. The world they lived in was a world known through their senses (despite the fact that Plato was somewhat skeptical of sensory impressions). The Greeks did not think of a world of the spirit or transspatial soul, as some think of today. Their world was a rather limited one. In a sense, we could call them isolationists. Their religion was primitive, with gods and goddesses having very human qualities.

19

Thus, the theme of this chapter is naturalism, as it relates to modern psychology. The Greeks wanted to learn about nature in its various aspects. Today, *scientific* psychology takes the same attitude, obviously in a much more sophisticated way. It is concerned with the nature of behavior and how an organism reacts to its environment. Like the ancient Greeks, this approach to psychology disregards the spirit, mind, or whatever name one wishes to attach to such unobservable phenomena. After the decline of Greek naturalistic thinking, two thousand years passed before psychology was able to explain its events again without making reference to things which do not exist as observable phenomena.

## The Hellenic Period (600–322 B.C.)

We begin our story in ancient Greece, in approximately the sixth century B.C. In those times, the country was politically divided and subdivided into small city-states. Athens was one such unit, and is our primary concern, because it became the ultimate center of Greek philosophy, science, and art.

The earliest period is usually referred to as the *cosmological* period because the scholars asked themselves such questions as: What is the nature of the universe? Is it made up of one or many things? If many, how are they to be accounted for?

One of the best expressions of Greek naturalism was in their science. The earliest scientist was Thales (*ca.* 600 B.C.), who not only predicted eclipses of the sun (possibly by accident), but who also had as his ultimate explanation of the cosmos that all things came from and were reduced to water (probably because it was essential to life).

Pythagoras, the great mathematician, thought that the ultimate explanations were to be found in numbers. Any high school sophomore studying geometry is familiar with the Pythagorean theorem. Incidentally, *Pythagoras* was one of the first to suggest that the world was a sphere, rather than flat.

Perhaps the finest example of the early Greek naturalistic psychology is to be found in Democritus (*ca.* 460–370 B.C.). He believed that all explanations were contained in nature which was made of tiny particles (atoms) constantly in motion. These particles differed in all matters of fashion—size, shape, angularity, and so on. Since they were constantly in motion, they bumped into each other; so obviously, there was constant change. He was the first Greek to give some detailed explanation of sensation. All sensation had to involve immediate contact. Taste, for example, involved atoms that were "small, angular, thin and winding."[1] Colors depended on the figure of the atoms. Seeing, in general, involved the sending of atoms through the air which touched the eye;

---

[1]R. S. Peters, *Brett's History of Psychology* (abridged one-volume edition) (London: George Allen and Unwin, Ltd., 1953), p. 44.

the eye would then receive a copy of the object seen. There was nothing in thought which had not passed through the senses.

What about the mental atoms or atoms of reason? The only difference lay in the fact that they differed in *degree* from the atoms of nature. They were smaller and moved at a more rapid rate.[2] Democritus' writings provide an excellent example of the naturalism we mentioned earlier. According to him, there was no dualism, no distinction between the mental and physical, mind or body. All events came out of the same substance, the atoms.

A final example of this attitude is to be found in the writings of the famous Greek physician Hippocrates (*ca.* 460–370 B.C.). He borrowed from Empedocles the four basic elements—earth, air, fire, and water—which correlated with his theory of humors within the body—phlegm (earth), blood (air), yellow bile (fire), and black bile (water). These accounted for the four basic human temperaments, as follows:

| blood | sanguine temperament | (cheerful) |
| yellow bile | choleric temperament | (fiery) |
| phlegm | phlegmatic temperament | (slow) |
| black bile | melancholic temperament | (sad) |

The humors could obviously be seen when a physician examined a patient, as in a head cold or cut in the skin. When the humors got out of balance, one might run into psychological difficulties, perhaps becoming a person with extreme melancholy or depression. Of particular interest is Hippocrates' explanation of epilepsy, which he dealt with in his work *On the Sacred Diseases.* He rejected the notion that epilepsy was due to anything other than natural causes. Epilepsy was caused by improper action of the organs that regulated the bodily fluids (humors), especially blood and phlegm. Although the explanations were primitive, he did not attribute epilepsy to super-natural powers, as many later writers did (see Fig. 1, page 22, for Objective-Subjective Cycle).

## Socrates (469–399 B.C.)

Beginning with Socrates, the kinds of questions the ancient scholars asked themselves began to shift; they became more concerned with *humans* than *matter.* Was there an absolute good? How must we account for the world of nature, for knowledge, and for morality?

What we know about Socrates comes mainly from the dialogues of Plato. Socrates' concerns were with political behavior, ethics, economics, and aesthetics. In a sense, he was one of the first social scientists. Socrates spoke of a *psyche* which, translated literally, means spirit or soul. Some historians of psychology, such as Watson,[3] suggested that his notion was similar to our modern concep-

---

[2]*Ibid.*
[3]R. I. Watson, *The Great Psychologists,* 4th ed. (Philadelphia: J. B. Lippincott, 1978).

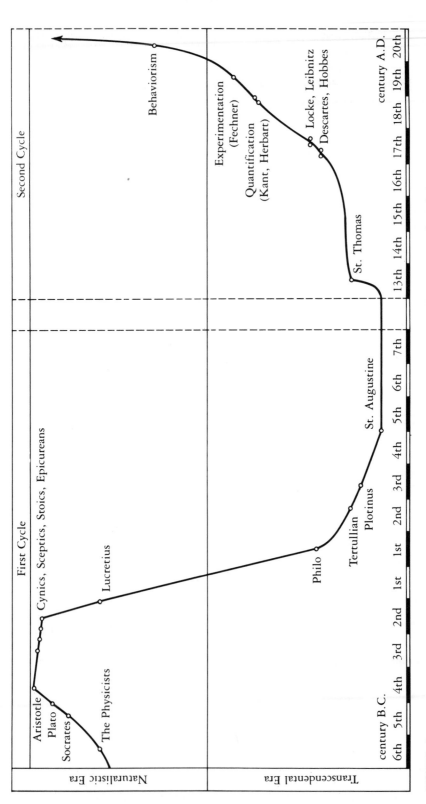

**FIGURE 1** *The Two Cycles in Psychological History.* (From J. R. Kantor, *The Scientific Evolution of Psychology*, Vol. I. Chicago: The Principia Press, Inc., 1963, p. 161. Reproduced by permission.)

tion of an ethereal substance which leaves the body at death as a shadow and goes to Hades. An alternate explanation, which was more in keeping with the *Zeitgeist* (spirit of the times) of Greek naturalism, was that modern scholars have imposed a Christian-like interpretation of a transspatial substance. This was not at all what Socrates had in mind. If one wished to "push a point" in terms of modern psychology as Wertheimer[4] has suggested, it might be found in Socrates' statement "Know thyself." This directive could be interpreted as the forerunner of the introspective method (looking into oneself and analyzing one's own experiences). However, in all probability, Socrates did not intend this interpretation. Introspection was not introduced into psychology until St. Augustine (see chap. 3).

## Plato (427–347 B.C.)

Our concern with Plato is not so much with his psychology, because it was somewhat fragmentary, but rather with his position as the predecessor of Aristotle, with whom ancient Greek psychology reached its height. Even more with Plato than with Socrates, later writers have imposed a Judeo-Christian interpretation of the nature of the soul on his writings.

Plato was born in Athens of a well-to-do family. He became a pupil of the great Socrates. At the age of forty he began to teach at the Academy, a place where scholars gathered. Most of his writings are in the form of dialogues, in which Socrates is the main speaker.

***Plato's Theory of Ideas.*** In one interpretation of the term, Plato was a dualist, in that he separated idea from matter. The basic reality became the idea. It was changeless, apart from matter, perfect and timeless.[5] Matter was imperfect, and we could only perceive it through our rather imperfect senses. Another way of looking at his theory is in terms of forms and their contents. Ideas constituted forms, and contents made up matter. Ideas, then, could be thought of as formulas or patterns.

Consider the idea of a perfect circle as an example. In the world of matter, one could draw many circles with various degrees of perfection. Some might be rough and very imperfect, others might approximate the perfect circle; but only in the world of ideas did the *real perfect circle* exist. From our vantage point in modern psychology, we might say that Plato's theory of the ideal constituted an overemphasis on constructs and an overevaluation of the process of abstraction. The whole theory might be summarized as a plan whereby things could be related to their patterns or models. A pattern was separate from the material from which it was made. Psychology today deals with many kinds of models, whether verbal, mathematical or pictorial.

---

[4]M. Wertheimer, *A Brief History of Psychology* (New York: Holt, Rinehart and Winston, Inc., 1970).
[5]A. Weber, *History of Philosophy,* trans. F. Thilly (New York: Charles Scribner's Sons, 1928).

Plato's ideas were eternal only in the sense that they lasted beyond the impressions they made. Like Socrates, Plato spoke of a psyche or soul. What Plato meant by psyche included: (1) moral human qualities, (2) thinking and (3) behavioral sources of many types of action. To think of Plato's dualism as a distinction between mind and body is to impose a construct quite foreign and unthinkable to the ancient Greeks.

Where did the ideas exist? "In the world beyond the heavens," said Plato, and this could very easily be misinterpreted in the light of the Christian doctrine of the divine. Nothing could have been further from Plato's thinking. Ideas existed only in the sense that one could think of a perfect circle as the abstract which would exist before and after we have come and gone from this world. Since Plato was somewhat skeptical of sensory data, his theory was an attempt to determine something more solid than what could be found in the experiencing sense.

Although we believe the above interpretation of Plato is closest to the facts as we know them in the light of the naturalism of the times, we should mention that our interpretation is not shared by all scholars. Plato's original writings (along with those of Aristotle) have gone through numerous translations from the original ancient Greek, through Arabic and Latin. Frequently, concepts are changed in translation, and new interpretations follow. Thus, there are those who interpret Plato's dualism in a different light. They would interpret the dualism as a separation of body and soul in the same sense that we discussed the mind-body problem in the previous chapter. Plato's "soul" could not be exactly of a Christian sort, for he lived many centuries before the Christian era. Nevertheless, these writers would point out a great similarity, and would maintain that the "world of ideas" could not be considered merely in a conceptual sense as we have suggested, but rather as a nonspatial or transspatial entity existing quite separate and apart from the world of reality.

In some passages of Plato's dialogues, it appears that he believed in a soul as immaterial and immortal in a more spiritual sense. Because Greek thought of the time was very naturalistic, this conception of a spiritual soul would have to be considered an exception to the beliefs and attitudes that prevailed at the time.

Evidence for this more spiritual interpretation can be found in Plato's doctrine of *reminiscence*. Knowledge existed in the soul prior to any actual experience. This is illustrated in a famous passage in the dialogue entitled the *Meno*. In it, Socrates questions an uneducated slave boy in such a manner that the boy appears to have knowledge of geometry, even though he had never had any acquaintance with the subject. The implication is that the knowledge existed in the soul prior to birth.

### Aristotle (384–322 B.C.)

Greek Hellenic thinking, and more particularly its psychology, reached a peak in the writings of Aristotle. He was the first real psychologist, and his natural way of describing psychological events bore a strong kinship to that of the *present-day psychologists* who treat psychology as a natural science of behavior.

Aristotle was born in Asia Minor. At the age of seventeen he became a pupil of Plato at the Academy in Athens, where he remained until Plato's death. Later, he became the tutor of Alexander the Great and then returned to Athens to found his own school. Alexander's death was followed by a hostile attack against Aristotle, and he was forced to flee to the island of Euboea where he died in 322 B.C.

Aristotle's psychology is found mainly in two works: the first being *De Anima,* translated to mean, *Concerning the Psyche* or soul. This is a reasonably systematic work, and we shall deal with it in more detail shortly. The second work, *Parva Naturalia,* is a series of essays on a variety of subjects, both psychological and biological. Some of the subjects are not of interest to us, such as "on youth and old age," "on respiration" or "on life and death." However, "on remembering" and "on dreaming" are of definite concern to us.

**Aristotle's Four Causes.** Aristotle believed in four kinds of causes: (1) formal, (2) efficient, (3) final, and (4) material.

Material causes refer to the matter of which a thing is made. For example, the material cause of a table is wood, and that of a statue is bronze. The efficient cause could refer to an immediate source or change or motion. An example could be, "Why did you go into the woods?" The answer, "To pick some daisies." This answer could also be the final cause because it refers to the purpose of the trip. The final cause refers to the essence or form of a thing. Daisies do not have the same form as trees, but as we shall see subsequently, form cannot be separate from matter. It should be noted that a single thing can function simultaneously as more than one cause.

**Aristotle's Metaphysics.** In order to understand Aristotle's psychology, we should mention a few words about his metaphysics. To Aristotle, things were made up of *form* and *matter,* but, unlike Plato's idea, the two were inseparable. It was *form* that made us humans rather than dogs or cats, but *matter* made us the particular individuals that we were. Form could not exist without matter, and there was no matter without form. Matter was what made things possible. The taking on of form was the actualizing of potentiality. For example, tin and copper were the matter for the form bronze, and at a higher level bronze became the matter for the actualizing of the form of a statue. All things could be organized hypothetically from pure form to pure matter. The position of anything on that scale depended on the degree of the form that had been actualized.

**De Anima.** In *De Anima* we had the first realization of the psyche or soul. A statue was made up of form and matter, but the form was not psyche. The psyche, as form, was never *separate* from the organism, but was merely a *function* of it. Psyche could be compared to the function of an instrument, like cutting was to an axe or, at a higher level of the psyche, like vision was to the eye. The psyche was neither physical substance nor mental stuff. We could think of psyche as one form of the organism, its action. The tissues and organs of the body constituted its matter. Their form constituted their function, but it was impossible for one to exist without the other.

*De Anima*[6] was divided into three main parts or books. The first part was an introduction in which Aristotle indicated what psychology was, its problems and a bit of history of what previous scholars had said. The main part dealt with psychological action and, in particular, the senses and their objects. The last part dealt with more complex activity.

In living organisms there was a hierarchy of psyches or functions. Since psyche was a function of all living things, there was no separation between biological and psychological functions. At the bottom of the hierarchy was the *nutritive* or *vegetative* psyche. It was common to all living organisms, plants and animals alike. Its functions were those of nutrition and reproduction. From our point of view, this really belongs to the subject matter of biology.

Next were the *sensing* or *perceiving* functions. They were common to both animals and humans, but not to plants. They served as the basis for gaining information about things. Each sense was associated with a particular organ of the body, the eyes for seeing, ears for hearing, and so forth. However, Aristotle did not ignore the objects that each organ sensed. There was a third factor which connected the sensing organism with the stimulus object, and that was the *media of contact*. Sensation functions allowed us to absorb the forms of things without ingesting their matter, in the same way that wax took on the seal of a signet ring without absorbing the matter from which the ring was made. Sensation was more than the passive reception of form; it was the actualization of the potentialities resident in the perceiving sense and the object perceived. For example, when the eye was shut, color was only potentially resident in the external object.

Aristotle discussed the five senses, their objects, and the media of contact which connected them. For taste and touch, flesh was the medium of contact. For smell, the media were both air and water, while for sight and hearing it was air.

To coordinate information coming from more than one sense at a time, Aristotle spoke of the *common sense*. (This was obviously not the meaning we ordinarily attribute to the term.) Every particular sense was oriented toward its own object. The common sense organized more than one sense. For example, the common sense allowed us to identify a cube through both the sense of touch and sight.

All living organisms were capable of *motion*, the third class of functions or psyches. Living bodies were self-moving and self-directing. In other words they need not move by some external force. Closely related to this function was appetite. In this case, it was the object of the appetite which gave rise to the movement toward it.

---

[6]Aristotle, *De Anima,* A. J. Smith and W. D. Ross, eds. (Oxford: Clarendon Press, 1940).

Both animals and humans had appetite. It was directed by the image of what was satisfying, leading to immediate pleasure. Because humans alone had reason, they could be moved (motivated) by what was right and wrong. Thus, humans could look to the future for more lasting benefits. Aristotle identified this kind of motivation as *wish*.

In the hierarchy of functions, *imagination* fell in an intermediary place. It was very closely related to sensation, and involved the highest function of all, *thinking* or *reasoning*.

What about *remembering* and *recollection?* Remembering belonged to the primary activities of sensing. If a thing were to be remembered, it first had to be sensed. But, another factor was involved—the passage of time. Remembering, then, involved objects previously reacted to in addition to an awareness of the time relationships between the past and the present. *Recollecting* was slightly different, and would be what we call *recall*. It involved an active search into the past. Whenever we recollected, it was necessary to awaken antecedent processes and continue these until we were able to call up the particular experience. We might begin with the sensation which was immediately encountered and search for the object. Today we call this *association*. From this, Aristotle arrived at the three laws of association: (1) *similarity* of things, (2) *contiguity* or togetherness, and (3) *opposites*. The whole concept of association became of utmost importance in the psychologies of the eighteenth and nineteenth centuries, as well as in modern learning theories of today.

At the top of the hierarchy was *reasoning,* which was limited only to human beings. It became a process or a means to an end. Reason made use of the material provided by the senses and then went beyond it. One must keep in mind, however, that reasoning was not separated from the organism that reasons. Reason dealt more with the abstract and ideal aspects of things, while sensing dealt with the concrete material characteristics. Reason's function was to know and reflect. It could take the material provided from the senses and refine it.

Although it was primitive in many ways, *De Anima* was an amazing work. It reflected a naturalistic psychology devoid of any dualism, just as an objective psychology of today does.

---

# The Hellenistic Period and the
# Decline of Greek Naturalism

With the death of Aristotle and the conquests of Alexander there was a gradual shift of thinking from Greece (in particular, Athens) to other parts of the world. The intellectual horizons of the Greeks became widened because of the conquests of Persia, India, and Egypt. Thus, there followed a breakdown of Greek naturalism into other ways of thinking. Athens still remained the center of philosophy, at least for a while, but with the museum and library at Alexandria, the latter became more the literary center of the ancient world. Eventually, the Roman conquests began in 30 B.C., and the rise of Christianity followed. Greek naturalism yielded to a new interpretation of the psyche that was both subjective and spiritual. The rise of the spirit will be dealt with in the next chapter.

The concerns of the post-Aristotelian thinkers were not so psychological. Much of what they said about psychology was a dilution of Aristotle's thinking. The schools shifted their interest to political and moral matters. The writings of the Stoics, Skeptics, Epicureans, and Cynics strove to achieve an independence for man from the world of nature.

The leader of the Epicureans was Epicurus (341–270 B.C.). His outlook was not what we generally associate with the name of the school—that is, pleasure through gastronomical delights. Rather, according to the beliefs, the pursuit of human beings should be the search for happiness. To achieve happiness was to avoid pain rather than merely to pursue pleasure. To avoid pain meant withdrawal from the strifes and maladies of the outside world. An active search for pleasure could result in pain when it was withdrawn. Of the schools after Aristotle, the Epicureans probably have the greatest relevance for modern psychology. Could one interpret what they called happiness in terms of the principle of reward or reinforcement in modern learning theory? Or, what about Freud's pleasure principle, the force striving toward fulfillment of the life instincts? Freud made it very clear that the pleasure principle could be interpreted as the relief of painful tensions.

The Cynics also advocated a withdrawal from civilized activity. They believed that society was full of hypocrisy, grief, envy, and hate.

The leader of the Skeptics was Pyrrho of Elis (360–270 B.C.). Like Plato, they did not trust sensory perception, but unlike Plato, they did not believe in pure form. What one might conclude from any particular sensory experience might be wrong in the light of later experiences. The modern term *skepticism* derives from this attitude of cautiousness about accepting what was known.

Probably the most widespread of the post-Aristotelian schools was that of the Stoics. Their leaders were Epictetus (A.D. 50–120) and the emperor Marcus Aurelius (A.D. 121–180). The school had been founded earlier by Zeno (333–262 B.C.). Their psychology was to "accept all things in a spirit of content." Today, a stoic is considered to be one who accepts misfortune without complaint. This attitude arose out of the belief that the universe was orderly and good. Along with this belief was a determinism that what will be will be. There was a causal ordering of the universe, so one must accept one's fate as part of that order.

## Suggested Further Readings

Dennis, W., *Readings in the History of Psychology.* New York: Appleton-Century-Crofts, 1948, chs. 1 and 2. Two selections from Aristotle, one from *De Anima,* the other, *On Dreams.* Both demonstrate Aristotle's naturalistic approach to psychology.

Hernstein, R. J., and Boring, E. G., *A Source Book in the History of Psychology*. Cambridge: Harvard University Press, 1966.

Kantor, J. R., *The Scientific Evolution of Psychology,* Vol. I. Chicago: The Principia Press, 1963, chs. 1–13. These thirteen chapters are devoted to an extensive discussion of the psychology of the ancient Greeks, as well as Greek science and mathematics. The entire naturalistic background of the Greeks is emphasized. Not easy reading, but the most scholarly presentation available of this era of early psychology.

Koch, S., and Leary, David L., eds., *A Century of Psychology as Science*. New York: McGraw Hill Book Co., 1985. A compendium of various articles written by a variety of distinguished authors on a variety of subjects relating to the history of psychology.

Leahey, T. H., *A History of Psychology: Main Currents in Psychological Thought,* 2nd ed. Englewoods Cliffs, New Jersey: Prentice-Hall, 1987. An excellent book, highly sophisticated, not the general "run of the mill" book on the history of psychology. Highly recommended.

Peters, R. S., ed., *Brett's History of Psychology* (abridged). London: George Allen and Unwin, 1953, chs. 2–5. Another discussion of the psychological aspects in ancient Greek writings. This book takes a much less naturalistic view than Kantor's.

Watson, R. I., *The Great Psychologists,* 4th ed. Philadelphia: J. B. Lippincott, 1978, chs. 1–4. These chapters cover Greek philosophy from its earliest beginnings with psychological interpretations. The writing style is easy to follow. A number of interpretations are different from those in the two texts cited above.

# CHAPTER

# 3

# *The Mind Route*

## I. The Rise of the Spirit

With the decline of Greek naturalism, the evolution of modern psychology took two routes: one was the route of the mind which traced psychology mainly through theology and philosophy, and the other was the route of the body which evolved through biology and other sciences. Some psychologists today still consider their subject matter to be the study of mind, mental phenomena, or mental life. These psychologists are called "mentalistic" or "dualistic" by those who differ with them. They still consider activities of both the mind and the body to be relevant, either operating independently of each other or by interaction.

Because the concept of mind or spirit has played such an important part in psychology even today, this and the following chapter are devoted to a number of issues concerning the nature of the mind: what its contents are; how it works; and how it can be related to body functions. These were the questions that concerned the early theologians and the more recent philosophers. The significance of the mind to modern psychology must not be underestimated. Many psychologists still maintain some concepts of mind regardless of what other terms they may substitute, and they are not ashamed to do so. They do not object to making an obvious division between the mental and the physical. Theirs is not the "hard-nosed" objectivism of the naturalistic Greeks or the modern experimentalists. Thus, the theme of this chapter and the next one is really the evolution of the concept of mind from the early theologians to the late nineteenth-century philosophers, who also considered themselves psychologists. We shall study the more recent concepts of mind in later chapters.

In early theological psychology, particularly Christian, the distinction was clearly made between the body, as a part of the world of nature, and the spirit or soul, which was nonspatial, made of a different essence, and which operated quite separately from the body in many cases. As time passed, explanations, which we today would call psychological, became the concern of philosophers, and the idea of a mind lost some of its more theological and spiritual qualities. Nevertheless, the nonspatial character of something existing apart from the physical world still remains. Because modern psychology is still strongly entrenched in mentalistic ideas, we shall consider in some detail how earlier thinkers have dealt with the problems encountered by presuming the existence of a mind or soul.

## The Rise of the Spirit

With the development and the spread of Christianity we entered a new era in the evolution of psychology, which we identified as the rise of the spirit. However, from its beginnings, the growth of the Christian church was often slow and painful. It took five centuries of strife and struggle before it attained acceptance and political dominance. It was opposed by such Roman emperors as Nero, Domitian, Hadrian, Marcus Aurelius, and many others. The last of the Christian persecutions occurred in A.D. 303 under Diocletian. By 395, Christianity had become the state religion of the Roman Empire. The new way of life involved a complete change of thinking about the relationship between people and the world. The human being was now made up of not only a physical being but also a spiritual entity. The spirit became independent of the laws of nature. That transcendent entity, the soul, involved a world of the invisible and the intangible, which could not be seen but only believed in. Despite the quarrels and differences among the Church Fathers (the so-called Patristics), several ideas of Christianity became firmly entrenched in Western culture.

1. The existence of one God, a personal being, creator of the Universe and all that was in it.

2. The divinity of Christ. Many theological problems were involved since God made human beings, but Christ became the Son of the Father through whose Grace salvation was possible.

3. The Holy Spirit, the third aspect of the Trinity. So we have God the Father, God the Son, and God the Holy Ghost. The notion of $x = 3x$ or three-in-one offered real difficulties for the early authorities, but, by the fourth century, the idea of a Trinity became reconciled. This third aspect of God, the Holy Spirit, existed in the world. God could guide people, make the holy presence known to them, and hear and answer their prayers.

### Plotinus (A.D. 205–270)

Although he was not a Christian, the doctrines of Plotinus, who lived in Rome for twenty-five years, present an excellent example of the new subjectivism which was to be further developed in the next several hundred years. The school of thought that Plotinus represented is often called neo-Platonism, for Plotinus inverted Plato. He took the latter's idea of *pure form,* which had meant merely the ultimate in perfection and harmony, and made it the new conception of the psyche (which now meant spirit). In Plotinus' writings we had a concept of soul as substance, existing without regard to spatiality and separate from the body. This concept was later reflected and refined in the writings of St. Augustine. Although Plotinus was a pagan, his thoughts and ideas lent support to the establishment of a Christian philosophy and psychology. Here we had one of the earliest statements of a spirit apart from the body. The spirit was later transformed into the mind, and this concept was to dominate psychology for centuries to come.

Plotinus started with the One (God). From the One was derived, by a process of emanation or spilling over, the universal intelligence or world soul (nous). The third and final emanation was the soul or spirit, which became the highest feature of humankind.

**The Soul.** The soul was immaterial and enveloped the body, but was quite separate from it. Its relation to the body was one of collateral existence. It did not mix with the body, but dwelled beside it, having an independent existence of its own, different from the body or other corporal things. The One was descended through the soul to the body. Plotinus, thus, presumed grades of being: the soul being superior to the body, and the other grades of being superior to it. The soul became indestructible and immortal. It performed certain classes of activity, which included (1) perceiving the world, (2) reflecting and thinking about what was known, and (3) pure contemplation, transcending the physical to dwell on eternal and timeless matters. This highest function was capable of experiencing the One. It remained for St. Augustine, the Christian, to perfect and adapt it to the Christian doctrine. The significance of Plotinus' doctrines was not so much that they showed how the soul worked in a psychological sense, but merely that they said that it existed.

## St. Augustine (A.D. 354–430)

With St. Augustine we had the complete triumph of the spirit. Science was abandoned in favor of an intense preoccupation with the nonmaterial world.

St. Augustine was born in North Africa of a pagan father and a Christian mother. After a youth of revelry, he became converted to Christianity at the age of 33. He later became the Bishop of Hippo in North Africa.

Scholars differ about how learned St. Augustine was. He believed that one should not be debauched by worldly affairs, for true knowledge was to come from God and *not* from an examination of the world of nature. In denouncing the flesh, one was free to create a spiritual world in agreement with the character of the true God. He believed that the activities of the pagan sciences offered us nothing. Here, we had a complete reversal of the Greek naturalistic doctrine, in favor of the other side of humankind, spirit as opposed to body.

St. Augustine's attitude toward God and humanity was made clear in his *Confessions*,[1] one of his major works. God was the creator of humankind, heaven and earth. God was in people and people were in God. This was a very personal God. The human soul was the image of God, and, for St. Augustine, it became magnified and the body minimized.

He was the last of the great Classical philosophers and the first great Christian philosopher. His view of humanity dominated philosophy until about 1300. In his philosophy, St. Augustine turned away from the physical world of pain and torment and replaced it with the spiritual world (heaven). Through introspection, the soul could know what was true and known by faith.

**The Soul**

The soul was a simple, self-contained, noncorporal substance without matter, having no physical dimensions. Soul was spaceless and known only by inner awareness and *introspection*. The representation of the Trinity was expressed in these three functions: (1) memory, (2) intelligence (understanding), and (3) will. Still like the Trinity, which was three in one, the soul was a single unity not divisible into parts. The soul was created by God at the time the body was created, in the same manner that Adam was animated. Through understanding, it was possible for the soul to know God.

In St. Augustine's writings we had a refinement of the soul or mind, which carries us into modern times. Of special importance for modern psychology was the introspective principle. One could only enter into the domain of consciousness by turning inward into one's own soul.

The implications of St. Augustine's introspectionism or "looking inward" for modern psychology are profound. In the structuralist psychology of the early twentieth century it became the main method of analysis of the mind or conscious experience (see chaps. 6 and 7). Later, Gestaltists used it with some variation in their study of perception (see chap. 14). Because perceptions and sensations tended to be private inward experiences, the main way to achieve understanding of them was through introspection. Modern psychoanalysis also uses the method as one of its main sources of data in a variant called "free association": "Tell me anything that comes to your mind." Finally, the phenomenological methods of humanistic and existential psychology are basically introspective (see chaps. 19 and 20).

## *The Arabic Period*

When the pagan schools in Athens were closed by the Emperor Justinian in A.D. 529, the Dark Ages began in the West. During St. Augustine's lifetime the light of science flickered. However, with the Dark Ages, it became extin-

---

[1]St. Augustine, *Confessions*, trans. W. Watts (London: Heinemann, 1912).

guished. By that time, the Roman Empire had collapsed and the West had become separated from the empire of the East. Corrupt government, civil wars, and the influx of the Barbarians all contributed to the decline. When Rome became the victim of the Vandals from the North, Constantinople became preeminent.

Then came a new religion called Islam. Mohammed, its founder, was born in Mecca, Arabia in A.D. 570. At about the age of thirty, he received a revelation from God that he had been chosen to be the new *Prophet*. In 622 he fled to Medina to escape persecution from those who opposed his teachings. Despite resistance, the spread of the new religion was rapid. The word *Islam* means "surrender to God."[2] Mohammed or "the sword" became the striving force of the Arabic conquests, and Arabia, Syria, Egypt and Persia were overthrown in rapid order. By 711 the Arabs had crossed the Strait of Gibraltar into Iberia (Spain).

With the onset of the Dark Ages in the West, many of the scholars fled to the East, taking with them not only what was left of Western science but also the writings of Plato and Aristotle. The leading mosques of Islam became the centers of learning. The Arabic culture at that time was an assimilation of the works of the Greek scholars. Through translations, the Arabs became acquainted with the medicine of Hippocrates, the mathematics of Euclid, and the astronomy and physics of Alexandria. Perhaps of most importance for psychology was the fact that Aristotle's *De Anima* was brought back into intellectual circulation. The Arabs did *not* impose on it the later Christian theology which we shall encounter in St. Thomas' writings.

The Arabs became the conservers of Greek science and philosophy. As they gained strongholds in Europe through conquests, their contacts with the Western world became reestablished. The conquests of North Africa and the Iberian peninsula, and war and trade in the eighth to tenth centuries, made these contacts firmer. By the eleventh and twelfth centuries, the Arab scholars had passed onto the West the translations they had made of the classical writings. The Crusades also helped establish these contacts.

## The Middle Ages

By the eleventh century, the social climate we identify as the Middle Ages had been established. With the rise of feudalism three social classes emerged: the clergy, the aristocracy, and the peasants. The Church was the dominant influence not only because of its authority over the spirit (which was still really important), but also because of its enormous land holdings and political power. The institutions of knighthood and chivalry became established. The peasants worked the land in return for the protection of their lords.

[2]R. I. Watson, *The Great Psychologists*, 4th ed. (Philadelphia: J. B. Lippincott, 1978).

As time passed, towns and cities grew. The population increased, and artisans carried on their work. Guilds served as protectors of the craft members. Another social class was established—the merchants.

In this setting, the great universities of the Middle Ages emerged. In the beginning, they started as schools that were fostered by religious institutions. However, in some instances, they were founded to further a particular branch of secular learning. For example, the University of Bologna in Italy was founded to teach the law. In the thirteenth century, the University of Naples (1224) and the University of Padua (1238) were founded by Frederick II. The University of Paris became an international stronghold where scholars came from many lands to study theology and other subjects. By the fourteenth century, the great German universities emerged—Vienna (1365), Heidelberg (1386), Cologne (1388). Of course, Oxford (1167) and Cambridge (1209) had been founded earlier. These became the centers of science (including astrology and alchemy), law, philosophy, and theology.

## St. Thomas Aquinas (*ca.* 1225–1274)

St. Thomas was born of an aristocratic family in a castle midway between Naples and Rome. He attended the University of Naples, and then joined the Dominican Order, much to the consternation of his family. He was abducted by members of his family and brought back to the family castle as a prisoner. After he regained his liberty, he again put on the habit of the Dominicans and went to Paris to study under the great Albertus Magnus.

In about 1265 he began his greatest work, *Summa Theologica*,[3] in which he placed his psychology in an unusual section, between a discussion of the six days of creation and a study of the original innocence of humankind.[4]

The psychology of St. Thomas transforms the ideas presented in Aristotle's *De Anima*. Even today Thomistic psychology is merely a modern recapitulation of St. Thomas' writings on Aristotle.[5] The aim of St. Thomas was to assimilate Aristotle's pagan and naturalistic ideas within the framework of Christian doctrine. St. Thomas described the human being as a highly specialized animal who moved, sensed, reasoned, and remembered, but who, unlike Aristotle's conception of humans, possessed a spirit.

It must be remembered that St. Thomas was primarily a theologian, so he was able to take Aristotle's naturalistic *psyche* or function and inject into it the soul in the Christian form. This was a distinctive event in the evolution of psychology. For us, the Christianized *De Anima* has never ceased to exert its influence, even in the twentieth century. What Aristotle considered reason, a function of a reasoning body, became the Christian soul for St. Thomas. The psyche was no longer a form of the body. The human being now consisted of a

---

[3]St. Thomas, *Summa Theologica*, Vols. I and II, A. C. Pegis, ed. (New York: Random House, 1944–1945).

[4]R. I. Watson, *op. cit.*

[5]R. E. Brennan, *Thomistic Psychology* (New York: The Macmillan Co., 1941).

body and a soul and, therefore, was a double being consisting of two separate entities. This kind of soul was found only in humans, who alone stood at the fringe of two universes, the world of matter and the world of the spirit. Humans were akin to the animals and neighbors to the angels. Because of its lack of matter, the soul was entirely simple. It was not made up of parts like a corporal substance, such as a body. It had no extension and no external contacts with the body. For St. Thomas, the soul's ultimate aim was to understand God and humankind's relation to God.

Many acts of the soul, however, had to be carried on by means of the body or a body part. For example, sensation involved both body parts, like the eye and the ear, and the soul. On the other hand, the ability to carry on such powers as willing and understanding was performed without the composition of the body, hence these functions were exclusively those of the soul. As a theologian, St. Thomas had to accept the universality of the soul.

What implications does St. Thomas' psychology have for us? In his writings we had the absolute inversion of Aristotle's naturalism as it was expressed in *De Anima;* we also had the full development of a dualistic psychology (mind and body) that is still prevalent today. What modern psychology has done in so many instances has been to treat the brain as the surrogate of the soul. Nevertheless, with the brain as the seat of the mind or soul, dualism is just as inevitable. From another viewpoint, we are all taught that each of us carries an internal world of private experiences, unique and known only to the beholder. There is the world of private experiences and the world of natural observations. Aristotle had simply treated the problem as *one* real organism interacting with a real object, but St. Thomas added the spirit. As a result of St. Thomas' writings, the mind-body problem was fully born and remains with us to the present.

It should be clearly understood that St. Thomas was trying to reconcile Aristotle's psychology with church dogma. Thus, the major shift was to take Aristotle's rational "soul" or thinking function (which was a direct function of the living organism) and make it immaterial and immortal.

St. Thomas adapted Aristotle's four functions or psyches to the spirit, so that they could be reconciled with the theology of the Christian church, as follows:

1. Aristotle's reasoning or rational function became the spirit or soul, completely separate from the body. This was the eternal and everlasting soul of the human being, the soul of theology. It contained both active and passive knowledge of the universe.

2. The locomotive soul sought good and avoided pain, resisted barriers and overcame obstacles.

3. The sensing or perceiving soul reacted in two ways: (1) the inner sense involved imagination, memory, and estimation, and included Aristotle's common sense; and (2) the external sense included Aristotle's five senses—sight, hearing, touch, taste, and smell.

4. The vegetative soul involved nutrition, growth, and reproduction.

## The End of the Middle Ages

Historians usually consider the Middle Ages to have lasted from approximately the eleventh century to the fifteenth century. Several factors led to the end of this period and thus to the beginning of the Renaissance. These factors included the growth of cities, the rise of capitalism, and the decline of feudalism. A great depression occurred, population declined, and crime and violence increased. The death blow probably came with the Plague of 1334 through the early 1350s, which wiped out one-third of Europe's population. Finally, a schism in the church led to further disruption.

## Suggested Further Readings

Brennan, J. F., *History and Systems of Psychology.* Englewood Cliffs, New Jersey: Prentice-Hall, 1982. For a good discussion of the medieval period, see chs. 2 and 3.

Watson, R. I., *The Great Psychologists,* 4th ed. Philadelphia: J. B. Lippincott, 1978, chs. 5 and 6. A very readable discussion of Plotinus, St. Augustine, and St. Thomas, as well as other Christian influences.

# CHAPTER

# 4

# *The Mind Route*

## II. Modern Philosophical Influences

$P$sychology broke away from philosophy, in a formal sense, in the late nineteenth century, at a point when scholars who were trained in philosophy and other disciplines decided to cast aside philosophical speculations and enter the experimental laboratory to test the theories that had been proposed. Many of these theories had been prominent themes in philosophical thinking.

Of course, in the history of modern philosophy (dating back several centuries to Descartes), there were many scholars who had little or no concern for psychological issues. In this chapter, we shall deal only with those who had a direct influence on modern psychological thinking.

This chapter is divided into four basic parts, each dealing with philosophers who were primarily concerned with a particular issue. These include: (1) the mind-body problem, (2) empiricism, (3) associationism, and (4) nativism. Before dealing with these themes and the philosophers who were concerned with them, a brief statement of each may be helpful in giving some coherence and relevance to the individuals and their ideas.

1. **The mind-body problem.** In the previous chapter we presented the development of the concept of a separation of mind (or spirit) and body. Although St. Augustine and St. Thomas believed wholeheartedly in a division between the two sides of human beings, the body and the spirit, they never were really concerned with the question of how the two might be related. This concern came after the Renaissance, with the continental philosophers Descartes, Leibnitz, and Spinoza. Each proposed a different solution. Of the three, Descartes was the most interested in psy-

38

chological issues, and has sometimes been called the founder of modern psychology.

2. **Empiricism.** As a revolt against the continental philosophies mentioned above, a movement arose which has had profound impact on modern psychology. This movement was represented primarily by three British philosophers: John Locke, the Englishman; George Berkeley, the Irishman; and David Hume, the Scotsman. Their basic premise was that all knowledge came from experience. Today, this idea may not seem to be a great innovation, since we accept it almost without question. At that time, however, it represented a revolt against the notion that ideas could be inherited, as Descartes had suggested, or that they might come from some other source outside the world of reality. The empiricist movement in philosophy influenced not only many brands of psychology, but also science in general.

Today, we speak of psychology in terms of experience and behavior. For example, the study of sensation is a very important field in psychology, and many introductory textbooks devote several chapters to how we know our world. The empiricist movement was also the forerunner of an objective approach to psychology—one which stressed the importance of learning rather than heredity.

3. **Associationism.** Arising out of the British empiricist movement was another very related movement which was also primarily British and which lasted until the end of the nineteenth century. The concerns of associationism, which had been touched upon by the empiricists, were how ideas could be hooked together and how many laws of association there should be. The principal associationists were: David Hartley, who was also concerned with the underlying brain activity in association, James and John Stuart Mill, Alexander Bain, and Herbert Spencer.

The principle of association is one of the most important in modern psychology. It is involved in many twentieth-century systems and theories, in particular, structuralism (see chap. 7) and modern learning theory (see chap. 13). Such psychologists as Ivan Pavlov and Edward Thorndike (see chap. 10) depended on association as a basic explanation for learning. In fact, they are considered today as modern associationists, and we have devoted a separate chapter (see chap. 10) to them.

4. **Nativism.** The issue of nativism was a reaction against empiricism. It implied that the way we perceived certain aspects of our world was not necessarily dependent on early experience or learning. In the history of psychology, nativism was presented primarily in the writings of Immanuel Kant. Its primary implications are to be found in modern Gestalt psychology, which began as a protest against structuralism.


Bearing in mind these issues that were taken from modern philosophy, let us continue our study with the Renaissance and the rebirth of knowledge in all areas.

### The Renaissance

The Renaissance in western Europe did not occur suddenly, but evolved over several centuries. It was a slow process, beginning first in Italy and then spreading throughout the Western world. The Renaissance bridged the gap for psychology between the medieval and the modern periods. Although scholars may differ about what constituted the most important factors which led to a revival of learning of all kinds, the following events may all be considered significant:

1. The invention of the printing press in 1450, which made the mass production of books possible.

2. The invention of gunpowder in the fifteenth century, which led to the collapse of the feudal system.

3. The age of discoveries with Columbus in 1492.

4. The introduction of the Copernican theory in 1543.

5. The fall of Constantinople in 1453, constituting an end to the Byzantine Empire and a shift of more culture back to the West.

6. The Protestant Reformation, which began in 1517 when Martin Luther nailed his ninety-five theses against the sale of indulgences to the church wall at Wittenberg.

Although there were no true psychologists during that period, the following scientific discoveries established the basis for a new attitude toward the importance of science during the Renaissance and later:

1. Copernicus' establishment of the heliocentric view of the universe. (The sun, rather than the earth, was the center of our planetary system.)

2. Galileo's improvements on the telescope, which helped to confirm the Copernican theory.

3. Newton's discoveries in optics and the laws of motion.

4. Kepler's laws of planetary motion. (For example, the planets had elliptical rather than circular orbits around the sun.)

5. Gilbert's discovery of magnetic fields.

6. Harvey's discovery of the circulation of the blood.

### The Mind-Body Problem

Both philosophers and psychologists who have accepted the idea of a basic division of the human being into the mental and the physical have pondered over the problem of how the two could be related. One solution that was offered by the early theologians (see chap. 3) was that the two were separate entities of very different substances, and that no statement other than that they were in coexistence was necessary. Another solution, not yet mentioned, was proposed by John Watson in the early twentieth century (see chap. 12). His proposal was simply a denial of the existence of mind, leaving only the body to be dealt with.

## The First Solution: Descartes' Mind-Body Interactionism

René Descartes (1596–1650), born of a wealthy family in La Haye, Touraine, a French province, had sufficient income to enable him to travel and study for the major portion of his life. He was educated at a Jesuit school, the College of La Flêche, and spent some time studying in Paris and Rome. Although he suffered from poor health, he entered the army of the Prince of Orange (Holland) in 1619. Twenty years of his life were spent in Amsterdam. In 1649 he was called to Sweden on the invitation of Queen Christiana to become her tutor. During this time he wrote his most significant psychological work, *The Passions of the Soul*.[1] However, as the historians tell us,[2, 3, 4] the severe northern winters and the demands of the Queen to rise at 5:00 A.M. for her early lessons were more than Descartes could bear, and he died of pneumonia in February 1650.

Today, we would call Descartes a Renaissance man because he was scholarly in many fields. He was a scientist, a philosopher, a mathematician, and a psychologist. He was, indeed, a gentleman-intellectual.

In considering Descartes' solution to the mind-body problem, we must first see how he planned the body functions.

***Descartes' Materialism.*** As a widely read scholar, Descartes was acquainted with the physiology of the time. He knew about the action of the muscles, nerves, and other biological structures. He knew that the muscles operated in opposing pairs, that the nerves were necessary for sensation and movement, and he was aware of Harvey's discovery of the circulation of the blood.

He compared the operation of the human body to a machine. In fact, he felt that animals were only machines with reflexes, instincts, and other automatic actions, and nothing more. He presumed the nerves were hollow tubes which contained the *animal spirits.* These, he considered to be gaseous substances derived from the blood by a process of distillation. He thought of the animal spirits as material substances which could move very quickly, like sparks shooting off from a flame.

[1]René Descartes, *The Passions of the Soul,* trans. G. T. R. Ross in *The Philosophical Works of Descartes,* Vol. 1 (Cambridge: Cambridge University Press, 1931).

[2]E. G. Boring, *A History of Experimental Psychology,* rev. ed. (New York: Appleton-Century, 1950).

[3]G. Murphy, *An Historical Introduction to Modern Psychology,* rev. ed. (New York: Harcourt, Brace, 1949).

[4]R. I. Watson, *The Great Psychologists,* 4th ed. (Philadelphia: J. B. Lippincott, 1978).

It is said[5] that Descartes originated his idea of the action of the nervous system from observing how fountains worked in the gardens of the great palaces. He likened the flow of water to the flow of animal spirits. These royal fountains were so arranged that they performed certain movements when someone stepped on their hidden pedals. A fountain in the form of a sea monster would squirt water, or Neptune would wave his trident to a passer-by.

**Descartes' Dualism and His Solution.** Many of the automatic actions of the human body operated in a purely mechanical way. The beating of the heart, respiration, and even walking seemed to be purely automatic actions of the body-machine. However, unlike the animals, the human being was endowed with a soul. The relation of the soul to the body was not the same as that described by St. Thomas or St. Augustine. Somehow, Descartes wanted to establish a direct connection between the body and the soul. Although they were connected in some way, they were still of different substances—the soul was unextended matter and the body was extended matter. In some activities, such as sensing and perceiving, both were operating.

How, then, did the interaction take place? Since body and soul were connected in some way, where was the point of connection? Descartes looked into the brain and the organs related to it. He observed that we have two eyes, two ears, and a brain divided into two hemispheres. However, there was only one little organ in the middle of the brain that had no duplicate: the pineal gland. This, then became the point of connection or interaction. Let us take sensation as an example to see how the operation worked. The images from the two eyes set up action in the animal spirits which converged on the pineal gland, making an impression on it. On the mirror of the soul or mind we would sense the impression.

Other activities operated in the reverse order. Suppose the soul desired to remember. It could activate the little gland which, in turn, could set in motion the animal spirits in the pores of the brain to discover traces left by the object when it was previously encountered. The relationship between body and soul can best be described in Descartes' own words from the *Passions of the Soul.*[6]

> Thus when the soul desires to recollect something, this desire causes the gland, by inclining successively to different sides, to thrust the spirits towards different parts of the brain until it comes across the part where the traces left there by the object which we wish to recollect are found.

The solution to the mind-body problem was that of interactionism.

**Significance of Descartes.** Although Descartes' knowledge of anatomy and physiology was primitive by our standards, at least to some degree, he thought of the human being as a living, behaving organism. Descartes could not, of

---

[5]*Ibid.*
[6]René Descartes, *op. cit.*, article 42.

course, cast off a spiritual soul, but he did attempt to bring it into some contact with the body. His psychophysical interactionism served as a model for several modern psychological schools—functionalism and psychoanalysis to name only two. With these systems interactionism was much more sophisticated, but it existed nevertheless (see chaps. 9 and 17).

## The Second Solution: Leibnitz and Parallelism

Gottfried Leibnitz (1646–1716) did not have a great deal to tell us psychologically, but what he offered us had considerable significance. His psychology was to be found in the theory of the *monad*.[7] A monad was a point of force, an element of all being, which was indestructible and immutable. Monads did not affect each other, hence there was *no interaction*. The differences which existed between monads lay in the degree to which they pictured or contained the apperception of other monads. God was the supreme monad, and the only one who could experience all the others' existence. A human individual, for example, was made up of many monads.

In his doctrine of apperception, Leibnitz wrote that individual monads had certain degrees of consciousness. By "degrees of consciousness," he meant the clarity with which a monad could reflect things in their totality. Since there were all degrees of consciousness, the poorer monads could be said to be unconscious, although they did possess action which might be so low as to be imperceptible. He called those with the low grades of awareness the *petites perceptions* (little perceptions).

Since monads did not interact, each was self-contained. What might appear to be an interaction was mere coincidence. Consequently, the activity of the monads was parallel. Spirit or mind monads could be parallel to body monads. To illustrate his view of parallelism, Leibnitz gave us the example of two clocks so constructed and set that they absolutely agreed in every respect. They ran parallel to each other, but never interacted. There was a *pre-established harmony* set up by God. This meant that the destination of all the monads was predetermined. Another way of illustrating the point was to consider a person striking a bell. The mind heard the bell. This was all one great coincidence and was part of God's pre-established harmony. The coincidences of all the careers of all the monads was part of God's order.

***Significance of Leibnitz.*** Two aspects of Leibnitz' theory have implications for modern psychology. The first is the degrees of consciousness or awareness that the monads contained. It was not Freud who created the idea of the unconscious (as some think) but rather Leibnitz whose ideas foretold it. Freud (see chap. 17), Jung (see chap. 18), and many of the psychoanalysts of today consider the degrees of consciousness and unconsciousness of great significance. For

---

[7]B. A. G. Fuller, *A History of Philosophy* (New York: Henry Holt, 1938).

Freud, the unconscious was the most important part of the mind. It was the seat of the instincts and ideas repressed from consciousness. Freud considered degrees of unconsciousness, but it remained for Jung who thought more specifically in degrees of unconsciousness to elaborate the concept. Jung proposed a division into a personal unconscious, that was particular to each one of us, and a collective or racial unconscious, that was shared by all humankind. For both Freud and Jung then, the mind consisted of degrees, from consciousness to the deepest unconsciousness.

The second of Leibnitz' theories that has implications for modern psychology is that of parallelism. In the concept of *psychophysical parallelism* we had two separate entities—mind and body—operating independently, but completely correlated with each other. The structuralism of Wundt and Titchener in the late nineteenth and early twentieth centuries, as well as Gestalt psychology, reflected this kind of attempt at a solution (see chaps. 6–7). These schools saw the mind and body as two separate entities which operated parallel to each other.

## The Third Solution: Double-Aspectism and Spinoza

According to Benedict Spinoza (1632–1677), the human being was but an aspect of God or nature, and mind and body could not be separated from each other. Mind and body simply became different aspects of the same substance. Spinoza identified the common substance, which presented itself under the twofold aspect, with God. Mental states did not affect bodily processes, nor did physical states produce changes in the mental, since they were simply different aspects of the same substance. This kind of mind-body relationship was called *psychophysical double-aspectism*. Take an apple and slice it down the middle and from side to side. What appears might look different from each position, but it is still the same apple. Perhaps, a more modern analogy would be to substitute a human brain, and cut it horizontally and vertically. What appears looks very different from each angle, but again it is the same brain. Thus, to Spinoza, soul or spirit was simply nature seen from one side. Matter was seen from a different angle.

These three solutions, *psychophysical interactionism, parallelism,* and *double-aspectism* have permeated the history of philosophy, as well as of more contemporary psychology. The earlier theorists, such as the structuralists (parallelism) and functionalists (interactionism), made their attitudes on the relationships fairly explicit. In more contemporary theories, the relationships must be inferred. However, when we come to these later theorists, we shall attempt to show how they have handled the problem.

***Significance of Spinoza.*** An example of double-aspectism that is more appropriate to modern psychology is the notion that mind and brain are one and the same but are simply viewed in two different ways. Their activities may be considered to be simple neurological processes or to be mental events such as thoughts. It is clear that Spinoza rejected the mind/body interaction of Descartes.

Thus, Spinoza anticipated the prevalent notion of nineteenth-century biologists as well as psychologists that the brain was simply the seat of the mind. The refusal to place the mind in some ethereal location led to its placement in the brain, a material substance.

## The Fourth Solution: Monism

Any attempt to solve the mind-body problem, as suggested in the first three solutions, can be considered to be *dualistic*. In some way the two entities, mind and body, are accepted as existing, and the solution is to be found in how they are related. There is a fourth possibility: to deny the existence of one or the other, leaving only one.

The early Greek naturalists of the cosmological period (beginning about 600 B.C.) were characteristically monists (the Greek root *monos* means "one"). For example, Thales reduced everything in the universe to water. At the height of Greek naturalism, Aristotle never separated form from matter. They were part of one entity, so in Aristotle's psychology, the various functions—vegetation, sensation, movement, and reason—were all functions of one organism. With the decline of Greek naturalism and the beginning of Christianity, a dualistic view entered into psychology, and soul (or mind) and body remained a basic distinction for over 2,000 years. With the emergence of the early behaviorism of John Watson beginning in 1913, a predominantly dualistic approach was questioned. Watson denied the existence of mind, consciousness, or mental functions. He left only a body that responded to stimuli. This same monistic approach was carried on by the later behaviorists: Edwin R. Guthrie, B. F. Skinner, and J. R. Kantor (see chap. 13). The behaviorists' solution was and is a monistic one, a complete denial of any concept of mind. Behavior is a function of a living body. Along the way, David Hume (1711–1776) is considered to be a monist, because he asserted that the only thing that existed was experience. There was no God, no mind, no body, only experience (see pp. 50–51). This has been identified as *subjective monism,* because experience as such is a private matter.

# *Empiricism*

*Empirical* means that one's facts are gathered from observation rather than from some other method, such as intuition or conjecture. The empirical attitude is basic to all science, for regardless of how much theorizing one might do, one has to depend in part on the events one observes in the world of nature. Many, but not all, psychologists today assume an empirical attitude. We gather our data from what we observe, whether it be in an informal way of watching something happen and then recording it, or through more formal experimentation under controlled laboratory conditions.

*Empiricism* began as a movement in Great Britain, and stressed the all-important idea of gaining knowledge from sensory experience. For the empiricists all knowledge came from experience, but this experience did not necessarily originate in the world of reality. What united the empiricists was their dependence on experience, rather than other things such as inherited ideas, as the source of knowledge.

As we have suggested earlier in this chapter, the empiricist movement had a profound effect on the development of later science, and especially psychology.

***Thomas Hobbes (1588–1679).*** Hobbes, like the later empiricists was British, having been born in Maimesburg, England. He is considered to be the founder of British empiricism and associationism. His views were set down in *Human Nature*[8] (1650) and *Leviathan*[9] (1651).

He was influenced by Galileo's concept of motion. Mental activity consisted of motions in the nervous system that resulted from motions in the outside world. Hobbes was a contemporary of Descartes but rejected his doctrine of the interaction between soul and body. Mental activity, for Hobbes, was merely the motion of atoms in the brain. Mental activity and motion coexisted, but Hobbes really never explained *how* they coexisted.

Hobbes introduced the concept of the association of ideas but left the details to the later empiricists and associationists. He considered associations to be "trains of thought." He distinguished two types: the first was unguided or rambling, whereas the second was orderly, as when two ideas were associated by some relationship, such as being similar in nature.

Historians generally agree that Hobbes had little influence on his successor, John Locke (see below), who was really responsible for establishing the empirical movement.

## John Locke (1632–1704)

Although Locke lived in the seventeenth century, his writings expressed more the spirit of the eighteenth century. The first of the British empiricists, Locke bridged the gap between the continental rational philosophers, such as Descartes, Leibnitz, and Spinoza, and a new attitude toward the nature of knowledge and the empirical tradition. Locke's influence on modern psychology cannot be overestimated.

John Locke was born in a small village in Somersetshire, England. Educated at Oxford, he dabbled in medicine, but never received a degree. He spent

---

[8]Thomas Hobbes, *Human Nature or Fundamental Elements of Policy* (London: Fra Boman of Oxon, 1650).

[9]Thomas Hobbes, *Leviathan.* Reprinted. (Cambridge, England: Cambridge University Press, 1904). (First published 1651.)

part of his life in politics and in minor governmental offices. When Locke was fifty-eight he wrote his main work *An Essay Concerning Human Understanding*.[10] This was revised several times, and the fourth edition appeared in 1670.

**Theory of Knowledge.** Locke had read Descartes, and in the first book of his *Essay* he attacked Descartes' theory that some ideas we have are inborn. His arguments were as follows: If ideas were innate, they should be constant in all minds, but neither the new-born nor the illiterate shared them. If innate, ideas should not show development, but they did. Finally, since ideas came from experience, they could not be inborn.

In his analysis, Locke wrote that all ideas came from experience. At birth the mind could be considered analogous to a blank sheet of paper, a *tabula rasa*. Basically, the mind was passive, and could do only two things. First, it could receive experiences from the outside world: this involved the act of sensing. Locke was actively concerned with the whole process of sensation, since it was the primary source of all knowledge. Second, the mind could *reflect upon itself*. It was basically through this process of reflection, or what we today might call introspection, that it became possible for people to engage in the process we call thinking. In stating that all knowledge came from experience, Locke was reiterating what Aristotle had said many centuries before.

When experiences came to us, they might be of two types, simple or complex. The first were very pure, and came only from sensation, like seeing the color red. Those of the more complex kind were made of up a combination of simple experiences or ideas.

Ideas as experiences might also have qualities. These qualities were *primary* and *secondary*. The primary qualities were inseparable from the object. Such qualities as movement, extension, shape, solidity, or number were of this sort. The secondary qualities, such as color, taste, and touch arose in the senses and were known apart from the object. It was through reflection that human beings gained knowledge of themselves, were able to think, made comparisons, and remembered.

The simple ideas seemed quite reliable because they seemed to correspond well with the real object. About complex ideas we were not so sure. We could get a rough approximation, but we might never know their real essence. For example, we would never be able to get at the nature of truth, which obviously was a complex idea.

Locke had no doubt about the existence of a real physical world, although he really could not experience its substance. However, he argued that you could not experience the qualities of things without there being something behind them. We knew there was something which gave us these qualities, but that something was "I know not what." We could experience ourselves as minds, but all we knew of our minds was that they existed.

---

[10]John Locke, *An Essay Concerning Human Understanding,* A. C. Fraser, ed. (New York: Dover Press, 1959).

**Association.** In the fourth edition of the *Essay,* Locke introduced the notion of the association of ideas. He exemplified the significance of association in his illustration of the "man born blind and suddenly made to see." Such a man could not identify a cube by sight if he had only experienced it through the sense of touch. Thus, the two had to be associated together. Once we experienced some ideas, through association with other ideas, the original idea might be brought back to mind when presented with the second.

**Locke's Dualism.** For Locke, there was no doubt that minds existed, but your mind with different experiences might be quite different from mine. At this point, it should be noted that by the time Locke came along, from a historical point of view, the theological conception of mind as soul had been somewhat extracted, leaving the mind apart from the body, but without spirit. Locke believed in God; not that he knew God through his senses, but through reflection. So, there *was* a real world (something he knew not what), and there also existed individual minds which received the experiences from the real world. Basically, Locke was not concerned with physiological or body correlates of mind and body as was Descartes. He merely presumed that both mind and body existed as separate entities; how one could get from one to the other did not seem to be an important issue.

**Locke's Significance.** Locke was concerned with what he could learn from his senses. He believed in a world of nature as the ultimate source of knowledge. This was a basic presupposition of all science, namely, that we were dealing with natural events. Locke believed in mind as separate from body, but this was part of a tradition which he never bothered to doubt. There were no inborn ideas, and the fact that God existed was accepted, but God was not the source of knowledge. The fact of a basic reality as the source of all knowledge was the significant point. Finally, Locke's introduction of the principle of association served as a basic principle of connection, which was held by many theories of psychology up to the present time.

## George Berkeley (1685–1753)

The second of the British empiricists was an Irishman who was educated at Trinity College, Dublin. A deeply religious man, Berkeley was ordained in the Anglican Church at the age of 24. His two principal psychological works are *An Essay Towards a New Theory of Vision,*[11] written in 1709, and *A Treatise Concerning the Principles of Human Knowledge,*[12] written a year later. Both were written when he was a relatively young man. In 1722 he attempted to found a

---

[11]George Berkeley, *An Essay Towards a New Theory of Vision,* in A. A. Luce and T. E. Jessop, eds., *The Works of George Berkeley,* Vol. 1 (London: Nelson, 1948).

[12]George Berkeley, *A Treatise Concerning the Principles of Human Knowledge,* in A. A. Luce and T. E. Jessop, eds., *The Works of George Berkeley,* Vol. II (London: Nelson, 1949).

college in Bermuda, but failed. For nearly three years he settled in the United States at Newport, Rhode Island. While there, he met Jonathan Edwards, the American theologian from Massachusetts who promoted a strict form of Calvinism in the area. For the last eighteen years of his life he became Bishop of Cloyne, County Cork, Ireland. As a result of the eventual "westward-ho" movement in the United States, a town in California was named after him. This presumably resulted from a poem he wrote on the theme, "Westward the course of an empire takes its way."

In his *Essay Towards a New Theory of Vision,* Berkeley introduced the question of how it was possible for us to perceive visually in three dimensions when, in actuality, our eyes experienced only two dimensions. The previous explanations which he referred to as the "angle argument" considered the angles of light which came from the object seen. However, since we could not actually *see* the angles, how was this any explanation at all for perceiving distance or the third dimension? He suggested that we judged the depth or distance of objects by *associating* the character of that distance. The size and shape of objects were associated by sight and by touch. Here, he included movement in space, for example, how far we could reach or could walk to the object. This became associated with its size. In Berkeley's writings we had an extension of the association previously introduced by Locke. However, Berkeley's association was more specific because it tied the two together by contiguity in space and time.

In his *Treatise Concerning the Principles of Human Knowledge,* Berkeley assumed a good deal of what Locke had already said. However, he took a new approach to the problem of how we got knowledge. Locke had said there was a real object and a sensation received in the mind from that object. As to the primary qualities of the object, Locke had said they existed in the object, but he could never really know the nature of that object. For Berkeley, all he knew was what he perceived, in other words his experiences. "Esse est percepi." Being is perceiving. There were no primary qualities, only secondary ones.

Reality was not the real world of nature, but consisted of a great many human minds. All we really knew of the real physical world was the impressions we had. In other words, we knew only our experiences. Berkeley presumed that we perceived nothing but our own experiences. By the existence of a thing, all we could say was that it was perceived. So we had individual minds and the experiences they perceived, nothing more. If this were so, where did we get our experiences from, if not the real world of objects? Ultimately, the ideas came from God. This belief that all of reality was merely minds and their experiences came to be known as *subjective idealism.* We had minds and their experiences and God and God's experiences. Here, our dualism had shifted to a higher level—minds and their experiences and God and God's experiences. If we all experienced the same room, God had given us all the same ideas.

For Locke, mind was a substance which received ideas from the real world. For Berkeley, anything outside the experiences in our minds must be within the mind of God.

***Significance of Berkeley.*** Berkeley was an empiricist in the sense that he said we know nothing more than our experiences. The problem was to find out where the experiences came from. Since he could not know the objects or the real world, they had to come from somewhere, and God seemed to be the answer. Berkeley's attention to association was a real step forward in explaining the perception of depth and distance or the third dimension by means of association.

## David Hume (1711–1776)

The third British empiricist was a Scotsman who was born in Edinburgh. He was, for the most part, self-educated. He never achieved a university professorship mainly because of his rather unorthodox religious convictions, which we shall soon discuss.

One of his earliest works, *A Treatise on Human Nature*[13] is probably of greatest concern to us. As with Berkeley, it is difficult to say that Hume really had a psychology as such, but his writings have some marked implications.

Locke had accepted objects, experiences, and the minds that received them. Berkeley had accepted God, minds, and experiences. For Hume, there were only experiences. A quotation from Hume's *Treatise* will make the point clear.[14]

> Mind is nothing but a heap or collection of different perceptions, unified together by certain relations and suppos'd tho' falsely to be endowed with a perfect simplicity and identity.

All we knew was that we had impressions (sensations) and ideas. We believed there was a real object only because our impressions tended to fit together. You could not prove a table existed in your salon after you had left the room.

Mind did not exist apart from impressions. We had no way of knowing that anything existed apart from experiences. All Hume found was a flowing stream of impressions and ideas.

Like his predecessors, Hume was concerned with association. Locke and Berkeley had suggested two laws of association, contiguity (togetherness) and similarity. Hume suggested three: resemblance (similarity), contiguity (togetherness in space and time), and cause and effect. To use his own examples, a picture led our thoughts to the original thing (similarity); on the mention of an apartment, one might mention other apartments (contiguity); and we associated a wound with the pain that follows it (causality).

But what about causality? Was there any necessary connection between any two events? One might have observed the sun to rise and set any number of

---

[13]David Hume, *A Treatise on Human Nature*, E. A. Selby-Briggs, ed. (Oxford: Clarendon Press, 1896).

[14]*Ibid.,* book 1, part 4, sec. 2.

times, but, said Hume, we had no way of knowing or being sure that it would rise again. We only got the idea because of these associations. So, what Hume did was to reduce cause and effect ultimately to contiguity; one thing followed another.

For Hume there was no evidence from experiences that God existed. Again, all we knew was our impressions and ideas. As far as minds or separate entities existing, we got that idea because of the assumption in filling in the gaps where no impressions were known. We got the idea that we existed as a self only because a group of impressions of the body came together.

**_Implications of Hume._** Hume has been considered the supreme skeptic by most philosophers. However, if one looks at Hume's theories from the viewpoint of psychology today, we can say he made a positive step in doing away with the mind, and consequently the dualism that existed from Locke and Berkeley. Since he had denied mind or soul, we had the first psychology without a mind as separate from the body since the time of the ancient Greeks.

On the other hand, Hume was completely subjective, as was Berkeley. In denying reality he made a revolutionary change that stressed the purely mental as opposed to the physical. In this sense, Berkeley and Hume took a step backwards.

## Associationism

The movement we refer to as associationism was a direct outgrowth of empiricism. Much of what the empiricists had said was taken for granted by the associationists. Locke, Berkeley, and Hume had all talked about the association of ideas. The associationists merely extended the point further. They argued about how many laws of association there should be, and, in the case of David Hartley, the first associationist that we consider, the underlying physiological explanations in the brain.

As associationism was gaining momentum, a minor revolt arose among a group of scholars in Scotland, which became known as the _Scottish School._ This deviation from the principles of association was an interesting sidelight in the history of psychology, and should not be ignored.

In psychology today, we do not speak so much of the association of _ideas,_ as of the association of stimuli and responses or the association of responses and rewards and punishments.

In a later chapter on modern associationism, we shall discuss some individuals who took the ideas of the older associationists and interpreted them in contemporary terms. For these people, association was a basic principle of learning. Such psychologists as Pavlov, Thorndike, and Guthrie accepted it as one of the most basic principles of their psychology.

### David Hartley (1705–1757)

A contemporary of Hume, Hartley has often been called the founder of British associationism. Others who followed him were James Mill and his son, John Stuart Mill, Alexander Bain, and Herbert Spencer. The latter two brought association psychology up to the twentieth century. We shall follow this thread in the history of psychology, even though we shall have to backtrack chronologically to include some other contributors, mainly from Germany.

Hartley's psychology was contained in his *Observations of Man,*[15] published in 1749.

Hartley was a physician and, unlike Locke, Berkeley, and Hume, he expressed a deep concern for the mind-body relationship. He was impressed by Newton's earlier observations that all physical things were forms of motion. Beginning with Newton's studies of motion and, in particular, the law of the pendulum, Hartley carried this idea of motion into the mental world.

When light struck the eye, the motion of particles or vibrations was changed from ether waves into vibrations in the nerves and the brain. Hartley called these smaller vibrations which occurred in the nervous system *vibratiuncles.* As long as the light continued to strike the eye, these little vibrations would continue to flow. When the light was cut off, the vibrations became weaker in strength. Memories then were the reactivation of the original vibrations.

Hartley presumed only one law of association, that of contiguity, and he proceeded to explain how this worked in the brain. When two sensations reached the brain, either together or in succession, they would set up vibrations in such a way that they became connected. Later, when one idea reactivated a vibration, the other vibration would also occur.

The parts of the brain were so connected that if a first stimulus was presented causing vibrations in a particular region, the arousal of the second brain region could occur without the need of the second stimulus. If a series or association such as *A, B, C, D,* occurred in succession, they left a trace of vibrations *a, b, c, d.* The reoccurrence of *A,* then would set off *b, c,* and *d* vibrations.

***Hartley's Significance.*** Hartley can be considered as one of the first physiological psychologists, although Descartes had tried to give some physiological explanation (although primitive) of how the nervous system worked in order to explain his mind-body interaction. Hartley attempted to relate the mental to the physical (ideas and vibrations), and to give a physiological explanation for the mental idea or image in terms of vibratory motions in the brain. Despite his naturalistic attempts at explaining the mental (experience in mind) in physiological terms, he was still a dualist. Psychophysical parallelism was the answer. What consisted of ideas and images on the mental side, were the correlated vibrations in the brain on the physical side.

---

[15]David Hartley, *Observations on Man, His Fame, His Duty, and His Expectations,* 4th ed. (London: Johnson, 1801).

## The Scottish School

For the moment we must interrupt our exposition of the British association movement to discuss another movement which arose in protest. The main protagonists were all teachers at Scottish universities who were solid Presbyterians. The important figures were Thomas Reid (1710–1796), Douglas Stewart (1753–1828), and Thomas Brown (1778–1820). In fact, it was Thomas Brown who attempted to bring the movement back to the stream of associationism, although he substituted the term "suggestion" for association.

Thomas Reid was the first of these scholars to object to the association laws of Hume. In his book *Essays on the Intellectual Powers of Man*[16] he stated that the mind *did* know more than its own processes. He proposed what today we would call a "faculty psychology," in which the mind was an organized entity with powers to perform various psychological activities. He was not the first to propose such a psychology, if we recall St. Augustine (p. 32). In any event, these faculties might include self-preservation, imitation, desire, self-esteem, pity, gratitude, duty, and imagination. There were also six intellectual powers: perception, judgment, memory, conception, moral taste, and will.

He not only objected to Hume's laws of association but also to Hume's idea that he doubted the existence of real objects. Reid said, "All mankind could not be wrong and go against the wisdom of the ages." We did experience sensations. There was no doubt, he told us, that we received experiences from real objects, and that God's wisdom added the plusses to turn sensation into human wisdom of the external world.

In Reid's psychology, we had, in a sense, a regression to medieval dogma. The faculty was a capacity of the soul. The fact that human beings were born with innate capacities is still a common concept today in such doctrines as the inheritance of intelligence, musical ability, or mechanical aptitude. On the other hand, he reinstituted the concept of a "real world," a fact that Hume had denied.

***Implications of Reid.*** Reid's psychology can be found not only in the Act psychology of Brentano (see chap. 6) but also in Wundt's psychology of content. In reacting to the empiricists' notion of the combination of experiences into ideas, Reid appealed to common sense. Perceptions are seen and known directly. He also anticipated two characteristics of Gestalt psychology (see chap. 14). First of all, experience is not a complex of simple sensations, but we are endowed with certain innate functions or principles of the mind that allow us to know the world. So in Reid we have not only a rejection of the empiricism proposed by Locke, Berkeley, and Hume, but also an anticipation of the later psychology of the Gestaltists—the idea that perceptions come to us as "wholes" not to be broken up into parts.

---

[16]Thomas Reid, *Essays on the Intellectual Powers of Man,* W. Hamilton, ed. (Edinburgh: Malcachian, Stewart, 1849).

When we come to Thomas Brown, a disciple of Stewart, we have an attempt to bring the Scottish psychology back to the association movement. In Brown's *Philosophy of the Human Mind*,[17] he still accepted the idea of a unitary soul or mind, but he needed some principle to explain how the mind functioned. Not daring to use the term "association," he substituted instead "suggestion," so as not to be thought of as reverting to the associationists and all they represented.

The primary laws of suggestion were contiguity, resemblance (similarity), and contrast. If one will recall Aristotle (pp. 24–27), these were the same laws he stated in *De Anima*. There were also secondary laws of suggestion. These could allow for variations such as duration (length of the original sensation), liveliness, frequency of presentation, recency, degrees of coexistence with other suggestions, and constitutional differences of mind or temperament.

However, we should remember that Brown did not revert completely and become another associationist. Mental life was not merely the accumulation of sensory experiences. To solve the objection of the existence of real things as proposed by Berkeley and Hume, Brown took the sensations from the object and added the muscle sense (today called kinesthetic or proprioceptive). Our belief in the existence of real objects was due to our feelings of muscular excitation. For example, we had the sensation of the rose from sight and smell. As soon as we discovered that the sensed rose required muscular effort to move it, the rose began to suggest real resistance. By such suggestion, the rose in our perception was turned into the concept of the real object. This really, then, turned out to be an extension of the concept of associationism.

## Back to Associationism: The Mills

James Mill (1773–1836) and his son John Stuart Mill (1806–1873) were primarily concerned with history and political theory, not psychology. They became intimately involved in a movement in nineteenth-century British philosophy called utilitarianism. They believed that by the usefulness of self, political, and legal action we could gain pleasure and avoid pain.

In his book, *An Analysis of the Phenomenon of the Human Mind*,[18] James Mill described his rather simple-minded associationism. The mind was made up of sensations and ideas. Ideas were derived from sensations. They were the primary states of consciousness. What James Mill meant by idea, we today would call image, although that term had not come into common use then. Perception was the process whereby a number of sensory bits were put together. For Mill, like Hartley, there was only one law of association—contiguity. However, he was very careful to point out that contiguity worked in two ways—associations could occur successively and simultaneously.

---

[17]Thomas Brown, *Lectures on the Philosophy of the Human Mind* (Edinburgh: Tait, 1820).
[18]James Mill, *An Analysis of the Phenomenon of the Human Mind* (London: Longmans and Dyer, 1829).

The idea we had of a real object was an addition of the original components put together by association. The idea of a window was made up of the ideas of glass, wood, and whatever else made up a window. The principle became known as "mental mechanics."

His son, John Stuart Mill, turned out to be a more important person in the history of human thought than his father. According to his writings and biographical references,[19] he was a child prodigy who learned Greek at the age of three and read Plato in the original at eight years. He had, for the most part, been privately taught by his father.

What we learn about his psychology is found in his *Logic* and in the edited and annotated edition of his father's book, *An Analysis of the Phenomenon of the Human Mind.* He accepted sensations and ideas as the basic elements of the mind. Unlike his father who believed the mind was passive, he concluded it to be active, that is, it could do more than accept the elements reflected upon it.

On the subject of association, he agreed with his father on contiguity, but added similarity and intensity.

Instead of accepting an additive process in combining the elements of sensation, he thought that the sensory elements could fuse so that what we had was a kind of "mental chemistry" where a new entity was not equivalent to the sum of its parts. Thus, the separate elements in the new fusion could no longer be distinguished. The loss of identity of the original elements was like the formation of a new combination in chemistry. Therefore, when a sensation was rearoused, the other parts of the combination would also be recovered.

## Alexander Bain (1818–1903)

Bain was a Scotsman who spent his whole life in Aberdeen. His principal works which concern us in psychology were *The Senses and the Intellect* (1855)[20] and *The Emotions and the Will* (1859).[21] These can be considered the first books on psychology as such. Prior to Bain, what we had gleaned as psychological implications had been from philosophical and theological treatises (except for Aristotle). Along with Herbert Spencer, Bain brought the whole British association movement to a conclusion. In *The Senses and the Intellect,* Bain stated that sensations and feelings could come together in close succession in such a way that when one of them was later brought to mind, the others were also likely to reoccur. This was much the same idea as stated by Hartley. For Bain, the solution to the mind-body problem was simply that of parallelism. Of course, Bain was not the first to take such a parallelist position, as we may recall from the works of Leibnitz and Hartley several centuries earlier.

Boring[22] has suggested that Bain was the first modern physiological psychologist. Bain actually brought very little that was new to psychology, except

---

[19]R. I. Watson, *op. cit.*
[20]Alexander Bain, *The Senses and the Intellect* (London: Parker, 1855).
[21]Alexander Bain, *The Emotions and the Will* (London: Parker, 1859).
[22]E. Boring, *op. cit.*

for his attempts at more modern physiological explanations as the correlates of mental events. For example, he described the sense organs and how they worked, he wrote of the reflex arc, and recounted what was known of how the brain worked. To Aristotle's five senses, he added the "organic" which was involved in hunger, thirst, or other internal conditions. He described how the muscles worked in opposing pairs. Thus, his explanations of physiology were more sophisticated than those of either Hartley or Descartes.

Bain, then, in one sense brought associationism to a conclusion. On the purely descriptive side, there was nothing to be added. On the other hand, he stood at the new threshold of psychology which stressed association in a more experimental context, as exemplified in the works of Pavlov and Thorndike (see chap. 10), Wundt (see chap. 6), and Titchener (see chap. 7).

## Herbert Spencer (1820–1903)

In 1870 Spencer wrote *Principles of Psychology*[23] in which he considered association to be the significant binding principle of psychology. What was new thus far was his theory of *evolutionary association*. He antedated Darwin, having started writing about evolution in 1850.

According to Spencer's theory, everything in the beginning of the universe was related to everything else in an expanding totality. Any kind of development, whether it referred to living or nonliving matter, involved a process of differentiation—that is, the emergence of recognizable and distinct parts. As humans evolved, their nervous systems became more complex and correspondingly allowed for the possibility of their being able to comprehend more complex experiences on the mental side. Along with greater differentiation, there was also an integrating principle which brought things back together. This was the principle of association, with which more and more complex types of experiences could be integrated.

Earlier in the nineteenth century, Jean-Baptiste Lamarck, the French naturalist, had proposed an evolutionary theory in which acquired characteristics could be passed on from one generation to another. Spencer applied this notion to associations, and this was probably the most novel aspect of his theory. He believed that when particular associations occurred often enough in an individual, they could be passed on to one's offspring. These associations would take on the form of instincts.

Spencer had developed his evolutionary doctrine in the years prior to the publication in 1859 of Darwin's theory of evolution as presented in *The Origin of Species*.[24] When Darwin's work appeared, Spencer jumped on the band wagon, and Darwin accepted him, calling him "our philosopher."[25]

---

[23]Herbert Spencer, *Principles of Psychology,* 2nd ed. (London: Williams and Norgate, 1870–1872).
[24]Charles Darwin, *The Origin of Species by Means of Natural Selection,* 6th ed. (New York: Appleton-Century, 1897).
[25]R. I. Watson, *op. cit.*

After Spencer and Bain, British associationism came to an end. In a sense, it could go no further. It remained for succeeding experimental psychologists to take over the basic principle.

---

## Nativism

To continue with the final major theme from the history of philosophy, we must backtrack to eighteenth-century Germany. In the beginning of this chapter, we spoke of nativism as a reaction to empiricism. We must now consider Immanuel Kant and his impact on modern psychology.

### Immanuel Kant (1724–1804)

Anyone who is familiar with the history of philosophical thought might wonder why the name of Kant should even be mentioned in this book. Although he was one of the greatest philosophers of all time, Kant was not a psychologist. In fact, he pointed out in his *Anthropology*[26] that psychology could never be a science; yet Kant fostered a scientific attitude.

In some ways, Kant set psychology back with his insistence on subjectivism. The mind could not be reduced to a brain or to bodily processes. It was impossible to use deductive methods to demonstrate the reality of the mind. Of course, this attitude was not new, since we have already encountered it with the Church Fathers.

By insisting on the unity of perception, however, Kant was attacking the associationism of the British empiricists as hard as he could. To Kant, experience was a unitary phenomenon. The presupposition that a perception could not be broken down into its divisible parts became the heart of the Gestalt psychology of the twentieth century. Here, then, was a first influence of Kant on modern psychology.

A second influence was to be found in his theory of *nativism*. By this, he meant that our tendency to perceive space and time as such was not entirely dependent on experience, but was native or inborn. The Gestalt psychology of the early twentieth century had also accepted this notion in a modified form when they spoke of the "primitive organization of experience." This was interpreted to mean that we tended to perceive things in natural ways which did not depend on learning. This notion was quite distinct from that of the British empiricists. Putting it another way, nativism implied that human beings had inherent or "given" ways of knowing things which were not dependent on experience.

---

[26]Immanuel Kant, *Anthropology,* in E. Cassirer, ed., *Immanuel Kant's Werke,* Vol. VIII (Berlin: B. Cassirer, 1922).

Other more recent implications of nativism are to be found in the studies of the animal ethologists and in studies of perception in human infants. We made reference to these in the section on basic issues in chapter 1. The ethologists have placed great emphasis on inborn or "innate" ways that animals perceive their environments. In the cases of human infants, there is evidence to indicate that they might have native depth perception by the time they are able to crawl. In these instances, infants would tend to avoid crawling over "visual cliffs," even though their mothers might be attracting them from the other side.

There is one final figure in the history of philosophy who, although he does not seem to fit into any of the four basic themes or issues mentioned in this chapter, had significant influence. He is Johann Herbart. He accepted some of Kant's ideas; yet he was not a nativist. However, since, like Kant, he was German, and since he also succeeded Kant in filling the university chair at Königsberg, we shall place him in this final section.

## Johann Herbart (1776–1841)

Herbart presumed to build a psychology based on experience, metaphysics, and mathematics. He believed that psychology could not be experimental but that it could be mathematical. Although Herbart agreed with Kant's notion of a unitary mind or soul, he did allow that the mind could be a composite of smaller units. He drew from Leibnitz the idea that there could be degrees of consciousness and unconsciousness. The mind could be thought of as an apperceptive mass, made up of psychic states which could cross the threshold of consciousness and enter the apperceptive mass. In the unconscious, ideas existed in a sort of static state. These psychic states or ideas had forces of various intensities. If the force were strong enough, they could overcome the counter forces already in the apperceptive mass and enter into consciousness. Herbart labelled this interaction of psychic forces in and out of consciousness "psychic dynamics."

We mentioned earlier that Herbart believed psychology could be mathematical. He calculated conditions which could determine what could and could not enter consciousness. First, there were the effects of opposing ideas on each other. One had to calculate the amount of one force that was going to oppose another force. Second, it was possible for two ideas to combine and suppress the ideas that were weaker.

The amount of assistance provided by one idea to another, which would enable it to get back into consciousness, could also be calculated. Herbart believed all this could be worked out mathematically.

***Implications of Herbart.*** Although he was committed to the doctrine of a soul, which he had borrowed from Kant, Herbart was interested in the idea of scientific psychology. His calculations were nothing more than fictions—purely hypothetical—nevertheless, he brought to psychology the idea that psychology could be quantified. He proposed that somehow his "psychic dynamics" (as mental phenomena) could be measured. The whole idea of measurement and quantification was an important basis for modern experimental psychology.

Other influences of Herbart will be understood later in the writings of Freud (see chap. 17) and Wundt (see chap. 6). It is clear by now that Freud did not invent the concept of the unconscious. However, Freud's notion of opposing forces between consciousness and unconsciousness was very important to his theory. Furthermore, it is well known from biographical sources[27] that Freud was acquainted with Herbart's writings.

It is difficult, without explaining the whole psychological systems of Freud and Wundt, to explain Herbart's influence. But, among other things, Wundt accepted the concept of the apperceptive mass (p. 83). When we come to an analysis of Wundt's system, we can reflect and see how he borrowed from Herbart, as well as from the British empiricists and associationists.

## Suggested Further Readings

Dennis, W., *Readings in the History of Psychology.* New York: Appleton-Century-Crofts, 1948, chs. 4, 8, 9, 10. Readings from Descartes' *The Passions of the Soul,* Locke's *Essay Concerning Human Understanding,* Berkeley's *New Theory of Vision,* and Hartley's *Observations on Man.*

Kantor, J. R., *The Scientific Evolution of Psychology,* Vol. II. Chicago, Illinois: The Principia Press, 1969, chs. 21–27 and 29. A consideration of Renaissance influences, the continental philosophers, the mind-body problem, the British empiricists, the Scottish School, and Kant. All very scholarly and edifying to the sophisticated reader.

Klein, D., *A History of Scientific Psychology.* New York: Basic Books, 1970. A treatment of the same individuals as those mentioned above, also at a rather sophisticated level.

Murphy, G., *An Historical Introduction to Modern Psychology,* rev. ed. New York: Harcourt, Brace and Co., 1949, chs. 2–4. A fairly elementary discussion of the seventeenth, eighteenth, and early nineteenth century philosophers and their psychological influences. Many of the same individuals mentioned above are discussed.

Robinson, D. N., *An Intellectual History of Psychology,* 2nd ed. New York: Macmillan Publishing Co., 1981. Emphasis is on philosophical influences from the ancient Greeks, through the scholastic period, to modern philosophical influences.

Watson, R. I., *The Great Psychologists,* 4th ed. Philadelphia: J. B. Lippincott, 1978, chs. 7–9. Readable discussions of the individuals mentioned in Kantor and Murphy, and easier reading than Kantor.

Wolman, B. B., ed., *Historical Roots of Contemporary Psychology.* New York: Harper and Row, 1968, chs. 2, 3 and 11. Contributed essays, each by a different author, on the psychological contributions of associationism, Herbart, and Kant.

---

[27]E. Jones, *The Life and Works of Sigmund Freud,* Vol. I (New York: Basic Books, 1953–1957).

# CHAPTER

# 5

# *The Body Route*

In the previous two chapters, we pointed out certain issues or themes from philosophical sources that have had a strong impact on modern psychology. In this chapter, we shall turn to major issues involving the body. Most of these issues have come from physics and from biology in its various branches. We shall point out two basic threads or themes that, in their evolution, have affected modern psychology. They are: (1) the development of neurophysiology and (2) psychophysics as the forerunner of experimental psychology. Each of these themes has had a distinctly different influence on modern psychology. They share the fact that they involve body activity in one way or another, although, in many cases, they do not ignore the mind. Secondly, for the most part, they did not evolve from philosophical thinking.

1. The first thread—the development of neurophysiology—is a long one. It began in the eighteenth century, and continued up to the twentieth. It involved the discovery of how nerves and muscles work, various theories about how the brain functions, as well as the physiology of vision and hearing, and their related theories. In modern psychology, the implications of this theme are for sensory and physiological psychology.

2. The second theme—psychophysics—involved the first attempts at real psychological experimentation. The main figures, Weber and Fechner, were not psychologists; although later experimental psychology, particularly in the areas of sensation, owes them a great debt. Psychologists through the twentieth century have often used their methods in the measurement of sensory responses in both animals and humans. Today, the methods of psychophysics are still very much a part of experimental psychology. Historically, psychophysical techniques led to the development of a true experimental psychology.

Even when we traced the historical antecedents through the mind route, we did not completely ignore the body. In Descartes' writings (p. 42), we saw an attempt to explain his soul-body interactionism through physiology. Later, with the beginnings of British associationism, David Hartley (p. 52) explained associations in terms of brain motions or vibrations as the correlates of mental events. In the nineteenth-century writings of Spencer and Bain (pp. 55–56), the physiological basis of mental functions was given a greater sophistication.

Before we begin examining our two main themes of this chapter, we must go back to the Hellenistic or Greco-Roman period of the first century A.D. As the Roman Empire developed with all its grandeur, it was amazing that no great philosophers or scientists had emerged. Rome was concerned with the law, and with political and military matters. The principles on which the Romans had built their roads, bridges, and magnificent buildings were borrowed from what had come before.

## Galen (A.D. 131–200)

The one exception to the failure of Roman science was Galen, who became a great physician. Of course, Galen learned much from his predecessor of several centuries before, the Greek physician Hippocrates, another proponent of Greek naturalism, whom we discussed in chapter 2.

Galen was actually a Greek subject to the Roman Empire, as he was born in Asia Minor. He studied for a time at Alexandria, and at the age of thirty-two, migrated to Rome to set up a practice of medicine.[1] He became the personal physician to the emperor, Marcus Aurelius. In addition to being an excellent practitioner, Galen learned a good deal about physiology. However, in keeping with the dualism which was emerging in ancient thinking, he located the seat of the mind in the brain and believed that the brain and the nervous system were important for higher mental processes, such as thinking. He held the ancient Greek notion of the animal spirits that flowed along the nerves and were essential for movement. This was later adopted by Descartes (see pp. 41–42). One of Galen's great discoveries was a distinction between sensory and motor nerves, an excellent observation which was later lost and had to be rediscovered by Bell and Magendie in the early nineteenth century.

Galen took Hippocrates' theory of the four humors (blood, phlegm, black bile, and yellow bile) and elaborated on it. Human beings were primarily cheerful creatures (because they had a predominance of blood in their bodies). Galen developed the system of pathological types, which occurred when the humors were out of balance. These balances and imbalances of the humors accounted for individual differences in the behavior of people.[2]

---

[1] R. I. Watson, *The Great Psychologists,* 4th ed. (Philadelphia: J. B. Lippincott, 1978).
[2] *Ibid.,* p. 80.

Galen was a prolific writer and was one of the great encyclopedists of ancient times. He codified all that was known about ancient medicine, anatomy, and physiology. Much of the information was in error, but the blame should not be put on Galen. He wrote what he knew and what he believed to be true at the time.

With Galen's death, the great interest in body functions and structures declined. This interest lay dormant, only to be revived by the great artists and sculptors of the Renaissance such as Leonardo da Vinci. During the Dark and the Middle Ages which followed, medicine became so garbled with theology that medical practice was hard to distinguish from it.[3] Demonology and witchcraft entered the picture, and many physical ailments were explained as a possession of evil spirits. For example, if one had a headache, a crucifix might be placed at the appropriate point. A little sprinkling of holy water might also help.

## Paracelsus (A.D. 1490–1541)

Paracelsus lived just after the Middle Ages, practicing his medical arts in both Germany and Switzerland. During the Dark Ages and Middle Ages, medicine had been pretty much reduced to theology and bloodletting. Paracelsus was one of the first since Galen to attempt a more scientific approach to the discipline. He first became interested in the actions of minerals and the diseases of miners. Out of this grew a view, not too dissimilar to that of Plotinus (see pp. 31–32), that mankind is an extension of the universe made up of three mystic elements: salt, sulphur, and mercury. A separation of these elements caused disease. Treatment consisted of mineral baths and the administration of various minerals, because human beings were made up of all the minerals. Paracelsus' writings are also filled with religious propositions and mysteries.

Related to psychology was Paracelsus' interest in magnetism. He believed that magnetic forces from heavenly bodies could affect human behavior. This notion was not too dissimilar to that promoted several centuries later by Anton Mesmer (1734–1816). In the late eighteenth century, Mesmer introduced the concept of animal magnetism (later identified as mesmerism or hypnosis). Mesmer believed he could induce magnetic forces from the planets into human beings and thereby treat a variety of mental disorders.

By Freud's time (around 1895), hypnosis was being widely used as a psychotherapeutic technique. In his early practice, Freud used hypnosis in psychotherapy but later abandoned it in favor of free association (see chap. 17, pp. 305–306).

Paracelsus was one of the first to identify what today we call hypnotic states—although, like Mesmer, his interpretation of the condition was incorrect.

---

[3]R. W. Lundin, *Principles of Psychopathology* (Columbus, Ohio: Charles E. Merrill, 1965).

# The Development of Neurophysiology

Many modern psychologists, in their desire for respectability, have linked psychology's origins to some branch of biology. In fact, some would consider psychology merely a branch of biology, rather than an independent discipline. Whatever one's biases might be about the importance of biology, to ignore its influence would be an unfair omission.

## Marshall Hall (1790–1856)

Hall was a Scotsman and a physician. On the basis of physiological experiments, he attempted to make a distinction between voluntary and involuntary movements of the body. Imposing the dualism of the times, as explained in the previous chapters, Hall thought of movements as being either conscious or unconscious. The conscious, or voluntary, movements seemed to depend more on the higher centers of the brain (in the cerebrum), while the involuntary, or unconscious, movements were a function of the lower centers, such as the cerebellum and even the spinal cord.

Hall's distinction exists today in a separation of the simple reflex acts which can be conditioned in a manner according to Pavlov, and in the more complex conditioned activity referred to as "instrumental" or "operant" learning (see chaps. 10 and 13).

## Sir Charles Bell (1774–1842)

Another Scotsman of about the same period, Bell was a brilliant physiologist. He rediscovered the distinction between sensory and motor nerves that had been made earlier by Galen but was lost for centuries. During the Middle Ages, dissection, of the human body in particular, was frowned upon by the church. The distinction between sensory and motor nerve functions became known as Bell's Law, and was later called the Bell-Magendie Law, because Magendie made the same discovery quite independently. The same nerves could no longer be thought of as operating in either direction, as had been supposed by Descartes. In the distinction presented by the Bell-Magendie Law, sensory nerves could only operate in a direction from the senses to the spinal cord or brain. However, the motor nerves, which were connected to the muscles, allowed activity from the nerves to the muscles, and the source had to come from within, as through the spinal cord. The law of "forward direction" in the nervous system followed, whereby the conduction of a nerve occurred only in one direction.[4]

---

[4]E. G. Boring, *A History of Experimental Psychology*, rev. ed. (New York: Appleton-Century-Crofts, 1950).

### Early Studies of the Nerve Impulse

Luigi Galvani (1737–1798) began his studies in 1791 on the stimulation of frogs' legs. He found that it was possible to produce a jerk of the leg by attaching the cut end of the nerve to two rods of different metals. If he took a frog's leg and suspended its nerve from a brass hook connected to a ground, with the foot touching a silver plate that was also grounded, the kick would be repeated indefinitely. This occurred because each kick broke the connection allowing the leg to return to its original position to complete the circuit again. From this classic experiment he concluded that animal tissues generate electricity.[5]

Alessandro Volta (1745–1827) insisted that the electricity was due to the use of two different metals, with the frog's muscle simply acting as a detector of electrical potential. Alexander von Humboldt (1769–1859) resolved the controversy by demonstrating that there were two related phenomena—intrinsic animal electricity and bimetallic electricity.

### Phrenology and Franz Joseph Gall

At about the same time that Bell and Magendie were making their discoveries, there appeared on the scene, first in Vienna and later in Paris, a man by the name of Franz Joseph Gall (1758–1828). Gall was much concerned with the localization of various psychological functions in the brain. Historians[6,7] wrote that even as a schoolboy he thought he observed a relationship between certain personality characteristics of his schoolmates and the bumps on their heads. Gall took the doctrine of the faculty psychology, as propounded by the Scottish school (pp. 53–54), and attempted to locate the various faculties in specialized parts of the brain. The doctrine of phrenology was born with Gall. Basically, it stated that if a particular trait were well developed in a special part of the brain, that part would expand and, consequently, push out a part of the skull next to it, causing a bump which could be measured at the surface of the head.

Gall's pupil, Spurzheim, carried on and elaborated on the idea. Basically, the doctrine could be considered in terms of three presumptions.[8]

1. The exterior of the skull corresponded to configurations in the interior part (the brain).

2. Faculty psychology was accepted, so the mind was analyzed into a number of separate powers or functions.

3. These faculties or powers of the mind were distinctly located in specific parts of the brain, so the superior function of any faculty or psychological function would be correlated with an enlargement of that part of the brain.

---

[5]*Ibid.,* pp. 32, 39–40.
[6]R. I. Watson, *op. cit.*
[7]E. G. Boring, *op. cit.*
[8]*Ibid.,* pp. 53–54.

In its time, phrenology was appealing and was widely accepted. People in all walks of life could find out what their special talents were by having the shapes of, and bumps on, their heads measured.

The concept of phrenology proved to be wrong, as later investigations on the localization of brain functions demonstrated. It was not generally accepted by the scientists of that day, and today, anybody who propounded the doctrine would be considered a fraud. However, because of its popular appeal phrenology "died hard." A journal devoted to its study, which first appeared in 1823, did not collapse until 1911.[9] Despite its falsity, perhaps the greatest benefits lay in the fact that it generated serious research on brain functions in the later nineteenth and twentieth centuries.

## The Physiology of the Brain

The theory of Gall and Spurzheim served as the impetus for Pierre Flourens (1784–1867) to embark on his extensive investigation of the brain functions by means of the method of extirpation, or removal of parts of the brain. He studied various brain parts and considered each as a separate unit. A part had to be removed carefully and as a whole, not just mutilated. Primarily, he used pigeons as his subjects. Flourens believed that by removing the cerebrum, thought and volition would be abolished. Beyond that, he believed that the cerebrum functioned as a whole, and not in many specific ways, as was suggested by Gall. From his observations Flourens concluded that the cerebellum (below the cerebrum) was the center for movement or locomotion. The medulla (atop the spinal cord) had a conservative function; without it, the body would die. Finally, sensation was located in the spinal cord.

According to Flourens, each part of the nervous system acted as a unit, and each represented basically a single function. He thus became a severe critic of the phrenologists, but from a psychophysical point of view. Like the phrenologists, he believed that the brain remained the seat of the mind.

***The Speech Area.*** In 1861 Paul Broca (1824–1880) announced to the world that the location of the center for speech was in the side of the left cerebral hemisphere, which was later known as Broca's area. His discovery was based on clinical observation rather than experimentation. At a mental hospital in Paris, a man whose only malady was that he was unable to talk came under Broca's care. Broca examined him and found that his vocal apparatus seemed in perfectly good working order. Five days later the patient died, and Broca performed an autopsy, discovering a lesion in the third frontal convolution of the left cerebral hemisphere.[10] In Broca's discovery, the pendulum had swung slightly back in the direction of brain specificity as propounded by the phrenologists. Today, it should be pointed out that neither Flourens' rather vague

---

[9]R. I. Watson, *op. cit.*
[10]E. G. Boring, *op. cit.,* p. 71.

functions of the total organs of the brain nor Broca's specific localization of speech seem to apply exactly.

**Motor and Sensory Centers.** Toward the last quarter of the nineteenth century, two German physiologists, Fritsch and Hitzig, believed they had discovered the localization of the motor area of the brain (locomotion of movement) by means of electrical stimulation on the cortex of a dog. They could see movement when the anterior portion of the cerebral cortex was stimulated. If the current were particularly strong, the dog would go into generalized convulsions. With weak current, they discovered different centers for different muscle groups.[11]

By the end of the nineteenth century, visual sensation had been located in the occipital region (rear) of the cortex, while hearing was located in the temporal lobes (side), and touch lay in the postcentral region behind the motor area.

Finally, it was Franz and Lashley in the twentieth century who showed how variable and temporary, as well as how inexactly, cortical functions might be located (see chap. 12).

## Müller and Specific Nerve Energies

In 1833, Johannes Müller (1801–1858) became professor of physiology at the University of Berlin. In its time, his *Handbuch der Physiologie der Menschen*[12] (*Handbook of the Physiology of Man*) was the standard work because of its exhaustive summary of what was known on the subject at that time.

Müller set forth his doctrine of specific nerve energies in the form of six separate laws, which can be briefly stated as follows:[13]

1. We were aware directly not of objects but of our nerves themselves. The nerves, thus, served as intermediaries between perceived objects and the mind.

2. There were five kinds of nerves, and each imposed its specific quality on the mind.

3. The same stimulus affecting different nerves gave rise to the qualities specific to that set of nerves.

4. Since the mind was located in the brain, there was an equivalence of internal and external stimuli. [Here was an attempt to make the psychic (mind) equivalent to the objective event.]

5. The senses had definite relationships to the physical stimuli.

---

[11]*Ibid.*, p. 74.
[12]Johannes Müller, *Elements of Physiology*, trans. W. Baly, 2 vols., 2nd ed. (London: Taylor and Walton, 1839–1842).
[13]E. G. Boring, *op. cit.*

**6.** The mind had a selective power over the energies; that is, we could still attend to part of a stimulus over other parts of it.

To summarize the doctrine, what Müller was saying was that each sensory nerve, regardless of how it might be stimulated, was going to lead to one kind of sensation and no other. The sensation's importance lay, not in the stimulus itself, but in the nerve connected to the sense organs and the brain center where the nerve terminated. For example, regardless of how we stimulated the eye—whether by light waves, pressure by the thumb on the eyeball, or by electricity—we still experienced a visual sensation.

As William James suggested in 1892,[14] if we would interchange the auditory nerve and attach it to the eye, then attach the optic nerve to the ear, we would see thunder and hear lightning!

Whether he knew it or not, Müller was expanding on Kant's notion of the innateness of perception. There had to be a source of the stimulus and a correlation between the external stimulation and the impression received. The nerves and the brain supported the mind and influenced the kind of ideas the mind would receive.

Although there may be those who still support the doctrine, from our vantage point, Müller's theory was wrong. Nerves do not have specific energies. He did nothing to resolve the mind-body problem; he only perpetuated it. If any good came out of Müller's theory it was that it served as a basis for later theories of hearing and vision (see below).

## Hermann von Helmholtz (1821–1894)

Helmholtz carried on the theme of sensory physiology that had been initiated earlier in the nineteenth century. Although he thought psychology belonged to philosophy, he made an exception in relating sensation to physiology. He followed the path of Müller in applying the latter's doctrine of specific nerve energies to his own theories of vision and hearing.

***The Speed of the Nerve Impulse.*** Prior to Helmholtz, it had been presumed by Müller and Halle that the speed of the nerve impulse was so rapid that it could not be measured. Estimates had been made that the impulse was many times the speed of light. Helmholtz disagreed and took the motor nerve of a frog's leg that was attached to the muscle (nerve-muscle preparation) and arranged the apparatus in such a way that both the moment of stimulation and the twitch could be recorded on a drum revolving at a designated speed. He thus measured the time between the stimulation and the twitch for nerves of different lengths. Knowing the speed of the drum motion, the time interval between stimulation and movement, and the length of the nerve, he could calculate the speed of the impulse. It turned out that the speed was much slower

---

[14]William James, *Psychology: Briefer Course* (New York: Henry Holt, 1923).

than anyone had thought previously—about ninety feet per second.[15] Later studies done with more accurate instrumentation indicated that the speed of the nerve impulse was a function of many variables, and that there was considerable variation. Nevertheless, it was Helmholtz who attempted the initial work and who demonstrated that the speed of the impulse is far slower than that of light.

*Theory of Vision.* Helmholtz used his discovery of nerve impulse speed to support his theory of specific fiber energies, which was an outgrowth of Müller's theory. To explain color vision, he revived an earlier theory proposed by Thomas Young (1773–1829). Young had postulated that there were three types of substances on the back of the eye, each of which was differentially sensitive to different wave lengths—basically, red, green, and blue (violet). Extending Müller's theory Helmholtz felt there must then be three specific kinds of nerve fibers within the optic nerve which would only be receptive to wave lengths of these three primary colors. Yellow could be accounted for by a mixture of red and green. Furthermore, when properly balanced, we could get white (or grey) from these three primaries. When the three primary colors were properly mixed we could get all other colors. Red or green color blindness could be explained as a deficiency in these appropriate structures. The theory has become known as the Young-Helmholtz theory.

*Theory of Hearing.* Helmholtz observed that the inner ear contained a small mechanism called the basilar membrane, which was capable of responding to all of the necessary variations in pitch and loudness that the human ear could discriminate. Thus, the membrane, despite its minuteness of structure, resembled the harp or piano which are also smaller at the top and wider at the bottom. He thought the membrane could vibrate "sympathetically" to whatever tones were heard. The membrane was attached to nerve fibers which terminated in the auditory area of the brain. Here again, we had a further elaboration of the doctrine of specific fiber energies, with each fiber capable of responding to a specific tone of a given pitch and loudness.

Another of Helmholtz's discoveries in the field of hearing was the way in which we know the timbre or quality of a tone. At the time, people knew that middle C played on the piano or on the B flat clarinet sounded different even though these notes were of the same pitch and loudness. The difference in their qualities was not, however, understood. Helmholtz discovered that the difference lay in the fact that different musical instruments produced the same fundamental frequency (256 cycles per second for middle C), but, in addition, they emitted different overtones (higher multiples of the fundamental frequency). (The vibration ratios differ for different instruments.) By varying the intensities of these overtones (higher frequencies) he could synthetically characterize the tonal qualities of various musical instruments.

Finally, of interest to the psychology of music was his theory of consonance

---

[15]R. I. Watson, *op. cit.*, p. 236.

and dissonance.[16] Dissonance was caused by a "beating," a kind of throbbing or waxing and waning of tones presented at the same time when their frequencies were only a few cycles apart. This beating could occur in the overtones as well. Consonance, then, was the result of an absence of the beating.

Helmholtz could not be called the founder of experimental psychology, although he dealt with issues which were certainly the forerunners of modern sensory psychology. His theories of hearing and vision are well known today, and appear in most elementary textbooks of psychology. He was a scientist in the true sense of the word. Since he was a careful experimenter, his procedures can serve as models for modern experimental design.

## Ewald Hering (1834–1918)

Like Helmholtz, Hering was concerned with sensory physiology. He was chiefly known for an alternate theory of color vision which he proposed in opposition to that of Helmholtz. He suggested that if we took white, which Newton said was the mixture of all wave lengths, in any theory that allowed for only three primary colors, as suggested by Helmholtz, we would encounter difficulties in explaining the possibility that we needed only two primary colors to give white. For example, if blue and yellow were mixed in proper proportions, they would give white. He thus felt that four primary colors must be needed for an adequate theory; red, green, blue, and yellow, in addition to black and white. Each color was presumed to produce a chemical change in the eye. He could thus presume three basic receptors—red-green, blue-yellow, and black-white. For example, yellow, when used as a stimulus, would produce an assimilative or anabolic function. Its opposite, blue, would produce a catabolic function. The chemical process would either be a building up or a breaking down process. In the same way, red-green or black-white could upset the chemical equilibrium in opposite directions, depending on the color used. One of the difficulties of the Helmholtz theory had been that a red-green color-blind person could still see yellow, which was not a primary color. By positing the three processes for red-green, blue-yellow, and black-white, Hering believed he had overcome this difficulty.

# Psychophysics: The Beginnings of Experimental Psychology

## Ernst H. Weber (1795–1878)

Weber was another important physiologist of his time. In about 1820, he began to teach physiology at Leipzig, where Wundt later established the first experimental psychology laboratory. He experimented in many areas of sensory phys-

[16]Hermann L. von Helmholtz, *On the Sensations of Tone*, trans. A. J. Ellis (New York: Dover, 1954).

iology. Weber's experiments on temperature sense led to the theory that a feeling of warm and cold was not directly the result of the actual temperature stimulation, but was due to a change in the temperature of the skin. For example, if you placed your hand in moderately warm water, the skin would adapt and the water would no longer feel warm. However, an increase or a rise in the temperature of the water would produce a feeling of warmth.

Another of Weber's experiments dealt with the sense of touch. If two separate pin points of stimuli were applied to a region of the skin, say the hand, one would ordinarily report feeling two different points. However, if the distance between the two points were gradually reduced, a point would be reached where one felt only one point, even though two stimuli were being presented. This has become known as the two-point threshold or limen. If the distance were below this, one would report only one point. A greater distance would be reported as two points. Weber further observed that the two-point threshold differed for various parts of the body; it was very small for the tips of the fingers and large for the back of the body. The threshold might also differ from one person to another.

Most important were Weber's studies of the muscle sense. One will recall Thomas Brown, who first recognized the muscle sense (p. 54) in detecting the resistance from an object if pushed or reached for. He gave this as evidence for the existence of a real world, which Hume and Berkeley had denied.

Weber was interested in how well one could discriminate differences in the weights of objects by lifting and comparing them with each other. He started with two series of weights, one with a standard for comparison of thirty-two ounces and the other with a standard of only four ounces.[17] He carried out many experiments and found that one's ability to tell the difference between standard and comparison weights was not absolute; one depended on the ratio of the magnitude of one weight to its standard in a given series. He found the threshold or point of "just noticeable difference" could be stated as a ratio, as in the case of weights of 1:40.[18] For example, if given a standard of forty ounces, I could just tell the difference between forty and forty-one. When given a standard of eighty, I would only be able to tell the difference between eighty and eighty-two ounces. In the case of a standard of forty, given weights less than forty-one but greater than forty would be below my threshold, or would not be a noticeable difference, but weights beyond forty-one could be discriminated as heavier than forty.

This was truly a psychological experiment, since a discrimination was measured. It led psychologists to attack genuine psychological problems in which measurement was involved. The principle Weber had demonstrated became known as Weber's Law. The law became the source of a great deal of further psychological research, even to the present day. Furthermore, Weber firmly

---

[17]G. Murphy, *An Historical Introduction to Modern Psychology* (New York: Harcourt, Brace and Co., 1949), chs. 8 and 10.

[18]D. Schultz, *A History of Modern Psychology* (New York: Academic Press, 1969), p. 33.

established that quantitative methods could be applied to psychological experimentation.

## Gustav Theodor Fechner (1801–1887)

Fechner was born in a small village in southeast Germany. He entered the University of Leipzig in 1817. It may seem paradoxical to state that Fechner, the real founder of psychophysics, a methodology still currently used in experimental psychology, was actually a mystic. Nevertheless, it is true, for Fechner's real interest in psychology was to find a solution to the age-old mind-body problem. During his life, he pursued many paths—philosopher, religious mystic, poet and writer, and dabbler in esthetics. For a detailed account of the various changes and facets in the course of his life, the interested reader may consult one of the basic histories of psychology, such as Boring.[19] Early in his career, Fechner began to take on an anti-mechanistic position, which eventually evolved into his "philosophy of nature." Later, as he developed the methods of psychophysics, he felt he had solved the riddle of the universe and the mind-body problem.

Under the *nom de plume* of Dr. Mises, he began to write a series of satires, even before he had graduated from the university. One of the earliest works was *Proof that Man Is Made of Iodine,* which was directed at the then-current medical fad for the use of iodine.

He shifted his interest many times throughout his career. After receiving his university degree, he became interested in physics. He developed a behavior disorder, presumably caused by overwork, which historians have called by many names. Murphy[20] called it a "nervous breakdown." Adding to this, he had injured his eyes by looking at the sun through improperly shaded glasses in an attempt to study after-images. He also became deeply religious and was intensely interested in the problems of the soul, which led to the development of his "philosophy of nature." There was nothing very new or outstanding about this view, and it brought him little fame. According to the theory, spiritual influences expressed themselves in physical ways. All parts of the universe could be considered a homogenous unity in one spiritual whole. In this mysticism, the world consisted of a series of souls which appeared to each other as bodies. All plants and animals were endowed with a kind of soul. The relation of the soul to the body was eventually to be stated in the psychophysical law.

*Psychophysics.* Psychophysics had begun with Weber's experiments with weights, but Weber had never written down the specific formula for his discovery. It was Fechner who stated the relationship as:

$$\frac{\Delta R}{R} = k$$

---

[19]E. G. Boring, *op. cit.*
[20]G. Murphy, *op. cit.*

in which the $\Delta R$ was the "just noticeable difference" in sensation stated in terms of a physical increment, $R$ was the standard stimulus used as the basis for the comparison, and $k$ was a constant. Using Weber's example of lifted weights, if $R = 40$ ounces and $\Delta R = 1$, we can see that it would take an increase of one ounce to be able to tell the difference between the two weights when the standard was 40. If we used a standard in which $R = 80$, then the "just noticeable difference" would be $\Delta R = 2$, and so on. The particular fraction would differ for different sense modalities. For this formulation, Fechner generously gave credit to Weber and called it Weber's Law.

In further observations, Fechner noted that if one increased the sensation magnitude of just noticeable differences in an arithmetical order of 1, 2, 3, 4, 5, the actual increase in physical magnitude to produce the just noticeable differences would increase in a geometrical order of 1, 2, 4, 8, 16, etc. Thus we were dealing with a logarithmic relationship. By a method of derivation of Weber's Law, Fechner emerged with a new equation:

$$S = k \log R$$

in which $S$ was the sensation magnitude and $R$ was the stimulus magnitude. Today, this has commonly been referred to as Fechner's Law.[21]

Fechner's extensive researches were published in 1860 in his *Elemente der Psychophysik*.[22] He believed he had made a mathematical equation to solve the mind-body relationship. In Fechner's original statement, then

$$\frac{\Delta R}{R} = k$$

the $\Delta R$ was the sensation or mental experience, and the $R$ equalled the physical or bodily event. Incidentally, students who are interested in the derivation of the formula may consult either Boring[23] or Kantor.[24]

This was not the whole history of psychophysics. The method used by Weber and refined by Fechner employed a set standard stimulus, given along with alternate series of stimuli differing in degree. Each was compared with the standard in random order. When the "just noticeable difference" was established, this became known as the *method of constant stimuli*. The standard was always compared with a series of greater and lesser magnitudes. The "just noticeable difference" was referred to as the *limen* or *difference threshold*.

Fechner also developed two other methods of psychophysics. In the *method of average error*, a person was given a standard stimulus and a variable stimulus which the person could adjust to meet or to be the same as the standard. If one

---

[21]E. G. Boring, *op. cit.*
[22]Gustav Fechner, *Elemente der Psychophysik*, 2 vols. (Leipzig: Breitkopf and Hartel, 1860).
[23]E. G. Boring, *op. cit.*, pp. 287–88.
[24]J. R. Kantor, *The Scientific Evolution of Psychology*, Vol. II (Chicago: The Principia Press, Inc., 1969), pp. 289–90.

were given a line of a standard length, along with another line that one could adjust, moving it back and forth until it was judged to be the same as the standard, no matter how carefully one might try, there would always be some error. Sometimes the adjustments would fall short, other times too long. After many trials, these errors could be averaged, and the degree of the error became the threshold.

The third of Fechner's methods has come to be called the method of just noticeable differences or, more commonly today, the *method of limits*. In this method, one was presented with two stimuli. One of them was increased or decreased until the subject detected a difference. These change points were then averaged to get the difference threshold or point of just noticeable difference.

The publication of *Elemente der Psychophysik* brought Fechner wide acclaim, and many later experimental psychologists, including Wundt, followed through with further psychological experiments and ramifications. For many decades these methods have applied. Carl Seashore, who developed the first test of musical talent in 1919 (later revised in 1937),[25] applied the basic principle to find how accurately his subjects could discriminate differences in pitch, loudness, time, rhythm, and timbre.

In the history of psychology, there was one great dissenter to Fechner—namely, William James—who thought the entire enterprise useless[26] (see chap. 8).

> Fechner's book was the starting point of a new department of literature, which it would be perhaps impossible to match for the qualities of thoroughness and subtlety, but of which, in the humble opinion of the present writer, the proper psychological outcome is just nothing.

James quoted the little poem:

> And everybody praised the duke
> Who this great fight did win,
> "But what good came of it at last?"
> Quoth little Peterkin,
> "Why, that I can not tell" said he,
> "But 'twas a famous victory."

***Significance of Fechner.*** There is no question that Fechner was an innovator. He placed the study of sensation on a quantitative basis and developed an experimental psychology. He certainly did not solve the mind-body problem. He was a mystic and a dualist. His theories themselves gave us nothing. His value lay in his methodology.

---

[25]Carl Seashore, *Seashore Measures of Musical Talents* (New York: The Psychological Corp., 1937, rev. 1960).

[26]William James, *Principles of Psychology*, Vol. 1 (New York: Henry Holt, 1890), p. 534.

## Suggested Further Readings

Boring, E. G., *The History of Experimental Psychology,* rev. ed. New York: Appleton-Century-Crofts, 1950, chs. 2–6, 14, and 15. One of the most referred-to texts regarding the influences of neurophysiology, phrenology, theories of vision and hearing, and psychophysics. Full of facts, with much detail including extensive biographical material. However, not the most exciting reading.

Boring, E. G., *History, Psychology and Science.* New York: John Wiley and Sons, 1963. Further elaboration of material in Boring's 1950 volume.

Kantor, J. R., *The Scientific Evolution of Psychology,* Vol. II. Chicago: The Principia Press, 1969, chs. 30, 32, 34, 35, and 37. Biological influences on psychology with philosophical implications.

Murphy, G., *An Historical Introduction to Modern Psychology.* New York: Harcourt, Brace and Co., 1949, chs. 8 and 10. Elementary discussions of nineteenth-century German physiological psychology.

Watson, R. I., *The Great Psychologists.* Philadelphia: J. B. Lippincott, 1978, 4th ed. Fechner and Helmholtz are extensively discussed.

# CHAPTER

# 6

# *Wilhelm Wundt: The Beginnings of Structuralism*

Wilhelm Wundt was unquestionably one of the great figures in the development of modern psychology. Some say the greatest.[1] Today we regard him as one of the pioneers who set psychology on its way. He can be considered the first psychologist of modern times. Wundt developed the first systematic approach to psychology, which was to be refined later by Titchener to become one of the dominant systems during the first three decades of this century. (Titchener's elaboration of the system will be discussed in the next chapter.)

Wundt's importance for us lies not only in his systematic approach to the "new" science but also in the fact that he "broke" with philosophy and took psychology into the laboratory where experiments could be performed. Although a question has arisen about who founded the first laboratory,[2] it has been generally credited to Wundt in the year 1879 at the University of Leipzig, Germany.

---

[1]D. B. Klein, *A History of Scientific Psychology* (New York: Basic Books, Inc., 1970).
[2]R. I. Watson, *The Great Psychologists,* 4th ed. (Philadelphia: J. B. Lippincott, 1978).

## *Antecedents*

Wundt was also a philosopher who wrote five books (plus revisions) on logic, ethics, and general philosophy. Today, his philosophy is of little concern to us. He was, like others of his time, a philosopher who turned psychologist.

The *Zeitgeist* was ready for Wundt. John Locke, two centuries earlier, had established the empirical tradition when he defied the continental rationalists and stated that all knowledge came from experience (see pp. 46–48). This was an important step not only in the history of science, but also in psychology. Wundt followed the tradition of defining psychology as the study of conscious experience.

Later, John Stuart Mill had talked about a mental chemistry in his association of ideas (see p. 55). For Wundt, psychology became a chemical analogy, because experience could be analyzed into its elements and compounds, and these could be synthesized as well. In *Logic,* Mill had suggested the possibility of an experimental psychology, but it remained for Wundt to make the idea a reality.

Other British associationists, such as Bain and Spencer, had developed the principle of association as far as it could go. Wundt, along with other early psychologists, used association as a basic principle of connection between the elements of experience. In addition, he studied associations in the experimental laboratory.

Then, there was Herbart, who had talked about apperception, the process whereby an idea could come into consciousness and combine with other ideas to form the apperceptive mass. Wundt paid considerable attention to this principle, both systematically and experimentally.

In Wundt's work, the mind and body routes to modern psychology merged. So far, in tracing the antecedents of Wundt's psychology, we have concentrated on the mind. But, there was a body side as well, for Wundt was also a physiologist who received a degree in medicine. In his book, *Grundzüge der physiologischen Psychologie*[3] (*Principles of Physiological Psychology*), Wundt devoted hundreds of pages to anatomy and physiology and included charts and diagrams.

Another aspect of the body route led to Wundt's reliance on Fechner's psychophysical methods as some basis for his laboratory experimentation. Through these techniques, one could study sensation experimentally, which constituted, for Wundt, one class of the basic elements of consciousness.

Early in his career, Wundt was an assistant to Helmholtz, a man considered to be the greatest physiologist of the times.

With Wundt, experimental psychology began as a formal science—one that was independent of the other sciences and of philosophy. He cast off the phil-

---

[3]Wilhelm Wundt, *Grundzüge der physiologischen Psychologie,* 5th ed., 3 vols. (Leipzig: Engelmann, 1902–1903).

osophical armchair analysis of mental phenomena and did what, at least in his own opinion, constituted experimental psychological research.

## The Life of Wilhelm Wundt (1832–1920)

Wundt was born the son of a Lutheran minister in a suburb of Mannheim, Germany in 1832. His childhood has been described as solemn and studious.[4] He was tutored by one of his father's assistants. The young Wilhelm developed a strong attachment to the vicar, and when the latter received a "call" to a parish in a neighboring town, Wilhelm accompanied him. Since the family was not wealthy, Wundt decided to study medicine. This course would enable him to support himself, and it would act as an opening to the study of science, including anatomy and physiology. He took his medical degree at the University of Heidelberg in 1856. For several years he was the assistant to Helmholtz, but became bored with the constant drilling of Helmholtz' students. His interest in physiology began to wane. This was, perhaps, a turning point in his career, for he began to look at the psychological problems posed by the earlier philosophers.

His first book, *Beiträge zur Theorie der Sinneswahrnchmung*[5] (*Contributions to the Theory of Sensory Perception*), was published in 1862. For the most part, the book is of little concern to us, except that in the preface he spoke of the need to create both an experimental and a social psychology.[6]

In 1875 Wundt was appointed to a chair in philosophy at the University of Leipzig, which he held until the time of his retirement in 1917. In 1879 he founded the first psychological laboratory there, which became known as the Psychological Institute. It began as a private operation, supported by Wundt's own funds until 1881. Then it was officially recognized by the university. It began as a simple operation consisting of only a few rooms (some historians say only one) but expanded over the years. In 1897 it moved to its own building, which was later destroyed during World War II. During the years 1873–1874, he published his *Grundzüge der physiologischen Psychologie*[7] (*Principles of Physiological Psychology*), which had six editions, the last in 1911. It was a large three-volume work, and in it he established psychology as a laboratory science, which became the "new psychology" in distinction to the older armchair speculations of the nineteenth-century philosophers. (Wundt's experimental methods will be discussed subsequently.)

---

[4]G. A. Miller, *Psychology: The Science of Mental Life* (New York: Harper and Row, 1962).
[5]Wilhelm Wundt, *Beiträge zur Theorie der Sinneswahrnchmung* (Leipzig: Winter, 1862).
[6]G. A. Miller, *op. cit.*, p. 16.
[7]Wilhelm Wundt, *Grundzüge der physiologischen Psychologie, op. cit.*

At Leipzig, he became a very popular lecturer.[8] To supplement his lectures on psychology, he frequently used demonstrations. He considered these demonstrations so important that he founded the first psychological laboratory in 1879. Initially, it consisted of only one room, but gradually it was expanded. As Wundt began to experiment, he attracted many students. Many of the great pioneers in psychology studied with him: G. Stanley Hall, James McKeen Cattell, Edward Scripture, and Charles Judd, who later translated Wundt's *Grundriss der Psychologie*[9] (*Outline of Psychology*) into English. Perhaps the most important of his students (although Wundt actually had little personal contact with him) was Edward Bradford Titchener, a Britisher who eventually took Wundt's psychology to America, to refine and popularize it, and give it the name *structuralism* (see next chapter).

As his experiments progressed, Wundt had to find a place to publish the results. So, in 1881 he founded the journal *Philosophische Studien.* In 1896 the *Grundriss der Psychologie*[10] appeared, which not only neglected the earlier physiological and anatomical sections of the *Physiological Psychology,* but also became a strictly psychological work in which his system was thoroughly outlined.

Much earlier, Wundt had stated the need for a social psychology. The first volume of his *Völkerpsychologie*[11] (*Folk Psychology*) appeared in 1900. It consisted of ten volumes, and was finally completed in 1909. Wundt thought of a collective folk mind which transcended all individual minds (a kind of group mind). The simpler mental functions—sensation, feeling, memory—could be studied in the laboratory, but for the higher mental processes, experimentation seemed impossible. *Folk Psychology* described the evolution of human mental development from primitive times.

During his life, Wundt was a prolific writer. According to Boring,[12] he wrote 53,735 pages or an average of 2.2 pages per day, from the years 1853 to 1900. His impact on psychology was tremendous. Scholars from all over the world flocked to study and work in his laboratory, and they returned to their respective countries to start their own laboratories. The most notable of these was Titchener, who came to Cornell University in America. Other laboratories sprang up quite independently. The *Zeitgeist* was right for the beginning of an experimental psychology.

---

[8]G. A. Miller, *op. cit.*
[9]Wilhelm Wundt, *Grundriss der Psychologie,* 1st ed. (Leipzig: Engelmann, 1896).
[10]*Ibid.*
[11]Wilhelm Wundt, *Völkerpsychologie,* 10 vols. (Leipzig: Engelmann, 1900–1920).
[12]E. G. Boring, *A History of Experimental Psychology,* 2nd ed. (New York: Appleton-Century-Crofts, 1950).

## *The Work of the Leipzig Laboratory*

Before considering Wundt's systematic position, let us examine the kind of experiments performed at the Leipzig laboratory. Wundt had spoken of a physiological psychology, using the methods and instruments of physiology.

Wundt was determined to study the contents of the mind or consciousness, and to do so, his methods involved *experimentation* and *introspection.* Introspection had had a long history. Plotinus and St. Augustine had introduced it as a soul-searching process, and it was the main method of the later philosophers. Descartes had thought of it as a kind of contemplative meditation, while the British empiricists were more content to introspect on the elementary experiences.

For Wundt, introspection took on a new meaning. This was not a naive process which anybody could perform. It had to be exercised by the *trained introspectionist,* and there were certain rules that had to be followed. These rules were:[13]

1. The introspectionist must be able to determine when the process was to be introduced.

2. The introspectionist must maintain a state of "strained attention."

3. The observation must be capable of repetition.

4. The conditions must be such that variations might be allowed—that is, the introduction or elimination of certain stimuli or variations in the strength or quality of the stimuli. Thus, the introspectionist must be capable of isolating the mental process at any moment.

Self-observation was not enough; it had to be accompanied by experimentation. The experimenter varied the conditions of the stimulus, and the introspectionist observed the changes in the experiences. For Wundt, experimentation and introspection went hand in hand.

Boring[14] has summarized the kinds of research that went on at the Leipzig laboratory.

### Sensation and Perception

We might expect that this was the major part of the output. In vision and hearing, as well as the other senses, psychophysical methods were used to determine absolute and difference thresholds (see pp. 71–73). There were also studies of color contrast, color mixing, eye movements, and after-images.

---

[13]R. I. Watson, *op. cit.,* p. 243.
[14]E. G. Boring, *op. cit.*

Touch was examined by determining the two-point threshold first developed by Weber (see pp. 69–71).

## Reaction Time

Reaction time had already been studied by Helmholtz and Donders. In Wundt's method, he attempted to develop a way of studying the stages which existed in a complex perceptual situation. In simple reaction time, one merely reacted as quickly as one could to a single stimulus. But in complex reaction time, more mental processes were involved. For example, one might be presented with two lights—red and green. One was to respond to the red one, but not the green one. Wundt thought that first one *perceived* the stimulus, then *apperceived* it (distinguished it as red or green) and, finally, one responded according to the instructions given.

It later turned out that subjects who were well trained in the procedure could not distinguish the three stages.

## Attention

For Wundt, attention was the clear perception of a narrow region of consciousness. The focus of attention became separate from the rest of consciousness. The range and fluctuation of attention were studied. James McKeen Cattell did the classic study of the span of attention, by finding out how many units (numbers, letters, words, dots) could be apprehended in a short exposure of the stimulus.

## Word Associations

As we have pointed out earlier, Wundt's psychology was strongly influenced by the concept of association. In the experiment, when a word was presented, the subject had to reply with another single word—the first word that came to mind. Also, the time required to make the response was measured. Wundt distinguished between "inner" and "outer" associations. Inner associations showed an intrinsic connection between words: for example, snake-reptile, light-dark, man-woman. The outer associations were more accidental. They might involve associations established through habits of speech, such as: George-king, fly-wheel, or tree-Christmas.

## Feelings

Feelings were studied by the method of paired comparison. In this method, each subject was required to compare every stimulus with every other one in a series. If one wanted to compare the pleasantness of a variety of tones, one would compare *A* with *B, C, D, E* and *F.* In each trial, the subject was required to state which of the tones was more pleasing to the ear. Eventually, an order of pleasantness could be established.

It is obvious from this survey that Wundt did not develop any really new kinds of experimental techniques.[15] Studies on the psychophysiology of vision and hearing had already been done by Helmholtz and others. Reaction time had been examined by Donders. The use of psychophysical methods had been introduced by Weber and Fechner. Wundt, however, introduced a program which consolidated these different methods of experimentation. During the period 1875–1919, Wundt produced one hundred and eighty-six doctoral candidates.[16] Of course, some were purely philosophical and not experimental. It must be remembered that although Wundt was first and foremost a psychologist, he held a chair in philosophy and had written extensively on that subject.

## Wundt's Systematic Psychology

Wundt's systematic position was most clearly outlined in *Outline of Psychology,*[17] from which the following discussion is taken.

### Definition and Subject Matter

To Wundt, there were certain contents of experience not to be found among the objects and processes of other sciences. These included sensations, feelings, emotions, ideas, and so on. Every experience had two aspects, the concrete object, and our experience of it. Thus, in nature, there were two kinds of experience, *mediate experience* (as in light and sound waves) and *immediate experience* (as in color or tone). The immediate experience was the concern of the psychologist.

Psychology was the study of the immediate experiences or consciousness. Wundt considered the elementary contents of consciousness to be psychical elements or atoms. They were of two classes: *sensations* and *feelings.* The sensations were the objective contents of consciousness, and the feelings were the subjective aspects. The content of consciousness, then, consisted of various combinations of these elements. The sensory elements came through any sensory modality—seeing, hearing, touching, tasting, smelling, and so on. The feeling elements had three dimensions: excitement-calm, pleasure-displeasure, and tension-relaxation. Every conscious feeling could be located in a three-dimensional space (see Fig. 2).

Sensations and feelings had two attributes—*quality* and *intensity.* The intensity attribute referred to the brightness of a color, loudness of a tone, or the amount of pressure in a touch. Its dimension could extend from zero to extreme

[15]R. I. Watson, *op. cit.*

[16]*Ibid.,* p. 250.

[17]Wilhelm Wundt, *Outline of Psychology,* trans. C. Judd (Leipzig: Engelmann, 1897).

**FIGURE 2** *Wundt's Tri-Dimensional Theory of Feeling.* Every feeling is supposed to be located somewhere in this space. (From *Psychology: The Science of Mental Life,* p. 21, Copyright © 1962 by George A. Miller. Reprinted by permission of Harper & Row, Publishers, Inc.)

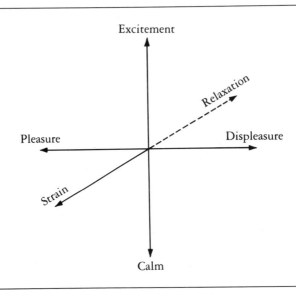

intensity. For feeling, the intensity attribute extended in either direction from the point of no feeling (where the axes cross in the figure), from no pleasure to extreme pleasure or extreme displeasure.

The attribute of *quality* referred to a particular pitch in sound such as F#, a specific color such as blue, a taste of sour, or something warm to the touch. The qualities of feeling referred to their specific dimensions. Wundt pointed out that feeling elements were much less clear and were harder to identify.

When the elements of sensation and feelings combined, the results were psychical *compounds.* Compounds could either consist of merely a cluster of simple sensations or feelings, or of a combination of both. *Ideas* constituted one such compound which could be broken down into its individual elements. The compound idea of a rose, for example, might consist of several visual sensations such as pink and green, a prickly touch, an element of smell, and a feeling of pleasantness.

A second class of compounds was *emotions.* Emotions constituted a complex of elements of different kinds of feelings. When feelings gave rise to an overt act we had *will.* A person might experience anger (a compound of feelings), which would result in will, culminating in the overt act of striking the object of the anger.

## Attention

This was referred to as a favorable recognition of a content of consciousness. It was clear comprehension designated as apperception. It amounted to a focusing of a particular element of consciousness. As the process of consciousness changed, compounds formed and re-formed. They might come into the field of consciousness, advance toward the focal point, and then fade away. Apperception was such a focusing. The sum of all the compounds as a whole at any given moment was the *apperceptive mass*. (Wundt borrowed this concept from Herbart, see p. 58.)

## Principles of Connection

One of the ways the elements were connected was by means of *association*. In a sense, association became the "glue" that held the elements of consciousness together. But Wundt went further. In anticipation of a doctrine later propounded by Gestalt psychologists, Wundt added the principle of *creative synthesis*. This had been anticipated in John Stuart Mill's "mental chemistry" (see p. 55). The principle constituted a chemical analogy in which two or more elements might form a compound, with the result being different from the mere sum of the component elements. Wundt also spoke of the law of *psychic relations*. This law was concerned with the problem of meaning or the significance of a particular event. Wundt never really dealt with the problem, and it remained for Titchener to elaborate the significance of meaning in his *context theory* (see next chapter).

Wundt's position on *learning* was taken more or less from the British empiricism of Locke, Berkeley, and Hume (see pp. 45–51). It consisted basically of the association of ideas in time and space: sensations call up the association of images. However, Wundt added the "law of psychic fusion," by which a new experience (see psychical compounds, p. 82) could be produced in which the components could not always be detected—a notion not dissimilar to J. S. Mill's "mental chemistry" (see p. 55).

Wundt's critics had maintained that memory was passive and merely the receptacle of experiences, but that, just as with learning, ideas were active processes. Experience was an event and *memory* was not the reconstruction of previous ideas but acted according to the rules, one of which was "creative synthesis" (see "Principles of Connection," above). Here complex events are based on simpler ones—the action of a higher synthesis into a higher unity. Also related to a memory was the act of attention, which could range from the fringe to the main focus of consciousness.

## Methodology

Earlier in this chapter, we discussed Wundt's method of observation through the use of *introspection*. Introspection was a skill to be developed. To become a trained introspectionist meant a long period of apprenticeship. Through introspection, one could analyze the conscious process to discover how the elements were arranged and synthesized.

## Mind-Body Problem

Those who have written commentaries on Wundt's psychology on this issue are in complete agreement. Wundt's solution was *psychophysical parallelism.* In his principle of psychical causality, he said that the brain was not the cause of experience. It should be remembered that Wundt talked about *immediate experience* and *mediate experience;* one was the physical, the other was the mental. These two existed side by side, and there was no interaction between them.

In his book *Outline of Psychology,* Wundt stated the principle clearly:[18]

> As a result of this relation, it follows that there must be a relation between all facts that belong at the same time to both experiences of the natural sciences and to the immediate experiences of psychology, for they are nothing but components of a single experience which is merely regarded in the two cases from different points of view. Since these facts belong to both spheres, there must be an elementary process on the physical side, corresponding to every such process on the psychical side. The general principle is known as the *principle of psychophysical parallelism.*

## *Völkerpsychologie*

In 1900 Wundt began the publication of his *Völkerpsychologie*[19] (Folk or Ethnic Psychology), an undertaking which continued until the year of his death in 1920. In it he developed what he considered the other half of psychology, the study of humans and society, in contrast to the individual, experimental psychology studied in the laboratory. Here the methodology was observational, not experimental. The Völkerpsychologie was the study of collective activity, in particular language, myths, and customs. He felt that the study of these phenomena would give greater insight to the higher workings of the human mind—something that could not be studied in the laboratory. In the Völkerpsychologie Wundt set forth his conception of the "group mind"—a synthesis or fusion of individual minds. Social phenomena, in general, resulted from fusion of the psychic elements of individual minds.

His studies of myths and customs, based on what he knew of their development through historical sources, were rather unspectacular. However, his discussion of language was more original. He divided language into "outer" and "inner." The outer consisted of the organization and associations of sounds as spoken or heard. The inner form consisted of the deeper cognitive processes

---

[18]*Ibid.,* pp. 317–18.
[19]Wilhelm Wundt, *Völkerpsychologie* (10 volumes), (Leipzig: Engelmann, 1900–1920).

in the speaker's thoughts, allowing the speaker to prepare utterances and enabling the listener to comprehend the meaning of what had been heard. The production of language involved the transformation of a thought into words. Thus the concept "red barn" becomes a sequence of words forming a sentence ("The barn is red.")

Wundt also described the origin of language, which he believed had evolved from involuntary, expressive sounds that eventually took on meaning (sometimes called the "bow-wow" theory). Further discussions involved primitive language and phonetics.

### Estimate of Wundt's Position

A final evaluation will be deferred until the end of the next chapter, since Titchener brought Wundt's psychology to America and founded a formal school called structuralism.

Wundt's great contribution to psychology was that he established it as an experimental science—one that remains today. Although the methods and theories are different, and experimental psychologists do not usually indulge in the introspection of Wundt's type, the attitude of an experimental science of psychology remains. Psychology no longer belongs to the "mental philosophy" of yesteryear, but exists as a separate and distinct discipline. Wundt accomplished this aim, and psychologists today have maintained it. According to Murphy:[20]

> Before Wundt published his physiological psychology and established his laboratory, psychology was little more than a waif knocking now at the door of physiology, now at the door of ethics, now at the door of epistemology. In 1879, it set itself up as an experimental science with a local habitation and a name.

## Wundt's Contemporaries

Although the time was right, it took a person of courage and tremendous fortitude, such as Wundt, to accomplish the task of starting a "new" psychology. As a number of historians have pointed out, in his time, Wundt was hard to criticize. He wrote endlessly. By the time a critic had raised a point, Wundt had changed his position and had literally out-written his critics.[21]

In retrospect, Wundt was undoubtedly the greatest psychologist of the late nineteenth century. There were others who shared some of his ideas, but who, at the same time, fostered different viewpoints. They should not be ignored as

---

[20]G. Murphy, *An Historical Introduction to Modern Psychology,* 2nd ed. (New York: Harcourt, Brace and Co., 1949), p. 159.
[21]D. P. Schultz, *A History of Modern Psychology* (New York: Academic Press, 1969).

contributing influences to modern psychology. Two of them, Brentano and Stumpf, opposed Wundt rather vigorously. Another, Külpe, agreed to some extent and tried to expand some of Wundt's ideas.

### Franz Brentano (1838–1917)

From a systematic point of view, Brentano was probably the most important critic of Wundt at the time. He was trained in the priesthood, but when the Vatican Council accepted the doctrine of the infallibility of the Pope, a doctrine which Brentano could not accept, he left the Church. His *Psychologie vom empirischen Standpunkt*[22] (*Psychology from an Empirical Standpoint*) was published in the same year as Wundt's *Principles of Physiological Psychology*. Also in the same year, Brentano accepted an appointment at the University of Vienna, where he remained for the next twenty years. He fostered an empirical psychology, not based on experimentation, but on observation.

Brentano objected to Wundt's psychology of content, which had fostered an analysis of the contents of consciousness. Instead, he set forth an *act psychology*. For him, psychological processes became significant only when they were thought of as acts. One must study the acts or processes of the mind, not its contents. If one saw a color or heard a tone, it was not in itself mental. The act of hearing or seeing made it mental. The mental acts always referred to objects. Thus, a division developed between Brentano and Wundt, a division between act and content, or between experience as a way of acting and experience as structure.

Psychic phenomena consisted of three kinds of acts: ideating, judging, and feeling. Brentano reached this conclusion by considering the possible relationships a subject had to its object. Ideating involved having an idea, whether it was real or imagined, past or present. In judging, there had to be an affirmation or denial of the object. In feeling, one might have attitudes about the object, accepting or repelling it.

As Titchener[23] put it, the mental processes (acts) could be described as follows:

**1.** Ideating (I see, I hear, I imagine.)

**2.** Judging (I acknowledge, I reject, I perceive, I recall.)

**3.** Feeling (I feel, I wish, I resolve, I intend, I desire.)

Each act had a content, but it was not contained within the act itself but rather was something beyond it. For example, the content in the act of seeing could be color, but color is in the domain of physics, not psychology. In the act, "I

---

[22] Franz Brentano, *Psychologie vom empirischen Standpunkt*, O. Kraus, ed., 2 vols. (Leipzig: Meiner, 1924–1925).

[23] Edward B. Titchener, "Brentano and Wundt, Empirical Experimental Psychology" (1921), in L. McAlister, *The Philosophy of Brentano* (Atlantic Highlands, N.J.: Humanities Press, 1976).

see a cat," the cat is the content, but for Brentano the content was far less important than the act.

Brentano and Wundt, as well as the later structuralists, were in total opposition. However, as we shall see subsequently, Brentano, in a rather indirect way, shared some of the same opposition that the functionalists raised against Wundt. The functionalists thought of psychological activity in terms of mental processes or functions rather than contents (see chap. 9). Likewise, the later Gestalt psychologists shared Brentano's objection to a psychology of elemental content.

## Carl Stumpf (1848–1936)

Stumpf was strongly influenced by Brentano, and can be considered also as belonging to the school of act psychology. Stumpf was primarily interested in music, but since no university gave formal degrees in music, he turned to philosophy and took his doctorate at Göttingen in 1868. His most important work was his *Tonpsychologie*[24] (*Tone Psychology*) (1883–1890). His writings were primarily on audition, and Stumpf can be considered one of the first psychologists of music. The psychological functions or acts consisted of perceiving, conceiving, desiring, and willing.

Stumpf developed a laboratory at the University of Berlin, where he had received a professional appointment. In those days, this was a prize appointment, and one which might well have gone to Wundt, since he was the more outstanding man at the time in the area of psychology. It has been suggested[25] that Wundt never received the appointment because of Helmholtz' objections.

In his laboratory, Stumpf carried out extensive research in hearing. At the time his work was rivaled by only that of Helmholtz.

A controversy arose between Stumpf and Wundt which emerged in a series of publications devoted to the introspective method in studying tones. The controversy revolved around the question of whether a trained introspectionist of the Wundtian variety was more qualified to make tonal judgments than a trained musician (Stumpf). It is interesting to note, however, that Stumpf, like Wundt, accepted the method of introspection.

## The Würzburg School:
## Külpe, Marbe, Watt, and Bühler

Oswald Külpe (1867–1915) began his career as a student and disciple of Wundt at Leipzig. His first book, *Grundriss der Psychologie*[26] (*Outline of Psychology*), followed in the Wundtian tradition. However, he withdrew from the Leipzig group because he considered Wundt's views to be too narrow.

---

[24]Carl Stumpf, *Tonpsychologie*, 2 vols. (Leipzig: S. Hirzel, 1883–1890).
[25]E. G. Boring, *op. cit.*
[26]Oswald Külpe, *Grundriss der Psychologie* (Leipzig: Engelmann, 1893).

In 1894 Külpe went to Würzburg, and two years later founded a laboratory which attracted a number of American students. Among them was James Angell, who later returned to the University of Chicago and became one of the founders of the functionalist school (see chap. 9).

In his *Outline,* Külpe had not mentioned "thought," but he became increasingly more convinced that thought processes must be part of the study of psychology. Wundt had ignored the "higher mental processes" and had relegated them to his *Völkerpsychologie.*[27] Külpe accepted Wundt's notion of conscious experiences and introspection, but tried to go beyond it. His investigations led him to the idea that thinking could occur in the absence of sensations and images. This became known as "imageless thought," which was interpreted to mean that thought did not have to involve any images. Students in the Würzburg school, in the course of their introspections, described how thinking about a definite problem could occur without the subject being aware of having any mental content of an image or sensory sort.

Others associated with the Würzburg school experimented more extensively with imageless thought. They included Karl Marbe (1869–1935), Henry Watt (1879–1935) and Karl Bühler (1879–1963).

Marbe asked his subjects to make judgments, such as telling which of two weights was heavier. Usually, the judgments were correct, provided that they were not too difficult to make. He then asked his subjects to introspect as to what was going on in their consciousness while making the judgments. The reply was that they could not really describe how the judgments were made. Thus, the judgments had to be more than mental content and were related to the attitudes of the subjects making the judgments. This "mental set" was interpreted as a new "imageless element" of the mind.

Watt, a student of Külpe's at Würzburg, experimented with word associations. He divided his approach into four stages: (1) instructions as to the nature of the task, (2) presentation of a single word, usually written on a card, (3) the search for an appropriate word for the reply, and (4) the actual verbal response. In each step he asked the subjects to introspect regarding their conscious processes. The subjects had no difficulty in responding with an appropriate word without any conscious effort. He concluded that the key to the problem was to be found in the instructions or task (*aufgabe*), which brought about a particular "set" in the minds of the subjects. The actual tendency was not present in the subjects' consciousness during the searching for and speaking of an appropriate word. The thought itself was imageless and could not be described introspectively. Thus, with proper preparation or instructions, the thought occurred automatically without any conscious content.

In 1907 Karl Bühler came to Würzburg and investigated the problem further. He presented his subjects with problems that required some "thought" before they could be solved. In their introspections, the subjects were to give as complete an account as they could of the steps they went through in arriving

---

[27]Wilhelm Wundt, *Völkerpsychologie, op. cit.*

at their solutions. Bühler explained that there were non-sensory thought processes. These constituted new types of structural elements—*thought elements.*

Wundt did not take kindly to the studies of imageless thought. He referred to the Würzburg studies as mock experiments, and objected to experimental studies of the higher thought processes, which he felt could only be understood by observing and interpreting them using his folk psychology.

The psychologies of Brentano, Stumpf, and Külpe never progressed very far. Their significance lay in their influences on later developments. However, Wundt's psychology survived at least for a while. It remained for Titchener to refine it and develop a system of structuralism, which we shall examine in the next chapter.

## Suggested Further Readings

Blumenthal, A. L., "A Reappraisal of Wilhelm Wundt." *American Psychologist,* Vol. 30 (1975), pp. 1081–1088. This article is an attempt to relate some of Wundt's basic ideas to contemporary psychology. Not for beginners.

Boring, E. G., "On the Subjectivity of Important Dates, Leipzig, 1879." *Journal of the History of the Behavioral Sciences,* Vol. 1 (1965), pp. 5–9. Interesting commentary on the founding of the Leipzig laboratory.

Bringmann, W. G., and Yweney, R. D., *Wundt Studies.* Toronto: C. J. Hogrefe, 1980. An excellent collection of papers, both original and reprinted, about Wundt, his career, and his impact on psychology.

Titchener, E. B., "Wilhelm Wundt." *American Journal of Psychology,* Vol. 32 (1921), pp. 161–78. Titchener's comments on the man he worked with and admired so much.

Wolman, B. B., ed., *Historical Roots of Contemporary Psychology.* New York: Harper and Row, 1968, ch. 13. The chapter on Wundt, written by George Humphrey, is a good exposition on Wundt, the man and his works.

Wundt, Wilhelm, *Outline of Psychology,* trans. C. Judd. Leipzig: Engelmann, 1907. By far, the best presentation of Wundt's systematic position, in his own words translated into English.

# CHAPTER

# 7

# *Structuralism*

Edward Bradford Titchener brought Wundt's psychology to America, where he refined and developed it into one of the leading systems or "schools" to compete with others during the first third of the twentieth century. Titchener propounded it, spread its ideas, gained adherents, and gave this school a name, *structuralism.* The system has had other names as well, *introspectionism* or *existentialism.* Introspectionism identified it by its main methodology. The term existentialism was dropped because it became confused with the French existential philosophy of Sartre, which had recently been expanded into a new existential psychology. But the existential psychology of today is quite different from what Titchener was talking about (see chap. 20).

It would be incorrect to say that structuralism dominated psychology in its prime, since other schools sprang up, usually in opposition. Some of these schools were: functionalism, behaviorism, and Gestalt psychology. In a sense, structuralism became the "whipping post" for the other psychologies, since almost everybody who did not agree with its tenets had something negative to say about it. Nevertheless, structuralism survived its attacks (at least for a while), developed many followers, and became an approach to psychology that was not to be dismissed lightly. Even before Titchener's death in 1927, the popularity of the system was beginning to wane, and by the mid-thirties it was finished as a unified separate approach to the nature of psychology. The reasons for its demise will be discussed in the concluding sections of this chapter.

## The Life of Edward B. Titchener (1867–1927)

Titchener was born in Chichester, England. Although his was an old established family, it had little money. Through scholarships, Titchener entered Malvern College and then Oxford, where he received his bachelor's degree in philosophy.

Rather dissatisfied with what he had learned in the course of his philosophical studies, he went to Leipzig to study with the famous Wundt. He remained at Leipzig for only two years, receiving his doctorate in 1892. Although he never had much personal interaction with the renowned scholar, partly because Wundt was a rather aloof person, the psychology that Wundt presented made a lasting impression on the young Titchener. As we have already indicated, scholars from other countries were at Leipzig at the time, many of them American. Eventually, they returned home to carry on psychology in different ways, but none of them held the allegiance to Wundt's position that Titchener did.

After leaving Leipzig, Titchener returned to Oxford, where he became an extension lecturer in biology. Titchener would have liked to have remained at Oxford, but the English were not ready for the "new" psychology. Therefore, he immigrated to America and to the then-new Cornell University at Ithaca, New York, where he remained for the rest of his life. He taught psychology and administered the new laboratory that had been established by James Angell just the year before. Titchener was then only twenty-five years old. In the next decade, he refined his system, wrote articles and books, and directed student research. During the thirty-five years that he was at Cornell, he directed fifty doctoral dissertations in psychology.

Titchener also made a number of translations of Wundt's enormous *Principles of Physiological Psychology*,[1] but as soon as he had finished translating one edition, Wundt had revised it. By the time Wundt wrote his fifth edition, Titchener translated only six of the chapters and quit.

He wrote less than a dozen books, but they were significant in outlining his position. Most of them were introductory and experimental texts. Some of them were: *An Outline of Psychology*[2] (1896), *The Primer of Psychology*[3] (1898), a four-volume *Experimental Psychology*[4] (1901–1905). The latter consisted of instructor's manuals and student workbooks. Then followed *Lectures in the Elementary Psychology of Feeling and Attention*[5] (1908), *Experimental Psychology of the Thought Processes*[6] (1909), and perhaps his most influential book, *Textbook of Psychology*[7] (1910).

He became the editor of the *American Journal of Psychology*, succeeding G. Stanley Hall. This journal did not serve exactly the same purpose as had Wundt's *Philosophische Studien*, but it did serve as one of the main outlets for the publication of his students' research.

[1]Wilhelm Wundt, *Principles of Physiological Psychology* (New York: The Macmillan Co., 1904).
[2]Edward B. Titchener, *An Outline of Psychology* (New York: The Macmillan Co., 1896).
[3]Edward B. Titchener, *Primer of Psychology* (New York: The Macmillan Co., 1898).
[4]Edward B. Titchener, *Experimental Psychology: A Manual of Laboratory Practices*, 4 vols. (New York: The Macmillan Co., 1901–1905).
[5]Edward B. Titchener, *Lectures on the Experimental Psychology of Feeling and Attention* (New York: Macmillan Co., 1908).
[6]Edward B. Titchener, *Lectures on the Experimental Psychology of Thought Processes* (New York: The Macmillan Co., 1909).
[7]Edward B. Titchener, *Textbook of Psychology* (New York: The Macmillan Co., 1910).

Titchener's relationships with the psychologists outside his own group were slight. In 1892 he was elected by the charter members of the American Psychological Association to its membership, but resigned a year later. He rejoined but never attended a meeting. When the association met one year at Ithaca, Titchener was "at home" for those who cared to visit him.

In 1904 Titchener organized his own group, "The Experimentalists." It was a rather informal group which met annually at various laboratories. As would be expected, Titchener dominated the meetings, deciding who was to come and what topics were to be discussed.[8] In 1913, when the group met at Yale, such eminent American psychologists as E. G. Boring, H. P. Weld, and H. S. Langfeld, who in their early days remained true to Titchener's position, were there. But there were also others there whose contributions became very diverse—such as Karl Lashley and E. C. Tolman (see chaps. 12 and 15).[9]

Titchener's lectures at Cornell were legendary. He wore his Oxford master's gown for he said, "It confirms the right to be dogmatic," and Titchener was.

Boring described the nature and atmosphere of Titchener's lectures in an article in the *American Journal of Psychology* following Titchener's death.[10]

In the first semester on Tuesday and Thursday at eleven he lectured to the undergraduates in the new lecture room in Goldwin Smith Hall, the room with a psychological demonstrational laboratory and an office built off it, and with the pitch of the seats determined by Titchener's stature. The demonstration was set out the hour before and Titchener arrived shortly after ten to inspect it. Later the staff gradually gathered in his office. When the time for the lecture arrived, he donned his gown, the assistant brushed his coat for fear of ashes from his ever present cigar, the staff went out the door for apparatus and took front seats and Titchener then appeared on the platform from the office door. The whole rite was performed pleasantly and sometimes jokingly, yet it was scrupulously observed. After the lecture the staff gathered in Titchener's office for an hour of talk and at one o'clock dispersed for lunch.

Although he was an Englishman who never gave up his British citizenship, Titchener has been described as being very Germanic and much like Wundt even to wearing a beard.[11] He never became Americanized or related to most of the other psychologists of his time.

---

[8]R. I. Watson, *The Great Psychologists,* 4th ed. (Philadelphia: J. B. Lippincott, 1978).

[9]A. A. Roback, *History of American Psychology* (New York: Library Publishers, 1952).

[10]E. G. Boring, "Edward Bradford Titchener, 1867–1927," *American Journal of Psychology,* Vol. 38 (1927), pp. 489–506, p. 500.

[11]E. G. Boring, *A History of Experimental Psychology,* 2nd ed. (New York: Appleton-Century-Crofts, 1950).

## *Structural Psychology*

### Elements of Consciousness

Titchener begins by posing three questions—the "what," the "how," and the "why" of psychology. The *what* refers to his systematic, introspective analysis of mental phenomena. The *how* refers to the problem of synthesis. How are mental events interrelated or combined? The *why* is to be found in the way mental events correlate with brain and nervous-system events. For Titchener, psychology was intended to study all conscious experience. As a matter of fact, he said, all science dealt with experience. Psychology was unique in that it dealt with *experience dependent on the experiencing individual.* In physics, the experience was independent of the individual. Titchener distinguished *consciousness* from *mind.* Consciousness considered all the elements present at any one *moment,* while mind consisted of all the experiences one had had from the day of one's birth.

Like Wundt, Titchener described the elements of consciousness. There were three basic classes: *sensations, images,* and *affections.* (Wundt had not included images as a special class.) The sensations were the elements of perceptions: the sights, sounds, tastes, smells, and the tactual and muscular sensations.

In *An Outline of Psychology*[12] he distinguished more than 42,415 different possible kinds of sensations as follows:

| Organ | Kinds of Sensations | Organ | Kinds of Sensations |
|---|---|---|---|
| Eye | 38,850 | Alimentary canal | 3 |
| Ear | 11,550 | Blood vessels | ? |
| Nose | ? | Lungs | 1 |
| Tongue | 4 | Sex organs | 1 |
| Skin | 3 | Ear (sense of balance) | 1 |
| Muscle | 1 | All organs (pain) | 1 |
| Tendon | 1 | | |
| Joint | 1 | | 42,415 |

Images were the elements of ideas. In some way, they represented patterns not actually present. Although Titchener had made a distinction between sensation and images, little space was devoted to images in his writings.

---

[12]Edward B. Titchener, *An Outline of Psychology* (New York: The Macmillan Co., 1896), p. 67.

The third basic class was affections, which became the characteristic elements of emotion. Affections were somewhat like sensations, but lacked the latter's clarity. Titchener dismissed Wundt's tri-dimensional theory of feeling and reduced affections to only one dimension, pleasantness–unpleasantness. He said that the other dimensions in Wundt's theory could be reduced to sensory elements, in particular, muscular and organic.

Like Wundt, Titchener considered the basic elements of experience to have attributes. There were *quality* and *intensity* (which Wundt had also proposed) but also *duration* and *clearness* and sometimes *extensity.*

*Quality* was the attribute that distinguished every elementary process from every other—hot, red, sour, or A#. Here, Titchener was following Wundt. *Intensity* placed a quality on a scale from lowest to highest; sensations were bright–dim, loud–soft, strong–weak, and so on.

*Duration* referred to the temporal attribute of the experience. It could be long or short, rise to a point and then fade away.

*Clearness* determined the place a particular process had in consciousness. Clarity meant that the experience was dominant and outstanding. Unclear experience faded in the background, and was considered to be at the fringe of consciousness. Affections *lacked* the attribute of clarity, since they were characteristically vague.

There was one more attribute, *extensity,* which belonged only to vision and touch. These experiences could be considered to be spread out in space. More recently, Stevens,[13] in his experiments on the dimensions of sound, has suggested that extensity could also be applied to tones. Loud, low tones were more extended or voluminous than soft, high ones.

The elements and their attributes constituted the whole structure of consciousness. In most of Titchener's texts, much space was devoted to discussions of the elements and their attributes. Each class of sensation was discussed in turn. The most space, of course, was devoted to vision. The sensations were typically described and related to their physiological correlates. There were references to classical experiments that often used the methods of psychophysics, also color mixing, studies in tonal discrimination, ways of determining the range of vision, and so forth. Titchener's discussion of sensation has become the prototype of present-day chapters on sensation in modern elementary psychology textbooks. Thus, he answers the "what," or what psychology is about.

## Attention

Like Wundt, Titchener gave considerable discussion to problems of attention. Attention constituted the arrangement of the conscious elements, and became the focus of consciousness, that which was in the foreground. Up to this point,

---

[13]S. S. Stevens, "The Attributes of Tone," *Proceedings of the National Academy of Science,* Vol. 20 (1934), pp. 457–59.

Titchener had followed Wundt's treatment fairly closely; but Titchener went further to describe three general stages of attention.

1. There was a kind of naive or involuntary attention. A sudden noise or flash of lightning quite naturally would command one's attention.

2. Voluntary or secondary attention was a purposeful focusing on some element in the state of consciousness. One might direct one's attention from one object to another.

3. There was what Titchener called "derived" or "habitual" attention. It was not naive but arose out of a repetition of similar circumstances. A mother attends habitually to the signals from her child.

## Perception

Titchener had considered sensations to be the most basic class of elements in conscious experience, but sensations, in themselves, constitute only raw experience. We do not at any one instant experience all the sensations that bombard us. Thus, perception involves experiencing a cluster or group of experiences that are selected out of all the possibilities presented. Titchener explained this selective process in terms of attention. What, in particular, was to be selected would be found in the determiners of attention.

"Perceptions are selected groups of sensations in which images are incorporated as an integral part of the whole process and it is in this—that perceptions have meaning."[14]

## Association

True to Wundt and the empirical tradition, Titchener accepted the principle of association. However, it was not so preeminent a principle as in other systems. Titchener's statement is as follows:[15]

> Let us try, however, to get a descriptive formula for the facts which the doctrine of association aims to explain. We then find this: that, whenever a sensory or imaginal process occurs in consciousness, there are likely to appear with it (of course, in imaginal terms) all those sensory and imaginal processes which occurred together with it in any earlier conscious present. . . . Now the law of contiguity can, with a little forcing, be translated into our own general law of association.

Thus, the "how" of psychology was to be discovered through understanding the processes of association.

---

[14]Edward B. Titchener, *Textbook of Psychology* (New York: The Macmillan Co., 1910), p. 367.
[15]Edward B. Titchener, *Textbook of Psychology, op. cit.,* pp. 378–79.

## Context Theory of Meaning

By 1915 Titchener had formulated his famous context theory of meaning. Wundt had touched on the problem, but never really dealt with it (see pp. 84–85).

In the context theory of meaning, *core* referred to raw experience, such as sensations of light, sound, touch, and smell. *Context* consisted of the associations that the raw experience would conjure up.

For Titchener, meaning was always context, that is, one mental process was the meaning for another mental process. Context was nothing more than the fringe of related processes that gathered around the central group, the core, of sensations and images. In perceptions and ideas which were more than simple sensations and images, there was core plus context. It was the context which gave meaning to the core. Titchener gave us several examples. In learning the meaning of some strange design, the core was the raw experience and the related fringe or associated experiences gave it the context or meaning.

In some cases, context was separated from core, such as when we repeated some word over and over again until the context disappeared and the word became meaningless. On the other hand, context could be added to core, such as when we learned the meaning of a foreign word.

Context and core might also be separated in time, as when we knew what we wanted to say but needed time to find the appropriate words.

The core, then, was the immediate, raw experience. Context was associated elements, typically reduced to kinesthetic or muscular sensations. Eventually, context might become verbal, as when we said something to ourselves about a stimulus.

## Emotion

The essential core of emotions is the feelings, or the affective aspects of experience. In order to understand how Titchener handled emotions, it is helpful to know how affections were studied in the laboratory. He suggested two methods: (1) impression and (2) expression. The impression method could involve making comparisons. For example, to study the affective characteristic of color, one might arrange a number of colors in descending order from the most pleasant to the most unpleasant; or one might use the method of paired comparisons, in which each color was paired with every other color, and in each pairing one color would be judged more pleasant than the other.

The expression method involved measuring bodily changes—breathing, heart rate, blood pressure, or the psychogalvanic response—that accompanied the affective experience. It is interesting that the measurement of the GSR (Galvanic Skin Response, as it is known today) had only recently been introduced into psychological laboratories at the time Titchener wrote his *Textbook* in 1910.

Titchener believed that emotions are simply intensified feelings arising from sensations inside the body. Here he referred to Darwin's theory of evolution: these organic aspects of emotion were carry-overs from an earlier period in human evolutionary development, a time when the more overt aspects were necessary for survival. Yet, Titchener still stressed the major affective mental components in emotions, along with the organic processes associated with those feelings.

## The Method of Introspection

Like Wundt, Titchener considered introspection and experimentation to be the methods of psychology. Introspection became one of the primary tenets of structural psychology. Science depended on observation, said Titchener, and introspection was one method of observation. Like Wundt, Titchener insisted on the "trained introspectionist."

In his *Outline of Psychology*,[16] Titchener gave several rules to follow if one were going to engage properly in the introspective process.

1. We must be completely impartial and unprejudiced. We must not be biased by preconceived ideas.

2. We must have our attention under control and not allow it to wander.

3. Our bodies and minds must be fresh. Fatigue, exhaustion, or drowsiness would prevent any sustained concentration.

4. Our general disposition must be favorable, that is, we should feel well, be of good temper, and be interested in the subject of our introspection.

One of the greatest problems Titchener encountered in the introspective process was what he called the "stimulus error." This meant to see the "thing" rather than its conscious content. The common example used by Titchener was to see a "table" and call it a "table." In this instance, one was reading into the conscious process what one already knew about the table. All that one's immediate experience told one was the color, brightness, and spatial pattern. The "stimulus error" consisted of reading unwanted meanings into what one was experiencing. As Wundt had insisted earlier, introspection could only be practiced by those who had had a rigorous training.

For Titchener, as for Wundt, introspection was part of the experimental process. Both insisted that it was experimentation that made psychology scientific. In the following quotation from Titchener's *Textbook of Psychology*, he expressed his attitude toward the need for experimentation. It should be kept in mind that Titchener's description of the experimental procedure included introspection as part of it.[17]

> An experiment is an observation that can be repeated, isolated and varied. The more frequently you can repeat an observation, the more likely are you to see

[16]Edward B. Titchener, *An Outline of Psychology, op. cit.,* pp. 38–40.
[17]Edward B. Titchener, *Textbook of Psychology, op. cit.,* p. 20.

clearly what is there and to describe accurately what you have seen. The more strictly you can isolate an observation, the easier does your task of observation become, and the less danger is there of your being led astray by irrelevant circumstances, or of placing emphasis on the wrong point. The more widely you can vary an observation, the more clearly will the uniformity of experience stand out, and the better is your chance of discovering laws. All experimental appliances, all laboratories and instruments, are provided and devised with this one end in view: that the student shall be able to repeat, isolate and vary his observation.

## Mind-Body Problem

When Titchener spoke of "experience dependent on the experiencing individual," he was stating his position of *psychophysical parallelism* which he adopted from Wundt. He clearly made a distinction between the mental and the physical. Neither caused the other, and they did not interact. A change in one accompanied a change in the other. The problem, as such, never became a real issue for him. He merely accepted it as a convenient explanatory device. He accepted it as a fact of expediency.[18] So, the parallelism between mind and body (in particular, the nervous system) constituted the "why" of psychology.

## *Evaluation*

### Criticisms of Structuralism

As one of the first systems to evolve, structuralism became the subject of the most vehement attacks.

1. First, Titchener had created a limited, "ivory tower" psychology. It was pure and self-contained, but it limited itself to the "immediate experiences of adult human beings." Titchener had no interest in applications at a time when other branches of psychology—child, social, animal, and abnormal— were beginning to emerge. Titchener simply ignored them.

2. A second major criticism came from those who objected to introspection as the main source of data. Those who opposed it considered it to be a most unreliable technique, although Titchener did not agree. Critics suggested that the mere act of introspecting might change the experience itself.[19]

   Another difficulty, mentioned by Boring in an article entitled "The History of Introspection,"[20] indicated that psychologists in different labo-

---

[18]E. Heidbreder, *Seven Psychologies* (New York: Appleton-Century Co., 1933), pp. 127–28.

[19]M. H. Marx, and W. A. Cronan-Hillix, *Systems and Theories in Psychology* (New York: McGraw-Hill Book Co., 1987), pp. 100–103.

[20]E. G. Boring, "A History of Introspection," *Psychological Bulletin*, Vol. 50 (1953), pp. 169–87.

ratories, using the same introspective techniques, were getting different results. The basic problem of the reliability of the data arose. Subjective data were always hard to verify. The same criticism had been levied against psychoanalysis (see chap. 17).

Finally, the question arose about just what the introspectionists were doing. They were trained in a certain way, with a special kind of vocabulary; but the question arose, was their vocabulary any more precise or special than any other? After all, in the final analysis, the introspective experience had to be translated into a verbal report. The introspectionists said they had their own vocabulary. The critics said theirs was no different from any other.

**3.** As psychology was evolving, it was becoming more and more concerned with objective, observable data. The animal psychologists and the behaviorists dismissed introspection because of its subjective nature. The structuralists' position was completely subjective. Further, they were completely content with a dualism of mind and body of a psychophysical sort. This bothered the behaviorists in particular. Psychology should study behavior, not consciousness. For the behaviorists and other objectively minded psychologists, consciousness was nothing more than "mental stuff," which had no place in a world of reality.

**4.** At a time when William James was pronouncing his pragmatism, and psychology was becoming more utilitarian and applied, the structuralists maintained an artificial attempt to analyze consciousness into its basic elements. But for what purpose? In the eyes of the pragmatists it was useless.

**5.** Finally, the Gestalt psychologists objected to the elementalistic kind of analysis (see chap. 14). They felt that a perception must be regarded as a whole, which was not divisible into its component parts. Their arguments will be discussed in more detail in the chapter devoted to their position.

## The Fate of Structuralism

Today, as a systematic position in psychology, structuralism is dead. It died because it had nowhere to go. It was limited; it defied application; it rejected objective data.

As late as 1933, Boring, in his book, *The Physical Dimensions of Consciousness,*[21] tried to correlate the attributes of experience—quality, intensity, clarity—with characteristics of the nerve impulses in the brain. But this was all purely hypothetical. According to Marx and Cronan-Hillix,[22] Boring dealt structuralism its final blow. Although Boring was still trying to salvage what was left of structuralism by defending consciousness as a legitimate study of psychology, his opponents were overriding him. In the early days, Boring had been an ardent student of Titchener's, and if structuralism had succeeded as a

---

[21]E. G. Boring, *The Physical Dimensions of Consciousness* (New York: The Century Co., 1933).
[22]M. H. Marx and W. A. Cronan-Hillix, *op. cit.*

system, Boring would have been Titchener's successor. But eventually, Boring realized the necessity of using objective, verifiable data as the subject matter of psychology and he acquiesced to its demise.[23]

## Contributions of Structuralism

What was left of structuralism has been absorbed into the mainstream of sensory psychology. Psychologists still study sensation, usually not through introspection, but through sophisticated laboratory instrumentation and quantitative analyses. Theories of vision and hearing persist, and the physiological psychologists still like to work with the physiological and anatomical correlates of the sensory processes. Psychologists still study vision, hearing, smell, taste, and pain.

In the previous chapter, we gave credit to Wundt for taking psychology away from the speculations of the arm-chair philosophers and establishing it as an independent experimental science. Titchener followed the tradition, and for several decades maintained faithful followers.

Titchener's system was neat and well defined. It set out to explore its intentions and, as such, it served as a model for other theories. It was self-contained. Its subject matter and methodology were well defined. It knew what its problems were, the "what," "how," and "why" of psychology. It pursued its problems in an orderly way to the bitter end.

Structuralism stimulated those who opposed it and originated new ways of thinking about psychology. One does not know how long it would have taken a more objective psychology to develop if it had not been for the subjectivity of structuralism.

Finally, perhaps the greatest impact of structuralism on modern psychology was its stress on the importance of experimental rigor, its attempt to carefully control its variables and to present a greater degree of theoretical sophistication than had previously been proposed.

## Suggested Further Readings

Boring, E. G., *The Physical Dimensions of Consciousness*. New York: The Century Co., 1933. A little volume in which Boring tries to correlate Titchener's attributes of experience with the nervous system and in particular with characteristics of the nerve impulse. With this book structuralism breathed its last breath.

Boring, E. G., "Edward Bradford Titchener, 1867–1927." *American Journal of Psychology,* Vol. 38 (1927), pp. 489–506. Boring's obituary to his mentor, in which he described many aspects of Titchener's personality and his work, not to be found elsewhere in general texts on history and systems.

---

[23]*Ibid.,* pp. 81–82.

Boring, E. G., "A History of Introspection." *Psychological Bulletin,* Vol. 50 (1953), pp. 169–87. One of the most illuminating discussions of the entire introspective movement in psychology up to the date of publication.

Roback, A. A., *A History of American Psychology.* New York: Library Publishers, 1952, ch. 16. A rather brief commentary on Titchener's life and works.

Titchener, E. B., *Textbook of Psychology.* New York: The Macmillan Co., 1910. Titchener's basic psychology. Probably the best exposition of his system in his own words.

# CHAPTER

# 8

# *William James: Forerunner of Functionalism*

William James (1842–1910) has played a unique and almost paradoxical role in the evolution of psychology. He was always a philosopher and a "sometime" psychologist. He has been considered by some[1, 2] to be the greatest psychologist to date. Looking back from our present-day position, this is a little hard to agree with. He *was*, however, one of the great pioneers in American psychology, and it is unquestionable that he exerted an influence on later trends in the field. In his objections to Wundt and the growing structuralist movement transplanted from Germany to America, James professed a new approach. This new approach led to the later functionalist movement that began at the University of Chicago (see next chapter). Chronologically, James was between Wundt and Titchener, but we have considered Titchener in the previous chapter because his structuralist system was a direct extension of Wundt's position.

For a time, James considered himself a psychologist, but he was never an experimentalist as were the structuralists, nor did he see experimentalism as the only solution to psychology's problems.

His psychology was not particularly systematic. His main position was set down primarily in the two-volume *Principles of Psychology*,[3] published in 1890.

[1]E. G. Boring, *A History of Experimental Psychology*, 2nd ed. (New York: Appleton-Century-Crofts, 1950).
[2]G. A. Miller, *Psychology: The Science of Mental Life* (New York: Harper and Bros., 1962).
[3]William James, *Principles of Psychology*, 2 vols. (New York: Henry Holt and Co., 1890).

It is possible to read it, chapter by chapter, not necessarily in order, without confusion. Nevertheless, there are certain themes or threads, both implicit and explicit, which appear throughout the work.

## The Man and His Works

James was born in New York City in 1842 at the Astor House, and his brother, Henry, the famous author, in the same city fourteen months later. His early education took place both in this country and in Europe. His family was well-to-do, so he traveled and was schooled in England, France, Switzerland, and Germany. As a result of this rather scattered education, it took time for him to settle down to what was to become his life's work. First, he tried painting for six months, and then, at the age of nineteen, entered Harvard University. He studied the sciences and in 1869 received his degree in medicine. His first position was teaching physiology at Harvard in 1872. Watson[4] argued that James established the first psychological laboratory in 1875. Wundt had usually been credited with that innovation at Leipzig in 1879, although prior to that date, Wundt was becoming organized. Whether James' endeavor was a real laboratory or merely a room with a few brass instruments is a matter of conjecture. History is often vague. In any event, James did get an appropriation from Harvard for $300 for use in physiology.[5]

In 1878 James signed a contract to publish his *Principles of Psychology*,[6] but the book was twelve years in preparation. During the following years, his academic position vacillated from that of philosopher to psychologist. At about the time of the publication of *Principles*, his title was changed to Professor of Psychology, and shortly thereafter, back to Professor of Philosophy. During his psychology years, the number of people he taught who were to become eminent psychologists was not large. His list could hardly match that of Wundt. Among them, however, were some very influential people: James Angell (see next chapter), Mary W. Calkins, Edward L. Thorndike (see chap. 10), and Robert S. Woodworth (see chap. 11). Angell, Thorndike, and Woodworth were all important figures in American psychology for the theories and systems they formulated. All these people turned out to have a profound effect on the psychology which was to come.

In 1899 James published *Talks to Teachers*[7] which, from the point of view of present educational psychology, was a kind of "Mickey Mouse" elucidation stressing the ideal of individual goals in education. His *Varieties of Religious*

---

[4]R. I. Watson, *The Great Psychologists,* 4th ed. (Philadelphia: J. B. Lippincott, 1978).
[5]*Ibid.*
[6]William James, *op. cit.*
[7]William James, *Talks to Teachers on Psychology: and to Students on Some of Life's Ideals* (New York: Henry Holt and Co., 1899).

*Experience*[8] (1901) was an attempt at a psychology of religion. He believed that there were basically three types of religious experience: a kind of shallow but *healthy-minded* experience; a denial of anguish—a kind of Christian Science; and, far more common, the "sick soul." The person with this second kind of experience came to grips with evil and anguished over it. There was always the possibility of overcoming despair and realizing that people were good. Nevertheless, evil might prevail as something to be constantly struggling with. The third type was *mystical.* Its description was ineffable, and one who has had the mystical experience would realize it intuitively. (Incidentally, James was a firm believer in psychic or extrasensory phenomena.)

In the field of modern philosophy, James is well known for his *Pragmatism*[9] (1909). The general idea stated was that ideas had to be treated in terms of their utilitarian consequences. An idea was true if it worked. Just what James meant by "worked" was subject to considerable controversy among philosophers,[10] but pragmatism became a very popular movement in the early part of this century.

## James' Psychology

James' psychology is primarily set down in his *Principles.* Today, the work is considered one of the great classics in psychology, and is read by all who presume to call themselves psychologists. In 1892 he published a condensed version called *Psychology: Briefer Course,*[11] intended as a basic text for beginning psychology students. It was intended by the publisher to be a "money-maker," and it was. In any event, both works enjoyed great popularity in psychology, because they investigated what psychology should be and because they were the first extended statements of what American psychology should be. The *Briefer Course* became popularly known as "Jimmy" to distinguish it from the larger two-volume work, the *Principles.*

Although the work was somewhat unsystematic, and disconcerting to some for that reason, there were at least two threads which ran through many of its chapters. The first was a kind of early functionalist psychology, to be elaborated on later. The second was James' position on the mind-body problem implicit in many of the chapters.

### Forerunner of Functionalism

We could say that James was the founder of functionalism only in an informal sense, but his influence on the later Chicago school of functionalism was un-

---

[8]William James, *Varieties of Religious Experience* (New York: Longmans, Green, 1902).

[9]William James, *Pragmatism: A New Name for Old Ways of Thinking* (New York: Longmans, Green, 1909).

[10]R. I. Watson, *op. cit.,* p. 328.

[11]William James, *Psychology: Briefer Course* (New York: Henry Holt and Co., 1892).

questionable. The theme of functionalism, taken from Darwin, was that behavior was adaptable, and in order to survive psychologically, one had to be able to adjust to one's environment. Sometimes the adaptation involved more of a bodily process. At other times, it became more the domain of the mind. It depended on what kind of behavior and what particular mental processes were involved. In any event, both mind and body were two different but related sides of life. For example, when we encountered a problem, reason served to solve it, and the solution was set into action. This might be the result of needs, purposes, or goals, but their satisfaction had *survival value*. As we examine the chapters in *Principles* more closely, this functionalist theme will be made evident.

## Mind-Body Problem

James, of course, was a dualist and, like his contemporaries and many of those who were to follow him, believed in the reality of both mind and body. His position was clearly that of *interactionism*. This was particularly interesting because it represented an explanation completely opposite to Wundt's parallelism—a position which James opposed on other grounds as well. His early training in physiology and anatomy led him to be concerned with neurological and other physiological processes. In fact, the first six chapters of *Principles*, Vol. I, dealt with physiology in order to clear the way for the psychology which was to follow. In those first chapters, he considered the most important aspects of neural activity that were necessary to *serve* mental life. In some later chapters, such as those on *habit* and *instinct*, the neurological and body processes were most important. In other chapters, such as *stream of consciousness, reason,* and *the self,* the mental took preeminence. In any event, there was an interaction between the two. Sometimes, the mind operated to serve the body and at other times, the body could take over more automatically, leaving the mind free for more useful things. As we examine the separate aspects of his psychology, we shall point out the inevitable examples of this *interactionist* position.

## Definition of Psychology

Quite clearly, James stated that "Psychology is the Science of Mental Life, both of its phenomena and of their conditions." By "phenomena" he referred to the subject matter found in experience. However, this should not be construed as the "experience" of the structuralists. The "conditions" meant that the bases for mental life were to be found in the body, particularly the brain. Although James was much concerned with consciousness, it was obvious that there was also a physical being as well.

## Methods and Snares

In his chapter on *Methods and Snares in Psychology,* James began by stating that psychology *is* a natural science, although he recognized that the problems of investigation that would be encountered by the psychologists were not going to be easy ones.

1. **Introspection.** This method was the most fundamental to psychology. Since psychology was the study of mental life, this obviously meant consciousness. The fact was that we had to examine our own mental activity, and introspection was the one way to do it. This was not, however, intended to be the introspection of the "trained introspectionist" of Wundt and Titchener. To James, it was a natural gift, and consisted in catching the moment of consciousness as it passed (see next section). Since consciousness changed, it was a fleeting thing. This was not the introspection of the laboratory aided by the brass instruments. James did not consider, as Brentano had, that introspection was infallible, but neither did he consider it impossible. It was beset with difficulties, but as a form of observation, it was most useful. By comparing reports of different observers, verification was possible.

2. **Experimentation.** Although he was not an experimentalist, James believed experimentation was a legitimate method of psychology. Although he had little use for the experiments of the Germans, Wundt or Fechner, he believed some kind of experimentation was possible. This he left to posterity to discover, since experimental methodology in the psychology of his time was in a rather primitive state. "Facts are facts," he said, and it was up to the experimenter to discover them.

3. **Comparative method.** This third topic was a subsidiary to the first two. It entered into the psychology of animals and children, of primitive peoples, and even mental defectives and the insane. He considered the comparative method somewhat inexact, and the investigator was left with his own common sense in using it. It should be noted at this time that psychology covered a broad scope of topics, in direct constrast to the limited area the structuralists considered psychology to cover.

The *snares* referred to the problems in executing the methods of psychology. The first of these was *language.* Words were used to convey the pragmatic needs of our everyday lives. The facts of consciousness could only be conveyed to others through the use of language, and there was not a very reliable relationship between what we could introspect, for example, and how we could make our introspections known to others. What if we had no word for a given mental event? Did we ignore it? In all probability, said James, the answer was "yes." Suppose we both observed the same mental event. How similar would our verbal descriptions be? It was a problem, and we were left to contend with it.

The second main snare was what James called the "psychologist's fallacy." Human beings were outside the mental states they observed. They were aware of their own mental states and the external objects of those states in the world of reality. Suppose one observed a tree. There was more in one's mental life regarding a tree than one's mere perception of it. What James was saying was that we tended to read into our perceptions more than what was actually there. James was urging people who presumed to be psychologists to report its subject matter (mental life) only at first hand and report only what was there. Although he was an opponent of the structuralists, the snare that James was describing amounted to the same thing Titchener had called the "stimulus error" (see p. 97).

## The Stream of Consciousness

Perhaps the crux of James' psychology is to be found in his chapter on the stream of consciousness. His functionalist position is well illustrated in this discussion.

> Consciousness, then, does not appear to itself chopped up into bits. Such words as "chain" or "train" do not describe it fully as it presents itself in the first instance. It is nothing jointed: it flows. A "river" or "stream" are metaphors by which it is most naturally described. *In talking of it hereafter, let us call it the stream of thought of consciousness, or of subjective life.*"[12]

In taking this position, James opposed the concept of consciousness as expressed by Wundt and the later structuralists. They had considered consciousness to be a more static state that could be broken down into its elements.

James described consciousness by its five basic characteristics, which together form the essence of mental life:

1. Consciousness was personal. The fact was that every thought tended to be part of a personal consciousness. A particular thought was *my* thought not *yours*, so there was a great gulf between one's own consciousness and that of others. Even though there might be what in abnormal psychology we speak of as multiple personalities or automatic writing, James did not think of secondary personalities.

2. Consciousness was always changing. This was basic to James' psychology, and distinguished him very explicitly from Wundt. Here, in a psychological way, he went back to Heraclitus who had spoken over a thousand years before of things being in a constant state of change. James applied this to mental life. No state of mind or idea, even if it recurred, could ever be identical with the first. Consciousness was like a constantly flowing stream, an unbroken affair. Sometimes it flowed very rapidly; at other times it seemed to hardly move.

3. Consciousness was sensibly continuous. There were no breaks or cracks in the stream. There might be interruptions in the continuity as during sleep, but in waking life there was no difficulty in making connections. Perhaps the description was best characterized in James' own words:

---

[12]William James, *Principles of Psychology* (New York: Dover Publications, 1950), Vol. 1, p. 239.

Like a bird's life, it seems to be made up of an alternation of flights and perch-ings. The rhythm of language expresses this, where every thought is expressed in a sentence, and every sentence closed by a period. The resting-places are usually occupied by sensoral imaginations of some sort, whose peculiarity is that they can be held before the mind for an indefinite time, and contemplated without changing; the places of flights are filled with thoughts of relations, static or dynamic, that for the most part obtain between the matters contem-plated in the periods of comparative rest. Let us call the resting place the "sub-stantive parts" and the places of flight the "transitive parts" of the stream of thought.

4. Consciousness dealt with objects other than itself. Here was a clearly stated dualism between the mind and the objects it dealt with. James pointed out that some psychologists have confused the objects of thought with the thoughts themselves. This was a version of the "psychologist's fallacy" mentioned earlier. Thoughts were unitary, no matter how complex they might be. If one were dealing with complex objects, the unity of their nature must also be recognized.

5. Consciousness was always selective or choosing. Sensation and perception were selective. In a sense, we selected what we wanted to see from a mass of stimuli surrounding us. We listened to the chirpings of a bird or looked for a lost object. We did not merely passively receive the experiences im-posed on our minds, but actively chose. At any time the mental stream was cluttered, and we did not attend to all of it.

## The Self

There was a consciousness of the self, or what James called the "me" or empir-ical self. This was the self as known, and it consisted of a hierarchy of aspects. What James referred to as the "self," we might translate into the term "person-ality." So then as now, personality became an integral part of psychology.

At the bottom of the hierarchy of aspects was the *material self*. This included not only our body but also its possessions—clothes, home, property, even money. In other words, all our personal possessions.

Second on the hierarchy was the *social self* or *social selves*. One had as many social selves as there were persons who responded to one or recognized or had opinions of one. I might have a somewhat different social self for my parents, my wife, my children, my minister, or my friends at the barroom. To the extent that we related to different social groups, we might have many or few social selves. The social selves tended to fall into classes, and to these we might exhibit different facets of our own personality.

Next, and at the top of the hierarchy, was the *spiritual self*. This was more intimate than the first two. The spiritual self consisted of psychological func-tions or what James called "all the psychic faculties or dispositions taken to-gether." This involved thinking, intellectual capacities, and willing, to name only a few. It should be pointed out that in this instance James did not mean spiritual in the sense of a "soul" of a theological nature.

James identified these three selves—the material, social, and spiritual—as the "me" or empirical self, the self as *known*. Over and above these was the *pure ego*, or self as *knower*, the "I." Just as we have described the selves as known, there had to be a self that did the knowing. There seemed to be a "something" which remained steadfast despite the transitory nature of flowing consciousness. This did not have to be transcendent or metaphysical. One could imply that what James really meant was a kind of "soul."

James' notion of *perception* was an attack on the fragmented, atomized nature of experience set forth by the British empiricists and associationists. His account of perception was in keeping with his concept of the *self*—the psychological self, the real object of thought, which in turn unites perceptions. Here James was referring to the self as *known* (the "me") and not the self as *knower* (pure ego).

## Habit

One of the most popular chapters in *Principles* is that on habit. It has often been referred to as the "wonderful chapter on habit," probably not so much for the significance of its content, but because of the elegance in writing style. The chapter not only illustrated James' strong bent for physiological explanations, but it discussed his dualism as well (interactionism). We have already described the stream of consciousness and some of the activities of mental life. Often, with continuous repetition, these mental functions became stabilized. When this occurred, pathways became established in the nervous system, particularly the brain. These pathways could account for the regularities of our lives—the ways we spoke, the things we did, and the places we went. Thus, in habitual activities, consciousness was allowed to lapse. Habit took over, and the traces of these habits were laid down in the brain. There was a real advantage to habit that illustrated James' functionalist position. As habits were laid down, the mind was left free to do other things and so one did not have to think about every action one took. Biologically speaking, habits resulted from an increased placidity of the neural matter, which made it easier for repeated activities to be continued.

The following famous quotation states his position clearly, and is one of the illustrations of the beauty of his writing.[13]

> Habit is thus the enormous fly-wheel of society, its most precious conservative agent. It alone is what keeps all within the bounds of ordinance, and saves the children of fortune from the envious uprisings of the poor. It alone prevents the hardest and most repulsive walks of life from being deserted by those brought up to tread therein. It keeps the fisherman and the deck-hand at the sea through the winter; it holds the miner in his darkness, and hails the countryman to his log-cabin and his lonely farm through all the months of snow; it protects us

---

[13]*Ibid.*, p. 79.

from invasion by the natives of the desert and the frozen zone. It dooms us all to fight out the battle of life upon the lines of our nurture or our early choice, and to make the best of a pursuit that disagrees, because there is no other for which we are fitted, and it is too late to begin again. It keeps different social strata from mixing. Already at the age of twenty-five you see the professional mannerism settling down on the young commercial traveller, on the young doctor, on the young minister, on the young counsellor-at-law. You see the little lines of cleavage running through the character, the tricks of thought, the prejudices, the ways of the "shop," in a word, from which the man can by-and-by no more escape than his coat sleeve can fall suddenly into a new set of folds. On the whole, it is best he should not escape. It is well for the world that for most of us, by the age of thirty, the character has set like plaster, and will never soften again.

## Instinct

In his discussion of instinct, James again stressed biological background. He was influenced by the animal psychologists of the time and considered humans also to be animals, likewise endowed with unlearned patterns of reacting. He considered the human to have a very large number of instincts, more than any other species. In stressing instincts as self-preservative, he reflected Darwin, and laid the basis for the functionalists. Babies had instincts for crying, biting, moving, and vocalizing, to name a few. Some of these grew in character, like locomotion and speech, while others died out. He included imitation, pugnacity, hunting, acquisitiveness, play, love, fear, and jealousy. Instincts were able to facilitate doing things the natural way.

Unlike the animal psychologists, James did not consider instincts to be "blind and invariable." They could be modified by habit. The important point was that they were nonrational. The fact that we possessed many opposing instincts (love-hate, pugnacity-sociability, bashfulness-vanity) indicated that with changing conditions antecedent to the onset of the instinctive act, the instinct itself might be variable and modifiable. It was, of course, McDougall and Freud who "jelled" the instinct doctrine in humans and made it the focal point of their systems.

## Emotion

In explaining emotions, James developed a theory that became his most widely known contribution to psychology. At about the same time, a Danish physiologist, C. G. Lange, published a similar theory; so today it has come down to us as the James-Lange theory of emotion.

Prior to the publication of this theory the classical or then-popular theory was that we perceived some object, experienced the emotion, and then responded to it. I saw a bear, I was afraid and I ran. The paradigm would read: $S$ (stimulus)—$E$ (emotion)—$R$ (response). James reversed the order. The following quotation explains his position clearly.[14]

---

[14]*Ibid.*, Vol. I, pp. 449–50.

Common-sense says, we lose our fortune, are sorry and weep; we meet a bear, are frightened and run; we are insulted by a rival, are angry and strike. The hypothesis here to be defended says that this order of sequence is incorrect, that the one mental state is not immediately induced by the other, that the bodily manifestations must first be interposed between, and that the more rational statement is that we feel sorry because we cry, angry because we strike, afraid because we tremble, and not that we strike, or tremble, because we are sorry, angry, or fearful, as the case may be. Without the bodily states following on the perception, the latter would be purely cognitive, in form, pale, colorless, destitute of emotional warmth. We might then see the bear, and judge it best to run, receive the insult and deem it right to strike, but we would not actually *feel* afraid or angry.

James thus made clear that the response which preceded the emotion followed directly from our perception of the object. The response included the running from the bear itself as physical movement, but also many internal reactions as well, such as increase in heart rate, blood pressure, flow of adrenaline, etc. In strong emotions such as fear, rage, or grief these were obvious. In the more subtle emotions, these might not be so easy to detect, but according to the theory they were still there.

The theory gave us one of the best examples of James' interactionist position between mind and body. One perceived the bear; this gave a mental impression which in turn caused the bodily activity of running and other physiological reactions. The perception of these was sent back up to the mind which experienced the emotion.

At the time of its conception, the theory generated considerable discussion and debate. It had its defenders and opponents. There are still dualistically inclined psychologists today who would take it seriously, and it still appears in many introductory texts along with Cannon's theory which opposed it.

Walter B. Cannon (1871–1945) was a Harvard physiologist who taught at the medical school there from 1899 until his death. He suggested that following the stimulus, the emotion (mental experience) and the visceral responses (in the body) occurred simultaneously. He argued that the visceral changes are not fast enough to be considered the actual source of the emotion.

Today, for all intents and purposes, the issue is dead. The James-Lange theory solved nothing, because emotions *are* responses. It is now considered important primarily in a historical context, as a theory that opposed the earlier "common sense" view.

## Reason

As a mental function, reason was of considerable importance to James. One aspect of reason, conceptualization, formed the "keel and backbone" of our thinking. Reason, however, had its foundation in nonrational needs (mind-body interaction again). Reason was also dependent on the machinery of the brain. It depended, likewise, on associations previously formed and stored in the brain somewhere. However, since it was dependent on associations, reason was subject to all the quirks and accidents that resulted from the forming of peculiar associations. Association by similarity was, of course, most helpful.

Because the mind was capable of choosing, it was capable of selecting (see stream of consciousness). Consequently, problems could be solved in an active way.

The anticipation of the later functionalists' psychology of a survival principle was evident in the human capacity to reason. Because humans could reason and were not driven by blind instincts, they had a better advantage for survival both physically and psychologically. So, again in reason, we had the two basic themes which ran through James' psychology, the mind-body interaction and the principle of survival.

### Memory

Remembering was a general characteristic of the brain structure, differing from one person to another. James was intrigued with the earlier notion set forth by the faculty psychologists that memory was a unitary function and could be improved with training. If one cultivated one's memory in one area, other areas could be cultivated as well. The only experiment he ever did[15] involved learning one kind of poetry to see if it would facilitate the learning of entirely different poetry. He used himself and a few of his students as subjects. His results indicated that his students did no better or worse on the second kind of material after having learned the first. Later, Thorndike and Woodworth[16] demonstrated that the faculty psychologists were wrong in their general mind-training idea, so that the degree of transfer from learning one set of materials to another depended on the similarity of material from one task to another (see chap. 10).

## William James: Some Unfinished Business

A series of lectures and discussions was held a few years ago as part of the commemoration of the seventy-fifth anniversary of the founding of the American Psychological Association. This series resulted in the publication of a small volume entitled *William James: Unfinished Business*.[17] Some of the issues raised are described below.

The stream of consciousness seems to be a model for modern phenomenological analysis (see chap. 20). Modern phenomenology is still actively concerned with man's inner experiences.

---

[15]*Ibid.*, Vol. I.

[16]Edward L. Thorndike and Robert S. Woodworth, "The Influence of Improvement in One Mental Function upon the Efficiency of Other Functions," *Psychological Review*, Vol. 8 (1901), pp. 247–61.

[17]American Psychological Association, *William James, Unfinished Business* (Washington, D.C., 1969).

James' psychophysical interactionism is still a model for much current research in physiological psychology. An interest in how the brain's function is interrelated with psychological activity continues to be a fertile area for research.

The instinct doctrine examined by James and further by McDougall fell into some disrepute with the advent of behaviorism (see chap. 11). However, there has recently been a considerable revival of interest, particularly among animal psychologists. Harlow,[18] in his discussion of the issue, stated that James' ideas on instinct held remarkably true in his own research with monkeys. James suggested that many instincts rose and then fell. Harlow has found this to be true in the maternal instinct of the mother as her infant matures.

James brought up many problems on levels of awareness, attention, consciousness, hypnosis, and daydreaming. These issues continue to command the attention of psychological research today.

Finally, James' humanism and concern with the problem of the "will" are of vital relevance for humanistic psychology today (see chap. 19). James, like the modern humanist, was concerned with matters of human purpose and values. He stressed the importance of "will," a matter which later psychologists partly abandoned in favor of such concepts as motivation or drive. But the existential and humanistic movements in psychology today maintain that the will cannot be ignored for it gives us self-direction, and it controls and integrates our activities.

Opponents of the "will" doctrine would consider it to be like a little "homunculus" or "little human" seated inside our brain, that directs our activity. Whether or not one agrees with the humanists on this issue is not important. What is significant, is that this issue, along with others cited above, is vital today, and was tackled earlier by James.

## Significance of James

Since James was not an experimentalist and his theories were not very systematic, the question arises as to why he has been so highly revered in a discipline which he later referred to as "that nasty little subject." He was more of a philosopher than a psychologist, and his main psychology was set forth in only one work, *Principles of Psychology*. Boring,[19] the oft-quoted historian of psychology, has suggested three reasons for James' eminence.

**1.** The first was personal. An obscure writer, or a crabbed personality might have said the same thing and gone unnoticed. His personality was charm-

---

[18]H. Harlow, "William James and Instinct Theory," in *William James, Unfinished Business, op. cit.*
[19]E. G. Boring, *op. cit.,* p. 512.

ing and magnetic. Also, he had an elegant writing style considered by many to be unequalled in psychological literature.

2. The second reason can be considered negative. He was opposed to the elementistic structuralism of Wundt and other Germans, such as Külpe. He offered an alternative approach to the nature of psychology at a crucial time when psychology was evolving from philosophy.

3. He was a pioneering American psychologist and, in a sense, he allowed psychology in this country to come into being. As the true antecedent of American functionalism, some of the ideas generated by him still remain with us.

But there are other reasons that have been suggested by a number of contemporary psychologists, including George A. Miller.

1. James popularized psychology and made scholars of the day recognize that a new intellectual discipline was evolving that had to be contended with. This, indeed was a most important contribution.

2. He was a *pragmatist*. Today, in modern experimental psychology, there is a trend toward questioning the usefulness of one's research. The days of "pure research," research for its own sake, are beginning to wane. Those agencies interested in funding the experiments of psychologists are asking, toward what useful purpose can the results of an investigation be put? The whole movement of applied behavioral analysis is one such example of the application of principles discovered in the laboratory for the betterment of human welfare (see chap. 13).

3. In recent years, a movement has evolved toward existential and humanistic psychology (see chaps. 19 and 20). Although some "hard-headed" experimentalists may consider this a regression to older times, nevertheless, the movement is gaining momentum. James' concept of the "stream of consciousness" is being rediscovered by these psychologists.

4. Finally, what we *can* say is that James launched psychology in America. And this we can say with great assurance.

Perhaps the significance of James is best summarized by Miller:[20]

> It is much easier to appreciate William James than to evaluate him. If one points to the thousands of students who read his books, to the inspiration he provided for Dewey and the functional psychologists at Chicago . . . , to the sensitivity with which he exposed to view a rich world of inner experience, to the intelligence of his arguments and the beauty of his prose, it is obvious that he was, and still is, the foremost American psychologist.

---

[20]G. A. Miller, *op. cit.*, pp. 77–78.

It should be pointed out that, although Miller's statement is beautifully phrased, one might wonder just how many psychologists today would share his conclusion that James still is the foremost American psychologist; probably not very many.

## Suggested Further Readings

American Psychological Association, *William James: Unfinished Business.* Washington, D.C.: American Psychological Association, 1969. A symposium presented at the seventy-fifth anniversary of the founding of the association. Many of the issues that James presented are still being considered but not necessarily resolved.

Hilgard, E. R., *Psychology in America: A Historical Survey.* Washington, D.C.: American Psychological Association, 1987.

James, W., *Principles of Psychology,* 2 vols. New York: Henry Holt and Co., 1890. James' basic psychology. Everyone who can should sample the elegance of James' writings. No psychologist has ever matched the beauty of his style.

James, W., *Psychology: Briefer Course.* New York: Henry Holt and Co., 1892. For those who prefer James in brief. A very popular beginning textbook in its day.

Wolman, B. B., ed., *Historical Roots of Contemporary Psychology.* New York: Harper and Row, 1968, ch. 8. Saul Rosenzweig's contributed chapter on William James and his stream of thought. Rather advanced.

# CHAPTER

# 9

# *Functionalism*

Functionalism arose as a protest against structuralism, but not in any dramatic way. As a system, it just grew without any great intention on the part of its founders. But, by 1925, when Harvey Carr published his book, *Psychology: A Study of Mental Activity,*[1] functionalism had established itself as a "school" at the University of Chicago, and was to flourish and influence later psychologies. Controversies existed between the two schools, and a lively battle ensued. By the time functionalism had reached its zenith, structuralism was beginning to diminish. When structuralism had vanished as a separate system, functionalism was also becoming absorbed by a growing American psychology.

## Antecedents

### The Theory of Evolution

In 1855 Herbert Spencer was fostering a philosophical theory of evolution which antedated Darwin by four years (see p. 56). For Spencer, evolution consisted of a change from indefinite homogeneity to definite heterogeneity, involving a continuous process of integration and differentiation. As humans had evolved, their nervous systems had become more complex, allowing for the possibility of more complex experiences. These changes allowed for a continuous process of greater adjustment to environmental conditions. The higher an organism was on the evolutionary ladder, the more complex and differentiated its responses became. Since the mind evolved along with the body, the greater the differentiation, the more *useful* experiences became.

---

[1]Harvey A. Carr, *Psychology: A Study of Mental Activity* (New York: Longmans, Green, 1925).

More psychological theories have been influenced by nineteenth-century evolutionary thinking than possibly any other intellectual (including scientific) movement of the time.

Darwin was not the first to present an evolutionary theory during the last century. Spencer, Darwin's contemporary, had posed a theory of a speculative sort, and when Darwin published his *The Origin of Species by Means of Natural Selection,*[2] Spencer jumped on the band wagon (see p. 56). Earlier, Lamarck (1744), both a botanist and a zoologist, had gathered such a mass of data on plants and animals that his theory, although controversial, could not be set aside lightly. He posed the question of why changes in the characteristics of organisms occurred from one generation to the next. In answer to this basic evolutionary question, one must consider the three main steps in his argument.[3]

1. When an organism confronted a physical environment certain adaptations had to occur.

2. These adaptations or adjustments caused the animal to exercise certain parts of its body.

3. Such exercise of a given part of the body caused an advancement of the adjustment process, which could cause that change to take place in his offspring. In other words, acquired characteristics of one organism could be passed on to one's offspring. A common example, although somewhat absurd to us today, explained why the giraffe had such a long neck: each generation had to reach higher and higher to get its food. On the other hand, a particular organ of the body might disappear if it were a hindrance or were useless. Snakes no longer had legs because they could get along without them.

## Charles Darwin (1809–1882)

As Darwin's theory began to gain acceptance, it tended to contradict and re-place that of Lamarck. However, the latter's theory was not completely aban-doned. As late as 1938, the psychologist William McDougall[4] was still attempting to establish the validity of Lamarck's hypothesis (see chap. 11). Even today in some biological and psychological circles, there has been some revival of Lamarckian thinking.

While on his trip to the South Seas (1831–1836), Darwin was able to collect and observe a tremendous number of plants and animals. In his later studies, after he had returned to England, he began to ask himself why certain

---

[2]Charles Darwin, *The Origin of Species by Means of Natural Selection* (New York: Appleton-Century-Crofts, 1897).

[3]G. Murphy, *An Historical Introduction to Modern Psychology* (New York: Harcourt, Brace and Co., 1949), chs. 8 and 10.

[4]William McDougall, "Fourth report on a Lamarckian experiment," pts. I–IV in *British Journal of Psychology,* Vol. 28 (1938), pp. 231–45, 365–96.

forms of life seemed so perfectly adapted to their present environment. He noted that in every generation there seemed to be a process of selection—that is, those best suited to that particular environment survived; the others died out.

Darwin had read Malthus's *Essay on Population,* in which the author pointed out that the number of offspring in a human population was greater than the number that could subsist. Therefore, there must be some struggle for survival.

Gradually, Darwin began to outline his theory in the following manner:

1. In most species the total number seemed relatively stable; yet there were many more offspring than parents. Darwin said, "The wastage is prodigious."

2. This led Darwin to the idea that those best suited to the environment would survive—the "survival of the fittest." In order to be "fit," the organism had to be capable of nourishing itself and warding off its enemies.

3. To be fit meant that one was capable of adapting to that environment. However, the survival of a species referred to a particular environment. A particular species might survive in one environment and not in another.

4. If, over the years, an environment changed, it followed that the organisms that remained would be those that could survive in the new environment.

5. Natural selection occurred from a *variation* that regularly occurred among the offspring of the same parents. With a change in the environment, natural selection would result in the evolution of a new species.

In 1859, after much study, Darwin published *The Origin of Species by Means of Natural Selection,*[5] generally referred to by the shorter title, *The Origin of Species.* Despite the fact that other theories of evolution had been propounded, Darwin's theory was taken seriously because of the mass of data he presented in support of his doctrine. In 1871 he published the *Descent of Man,*[6] in which he emphasized the similarity of human characteristics (including psychological) and those of the higher animals, from which came the false notion that humans were direct descendants of the apes. With an even greater psychological bent, *The Expression of Emotions in Man and Animals*[7] was published in 1872; in this work he suggested that humans resembled animals in facial and postural expressions during emotional activity.

***Implications of Darwin's Theory.*** Darwin's influence on psychology was not only general for the entire discipline as a whole, but it was also specific with regard to more particular theories that emerged.

---

[5]Charles Darwin, *op. cit.*
[6]Charles Darwin, *The Descent of Man* (New York: Appleton-Century-Crofts, 1871).
[7]Charles Darwin, *The Expression of Emotions in Man and Animals* (London: Murray, 1873).

Darwin was a dualist and applied his theory of evolution to both mind and body. This was most evident in his latter two works. In these it was clear that animals had minds and engaged in thought processes, but to a lesser degree than humans. The lower one descended on the scale to the more primitive creatures, the less significant the mental functions were. However, Darwin's theory dealt a crushing blow to the philosophical notion that humans were distinct from lower forms, since they had been endowed with minds or souls, which the lower forms lacked. The Christian Church was upset, as today, in the more fundamentalist sects, it still is.

Since Darwin accepted a mind-body dualism, the inevitable controversy followed about whether animals had consciousness and, if so, to what degree; and how low must one go to simpler forms before consciousness ceased. The controversy ended in a stalemate, only to be resolved by later animal psychologists and the behavioristic movement. This movement concluded that the study of mind was impossible, and one might better look to the observable behavior and forget about whether or not minds existed.

A second major influence led to a serious consideration that animals were worth studying for their behavioral as well as their biological aspects. Thus, with Darwin, was born a sincere and lasting attitude that the behavior of animals was worth studying and, consequently, the whole field of animal psychology evolved. The more specific influences of the animal psychologists will be discussed in later chapters. Since human beings were kin to the animals, not only was animal behavior worth studying for its own sake, but also for what implications it might have for humans.

More specifically, evolutionary theory had profound influences on the psychology of William James[8] and the later functionalists (see chap. 8). James considered that the mind and the body interacted, and one of the great advantages of humans was that their highly developed minds could aid in the survival of their bodies.

The later functionalists stressed the significance of psychological adaptation or adjustment to the environment. The whole concept of adjustment for good psychological survival and good mental health was presented as a necessity, as opposed to the idea of maladjustment which would lead to a psychological breakdown.

Darwin's influence on Freud and the entire psychoanalytic movement cannot be overlooked (see chap. 17). Freud paid tribute to Darwin in stressing the animal nature of humans and opposed the rationalists of his time, who considered the human being to be primarily a thinking and reasoning creature. Freud stressed the animal nature of humans, as a species which shared the same instincts and basic nature as lower forms. The life instincts operated primarily for human survival. According to Freud, human activity inevitably could be reduced to the fulfillment of instinctual desires.

---

[8]William James, *Principles of Psychology,* Vol. 1 (New York: Henry Holt, 1890), p. 534.

## Sir Francis Galton (1822–1911)

Darwin was a biologist whose psychology simply reflected the dualism of the times, and it never occurred to him to abandon it. It remained for Darwin's cousin, Francis Galton, to apply evolutionary thinking more specifically to psychology. In 1869, only a decade after the publication of the *Origin of Species,* Galton published his *Hereditary Genius,*[9] in which he attempted to show that an individual's greatness would follow certain family lines with such certainty that it would be absurd to look to environmental influences. He took the idea for inheritance of such powerful mental functions from his studies of eminent families—jurists, scientists, and authors. Galton thought very specifically of the kind of gifts that could be passed on from one generation to another in the fields of the law, medicine, and so forth. Like Darwin, Galton presupposed that there must have been some time in the past when great variations of mental ability occurred in these families, and the superior ones were best able to survive.

Again, following Darwin's thesis, he believed that a constant variation from one generation to the next existed, so *individual differences* would always be present. The concept that people varied greatly not only in physical traits but also in mental ones, had been generally ignored by the earlier philosophers and those who dabbled in psychology.

Galton's concern for individual differences led him into areas of psychological statistics and the measurement of mental abilities.[10] In fact, he was the first to develop psychological tests and measurements. Following the lead of the British empiricists (see chap. 4), who believed that all knowledge came from experience, Galton concluded that human intelligence might best be measured by examining sensory capacities. His supposition was that the keenest sensory capacities would be found among the most intelligent individuals. He contrasted the sensory capacities of those he considered to be the most able individuals with those referred to in those days as the idiots and imbeciles— that is, the mentally retarded. In 1882 Galton developed a small laboratory in London where, for the payment of a small fee, a person could take a variety of tests: physical measurements, reaction-time measurements, and measurements of sensory capacities.

Furthermore, in order to handle the data gleaned from his measurements, it was necessary to develop certain psychological statistics. These included ranking individuals from highest to lowest according to their performance on any specific test and then grouping them in order of merit (percentile ranking), as well as the correlation by which one group of individuals could be compared with another to see the degree of relationship (high or low).

Finally, Galton presumed to point out that different races of people survived in different parts of the world because of their adaptation to that partic-

---

[9]Francis Galton, *Hereditary Genius* (London: Macmillan, 1869).
[10]Francis Galton, "Psychometric experiments," *Brain,* Vol. 2 (1879), pp. 49–62.

ular environment. This was true of nationalities also. For example, the culture of ancient Greece was the result of a favorable variation in the Hellenic stock.

Darwin's theory of evolution influenced the psychology of William James. But more importantly, in terms of contemporary psychology, Darwinism strongly influenced functionalism, many traces of which are found in psychology today.

### William James

As indicated in the previous chapter, James and his theories were the most immediate predecessors to functionalism. James had spoken of *adjustment* and *adaptation*. Sometimes the mind aided the body in its survival, when it was capable of reasoning. As it developed, habit also allowed the mind greater freedom for adaptive activities. At other times the body was preeminent, such as when the main survival function in emotion might be to run away from a frightening object.

A second aspect of James' thinking had a direct influence on functionalism—namely, his pragmatism. Above all, James was a philosopher. To him, knowledge was relative, and the validation of any knowledge was to be found in terms of its consequences, indeed, its usefulness. The functionalists carried James' pragmatism into psychology. James had popularized pragmatism, and John Dewey, the first of the University of Chicago functionalists, applied it to social problems and education. Functionalism was in favor of psychological applications.

## *Protests of Functionalism*

Although functionalism did not develop specifically and intentionally as a protest against the other psychologies of the day, in particular structuralism, it conceived of a new way of looking at psychology. William James, as we learned in the previous chapter, had paved the way.

1. Functionalism intended to study *mental processes* or *functions*, not the elements of a static consciousness.

2. Functionalism was concerned with utilitarian, common-sense issues in psychology. It was interested in applications and not in a simple "pure analysis" of the mind. The functionalists asked the question, what do mental processes accomplish in the world? It should be remembered that structuralism, at all costs, wanted to remain pure and avoided any attempts to apply its findings.

3. The structuralists had maintained that functions could not appear directly in consciousness, and thus could not be the object of true introspective analysis. A difference arose not only in the nature of the subject matter,

but also in the methodology. Functionalism did not dismiss introspection as a method of gathering data. It merely maintained that introspection was not the only method. Furthermore, functionalism did not maintain the same attitude of the "trained introspectionist" as had the structuralists.

In 1899 Titchener had published an article entitled *"The Postulates of a Structural Psychology."*[11] In it, he made a distinction between structural and functional psychology and, as such, he named both schools. Although maintaining the structuralist position, he allowed that the future might make room for a functional psychology, even though at the time of his writing, he was not very optimistic. In an article published the next year,[12] Titchener took a stronger position against functionalism. Among other things, he criticized the functionalists' type of introspection as being unscientific.

## Functionalism as a School

As a school, functionalism is probably the most flexible and eclectic of any of the systems we shall study. It drew its propositions from many sources. Its early proponents, Dewey, Angell, and Carr, did not align themselves to a single philosophical tradition and were less tied to any particular formal doctrine.[13]

Before considering the contributions of the three main founders, let us attempt to find some common threads that characterized functionalism and gave it the right to be called a "school" or system of psychology.

1. Psychology dealt with mental functions rather than contents. In a sense, functionalism owed a debt to Brentano and his act psychology. However, Brentano limited himself to mental acts, while the functionalists, particularly as the school reached its maturity in Carr, were not limited to the mental, but involved in the physical as well.

2. Psychological functions were adjustments or adaptations to the environment. They served the organism in its attempt at survival. Where Darwin had stressed physical and biological survival, the functionalists stressed the psychological. The organism's ability to make changes according to its changing relationship to its environment was of utmost importance.

3. Psychology had to have utilitarian aspects. It had to allow for practical applications to children, animals, education, and other fields.

---

[11]Edward B. Titchener, "The Postulates of a Structural Psychology," *Philosophical Review,* Vol. 7 (1898), pp. 449–65.
[12]Edward B. Titchener, "Structural and Functional Psychology," *Philosophical Review,* Vol. 8 (1899), pp. 290–99.
[13]J. R. Kantor, *The Scientific Evolution of Psychology,* Vol. II (Chicago: The Principia Press, Inc., 1969).

4. There was no break between the stimulus and the response. Mental activity was part of the whole world of activity that included both mental and physical.

5. Psychology was closely related to biology. It evolved out of biology. An understanding of the anatomical and physiological functions was helpful in understanding the mental.

## The Founders

Functionalism was the first truly American school. Although William James prepared the way, and the functionalists borrowed heavily from him, James could not be considered to have founded a formal school which gained adherents in the same way that other schools did.

We have tried to point out some of the basic tenets which held functionalism together. But, because of its rather nebulous and eclectic nature, the best understanding can be had by considering the main contributions of the three founders: John Dewey, James Angell, and Harvey Carr, each in order.

### John Dewey (1859–1952)

Dewey had a rather undistinguished early career. He taught high school for a while and, in 1884, received his Ph.D. in philosophy from Johns Hopkins University. He was invited to join the faculty at the University of Chicago in 1894. He is usually credited with sparking the movement which we call functionalism. During the years he remained at Chicago, Dewey fostered psychology. In 1904 he went to Columbia University, where he remained until his retirement, and became more concerned with educational and philosophical issues.

Dewey's main contribution to functionalism is to be found in a paper he published early in 1896 called "The Reflex Arc Concept in Psychology."[14] This constituted the initial push that started functionalism on its way. He pointed out that psychological activity could not be broken down into parts or elements, but had to be considered as a continuous whole. Like James, he was attacking the psychological elementalism of the structuralists. In the traditional concept of the reflex arc, a distinction was made between the sensory, central, and motor aspects. Dewey contended that the distinction between the stimulus and the response was based not on differences existing in reality, but on the different functions played by each in the whole event.

He used the familiar example of the child who saw a flame, reached into it, and burned his or her fingers. The act was not a simple sequence of three

---

[14]John Dewey, "The Reflex Arc Concept in Psychology," *Psychological Review*, Vol. 3 (1896), pp. 357–70.

discrete events—seeing, reaching, and being burned. The description of these discrete elemental units did not give us the full story. After an experience of this sort, the child's perception of the flame that first invited the child to reach out, would be completely changed. The stimulus, the flame, would have an entirely new function, one of withdrawal rather than attraction. Dewey argued for a unitary act—from sensation to movement to a new sensation which arose out of that movement. He argued that the earlier distinctions usually made were artificial. His concern was with the act as a *function*; and in this case an *adaptive* function was formed. Further, he mentioned that we should think of molar units of analysis (as opposed to the structuralists' molecular).

This paper was Dewey's only major contribution to functional psychology. During his stay at Chicago and later at Columbia, he became involved in the application of pragmatism to education, the idea that education should be student-oriented rather than subject-oriented.

Dewey's contribution to functionalism, then, was that we must not treat psychological events as artificial constructs, but should stress their significance in helping the organism adapt to its environment.

Dewey was also a social philosopher and was deeply concerned with human welfare. In his pragmatism, he argued that knowledge could operate to maintain human survival. Consequently, knowledge operated in the adjustmental process. In this attitude, Dewey made a further contribution to the functionalists' pragmatic position.

## James Rowland Angell (1867–1949)

Angell came from an academic family. His grandfather had been president of Brown University, and his father was president of the University of Vermont and later the University of Michigan. While Dewey had been at Michigan before coming to Chicago, Angell had studied with him. He then received his M.A. under William James at Harvard. He never received a Ph.D., although in the course of his career, he was granted twenty-three honorary doctorates. By the time he came to the University of Chicago, the grains of functionalism were well established. He became chairman of the department of psychology, a position he held for over twenty-five years. When Angell took over the department of psychology at Chicago, functionalism was becoming a growing concern. An active laboratory developed, with a growing body of research and an enthusiastic group of graduate students. Angell built up the department and made it the center of functionalism. By 1921, when Angell left to become the president of Yale University, functionalism was extremely popular.

In 1903 Angell published his first views on functional psychology.[15] In attacking structuralism, he stated, "sensation is no discrete psychological entity compared with other similar entities into the complex we call perception." He

---

[15] James R. Angell, "The Relation of Structural and Functional Psychology to Philosophy," *Philosophical Review*, Vol. 12 (1903), pp. 243–71.

pointed out the disparity between structure in biology and in psychology. No psychological event was comparable to the cell of biology. Sensation was merely an artifact when divorced from the whole complex of reality.

In 1904 he published *Psychology: An Introductory Study of the Structure and Function of Human Consciousness.*[16] The book was extremely successful, having four editions by 1908. Although the book was somewhat eclectic, it was an assemblage of what was known about psychology at the time. Psychology was defined as the "science of consciousness," and various chapters were devoted to the nervous system, sensation, perception, judgment, feeling, emotions, and will.

The flavor of functionalism can be seen in the following quotation, which includes excerpts from the preface and the first chapter.[17]

> Psychologists have hitherto devoted the larger part of their energy to investigating the *structures* of the mind. Of late, however, there has been manifest a disposition to deal more fully with its functional and genetic phases. To determine how consciousness develops and how it operates is felt to be quite as important as the discovery of its constituent elements. . . .
>
> We shall discover, as we go on, abundant reasons for the belief that conscious processes and certain nervous processes are indissolubly bound up with one another in the human being. But at this point, without attempting to justify the assertion, we may lay it down as a basal postulate that the real human organism is a psychophysical organism and that the mental portion of it is not to be completely or correctly apprehended without reference to the physiological portion. . . .
>
> Mind seems to be the master device by means of which these adaptive operations of organic life may be made most perfect. We shall consequently attempt to see in what particulars the various features of consciousness contribute to this adaptive process. . . . Our adaption of the biological point of view . . . will mean not only that we shall study consciousness in connection with physiological processes, whenever possible, but it will also mean that we shall regard all operations of consciousness—all our sensations, all our emotions, and all our acts of will—as so many expressions of organic adaptations to our environment, an environment which we must remember is social as well as physical.

His clearest exposition of the functionalist position is found in his presidential address (1906) to the American Psychological Association entitled "The Province of Functional Psychology."[18] In it, he outlined three separate conceptions of functional psychology.

**1.** Functional psychology was the study of mental operations as opposed to elements. Here, he was stating his opposition to structuralism, which was

---

[16]James R. Angell, *Psychology: An Introductory Study of the Structure and Function of Human Consciousness* (New York: Henry Holt and Co., 1904).

[17]*Ibid.*, pp. 6–7.

[18]James R. Angell, "The Province of Functional Psychology," *Psychological Review,* Vol. 14 (1907), pp. 61–91.

beginning to take a prominent place in American psychology. The task of functional psychology was to discover *how* a mental process worked. A mental function, unlike any glimpse of a momentary consciousness as studied by the structuralists, was an enduring function, similar to the functions found in biology.

2. Functional psychology could be considered as a "psychology of the fundamental utilities of consciousness." The mind was engaged in mediating between the environment and the needs of the organism. A psychological function should thus be an accommodating one. Mental processes were not isolated events but were part of a larger functioning organism. By adapting to the demands of the environment, mental functions enabled an organism to survive. Habits could take care of the familiar, but when the environment presented a novel situation, consciousness had to take charge of the adaptive process.

3. Functional psychology had to be concerned with the entire psychophysical relationship between the organism and its environment. Functionalism was concerned with the totality of relationships between mind and body. Mind and body could not be separated, but belonged to the same whole. There was a constant interaction between the two.

Angell suggested that the first two of these points restricted functional psychology to the study of conscious experience. In this sense, possibly they were too narrow; but the third, he found most satisfactory. However, he did feel that all three were interrelated.

### Harvey A. Carr (1873–1954)

When Angell went to take over the presidency of Yale University in 1921, Carr, who had received his Ph.D. at Chicago in 1904, became the head of the department of psychology at Chicago. By this time, functionalism had settled down and was one of the dominant systems of the day. It was no longer a mere counter-attack against structuralism, but was a recognized school. Carr equated functional psychology with American psychology, and functionalism reached the peak of its popularity under Carr's leadership.

Carr's book, *Psychology: A Study of Mental Activity*,[19] published in 1925, expressed functionalism in its most refined form. Carr's psychology began to take on more of a behavioristic flavor, since he placed more emphasis on behavior than Angell had. However, Carr still considered adaptation as one of the main tenets of functional psychology, and introspection was not eliminated as a method.

---

[19]Harvey A. Carr, *op. cit.*

## Definition and Subject Matter

Psychology was the study of *mental activity*—in other words, adaptive behavior. It involved such processes as perception, memory, feeling, judgment, and will. We acquired, retained, organized, and evaluated our experiences for subsequent utilization in the guidance of adaptive and adjustive behavior. Psychology did not deal with elements or content but with processes. Mental activity had to be concerned with what it accomplished.

### The Adaptive Act

The fact that behavior was adaptive was one of the main tenets of functionalism. For Carr, it became the main concern of psychology. The adaptive act had three characteristics: (1) a motivating stimulus, (2) a sensory stimulus, and (3) a response that altered the situation in a way that should satisfy the motivating stimulus. When a hungry person reached for food and ate to the point of satiation, this was a demonstration of the adaptive act. Hunger was the motivation, food was the sensory stimulus, and eating was the adaptive response.

1. The motive as stimulus remained relatively persistent until the organism acted in such a way that the motive no longer affected it. The motive aroused and directed the activity. In the illustration, a person who was not hungry would not seek food.

2. The sensory stimulus was of equal importance. The adaptive act was determined not only by the motive, but also by the object toward which it was directed. Carr referred to the stimulus as an incentive or a goal.

3. The response culminated the whole process. Activity continued until the motivating conditions were satisfied and the motivating stimulus was no longer effective. In this instance, finding and eating the food brought the adaptive act to a close.

There were other ways the adaptive act might be brought to a close. The actual continuance of an act might alter the motivating stimulus. A person cutting the lawn in the hot sun might quit out of sheer exhaustion. Further, the act might lead to sensory consequences that could disrupt it. A person reaching for a hot kettle on the stove might drop it because of the pain it caused. When an act came to a close, it was always because the situation had changed.

The adaptive act was a function of the entire situation. There was a difference between the way we reacted to a bear at the zoo and when we encountered it in the wild. The adaptive act was not necessarily a simple one, as used in the previous illustrations. If an act were repeated over and over again, it might alter the situation that originally initiated it. An altered situation called for altered reactions to it. With repetition, we made new adjustments and viewed the situation in a different light.

In higher organisms such as humans, Carr divided the adaptive act into two stages. The first stage involved attentive adjustment. This would include the initiation of motor sets and adjustments of the sense organs. These shut off distracting influences and prepared the organism for the most efficient response. The second phase was the consummation of the act in achieving the goal.

Carr also made a distinction between two kinds of consequences of the adaptive act. We have already mentioned the first in the satisfaction of the motivating stimulus. The second involved certain auxiliary results. Eating satisfied hunger, but also involved the fulfilling of a body need, as in nourishment. We should not explain an act in terms of the ulterior consequences, but in terms of the motive itself, in this case, hunger not nourishment. Basically, we ate because we were driven by hunger.

The adaptive act, then, was the basis of Carr's psychology. It involved the adjustments of an organism to its environment.

## Perception

Carr defined perception "as the cognition of a present object in relation to some act of adjustment."[20] True to the functionalist position, he considered perception to be another example of the adaptive act. To begin with, he viewed perception as a selective process, in which an organism responded to certain aspects of the incoming sensory stimuli rather than others. Perception differed from sensation in that it added meaning to the experience. Meaning involved recalling the memory of relevant past experiences. As these appropriate past experiences became associated with the present experiences, the perception took on meaning. Carr believed that perceptions were influenced by variables other than past experiences: the perceiver's particular needs, current attitudes, and purposes and future goals. Carr's interpretation of perception provided a basis for later studies on the influence of personality variables on the ways certain experiences are perceived.

## Learning

In Carr's discussion of the adaptive act, learning was certainly significant. But Carr went further. He adopted the principles of association taken from the earlier psychologists. Carr made a distinction between what he called *descriptive* and *explanatory* laws of association. A descriptive law would be that of similarity, where one idea of an object brought to mind the idea of a similar one, such as table-desk. Explanatory laws were more important, for example, contiguity where antecedent conditions were followed by consequent ones. These explanatory laws could further be divided into two categories—*origin* or *function* of

---

[20]*Ibid.*, p. 110.

associations and *functional strength* of associations. Contiguity conformed to the first class. Functional strength explained why some associations were stronger than others. The law of frequency was a specific example. Quite obviously, associative strength increased with greater repetition of the association. There was a point, however, when further frequency or repetition did not increase the strength. This was the point of diminishing returns.

Hilgard and Bower[21] have summarized the more recent functionalist position on learning. The basic principles in the learning process involve: (1) the fact that there are individual differences in the capacity of the learner; (2) different kinds of practice leading to different forms of learning curves; (3) some concept of motivation that is usually present; (4) the degree of meaning as one dimension of which materials can be scaled from the most meaningful to the most nonsensical.

## Emotion

Following the functionalist's tradition, Carr defined emotions as *organic readjustments.* Anger occurred when a person confronted obstacles that interfered with his or her freedom of movement. In this instance, the organism readjusted by an increase in energy, enabling it to overcome the obstacles which had come in its way. This energy stemmed from increased internal activity, such as greater heart rate, rise in blood pressure, heightened respiration, and so on. Some emotions, such as fear and anger, were biologically useful. Sorrow and envy did not seem to have any utilitarian value.

Emotions arose when there did not seem to be appropriate avenues for motor adjustment. When the person was able to react to the situation, such as in overcoming an obstacle or running away from a dangerous threat, the emotion would die out.

Carr presented the James-Lange theory, but pointed out some of his disagreement. He did not agree that the emotions were merely explained by the perception of the organic and motor process. In other words, Carr was reverting, in part, to the more classical theory that a conscious awareness of the emotionally arousing events frequently preceded the actual physiological and motor processes. The conscious experience, furthermore, could be independent of the physiological correlates. However, he did follow James in stating that emotions were basically psychophysical adjustments occurring when certain situations arose.

## Thinking

Carr discussed thinking in a section of his *Psychology* entitled "The Function of Ideas."[22] Ideas were substituted for stimuli previously responded to through the

---

[21]E. R. Hilgard and G. H. Bower, *Theories of Learning,* 3rd ed. (New York: Appleton-Century-Crofts, 1966).
[22]H. A. Carr, *Psychology: A Study of Mental Activity* (New York: Longmans, Green, 1925).

mental function of perception. Ideas or thoughts could arouse responses that had adaptive value. For example, the thought of an upcoming event, such as an examination, ought to induce the student to prepare for it. A person walking home at night could use thoughts to select the safest possible route. Thoughts were used in setting a plan for the future. They could also act as the basis for creativity. Such planning would result in creative ideational adaptive behavior.

Although Carr discussed reasoning in a separate chapter from the one on the function of ideas, there is considerable similarity in the discussions. A person's awareness of a problem could be the result of an actual perception of the real world or it could be initiated by an idea. In either case, the solution involved "an analytical ideational attack" until a solution was discovered in a more or less accidental manner. Reasoning, like thinking, had adaptive value, because appropriate solutions had survival value.

## Methodology

Carr accepted various methods for studying mental activity. Although functionalism had arisen as a protest to structuralism, it accepted introspection but added observation. Experimentation was the most desirable method of gathering data, but in human studies Carr thought complete controls were extremely difficult. However, he did not rule out "common observation" as a means of gaining knowledge about an event.

Much of the research at the University of Chicago was of an experimental nature, and had the objectivity that structuralism lacked. More recent functionalists have relied on carefully controlled laboratory experimentation.

Functionalism, then, did not adhere to any one specific method. The best method to use depended on the problem to be investigated.

## Mind-Body Problem

Carr described mental activity as being psychophysical. The psychic part referred to consciousness of one's activity. We did not perceive, reason, or will without being aware of it. The physical aspect referred to the reactions the organism made. Carr made no issue of the relationship of the mental and the physical. He simply accepted it as a matter of fact. In the adaptive act, we had a totality of the mental and the physical. The mental did not exist as a separate entity as it did for the structuralists. The mental could not be separated from the physical any more than one could separate the grin from the Cheshire cat.

The fact that Carr talked about a psychophysical process implied a definite dualism. Angell[23] in his article, "The Province of Functional Psychology," took the same position as James did and left no doubt that the relation was one of *psychophysical interactionism.* However, for Carr, the solution seemed more to be one of *double-aspectism;* and the issue was of no metaphysical importance.

---

[23]James R. Angell, "The Province of Functional Psychology," *op. cit.*

## The Fate of Functionalism

Like structuralism, functionalism no longer exists as a formal system in psychology. It never was a tightly knit system. Its first adherents were all at the University of Chicago. John Dewey started it, James Angell fostered it, and Harvey Carr brought it to its fruition. Of course, William James had set the stage. A number of historians[24], [25], [26] have stated that Robert S. Woodworth brought functionalism to Columbia University. (Woodworth's position will be described in chapter 11.) His psychology certainly had a functionalist flavor, but he departed enough from the functionalist position to develop a separate system, one which he called *dynamic psychology.*

Although functionalism has been absorbed into the mainstream of psychology, certain contemporary psychologists, such as J. A. McGoech,[27] Andrew Melton, and Benton J. Underwood,[28] make use of functionalist ideas in their study of human learning. They have undertaken large research projects in order to study different variables involved in the learning process. In particular, Underwood and his colleagues have studied proactive and retroactive inhibition (how previous and subsequent learning affects the recall of verbal material), factors involved in the rate of verbal learning (such as massed versus distributed practice), the optimum amount of material to be presented for the most efficient learning, the importance of recitation and factors involved in the transfer from one learning situation to another. The emphasis on association in the learning process ties these more recent studies to the earlier functionalist position.

## Functionalism and the Testing Movement

Although interest in the measurement of mental abilities did not start with functionalism, the school's proponents gave testing a new emphasis. Among the first functionalists to research testing was James McKeen Cattell. A student of Wundt, Cattell was especially interested in testing the acuity of the senses. In his work, Cattell attempted to measure such mental abilities as "the span of apprehension," a term that referred to the number of elements the mind could hold at one instant. Cattell first used the term "mental test" in an 1890 article in the journal *Mind,* called "Mental Tests and Measurements."

Intelligence testing, as we know it, began in France with the work of Alfred Binet in the early twentieth century. Binet criticized the intelligence tests of his day, calling them unusually simple and unable to measure anything but specialized abilities. He also thought they were focused on sensory abilities

[24]E. G. Boring. *A History of Experimental Psychology,* 2nd ed. (New York: Appleton-Century-Crofts, 1950).

[25]M. H. Marx and W. A. Cronan-Hillix, *Systems and Theories in Psychology* (New York: McGraw-Hill Book Co., 1987).

[26]D. P. Schultz, *A History of Modern Psychology* 4th ed. (New York: Harcourt Brace Jovanovich, 1987).

[27]J. A. McGoech, *Human Learning* (New York: Longmans, Green, 1937).

[28]Benton J. Underwood, *Psychological Research* (New York: Appleton-Century-Crofts, 1957).

rather than intelligence. In 1904, Binet developed an intelligence scale as part of a study of the education of retarded children in Paris schools.[29] He released a final edition of the scale in 1911, the year of his death. Subsequently, translations and adaptations appeared in many languages.

Louis M. Terman standardized an American version of the Binet test at Stanford University in 1916. Called the Stanford Binet Measure of Intelligence, this test measures the intellectual functioning of children at various ages. It is used to predict scholastic aptitude. Although the original version of the test was standardized using children from Californian schools, later versions drew upon a more highly diverse group of children.[30]

In 1942 David Wechsler devised a similar test to assess the intellectual functioning of adults. Called the Wechsler Adult Intelligence Scale (WAIS), the test measures vocabulary, comprehension, and mathematical skills.

## *Evaluation*

### Criticisms of Functionalism

1. The first criticism was levied by the structuralists, who preferred content to functions. We have already considered the attacks and counterattacks of both schools. Although the criticism is not so relevant today, it should at least be mentioned, because, in its day, it was considered of utmost importance.

2. One of the most common criticisms referred to functionalism's rather vague nature. According to Kantor,[31] the functionalist system was so formless that the historian of psychology found it difficult to set down its tenets in any orderly way (although we have tried). In fact, many texts[32, 33] devote only a few pages of exposition to functionalism. Still, functionalism did exist as a school and has influenced the thinking of American psychology. Part of the vague nature of functionalism, as mentioned by its critics, was that the functionalists never explained what they meant by "function."

3. With its emphasis on goals and utilitarian aspects, functionalism has been accused of being teleological (the future determines the present). This, of

[29]A. Binet and T. Simon, "Methods Nouvelles pour la Diagnostic Intellectual des anormaux," *Année Psychologie,* 1905, 11, pp. 191–224.

[30]R. L. Thorndike, L. P. Hagen and J. L. Salter, *Manual for the Stanford-Binet Intelligence Test,* 4th ed. (New York: Riverside Publishing Co., 1986).

[31]J. R. Kantor, *op. cit.*

[32]B. B. Wolman, *Contemporary Theories and Systems in Psychology* (New York: Harper and Bros., 1960).

[33]Robert S. Woodworth, *Contemporary Schools of Psychology,* rev. ed. (New York: The Ronald Press Co., 1948).

course, was objectional to the determinists, but it was not an uncommon position. McDougall (p. 159) and Tolman (p. 272) were teleological, as were the later analysts, Adler and Jung (see chap. 18).

4. Henle has criticized functionalism as being too eclectic. Eclecticism is a patching together of a little from this system and a little from that. From the viewpoint of a pure systematist, eclecticism attempts to reconcile conflicting views, but in so doing, ends up with a mixture which turns out to be "vapid and nondescript."[34] The rather easy attitude of functionalism in picking and choosing various kinds of techniques and problems has caused difficulty. However, functionalism never really attempted to become a strict school as did structuralism, behaviorism, or Gestalt. It grew and evolved into a flexible system that was held together by a few important tenets, as mentioned early in this chapter.

The fact that other schools such as behaviorism and Gestalt were more aggressive, did not help functionalism. Watson, the founder of behaviorism, was "raised" at the University of Chicago in the functionalist tradition, but rejected it because of its rather nebulous position and because of its dualism (see chap. 12).

## Contributions of Functionalism

1. Functionalism's main contribution to psychology was its unfailing attempt to broaden its scope and remove itself from the limited focus of the earlier psychologies. The functionalists were concerned with animal and child psychology, problems of abnormal psychology, and psychological testing. Unlike the structuralists, they were willing to accept individual differences and the applications of psychology. The whole intelligence test movement, in particular the work of Lewis M. Terman in developing the Stanford-Binet Scale, had a functionalist flavor.

2. Functionalists began with mental activity that, in itself, was dualistic. As the system evolved, more and more emphasis was placed on overt acts of the organism (behavior). It was not difficult for Watson and later behaviorists to take the next step and define behavior more precisely.

3. The concept of adjustment has become an integral part of abnormal psychology and mental hygiene. It is the mal-adaptive act that causes problems, and the role of the mental hygienist is to promote adjustive behavior. The abnormal psychologist studies the causes of mal-adjustment, and the function of the therapist is to lead the individual to more appropriate behavior.

---

[34]M. Henle, "Some Problems of Eclecticism," *Psychological Review,* Vol. 64 (1957), pp. 296–305.

Functionalism was phased out, but it left its mark. It was a truly American psychology which led to further developments and refinements. In a sense, functionalism set a direction, which many American psychologists were to follow.

In conclusion, it should be re-emphasized that functionalism was not so much rejected as it was absorbed into the general fabric of American psychology.

## Suggested Further Readings

Carr, Harvey A., *Psychology: A Study of Mental Activity*. New York: Longmans, Green, 1925. Carr's most complete statement of functionalism at the height of its popularity. Much of our discussion of Carr has been taken from this text.

Carr, Harvey A., "Functionalism and Its Historical Significance," in Murchison, C., ed., *Psychologies of 1930*. Worcester, Mass.: Clark University Press, 1930. A further, but condensed, statement of Carr's functionalist position.

Dewey, John, "The Reflex Arc Concept in Psychology." *Psychological Review*, Vol. 3 (1896), pp. 357–70. The beginnings of functionalism.

James, William, "The Chicago School," *Psychological Bulletin*, Vol. 1 (1904), pp. 1–15. James' commentary on the beginnings of the Chicago school of functionalism.

# CHAPTER

# 10

# Modern Associationism

Associationism never existed as a formal school of psychology like structuralism, functionalism, behaviorism, or Gestalt psychology. It served rather as a principle, forming the basis for research and explanation by several psychologists who operated quite separately. Ivan Pavlov and other Russians applied it to the conditioned reflex, and Edward L. Thorndike considered it of great importance in his studies of learning. It is interesting to note that, although these two men worked quite separately and used different techniques, in 1923 Pavlov acknowledged the great significance of Thorndike's work (see pp. 142–149).

Association also became a significant principle for later learning theorists such as Edwin Guthrie, Clark Hull, and B. F. Skinner (see chap. 13). We have already seen how Titchener and Wundt applied it to their systems.

## Philosophical Antecedents

The principle, of course, has had a long history. In chapter 4, we traced in some detail what various philosophers and other writers of the eighteenth and nineteenth centuries wrote about its nature as a functional principle as well as the number of laws there ought to be. Table 1 gives a summary of the laws of association proposed by these early writers.

Aristotle was one of the first to talk about association (p. 27), although Plato spoke of similarity and contiguity without elaborating on them. The matter was not considered again until John Locke, the first of the British empiricists, introduced it in the fourth edition of his *Essay Concerning Human Un-*

**TABLE 1**                       **Laws of Association**

| Writer | Dates | Contiguity | Similarity | Contrast | Causality |
|--------|-------|------------|------------|----------|-----------|
| Aristotle | (384–322 B.C.) | X | X | X | |
| Locke | (1632–1704) | X | X | | |
| Berkeley | (1685–1753) | X | X | | |
| Hume | (1711–1776) | X | X | | X* |
| Hartley | (1705–1757) | X | | | |
| J. Mill | (1773–1836) | X | | | |
| J. S. Mill | (1806–1873) | X | X | | |
| Bain | (1818–1903) | X | X | | |
| Spencer | (1820–1903) | X | X | | |

From *Systems and Theories in Psychology* by M. H. Marx and W. A. Cronan-Hillix. New York: McGraw-Hill Book Co., 1987, p. 109. Used with permission of McGraw-Hill Book Company.
*Later reduced to contiguity.

*derstanding.*[1] Locke's concern was how experiences could be formed into ideas. He suggested that some ideas seem to hang together logically while others become associated by mere chance (see pp. 47–48).

George Berkeley used the concept of association to explain how we were able to perceive distance even though images on our eyes came only in two dimensions (see p. 49).

David Hume, the last of the empiricists, furthered the idea by suggesting that similarity, but more often contiguity (togetherness), accounted for how ideas stuck together. He also proposed cause and effect as a third principle or, what seemed to him, to be a "necessary connection" between events. Later, however, he considered that these habitual connections amounted to nothing more than contiguity. For example, throwing water might put out a fire (see pp. 50–51).

Following the empirical tradition, a group of researchers called the British associationists paid even greater attention to the principle of association.

The first of these was David Hartley, who attempted a physiological explanation of association in terms of brain vibrations (see p. 52).

Later, James Mill proposed a kind of "mental mechanics," a principle whereby any idea we had was an addition of its original components put together by association (see pp. 54–55).

His son, John Stuart Mill, instead of accepting the additive process his father had proposed, suggested a kind of "mental chemistry," by which ideas fused so that a new entity might be formed that was more than the sum of its parts. Association was, nevertheless, the basic adhesive process.

---

[1]John Locke, *An Essay Concerning Human Understanding,* A. C. Fraser, ed. (New York: Dover, 1959).

Alexander Bain and Herbert Spencer brought the concept of association, from a philosophical standpoint, as far as it could go. They offered little that was new so far as the principle itself was concerned. From that point, it remained for the experimental psychologists to take over. This concern will constitute the remainder of this chapter.

## An Early Experimental Look at Associationism

***Hermann Ebbinghaus (1850–1909).*** In 1885 Ebbinghaus published his famous work on memory.[2] This began the first experimental work on the subject. Some of these findings are discussed in the paragraphs that follow. He was concerned with the problems of forming associations and then later testing their strength by recall. Prior to his studies, the procedure used by the early philosophers had been to begin with associations already established and to infer backward about the process of how they were formed. Ebbinghaus approached the problem from the opposite direction. He studied the conditions under which they could be established and, so, introduced the concept of learning into experimental psychology.

Although his major interest was memory, Ebbinghaus realized that in order to remember, one must first learn something. To minimize the effects of associations that had already been established between words, he introduced the nonsense syllable. A nonsense syllable ordinarily consisted of two consonants separated by a vowel—DIB, WOX, ZAK, etc. To be "nonsense," a syllable could not be a three-letter word in the language. For example, BED and FUR would not qualify.

By using the nonsense syllable, Ebbinghaus thought that he would be able to obtain more reliable forgetting curves. When real words were used, prior associations with these words might skew results.

If materials were to be learned and remembered, and if associations were to take hold, Ebbinghaus realized that the materials had to be repeated. In other words, frequency of presentation seemed to be the key process for the "stamping in" of associations. In many of his experiments, he used himself as the subject. He placed on cards the syllables to be learned and read them through in order at a uniform rate, which he timed by the ticking of his watch. After each reading, he paused and then began again. When he felt he could recite the list, he spoke them from memory and made a record of his mistakes. He continued this procedure until he had attained "complete mastery," that is, reproducing the list without error. To test his memory, he would find out how many syllables he could recite. He then varied the length of time between original learning and first recall. From this, he derived the famous Ebbinghaus forgetting curve, familiar to all beginning students of psychology. He found

---

[2]Hermann Ebbinghaus, *Über das Gedächtnis* (1885), trans. H. A. Ruger and Charles Bussenus, *On Memory* (New York: Teachers' College, Columbia University, 1913).

that material was forgotten very rapidly during the first hours after the original learning and then more and more slowly thereafter. When plotted on a curve, he found that forgetting dropped very rapidly in the beginning and then gradually tapered off.

Ebbinghaus did not publish a great deal in psychology, but what he did publish was important; and his experiments have served as models for procedures in verbal learning studies up to the present time. Before him, the associationists had only speculated about how associations occurred. Ebbinghaus put the process to an experimental test and then measured resistance of associations by testing later recall.

## Ivan Pavlov (1849–1936)

Ivan Petrovich Pavlov was born in a provincial town in central Russia. He obtained a degree in animal physiology at the University of St. Petersburg in 1875 and completed medical training in 1883. He studied for two years in Germany and, at the age of forty-one, was appointed to the St. Petersburg Military Medical Academy as professor of pharmacology and later physiology. Throughout his life, he was an ardent researcher in physiology. Although his studies have profound implications for psychology even today, he never considered himself in any sense a psychologist and, in fact, had little use for the psychologists of his time.

In his early work, he was concerned with the physiological processes involved in digestion. This brilliant work earned him the Nobel Prize in 1904.

As with many breakthroughs in science, Pavlov's research into an area we would consider psychological came somewhat by accident. He had developed a surgical technique whereby he could expose the salivary glands of a dog. The surgical technique permitted the secretion of a particular gland to be diverted through a tube outside the body of the animal where the exact amount of secretion could be measured without damaging the nerves or blood supply. He then noted that when meat or bread was placed in the dog's mouth the saliva would flow quite naturally. He noted that saliva would also flow in anticipation, when the dog *saw* the food dish or *heard* the footsteps of the approaching attendant. The reflex of salivation also occurred to stimuli that had been associated with the natural stimulus. Pavlov realized that this "psychic secretion"[3] also occurred in the absence of the natural stimulus (the food), once the two had originally been paired together.

At first, Pavlov had some doubts about whether or not he should pursue this line of investigation, which seemed to be of a "psychical" or psychological nature. He finally decided that since the explanations were invariably physiological in nature, he would continue. He also discovered that a variety of other

[3]Ivan P. Pavlov, *Conditioned Reflexes* (London: Oxford University Press, 1927).

stimuli associated with food could elicit the salivation—such stimuli as a buzzer, a light, or the clicking of a metronome. This response to associated stimuli he labeled the *conditioned response*[4] (CR), while the natural response of salivation to food became the *unconditioned response* (UR). On the stimulus side, the natural stimulus (food) became the *unconditioned stimulus* (US) and the other stimulus (sight of dish, footsteps, bell, etc.) became the *conditioned stimulus* (CS). The conditioned response was obviously *learned,* but Pavlov, still remaining the physiologist, attributed it to "higher nervous activity" in the brain. In other words, the cerebral cortex, rather than the spinal cord, must be involved.

In one of his experiments,[5] Pavlov subjected the dog to the ticking of a metronome for a 30-second period before presenting the meat. On further trials, he noted that when the metronome started to tick (having been associated with food), the dog would salivate in anticipation. There seemed to be some exciting effect. With further pairings and trials, however, the dog would not begin to salivate immediately, but would wait, indicating some inhibiting or depressing effect. (This procedure ordinarily was called the *delayed CR.*) Such excitations and inhibitions were caused by processes in the brain.

In any event, Pavlov believed he had found out how to produce two different brain states—one, the excitation of nerve impulses, the other, an inhibition of them. In the delayed *CR*, we had first an inhibition and then an excitation.

Pavlov also observed that when the *CS* was presented time after time without the *US* (food), the conditioned response that had been established earlier tended to die out or become *extinguished.* He also noted that during this extinction period the dog often became drowsy or even fell asleep, so the inhibitory process was taking over. However, after a lapse of time, the next day for example, when the *CS* was again presented, there was further excitation in saliva flow. This became known as *spontaneous* recovery. Thus, the *CR* had not become completely extinguished on the first day.

Pavlov also observed that once a conditioned response had been established to a specific stimulus, other stimuli similar in nature to the original one might also elicit the response. For example, when one particular rate of beating of a metronome was used to establish the *CR*, then, other rates of beating although of a smaller magnitude would also elicit the response. There was a *generalization* of the stimulus. To explain this process in terms of brain functions, he presumed a spread of effect to other parts of the brain that he called *irradiation.*

By a technique of selective reinforcement (and Pavlov introduced the term *reinforcement*), he found he could produce an effect that was the opposite of generalization. If he continued to reinforce (present food) to a particular tone or beat of the metronome and *not* reinforce other tones or rates of beating, the animal could develop a *discrimination.* That is, salivation would occur to a given, specific tone and not to other tones. However, he realized that sometimes he could stress the discrimination too far, and when this happened, not only was the discrimination, earlier established, destroyed, but also the dog's

[4]*Ibid.*

[5]Ivan P. Pavlov, *Lectures on Conditioned Reflexes* (New York: Liveright, 1928).

general behavior would become disorganized. It would bark, wrestle with the harness, and become generally unmanageable. This observation he called the *experimental neurosis*. Through experimental manipulations, the dog was made to become neurotic.

Pavlov never wavered from the idea that his problems were physiological and not really psychological. (We, obviously, would disagree.) As to what psychologists were doing, Pavlov remained skeptical. In fact he considered the field of psychology to be "completely hopeless."[6] However, later in his career, Pavlov graciously acknowledged the work of Thorndike.

## Mind-Body Problem

Pavlov considered the brain as a mosaic of neural excitations and inhibitions. Each point on the brain corresponded to some stimulus in the external environment. For each stimulus or stimulus pattern, there was a corresponding brain pattern of excitations and inhibitions. To begin with, there were corresponding patterns between unconditioned stimuli and unconditioned responses. Corresponding patterns also developed between conditional stimuli and conditioned responses. The connections between stimuli and unconditioned responses were fairly fixed, but the patterns between conditioned stimuli and responses could change, depending on changes in the environmental conditions (conditioning, extinction, discrimination, and so on). In the early stages of conditioning the pattern was fairly generalized, so the irradiation of nerve impulses covered a fairly large portion of the cerebral cortex. Likewise, the inhibitory impulses also covered a large portion of the brain. As conditioning proceeded, the excitations and inhibitions became more concentrated in specific brain areas, so a *dynamic stereotype* developed. This amounted to a neural mapping of what was going on in the environment.

Pavlov's neurological explanations of various aspects of conditioning and extinction represent an excellent example of *psychophysical parallelism* as an explanation of the mind-body problem. Here the environmental events had a parallel in the activity of the brain.

## Implications of Pavlov

Before considering the implications of Pavlov, one might make a passing reference to Ivan M. Sechenov (1829–1905), another eminent Russian physiologist, whom Yamoshevski considered the founder of objective psychology.[7] Sechenov believed there was a physiological basis for all psychological processes. He considered the "psyche" as not being independent of the body, but seated in the brain. Reflexes could be learned as well as unlearned, and all "psychical

---

[6]R. I. Watson, *The Great Psychologists from Aristotle to Freud* (Philadelphia: J. B. Lippincott, 1963).

[7]M. B. Yamoshevski, "I. M. Sechenov—The Founder of Objective Psychology," in B. B. Wolman, ed., *Historical Roots of Contemporary Psychology* (New York: Harper and Row, 1968).

processes" could be explained in one way or another as reflexive activity. It remained for Pavlov, who gave much credit to Sechenov, to test the idea. Although Pavlov never succeeded in proving the theory, he did develop a methodology of tremendous importance, as we have seen.

Like Ebbinghaus and in a more precise way, Pavlov took associationism out of the realm of philosophical speculation and began to experiment. He was a careful researcher, and his quantification of the conditioned reflex was carefully executed.

Although Pavlov had some disdain for psychology, his influence today cannot be overestimated. He established a technique for studying a form of learning that is as popular today as ever. John Watson, the founder of behaviorism, was much impressed with Pavlov's paradigm of learning, and incorporated it into his own explanation of more complex learning (see chap. 12). In this sense, Watson oversimplified the problems in learning and overgeneralized learning, presuming that more complex activity could be explained by a simple operation.

However, modern learning theorists have recognized the kind of learning Pavlov demonstrated, and refer to it as classical, Pavlovian, or respondent conditioning, as opposed to instrumental or operant conditioning (see chap. 13).

## *Vladimir Bekhterev (1887–1927)*

A fellow countryman of Pavlov's and also a physiologist (and psychiatrist), Bekhterev took a more positive attitude towards psychology. He was interested in applying the conditioned reflex to humans as well as to animals. He preferred to use the term "associated reflex." In fact, he was interested in establishing a whole science of what he called "human reflexology." Instead of merely studying salivation and other digestive secretions, he turned his attention to motor responses. By this he suggested the withdrawal of the finger or hand from an electric shock. The experiment for which he was best known involved this procedure. The shock, when applied, became the unconditioned stimulus (*US*) and the withdrawal of the finger or shocked limb became the unconditioned response (*UR*). He carefully measured the contractions of the skeletal muscles. With the shock, he paired some neutral stimulus, such as a bell or buzzer (*CS*), and eventually the subject would withdraw (*CR*) merely to the sound. These newly established reflexes were not the result of mental operations, but remained observable responses. He felt that the reflex principle could be applied to more complex human behavior, even speech. His main book, originally written in Russian in 1907, was finally translated into English in 1922[8] under the title, *General Principles of Human Reflexology*. His experiments involved a great number of motor responses. Speech became a complex symbolic reflex which

---

[8]V. M. Bekhterev, *Human Reflexology*, trans. W. H. Gantt (London: Universities Press, 1922).

grew out of simpler reflexes acquired earlier in an organism's conditioning history. Whatever the process, it ultimately involved a flow of energy in the nerve cells and tissues. Bekhterev stayed with the notion of a psychology based on physiology, but rejected the subjective approach to psychology fostered by Wundt and the structuralists. His psychology became a forerunner of behaviorism as he rejected subjective or mentalistic explanations. He believed that thinking, learning, and motivation could be ultimately reduced to mechanistic functions.

## Edward Thorndike (1874–1949)

During the approximately fifty years that Edward Lee Thorndike was actively associated with psychology, he developed a highly systematic theory of associationism, indeed one of the first organized theories of learning.[9] Like Ebbinghaus and Pavlov, he took the concept of association out of the realm of the philosophers' "ideas" and began to experiment. Also like Pavlov, but quite independent of him, Thorndike recognized what we might consider the importance of reward or reinforcement. Pavlov had stated his own law of reinforcement in 1902, and Thorndike first stated what he called the "law of effect" in 1898.[10]

While an undergraduate at Wesleyan University, he first became exposed to William James' *Principles of Psychology*.[11] He went to Harvard, studied under James, and began his first studies in the field of animal learning. His first research involved baby chicks, whom he taught to run mazes that he improvised by arranging books together.

Boring[12] told the story of the problems encountered by Thorndike in housing his little birds. Thorndike's landlady objected to having chicks in his room, and James tried to find space in the laboratory and museum at Harvard without success. The problem was finally solved by placing the birds in the cellar of James' house, much to the delight of the James children. Thorndike then went to Columbia at the invitation of and with the financial help of James McKeen Cattell. Thorndike took his two best trained chicks with him. At Columbia, he worked with cats and dogs in different kinds of puzzle boxes. His dissertation, *Animal Intelligence: An Experimental Study of the Associative Process in Animals*,[13] was published in 1898, and is one of the classic treatises on animal

---

[9]E. R. Hilgard, *Theories of Learning,* rev. ed. (New York: Appleton-Century-Crofts, 1956).

[10]Edward L. Thorndike, "Animal Intelligence: An Experimental Study of the Associative Process in Animals," *Psychological Review Monograph,* 1898, No. 8.

[11]William James, *Principles of Psychology,* 2 vols. (New York: Henry Holt and Co., 1890).

[12]E. G. Boring, *A History of Experimental Psychology,* rev. ed. (New York: Appleton-Century-Crofts, 1950).

[13]Edward L. Thorndike, *op. cit.*

learning. It was later revised to include further experiments, and was published in 1911.[14] Early in his career, he became interested in educational and social psychology which took him to Teachers' College, Columbia University, where he remained until his retirement in 1949.

## Definition of Psychology

As Marx and Cronan-Hillix[15] suggest, Thorndike's definition of psychology was implicit in his writings. Psychology was first and foremost the *study of stimulus-response connections* or *bonds*. In his last book, *Selected Writings from a Connectionist's Psychology*,[16] Thorndike took a rather broad view of what he meant by connections. Connections might occur in a long series, in which the response to one situation became a situation for producing another response, and so on. They could originate from parts or elements of a situation or from the situation as a whole. They could be determined by immediately preceding stimuli, or by the attitude of a person, or conceivably by a person's entire makeup.

Thus, we had a strictly *S–R* (stimulus-response) psychology in which the bond that held the two together was *association*.

## Thorndike's Early Position (1898–1930)

Thorndike was a prolific researcher and writer. Since, in his later writings, he altered his position on certain issues, it seems appropriate to discuss his early thinking, much of which remained unchanged, and then point out where he later altered his ideas as the result of further experimental findings.

His early experiments involved placing hungry cats in a puzzle box.[17] He constructed a number of different kinds of boxes. In some, the cat was required to pull a rope, flip a switch or press a pedal, which caused the door to the box to fly open and allowed the cat to escape to get a bit of food. In some of the boxes, more complicated situations required the animal to perform a series of three consecutive responses before it could escape. The measure of learning was the time it took the cat, after having been placed in the box, to make the appropriate response that would lead to its getting out and receiving food. Although the time per trial tended to be somewhat erratic (time varied from one trial to another), eventually, the latency was reduced to a minimum, so that as soon as the cat was placed in the box, it rather quickly flipped the switch (or whatever the mechanism was), freed itself from the box, and was rewarded with food.

---

[14]Edward L. Thorndike, *Animal Intelligence*, rev. ed. (New York: The Macmillan Co., 1911).

[15]M. H. Marx and W. A. Cronan-Hillix, *Systems and Theories in Psychology* (New York: McGraw-Hill Book Co., 1987).

[16]Edward L. Thorndike, *Selected Writings from a Connectionist's Psychology* (New York: Appleton-Century-Crofts, 1949).

[17]Edward L. Thorndike, *Animal Intelligence, op. cit.*

*Trial-and-Error Learning.* In the puzzle box situation, the cat was observed to do a great deal of clawing, biting, and dashing about before the latch was moved. Eventually, the right response was "stamped in" and the other useless responses were eliminated. The process seemed to be a gradual one in which the errors or wrong responses were eventually eliminated. This seemed to be a random process. Learning tended to be blind, rather than insightful, as suggested later by the Gestalt psychologists. So, Thorndike called it trial-and-error learning.

From his early observations, Thorndike formulated three laws of learning: (1) readiness, (2) exercise, and (3) effect.

*Law of Readiness.* The law of readiness is not very relevant to our discussion since it involved a kind of physiological substratum for the more important *law of effect*. It stated the circumstances under which a learner would be satisfied or annoyed. For example, what if the animal were not hungry (deprived of food)? Was it ready to learn? Thorndike did not fuss a great deal about the neurological and physiological details. However, as he became more interested in educational psychology,[18] he wrote about a kind of "reading readiness" (still popular today), that referred to a child's level of maturity appropriate to his or her ability to begin to learn to read. This seemed to be a kind of physiological matter determined by maturation.

*Law of Exercise.* This law referred to the strengthening of connections, or S–R bonds, through *use* or *practice* and a weakening of other responses caused by a lack thereof (law of disuse). The law applied to repetition, habits, rote memorizing, and so on. It appeared that the more one practiced a task the stronger the bonds became.

*Law of Effect.* Perhaps the most significant effect was the strengthening or weakening of a connection by its *consequences*. A response became "stamped in" because it was followed by a "satisfying state of affairs." The greater the satisfaction, the better the bond. The other half of the law of effect stated that responses that led to unsatisfying consequences were "stamped out."[19]

> By a satisfying state of affairs is meant one which the animal does nothing to avoid, often does things which maintain or renew it. By an annoying state of affairs is meant one which the animal does nothing to preserve, often doing things which put an end to it.

Two objections were leveled against such a statement. First, the term, "satisfying," seemed to be a completely subjective one. How did one know if the

---

[18]Edward L. Thorndike, *Educational Psychology* (New York: Lemcke and Buechner, 1903).
[19]Edward L. Thorndike, *The Psychology of Learning* (New York: Teachers' College, Columbia University, 1913), p. 2.

animal were satisfied or annoyed? Could you ask it? The answer, of course, was that one had no way of knowing.

The other objection involved the implications of a *backward* effect. How could something which happened now (getting the food) have an effect on what happened before? If one thinks for a moment, however, the criticism was really unjustified, for what Thorndike was considering was the effect on the probability of occurrence of the *next* or following response. The criticism was that Thorndike was teleological, that the future (effect) determined the present. This, of course, was not what Thorndike really meant. It remained for Skinner,[20] in his *principle of reinforcement*, which he modified from Thorndike, to make the matter clear. A reinforcement, if positive, merely increased the probability of the same response occurring again, thus stating the matter in operational terms.

***Theory of Transfer.*** Prior to Thorndike's studies on transfer of training in learning, there had existed in educational psychology a theory that has been called the "doctrine of formal discipline." The theory stated, for example, that the study of certain academic subjects, such as mathematics, Latin, Greek, and so on, was very worthwhile because they tended to "train the mind" so there could be a great deal of generalization to other disciplines. This would, in effect, make one's mind sharper, so that other quite unrelated materials could be learned quite easily. Thorndike proposed an alternate theory that developed out of an experiment he did with Woodworth in 1901;[21] it was more formally stated in his *Educational Psychology* in 1903.[22] The theory stated that transfer from one situation to another depended on *identical elements* being present in the original learning situation that could be transferred to a new learning situation, thus, making the new learning easier. The degree of transfer or facilitation would depend on how much the two situations (new and old) had in common. The substance of two different school subjects such as English and French might be different, but there might be many words that were the same, such as *table,* or grammatical principles (both languages use "s" to make nouns plural), which were also common. One learned English for the first fourteen years of one's life, but it did not require an equal number of years to master the French language. Likewise, there were similar procedures for looking things up in a dictionary, cookbook, or handbook—all of which had much in common, even though the contents of these books were quite different.

As an educational psychologist, Thorndike became very involved in the mental test movement, which was very popular at the time, and suggested that

---

[20]B. F. Skinner, *The Behavior of Organisms: An Experimental Analysis* (New York: Appleton-Century-Crofts, 1938).

[21]Edward L. Thorndike and Robert S. Woodworth, "The Influence of Improvement in One Mental Function upon the Efficiency of other Functions," *Psychological Review,* Vol. 8 (1901), pp. 247–61.

[22]Edward L. Thorndike, *Educational Psychology, op. cit.*

intelligence as measured by many of the current tests was really a measure of the transfer-capacity of the individual taking the test.

## Thorndike's Later Position (1930–1949)

*Modification of the Law of Exercise.* The kind of experiment that led Thorndike to alter the law of exercise was something like the following: with the repetition of a task in which the law of effect was not applicable, improvement did *not* seem to take place. For example, if one were blindfolded and asked to draw a line four inches long and one were not given any knowledge of results, one would not do better at the end of the practice session than at the beginning. According to Thorndike, practice worked only when other factors could be made effective. Thus, he did not completely repeal the law of exercise, but thought that the amount of strengthening obtained through mere repetition was negligible. For practice to work, there had to be some *effect* involved. In the previous illustration there was none, and consequently, learning was not improved.

*Modification of the Law of Effect.* In his original statement of the law of effect, he had said that satisfying consequences tended to "stamp in" and dissatisfying consequences "stamped out" responses. In other words, punishment seemed to be the opposite of reward. A number of experiments gave data contrary to the supposition. He did one of these experiments with chicks.[23] A simple maze had three pathways, one of which led to "freedom, food, and company," that is, an open box in which there were other chicks eating. A wrong choice led to confinement for thirty seconds. He found that rewarding a connection always strengthened it, but punishment (confinement) did not necessarily weaken the connection.

*The Spread of Effect.* In 1933 Thorndike reported experiments to support an extension of his law of effect. This meant that the influence of a particular positive consequence acted to strengthen not only the S–R connection to which it belonged but also adjacent connections both before and after the rewarded connection. The degree of the effect would diminish with each step that the connection was removed from the original rewarded one. In other words, there was a kind of generalization both forward and backward.

In one experiment, a subject was asked to say a number anywhere between 1 and 10 in response to a stimulus word given by the experimenter. The experimenter then called out "right" or "wrong." These responses were contrived by a pre-arranged assignment of correct numbers to each word. The lists were so long that the subjects could not recall on the second run through just what they had done on the first. After the lists were read numerous times, subjects'

---

[23]Edward L. Thorndike, "Rewards and Punishment in Animal Learning," *Comparative Psychology Monographs*, Vol. 8 (1932), No. 39.

responses were classified. When the number of responses repeated was analyzed, the results showed that the rewarded responses, "right," were repeated more often than the "wrong" responses, *and* with greater than chance expectancy if they occurred *near* in time to a response called "right."

Thorndike also found that the effect diminished with the distance (before and after) between the word that was rewarded and other words near it on the list. The rewarded response (correct number corresponding to a word) had the greatest probability of occurring again, but also there was an increased probability of responding with the same number to neighboring words, even though those words had not been rewarded.

## Education

Throughout most of his career, Thorndike was concerned with the problems of education and the application of the principles he had developed to the process of human learning and teaching.

We have already noted Thorndike's rejection of the "doctrine of formal discipline," which advocated the general training and shaping of the mind by studying the classics, mathematics, and logic. He felt that if there were advantages in studying certain subjects, it was not that they "trained the mind" but that certain "identical elements" learned in one subject could be carried over to the new subject. However, something had to be transferred, whether it was a specific term or principle.

Thorndike also objected to the traditional lecture method in teaching, because the lecture did not necessarily let the student know exactly what he or she was supposed to learn. "But telling a fact to a child may not cure his ignorance of it any more than patting him will cure his scarlet fever."[24] Thorndike was saying that the teacher must carefully define the educational objectives.

In 1922 Thorndike formulated seven rules for proper teaching of arithmetic,[25] which could also apply to the teaching of other subjects:

1. Consider the situation the pupil faces.

2. Consider the response you wish to connect with.

3. Form the bond; do not expect it to come by a miracle.

4. Form no bond that will have to be broken.

5. Do not form two or three bonds when one will serve.

6. Form bonds in such a way that they will make appropriate connections when they are used.

---

[24]Edward L. Thorndike, *Education: A First Book* (New York: Macmillan, 1912), p. 61.
[25]Edward L. Thorndike, *The Psychology of Arithmetic* (New York: Macmillan, 1922), p. 101.

**7.** Favor the situations that life itself will offer and the responses that life itself will demand.

Finally, Thorndike objected to the theory of intelligence as consisting of a general mental ability. He rejected the idea of an overall mental capacity in favor of one that stressed synthesis. Thus, intelligence depended on the "number of connections in a person's brain." He distinguished three types of intelligence:

**1.** Abstract intelligence, which dealt with symbols, words, and concepts.

**2.** Social intelligence, an ability to deal properly with social relations (tact, leadership, and other social abilities).

**3.** Mechanical intelligence, which was related to the manipulation of objects, tools, and machinery.

He opposed Alfred Binet's tests of intelligence, later revised by Louis M. Terman (Stanford-Binet Scale) because they assumed a general mental capacity. He substituted his own test, the *Intellect CAVD* (Completion, Arithmetic Reasoning, Vocabulary, Directions). These were four tests that measured relatively unrelated abilities that, taken together, represented abstract intelligence.

## Evaluation of Thorndike

Thorndike, like Pavlov, has had a profound influence on modern learning theory. His law of effect has been reinterpreted by Hull[26] and Skinner[27] in terms of *reinforcement,* namely that behavior is strengthened by its consequences. Although Guthrie[28] minimized reinforcement as the significant variable, S–R connections remained the central core of his theory. Thus, Guthrie formalized a systematic association theory. Estes,[29] in his mathematical models, has also stressed a statistical association theory.

Thorndike initiated systematic experimental studies in both human and animal learning. His experiments with cats in the puzzle box have become the prototype of modern learning experimentation, whether the apparatus be a runway or an operant conditioning chamber (Skinner). He became an active leader in the fields of mental testing and educational psychology, the latter through his extensive experiments in human learning.

Thorndike's position had declined over the past two decades as more sophisticated learning theories have evolved. Although some may substitute the

---

[26]Clark L. Hull, *Principles of Behavior* (New York: Appleton-Century-Crofts, 1943).
[27]B. F. Skinner, *op. cit.*
[28]Edwin R. Guthrie, *The Psychology of Learning* (New York: Harper and Row, 1935).
[29]W. K. Estes, "Toward a Statistical Theory of Learning," *Psychological Review,* Vol. 57 (1950), pp. 94–107.

terms "contiguity" or "functional relationship," the concept of association still remains.

Thorndike, of course, had his critics. The Gestalt psychologists objected to the idea of blind or haphazard "trial-and-error" learning, in favor of a more organized concept of insight learning. They further objected to the connectionism and transfer of identical elements. For Gestaltists, psychology had to deal with "wholes," not with little elements of behavior.

The behaviorists objected generally to Thorndike's dualism, which was implicit in his system. He commonly used the terms "mind" or "mental." His statement of the law of effect involving "satisfying consequences" was violently objected to as being completely dualistic and subjective. Thorndike was a dualist, there is no doubt, but it never bothered him. He sought no solution to the mind-body problem, but merely ignored it.

We have devoted this chapter primarily to the work of two researchers, Pavlov and Thorndike, who operated quite independently but shared the basic principle of associationism.

It might be appropriate to conclude with a quotation from Pavlov's *Lectures on Conditioned Reflexes* in which he, a physiologist, acknowledges the significant work of the psychologist, Thorndike.[30]

> Some years after the beginning of the work with our new method I learned that somewhat similar experiments had been performed in America, and indeed not by physiologists but by psychologists. Thereupon I studied in more detail the American publications, and now I must acknowledge that the honour of having made the first steps along this path belongs to E. L. Thorndike. By two or three years his experiments preceded ours, and his book (*Animal Intelligence: An Experimental Study of the Associative Process in Animals,* 1898) must be considered a classic, both for its bold outlook on an immense task and for the accuracy of its results.

## Suggested Further Readings

Hilgard, E. R., and Bower, G. H., *Theories of Learning,* 3rd ed. New York: Appleton-Century-Crofts, 1966, ch. 2. An excellent summary of Thorndike's basic position on learning.

Pavlov, Ivan P., *Conditioned Reflexes.* London: Oxford University Press, 1927. Basic readings in Pavlov. The best place to begin if one wishes to read Pavlov.

Postman, L., "The History and Present Status of the Law of Effect." *Psychological Bulletin,* Vol. 44 (1947), pp. 489–565. The title gives a good indica-

---

[30]Ivan P. Pavlov, *Lectures on Conditioned Reflexes,* trans. W. H. Gantt (New York: International Press, 1928), pp. 39–40.

tion of what the article is about. The significance lies in the many diverse but, in many ways, similar interpretations of the law.

Thorndike, Edward L., *Selected Writings from a Connectionist's Psychology*. New York: Appleton-Century-Crofts, 1949. A Thorndike sampler.

Warren, H. C., *A History of Association Psychology*. New York: Charles Scribner's Sons, 1921. Just what the title implies.

# CHAPTER

# 11

# *Hormic and Dynamic Psychology*

An Englishman by birth, William McDougall (1871–1938) received his medical training at Cambridge University and the University of London. During the period between 1899 and 1900 he was a member of the Cambridge Anthropological Expedition to the Torres Straits. On his return to London, he became a "reader" at University College, London. Between 1904 and 1920 he was appointed "Wilde Reader in Mental Philosophy" at Oxford. During this so-called "British period" he wrote some of his most significant works and developed his system of hormic psychology. McDougall served in the British Medical Corps during World War I, working with patients with behavior disorders. These studies led to his writing a text on abnormal psychology.[1] In 1920 he was called to Harvard University to fill a chair once occupied by William James, a man for whom McDougall had considerable admiration. In 1927 he was asked to become the head of the department of psychology at Duke University, where he remained until his death in 1938.

---

[1]William McDougall, *Outline of Abnormal Psychology* (New York: Charles Scribner's Sons, 1926).

## McDougall's Hormic Psychology

### Definition of Psychology

Although John Watson founded behaviorism as a movement in psychology in 1913 and defined psychology as the *science of behavior*,[2] he was not the first to do so. In McDougall's first book, *Physiological Psychology*[3] (1905), he defined psychology as follows:[4]

> Psychology may be best and most comprehensively defined as the positive science of the conduct of living creatures.

Later, in *Introduction to Social Psychology*[5] (1908), he considered conduct to be fairly synonymous with *behavior*. However, what McDougall had intended was quite different from what Watson was dealing with, as we shall see in the next chapter. McDougall wanted to account for the fact that mental processes *resulted* in the activity of living organisms, and that they had to be studied by methods other than introspection, as was proposed by the structuralists. Furthermore, in this book he laid the framework for a new social psychology, based on his doctrine of instincts (see below).

### Purposivism or Hormic Psychology

McDougall took the word "hormic" from the Greek "hormé," which meant an "urge." The urge had a purpose. The central idea was that an end or purpose drove us on to action without our necessarily having any real knowledge of its nature, although a vague kind of foresight might be involved.

Purposive behavior was goal-seeking. This striving to achieve an end became the central core of a psychology involving all living organisms.

In *Introduction to Social Psychology*,[6] he described what constituted striving or goal-seeking behavior.

1. It was spontaneous. A cat lying in wait leaped on its prey when the occasion was appropriate.

2. It persisted. The behavior might start with some stimulus, but it would continue long after the stimulus had been removed.

---

[2]John Watson, "Psychology as the Behaviorist Views It," *Psychological Review*, Vol. 20 (1913), pp. 158–77.
[3]William McDougall, *Physiological Psychology* (London: J. M. Dent, 1905).
[4]*Ibid.*, p. 1.
[5]William McDougall, *Introduction to Social Psychology*, 14th ed. (London: Methuen and Co., Ltd., 1919).
[6]William McDougall, *Introduction to Social Psychology*, 5th ed. (London: Methuen and Co., Ltd., 1912).

**3.** Even though persistence was inevitable, the duration of the activity would be variable. If an organism could not find its goal in one way, it would attempt one variation or many until that final goal was reached.

**4.** A particular act would terminate once the goal had been found. There would then follow some other act which might lead to another goal, and so on.

**5.** There was improvement with repetition. Thus, learning was involved. However, McDougall certainly did not stress the importance of learning in psychology as did the later behaviorists.

These formulations did not appear until the fifth edition of *Introduction to Social Psychology* was published in 1912.[7]

If activity were to lead to an end or a goal, there had to be some kind of energy involved. McDougall had had considerable training in biology, so he felt it necessary to establish some kind of physiological foundations for his purposive theory. He labeled this "instinctive energy" (see theory of instincts below). There was a potential psychophysical energy stored in the tissues in a chemical form, which could be transformed into a kinetic or electrical form. Any activity of an organism involved either a discharge or redistribution of this energy.

## Theory of Instincts

In *Introduction to Social Psychology*, McDougall first set down his instinct theory. Prior to that time, there had been no true social psychology. What had been written earlier was the result of the work of historians, economists, and other "social scientists." Experimental psychologists of the time (1908) had concerned themselves with problems of sensation, perception, learning, memory, and reasoning. For McDougall this seemed very much an intellectual state of affairs. He considered the psychology of the time a kind of one-sided intellectualism. The assumption had been that human behavior was rational. Of course, Freud had introduced the pleasure principle and was also developing an instinct doctrine but, in the beginning, McDougall was unaware of it. When McDougall became acquainted with Freud's writings on instincts, he reacted favorably.

The fundamental assumption for hormic psychology was that there had to be a certain number of fundamental instincts that were inherent in all people. For McDougall, an instinct was not merely a mechanical set or chain of reflexes, but was a vital, urging force striving for some sort of goal.

The instinct had three aspects:

**1.** A perceptual predisposition to notice certain stimuli when encountered— for example, as to perceive food odors.

---

[7]*Ibid.*

2. A predisposition to make certain movements that would lead to or approach the goal.

3. In the middle, between the perceptual predisposition to notice and the final movements to the goal, was the emotional core.

Sometimes it was difficult to distinguish between the latter two. The three aspects were referred to as: (1) cognitive (perceptual), (2) conative (goal seeking), and (3) affective (emotional core). Combined, these constituted the complete mental act. The emotional core involved the energy of the instinct, that which could give rise to the activity once a stimulus was presented to trigger the reaction.

It should be made clear that McDougall's interpretation of the instinct was not a "hedonistic" one, to be interpreted as involving satisfying or pleasurable consequences. As human organisms, we were so conceived that we inherently strove toward certain goals. Our human nature was based on a series of inborn tendencies that were all essential and shared. To some degree, these resembled the instincts of animals.

In 1908 he listed twelve major instincts in the first edition of *Introduction to Social Psychology*. In further editions, he revised the list, and by 1932 the list had grown to contain seventeen. Besides these major instincts, he also listed some minor tendencies, such as the urge to breathe when out of breath, to cough, to sneeze, to eliminate, and so on. By the time McDougall wrote *Energies of Men*[8] in 1932, the term "instinct" had come into some considerable disfavor, particularly insofar as human behavior was concerned. McDougall substituted the term "propensity," but the basic idea remained the same.

This was his original list.

| | |
|---|---|
| Hunger | Maternal (paternal) |
| Rejection of certain substances | Gregariousness |
| | Self-assertion |
| Curiosity | Self-abasement |
| Escape | (submission) |
| Fight (pugnacity) | Construction |
| Sex | Acquisition |

In the fifth edition of *Introduction to Social Psychology* in 1912,[9] he listed what he called the seven basic instincts and their emotional cores.

| Instinct | Emotional Core |
|---|---|
| Rejection | Disgust |
| Curiosity | Wonder |

---

[8]William McDougall, *Energies of Men, A Study of the Fundamental Dynamics of Psychology* (London: Methuen and Co., Ltd., 1932).
[9]William McDougall, *Introduction to Social Psychology*, 5th ed., *op. cit.*

Escape                    Fear
Fight                     Anger
Self-assertion            Elation
Self-abasement            Subjection
Maternal (paternal)       Tender emotion

Other instincts listed in the original group, such as sex, gregariousness, hunger, acquisition and construction, did not seem to have any well-defined emotional accompaniment.

By 1932, the list had grown to seventeen. The following five were added to the original twelve:

Appeal (cry aloud for assistance)
Laughter
Comfort
Rest or sleep
Migration

The significance of the instinct doctrine represented the fundamental structure of the entire system. This can be understood in the following quotation from the first edition of *Social Psychology*.[10]

Directly or indirectly the instincts are the prime movers of all human activity . . . determine the ends of all activities and supply the driving power . . . and all the complex intellectual apparatus of the most highly developed mind is . . . but the instrument by which thier impulses seek their satisfaction.

## Native Capacities

All human beings had many native capacities or abilities. However, unlike the instincts, the capacities had no driving force in themselves, but had to be driven by the instincts (propensities) or had to be sentiments derived from the instincts (see below). One might have a great capacity for music or intelligence but, if no driving force energized it, the capacity would be unfulfilled.

## Learning

It became obvious to McDougall early in his writings that instincts could be modified. This fact was mentioned in the fifth edition under the basic characteristics of psychological activity (see pp. 152–153). The main point was that activity improved with repetition. For example, when an infant was restrained, the urge to fight emerged. Later in the child's experience, parental commands of restraint might elicit the impulse. With practice, the fulfillment of an instinct was improved. Thus, both the perceptual and activity parts of the entire

---

[10]William McDougall, *Introduction to Social Psychology*, 1908, p. 44.

instinct might be subject to modification, but the emotional core (if it could be identified) would remain unchanged.

## Sentiments

There could be another kind of modification of the instincts. Tendencies could combine into what he called the "sentiments." This occurred when two or more instincts became attached to the same object. A man's love for his wife might include both the sex instinct and a maternal or mothering instinct. What we referred to as patriotism involved many instincts and their cores. Danger to one's country aroused fear. An attack gave rise to anger. Rivalry with another country aroused self-assertion. McDougall, as cited by Woodworth, believed that the self-assertive instinct was involved in many sentiments, including one's school, one's religion, and other objects with which one might identify.[11] Much human activity was explained by the sentiments that were derived from the instincts and that still possessed the emotional core of the instincts. Most of our social behavior was explained in this way. There was no single social instinct, but as the result of instincts combined into sentiments, we were very much social animals. Such a combination might include self-assertion, gregariousness, and the maternal instinct.

## The Group Mind

McDougall wrote *The Group Mind*[12] in answer to the criticism levied against him, particularly by the behaviorists, that in his *Social Psychology* he had not adequately explained how individual instincts operate in explaining the behavior of crowds and other aggregates of people. Any group of people—a crowd, a church congregation, a union of workers, an audience in a theater—could possess a group mind that operated above and beyond the individual minds that comprised it.

He defined the group mind in the following way:

> It consists of the same stuff as individual minds, its threads and parts lie within these minds: but the parts in the several individual minds reciprocally imply and complement one another and make up the system which consists wholly of them.[13]

Thus, in the group mind there were interactive effects among the individuals who constituted the group. The question may be asked, What factors or conditions bind the individual minds together to constitute the group mind? McDougall's reply was the *intensity* of the emotions involved. In the behavior

[11]Robert S. Woodworth, *Contemporary Schools of Psychology*, rev. ed. (New York: The Ronald Press Co., 1948).
[12]William McDougall, *The Group Mind* (New York: Putnam, 1920).
[13]*Ibid.*, p. 15.

of a crowd, for example, the emotions reached a pitch that could seldom, if ever, be attained in a single individual. The individuals were caught up in a great wave of emotions in which the participating persons lost their individuality. This explained the often-violent behavior of a mob rioting in a large city. According to McDougall, "It is a notorious fact that, when a group of men think and feel and act together, the mental operations and the actions of each individual of the group are apt to be very different from those he would achieve if he faced the situation as an isolated individual."[14]

In accounting for the panic of a crowd caught in a dangerous situation, such as a theater fire, McDougall compared their behavior to that of a herd of mindless animals acting instinctively, trampling each other to escape the threat of impending doom.

McDougall devoted a great deal of space in comparing the group behavior of primitive people to the groups in a modern industrial nation, such as the United States. Here he appealed to his instinct theory by which human beings, whether primitive or civilized, still shared the same common instincts. In the sharing of similar instincts, mass migrations, the character of a nation or the development of lasting social institutions could be explained.

McDougall considered *The Group Mind* to be his *magnum opus*. At the time his instinct theory, as set forth in his *Social Psychology,* was very popular, but his theory of the group mind did not fare so well. It was considered descriptive rather than explanatory. The behaviorism of John Watson was gaining greater appeal. This was an approach to psychology for which McDougall had no use. Behaviorism was attempting to demolish any conception of the existence of individual minds, let alone a group mind (see chaps. 12 and 13).

## The Lamarckian Experiment

In the same year that McDougall published *The Group Mind* (1920) he undertook a long-range experiment designed to support the Lamarckian theory of the hereditary transmission of acquired characteristics. This was at a time when Darwin's theory of natural selection was becoming extremely popular. His procedure was to train a group of white rats to select the correct escape platform in a tank of water. The tank had three parallel alleys and the rats were placed in the middle one and required to swim its length, then turn either to the right or left. At each exit there was a platform, one brightly, the other dimly, illuminated. In order to avoid drowning, the rats were required to climb onto one of the platforms. The correct exit was at the dimly illuminated platform. If the rats chose the more brightly illuminated one, they received an electric shock. In each generation only half the rats received the training. The experiment continued through twenty-four generations. Ten years later, in 1930, McDougall was convinced that the experiment demonstrated a clear-cut proof of the reality of the Lamarckian theory. In each generation the average number of

---

[14]*Ibid.,* p. 31.

errors was calculated. In the last report, the rats in the untrained group made an average of 125 errors before they learned to escape from the appropriate exit while those in the trained group made an average of only twenty-five errors.[15]

The study, however, had its difficulties. Rats died and had to be replaced. Other independent investigators attempted to replicate McDougall's procedures but failed to verify his findings. Criticisms were centered around McDougall's experimental procedures and selective breeding techniques. William Sahakian, a historian of psychology, has called the study an "abortive effort."[16] Unquestionably, the whole operation strongly hurt McDougall's status in the eyes of his fellow psychologists.

Today, however, there has been a modest revival of the Lamarckian theory. It is difficult to explain certain changes in species development merely by means of natural selection, so it is possible that McDougall was not 100 percent wrong.

## Mind-Body Problem

In his earliest writings in 1898,[17] McDougall, then very much a biologist, was concerned with the relationship between mind and body. He concluded that consciousness was an accompaniment of the neural processes. Most of what went on in the nervous system was usually of an unconscious nature. Only a new process became conscious. Later, he focused on the synapse (the point of connection between neurons) as the point where conscious mental activity occurred (1901).[18] Thus, McDougall reiterated in a more precise way what the physiologists of the nineteenth century had accepted—that the brain was the seat of the mind.

By 1911, in his book *Body and Mind*,[19] the "soul" doctrine was introduced. The soul was a process or the sum of definite capacities for psychophysical interaction.

Furthermore, in this book, he advocated a doctrine of animism, which was merely an extension of the "soul" doctrine. He believed there was a bit of "soul" even in inorganic matter. Through evolution, organic matter developed a greater degree of "soul," and this increased as one proceeded from the lowest form of life to humans. This animistic notion never became very popular at the time when psychology was fighting vigorously to cast off any theological implications.

---

[15]William McDougall, "Fourth Report on a Lamarckian Experiment," pts. I–IV, *British Journal of Psychology*, Vol. 28 (1938), pp. 321–45, 365–95.

[16]William Sahakian, *History and Systems of Psychology* (New York: Halsted Press, Division of John Wiley and Sons, 1975), p. 79.

[17]William McDougall, "A Contribution Towards an Improvement in Psychological Method II," *Mind*, Vol. 7 (1898), pp. 159–78.

[18]William McDougall, "On the Seat of Psychological Processes," *Brain*, Vol. 24 (1901), pp. 577–630.

[19]William McDougall, *Body and Mind: A History and Defense of Animism* (London: Methuen and Co., Ltd., 1911).

In addition to the "soul" doctrine, McDougall was a firm believer in psychic phenomena (extrasensory perception). When he assumed the chairmanship of the department of psychology at Duke University, he furnished a fertile and sympathetic background for the psychic research of J. B. Rhine's studies in mental telepathy (direct mind-to-mind communication), precognition (foretelling the future) and psychokinesis (manipulation of material objects through mental effort alone). Although a few respectable psychologists have taken Rhine's research seriously, the vast majority of them have been extremely skeptical.

## McDougall's Support for Unpopular Causes

It should be clear by now that McDougall had become the champion of many unpopular causes:

**1.** He advocated a doctrine of the soul and an anti-mechanistic attitude at a time when behaviorism, which denied the mind, was beginning to make headway.

**2.** He supported psychic research, an endeavor that was never very popular in America. His support of J. B. Rhine's extrasensory research left a scar on the psychology department at Duke University for many years after McDougall's death.

**3.** He fostered a teleological psychology in his theory of instincts and purposivism, an attitude that was highly questionable among deterministic psychologists.

**4.** Perhaps most unpopular of all was his attempt to prove the Lamarckian theory of the inheritance of acquired characteristics, a cause he championed until his death. The whole concept was implicit in his theory of instincts. In the evolution of instincts, learning had to be taken into consideration. Thus, if society were to evolve as it had, the changes would be transmitted from one generation to another according to Lamarckian principles.

## Evaluation of McDougall

In the early years while he was still in England, McDougall's theories received considerable acceptance. His new approach and the development of a dynamic psychology were only paralleled by Freud. He developed a new social psychology and influenced thinking in the fields of politics, economics, and anthropology. His influence on psychology stressed the reality of instincts and goal-seeking behavior, a matter already widely accepted by animal psychologists. He reacted against the "intellectualism" in psychology and followed an evolutionary doctrine that advocated that man was very much akin to the animals.

However, during the latter part of his stay in America, his popularity began to wane. He was opposed by the behaviorists, who objected to his dualistic and anti-mechanistic views. As behaviorism began to take hold, McDougall's "star began to fall." Many critics said that his theories could not be tested, as indeed was true. The sociologists and later social psychologists felt that the social nature of human beings was a product of culture and environment, not of instincts.

McDougall struck back. Of structuralism he wrote, "A quagmire of pedantry, a mass of confusion and error, lacking even the modest merit of internal consistency."[20] With regard to Gestalt psychology he wrote, "The name is a novelty; but the principle has long been recognized."[21] About behaviorism he wrote, "I regard Dr. Watson as a good man gone wrong . . . a bold pioneer whose enthusiasm in the cause of reform in psychology has carried him too far . . . and landed him in a ditch. . . ."[22]

However, McDougall's influence on modern psychology is still felt. Although he was a learning theorist, Tolman[23] developed a psychology of "purposive behaviorism" (see pp. 272–274). With the recent movement in animal psychology, and in particular with such ethologists as Tinbergen[24] and Lorenz,[25] instinct theory has been revived, at least insofar as animal behavior is concerned (see below).

## Current Instinct Doctrine

With the decline of McDougall's psychology, the concept of instinct had practically disappeared from psychology, probably due to the attacks of the behaviorists (see chaps. 12 and 13). However, largely as a result of the works of two European zoologists, there developed a new branch of biology called *ethology*, the study of animals in their natural habitat. This new endeavor began largely as a result of the works of Konrad Lorenz in Germany and Niko Tinbergen in England. Tinbergen's book *The Study of Instinct*[26] and Lorenz's *King Solomon's Ring*[27] stimulated interest in this new field of study both in Europe and in America.

Early studies were directed at what ethologists call *species-specific* behavior, which means that certain patterns of behavior are characteristic of one species but not of another. Work by Tinbergen and Lorenz resulted in the formulation of the concepts of *releasers* and *imprinting*. A releaser is a highly specific stimulus

[20]William McDougall, "Experimental Psychology and Psychological Experiment," *Character and Personality*, Vol. 1 (1932–33), pp. 195–213, p. 197.

[21]William McDougall, *Energies of Men, A Study of the Fundamental Dynamics of Psychology*, p. 46.

[22]William McDougall, "Fundamentals of Psychology," *Psyche*, Vol. 5 (1924), p. 14.

[23]E. Tolman, *Purposive Behavior in Animals and Men* (New York: Century Co., 1932).

[24]N. Tinbergen, *Social Behavior in Animals* (New York: John Wiley and Sons, 1953).

[25]K. Lorenz, "The Comparative Method in Studying Innate Behavior," *Symposia for the Study of Experimental Biology*, Vol. IV, pp. 221–68.

[26]Niko Tinbergen, *The Study of Instinct* (New York: Oxford University Press, 1951).

[27]Konrad Lorenz, *King Solomon's Ring* (New York: T. Y. Crowell, 1952).

that "triggers" or initiates a species-specific behavior. For example, the sight of a mother duck releases a *following* reaction in her ducklings at about sixteen hours after hatching. If another object is presented at the appropriate time, the ducklings will follow that object. Lorenz found that if the mother duck were removed and he placed himself in her stead, the ducklings would follow him. This new process was designated as *imprinting*. Very important to imprinting was the *critical period*. In the case of the ducklings, the critical period was between 8 and 20 hours after hatching. If the stimulus were presented before or after the critical period, imprinting did not take place.

For present day ethologists, instincts must refer to limited forms of behavior. If the behavior is more complex, learning is also operating. Of course, McDougall had recognized that instincts could be modified by learning. The phylogenetic level of the species is related to the relative importance of instincts. Insects, for example, must rely primarily on their instincts for capturing their prey, mating, and nest building. Instincts are characteristically highly specific and stereotyped patterns of adaptation. Ethologists speak of a number of critical factors. The first factor is sensory coding, followed by maturational readiness and internal drive states. The latter are postulated as states that interact with the sensory coding to bring about the response. If considered broadly enough, these newer concepts show some correlation with McDougall's three characteristics of an instinct: (1) perceptual readiness (sensory coding), (2) predisposition to make certain movements (the response aspect of the instinct), and (3) emotional core (internal drive states).

## Woodworth's Dynamic Psychology

Robert Sessons Woodworth (1869–1962) was both a contemporary and a successor to McDougall, a successor in that he continued to foster a psychology based on motivation and drive.

Many psychologists have considered him to be basically a functionalist (Boring,[28] Schultz and Schultz,[29] and Marx and Cronan-Hillix[30]). To be sure, he did share many of the ideas of the Chicago functionalists, but these did not constitute his major or unique contributions to psychology.

Woodworth received his A.B. degree from Amherst College and his A.M. from Harvard University, where he was exposed to William James and liked what the latter had to say. He then went on to Columbia University to receive his Ph.D. in 1899. After a brief sojourn to teach physiology in New York hospitals and to study

---

[28]E. G. Boring, *A History of Experimental Psychology*, rev. ed. (New York: Appleton-Century-Crofts, 1950).

[29]D. P. Schultz and S. E. Schultz, *A History of Modern Psychology*, 4th ed. (New York: Academic Press, 1969).

[30]M. H. Marx and W. A. Cronan-Hillix, *Systems and Theories in Psychology* (New York: McGraw-Hill Book Co., 1987).

a year in England with the famous physiologist Sherrington, he returned to Columbia to spend the rest of his career (he retired in 1945).

His systematic position was first set down in *Dynamic Psychology*[31] published in 1918. In 1921 he wrote what was to become one of the most popular introductory texts in psychology (it had its fifth edition in 1947). For twenty-five years[32] this text dominated the field. During the decades of the twenties and thirties, its competition was minimal. Woodworth's *Experimental Psychology*[33] was the major handbook in the field of experimental psychology, published in 1939 and later revised by Harold Schlosberg in 1954.[34] He received the first Gold Medal Award from the American Psychological Foundation, being cited for "unequaled contributions to shaping the destiny of scientific psychology." Other statements of his theoretical position are to be found in Murchison's *Psychologies of 1925,*[35] and *Psychologies of 1930,*[36] and in Woodworth's *Dynamics of Behavior*[37] in 1958.

Woodworth himself wrote that it was not his intent to establish a formal system. But, like McDougall, he was strongly interested in fostering a psychology of motivation (hence, the term "dynamic"). However, he differed with McDougall on many issues, as we shall see. Although Woodworth did not actually engage in the squabblings between theorists of the time, he did deplore Titchener and Watson, whom he called his "bogey men."

## Subject Matter of Psychology

To begin with, he was very much concerned with cause-effect relations—namely, the response and what events caused it to occur. One could consider him to be one of the early *S-R* (stimulus-response) psychologists, since those relationships were very important to him. However, his theory was not quite that simple, since he considered the organism and what went on inside it as being very important in determining the response. Thus, he presented the paradigm *S-O-R,* which was one of his main tenets throughout his writings. Woodworth preferred to begin with the *response* and then investigate the antecedent conditions. The stimulus was not the only cause, but was simply part of it. There was the organism with its store of energy, as well as other physiological events. He compared the relationship of *S-O-R* to that of a loaded gun. The action was not only determined by the stimulus (pulling the trigger) but also by the structure of the gun and its stored energy (the gun powder). The action was as much the result of the structure and conditions of the organism as it was of the stimulus that instigated it. So also, inside the organism there were other stimuli at work, including the machinery of the nervous system.

---

[31]Robert S. Woodworth, *Dynamic Psychology* (New York: Columbia University Press, 1918).

[32]Robert S. Woodworth, *Psychology* (New York: Henry Holt & Co., 1921).

[33]Robert S. Woodworth, *Experimental Psychology* (New York: Henry Holt & Co., 1939).

[34]Robert S. Woodworth and H. Schlosberg, *Experimental Psychology,* rev. ed. (New York: Henry Holt & Co., 1954).

[35]C. Murchison, ed. *Psychologies of 1925* (Worcester, Mass.: Clark University Press, 1928).

[36]C. Murchison, ed. *Psychologies of 1930* (Worcester, Mass.: Clark University Press, 1930).

[37]Robert S. Woodworth, *Dynamics of Behavior* (New York: Holt, Rinehart and Winston, 1958).

## Definition of Psychology

In defining psychology, however, Woodworth felt obliged to include both *behavior* and *consciousness*. Even though one might observe the eventual results in an overt act, something usually came before that was also part of the event—namely, consciousness that might only be discovered through introspection. He was not enthusiastic about the introspection of the structuralists, but nevertheless felt it was a necessary part of psychological methodology, although it was not the only distinctive method. He felt that to limit oneself merely to a series of motor events, as the behaviorists did, was not a complete account. A complete analysis of the event must also include the organism and its physiology.

## Mechanism and Drive

The crux of Woodworth's theory lay in his account of mechanism and drive. Mechanism referred to *how* a thing was done and drive referred to *why* it was done. Consider an automobile. The mechanism referred to that which made it go. The drive was the power applied.

In the early days at Columbia, Woodworth was acquainted with Thorndike and his experiments with the cats in the puzzle box. Applying Woodworth's distinction to this series of experiments, the animals' clawings, scratchings, biting, and pushing constituted the mechanism, in this case, behavior (see pp. 143–145). The drive was hunger. In this example, mechanism was separate from drive. However, it was possible in the eventual history of an organism for a mechanism to acquire its own drive function. What started out to be merely mechanism might also involve drive or become a drive for other activities.

Consider the businessman who had worked for many years and was driven by his needs to fulfill biological necessities to maintain himself and his family. Once he acquired an adequate estate, indeed, all the money he could possibly use to fulfill these needs, he could retire; but did he? No, he continued to work. In this instance, his mechanism of working took on the function of its own drive. He worked for the sake of working. Later, the eminent personality theorist, Gordon Allport, presented his theory of the "functional autonomy of motives."[38] By this, Allport meant that behavior that initially required motivation or drive to initiate it and carry on its function could take on its own motivating function. One might need a push to start sliding down a hill on a sled, but once the action started, it had its own drive to carry on by means of its own motion. As children, we might have eaten (mechanism) only when hungry. As adults, eating was not always dependent on hunger, as in the compulsive eater or drinker. The drive, then, could be either an organic state, as in hunger (S-O-R), or it might be a mechanism that had taken over that function.

---

[38]Gordon W. Allport, *Personality: A Psychological Interpretation* (New York: Henry Holt & Co., 1937).

## Learning

Other activities, such as learning and memory, might also be evaluated by the principle of mechanism and drive. In learning, we had the explanation of how the enormous additions of behavior occurred through practice and exercise. Both heredity and environment had to play their part. A particular S-O-R connection was established through exercise. However, new stimuli might also become associated, as in the conditioned response. Learning, as a mechanism, might have needed drive to start it, but through practice the learning itself took on its own driving force. Similarly, a connection might be broken through pain (punishment), failure (extinction?), or negative adaptation.

## Woodworth versus McDougall

Woodworth and McDougall agreed on the necessity of developing a psychology based on motivation. Woodworth called these states "drives," while McDougall used the term "instincts." Both concepts had much in common. However, for Woodworth, the drives were far less specific, and they had no specific built-in power of direction. For McDougall, an instinct had to have a driving force (emotional core). Therefore, no concept of mechanism in Woodworth's sense was possible, since an instinct could not take on its own motivational state. It already had it.

Both believed that human beings were born with certain native capacities. These were inborn "gifts" or "abilities." For McDougall, these capacities needed some instinctive force to energize them to their fulfillment. If no instinct ever came into operation, the capacity might always remain only potential. For Woodworth, this was not necessarily the case. A gifted person could readily respond to particular classes of stimuli, such as sounds for the musician or visual stimuli for the artist. So, for McDougall, the capacities would be dormant unless activated by some instinctual force. For Woodworth, the gifts and capacities could be compared to the drives themselves. Like drives they had the native power for action. In other words, they could become mechanisms with their own driving power for fulfillment. The starving artist continued to paint. The drive to paint had become the artist's mechanism.

In the later statement of this theory in *Dynamics of Behavior*[39] (1958), Woodworth's system was brought up to date. The book was far more eclectic than his earlier systematic view. He took cognizance of contemporary learning theorists such as Hull and Skinner, whose systematic writings were not available in the twenties. There was some attempt at integration along with experimental evidence. But the basic facts remained the same. The S-O-R paradigm remained. Four chapters were devoted to motivation (drive). The concept of mechanism was incorporated within the sections on drive. The rest of the book was devoted to the research on perception and learning, much of which was taken from *Experimental Psychology*.[40]

---

[39] Robert S. Woodworth, *Dynamics of Behavior, op. cit.*
[40] Robert S. Woodworth and H. Schlosberg, *Experimental Psychology*, rev. ed., *op. cit.*

## Evaluation of Woodworth

Woodworth's systematic position has not had the impact on psychology that many of those that preceded or followed it have had. Along with McDougall, Woodworth firmly established motivation in psychology and made the later learning theorists strongly aware of its importance. He lived to be ninety-three and devoted seventy of those years to psychology. For decades, his introductory text had no equal in popularity and many beginning students who studied it would always remember his emphasis on the *O* along with the *S*. Certainly, with his emphasis on the organism, he stimulated people to pursue investigations in physiological psychology. Even as late as 1940, there were few texts in that field. Today, the situation is changed. His *Experimental Psychology* was encyclopedic for its time, and for several decades was considered the best summary of data in the general experimental area. Since its revision, it has continued to be a very popular text and reference source.

## Suggested Further Readings

McDougall, William, *Introduction to Social Psychology,* 5th ed. London: Methuen, 1912.

McDougall, William, "The Hormic Psychology," in Murchison, C., ed., *Psychologies of 1930.* Worcester, Massachusetts: Clark University Press, 1930. Both references give a basic introduction to McDougall's instinct theory.

Robinson, A. L., *William McDougall, A Bibliography Together with a Brief Outline of His Life.* Durham, North Carolina: Duke University Press, 1943. For those who wish to look into McDougall's experimental program via the references given, as well as to learn about other areas in psychology in which he wrote, such as abnormal, physiological, and so on.

Wolman, B. B., ed., *Historical Roots of Contemporary Psychology.* New York: Harper and Row, 1968, ch. 6. Harold McCurdy's chapter on McDougall is an interesting supplement to the material presented in this chapter.

Woodworth, Robert S., *Dynamic Psychology.* New York: Columbia University Press, 1918. Woodworth's first full statement of his *S-O-R* psychology.

# CHAPTER

# 12

# *Early Behaviorism*

No movement in psychology is without its antecedents, and behaviorism is no exception. Although we generally credit John B. Watson as its founder in 1913, behaviorism had strong antecedents.

Before we consider Watson's systematic position as well as the positions of his contemporaries, let us recall some earlier influences that were both direct and indirect. The most important of these include: (1) Greek naturalism, (2) French materialism of the eighteenth and nineteenth centuries, (3) Darwin and the animal psychologists of the late nineteenth century, (4) Pavlov and the conditioned reflex, and (5) functionalism, the school that Watson "grew up" with.

## Antecedents

### Greek Naturalism

Over two thousand years passed from the time of Aristotle's naturalistic psychology until Watson presented a position that, in one stroke, threw the "mind" out of psychology. In a sense, Aristotle was the first "behaviorist," since in *De Anima,* he considered the body and the functions that it performed (see chap. 2). These functions were acts of the body and not separate from it—digestion, sensation, movement, and reason. The significance of Aristotle and the ancient Greeks was that they presented a kind of psychology (although primitive) that consisted of objective, observable phenomena. Watson also maintained this same attitude in the best way he could. From the fall of Greek naturalism until Watson, psychology was dominated by a dualism, a separation of mind and body. This dualism still exists today in many psychological theories. Watson had studied philosophy in his early years, and he was familiar with ancient Greek naturalism, although he made no reference to it in his writings. Nevertheless, the influence was there, although indirect.

## French Materialism

***Julien de la Mettrie (1709–1751).*** La Mettrie developed the doctrine of hedonism, the concept that pleasure was the chief goal of life. Hedonism in itself was not particularly significant for the early behaviorists as it possibly was for later behaviorism and for psychoanalysis. The important influence of La Mettrie was his emphasis on materialism as opposed to spiritualism—namely, that a human being was really a machine. His influence on psychology was his belief that there could be a physical interpretation of the mind. Of course, Descartes had considered both animals and the human body to be machines, but he could not depart from his concept of a soul separate from the body and interacting with it.

***Pierre Cabanis (1757–1805).*** Cabanis accepted much of La Mettrie's materialism. From a historical point of view, he can be considered one of the earliest physiological psychologists. One of the questions that philosophers and other writers of his time pondered was whether victims of the guillotine suffered any pain after losing their heads. In 1795 he wrote an essay in which he addressed the problem. In so doing he attempted to relate the mind to the body. He believed there could be no mental activity unless the brain were involved. Any functions of the body that did not involve the brain were merely mechanical functions of lower parts of the body. Cabanis concluded that the brain was the organ of consciousness, just as the stomach was the organ of digestion. So he defined "mind" in terms of brain functions. In answer to his original question of whether or not a person suffered pain after decapitation, he concluded that the guillotine was not painful. With the loss of the head, a person was no longer conscious. Any movements that occurred in the body after the head fell from it were merely reflexes at a nonconscious level of functioning.

***August Comte (1798–1857).*** Beyond the materialists' point of view that the human being was a machine, Comte founded another movement called positivism.[1] Positivism was to dominate a good bit of behaviorism well into the twentieth century. According to this point of view, only objective and observable knowledge was valid. In rejecting introspection, which stressed the inner analysis of conscious experience, private knowledge could not be valid. Here we note that almost a century before behaviorism began, introspection had been rejected. In Comte we have a rejection of mentalistic and subjective approaches

---

[1]E. G. Boring, *A History of Experimental Psychology,* rev. ed. (New York: Appleton-Century-Crofts, 1950).

to psychology. He stated that "in order to observe, your intellect must pause from activity and yet it is this very activity you want to observe: if you do not effect it there is nothing to observe. The results of such a method are in proportion to its absurdity."[2]

## Animal Psychology

We have already discussed the influences of Darwin in several previous chapters. What concerns us here are his great many observations on animals that influenced later animal psychology. In *Expression of Emotion in Man and Animals*,[3] he drew close relationships between expressed emotions in humans and lower species, for example, the grinding of teeth, frowning, and so on.

*George John Romanes (1848–1894).* One of the earliest of the animal psychologists of the nineteenth century, Romanes was a personal friend of Darwin and was sincerely interested in finding out about the behavior of animals from whatever sources he could gather. He collected stories, both popular (and often unreliable) and more scientific, and put them together in his book, *Animal Intelligence*,[4] which was published in 1886. Psychologists remember him best for a method of gathering data called the *anecdotal method*. Despite his attempt at objectivism, he reverted into accepting data from stories or anecdotes. Another trap he fell into was *anthropomorphism*, which meant attributing human traits such as reason, intelligence, will, or pleasure to animals. Of course, Darwin had done this, too. Today, behavioristic psychologists abhor both methods. However, we must credit Romanes for stimulating the initial study of the behavior of animals as a legitimate course of intellectual investigation and preparing the way for later more objective and experimental studies.

*C. Lloyd Morgan (1852–1936).* Another important figure in animal investigation, Morgan wrote several books on animal behavior; and, in *Introduction to Comparative Psychology*,[5] he dealt in detail with the comparisons of the behavior of lower forms with humans. His observations were of a semi-experimental type, half way between naturalistic observation of animals in their own native habitat and the controlled conditions of the laboratory.

He is best remembered by comparative psychologists for what was known as "Lloyd Morgan's canon." This was a reaction against Romanes' anthropomorphism and was an application of the "law of parsimony" or Occam's Razor. He stated that we must not interpret an action as demonstrating a higher psychical process if it could be interpreted as the outcome of one that stood lower in the psychological scale. For example, rather than talk about the intelligence of animals, it was better to speak of their habits. Like Thorndike, he chose to

---

[2]Auguste Comte, *The Positive Philosophy,* trans. H. Martineau (London: G. Bell, 1896, p. 11).
[3]Charles Darwin, *Expression of Emotion in Man and Animals,* 2nd ed. (London: J. Murray, 1872).
[4]George J. Romanes, *Animal Intelligence* (London: Kegan, Paul, 1886).
[5]C. L. Morgan, *Introduction to Comparative Psychology* (London: W. Scott, 1891, rev. ed., 1899).

explain learning on the basis of a few simple principles rather than become involved in complex, higher mental processes.

***Jacques Loeb (1859–1924).*** A third major figure in animal psychology, Loeb was a German biologist who came to the United States in 1891. Watson studied under him while at the University of Chicago. Loeb became involved in the realm of psychology when he argued that the activity of animals was comparable to the tropisms of plants. Animals were so structured that they would react selectively to certain kinds of energy—mechanical, chemical, and so on. Most of his examples involved very low forms such as jellyfish, starfish, and worms, and, theoretically, he extended his idea to higher forms. Although he did not ordinarily attempt to deal with the problems of human behavior, he dabbled with the human problem of consciousness. His concern, along with that of other animal psychologists, was to determine at what point in the evolutionary scale animals had consciousness. The criterion he set down was whether or not a particular species was capable of associative memory. If so, it had consciousness.

We have already dealt extensively with Edward L. Thorndike, who began his work in animal psychology in the late nineteenth century (see pp. 143–146). Two other individuals might be mentioned, W. S. Small and Robert Yerkes. Small introduced the animal maze in 1900, which was used for decades as a basic apparatus for animal research. Yerkes also began his animal investigations in the same year. He worked with a variety of species—crabs, turtles, rats, worms, birds, monkeys, and apes. At one time, he collaborated with Watson in developing a visual testing apparatus. He is perhaps best known for the establishment of the Yerkes Laboratories of Primate Biology in Orange Park, Florida, which involved a great deal of investigation with anthropoid apes, for the most part, chimpanzees. Finally, and quite a departure from his sub-human concerns, was the fact that during World War I he was chief of psychological services that tested the intelligence of the large drafted army.

## The Conditioned Reflex

We have already discussed Pavlov and Bekhterev, who developed conditioning procedures in both lower forms and humans. The significance of the conditioned reflex for behaviorism is twofold. First, it served as an objective method for the development and modification of behavior. The conditioning paradigm served as an explanation for all types of behavior. Second, as we shall see subsequently, Watson was very impressed with Pavlov's work and used his simple conditioning procedures as models for explaining all kinds of human learning.

## Functionalism

The influence of functionalism need not be belabored, since we considered it as a system in a previous chapter. Watson, whom we can call the formal founder of behaviorism, was a student of Angell. He wrote his doctoral dissertation under Angell and Donaldson at Chicago, so Watson was thoroughly entrenched in the functionalist movement. Since Watson founded behaviorism partly as a reaction against the functionalists, in this sense we might consider the influence of functionalism to be negative. Of course, Watson objected to the structuralists, too. Stated simply, Watson saw a need for a greater objectivity than functionalism had to offer. Nevertheless, there were strong evidences of functionalism in Watson's ideas. Both schools were concerned with activity rather than with mere elements of consciousness. Like the functionalists, Watson desired a wider application of psychology in the fields of animal and child psychology than the structuralists' "ivory tower" would permit.

## John Watson (1878–1958)

### The Man and His Works

Watson was born on a farm in Greenville, South Carolina. According to his own account, he was not a scholar in his early years. He attended Furman University in his hometown, studying such formal subjects as Latin, Greek, mathematics, and philosophy. In 1900 he earned his master's degree. He then entered the University of Chicago. At the beginning, he was more concerned with philosophy than with psychology, but it was Angell who first introduced him to psychology. He studied biology and physiology under Jacques Loeb and H. H. Donaldson, a neurologist. Under the direction of Angell and Donaldson, his doctoral dissertation used both neurological and psychological techniques, correlating behavior with the growth of medullation in the central nervous system of the white rat. The title of his thesis was *Animal Education: The Psychical Development of the White Rat*. He completed it in 1903. After receiving his degree, he remained at Chicago. In 1907 he published a monograph on "kinesthetic and organic sensations of the white rat,"[6] in which he investigated what cues a rat used in learning mazes.

The following year, Watson moved to Johns Hopkins University, where he became director of the psychological laboratory. The years between 1908 and 1920, before he left the academic world, were his most productive. In 1912 he gave a series of lectures at Columbia University, which contained the contents of an article that was published in 1913 in the *Psychological Review* under the title "Psychology as the Behaviorist Views It."[7] This set behaviorism afire and became known as the behaviorist's manifesto. (It is interesting to note Watson

---

[6]John B. Watson, "Kinesthetic and Organic Sensations: Their Role in the Reactions of the White Rat to the Maze," *Psychological Monographs*, No. 33, 1907.
[7]John B. Watson, "Psychology as the Behaviorist Views It," *Psychological Review*, Vol. 20 (1913), pp. 158–77.

obviously had no difficulty in having the article published, since he was an editor of the journal at the time.)[8]

The behaviorist's manifesto began as follows:

> Psychology as the behaviorist views it is a purely objective experimental branch of natural science. Its theoretical goal is the prediction and control of behavior. Introspection forms no essential part of the methods, nor is the scientific value of its data dependent upon the readiness with which they lend themselves to interpretation in terms of consciousness. The behaviorist, in his efforts to get a unitary scheme of animal response, recognizes no dividing line between man and brute. The behavior of man, with all of its refinements and complexity, forms only a part of behaviorism's total scheme of investigation.

In the same article, he set down what he considered to be the basic tenets of behaviorism:

1. Psychology thus far has failed to make good its claim as a natural science.

2. Psychology for the behaviorist is a purely objective, experimental branch of natural science that has as little use for introspection as do the sciences of chemistry or physics.

3. The elimination of states of consciousness as the proper subject for investigation will remove a barrier from psychology that exists between it and other natural sciences.

4. The proper subject matter for psychology is behavior.

In the following year, Watson wrote his first book, *Behavior: An Introduction to Comparative Psychology.*[9] At this time in his career he was very much an animal psychologist. He argued that animal psychology should be a significant specialty in the broad field of psychology. He felt that using animals as subjects allowed for more complete control of the experimental situation.

In 1918 Watson had begun experimenting with children. One of his investigations involved the study of hand preference, in which he used very young infants as his subjects. He measured the anatomical structure of the arm and the length of time the infant would hold onto a suspended bar with each hand. He also measured the amount of activity in each hand, such as slashing about or reaching for an object. Watson concluded that handedness was not inherited, but was a matter of cultural pressure that was actually conditioned, since we lived in a right-handed society.

---

[8]*Ibid.*, p. 158.
[9]John B. Watson, *Behavior: An Introduction to Comparative Psychology* (New York: Henry Holt & Co., 1914).

His most significant book, *Psychology from the Standpoint of a Behaviorist,*[10] first appeared in 1919 and was revised in 1924 and in 1929. In 1925 he wrote *Behaviorism,*[11] which was revised in 1930. In these later works, his main concern was to carry over the principles learned from animal psychology to human behavior.

In 1920 Watson left Johns Hopkins University and the academic world. His wife had sued him for divorce and this became so sensationalized that he was asked to resign from the University. Following the divorce, he married Rosalie Raynor, with whom he had collaborated in the classic study of conditioned fear in an infant named Albert B (see p. 175). Watson entered the advertising firm of J. Walter Thompson in New York. He did not abandon psychology completely, for in the ensuing years he continued to write. In 1928 he wrote a manual on child and infant care called *Psychological Care of the Infant and Child.*[12] By 1930 Watson's career as a contributor to psychology was almost ended.

## Watson's Psychology

In the clearest sense, Watson's system was an *S-R* (stimulus-response) psychology. The stimuli might be simple or complex, and if complex it would be perfectly proper to speak of a stimulus situation that could be ultimately reduced to smaller units. The following quote from *Behaviorism* (1925) states this position:[13]

> By stimulus we mean any object in the general environment or any change in the tissues themselves, due to the physiological condition of the animal, such as the change we get when we keep an animal from sex activity, when we keep it from feeding, when we keep it from building a nest. By response we mean anything the animal does—such as turning toward or away from a light, jumping at a sound, and more highly organized activities such as building a skyscraper, drawing plans, having babies, writing books and the like.

The mechanisms of responses were the activities of the smooth and striped muscles and the secretions of glands, both internal (adrenal, thyroid, pituitary) and external (perspiring, tearing, salivating).

Responses were classified as learned and unlearned, overt and covert (implicit). Overt, learned responses included much of what we obviously do: talking, walking, building a house, playing a game. Implicit, learned responses included thinking (subvocal speech) and perceiving, as well as certain conditioned emotional responses in which internal physiological activity was in-

---

[10]John B. Watson, *Psychology from the Standpoint of a Behaviorist* (Philadelphia: J. B. Lippincott, 1919).

[11]John B. Watson, *Behaviorism* (New York: W. W. Norton and Co., 1925, rev. ed., 1930).

[12]John B. Watson, *Psychological Care of Infant and Child* (New York: W. W. Norton and Co., 1928).

[13]John B. Watson, *Behaviorism, op. cit.,* pp. 6–7.

volved. Overt, unlearned responses included all natural reflexes: eye blinking, tearing, coughing, sneezing, the knee jerk, and breathing. Finally, covert, unlearned responses included digestion, blood pressure, and heartbeat.

## The Methods of Behaviorism

Since psychology was an objective science it had to use empirical methods. Watson allowed basically for (1) observation, (2) conditioning, (3) testing, and (4) the verbal report.

As an experimentalist, he saw great value in the experimental method of the laboratory. However, he did not frown on naturalistic observations of the S-R relationships in the field outside the laboratory.

The conditioned reflex technique as adopted from Pavlov and Bekhterev was also useful, particularly in the study of learning. It is interesting that Watson listed this technique as separate from observation.

The verbal report merits special attention. As indicated in the quote from the behaviorist's manifesto (see p. 171), it was clear that Watson was violently opposed to introspection. Speech reactions were observable phenomena and were obviously of use to the behaviorist. Sensations and feelings as such had to be rejected since we had no way of observing them directly. On the other hand, I could *tell* you that I felt warm or cold or saw red or green. For Watson, psychology was the study of behavior, *not* experience. This was obviously an attack on structuralism, whose system depended strongly upon sensation. The structuralists replied and pointed out that their most precious method, introspection, was in Watson's term the same thing as the verbal report. According to Watson, this was not the case. The structuralists were investigating almost exclusively subjective phenomena—the contents of consciousness—that were not permitted in Watson's system.

## The Mind-Body Problem

Before proceeding further into Watson's systematic position, we should clarify his position concerning the mind. One of the major statements in the behaviorist's manifesto was a denial of consciousness or mind. Watson stated:[14]

> The plans that I must favor for psychology lead practically to the ignoring of consciousness in the sense that that term is used by psychologists today. I have virtually denied that the realm of psyches is open to experimental investigation. I don't wish to go further into the problem at present because it leads inevitably over into metaphysics. If you will grant the behaviorist the right to use consciousness in the same way as other natural scientists employ it—that is, without making consciousness a special object of observation—you have granted all that my thesis requires . . .

---

[14]John B. Watson, "Psychology as the Behaviorist Views It," *op. cit.,* p. 174.

In this quotation, Watson showed some confusion about behavior and consciousness. This would indicate that he was taking a stand that is today called *methodological behaviorism*. This position would admit that the facts of mind or consciousness might exist but were not to be studied or explained by the techniques of science. In other words, they went beyond the scope of psychology.

A stronger position, which Watson adopted in 1919, is identified today as *radical behaviorism*. This denied all aspects of the existence of mind or consciousness in any respect inside or outside the realm of psychology. It was expressed in the following quotation from Watson:[15]

> He then who would introduce consciousness, either as an epiphenomenon or as an active force interjecting itself into the physical and chemical happenings of the body, does so because of spiritualistic and vitalistic leanings. The behaviorist cannot find consciousness in the test tube of his science. He finds no evidence anywhere for a stream of consciousness, not even for one so convincing as that described by William James. He does, however, find convincing proof of an ever-widening stream of behavior.

The denial of consciousness, mind, or soul was the hallmark of behaviorism. With one thrust it struck at all mentalistic systems, either in the naive statement of the structuralist's parallelism or in the more sophisticated theorists such as Tolman, who substituted "intervening variables." The dualism was still there.

Watson and the other behaviorists were clearly monists, one body no mind. With Watson, we had the first complete denial in formal psychology of the "other universe." From the time of Aristotle and the ancient Greeks until Watson, in one way or another, psychology had accepted a dualism of mind and body, regardless of the statement of the relationship, if any. With the demise of the mind, the mind-body problem no longer remained a problem for the behaviorist. All that remained was a behaving organism.

Furthermore, Watson was not concerned with the intervening brain processes (not true of all behaviorists), for he considered the brain as a "mystery box." The true study of psychology was that of responses of muscles and glands to stimuli.

At the beginning, this position came under attack from various sources. But, as time elapsed, behaviorism gained in popularity. According to the behaviorist, the science of psychology should only deal with physical events which exist in space and time.

## Instinct

Robert I. Watson, in his book *The Great Psychologists*,[16] pointed out that John Watson's views about instincts passed through three phases. In his first book,

---

[15]John B. Watson and William McDougall, *The Battle of Behaviorism* (New York: W. W. Norton and Co., 1929, p. 26).
[16]Robert I. Watson, *The Great Psychologists* (Philadelphia: J. B. Lippincott, 1978).

*Behavior: An Introduction to Comparative Psychology*[17] (1914), a considerable discussion was devoted to instinct. Instinct consisted of a series of reflexes joined together as unlearned. By 1919, in *Psychology from the Standpoint of the Behaviorist,*[18] such unlearned behavior could be seen only in infants because this behavior was soon covered over by habits. Finally, by 1925 in *Behaviorism,*[19] the concept of instinct at the human level was completely rejected. A catalogue of simple reflexes became the only allowable unlearned behavior. These reflexes included sneezing, crying, eliminating, sucking, or crawling. The ways in which these simple reflexes were performed differed slightly according to the structure of the organism.

## Learning

Crucial to Watson's position and that of the later behaviorists was the strong emphasis on learning. To Watson, habits were the products of learning and were formed by means of two basic laws, *recency* and *frequency.* These held true for simple maze learning as well as complex human problem solving. Watson erred in ignoring Thorndike's *law of effect,* which he considered to be "highly figurative," probably because of its subjective nature—"satisfying consequences" (see pp. 144–145). Fortunately, later behaviorists, such as B. F. Skinner, reformulated the law of effect into the *principle of reinforcement,* removing its dualistic and subjective implications.

As mentioned earlier in the section on methods, by 1915 Watson was very impressed with the work on the conditioned response. He felt it could be applicable not only to human learning but also to thinking and emotions. Habit, then, became nothing more than complex conditioned responses.

One of the classic experiments in psychology, performed and published by Watson and Raynor in 1920,[20] involved the conditioning of a fear response in a young infant, Albert, an eleven-month-old boy raised in a hospital where his mother was a wet nurse. For the conditioned stimulus they used a laboratory white rat and for the unconditioned stimulus a steel bar that was struck to give a loud noise. As the conditioning proceeded, Albert jumped, fell forward, and cried. Eventually, these responses occurred without the unconditioned stimulus—when the white rat was presented alone. This response was interpreted as a conditioned fear. They also demonstrated the process of the generalization of the response. Without further trials, Albert also exhibited the fear reaction to a dog, fur coat, wool, and even a Santa Claus mask.

As time has passed, we have come to realize that Watson's ideas on learning had many flaws. He depended on frequency and recency, which modern behaviorism does not consider to be as crucial as reinforcement, which Watson ig-

---

[17]John B. Watson, *Behavior: An Introduction to Comparative Psychology, op. cit.*
[18]John B. Watson, *Psychology from the Standpoint of a Behaviorist, op. cit.*
[19]John B. Watson, *Behaviorism, op. cit.*
[20]John B. Watson and R. Raynor, "Conditioned Emotional Responses," *Journal of Experimental Psychology,* Vol. 3 (1920), pp. 1–14.

nored. Further, he over-extended Pavlov's conditioning paradigm, applying it to all learning. It was for later behaviorists to distinguish between classical conditioning of the Pavlovian sort and instrumental or operant learning (see Chap. 13).

## Memory

Watson criticized earlier psychologists who considered memory to be a faculty of the mind. William James, who Watson regarded highly in many ways, had defined memory in terms of consciousness and then defined consciousness in terms of memory. For Watson there really was no mystery about the process. His interpretation of memory involved a threefold process. First of all, there had to be learning of some skill or verbal habit. Secondly, there was a loss of performance due to disuse. Finally, there could be relearning involving the effort and amount of time necessary to regain the task. This process held both for motor as well as verbal memory. A failure to recall something was due to a breaking up of certain motor systems that had been built up during the original learning process. Often this disintegration of muscular systems was a godsend, for it saved us from carrying around a host of useless verbal and motor organizations.[21]

## Emotion

Like other kinds of behavior, emotions involved strictly bodily reactions. In denying consciousness, Watson cast away any notion of emotions or feelings as subjective experiences, which had been presumed by the structuralists and William James. Various kinds of stimuli could evoke different emotions. Much of emotional activity might be implicit, involving visceral activity of the internal involuntary muscles and glands. Of course, part of the emotion could be overt and directly observable through facial expressions, postures, and gestures.

In 1919 Watson mentioned that there were three innate emotions found in human infants—fear, rage, and love. Other more complicated emotions were acquired through conditioning. Each of the three primary emotions could be set off by a specific stimulus or set of circumstances. Fear was aroused by sudden, loud noises or by sudden loss of support. Rage was produced by restraint or hampering of the infant's movements, and love was produced by soft stroking of the body, as in cuddling, rocking, or gentle patting. On the response side, fear involved a startle, catching of the breath, clutching, crying, and rapid breathing. In rage the body stiffened, breath was held, and there were slashing movements in the arms and legs. Love responses typically involved smiling, cooing, or gurgling.

As one developed into adulthood, these simple hereditary patterns broke down, although the basic elements remained. Shame, for example, developed

---

[21]John B. Watson, *The Ways of Behaviorism* (New York: Harper and Bros., 1928).

out of punishment for various activities including sex. Jealousy arose out of interference with sexual arousal.

Watson's theory of the three primary emotions turned out to be somewhat weak. For example, later investigations by Sherman[22] failed to confirm Watson's observations. When the observers were asked to identify the behavior without knowing what the prior stimulating conditions were, they were in great disagreement.

## Thinking and Speech

Speech arose as a learned activity out of the infant's random vocalizations and babblings. In its acquisition, speech eventually became an entirely overt activity. Words were substituted for explicit manual movements. Other kinds of movements became substituted for verbal communication, like frowning or grimacing, shrugging the shoulders, nodding the head, and so on. As the child learned to speak he talked out loud to himself, but frequently others in his environment would tell him to be quiet, thus reducing his overt speech to a whisper. The speech gradually became implicit, involving only minute muscle movements in the vocal apparatus. This resulted in thinking, which then was nothing more than *subvocal talking.* The inaudible thinking was nothing but talking to ourselves. All thinking did not have to be merely implicit subvocal action of the vocal apparatus. Watson allowed that the other parts of the body might also be involved. The deaf mute thought with his fingers. Nevertheless, the vocal apparatus was the most important organ of thought. In order to avoid introspection, thinking was reduced to tiny movements in the mouth, lips, tongue, and larynx.

As Watson[23] put it:

> The child talks incessantly when alone. At three he even plans the day *aloud,* as my own ear placed outside the keyhole of the nursery door has very often confirmed. Soon society in the form of nurse and parents steps in. "Don't talk aloud—daddy and mother are not always talking to themselves." Soon the overt speech dies down to whispered speech and a good lip reader can still read what the child thinks of the world and of himself. Some individuals never even make this concession to society. When alone they talk aloud to themselves. A still larger number never go beyond even the whispering stage when alone. Watch people reading on the street car; peep through the keyhole sometime when individuals not too highly socialized are just sitting and thinking. But the great majority of people pass on to the third stage under the influence of social pressure constantly exerted. "Quit whispering to yourself," and "Can't you even read without moving your lips?" and the like are constant mandates. Soon the process is forced to take place behind the lips. Behind these walls you can call

[22]M. Sherman, "The Differentiation of Emotional Responses in Infants," *Journal of Comparative Psychology,* Vol. 7 (1927), pp. 264–84; 335–51.

[23]John B. Watson, *Behaviorism,* rev. ed. (New York: W. W. Norton and Co., 1930), pp. 240–241.

the biggest bully the worst name you can think of without even smiling. You can tell the female bore how terrible she really is and the next moment smile and overtly pay her a verbal compliment.

As more sophisticated apparatus was developed, Watson's theory was subsequently subjected to experimental tests that could detect the minute muscular activity. In 1932 Jacobson[24] found that with great amplification tongue muscles were active during silent speech and, in 1937 Max[25] found similar small muscle movements in the arms and hands of deaf mutes when they were "thinking." Today, these studies are considered an over-simplification of the thinking process.

## Personality

At the time Watson was developing his system, Freud and those associated with the developing psychoanalytic movement made elaborate explanations of the human personality, which made use of dualistic distinction between mind and body (see chaps. 17 and 18). Watson felt that the concept of personality could not be ignored, and the behaviorist had to handle it. He proposed that personality constituted a rather straightforward cataloging of habits and other established activities. Personality included all our actual and potential reactions including speech, abilities and skills, and even our internal and visceral activity. Habit systems, as Watson called them, involved groupings of smaller units, clustered together around a particular event. These events could involve a person's trade, family relationships, religion, attitudes towards country, even the person's information system. For each person, the "personality" would be different.

Personality, as such, was quite consistent for a particular individual. However, it could be changed. Through further conditioning, old habits were lost and new ones acquired. No one remained the same throughout life. The modifications usually occurred rather slowly, however.

In Watson's discussions of personality, he became involved in the problems of how human beings might better themselves. Here, psychology could be applied. Unfortunately, Watson did not spell out the techniques for appropriate behavior modification as we know them today. He spoke of education in a general sense, but it remained for the later behaviorists, in their applied behavioral analysis, to deal with specific procedures.

## Watson's Environmentalism

In his early writings in 1914, he spoke of the importance of hereditary tendencies (see the section on instinct). By the 1920s he became an ardent environmentalist. Instincts were reduced to simple reflexes, and our abilities, habits,

---

[24]E. Jacobson, "Electrophysiology of Mental Activities," *American Journal of Psychology,* Vol. 44 (1932), pp. 677–94.
[25]L. W. Max, "Action-Current Responses in the Deaf During Awakening, Kinesthetic Imagery and Abstract Thinking," *Journal of Comparative Psychology,* Vol. 24 (1937), pp. 301–44.

and general behavior were dependent on the ways our environment treated us. Watson completely overemphasized his denial of hereditary factors and his stress on a most extreme environmentalism.

In 1925, in *Behaviorism,* he offered us the following (now a famous quotation):[26]

> Give me a dozen healthy infants, well-formed, and my own specified world to bring them up in and I'll guarantee to take any one at random and train him to become any type of specialist I might select—doctor, lawyer, artist, merchant-chief and, yes, even beggar-man and thief, regardless of his talents, penchants, tendencies, abilities, vocations and race of his ancestors.

This was as extreme a position on the importance of environment as could be found in psychology.

From his study of Albert, Watson was convinced that later personality disturbances went back to earlier infant and childhood training and, if learned, the behavior could also be improved by better environment.

This led him to suggest a plan for social improvement that he called "experimental ethics," based on his own behavioristic principles. It was a visionary program for rehabilitation and re-education. Of course, some criminals were beyond repair and if they could not be re-educated, they had to be kept from society, either under restraint or put away. The punishment for a criminal should not be for retribution by society, but for the protection of society.

## Determinism

From the above discussion, it should be clear that Watson believed that behavior was determined and was not the product of caprice or "free will." Although it was not universal, the principle of determinism has tended to characterize many behavioristic systems. Paradoxically enough, Freud, who developed many theories in complete contrast to behaviorism, was an absolute determinist.

## Reactions to Watson

Any new approach to psychology was bound to be heralded as a new solution to psychology's ills. The first edition of *Behaviorism* received rave reviews in leading New York newspapers. It was also damned by those who held opposing views. Watson harshly attacked the existing psychology in his denial of the mind, rendering those ideas are useless as monk's lore and old wives' tales. But other protagonists of the time did not accede to Watson.

One of Watson's most ardent opponents was William McDougall. By 1925 Watson had almost completely disavowed the instinct doctrine that was the foundation of McDougall's psychology. In 1929 they published jointly, *The Battle of Behaviorism.*[27] McDougall attacked Watson on many grounds. He said

---

[26]John B. Watson, *Behaviorism, op. cit.* p. 82.
[27]John B. Watson and William McDougall, *The Battle of Behaviorism, op. cit.*

a denial of consciousness and introspection eliminated a good deal of the legitimate data of psychology. It should be recalled that at the time Watson published the behaviorist's manifesto, McDougall's instinct theory was highly regarded by many psychologists and social scientists. As Watson gained in popularity, McDougall lost more and more support.

Watson's denial of consciousness was not taken well by other psychologists. As late as 1948, Robert Woodworth[28] (who had never liked Watson from the beginning) stated that such objectivity would squelch future research in the areas of sensation and perception. The substitution of the "verbal report" for introspection was wholly inadequate. It was true, of course, that Watson had great difficulty in handling the problems of sensation and other aspects of the private or internal world of individuals. Watson suggested a kind of discrimination training for detecting differences in light waves by the use of shock when the stimuli were out of the range of normal vision, as in infra-red and ultra-violet. The problems of sensation were left for the later behaviorists to solve in their studies of discrimination.

Watson was also criticized for his determinism. The "free will" psychologists believed that he had rejected personal responsibility—the idea that humans could be the masters of their own fate and not merely the products of their environment.

From the point of view of contemporary psychology, many people believe that Watson "went overboard" in his extreme environmentalism. He literally dismissed hereditary factors as being of no consequence. What we consider today as being biological participants or limitations were not even discussed. Thus, whatever individual differences in behavior existed for him had to be explained entirely in terms of environmental differences.

His theory of learning was in many ways inadequate, and he failed to see the positive implications of Thorndike's law of effect. In many ways, his ideas were primitive. He spoke of education in his "experimental ethics" but never spelled out any specific principles.

## Positive Contributions of Watson

Watson proposed and insisted upon a completely objective science of behavior. He believed that behavior was lawful, and the aim of psychology should be the prediction and control of behavior, as was stated in the second sentence of his behaviorist's manifesto.[29] These tenets are held today by many objective and experimental psychologists. If there were no laws of behavior, how could psychology ever be a science? Presuming behavior was lawful and determined, then it could also be applicable to practical situations.

By his denial of mind and consciousness, he reawakened an objectivism that had been lost since the fall of ancient Greek psychology. He established

---

[28]Robert S. Woodworth, *Contemporary Schools of Psychology* (New York: The Ronald Press Co., 1948).
[29]John B. Watson, "Psychology as the Behaviorist Views It," *op. cit.*

psychology on a firm footing and paved the way for later experimental psychologists to expand and to follow lines of empirical research leading to new discoveries and more carefully controlled experimentation.

## Other Early Behaviorists

### Albert P. Weiss (1879–1931)

Weiss was born in Germany and came to America at an early age. In 1916 he received his Ph.D. at the University of Missouri. The remainder of his career was spent at Ohio State University. His principal work, *A Theoretical Basis for Human Behavior*[30] (1925), stated his program for what he called a biosocial behaviorism. Because of his untimely death, he did not elaborate the ideas established in his work.

Weiss proposed a completely objective behaviorism, denying consciousness, mind, and introspection. He interpreted the entire function of the organism as a physiological process and an interaction with the environment (hence, the term biosocial). Weiss proposed a most radical kind of reductionism. Basically, all psychological processes were reduced to the same elements that physics dealt with. Protons and electrons constituted the elements of physics and, since mind was denied, all that remained was a physical world.[31]

> The universe is the sum of the movements of its fundamental elements, the electrons and protons. The electron is defined as the smallest unit of negative electricity and the *mobile* constituent of the atom. The proton is defined as the smallest unit of positive electricity and the *stable* constituent of the atom.

Considering the organism itself, Weiss found it to be made up of a relatively permanent organization of atoms, molecules, and tissues. Changes within the organism were correlated with electron-proton changes in the environment. There was an interaction between the organism and the environment that Weiss grouped under abstract terms of growth, nutrition, and metabolism—life.

At this point, he progressed to the biological level. Here, psychology became a branch of biology, which was ultimately a branch of physics. The newborn was a biological entity, but as he grew, behavior began to occur.

Human behavior, then, was analyzed into biophysical and biosocial stimuli and reactions. A biophysical stimulus was any form of energy releasing its function in a sense organ. The biosocial stimulus (also a biophysical one) had become a socialized substitute for other forms of stimulation. The biophysical response involved the network of motor neurons ending up with a muscular or glandular

---

[30]Albert P. Weiss, *A Theoretical Basis of Human Behavior* (Columbus, Ohio: Adams, 1925).
[31]*Ibid.*, p. 427.

response. A biosocial response (also a biophysical one) was one in which the muscular activity produced a socialized stimulus.

Psychology studied the impact of social forces on human behavior. It was clear that behavior was both biological and social because other people acted as stimuli. Learning occurred when new responses occurred to a changing social situation. Weiss went on to consider group behavior, social organization, and finally civilization as the highest sort of sensory-motor interchanges among individuals. Civilization became the cumulative effect of the behavior of the individual in the group toward achieving the totality of electron-proton movements outside the locus of the movements defined as the individual.

## Karl Lashley (1890–1958)

Lashley was a student of Watson's at Johns Hopkins, where he received his Ph.D. in 1915. His many distinguished appointments included the University of Minnesota (1917–1926), University of Chicago (1929–1935), Harvard University (1935–1952), and finally the Yerkes Laboratory of Primate Biology.

Lashley became an ardent supporter of behaviorism and spoke highly of Watson, although they differed on some very basic issues. In the main, however, Lashley saw no use for consciousness or mind, or for introspection as a method of psychology. He did not formulate a detailed systematic psychology, but supported the behaviorist's position through his research in physiological psychology. He considered introspection as "an example of pathology of scientific methods."[32]

On the other hand, Lashley did not accept Watson's dependence on Pavlov's paradigm for conditioning. For example, he felt that generalization was less a function of the stimulus and was more dependent on the organism.

Lashley is best known for his extensive research in physiological psychology. Unlike Watson, who considered the brain as a "mystery box," Lashley wanted to dig, literally, into the brain to see what happened to behavior when parts of the brain were removed.

***Mass Action.*** Collaborating with Shepard I. Franz, a former professor of his, Lashley engaged in a series of experiments, using cats and monkeys in an apparatus similar to that developed by Thorndike. After the animals had learned to escape from the apparatus, various parts of the cortex of the brain were cut away (method of extirpation). As soon as the animals had recovered from the operation and were put back in the box, the investigators found that the animals could no longer perform the required task. With further training, however, the task could be relearned, even in cases where both frontal lobes had been removed.

---

[32]Karl Lashley, "The Behavioristic Interpretation of Consciousness," *Psychological Review,* Vol. 30 (1923), pp. 329–52.

In further experiments, Lashley used white rats as his subjects.[33] He first trained them to make light-dark discriminations. In various experiments he removed different parts of the rats' brains, practically every possible part in one experiment or another. In no case did the rats lose what they had previously learned. He concluded that the brain functioned as a whole, and the remaining parts were able to take over for the damaged or removed areas.[34]

From these findings, Lashley proposed (along with Franz) what he called the law of *mass action*. Thus, learning did not depend on specific neural connections in the brain, but on the brain as a whole. The rate of learning (in mazes) turned out to be a function of the total mass of brain tissue available. Furthermore, what he found to be important was the *amount* of brain tissue left. The greater the amount of undestroyed tissue, the better was the retention of the original task. These observations opposed other theories of specific localization of functions in the brain.

**Equipotentiality.** Accompanying the principle of mass action was the fact that each part of the brain was just as important as the other, or they were *equipotential*. Learning was a process in which the entire mass of the nervous system was involved. If some parts were missing, others had the equipotentiality to carry on functions that originally might have been more important in a more specific area. For example, when the visual area was removed, although patterning was lost, rats could still discriminate differences in light intensity, follow lights, and so on. Although he was an ardent behaviorist, it has been suggested by several theorists[35, 36] that Lashley's studies tended to support Gestalt psychology's theories of wholes and configuration (see chap. 14).

According to the Gestalt theory (see chap. 14), when one had a perceptual experience, it corresponded to an isomorphic map laid down in the brain field. In a sense, there was a correspondence or parallel between the perception and what appeared in the brain. Lashley actually attacked this Gestalt idea as originally proposed by Köhler, and gave experimental evidence to support his objection. In this experiment, Lashley and his associates[37] placed silver foil on the animal's cortex, thus shortcircuiting such supposed "brain fields" without destroying the discrimination that, according to the Gestalt theory, should have depended on those fields.

Unlike Thorndike, who considered learning much of a trial and error affair, Lashley supported a principle of organization; that is, animals did not act randomly, but selected the appropriate cues to which to respond. In any learning

---

[33]Karl Lashley, *Brain Mechanism and Intelligence* (Chicago: University of Chicago Press, 1929).
[34]*Ibid.*
[35]B. B. Wolman, *Contemporary Theories and Systems in Psychology* (New York: Harper and Bros., 1960).
[36]M. H. Marx and W. A. Cronan-Hillix, *Systems and Theories in Psychology* (New York: McGraw-Hill Book Co., 1987).
[37]Karl Lashley, K. L. Chow and J. Semmes, "An Examination of the Electrical Field Theory of Cerebral Integration," *Psychological Review*, Vol. 58 (1951), pp. 123–36.

series, the components of the stimulating situation that were dominant in the organization became effective.

Although he was a behaviorist, Lashley did not support the idea of an *S-R* psychology such as Watson's. Like Weiss, he was a reductionist. Weiss had reduced behavior to the activity of electrons and protons. Lashley was content to reduce it only to neurophysiology.

### Walter S. Hunter (1889–1953)

Hunter was a product of the University of Chicago functionalists, having received his Ph.D. there in 1912. He soon joined the behaviorists in rejecting dualism and accepting psychology as the science of behavior. He actually wished to abandon psychology's heritage to philosophy in the name of the new science. The term, psychology, involved the Greek word "psyche" which had referred to "soul." He substituted the term "anthroponomy" as a more appropriate synonym for behaviorism. "Anthropo" means human and "nomes" refers to the study of the laws of humans. It was quite obvious that his suggestions never caught on.

Hunter is also well known for his studies with the delayed-reaction apparatus. With this, it was possible to study the process of remembering in animals, a matter previously limited to human remembering.

In his experiments, an animal was first given a visual stimulus that indicated in which of a series of boxes food could be obtained. After the preliminary discrimination learning, the light for the appropriate box was presented and then turned off. Meanwhile, the animal was restrained; the problem was to determine how long it could "remember" which was the right door leading to the box where food was presented. Hunter found that in many species the animals would maintain a bodily posture that kept them oriented in the right direction.

### Edwin B. Holt (1873–1946)

Holt received his Ph.D. at Harvard in 1901, remaining there until 1917. After some time out for writing he taught at Princeton from 1926 to 1946. Like other early behaviorists, Holt stressed psychology as the study of behavior, or what he called "the specific response relationship." However, unlike Watson's molecular or "muscle twitch" psychology, Holt considered the response system to involve a whole unit of activity. This is ordinarily called "molar" behavior. Watson's molecular approach would have analyzed a person walking down the street in terms of each step. For Holt the event was to be considered as "walking to the grocery store." The entire event was one unit from beginning to end. Furthermore, there was a purpose to this walking—namely, going to the grocery store. Holt's psychology was the forerunner of Tolman's "purposive behaviorism" (see chap. 15). Behavior was molar, purposive, and cognitive. The cognitive aspect, for Holt, involved meaning. When a response specified something, that constituted its meaning.

There was a certain dynamic principle in the event, which Holt called "wish." In his book, *The Freudian Wish and Its Place in Ethics*[38] (1914), Holt stated that Freud had given psychology back its will. The wish became the purpose of behavior. It was the mechanism by which an organism could set out an action that was directed toward a goal. In Holt's psychology we find a restatement of McDougall's concept of purpose as well as an anticipation of Tolman's purposive behaviorism, which was to follow.

## Summary of Early Behaviorism

One cannot set a date where early behaviorism left off and later behaviorism began. It was all a continuous movement. Behaviorists have shared certain common characteristics. Perhaps the most important of these involved the denial of mind and consciousness and the substitution of the activity of living organisms, animals, or humans as the legitimate study of psychology. The method of experimentation seemed to be the best way to discover the facts about behavior. Introspection was generally rejected. By and large, the early behaviorists found animals to be the most useful subjects for their inquiries. Through animal experimentation, legitimate principles could be established. Of course, they did not limit themselves to animals, nor were the behaviorists the exclusive users of animals for their experimentation.

Some of the early behaviorists, like Weiss and Lashley, were reductionists, while others were not. The same is true today. Then, as now, there were many brands of behaviorism. The early behaviorists had a strong impact on psychology in leading it in the direction of a natural science. It had and has had its opponents.

In the next chapter, we shall consider further variations of behaviorism, whose adherents have had just as diverse opinions as the early behaviorists had.

The reader might well ask on what grounds or by what criteria we distinguish the early from the later behaviorists, since they follow each other chronologically, and there was no specific time gap.

In the first place, the ideas of the later behaviorists are all contemporary— that is, they are all still seriously considered, at least by those who adhere to a particular position; the ideas are not merely of historical interest. We might still accept some of Watson's basic tenets, but the system as a whole is no longer strictly adhered to.

Secondly, the theories of the later behaviorists were more sophisticated and the experimental evidence used to support them was, for the most part, better controlled.

---

[38]Edwin B. Holt, *The Freudian Wish and Its Place in Ethics* (New York: Macmillan, 1914).

Finally, the later behaviorists tended to present more limited theories mainly centering around the basic issues involved in learning and motivation. However, this was not altogether the case, as we shall see.

## Suggested Further Readings

Bergman, G., "The Contributions of John B. Watson." *Psychological Review,* Vol. 63 (1956), pp. 265–76. A commentary on Watson's contribution to psychology with strong philosophical overtones.

Skinner, B. F., "John Broadus Watson, Behaviorist." *Science,* Vol. 129 (1959), pp. 197–98. Skinner, a later behaviorist, acknowledges his debt to Watson.

Warden, C. J., "The Historical Development of Comparative Psychology." *Psychological Review,* Vol. 34 (1927), pp. 135–68. Relevant to this chapter because of the importance of animal psychology in the development of behaviorism.

Watson, J. B., *Behaviorism,* rev. ed. New York: W. W. Norton and Co., 1930. A statement of Watson's full system, particularly with regard to human behavior. Written in layman's language, it became one of Watson's most popular works.

Watson, J. B., "Psychology as the Behaviorist Views It." *Psychological Review,* Vol. 20 (1913), pp. 158–77. Watson's first statement of behaviorism which shook up quite a few people.

Weiss, A., *A Theoretical Basis of Human Behavior.* Columbus, Ohio: Adams, 1925. An alternate version to Watson's of early behaviorism. Students interested in the evolution of behaviorism should at least attempt parts of the book.

# CHAPTER

# 13

# *Later Behaviorism*

For all intents and purposes, by 1930 Watson had stopped writing and theorizing about psychology, but his influence continued to be widely felt. In the tradition of behaviorism, many prominent researchers emerged who developed their own theories but still remained within the broad behavioristic framework. This chapter will discuss five of these significant figures as expressing part of the later development of the behavioristic movement: Edwin R. Guthrie, Clark L. Hull, B. F. Skinner, Albert Bandura, and J. R. Kantor. The first four of these have emphasized the problems of learning. However, although he stressed learning, Skinner and his followers have broadened the scope of their concept of psychology to include many areas other than simple laboratory experimentation. Kantor maintained a systematic approach true to the early meaning of the term *system*. Like Watson and Thorndike, already mentioned (see chaps. 10 and 12), Guthrie, Hull, and Skinner retained the concept of an S-R (stimulus-response) psychology. Kantor, on the other hand, maintained a more molar, a wholistic, approach. Although Guthrie, Hull, and Skinner are no longer living, their influence is still felt on the contemporary behavioristic scene. Bandura, the youngest of the five, maintains a fairly wide following today. Kantor never attained as wide a following, but his influence seems to be growing.

## Edwin R. Guthrie (1886–1959)

Guthrie received his Ph.D. in 1912 from the University of Pennsylvania, and shortly thereafter went to the University of Washington, where he remained until his retirement in 1956. In 1958, the year before his death, he received the Gold Medal Award from the American Psychological Foundation for outstanding contributions to psychology.

Like Watson, Guthrie maintained that psychology was the study of observable behavior that should be measurable and subject to experimental methodology. His earliest book, in collaboration with S. Smith, was entitled *General Psychology: In Terms of Behavior.*[1] It definitely was in the Watsonian tradition, although it paid much less attention to physiological details. Unlike Watson, Guthrie did not follow the Pavlovian paradigm for learning, but rather considered it to be a matter of associative connections. His other significant books include: *The Psychology of Learning* (1935),[2] (1952)[3] and *The Psychology of Human Conflict* (1938).[4] He also wrote an elementary text in collaboration with A. L. Edwards called *Psychology: A First Course in Human Behavior* (1949),[5] which maintained a strong behavioristic orientation. However, in contrast with other beginning books of the time, such as Woodworth's, it never attained great popularity.

## Guthrie's Theory

Guthrie's theory is one of the simplest and most easily understood of all those considered in this text. This simplicity has been one of its most appealing characteristics, but also the main target of its critics.

Guthrie started with one simple law of learning—namely, that of associative contiguity in time. "A combination of stimuli which has accompanied a movement will on its recurrence tend to be followed by that movement."[6] A similar statement in 1959, the year of his death, is as follows: "What is being noticed becomes a signal for what is being done."[7] No notion of drive or motivation was involved, simply an *S-R* connection. In stressing association, Guthrie was following Thorndike, but without the law of effect. As a subprinciple Guthrie later stated: "A stimulus pattern gains its full associative strength on the occasion of its first pairing with a response."[8] This was a kind of recency principle which was especially important to the theory—for that which was last done in the presence of a stimulus combination would be what would be done again when that particular stimulus combination reoccurred. This was called *one-trial learning*. When a particular *S-R* connection occurred, it would remain in the organism's repertoire in full strength and indefinitely unless some suc-

[1]S. Smith and Edwin R. Guthrie, *General Psychology in Terms of Behavior* (New York: Century Publishing Co., 1921).

[2]Edwin R. Guthrie, *The Psychology of Learning* (New York: Harper and Bros., 1935).

[3]Edwin R. Guthrie, *The Psychology of Learning*, rev. ed. (New York: Harper and Bros., 1952).

[4]Edwin R. Guthrie, *The Psychology of Human Conflict* (New York: Harper and Bros., 1938).

[5]Edwin R. Guthrie and A. L. Edwards, *Psychology: A First Course in Human Behavior* (New York: Harper and Bros., 1949).

[6]Edwin R. Guthrie, *The Psychology of Learning*, op. cit., p. 26.

[7]S. Koch, ed., Vol. 2, *General Systematic Formulations in Psychology: A Study of a Science* (New York: McGraw-Hill Book Co., 1959), p. 186.

[8]Edwin R. Guthrie, "Conditioning: A Theory of Learning in Terms of Stimulus, Response and Association," in *The Psychology of Learning* (National Society for Studies in Education, 41st Yearbook, 1942), p. 30.

ceeding event occurred to destroy or replace it. More complicated forms of learning, such as problem solving, could be reduced to the basic principle of association by contiguity.

If this matter of *simultaneous* association between stimuli and movements was the crux of learning, how did Guthrie account for possible delays between the presentation of stimuli and movements where learning still occurred? His answer was that a stimulus gave rise to movements, and those in turn produced other stimuli, which in turn produced other movements that filled in the gaps.

## Why Improvement with Practice?

If one took Guthrie's statement at face value, the implication was obvious that any *S-R* connection gained its full strength on first pairing, and practice would not be necessary for further improvement. But anybody who has learned a given task knows that improvement does occur with repetition. In order to untangle what appears to be a paradox, one must realize that Guthrie distinguished *movements* from *acts*. A movement was a pattern of motor or glandular responses. An act was a movement or series of movements that brought about some end result. The act was then to be considered on a larger scale. An act was a movement, but the reverse was not true.

An understanding of how improvement seemed to occur with practice was to be found in Guthrie's favorite example of learning a skill such as basketball. One act in the skill was throwing the ball into the net. This was made up of several movements that were connected with several stimuli. Therefore, the skill involved many movements occurring under a variety of different stimulus circumstances. Any movement might be learned in a single trial, but there was an almost endless number of possibilities or connections to be acquired: for example, whether one was near or far from the basket; whether one approached it from left, right, or center; whether one was shooting in free play or for an extra point; the presence and arrangements of other players on the floor; whether or not there was a guard nearby; and so on. Practice improved performance not because of sheer repetition, but because of the multiplicity of *S-R* associations of cues and movements that had to be built up. The more complex the performance to be acquired, the greater the number of stimuli involved that must be connected with a variety of movements. In learning to play the piano or to type, the same problems were involved. There was an endless number of combinations in the arrangements of notes or letters, along with different responses to each.

***Movement-Produced Stimuli.*** Although the principle of contiguity between environmental stimuli and the resulting behavior is a cornerstone of Guthrie's theory, there is more to the situation than the simple S-R connection between the environment and movements. Often a long time might elapse between the presentation of an external environmental event and the resulting overt responses. To fill in the gap, Guthrie postulated the existence of *movement-produced stimuli*. Following an external stimulus—such as a telephone ringing, for example—the movements we make in going to the phone produce stimuli (called proprioceptive stimuli) in our muscles, tendons, and joints for other movements to occur.

> When the telephone bell rings we rise and make our way to the instrument. Long before we have reached the telephone the sound has ceased to act as a stimulus. We are kept in action by the stimuli from our movements to the telephone. One movement starts another, then a third, the third a fourth, and so on. . . . These movements and their movement-produced stimuli make possible a far-reaching extension of association conditioning.[9]

## Extinction and Forgetting

According to Guthrie, when a particular S-R connection was made, it should remain indefinitely. Yet, we know that behavior was often weakened by forgetting or extinction. Pavlov first discovered that a response such as salivation was conditioned when the conditioned stimulus (the bell) was paired with the unconditioned stimulus (food), the latter considered to be a reinforcement. He then observed that when the unconditioned stimulus, food, was withheld, the response to the conditioned stimulus gradually died out or was extinguished because of the removal of the reinforcement. Guthrie, it should be noted, made no use of the concept of reinforcement as a basic explanatory principle. To explain extinction then, Guthrie introduced the concept of *associative inhibition*, which meant that an incompatible response had been learned that interfered with the previous one. Thus, no new learning principle was necessary. It was simply the development of succeeding associative connections that interfered with the previously established ones. That is, something else was learned (an S-R connection) which replaced what was previously learned and interfered with it. Forgetting followed the same principle. Without the interference of succeeding events, there would be no forgetting.

## Breaking Habits

A habit is a well-established set of movements that has been associated with a large number of stimuli or cues. The greater the number of stimuli that have caused the responses, the stronger the habit will be. For some people, smoking is a very strong habit, because it has been associated with so many different cues—after a meal, with a cup of coffee or drink, or in the dining room, parlor, or on the street—in the presence of so many different conditions.

Guthrie has suggested several methods by which habits can be broken:

1. **Threshold method.** This method involves presenting the stimulus that has been associated with the movements in such a manner that the response will not occur. Thus, the stimulus presented is so weak that it does not cause the response to occur. For example, in breaking a fear habit, the

---

[9]Edwin R. Guthrie, *The Psychology of Learning* (New York: Harper and Bros., 1935), p. 54.

feared object could be placed far enough away so that the fear would not be elicited. Or, if a father had a habit of making an emotional outburst when told about family expenditures, it might help to "break the news to him gently."

2. **Fatigue method.** Here the stimulus is presented so frequently that the response is exhausted, allowing for new alternate responses. The example of horse training would apply here. A horse is ridden until it gives up its bucking, and the fatigue causes it to do something else, such as walking calmly. Guthrie cites the example of the little girl who had the habit of striking matches. She was required to strike one match after another until it was no longer any fun. To cure the smoking habit, one might smoke one cigarette after another until it was no longer enjoyable.

3. **Incompatible response method.** In this method, stimuli for the undesirable response are presented along with other stimuli that are incompatible with the undesirable response. Here again, to break the smoking habit, one might offer the smoker a cigarette while the smoker is eating corn on the cob. One of Guthrie's favorite anecdotes about this method told of breaking a dog of the habit of catching and eating chickens by tying a dead chicken around the dog's neck.

*Sidetracking Habits.* This is not the same as breaking a habit. Sidetracking a habit is achieved by avoiding all the cues that elicit all the aspects of the undesirable habit. This involves leaving the situations in which the habits are most likely to occur. An example might be going into a new environment to get a fresh start. There, most of the old associations would be absent. However, it is possible that even in a new environment, some of the old stimuli might still be present. An example might be to stop smoking when one goes on a vacation, a situation in which most of the old stimuli that elicit smoking would be absent.

## Motivation and Reward

Other theorists, whom we have encountered and shall encounter later in this chapter, have placed strong emphasis on the role of motivation and reward in learning. We have already noted Thorndike's law of effect, and we shall soon learn how Hull and Skinner handle the closely related principle of reinforcement. Since Guthrie's theory did not make use of this concept, what alternate explanations could be given to account for what appeared to be the importance of motivation and reward in learning? The only significance of motivation (food deprivation) to Guthrie was that it increased the number and vigor of movements that could achieve associative connections with stimuli. A hungry cat made more movements than a satiated one. With greater movement there was a greater opportunity to make more associative connections with stimuli.

The only significance of reward (reinforcement) was that it amounted to a mechanical arrangement in which reward was given following a series of acts, and that reward removed the organism from the stimuli that acted just prior to it. Thus, being removed from these stimuli preserved the act. Behavior was *not* strengthened by the reward, but it allowed the behavior from the previous situation to remain unchanged. Reward appeared to work because it removed the organism from the stimulus situation in which a correct *S-R* connection had already been established, thus preventing the weakening of the response by associative interference. No new movements could become attached to the situation that originally led to the correct or desired response.

## Punishment

Punishment was considered similar to motivation. For example, mild punishment might lead to greater activity, allowing for more *S-R* connections. Moderate punishment might break up *S-R* connections leading to the development of alternatives. Continuous punishment might function in keeping an organism active until the punishment was terminated. Punishment could also change the situation just as reward did, so other antecedent behavior would be kept intact and new learning would be inhibited.

Thus, if punishment is to work it must (1) cause behavior that is incompatible with the punished behavior, and (2) be applied in the presence of the stimuli that caused the punished behavior. If these two conditions are not met, the punishment either will be ineffective or may even strengthen the undesired responses.

## Experimental Evidence

Thus far we have considered Guthrie only in terms of his theoretical position. Basically, throughout his career, Guthrie preferred to theorize, and depended on anecdotes to support his position. However, one significant exception was found in a series of experiments published in collaboration with Horton.[10] Horton and Guthrie observed the behavior of cats as they escaped from a puzzle box. The box was designed so that the behavior of the animals could be observed at all times, and this behavior could be photographed. In the center of the box was a pole mounted on a hemisphere. If the pole were touched or moved in any direction, it would return to its original upright position. On each trial, the cat entered the box from a tunnel at the rear of the cage. If the pole were touched in any manner, the front door opened, allowing the cat to escape and receive a piece of salmon.

The results indicated a very repetitious and stereotyped response in various subjects. If a cat hit the pole the first time, it tended to continue the same response on successive trials. Other cats might back into the pole, paw it, or roll against it. The significant findings in support of the theory indicated that the method of escape used on successive trials tended to be the same as that used on the original or initial trial. Rather than being variable, the stereotyped

---

[10]Edwin R. Guthrie and C. P. Horton, *Cats in a Puzzle Box* (New York: Henry Holt and Co., 1946).

nature of the response persisted. Of course, there were some variations in certain instances, but these were attributed to artifacts of the experiment, such as a change in the stimulus situation. There could be accidental distractions—remaining in the box too long or a failure to operate the release mechanism (the pole)—but according to the theory these constituted new stimuli.

Those who have criticized the theory in favor of one that supported greater variability in learning, suggest that the stereotyped behavior appeared because the problem was so simple. It could be mastered in a single trial. Easy learning took place promptly, and was repeated if there were nothing to break it up, and if there were reinforcement to sustain it.[11]

In another experimental support of the theory, Voeks[12] studied the particular responses human subjects made at choice points in a raised relief finger maze. Fifty-six of fifty-seven subjects tended to make the same choice at a point that had been made on the previous trial. She referred to this as postremity, as opposed to frequency. That is, the prediction of what choice a person might make was better made from the previous trial than from observing the overall frequency of that particular choice over the trials.

Voeks had also attempted to reformulate Guthrie's theory in terms of four basic postulates. Actually, this formulation adds nothing to our understanding of the theory, so it will not be elaborated here. The interested reader may look into the appropriate reference.[13]

## Prediction and Control

Like Watson and other contemporary learning theorists, Guthrie asserted that the aims of psychology should be the prediction and control of behavior. In the last statement of his theory in 1959 he maintained this attitude.[14]

With regard to these problems he gave some practical advice.

1. If one wished to establish a particular kind of behavior and discourage another, one should arrange the stimuli so that the desired behavior would occur in its presence, or arrange the stimuli so that the undesirable behavior did not occur. In this instance, Guthrie related one of his many anecdotes:[15]

   > The mother of a ten-year-old girl complained to a psychologist that for two years her daughter had annoyed her by a habit of tossing coat and hat on the floor as she entered the house. On a hundred occasions the mother had insisted that the girl pick up the clothing and hang it in its place. These wild ways

---

[11]E. R. Hilgard, *Theories of Learning,* 2nd ed. (New York: Appleton-Century-Crofts, 1956), p. 68.

[12]V. W. Voeks, "Acquisition of S-R Connections: A Test of Hull's and Guthrie's Theories," *Journal of Experimental Psychology,* Vol. 47 (1954), pp. 437–47.

[13]V. W. Voeks, "Formulation and Clarification of a Theory of Learning," *Journal of Psychology,* Vol. 30 (1950), pp. 341–63.

[14]Edwin R. Guthrie, "Association by Contiguity," in S. Koch, *op. cit.*

[15]Edwin R. Guthrie, *The Psychology of Learning, op. cit.,* p. 21.

were changed only after the mother, on advice, began to insist not only that the girl pick up the fallen garments from the floor, but that she put them on, return to the street, and re-enter the house, this time removing the coat and hanging it up promptly.

Thus, for the desired behavior to become associated with the proper cues, the child had to go outside the house. Entering the house then became the stimulus for hanging up the coat.

**2.** Guthrie also suggested using as many stimulus supports for desirable behavior as possible. The more stimuli that could be associated with desirable behavior, the less likely it would be that other stimuli or competing responses would operate. For example, there would be fewer lines "muffed" in amateur theatrical performances if more dress rehearsals were allowed, because the stimuli (cues) would come from so many different aspects of the situation—the stage, actors, costumes, setting, and so on.[16]

## Criticisms of Guthrie

Guthrie's theory had been both praised and damned for its simplicity. Those who opposed it on this ground claimed that he had attempted to explain too much on the basis of too few principles. A great deal had to be taken on assumption. Mueller and Schoenfeld[17] claimed that Guthrie had failed to be explicit on too many basic issues.

A second major criticism was a failure to present sufficient experimental proof for the theory. In comparison to other learning theories such as Hull and Skinner (see next sections), Guthrie's experimental evidence was sparse. As mentioned earlier, Guthrie depended on anecdotes. Furthermore, he preferred theory to facts and claimed that it was the theory that survived. Although Guthrie's anecdotes were interesting and often quite convincing, those who opposed him claimed that they were no proper substitute for more rigorous experimentation.

Psychologists who supported the position that stressed reward or reinforcement, wondered in amazement how Guthrie could maintain a theory that almost completely ignored it, since they felt it was a crucial aspect of learning. They felt he had sidetracked the issue. With the overwhelming experimental evidence in support of reinforcement, it was hard to accept a theory of learning that ignored it.

Finally, in his insistence on the stereotyped nature of behavior, his opponents claimed he had ignored the aspect of individual differences. They claimed that variability was a basic characteristic of most all behavior, particularly in the learning process. Furthermore, because of a variety of previous conditioning histories, people or animals simply did not always behave in the same way, and

---

[16]E. R. Hilgard, *op. cit.,* p. 64.
[17]C. G. Mueller and W. N. Schoenfeld, "Edwin R. Guthrie," in W. K. Estes et al., *Modern Learning Theory* (New York: Appleton-Century-Crofts, 1954).

there was more to basic individual differences in behavior than simply differences in the S-R connections that were attained.

## Contributions of Guthrie

If we turned the coin around, we might say that the simplicity of the theory was one of its major attributes.

People who comment about theories (particularly psychologists) tend to like those theories that are parsimonious, which depend on only a few basic principles that are simple and easy to understand. One should have no difficulty in grasping the major concepts involved in Guthrie's position.

Although lacking the abundance of experimental supports that some would like, much of Guthrie's theory is hard to disprove. It has stood the test of time, and Guthrie has maintained a position as one of the major learning theorists of our time. The theory is more than of historical interest, and is considered seriously today by many contemporary psychologists interested in the general field of learning.

Finally, for those who support an anti-dualistic position, Guthrie had maintained a strong behavioristic position throughout his career. There was no reference to unknowns "inferred" or "internal states" of the organism. From the beginning, Guthrie had never waivered from a position based on observable relationships.

## Clark L. Hull (1884–1952)

As Guthrie's theory was marked by its simplicity, Hull's was quite the opposite. If properly understood, it is probably the most complex one that the reader will encounter in this book. Because of its complexity, it is difficult to do justice to it in the space provided; and yet, because of its great importance, it cannot be ignored. It has been one of the most dominant in the field of learning up to the present time and still has many faithful adherents. Its main contender at the present time is the theory of B. F. Skinner, which will be considered in a later section. Those who follow Skinner's position, which is continuing to gain popularity, claim that Hull's theory is on the wane. However, there is no universal agreement in this respect.

Unlike Guthrie's theory, Hull's has generated a vast quantity of research, and continues to do so. Those who are faithful to it, along with many of those who are critical of it, would still agree that it constitutes one kind of model of careful, precise, and logical theory construction.

## Hull's Career

During his early life, Hull was plagued by poor health and, in particular, poor eyesight that troubled him throughout his life. Despite these handicaps, he attended the University of Michigan, in the state in which he was raised. In

1918 he received his Ph.D. in psychology at the University of Wisconsin where he remained for the following ten years. His doctoral dissertation was in the area of concept formation, and it has been considered a masterpiece in good experimental design and execution.

One of his early experiments, often cited in texts of readings in experimental psychology,[18] concerned the effects of tobacco smoking on efficiency in performing certain psychological tasks. It exemplified the careful use of experimental controls of sensory factors. The control group (blindfolded) actually breathed in hot air. However, all other factors were kept constant, such as the heat of the pipe and so on.

Hull's next major effort was in the field of aptitude testing, in which he wrote one of the early texts in 1928.[19] He abandoned this area of psychology because he failed to see much future in it. (Present day psychological testers would certainly disagree!)

His early experiment on tobacco smoking led him to develop an interest in suggestibility, and for the next ten years he devoted himself to a study of hypnosis and suggestibility. Many experiments were performed by him and his students, which resulted in the publication of *Hypnosis and Suggestibility*[20] in 1933. For many years this book was considered the most authoritative text in the field, and it still remains a classic.

Even before this, Hull had been interested in the field of learning, and in 1929 he became research professor at Yale. He remained there for the rest of his career, devoting his efforts to developing a theory of learning along with experimental research to support it. In 1940 he and a number of his colleagues published *A Mathematico-Deductive Theory of Rote Learning*.[21] This was considered a masterpiece in theory construction, but so few people could understand it, that it never gained much popularity. The first (and most understandable) formulation of his more complete theory appeared in 1943 in *Principles of Behavior*.[22] Revisions followed in *Essentials of Behavior*[23] in 1951 and *A Behavior System*[24] in 1952, the latter being formidable reading for those who are unsophisticated in mathematics and learning theory.

## Hull's System

The development of Hull's ideas was marked by influence from a variety of sources, all of whom we have some acquaintance with so far. They include:

[18]W. L. Valentine and D. D. Wiggins, *Experimental Foundations of General Psychology* (New York: Rinehart and Co., 1949).

[19]C. L. Hull, *Aptitude Testing* (Yonkers-on-Hudson: World Book Co., 1928).

[20]C. L. Hull, *Hypnosis and Suggestibility: An Experimental Approach* (New York: D. Appleton-Century Co., 1933).

[21]C. L. Hull, *Mathematico-Deductive Theory of Rote Learning* (New Haven: Yale University Press, 1940).

[22]C. L. Hull, *Principles of Behavior* (New York: Appleton-Century-Crofts, 1943).

[23]C. L. Hull, *Essentials of Behavior* (New Haven: Yale University Press, 1951).

[24]C. L. Hull, *A Behavior System: An Introduction to Behavior Theory Concerning the Individual Organism* (New Haven: Yale University Press, 1952).

Darwin, Pavlov, Watson, Woodworth, and Thorndike. Watson's influence was that of a behaviorist, and like Watson's and others, Hull's system can be considered an *S-R* psychology of the behavioristic variety. Hull was also impressed with Pavlov's work on the conditioned reflex, which he considered a simple form of learning on which more complex kinds of learning could be built. Pavlov had also introduced the concept of reinforcement that was to be crucial to Hull's system. Similarly, his debt to Thorndike was to be found in the concept of reinforcement as one of the primary variables in learning. However, for Hull the reinforcement or reward was not successful because it *satisfied,* but because it operated in the *reduction of drives.* Hull's was very much a drive theory. Thus, anything that satisfied needs or reduced drives could be considered a reinforcer. Today, Hull and Skinner are considered the two most important reinforcement theorists. Although their theories differ in many other respects, they have both agreed that without reinforcement learning could not occur. This was certainly contrary to Guthrie's position stated in the previous section.

It will be recalled that Woodworth (see chap. 11) presented the *S-O-R* paradigm where the stimulus (*S*) affected the organism (*O*) and the consequent response (*R*) depended on both the *S* and the *O*. Spence[25] has suggested that Hull's system was a Herculean elaboration of Woodworth's ideas. For Hull, the *O* was stated in a complex set of intervening variables. However, because Hull made such wide use of these inferred or internal states, behaviorists such as Kantor and Skinner (see next sections) have considered Hull to be a dualist, and thus not really a true behaviorist. We have included Hull in this chapter because he considered himself a behaviorist, as have many others. Because there appear in Hull's intervening variables obvious inferences to internal states that are not likely to be demonstrable in the near future, the dualism appears quite obvious. We might, therefore, call him a "so-called" behaviorist.

Hull spoke of the environmental influences on an organism as the *input,* and a measure of the organism's responses as the *output.* What went on within the organism must be inferred, and to account for these inferences he postulated the intervening variables, which were most crucial to his system. He felt that if we could tie these inferences to the input-output variables by means of quantitative mathematical statements (which he did in his postulates), nothing was lost, and something could be gained in deducing new facts.

Hull's final debt was to Darwin, in his stress on the importance of an individual's biological adaptation to the environment. Organisms developed needs that involved a deviation from the optimal biological conditions necessary for survival. Learning took place when these needs were satisfied and a biological equilibrium was established. Therefore, drive, motivation, and reinforcement (mentioned earlier), were crucial to his theory. Hull's system was almost as much a theory of motivation as it was a theory of learning.

---

[25]K. W. Spence, "Clark Leonard Hull (1884–1952)," *American Journal of Psychology,* Vol. 65 (1952), pp. 639–46.

## A Hypothetico-Deductive Theory

Hull began to develop his theory of learning as early as 1915, and by 1943 it was published in *Principles of Behavior.*[26] This was a tremendously important volume, for it stimulated a vast amount of research and drew attention to his theory from many sources. Later revisions have already been cited.

Hull followed the deductive method used by Newton and applied it to psychology. Accordingly, he defined his theory as "a systematic deductive derivation of the secondary principles of observable phenomena from a relatively small number of primary principles or postulates. . . ."[27] For him, psychology did *not* begin with basic well-established laws based on observation, but observation and theory went hand in hand. The observation acted as a check on the validity of the internal postulates formalized by deduction. The hypothetico-deductive method involved the postulating of intervening variables, the *O* facts, which were used to account for the observable events. In its final form, Hull's system[28] constituted eighteen postulates and twelve corollaries. These were stated in both mathematical and verbal forms.

Hull's final version of his theory, *A Behavior System,* is so difficult to understand that unless one is well versed in both mathematics and learning theory, it becomes incomprehensible. However, for those sophisticated psychologists it becomes a stimulating and highly intelligent statement of learning principles.

In the discussion that follows, we shall lean primarily on Hull's earlier position since there was much similarity between the two, even though Hull continued to revise his earlier position. We shall not present all the postulates and corollaries in Hull's original statements, and those we do present will be stated in simplified form. This may not do justice to Hull's highly sophisticated theory, but our discussion is for readers who are gaining their first full-scale acquaintance with psychological theory. More detailed statements and extensive elaborations can be found in Hilgard and Bower's *Theories of Learning*[29] or in Koch's book, *Psychology: A Study of a Science,* Vol. 2.[30] From there, the interested reader can go to the original sources.

The system was stated in a series of postulates and corollaries. The first two postulates dealt with the importance of neural activity in the brain following a sensory input. The fact that there was a gradual decay in neural excitation allowed for contiguous association. Also, when more than one sensory impulse occurred at the same time, in the process of their interaction, one might modify the other.

The third postulate dealt with a very important aspect of the theory, that of reinforcement. In simplified form, it can be stated as follows:[31]

---

[26]C. L. Hull, *Principles of Behavior, op. cit.*
[27]*Ibid.,* p. 2.
[28]C. L. Hull, *A Behavior System, op. cit.*
[29]E. R. Hilgard and G. H. Bower, *Theories of Learning,* 4th ed. (New York: Appleton-Century-Crofts, 1966).
[30]S. Koch, *op. cit.*
[31]E. R. Hilgard, *Theories of Learning, op. cit.,* p. 154.

When a response (R) is closely associated with a stimulus trace (s) and the stimulus-response conjunction is associated with a rapid decrease in drive-produced stimuli ($S_D$), there will result an increase in the tendency for that stimulus trace (s) to evoke that response (R).

The rapid decrease in goal stimulus ($s_G$) is also reinforcing.

It should be noted that for both Hull and Guthrie a contiguous S-R connection occurred. For Guthrie it became fixed simply because it occurred. For Hull, it was strengthened because it was associated with reinforcement. In this instance, the reinforcement was considered primary, as in hunger or thirst. The postulate concerning drive (D) will be considered shortly. Along with this postulate of primary reinforcement, two corollaries followed that dealt with secondary drive and secondary reinforcement. A secondary reinforcer was a stimulus that acquired its function to reinforce by its association with a primary one. An example of a secondary drive would be fear. An animal placed in a shuttle box was shocked in one compartment until it escaped to another in which no shock was presented. On later occasions, when placed in the original compartment, in the absence of shock it would maintain the same escape response. Thus, the secondary drive for escaping was postulated. Furthermore, aspects of the nonshocked compartment took on a secondary reinforcing function.

The fourth postulate was also crucial to the system because it dealt with the building up of response strength, or what Hull called "habit strength."[32]

> Habit strength (the tendency for a stimulus trace to evoke an associated response) increases as a positive growth function of the number of trials, provided that trials are evenly spaced, reinforcement occurs on every trial, and everything else remains constant.

Habit strength referred to the intervening variable for learning. As stated in the postulate, it depended on the number of reinforced trials. It could also be a function of a number of other variables, such as strength of the drive, the delay between response and reinforcement, and the time interval between stimulus and response.

The fifth postulate dealt with primary drive.[33]

> A. A primary drive (at least that resulting from food deprivation) consists of two components: (1) the drive proper, which increases with number of hours of food deprivation, and (2) an inanition component which reduced drive as starvation continues . . .
> B. Each drive condition generates a characteristic drive stimulus ($S_D$) which is an increasing function of the drive condition.
> C. Some drive conditions may initiate action habits set up on the basis of different drive conditions.

[32]*Ibid.*
[33]*Ibid.*, p. 155.

Drive activated habit strength into reaction potential, and could be stated as follows $_sE_R$ (reaction potential) $= D \times {_sH_R}$ (habit strength).

As mentioned earlier, drive was particularly significant in Hull's theory. Without drive the primary reinforcement had no function. The importance of the reinforcement was that it reduced drive. Further, each drive activated habit strength into reaction potential; without drive there could be no response.

The sixth and seventh postulates were concerned with stimulus intensity (V) and incentive motivation (K). These referred to the influences of the intensity of initiating stimuli and the amount of reinforcement.

The eighth postulate was particularly significant because it dealt with the concept of the reaction potential referred to earlier.[34]

> When conditions have been constant throughout learning and response-evocation, the reaction potential ($_sE_R$) is determined by the habit strength ($_sH_R$) multiplied by (1) the drive (D), (2) the stimulus-intensity dynamism (V), and (3) the incentive motivation (K). The general equation becomes: $_sE_R = D \times V \times K \times {_sH_R}$.

This postulate was a combination of the previous three. Reaction potential could be considered as the *probability of a response occurring,* which depended on the amount of drive, the stimulus intensity, the amount of incentive, and the already present habit strength of that response. (This latter statement came from the 1952 version.)

The ninth postulate dealt with inhibitory potential. In many learning theories inhibition is expressed in terms of extinction. Guthrie explained it as a result of competing responses. For Skinner, it merely resulted from a failure to present the reinforcing stimulus. Hull found it necessary to postulate two kinds of inhibition—reactive inhibition and conditioned inhibition. To him, extinction was due to a building up of both conditioned and reactive inhibitions. Reactive inhibition was generated whenever a response occurred. This could be likened to tissue injury, fatigue, or pain. It thus interfered with repetition, inhibiting reaction potential.

The concept can best be understood in a simplified restatement of the postulate:[35]

> A. The occurrence of a response produces reactive inhibition ($I_R$) which both inhibits reaction potential and acts as a negative drive.
>
> B. Reactive inhibition ($I_R$) dissipates spontaneously with the passage of time as a simple decay function of elapsed time.
>
> C. As a given response is repeated, increments of reactive inhibition summate. The resulting $I_R$ also summates with conditioned inhibition $_sI_R$ to produce the aggregate inhibitory potential ($I_R$).

---

[34]*Ibid.,* p. 155.
[35]*Ibid.,* p. 155.

D. When nonreinforced responses follow each other at short intervals, the aggregate inhibitory potential $(I_R)$ increases with the magnitude of work involved in each response, the greater the work involved the fewer the number of unreinforced responses to a criterion of experimental extinction.

Our discussion of these postulates so far should be sufficient to give the reader an adequate introduction to the system. Other postulates dealt with the generalization of stimuli (postulate ten), behavior oscillation (postulate twelve), reaction potential as it related to a number of variables such as reaction threshold (postulate thirteen), as a function of latency (postulate fourteen), as a function of reaction amplitude (postulate fifteen), and total response to extinction (postulate sixteen).

Postulate seventeen dealt with the problem of individual differences, and could easily be understood as follows:[36]

> The constant numerical values appearing in the equations stated in the basic postulates and corollaries vary from species to species, from individual to individual, and from some physiological states to others in the same individual at different times.

By way of summary, we can consider that Hull's system consisted of a series of postulates and corollaries that centered around the concepts of drive, response strength (habits or learned behavior), and reinforcement. Pure repetition of a task simply generated inhibition. What strengthened behavior was the reinforcement that reduced the drive. The reduction of drive was positive when food was given or negative when an animal escaped from shock. The number of reinforcements was crucial to acquiring greater response (habit) strength.

Drive operated in a complex way in learning. It operated in conjunction with both primary and secondary reinforcement. It also activated habit strength in the reaction potential and provided a variety of internal stimuli that directed behavior.[37]

## Experimental Support

As one example of how Hull and his followers experimented in an attempt to verify the theory, we may cite corollary iii, which dealt with delay in reinforcement. The second part is stated as follows:

> For a response, the greater the delay in reinforcement, the weaker the reaction potential according to a gradient that falls off rapidly at first and then more slowly.

---

[36]*Ibid.*, p. 155.
[37]*Ibid.*, p. 175.

In an early experiment, Hull[38] trained rats to run down a specially constructed alley for food. His measurements indicated that the rate of running was one of positive acceleration—that is, the closer to the goal they were, the faster the rats ran. In another experiment,[39] Hull tested the order in which rats eliminated blind alleys in learning a maze. He found that those blind alleys nearest the goal were the first to be eliminated. Further, a long blind alley was eliminated sooner than a short one, since the former involved a greater temporal delay in reinforcement.

In a later study, Arnold[40] trained rats in a special push-button apparatus to get the reinforcement of a pellet of food. Prior to the experiment proper, any one of four buttons pushed would yield a reinforcement delivered by a little car running by the window of the experimental cage. Later, all four buttons had to be pressed before reinforcement was delivered. As each button was presented he found an increase in the speed of pushing with a particular gain in the last button, the one that was directly followed by reinforcement.

In these instances, the experimental findings were stated as bearing a close relationship to the theoretical proposition. These were only a few examples of the methods by which Hull and his followers tested their hypotheses. The interested reader can go to earlier references cited in this chapter for further examples.

In conclusion by using his set of proposed postulates Hull tried to show that behaviorism could be accounted for mathematically. Like Euclid, psychology could be accepted as a science and accounted for by a set of postulates from which predictions of actual behavior could be accurately tested by means of observation and experimentation. Furthermore, specific details could be observed. Some of it worked, but some of it didn't.

## Criticisms of Hull

Hull's system has been criticized by those who prefer simpler statements as being unnecessarily complicated. Whether or not the criticism was legitimate depended, in part, on how knowledgeable one was in the matters that Hull presumed one must understand before one could grasp the system. Hull dealt a great deal with mathematics in his postulates and corollaries. (We have intentionally omitted most of these aspects in our discussion, because an elaboration of them would make this section interminably long and difficult for many.) On the other hand, many critics have indicated that Hull was obsessed with mathematics, which he loved, and his statements could have been made

---

[38]C. L. Hull, "The Concept of Habit Family Hierarchy in Maze Learning," *Psychological Review*, Vol. 41 (1934), pp. 33–54.

[39]C. L. Hull, "The Rat's Speed of Locomotion Gradient in the Approach to Food," *Journal of Comparative Psychology*, Vol. 17 (1934), pp. 398–422.

[40]W. J. Arnold, "Simple Reaction Chains and Their Integration I. Homogeneous Chaining with Terminal Reinforcement," *Journal of Comparative and Physiological Psychology*, Vol. 40 (1947), pp. 349–63.

just as useful by the omission of mathematics. Putting aside the mathematical problems involved in understanding the theory, the system was still inordinately involved—with all its postulates, corollaries, and theorems deduced from them. The critics stated simply that Hull could have made his points in a far easier manner given the same experimental results. A good experiment, properly designed and executed, can stand on its own in stating functional relationships, without the need to relate to such complicated statements of intervening variables, as were used in Hull's system. This was basically an antitheoretical position, taken by Skinner.[41]

A second criticism levied against Hull, as well as Tolman and others who leaned on inferred states and internal variables, was that they could never really be demonstrated or directly proven. The demonstration was only made by inference. For example, nobody had ever seen a *stimulus trace,* and a *secondary drive* made no reference to observable operations. To speak of "fear" as an acquired drive, as the Hullians were inclined to do, only clouded the issue. The fact that a rat escaped from a box was a simple enough observation, without postulating that it did so because of an acquired drive of "fear."

In essence, Hull's theories required a very sophisticated kind of dualism. As we have indicated earlier, to consider oneself a behaviorist and still deal in dualistic concepts was a complete contradiction in terms. Of course, Tolman and others who dealt in intervening variables were equally guilty.

Another criticism was that Hull's theory was overly particularistic; that while he intended his system to be one that could apply to all mammalian behavior, he and his associates primarily directed their research to the white rat. This was not entirely true, since they studied the human eyelid reflexes and other kinds of human behavior. In postulate seventeen, Hull allowed for individual differences among species as well as within species. But, many of his other postulates seemed to depend primarily on the rat's behavior in a runway or some other kind of apparatus.

Finally, Hull's system had been praised by many because of its logical nature. The question was, how logical was it really? A careful examination of the logical flaws is beyond the scope of this discussion. However, Koch[42] has given an analysis of Hull's logical difficulties. He points out, for example, that Hull's supposedly quantifiable postulates were based on "remote inferences by combining arbitrary calculations."

## Contributions of Hull

Even though Hull has been the subject of the severest attacks, at least he has not gone unnoticed. He formulated a theory so precise and detailed that it could not be ignored. It was this precision that enabled it to be tested. Other more generalized theoretical statements such as Guthrie's were hard to prove or dis-

---

[41]B. F. Skinner, "Are Theories of Learning Necessary?" *Psychological Review,* Vol. 57 (1950), pp. 193–216.

[42]S. Koch, *op. cit.*

prove. Hull subjected his system to constant revision. When particular theoretical statements proved to be inadequate, he modified them.

A good theory is one that can be put to the experimental test. The vast amount of experimental research generated by Hull's theory represents a considerable advancement in understanding problems of learning. The only other modern learning theorist whose system has provoked so much research has been B. F. Skinner, who will be considered in a later section. Whether or not one accepts Hull's theoretical constructs, the results of his experimentation remain as lasting contributions to psychology. Because Hull insisted on quantification, a great many experiments were rigorously and carefully executed. They stand as models of how proper experiments should be performed.

Hull had intended to broaden his system to include wider areas of psychology, but he did not live to do so. However, such theorists as J. S. Brown, John Dollard, N. E. Miller, and Kenneth Spence have followed in his tradition, although they developed some alternative views. They have applied some of Hull's basic ideas not only to more complex forms of learning but also to other fields as well, such as social psychology, personality, and psychotherapy.

In particular, the extensive work of Kenneth W. Spence served as an extension of Hull's theory. Spence accepted some of Hull's basic ideas and rejected others. For example, he saw less need to stress drive reduction, and preferred to emphasize contiguity. Space does not permit an elaboration of his theory, but the interested reader is referred to his book, *Behavior Theory and Conditioning*.[43]

## Interbehaviorism of J. R. Kantor

As a system, interbehaviorism exists today in the original sense of the term. It attempts to encompass the wide field of psychology within its framework, and has a group of faithful adherents (although not very large) who follow its basic tenets and communicate with each other through the *Interbehaviorist*, a quarterly journal.

J. R. Kantor (1888–1984) received his Ph.D. at the University of Chicago in 1917, at a time when functionalism was in its prime. He taught at the universities of Minnesota and Chicago for a short time. Then, in 1920 he went to Indiana University, where he remained until his retirement in 1959. On two successive occasions during this period he served as chairman of the department of psychology. Subsequent to his retirement, he has taught at the University of Maryland, New York University, and the University of Chicago. His first major work in which he outlined his systematic approach was a two-volume, *Principles*

---

[43]Kenneth W. Spence, *Behavior Theory and Conditioning* (New Haven: Yale University Press, 1956).

*of Psychology*[44] (1924–1926). Subsequent works include: *An Outline of a Social Psychology*[45] (1929), *A Survey of the Science of Psychology*[46] (1933) (an introductory text), *Problems of Physiological Psychology*[47] (1947), and *Interbehavioral Psychology*[48] (1958), a restatement of his original position. One of his more recent and probably most scholarly works is the two-volume history of psychology written within the framework of his own viewpoint, *The Scientific Evolution of Psychology*[49] (1963–1969). His most recent books are *Psychological Linguistics* (1977)[50] and *Cultural Psychology*[51] (1982).

## Interbehavioral Psychology: Some Basic Considerations

Throughout his long career Kantor has developed a system that falls within the basic framework of behaviorism. However, Kantor has preferred to call his approach *interbehaviorism* so as not to confuse it with that of Watson or of later *S-R* theorists.

Kantor has maintained that psychology is one of the natural sciences dealing with events that exist within a framework of space and time. He allows that psychology is related to other sciences, but that it has a basic subject matter of its own. Throughout his writings, he has maintained a strong anti-dualistic position, and many of his writings have been directed against other psychologists who use dualistic or mentalistic concepts.

Kantor feels that other theories of a behavioristic sort have placed too much emphasis on studying the responses of the organism and have neglected the equal importance of the stimulus object. Thus, for him, the subject matter of psychology is the *interactions of organism and stimulus objects*.

Although highly theoretical in nature, Kantor's system emphasizes that constructs developed in theory must always be directly related to basic observable events. In other words, he rejects intervening variables. Further, these constructs must be derived and made applicable to the original events and should not be built out of prior biological or physical constructs.[52] Thus, Kantor maintains a basically nonreductionistic view of psychology.

---

[44] J. R. Kantor, *Principles of Psychology*, 2 vols. (New York: Alfred A. Knopf, 1924–26. Reprinted, Chicago: The Principia Press).

[45] J. R. Kantor, *An Outline of a Social Psychology* (Chicago: Follett Publishing Co., 1929).

[46] J. R. Kantor, *A Survey of the Science of Psychology* (Bloomington, Ind.: The Principia Press, 1933).

[47] J. R. Kantor, *Problems of Psychological Psychology* (Bloomington, Ind.: The Principia Press, 1947).

[48] J. R. Kantor, *Interbehavioral Psychology* (Bloomington, Ind.: The Principia Press, 1958).

[49] J. R. Kantor, *The Scientific Evolution of Psychology*, 2 vols. (Chicago: The Principia Press, 1963–69).

[50] J. R. Kantor, *Psychological Linguistics* (Chicago: The Principia Press, 1977).

[51] J. R. Kantor, *Cultural Psychology* (Chicago: Principia Press, 1982).

[52] J. R. Kantor, *Interbehavioral Psychology* (Bloomington, Ind.: The Principia Press, 1958).

## Psychological Interactions

The basic components of Kantor's systematic position can be understood by referring to Fig. 3. His has often been classified as a "field theory," which indeed it is. The basic unit for analysis is the *behavior segment*. More complex psychological activities constitute a succession of these behavior segments. In a "segment" we have an organism interacting with a stimulus object. It is clear that both the stimulus and the organism are of equal importance, and one should not be glorified over the other. The stimulus may be an object, a person, or some other kind of event. The relationship between the object and the organism is a reciprocal one, so both constitute the elements of the interaction.

The stimulus object has certain functions. A simple acquisition of a stimulus function can be illustrated in Pavlov's conditioning experiment. The orig-

**FIGURE 3**   *The Interbehavior Field. RB* stands for reactional biography or the individual's part in developing a response function. *SE* (stimulus evolution) refers to the process by which an object develops a stimulus function. *M* is the contact medium—i.e. light, in vision. (From J. R. Kantor, *Problems in Physiological Psychology,* Chicago: The Principia Press, 1947, p. 117. Courtesy of The Principia Press.)

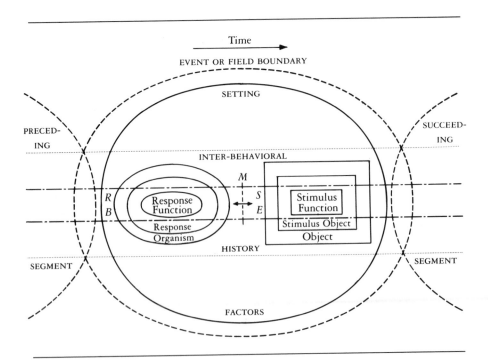

inally neutral stimulus, the bell, acquires the *stimulus function* of eliciting a salivatory response. The mere physical object (or event) can be distinguished from the function it serves.

*Universal stimulus functions* are based on the natural properties of the objects themselves. They are universal because they serve the same function for all members of a given species. They are also related to the biological condition of the responding organism. For example, a hot object stimulates a person to jerk his or her hand away from it.

*Individual stimulus functions* are more unique and particular to a person. Seeing a particular stone during an exploration, one person might simply kick it aside, while another might pick it up and add it to his or her collection.[53] The individual stimulus function will depend on the previous contacts or interactions a person has had with that object.

*Cultural stimulus functions* are identified in such a way that they call out similar reactions in a group of people. They are not universal, but may be shared by a community of individuals. For most of us, an apple has the stimulus function of an object to be eaten, but for some people it may merely be used for decorative purposes. Like individual stimulus functions, cultural functions acquire characteristics from previous interactions.

On the other side of the interaction, we have the organism and the response functions it performs. Kantor stresses the fact that psychological response, which is a function of the organism, typically involves the activity of the entire organism, thus maintaining a molar rather than a molecular approach. However, in some instances it may be useful to study more specific response patterns, depending on the types of psychological activity involved. The variety of responses that an organism is capable of performing is very wide, including perceiving, thinking, feeling, learning, remembering, reasoning, and so on. Kantor is willing to undertake the study of all possible kinds of psychological activity.

## Interactional Setting (S) (Setting Factors)

Any interaction between an organism and a stimulus does not occur in a vacuum since there are other setting factors that have to be taken into account. The setting factors constitute the background against which the interactions take place. They constitute the general surrounding circumstances that operate to inhibit or facilitate a particular interaction. These may include motivational conditions when an organism is deprived or satiated, its age, and the presence of other objects. However, they should not be interpreted as intervening variables.[54]

[53] J. R. Kantor, *A Survey of the Science of Psychology.*
[54] J. R. Kantor, *Interbehavioral Psychology.*

## Media of Contact (M)

In order for psychological interaction to take place, the organism must come in contact with the stimulus object. For example, it is impossible to perceive visual objects in the absence of light. Thus, light and sound do not actually act as the stimuli (as they do in some systems), but simply serve as media whereby interactions can take place. If you will recall Aristotle's psychology in chapter 2, you will note Kantor's similarity to the Greek philosopher.

## Interbehavior History (H)

The interbehavior history constitutes the reactional biography (*RB*) and the stimulus evolution (*SE*). The reactional biography has remained one of Kantor's most popular concepts, and is borrowed by other experimenters in their psychological explanations. Basically, it refers to the history of interactions an organism has had with various stimulus objects. The reactional biography is gradually built up, like building blocks, resulting in a history of interactions that Kantor calls an organism's *behavior equipment.*

Finally, there is the stimulus evolution (*SE*) that is the process of stimulus-function development of objects in psychological interbehavior. On the stimulus side, it corresponds to the development of the reactional biography on the response side.

Putting these events all together, Kantor suggests that the psychological event (*PE*) = f *SF* (stimulus function), *RF* (response function), *H* (interbehavior history), *S* (setting factors), and *M* (media of contact).[55]

## Learning

It should be obvious from our previous discussion that in an organism's acquisition of response functions to stimuli, learning is very important. Like all other forms of psychological activity, learning involves organism-stimulus-object interaction. In his discussion of learning, Kantor tends to follow the functionalist position, since he considers that the primary occupation of a psychological organism is to adapt to its surroundings. As humans we must adjust to things as they are, as well as allow for a possible reconstruction of the environment. Learning, thus, involves a coordination of responses to appropriate stimulus situations. Such contacts are often of a casual sort. On the other hand, learning may involve arrangements of a more contrived sort, such as in classroom learning, learning a skill, and so on.

Learning is basically rooted in six characteristics that Kantor describes as unique psychological responses. They differentiate the subject matter of psychology from other disciplines. The characteristics are: differential, variable, modifiable, integrative, delayable, and inhibitive.

---

[55]J. R. Kantor, "The Aim and Progress of Psychology," *American Scientist,* Vol. 34 (1946), pp. 251–63.

Kantor, thus, does not present an overwhelmingly new approach to learning. However, it is crucial to the development of the reactional biography of interbehavioral history discussed earlier.

## Implicit Interactions

Implicit interactions include such behavior as thinking, judging, imagining, reasoning, and so on. Superficially, one may be given the impression that one is reacting to stimuli that are not present, such as when a person appears preoccupied in daydreaming. But, as Kantor believes, every interaction constitutes an interaction of at least two things—the organism and the stimulus object. Therefore, the stimulus typically involved in implicit behavior is called a *substitute stimulus*. Common examples of substitute stimuli involve the use of maps, diagrams, or pictures that substitute for the object or persons they refer to. A good example is the traveler who reviews his color slides, thereby, in a sense, implicitly reliving the original trip in which he overtly interacted with physical objects and people.[56]

Kantor points out that all implicit behavior originates from direct contact with things. Imaginative creative acts are the product of previous more specific interactions. For example, inventions are the result of principles and objects that have been encountered at some earlier time. The most fantastic imagination involves previous contacts with real things.

Implicit activities are often very subtle and difficult to observe. If one can identify the substitute stimulus, one may be in a better position to appreciate what another person is thinking about. But this is not always possible, and one may merely conjecture what another person is reflecting upon. Another example may make clear just how implicit interactions work and how they are related to the substitute stimuli that initiate them. Consider the case of a young intern who is called in to complete an operation at a time when the attending surgeon is called out of the operating room. After completing the operation, which was a series of behavior segments involving a series of observable interactions, the intern goes home and relives what has happened. He may look at his hands (substitute stimuli) which, in this case, were intimately involved in the original interactions. At this point, the young intern relives all the aspects of the operation. Some of it may be slightly observable to another person in viewing his facial expressions or his slight motor movements.[57]

Implicit interactions involve a wide range of responses. They may be quite similar to the acts previously performed in the original situation, as in the case of the young intern, since the series of implicit interactions so closely followed the original overt behavior segments. On the other hand, they may be quite unrelated. In other cases, the original stimulus may have been quite a complex situation where the implicit reactions are of a more inventive sort, as in problem

---

[56]H. C. Mahan, *The Interactional Psychology of J. R. Kantor* (San Marcos, Calif.: Project Socrates Press, 1968).

[57]J. R. Kantor, *A Survey of the Science of Psychology.*

solving and conceptualization. Often, only a slight clue may be necessary to set off the chain of implicit interactions.

In many cases the exact nature of the implicit behavior can only be inferred. In others, it may become observable. Through the verbal report, we may understand these implicit behaviors by their outcome, as in the behavior of planning or problem solving. One might ask "Just how did you do that?" The responder then makes the various aspects of his or her implicit planning overt through verbal responses. In any event, the private nature of implicit behavior does not seem to be a compelling issue for Kantor. In most psychological activity the whole organism is involved, and it is unnecessary to identify specific aspects of the actual responses. The basic operation involved in implicit behavior is the use of the substitute stimulus as we have described it above. This differentiates implicit interactions from other kinds.

## Feeling or Affective Interactions

In feeling or affective interactions, the object takes on a greater importance and *acts upon the organism.* The object, thus, produces a change in the organism, but the person does nothing to the object. Take the simple example of a student looking at his or her final grade posted on a bulletin board. If it is an A, the student may smile and make certain vocal responses. An F, on the other hand, may result in quite opposite behavior. Very frequently affective interactions involve responses of the organism that are of an internal or visceral sort. The basic characteristic of feeling interactions is that instead of an organism doing something to the stimulus, as in effective interactions (operant in Skinnerian terms), the organism is *affected by the stimulus.* Affective interactions amount to more than just biological activity, which may be only a part of them. These affective interactions, like others, involve the whole organism, and the physiological functions are only a part of the entire response picture. The category of affective interactions involves a wide variety, including sorrow, joy, hate, anger, jealousy, fear, and so on. When an organism does something to the stimulus, as in striking one's enemy, the interaction no longer belongs in the affective class. It may be an ensuing behavior segment that follows the original affective one.

## Emotion

Emotion constitutes a particular kind of psychological interaction that Kantor designates as a "no response" behavior segment. An analysis of the entire emotional event would include:

**1.** The pre-emotional behavior segment that constitutes those interactions which go on prior to the presentation of the emotional stimulus.

**2.** The emotional segment proper, which may be very much related to that which preceded it. The emotional segment involves a complete disruption of ongoing activity, and may be thought of as a kind of psychological "freezing." Such instances are noted when one's car stalls on a railroad track and in sight of an oncoming train, but one does nothing but remain stuck to the seat. Or, one may be so stunned by some remark that one is rendered speechless.

3. In the first post-emotional segment, a new stimulus is presented that brings about a recovery or initiates a new interaction. In the instance cited above of a person frozen to the wheel of an automobile, some passer-by may quickly call to the person to "get out" or actually pull the driver from the car.

4. The second post-emotional segment is one in which the person may simply state, "That was a lucky escape." In general, this behavior may also be described as a reflection on what has just happened.

It should be pointed out that for Kantor there are no classifications of emotions as there are in feelings. There is only one kind of emotional activity—the descriptive act we have just discussed. It may occur under different circumstances, as a mild emotion where one makes a *faux pas,* or a more violent emotion when one is caught in a burning building but fails to jump to safety.

## Remembering or Memorial Interactions

If one makes an appointment for some future time and the appointment is kept, a memorial or remembering act has occurred. A failure to keep the appointment would usually be construed as forgetting. Memory, then, involves a delay in time between an initial phase or behavior segment and a finalization of the behavior. Rather than being a backward-looking reaction as considered in most systems, remembering is forward-looking. An act once begun is not completed until some future time. Thus, memorial behavior consists of three phases: (1) initiation, (2) delay, and (3) consummation. For the initial phase, an interaction occurs, as in making the appointment. To assure consummation, one must set up or project some *substitute stimulus* that will then be encountered at some future time to complete the act. For example, if I write the appointment down on my calendar and so contrive the situation that I will encounter the substitute stimulus at the future time when the appointment will be kept, the act will be consummated. If I fail to encounter the substitute stimulus, one might say that I have forgotten. The projection of the substitute stimulus may be quite intentional, as in writing down an appointment, making a shopping list, or tieing a string around one's finger, and so on. On the other hand, it can be quite incidental, and on hearing some remark or some other stimulus, one may say, "Oh, that reminds me, I must . . ." Such acts of forgetting occur because of the failure either to set up some substitute stimulus, or to encounter another less intended one. The best way to avoid forgetting is to connect the consummatory response with as many substitute stimuli as the situation warrants. Sometimes we are preoccupied at the time or we may move out of the range of the substitute stimulus. It then fails to function.

The period of delay may be quite brief or it may extend over a long period of time. In the latter case, forgetting does not occur because of the passage of time but because of a great difficulty in encountering appropriate substitute stimuli.

## Biological Participants in Psychological Interactions

The role of biological events in an organism's interbehavior is not intended to give any explanatory principles. As we have seen earlier, Kantor recognized that physiological functions may be part of the interbehavioral event. However, they are not intended as causative. In the case of a brain-damaged child, the fact of his damage may be a limiting function on the kinds of the interactions he may acquire. As an influence on behavior, however, physiological functions cannot be ignored. In the case cited, a certain damage or other interfering factors of a biological nature may make it impossible to come into contact with certain stimulus objects and acquire reactions toward them. The same would be true for one who is deaf or blind. In some cases, these biological participants may completely leave the psychological counterpart at a stand-still, as in the case of a vegetative idiot.

## Criticisms of Interbehaviorism

Kantor has been criticized for having taken a basically negative view of psychology. Many of his articles and books have been primarily intended as attacks on alternate viewpoints. His criticisms have often been devastating and have hindered him in gaining the recognition that his sympathizers feel he deserves. Although he has taken a positive approach in developing an alternate system, it may be claimed that too much of his time has been devoted to tearing down other systems. He has continually harped on dualism, the ineptitudes of physiological psychologists, as well as theories and movements that are of a more limited nature.

Many of his critics claim they simply do not understand what he is trying to say. Actually, the system is much less difficult than it would appear to the uninitiated reader. Nevertheless, his writings have often been obscure. His style is excessively wordy and often difficult to follow. The level of his exposition is often so erudite that it is directed only toward graduate students and professional psychologists.

Kantor has also been criticized for developing a highly theoretical system that has failed to generate much significant experimental research. Throughout his career, Kantor has remained a complete theoretician, and a review of his complete bibliography discloses only one actual experimental report. Furthermore, much of his writing appears to be more philosophical than psychological. However, a recent book of readings edited by N. H. Pronko, *Panorama of Psychology*,[58] intended for the introductory student, presents appropriate experi-

---

[58]N. H. Pronko, *Panorama of Psychology* (Belmont, Calif.: Brooks Cole, 1969).

mental and clinical evidence integrated in such a manner as to support Kantor's theoretical position.

A more recent book by Pronko, *Psychology from the Standpoint of an Interbehaviorist*[59] (1980), is a very readable introduction to Kantor's systematic position.

### Contributions of Interbehaviorism

Among psychologists today, there are few who are as scholarly in their output as Kantor. Perhaps the best example of this is to be found in his book, *The Scientific Evolution of Psychology*,[60] a history of psychology beginning with the ancient Greeks. The work was many years in preparation. All sources are primary, and references are given in the language of the original writers. In all his works, Kantor has followed the same careful pattern of research. Also, in his writings he has shown his wide understanding of other sciences—mathematics, social science, and philosophy. One cannot deny his amazing mastery of these other fields.

Much of Kantor's influence on modern psychology has been indirect. He has presented many innovative ideas that were often borrowed by others, sometimes without acknowledgment. He has held steadfastly to the tradition that psychology should be a natural science. Although his attacks on dualistic systems have been highly critical, they are nevertheless very carefully organized and logically executed. His influence on other behaviorists, notably those who follow the lines of Skinner, has been accepted and acknowledged.

Finally, in developing a broad systematic approach to psychology as a system in the original sense (see pp. 1–2), Kantor has not been afraid to tackle a vast variety of psychological issues, including perceiving, learning, remembering, and implicit activity of all sorts, which are considered within the range of general psychology. Further, he has devoted himself to such other fields as social psychology, abnormal psychology, and physiological psychology.

## *Burrhus Frederic Skinner (1904–1990)*

Because of its scope and wide range of applications, Skinner's position becomes more a system of psychology than a mere theory of learning, although he has typically been placed in the group of modern learning theorists along with Guthrie, Hull, and Tolman.

---

[59]N. H. Pronko, *Psychology from the Standpoint of an Interbehaviorist* (Monterey, Calif.: Brooks/Cole Publishers, 1980).
[60]J. R. Kantor, *The Scientific Evolution of Psychology*.

## Skinner's Career

Like Hull, Skinner had a long and widely influential career. His contributions were varied, and he did much to change the course of American psychology. In terms of his influence, he may be considered as one of the most important figures in twentieth-century psychology, along with others such as Pavlov, Watson, and Freud.

Skinner was born in Susquehanna, Pennsylvania on March 20, 1904. He received his A.B. from Hamilton College in 1926 where he majored in English and the classics. (In his time, there was no psychology department at Hamilton.) He received his M.A. in 1930 and his Ph.D. in 1931 from Harvard. After several years of post-doctoral fellowships, he worked at the universities of Michigan and Minnesota from 1936–1945. In 1945 he was asked to be chairman of the psychology department at Indiana University where he remained until 1948. After that, he returned to Harvard, where he spent the rest of his career.

During the thirties, Skinner's earliest research efforts were devoted to developing a set of learning principles using primarily the white rat as his subject in a specially contrived apparatus of his own invention, often called a "Skinner box" (a term Skinner himself deplored). He preferred that it be called an operant conditioning chamber. The box, in its earlier form, consisted of a relatively small chamber, large enough for the rat to move about in, but small enough to limit its behavior to the particular response Skinner wanted to study. Mounted on one side was a small metal bar that the rat could press to receive a food pellet in a tray below. Other additions included more than one bar, cue lights to which the animal could respond, and a shock grid on the floor for studies of escape and avoidance behavior. The box has proven so versatile that literally thousands of different experiments have been performed with it. To record the response of the rat, Skinner invented what he called a "cumulative recorder," whereby the *rate* of response could be recorded. The advantage of this technique was that the experimenter could see the performance of the animal as it occurred. The rate of responding has been the primary measure, but various other aspects of the shape of the curve could be seen (see Fig. 4, p. 219). As the animal continued its response, the pen of the recorder always moved in an upward direction (hence, the term "cumulative").

During the forties, Skinner began using pigeons as his experimental subjects. Consequently, he altered the form of his apparatus, and the basic response to be studied was pecking on a disc that was mounted on one side of the cage. Food was delivered in a tray below the disc. Skinner found several advantages in using pigeons—faster response rates could be established, and the animals lived longer (if one were interested in long-term studies). Later adaptations of Skinner's basic technique have been applied to monkeys that were placed in a restraining chair, where they could press a key. For human experimentation, a plunger (like that used in a candy or cigarette machine) was the basic manipulandum which could be pulled so that appropriate reinforcement would be given (in the form of candy or a variety of tokens such as money).

Among Skinner's other early innovations was a "baby tender," an air-conditioned box that acted as a crib in which the infant could live during the early part of his life. He raised his second daughter in the apparatus for the first two and one-half years of her life. Although the apparatus was commercially available, it never really became popular. Critics have claimed that the apparatus made his daughter neurotic, but Skinner categorically denied this.

Skinner's next innovation, in the late fifties, was the invention of the teaching machine and the development of programmed learning. The application of this invention to education will be discussed in more detail in a later section. More recently, Skinner devoted himself to the problems involved in the design of a culture in which people would live, applying appropriate psychological principles for a Utopian kind of life. Such model communes are now a reality in several parts of this country.

Skinner's first major book was *The Behavior of Organisms*[61] (1938), in which he not only outlined the basic tenets of his system but also gave many experimental examples from his own research.

In 1948 he wrote a Utopian novel, *Walden II,*[62] a book used more often in psychology courses than in English classes. The book outlined an ideal psychological community. At first the book aroused much skepticism, but it has since sold over a million copies. The idea of developing a Utopian culture was a compelling interest of Skinner's.

In 1953 he wrote *Science and Human Behavior,*[63] designed as an introductory text, in which he applied his principles to matters outside the laboratory—to social issues, education, law, government, religion, and even psychotherapy. In 1957 he published *Verbal Behavior,*[64] as he recognized that a system should include an analysis of language. Skinner's analysis did not meet with much favor among linguists. In the same year, in collaboration with C. B. Ferster, he published a huge volume entitled *Schedules of Reinforcement*[65] (see below). One of Skinner's publications in the 1970s was *Beyond Freedom and Dignity,*[66] a rather controversial volume in which he proposed to design a culture, indeed the entire world, based on the principles he had developed (see following). Skinner also completed a three-volume autobiography: *Particulars of My Life*[67] (1976), *The Shaping of a Behaviorist*[68] (1978), and *A Matter of Consequence* (1983).[69] Too, in collaboration with M. Vaughan, he wrote *Enjoy Old Age* (1983).[70]

[61]B. F. Skinner, *The Behavior of Organisms: An Experimental Analysis* (New York: D. Appleton-Century Co., 1938).
[62]B. F. Skinner, *Walden II* (New York: The Macmillan Co., 1948).
[63]B. F. Skinner, *Science and Human Behavior* (New York: The Macmillan Co., 1953).
[64]B. F. Skinner, *Verbal Behavior* (New York: Appleton-Century-Crofts, 1957).
[65]C. B. Ferster and B. F. Skinner, *Schedules of Reinforcement* (New York: Appleton-Century-Crofts, 1957).
[66]B. F. Skinner, *Beyond Freedom and Dignity* (New York: Alfred A. Knopf, 1971).
[67]B. F. Skinner, *Particulars of My Life* (New York: Alfred A. Knopf, 1976).
[68]B. F. Skinner, *The Shaping of a Behaviorist* (New York: Alfred A. Knopf, 1978).
[69]B. F. Skinner, *A Matter of Consequence* (New York: Alfred A. Knopf, 1983).
[70]B. F. Skinner and M. Vaughan, *Enjoy Old Age* (New York: W. W. Norton, 1983).

In 1958 Skinner received the American Psychological Association's Distinguished Contribution Award, and in 1968 he received the National Medal of Science Award, the Federal Government's highest award for distinguished achievement in science, mathematics, and engineering. To date, only one other psychologist has ever received the award. In 1971 he received the Gold Medal Award of the American Psychological Foundation.

## Skinner's System:
## Some Basic Considerations

The influence of Watson is clearly seen in Skinner's *S-R* psychology. His approach was to take a small "bit" of behavior, such as a bar press, and study it under carefully controlled conditions. By manipulating the independent variables in a systematic fashion, he could observe what happened to the dependent variables. When done properly, a "functional relationship" was established. Skinner's approach was completely descriptive and has often been called *descriptive behaviorism.* His method was inductive rather than deductive. There was no reference to inferred states or intervening variables. The approach can be called an "empty organism" approach, because Skinner was not concerned with what goes on inside. He maintained that the execution of a properly controlled experiment would yield valid and observable relationships, and that this would become the legitimate data of psychology. Thus, the subject matter of psychology is the behavior of living organisms.

As opposed to Hull and Tolman (see earlier and chap. 15), Skinner was inclined to take an atheoretical position. In his article "Are Theories of Learning Necessary?" Skinner answered no. He did not object to theory, *per se.* What he did oppose were theories based on hypothetical entities that had no way of being proven. These he considered "fictions."

Skinner did, however, make use of theory. For example, in his extrapolation of principles from the laboratory to the world at large, as expressed particularly in *Science and Human Behavior,* a great deal of theorizing was involved. Furthermore, in his proposal to design an ideal culture, the problem was entirely theoretical. However, although Skinner had been ranked as one of the leading learning theorists, he would have claimed that he was not a "theorist" in the usual sense of the word.

Another unique aspect of Skinner's methodology was his reluctance to use the statistical analyses of his data. He maintained that large masses of subjects and complex statistics only acted to cover up for sloppy experimentation and failure to use proper controls. Thus, he stressed the importance of the "single organism." Under carefully controlled conditions, one can reach appropriate conclusions based on the records of one or at least only a few subjects. If one reads the reports in the *Journal of the Experimental Analysis of Behavior,* a journal devoted to Skinnerian research, one will find this use of only a few subjects characteristic of the reports. The lack of complex statistical analyses may be appealing to those who have an aversion for mathematics.

## Conditioning

***Operant and Respondent Behavior.*** Early in his writing,[71] Skinner maintained a distinction between two kinds of conditioning—type *S* and type *R*. Type *S* has been called *respondent,* and follows the classical Pavlovian paradigm. In this instance, a stimulus elicits a response, as when the bell is rung the dog salivates. Further, the reinforcement (food) as the unconditioned stimulus comes *before* the response. Skinner allowed that this is a legitimate form of learning, but one that is limited in nature. Just how many unconditioned reflexes can be conditioned? In general, those who follow Skinner's position consider *respondent behavior* to consist of unconditioned and conditioned reflexes.

Far more important is that larger class of behavior called *operant.* It is so named because the organism *operates on* the environment. The simple experimental examples of a rat's bar pressing and a pigeon's key pecking would be considered operants. By calling this class type *R,* Skinner draws our attention to the significance of the consequences of the response—namely, the *reinforcement* that *follows* the response. If the food acts as a reinforcement, it will be shown as strengthening the response by increasing the probability of that response occurring again.

In his emphasis on *reinforcement* as one of the crucial aspects of learning, Skinner acknowledged his debt to Thorndike.[72] However, Skinner reformulated Thorndike's law of effect as follows: "If the occurrence of an operant is followed by the presentation of a reinforcing stimulus, the strength is increased."[73] However, for Skinner, the reason the reinforcement worked was not the same as it was for Thorndike or Hull. The reader will recall that Thorndike considered the satisfying consequences and Hull stressed drive reduction. Since Skinner's is purely a descriptive system, the simple observed relationships are enough. When certain stimuli are presented, they strengthen behavior. This can be observed and measured.

***Positive and Negative Reinforcers.*** What we have described so far have been positive reinforcers—namely, those stimuli, such as food and water, that strengthen behavior when they are presented. Negative reinforcers are identified as stimuli that strengthen behavior *when they are removed.* A rat may be placed in an operant conditioning chamber, and the shock from the grid floor is turned on. When the rat presses the bar the shock is turned off. On further occasions, the latency of this response is greatly reduced, so immediately when the shock is applied the bar is pressed. The shortening of the latency is an indication that the response is being strengthened. (This operation of negative reinforcement is also called escape.)

---

[71]B. F. Skinner, *The Behavior of Organisms, op. cit.*
[72]B. F. Skinner, *Science and Human Behavior, op. cit.*
[73]B. F. Skinner, *The Behavior of Organisms, op. cit.,* p. 21.

Simple examples of the effect of both positive and negative reinforcement can be found in human activity. A child asks for candy. If it is given, the child is more likely to ask again. We sit down at the dinner table because we receive food. On the negative side, we put on sunglasses to escape the glare of the sun; we kick off a tight shoe or put up an umbrella when it starts raining.

***Extinction.*** Extinction is found in both operant and respondent behavior. In operant behavior, it occurs simply by the removal of the reinforcer. The organism may continue to respond for a while until the response simply dies out. Skinner often used the resistance to extinction as a measure of response strength. A strong response is slow to extinguish. Extinction is a most effective way to get rid of undesirable behavior, although the process may be a long one if the previously conditioned response is strong. One way to rid a child of temper tantrums is simply to ignore them. Note that Skinner did not postulate any inhibitory potentials, but depended simply on his observations.

***Schedules of Reinforcement.*** One of the unique features of Skinner's apparatus is that it lends itself to the possibility of presenting reinforcements in an intermittent manner. The effects of various schedules on the characteristics of the response has been a fruitful area of Skinnerian research. Ferster and Skinner's *Schedules of Reinforcement*[74] is a large volume reporting massive data on a variety of schedules often of a very complex nature. We shall limit our discussion to a consideration of the four basic schedules: fixed interval, variable interval, fixed ratio, and variable ratio.

In fixed interval (*FI*), the reinforcement becomes available after a designated period of time, regardless of what the organism is doing in the intervening period. For the reinforcement to be delivered, a response has to occur, at or after the time interval designated. The characteristic of the response curve after considerable conditioning on this schedule results in a kind of temporal discrimination. Shown on the curve, this takes the form of a kind of "scalloping" (see Fig. 4). Following a reinforcement, the organism learns that another one is not going to be delivered immediately, so its rate of responding is relatively slow at the beginning of the interval. As the time for reinforcement approaches, the curve becomes positively accelerated, so that the most rapid rate of response comes just before the reinforcement.

In variable interval (*VI*), the reinforcement becomes available intermittently on some average time schedule. In a *VI* of one minute, the organism receives its reinforcement for responding on the average of once a minute. Sometimes it may come after fifteen or forty-five seconds; at other times the interval may be as long as a minute and a half. Since these reinforcements are delivered in a random manner, the characteristic of the curve is one of a rather steady rate of response (see Fig. 4). It should be noted that in interval schedules the reinforcement is dependent on the experimenter or some other outside agency.

---

[74]C. B. Ferster and B. F. Skinner, *op. cit.*

**FIGURE 4**  *Ideal Samples of the Four Main Schedules of Reinforcement.*

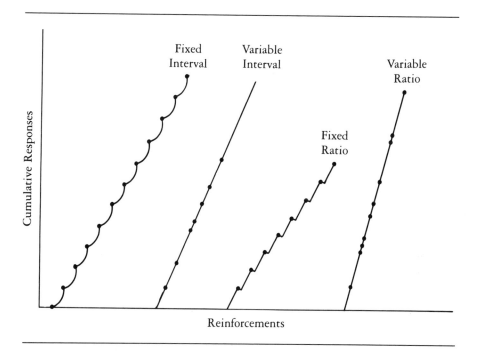

In fixed ratio (*FR*), the reinforcement is delivered after a given fixed number of responses. For example, in an *FR*:10, every tenth response is reinforced. As the behavior is strengthened, the ratio may be gradually stepped up so that ratios of 1000 or more can be established. Once the behavior is established, the characteristic of this curve is like a series of steps (see Fig. 4). The animal makes a rapid run, receives its reinforcement, and takes a break. This is followed by another rapid run and a break and so on. The length of the break is a function of the ratio. Long ratios will be followed by long breaks.

Variable ratio (*VR*) follows the same principle as variable interval, except that the ratio is expressed in average number of responses made and not time. A *VR*:10 means that on the average the organism will be reinforced for every tenth response. This schedule can yield very rapid rates of response.

Applications of intermittent reinforcement can be found in many aspects of human behavior. One may be paid by the week (*FI*) or by the amount of work one does (*FR*). Most gambling devices operate on a *VR* schedule, since the player does not know exactly when he will be paid off.

***Discrimination.*** So far in our discussion, we have not mentioned antecedent stimuli in operant conditioning. We waited until an organism made a particular response in an experimental situation, and when and if it occurred "spontaneously," it was reinforced. Like Watson, Skinner was very much concerned with the prediction and control of behavior. One way to control behavior is to reinforce responses we want strengthened and not reinforce (extinguish) those responses we wish to have weakened. Another kind of stimulus that is very significant in control is a discriminative one, designated by $S^D$. In a simple experiment on discrimination with a pigeon, the bird is trained to peck at a red disc (pigeons have color vision). When a green disc is presented, no reinforcement is given. In other words, the formation of a discrimination involves both conditioning and extinction. When the discs are presented randomly, the red is usually always reinforced while the green is never reinforced. Because of a phenomenon called *generalization*, in the beginning of the experiment, the pigeon may peck equally at both discs, but as the discrimination becomes formed it pecks less frequently on the green disc and more frequently on the red one. Eventually, responses to the green disc are completely extinguished or eliminated. When the discrimination is well formed, the bird will peck only at the red disc. When the green disc is presented, the pigeon either does nothing or engages in some alternate behavior.

Discriminative control is very important in all forms of human behavior. We stop at red lights, go at green ones. Mother comes when the baby cries, because the crying is a discriminative stimulus. In picking strawberries, we choose the ripe ones and leave the others alone. Complex learning, such as concept formation, also involves the two processes of discrimination and generalization. Concepts involve discriminating between classes of stimuli and generalizing within a given class. Take a simple concept of discriminating a dog from a cat. There are many varieties of dogs and cats (generalization), but we are able to discriminate the two classes because of certain distinctive stimulus properties of each.

**Differentiation.** In discrimination, emphasis is placed on the stimulus side. We discriminate among stimuli. In differentiation, the response side is emphasized. A simple example of differentiation is found in training a pigeon to peck at a disc. In this case, if we simply waited until the bird did it "spontaneously," we might wait a lifetime. Therefore, a process of differentiation or "shaping" must be involved. This makes use of reinforcing successive approximations to the final desired response. We might begin by reinforcing only those responses made on the side of the cage nearest the disc, then only those responses that come closer and closer to the disc until the final response of actually pecking at the disc is made. In using the method of successive approximations, less approximate responses become extinguished. And finally, this would be the only response that would be continuously reinforced.

Skinner did not agree with Guthrie on the stereotyped nature of the response. He felt that even in the most highly executed skills, there would always be some degree of *variability*. It is this variability of responses that makes shaping possible. In a variability of responses, we select the one nearest the desired one and then continue in that direction by more and closer successive approximations. As shaping continues, variability is decreased, but even the most expert golfer might miss a shot or the pianist might strike a wrong note.

Thus, in his concepts of differentiation and variability, Skinner denies the law of exercise—that practice in itself improves a task. It is through the use of selective reinforcement out of a variability of responses that a skill is developed. The undesirable responses go unreinforced and are extinguished, while the more desirable ones continue to be strengthened. It is the selective reinforcement of the most appropriate responses that is crucial to the development of a skill.

***Secondary (Conditioned) Reinforcement.*** Like Hull, Skinner makes use of the concept of secondary reinforcement—that is, those stimuli that become associated with primary ones, such as food and water, can take on a reinforcing function of their own. For Skinner, however, a secondary reinforcer acquires its function in a very special way. It must first have acquired the function of being a discriminative stimulus. Once this is established, it can then be used to reinforce other responses. Let us take a simple experimental example of training a rat to press the lever to the discriminative stimulus of a white light. In training, all responses made in the dark have been extinguished, so the discrimination has been formed to respond to light only. Now, for the first time, a chain is lowered into the cage. The rat pulls the chain with its teeth and is reinforced by the mere presentation of the light. The rate increases, thus demonstrating that the light has a reinforcing function. Summaries of other experiments demonstrating secondary reinforcement can be found in Skinner,[75] Keller and Schoenfeld,[76] and Lundin.[77]

Another aspect of the secondary reinforcer is its great generality of function. Once it has been established, it will reinforce other responses in equal strength. In human affairs, secondary reinforcers are very important. We are reinforced by the attention, approval, and affection of others or by such tokens as money, grades, or diplomas. Almost anything that interests us can be considered a secondary reinforcer.

***Aversive Conditioning.*** In Skinner's system, much emphasis is placed on the importance of positive reinforcement. In his Utopian society, described in *Walden II*,[78] the use of positive reinforcement as opposed to aversive conditioning is the crux of the society's success. Yet, Skinner recognizes that aversive control is frequently used and can be demonstrated experimentally.

Punishment is a very common example. In one of his early experiments, Skinner[79] demonstrated how punishment works. Further experiments by Estes[80]

---

[75]B. F. Skinner, *The Behavior of Organisms, op. cit.*

[76]F. S. Keller and W. N. Schoenfeld, *Principles of Psychology* (New York: Appleton-Century-Crofts, 1950).

[77]R. W. Lundin, *Personality: A Behavioral Analysis,* 2nd ed. (New York: The Macmillan Co., 1974).

[78]B. F. Skinner, *Walden II, op. cit.*

[79]B. F. Skinner, *The Behavior of Organisms, op. cit.*

[80]W. K. Estes, "An Experimental Study of Punishment," *Psychological Monographs,* Vol. 57 (1944), No. 263, pp. iii–40.

and, more recently, Azrin[81] have explored a number of variables of which punishment can be a function, such as the strength of the punishment, the schedule on which it is applied, and so on. Because of space limitations, we shall confine ourselves to Skinner's original experiment. After conditioning animals, he put them in extinction. During the first ten minutes of extinction, the animals were punished by a "snap back" of the bar that they had been pressing. The rate was obviously sharply decreased, but following the cessation of punishment, the rate of responding gradually recovered to match the control group, which received no punishing stimuli. Thus, Skinner demonstrated that, at least for moderate punishment, the punishing stimulus does not *eliminate* the behavior but merely *suppresses* it. It should be noted here that punishment is not the same as negative reinforcement (escape), because negative reinforcement strengthens behavior.

Another form of aversive conditioning is avoidance. Like punishment and escape, avoidance involves the use of aversive stimuli. In avoidance behavior, a warning signal is given that acquires the function of a discriminative stimulus. If a response does not occur in a specified period of time to terminate the warning signal, the aversive stimulus, such as shock, is presented. Eventually, the animal learns to respond by pressing the bar before the shock is presented, thus avoiding it. In this instance, the warning signal also takes on the function of a *secondary negative reinforcer* because of its original pairing with the shock before avoidance behavior has been established. In this case, the reinforcement comes from the removal of the secondary negative reinforcer, just as in escape the reinforcement came from the removal of a primary negative reinforcer.

## Superstitious Behavior

Typically in operant conditioning a response is contingent upon—that is, related to—another response or reinforcement. A rat presses a lever and is reinforced with food. The response is strengthened, whether the reinforcements are delivered continuously after each response or on some intermittent schedule.

Suppose the situation were so contrived that regardless of what an organism was doing, a reinforcement might be delivered, say, every 15 seconds. In this situation the reinforcement would be independent of the animal's behavior and would be *noncontingent*. This is the way Skinner defined superstitious behavior— that is, the behavior develops by being accidentally reinforced. Suppose a tribe of Native Americans happened to do a dance, which also happened to be followed by rain. An accidental contingency could be set up, and although there was absolutely no direct connection between the dance and the rain that followed, the probability that another rain dance might occur would be great. Or take the case of a baseball player who adjusted his cap in a certain way and then hit the next pitch for a home run; the probability is great that the cap-adjusting behavior would increase, and a superstitious response would be established.

---

[81]N. H. Azrin and W. C. Holz, "Punishment," in W. Honig, ed., *Operant Behavior: Areas of Research and Application* (New York: Appleton-Century-Crofts, 1966).

Nonetheless, reinforcement of hitting a home run was not contingent upon the cap adjustment.

## Drive

Since Skinner's system did not involve inferred states or intervening variables, the question arises as to how he could account for drive or motivation, which is so crucial to other systems. He did it in a rather simple manner, by defining drive operationally, either in terms of the hours of deprivation (such as food) or the percentage of an animal's normal body weight. In either case, the drive operations refer to completely observable events. Skinner showed little or no concern for internal functions, for he maintained a nonreductionistic position that psychology has its own data to deal with and does not need to depend on internal conditions as explanatory principles.

## Emotions

Skinner handled emotions in a manner similar to drive, in terms of particular operations performed. Emotions are defined specifically with respect to the circumstances that affect the probability of a given response occurring or not occurring. Depression or sorrow result typically from the removal of conditioned positive reinforcers, such as following the death of a member of one's family who has been the source of much secondary positive reinforcement. Joy, on the other hand, occurs when an absent secondary positive reinforcer is re-presented, as in seeing an old friend again. Anxiety is defined in terms of warning signals that are inevitably followed by aversive stimuli from which an organism cannot escape. In an experiment by Estes and Skinner,[82] rats were trained to press a bar on an intermittent schedule of positive reinforcement. After the basic rate was established, superimposed on it was the presentation of a continuous tone followed several minutes later by an electric shock. As the experiment continued, the animals ceased responding when the tone was presented and cowered in the corner of the cage. After the shock was eventually presented, they resumed their bar-pressing behavior until the next tonal presentation. This experimental operation was designated as anxiety. In humans, the situation is similar. Anxiety is expressed when some threats, such as warning signals (like the tone), are given that are followed by some kind of aversive stimulus from which one cannot escape. The basic characteristic of the anxiety operation is its inescapability; in other words, one simply has to wait for the event to occur.

## Verbal Behavior

Language is one of the clear characteristics that distinguishes humans from lower forms. If one stops to think for a moment, one can realize just how much

---

[82]W. K. Estes and B. F. Skinner, "Some Quantitative Properties of Anxiety," *Journal of Experimental Psychology*, Vol. 29 (1941), pp. 390–400.

of one's own behavior is verbal. Skinner maintained that speech, like other behaviors, is subject to the contingencies of reinforcement. His analysis was quite complex, so we can describe only a few main points here. Skinner found it necessary to make a distinction between two main functions of language. The first of these is the *mand* (from command or demand). Very frequently this is related to primary reinforcement. Furthermore, the reinforcement is quite specific. For example if one says, "Pass the butter," this verbal statement is specifically reinforced by receiving the object requested. Mands also represent some of the earliest forms of language development, for example when the baby asks for "water" or "a cookie."

The second and much wider function is the *tact*. When people are *tacting*, they are describing the world about them. Tacts are characteristically related to discriminative stimuli in the environment, and the reinforcements are more generalized. One might say, "It's a beautiful day today." The discriminative stimuli represent the conditions of the weather and the physical environment. The reinforcement would typically be generalized, as in approval from the person with whom one is speaking. Of course, there are *false tacts,* as in when one is telling a lie or making inappropriate discriminations with regard to the environment.

Self-descriptions are statements that fall into the same class: "I am beautiful," or "I am intelligent." This is the nearest that Skinner came to any concept of "self."

Skinner defined other forms of verbal behavior, such as autoclitic, echoic, and textual behavior. Autoclitics exhibit verbal behavior based on other verbal behavior. Their main function is to qualify responses and express relations. Unlike mands and tacts, which are controlled by overtly observable stimuli, autoclitics may be controlled by stimuli known only to the speaker. For example, a person might say, "I was about to say that . . ." or "I am not sure whether I like this painting placed over the fireplace."

In echoic behavior, the responses are reinforced when another person's responses are repeated verbatim. Echoic behavior is frequently a prerequisite for more complex verbal behavior. In the early stages of speech acquisition, children frequently engage in such echoic utterances. They will repeat words or expressions before they have learned how these words are related to environmental events. When this occurs, it can become the antecedent for more complex verbal relationships. Examples might include "oh-oh" or "hoo-hoo," which call attention to more meaningful verbal behavior that is to follow.

Textual behavior refers to reading aloud or silently from a script, a book, or any other written material.

Extinction also entered into Skinner's verbal analysis. If one wishes to be rid of another's annoying verbal behavior, he or she can withhold the reinforcement of attention by ignoring what the other person is saying. But what about the bore who continues to talk, despite the fact that nobody is listening? Skinner suggested that the bore is being reinforced by hearing himself or herself talk. For a critique of Skinner's analysis of verbal behavior, see Chomsky's review of Skinner's book (see pp. 290–291).

## Programmed Learning

As indicated earlier in this chapter, programmed learning was one of Skinner's significant innovations. He was distressed by traditional educational techniques of constant drilling, and by the teacher's use of so much aversive control. Skinner's technique involved the basic principles of shaping and continuous reinforcement. The subject is presented with a set of material in which statements are given, and the subject is to fill in answers. After filling in each answer, the subject checks to see if the answer is correct. He or she then goes on to the next bit of material, called a "frame." The material is presented in small steps, with each frame following from the preceding one in a systematic fashion. A good program should be so designed that the student's chance of error is very slight. Having a right answer is considered to be reinforcing. Programs are designed so that students can work at their own rates—some faster than others. In the end, a test of the material learned shows that the rapid worker and the slower worker have both mastered the material.

Programs have been developed in numerous areas from teaching elementary English and arithmetic to more complex subjects, such as calculus, physics, electronics, or music. Holland and Skinner[83] developed their own program to teach the basic principles of Skinner's system. Another program on the basic principles of operant and respondent conditioning has been developed by Geis, Stebbins, and Lundin.[84] In the development of a program there must be constant revisions. A bad frame (one that is frequently missed) must be replaced by a more appropriate one. Continuous error analyses are made. The program cannot progress so rapidly that constant mistakes are made when too much material is assumed; nor should it move so slowly that the method becomes monotonous or boring. Programs may be presented in simple book form, where the subject works down the page using a card to cover up the answers until it is time to look at them, or programs may be presented more mechanically by means of teaching machines. For a more detailed discussion, see Skinner's book *The Technology of Teaching*.[85]

## Behavior Modification

The most recent application of Skinner's principles has been in the area of changing undesirable behavior. The technique is often referred to as behavior therapy. Basically, it involves shaping and selective use of positive reinforcement, either primary or secondary, as well as extinction. It has been applied to all kinds of behavior problems. Autistic children have been taught to speak, behavior of mental defectives has been improved, and schizophrenic symptoms have been modified or eliminated. The technique can also be applied to more

[83]J. G. Holland and B. F. Skinner, *The Analysis of Behavior: A Program for Self-Instruction* (New York: McGraw-Hill Book Co., 1961).

[84]G. L. Geis, W. C. Stebbins, and R. W. Lundin, *The Study of Behavior,* Vol. I., *Reflex and Operant Conditioning* (New York: Appleton-Century-Crofts, 1965).

[85]B. F. Skinner, *The Technology of Teaching* (New York: Appleton-Century-Crofts, 1968).

minor disorders, such as thumbsucking in children. The research in this area has been "mushrooming," to the degree that several journals have been established to report research findings. One journal devoted particularly to research following Skinner's principles is *The Journal of Applied Behavior Analysis*. The literature is so vast that only a few simple examples may be cited. In one study, Baer[86] wished to eliminate thumbsucking in children. He began by showing a child a series of cartoons. As soon as the thumb was placed in the mouth, the film was turned off. When the thumb was removed from the mouth the film continued. He found this technique, at least during the experimental sessions, to be effective in the elimination of the undesirable behavior. In another study that illustrates more specifically the process of shaping, Isaacs, Thomas, and Goldiamond[87] shaped out vocal responses in a schizophrenic who had been mute for nineteen years. First, they placed a piece of chewing gum before the patient. When he noticed it, it was given to him and he was allowed to chew. Next, the therapist waited until the patient made lip movements before he was allowed to receive the gum. In succeeding weeks, gum was held up to the subject and he was instructed to say, "Gum." Obtaining the gum was contingent upon vocalizations that successively approximated the word *gum*. Thereafter, other vocal responses were shaped, then vocal responses were demanded in the presence of other persons. It was subsequently possible to get the patient to speak in group therapy sessions.

## Beyond Freedom and Dignity

Skinner's book *Beyond Freedom and Dignity* (1971) aroused considerable controversy, particularly among those who opposed his position as well as those who did not understand what he was talking about.[88] The work is a kind of social philosophy, an attempted to go beyond the laboratory and apply his ideas to a contemporary society. Skinner attempted to reinterpret many concepts that had previously been characteristically mentalistic in the light of a behavioristic psychology.

To begin with, Skinner suggested that in the effective solution of human problems one must apply some sort of technology. This is not a mechanical or physical technology, but a technology of behavior. Many people resist such an idea and prefer the notion of what Skinner called the "autonomous man," one who is a self-composed "inner man" free to do whatever the will dictates. This fiction of the "autonomous man" has its counterparts in many current concepts of the "self," particularly as found in the humanistic movement (see chap. 19).

However, Skinner maintained that we are the product of our genetic endowment and the external stimuli in our environment. If this is the case, a

---

[86]D. M. Baer, "Laboratory Control of Thumbsucking by the Withdrawal of Reinforcement," *Journal of the Experimental Analysis of Behavior*, Vol. 5 (1962), pp. 525–26.

[87]W. Isaacs, J. Thomas, and I. Goldiamond, "Shaping Vocal Responses in Mute Catatonic Schizophrenics," *Journal of Speech and Hearing Disorders*, Vol. 25 (1960), pp. 8–12.

[88]B. F. Skinner, *Beyond Freedom and Dignity* (New York: Alfred A. Knopf, 1971).

conception of control is a necessary part of the technology. As a determinist, Skinner suggested that earlier mystical ideas of freedom and dignity need to be either redefined or abandoned. Freedom really means to be free from aversive controls in our environment. But some kind of control is inevitable, so the control should be that of positive reinforcement. The old notion of a "sense of dignity" supposedly means what is attributed to an individual or what one attributes to oneself. When aversive controls are eliminated, the idea of "dignity" becomes irrelevant because in Skinner's thinking this kind of behavior had already been explained.

The key to a technology of behavior is to be found in contingencies of reinforcement. The objectives of these contingencies are to be found in three types of values or "goods": those things that have biological survival, those things that help others, those things that help a culture to survive.

In the evolution of a culture, those aspects that will survive are the ones that bring the individual under the fullest consequences of his or her behavior. Whenever we arrange the environment to affect others, we are engaging in control. What we need is to be clear about the means and objectives of our control. In speaking of control, Skinner did not deny the possibilities of self-control. If it is true that we are under the control of our environment, then self-control simply means that we arrange or rearrange these controlling environmental stimuli.[89]

> He (man) is indeed controlled by his environment, but we must remember that it is an environment of our own making. The evolution of a culture is a gigantic exercise in self-control. . . . We have not seen yet what man can make of man.

Even up to the time of his death, Skinner continued to lecture and write. His later books contained articles previously published in professional journals and magazines. There was nothing really new except his concern for a better psychological society. He had become more of a social philosopher than a psychologist, but as a true behaviorist, he continued to abandon concepts of mind and consciousness. He continued to be disturbed by the growth of cognitive psychology.

Although we can say that Skinnerian behaviorism is alive and well, it does not have the hold on American psychology that it had a decade or two ago. Operant conditioning apparatus is still being manufactured, and the Skinnerian journals still survive. To his great credit, a whole issue of the *American Psychologist,* the official organ of the American Psychological Association, was devoted to Skinner's essays on and studies of psychology.[90] Since that journal was founded in 1946, no other psychologist, living or dead, has had an entire issue devoted to his or her work.

---

[89]*Ibid.,* p. 215.
[90]*American Psychologist,* "Reflections on B. F. Skinner and Psychology," Vol. 47 (1992), No. 11.

Much to Skinner's dismay, cognitive psychology (see chap. 16) has continued to gain in popularity. It has brought back into psychology such concepts as mind and consciousness, with absolutely no hedging or apologies.

Psychology began in the late nineteenth century with Wundt's "consciousness" and James' "science of mental life," and now, more than a century later, it has come full circle, only with much more sophistication. As Empedocles, the ancient Greet philosopher, stated, "things are constantly changing."

## Criticisms of Skinner

1. One of the most frequently cited criticisms levied against Skinner and his followers has been their atheoretical or even anti-theoretical approach to the problems of psychology. At least with regard to experimentation, particularly in learning and with subhuman subjects, Skinner maintained a strict position of descriptive observation of whatever functional relationships he observed. He found no need for theory as "extra" explanations. However, theory is most crucial to science. What would Einstein have done without theory? Of course, the criticism is not entirely justified, since Skinner employed theory in his extrapolation of principles discovered in the laboratory to a wide variety of circumstances in the world of human activity at large. In *Science and Human Behavior*,[91] he discussed in detail the many applications to a variety of human endeavors. These have been mentioned earlier. In the final analysis, it depends on how one cares to define theory.

2. A second criticism concerns the limited nature of the behavior he chose to study, such as a bar press or a key peck. This is indeed a molecular approach to data analysis. All other aspects of the behavior of the organism have been largely ignored.

    Related to this criticism is the failure of the Skinnerians to attempt to deal with many other aspects of behavior that are psychological and particularly human in nature. Kantor, in an invited address to Division 25 of the American Psychological Association (the division of The Experimental Analysis of Behavior), otherwise known as the Skinnerian's division, states:[92]

    > I propose that TEAB (The Experimental Analysis of Behavior) should attempt to disclose the salient components of feeling and emotional behavior . . . the creative process of imagination as well as behavior called inventing, thinking, problem solving, and reasoning in whatever situation they are performed.

---

[91]B. F. Skinner, *Science and Human Behavior, op. cit.*

[92]J. R. Kantor, "An Analysis of the Experimental Analysis of Behavior," *Journal of the Experimental Analysis of Behavior*, Vol. 13 (1970), pp. 101–108, 105. Copyright 1970 by the Society for the Experimental Analysis of Behavior, Inc.

In criticizing Skinner and the whole TEAB movement, Kantor based his comments on Skinner's earlier approach, which involved a simple learning theory not intended to encompass the whole field of psychology. Thus, the use of a simple bit of behavior as the basic datum of psychology appears to be a gross oversimplification of the problem. However, at least in theory, Skinner attempted to broaden the scope of his system to include other aspects of psychology besides simple learning.

3. Skinner has been criticized for proposing a theory that is purely descriptive and not explanatory. This kind of criticism is levied by people who want to look for the roots of behavior in "inner causes." Skinner intentionally avoided references to physiological principles as explanations, whether they be involved in biological drives or in the nervous system. Skinner's "empty organism" is not appealing to those who feel the O (organism) must be taken into account to explain the whole picture of psychology. Thus, Skinner was very much of a nonreductionist.

4. The question arises as to the validity of extrapolating so freely from non-human experiments to the vast array of human behavior. Again, Kantor[93] suggests that the TEAB movement has put far too much stress on subhuman subjects. The criticism would have been more valid when Skinner and his co-workers limited themselves almost exclusively to the white rat and the pigeon. However, within the past fifteen years, the amount of careful research using operant techniques with human subjects has multiplied at an astonishing rate. The entire field of behavior modification is an example of this.

5. In taking the "empty organism" approach, in which behavior is entirely a function of environmental conditions and genetic endowment, his critics feel that Skinner ignored other biological participants in the determination of behavior. He ignored legitimate organismic conditions that participate in the psychological explanations. Such conditions as fatigue, glandular imbalance, or brain damage can limit behavioral possibilities. On the other hand, there are biological *advantages,* such as a healthy physique or better-than-normal eyesight or hearing,[94] that can improve behavioral possibilities.

6. Those who are inclined toward a cognitive approach—which includes intervening mental states such as ideas, cognitions, expectancies, or feelings—believe that these mental events interact with the environment and behavior to determine the final result. (See the following section on Bandura's social learning theory.)

7. Other criticisms levied against Skinner include his inadequate analysis of verbal behavior (see Chomsky, pp. 290–291) and his design for a culture

---

[93]*Ibid.,* pp. 101–108.
[94]Parker E. Lichtenstein, "Skinner's radical environmentalism," *Denison Journal of Biological Science,* Vol. 9 (1972).

(pp. 226–227), which his opponents consider to be antidemocratic and fascistic.[95]

## Contributions of Skinner

If most psychologists were asked to name four or five of the most eminent psychologists of the twentieth century, they would find it hard not to include Skinner's name in their list. His influence, which was great during the early forties, is far greater today. Many educated people outside the field of psychology recognize his name as being as familiar as that of Freud or Pavlov. No other system has two journals exclusively devoted to Skinnerian research.

Skinner developed a set of psychological principles, based not just on theory, but on rigorous and carefully controlled observation. Experimental demonstrations of the principles of operant conditioning have been developed in a variety of species, from cockroaches and goldfish to monkeys and humans. The importance of reinforcement as the basic principle of control has been demonstrated in a vast number of species. In all instances it works. Furthermore, a fixed interval schedule curve will look very similar whether the subject is a pigeon, a rat, a monkey, or a child working for candy.

As an imaginative and creative innovator, Skinner was perhaps second to none in psychology. Although Hull developed a highly sophisticated learning theory, the apparatus he used was traditional—the maze, the runway, and so forth. The Hullians even borrowed the "Skinner box" as an apparatus for their investigation. Early in his career, Skinner developed new forms of apparatus whereby the most precisely controlled experiments could be pursued. His influence on education, in the development of programmed learning and the teaching machine, shook up very traditional educators. Finally, although Skinner was not so personally involved in psychotherapy through behavior modification, this approach to the treatment of various psychological problems is a credit to Skinner in applying the principles he developed.

By his purely objective and anti-dualistic position, he, perhaps more than anyone, demonstrated that psychology can be a science—a science whose methodology and precise control of relevant variables is comparable to any of the natural sciences.

---

## Albert Bandura (1925–      )

Bandura was born in Mundara, Alberta, Canada, in 1925. He received his B.A. at the University of British Columbia and his Ph.D. from the University of Iowa. Since 1953 he has taught at Stanford University, and in 1974 he served as president of the American Psychological Association.

---

[95]*Ibid.*

He has developed a theory founded upon a behavioristic position that stresses social learning as the main basis for behavior acquisition. His research has been closely tied with behavior modification and, in particular, modeling. His first books, *Adolescent Aggression*[96] (1959) and *Social Learning and Personality Development*[97] (1963), were written in collaboration with Richard Walters. A more recent work, *Social Learning Theory*[98] (1977), gives the most complete statement of his theory.

Bandura believes human behavior can be best understood as a reciprocal interaction between behavioral, cognitive, and environmental influences. In this assertion, he stresses the role of environmental influences in psychological development, but at the same time he believes that our environment is of our own making. Further, there are certain cognitions, which can also act as causes of behavior. Here we have a "soft" behaviorism that allows for the mental factors. Thus, there are certain internal events, such as thoughts and expectations, that interrelate and regulate each other. This contrasts with the "hard," or radical behaviorism of B. F. Skinner, who allowed for private events but insisted that they must be interpreted as behavior and not some intervening mental processes.

Observational learning, or modeling, plays a key role in personality development. Bandura believes the vast majority of our behavior is acquired by copying what others do. The behavior need not be actually performed in order for learning to take place. Simply observing the behavior of others and its consequences is sufficient for new behavior to be learned. For example, a child can become aggressive, cooperative, or competitive simply by watching other children engaging in those behaviors. Likewise, the modeling can occur in symbolic form, as when people acquire behavior by watching television or seeing a movie. Bandura has been much concerned with violence, as seen in movies and television, and its effects on the behavior of our youth.

He does not deny that behavior can be maintained and strengthened by external reinforcing stimuli, whether they are in the form of food, drink, praise, or approval, but he goes further in stressing the importance of *vicarious reinforcement*. Using his example, a waitress in a restaurant observes another being generously tipped for efficient and polite service. This observation can increase the possibility that the observing waitress will do likewise. Observing the vicarious consequences of another's behavior will play an important part in strengthening the behavior of the observer. The vicarious consequences of watching others being rewarded will incline a person to model what he or she has seen. The converse situation also holds: observing others being punished will inhibit the observer's repeating the punished act. Observational learning occurs primarily through our cognitions. We project ourselves into situations that we observe and then think about the consequences. Likewise, certain char-

---

[96] Albert Bandura and R. H. Walters, *Adolescent Aggression* (New York: Ronald Press, 1959).

[97] Albert Bandura and R. H. Walters, *Social Learning and Personality Development* (New York: Holt, Rinehart and Winston, 1963).

[98] Albert Bandura, *Social Learning Theory* (Englewood Cliffs, N.J.: Prentice-Hall, 1977).

acteristics of the model will affect behavior. If the model has high status, is attractive, or is similar to the observer in age and sex, the probability that modeling will occur is increased.

Besides using external and vicarious reinforcements, the observer can engage in *self-reinforcement.* An example of this is the feeling of satisfaction or pride one has in a job well done, even if nobody else has told one so (external reinforcement) or in observing another being thus reinforced (vicarious reinforcement). It is characteristic of humans to develop certain standards of conduct. By exceeding these standards, people reinforce themselves in the absence of external rewards. Likewise, in doing a mediocre job, we can perceive our action as substandard and consequently punish ourselves, possibly by experiencing feelings of guilt. This concept has some relationship to the Freudian notion of the superego, which rewards or punishes the ego for what it does or thinks.

These self-reinforcing systems are acquired by the same learning principles that are involved in learning other types of behavior. Unlike some other behavioristic approaches, Bandura believes in the self-regulatory aspects derived from our own behavior. This involves self-observation, self-judgment of one's own performance, self-evaluation, and self-response.

In *self-observation,* we note the quality and proficiency of our own performances. The criteria we set for ourselves depend on the kinds of actions we are performing. Good golfers note the accuracy of their strokes, and good writers note the correctness of their grammatical constructions.

*Self-judgment* depends on the internal standards we have set for ourselves as poor, average, good, or excellent. In the beginning, we do not expect as much of ourselves as we do after we have achieved greater proficiency.

*Self-response* typically involves *self-evaluation.* In a sense, we are criticizing ourselves. If we do it well, we feel good. Doing it poorly brings on self-punishment ("I did a rotten job").

Finally, Bandura believes that self-reinforcement or self-gratification can be delayed or postponed in favor of a larger and more valuable one in the future. Thus, rather than spending money on an immediate pleasure, we can postpone the act by saving up more money for a greater pleasure. For example, we could eat out at an average restaurant once a week, but we might prefer to save our money and go to an elegant dining establishment only once a month.

Much of the research available involves verification of the concept of modeling. An experiment by Bandura, Ross, and Ross[99] demonstrates the role of vicarious reinforcement in modeling. In this study, children were shown television films in which they observed other children as models exhibiting both verbal and physical aggression. One group saw children's aggressive behavior being positively reinforced, another group saw the models' aggressive behavior being punished, and a third group saw the models' aggressive behavior being neither reinforced nor punished. After seeing the films, the children were

---

[99]Albert Bandura, D. Ross, and S. A. Ross, "Vicarious Reinforcement and Imitative Learning," in W. A. Staats, ed., *Human Learning* (New York: Holt, Rinehart and Winston, 1964).

placed in a play situation in which their own aggressive behavior was rated by the experimenters. Results indicated that the group that saw aggression being positively reinforced showed much more aggression than the group that saw it punished.

Bandura's approach is similar in many ways to the operant conditioning approach of B. F. Skinner. Both stress the significance of learning in psychological development through the use of positive reinforcement. Besides emphasizing external reinforcement, as Skinner typically did, Bandura adds the possibilities of vicarious and self-reinforcement. Although Skinner allowed for modeling, he placed the largest thrust on learning by doing, while Bandura believes that the vast majority of human behavior is learned by observation or by watching others perform. As mentioned earlier, Bandura is considered a "soft" behaviorist, because he makes use of internal causes in cognitive processes. Skinner's "hard" behaviorism gives no credence to inner causes.

In his approach, Bandura generally opposes psychoanalysis or other neo-Freudian approaches that make use of numerous hypothetical constructs, such as libido, psychic energy, or cathexes.

Unlike some other theories, such as Freud's, Bandura's theory is supported by a good bit of careful experimental research.

Like the psychodynamic and other behavioristic approaches, Bandura's approach stresses the longitudinal, or developmental, processes in behavior acquisition.

## Contributions of Bandura

Bandura has proposed a "new" kind of behaviorism that places great emphasis on the role of observational learning. His supporters believe that, because so much of our learning is by observation, this important aspect of the learning process has been neglected by other behaviorists. His addition of the concepts of vicarious reinforcement and self-reinforcement gives a more complete picture of the complex reinforcement process than theories that rely solely on external reinforcement to explain behavior.

Bandura's theory is not just theory but is substantiated by experimental studies that support his contentions.

Those who favor a more cognitive approach feel that Bandura tells a more complete story about the causes of behavior. Our behavior is not only the result of antecedent environmental conditions but also is affected by the intervening cognitions, which must also be taken into account.

## Criticisms of Bandura

Most of the criticisms of Bandura come from the "hard" behaviorists, who put no credence in intervening variables, such as cognitions or expectations. These are labeled as "mentalistic" constructs that have no reference to events occurring in space and time. The more traditional behaviorists feel that behavior can be best understood in terms of the functional relationships between the antecedent environmental events and the resulting behavior of the organism. A reference to intervening processes as "mental stuff" adds nothing to our understanding of behavior.

The traditional behaviorists feel that Bandura has deserted the cause of scientific behaviorism in favor of the more cognitive approach to psychology. Bandura can be considered a "cognitive behaviorist." For more reference to Bandura's cognitive approach see also chap. 16 on cognitive psychology, pp. 297–298.

## Suggested Further Readings

Bandura, A., *Social Learning Theory.* Englewood Cliffs, New Jersey: Prentice-Hall, 1977. The most complete statement of Bandura's theoretical position. There are plenty of good examples and experiments.

Bandura, A., *Principles of Behavior Modification.* New York: Holt, Rinehart and Winston, 1969. One of the first books to survey methods of behavior modification. Studies of modeling as a means of behavior change dominate the work.

Bandura, A., *Social Foundations of Thought and Action: A Social Cognitive Theory.* Englewood Cliffs, New Jersey: Prentice-Hall, 1986.

Broadbent, D. E., *Behavior: A Survey of Twentieth Century Behavioristic Psychology.* New York: Basic Books, 1963. Just what the title implies, but it demonstrates that despite its differences, behaviorism is very much alive today.

Estes, et al., *Modern Learning Theory.* New York: Appleton-Century-Crofts, 1954, chs. 1, 3, and 5. A critical evaluation of three behavioristic theories of learning: C. L. Hull by Sigmund Koch, B. F. Skinner by W. S. Verplanck, and Edwin R. Guthrie by C. G. Mueller and W. N. Schoenfeld.

Ferster, C. B., and Perrett, M. C., *Behavior Principles.* New York: Appleton-Century-Crofts, 1968. An exposition for beginning students of basic Skinnerian psychology.

Guthrie, Edwin R., *Psychology of Learning,* rev. ed. New York: Harper and Bros., 1952. Guthrie's basic position with many interesting anecdotes.

Hilgard, E. R., and Bower, G. H., *Theories of Learning,* 3rd ed. New York: Appleton-Century-Crofts, 1966, chs. 4, 5, and 6. Good discussions of the theories of Guthrie, Hull, and Skinner, particularly with regard to learning. Much experimental support is presented.

Hull, C. L., *Principles of Behavior.* New York: Appleton-Century-Crofts, 1943. Not easy going, but the best place to begin if one wants to read Hull as a primary source.

Hull, C. L., *Essentials of Behavior.* New Haven: Yale University Press, 1951.

Hull, C. L., *A Behavior System: An Introduction to Behavior Theory Concerning the Individual Organism.* New Haven: Yale University Press, 1952. The whole system, but tough going.

Kantor, J. R., and Smith, N. W., *The Science of Psychology: An Interbehavioral Survey.* Chicago: The Principia Press, 1975. A revision of Kantor's earlier *A Survey of the Science of Psychology* (1933). The book is an introduction to

Kantor's basic system aimed at the undergraduate reader. For one who knows nothing about Kantor's system, this is the place to begin.

Skinner, B. F., *Science and Human Behavior.* New York: The Macmillan Co., 1953. Skinner takes his psychology out of the operant conditioning laboratory and applies it to a variety of problems encountered by individuals and society. Meant as a basic text for Skinner students.

Skinner, B. F., "Behaviorism at Fifty." *Science,* Vol. 140 (1963), pp. 951–58. Skinner discusses the evolution of behaviorism from Watson's time to his own position.

Skinner, B. F., *Beyond Freedom and Dignity.* New York: Alfred A. Knopf, Inc., 1971. Skinner hits the best seller list with a short but highly controversial book in which he attempts to explode previous notions of value, freedom, and dignity. Basic Skinnerian principles are substituted for what Skinner considers outmoded ideas.

# CHAPTER

# 14

# *Gestalt Psychology*

In 1912, the same year that Watson gave the lectures at Columbia which set behaviorism in motion, Max Wertheimer[1] published a series of experiments in Germany on apparent motion. These experiments were to serve as the basis for an entirely new kind of psychology which was much at variance with the existing psychologies of the time and those that were to evolve alongside it. This new school took on the name *Gestalt,* a term which has no literal translation in English although the words "form," "shape," or "configuration" have most frequently been used as the nearest translations. In Köhler's book, *Gestalt Psychology,*[2] he noted that the term was used in two different ways in German. The first denoted the shape or form as a property of perceived objects. The second sense referred to the more concrete form of an object, such as a triangle. Thus, we could refer, in the first sense, to the attribute of triangularity and in the second, to the triangle itself. The early contributions of Gestalt psychology were in the field of perception, particularly visual, although auditory perception was not ignored. Later, it spread its principles to the fields of learning, thinking, and memory, so that by the mid-1930s Gestalt psychology was a well-established system of psychology.

## Antecedents

Like many of the other schools which began in the early twentieth century, Gestalt psychology has had a rich heritage. Many names and ideas could be mentioned, but we shall try to limit ourselves to the most important ones.

---

[1]Max Wertheimer, "Experimentelle Studien über das Sehen von Bewegung," *Zeitschrift für Psychologie,* Vol. 61 (1912), pp. 161–265.
[2]Wolfgang Köhler, *Gestalt Psychology* (New York: Liveright, 1929).

## Immanuel Kant

A number of writers on systematic psychology have ignored the contributions of Kant, but as the reader will recall in chapter 4, Kant's main influence on psychology was on the Gestalt movement (see p. 57). In 1781 he published one of his most important works, *Critique of Pure Reason.*[3] Kant agreed with Locke and the other empiricists that knowledge came from sensations, but said that our perception did not give us knowledge of the things themselves except as they appeared to us as phenomena. Things themselves might exist, but we perceived them only in the way our minds were capable of perceiving them. Thus, there was a sharp difference between the perception of the object and the object itself. We perceived phenomena only in a manner determined by our minds. The mind was not like a photographic camera; it ordered its perceptions. Time and space existed inherently in the human mind. Without a mind to perceive it, the entire corporal world would vanish. Thus, wrote Kant, the world as perceived involved the sensory perception of the object and the *a priori* forms of the mind's function.

Two points from Kant are represented as basic tenets of Gestalt psychology. First, the world as we perceive it was not the same as the real world. Second, certain of our perceptions of objects came naturally as primitive organizations quite independent of learning. This was the nativism of Kant that we referred to in chapter 4 as one of the themes in the history of psychology which has influenced modern thinking.

## John Stuart Mill

We will recall in chapter 4 that although Mill was an associationist, he had developed the idea of a mental chemistry in which ideas were not merely the sum of the individual elements, but could evolve into a new whole which was more than the sum of its parts.

## Franz Brentano and Carl Stumpf

Discussed earlier in relation to structuralism, these men had opposed the idea of a passive mind that merely received experiences, and had stressed the *act* of perceiving or sensing rather than the analysis of the various elements. This anti-analytical attitude has been firmly held by the Gestaltists.

## Ernst Mach (1838–1916)

Mach offered a more direct influence. Although he was a physicist, he insisted that sensations served as the basis for all science. To the simple summation of sensations he added the possibility of a *space-form* dimension as illustrated in a triangle or any other kind of geometrical figure, as well as a *time-form* dimension

---

[3]Immanuel Kant, *The Critique of Pure Reason* (New York: The Macmillan Co., 1929).

as heard in a melody. He considered these space- and time-forms to be independent of their elements. A triangle could be blue or white, large or small, but it still retained its quality of being a triangle. Likewise, a melody was the same melody regardless of the key in which it was played, and it did not lose its time-form dimension in the transposition. The implications of the concept of "form" for Gestalt psychology are considered in the term itself, and it will be elaborated shortly.

### Christian von Ehrenfels (1859–1932)

As a philosopher Ehrenfels elaborated on Mach's ideas. He believed that there were qualities in experience which went beyond those generally recognized in our sensations. These he called the *Gestaltqualitäten* or form-qualities. In a melody, there was a temporal pattern that was independent of the individual sensational tones which were the elements out of which it was composed. The same was true for visual form in a manner similar to that stated by Mach. For Ehrenfels and the Austrian Graz school, the problem of form in itself was an element, but not merely an element of sensation. It existed as a new element created by the mind to be added to the sensation elements. The new elements were present in the mind but were not in physical things. Actually, Mach and Ehrenfels still retained the elemental sensational position. They merely added more elements. Although they obviously had an influence on early Gestalt psychology, the early proponents denied it, since Mach and Ehrenfels were still thinking in an additive manner as had Wundt and Titchener. However, the concept of the "form quality" became integrated into Gestalt psychology.

## The Founding of Gestalt Psychology

### Max Wertheimer (1880–1943)

Wertheimer was the official founder since he did the initial experiment, although Wolfgang Köhler (1887–1967) and Kurt Koffka (1887–1941), who served as subjects, can certainly be considered co-founders. Wertheimer took his degree in philosophy in 1904 under Külpe at Würzburg. In 1910 he arrived at the University of Frankfurt after having attended lectures by Ehrenfels.

Koffka and Köhler had received their degrees at Berlin in 1908 and 1909, respectively. They were already assistants at the Psychological Institute at Frankfurt.

In the year 1910, Wertheimer happened to be traveling from Vienna to Germany by train for a holiday. When the train made a stop at Frankfurt, he bought a stroboscope, which in those days was a toy used by children. The stroboscope is an instrument that allows still pictures to be exposed alternately so that apparent movement is perceived. This principle is the same one on which motion pictures operate. From Wertheimer's initial observation, he got the idea which was to be the beginning of Gestalt psychology, namely that what we perceive does not necessarily conform to what actually happens in the real world.

Wertheimer's initial experiment[4] involved an apparatus called a tachisto-scope. By means of it, visual stimuli could be presented for any given period of time, long or short, and in succession. Wertheimer presented two different vertical lines in separate places on the face of the apparatus—one on the right side, the other on the left side. Each presentation alternated with the other and was separated by an interval of time. Wertheimer found that if the interval of time between the exposures was as long as one second, his subjects saw first one still line on the left, then another still line on the right. This perception corresponded to the physical event. As the time interval between presentations was shortened, his subjects began to see something moving from one position to the other. At one-fifteenth of a second, the subjects saw not two lines but a single line appearing to move across the screen from left to right. However, with even shorter intervals the motion became less apparent, and at one-thir-tieth of a second, his subjects reported no movement but merely saw two lines standing still side by side.

Variations of the experiment involved a vertical line followed by a horizon-tal line. With the appropriate time interval, the line tended to move down and back up, again apparent motion. In another experiment, he presented a vertical line followed by horizontal lines both at the right and left of the middle ver-tical. In this instance, the movement appeared in both directions, just as in a motion picture two figures can be seen to move in opposite directions. These experiments were published in 1912, and the illusion became known as the Phi phenomenon. This was an important discovery for Gestalt psychology. Of course, the illusion of apparent movement had been known before Wertheimer's experiment, and a number of explanations had been given to account for it. Wundt had explained it in terms of movements of the eyes, but Wertheimer's experiment, where the lines moved in opposite directions, ruled this out since even both eyes could not move in two directions at once.

Another explanation had been that one merely inferred movement. Wert-heimer pointed out that at certain time exposures one merely saw two figures alternating, and at faster exposures the figures appeared simultaneously again without movement. Why not infer movement under these circumstances? Wertheimer's explanation seemed to be that the movement actually took place in the brain (see Isomorphism, pp. 244–248).

## Implications of the Phi Phenomenon for Gestalt Psychology

For Wertheimer, the apparent movement seen in his experiment did not cor-respond to the physical event of two lines flashing back and forth. In other

---

[4]Max Wertheimer, *op. cit.*

words, what his subjects saw was something different from what actually happened. A new interpretation of the basic nature of sensation was necessary. The explanation by Ehrenfels and the *Gestaltqualitäten* was insufficient.

**The "Whole" Attitude.** In the experiments, the subjects were perceiving a whole or Gestalt rather than a succession of isolated sensory elements. This perception of the whole was inherent in the sensory process, for the whole was a primary and unanalyzable experience. The whole, then, was *not* the sum of its parts. This became a very basic tenet for Gestalt psychology. The Gestalt psychologists objected to the analysis into single, simple elements. If there were parts, they were to be dependent on the whole. Wertheimer considered how a melody was heard as a single, whole experience. If one broke it down into its single notes, something was lost. The melody stood as a whole, not analyzable into its single tones.

**The Phenomenological Field.** In perception, one experienced a field or environment that would be destroyed through elementalistic analysis. This did not mean that the Gestalt psychologists denied any form of analysis. If an analysis were made, it had to be meaningful to the whole. In 1935 Koffka[5] suggested that psychology should not be regarded as merely the study of responses to stimuli, but rather as a reaction governed by a field of interacting forces which was self-organized into definite patterns. These patterns, of course, were capable of changing. The field as we perceived it (Koffka also called it the behavioral environment) was a phenomenological one. It was not merely an assemblage of individual stimuli but was organized; and our actions were governed by the organized field, not merely the specific stimuli in it. Thus, psychology became the study of the whole *immediate* experience. The early studies primarily involved perception, but Gestalt psychologists later expanded their principles to learning, thinking, and memory (see below). Their methods involved an emphasis on introspection—a more naive kind of introspection and not the same as the trained introspectionism of the structuralists—and on experimentation. Some of these methods will be described in the sections that follow.

## The Protests of Gestalt Psychology Against Other Schools

Certainly the development of Gestalt psychology was not unique among psychological schools arising at the time. Before continuing with more of the basic principles of Gestalt psychology, we should pause to see what objections Gestalt psychology had to the ideas which preceded it and to those which were evolving at the same time.

---

[5]Kurt Koffka, *Principles of Gestalt Psychology* (New York: Harcourt, Brace and Co., 1935).

**_Elementalism._** Since Gestalt psychology took a firm stand, as we have already seen, on the uniqueness of the whole as not being the sum of its parts, a strong objection was raised against a kind of psychology that would analyze its data into elementary parts. The perception as we experienced it was not merely a core of sensations or a clustering of elements. The experience could not be broken down into its individual elements. For the Gestaltists, such an analysis ignored the situation as it really was. In their attempt at analysis, such systems as structuralism had altered or destroyed the full and unique character of the experience.

**_Association._** A second objection was aimed directly at those systems that depended on the principle of association. Wertheimer referred to the bonds of association used both by the structuralists and by Thorndike as the "bundle hypothesis." The Gestalt psychologists felt that association was merely an artificial means of lumping elements together. Since experience (and behavior) consisted of a whole or was molar in nature (as opposed to molecular), it needed no principle of connection to bind the parts together. It followed that this general principle used by the structuralists and associationists had to be rejected.

**_The Constancy Hypothesis._** The constancy hypothesis held that there was a one-to-one relationship between the physical and the mental event. This was expressed in the psychophysical parallelism of the structuralists. According to early Gestalt experimentation, this simply was not the case in the Phi phenomenon. A rectangular table was judged as a rectangle even though we viewed it from various angles. We still called it a rectangle regardless of the fact that the image given from viewing it from various angles was not rectangular. Similarly, in optical illusions, what we perceived was not the same as what was there physically.

**_S-R Psychology._** As might be expected, just as the Gestalt psychologists had objected to elementalism and associationism, so they were diametrically opposed to a theory that broke down its subject matter into simple and discrete stimulus-response units, typical of Thorndike and the early behaviorists. In a further elaboration of the Gestalt principle, we shall note with considerable interest how such diverse schools could exist at the same time alongside each other.

Another objection that Gestalt psychology had to S-R psychologies such as behaviorism was the latter's denial of consciousness. For Gestalt, psychology dealt with both behavior and consciousness. Because of its strong emphasis on the study of perception, psychology had to be very concerned with the immediate experience (consciousness), but not in the manner suggested by the structuralists.

Finally, the Gestalt psychologists objected to the kind of physiology used by other schools when physiology was involved in its explanatory principles. Traditionally, the nervous system had been treated as a complex series of connected neurological units. Neurological circuits ran from designated points of stimulation along definite patterns in the nervous system. By analogy, the nervous system could be conceived of as operating like a telephone system. The neurological explanations of the Gestalt psychologists will be elaborated later, in the section on isomorphism. Its conception was more of a patterning of cohesive and restraining forces which gave a picture in the brain, like a map, of whatever was perceived.

## Principles of Organization

In an article published in 1923,[6] Wertheimer set forth a group of principles as illustrations of how the perceptual field could be organized. It should be remembered that these ways of organization were quite natural or native and often have been referred to as "primitive organization." Generally, the Gestalt psychologists have deemphasized the role of learning in perception, as stated by Köhler in 1947.[7] The grouping seen will tend to be quite natural (nativism again).

### Principle of Proximity

Here, elements which were close together either in time or space would tend to be grouped together, as seen in the following illustration:

OO        OO        OO        OO

In this example we perceive groups of two's, instead of some other random order.

### Principle of Similarity

Elements that were alike in their structure would tend to be perceived together, unless there were other factors in the field overriding them.

XXX    OOOXXXOOO    XXXOOOXXX

The X's tend to be grouped together, and the O's appear in a similar fashion.

---

[6]Max Wertheimer, "Untersuchungen zur Lehre von der Gestalt II," *Psychologische Forschung,* Vol. 4 (1923), pp. 301–50.
[7]Wolfgang Köhler, *Gestalt Psychology: An Introduction to the New Concepts in Modern Psychology* (New York: Liveright, 1947).

## Principle of Objective Set

If one saw a particular kind of organization and got a mental "set" for it, it might be possible to continue to see that organization even though the stimulus arrangements might be slightly altered. Consider the following illustration:

OO   OO   OO   OO   OOOOOOOO

In looking at the O's at the left-hand grouping, they obviously group by proximity. As one continues to look to the right where the O's become more evenly spaced, it might still be possible to group them as one did in the first series.

## Principle of Continuity (Principle of Direction or Good Continuation)

According to this principle, the stimuli that have continuity with each other are perceived as flowing in the same direction or following the same pattern, and will be seen as a figure. In the illustration following, the straight line and the wavy line are perceived as continuous, even though one is broken by the other.

## Principle of Closure

When certain parts of our perceptual organization were left out, there was a tendency to "fill in the gaps," in other words, to make the Gestalt complete. If a figure were shown in which the lines were incomplete, as in certain sketches or water color paintings, the perceiver was inclined to complete it.

## Principle of Prägnanz

Actually, closure was merely a special case of the more general law of Prägnanz—"good form" or "good Gestalt." If one were to draw a star in which the lines were not completely connected, one would still tend to see it as a star instead of as some other odd geometrical figure. One would connect the lines at the five points because that made the best form. The same would hold true for a circle or a square in which the actual lines were broken (see Fig. 5).

## Principle of Figure and Ground

This was one of the most important principles of "primitive organization." It stated that any perception would tend to organize itself into a figure that stood out from its background. An instructor sitting at a desk in front of a class would be perceived as the figure, and other objects such as the blackboard or window in the rear would constitute the ground. In a reversible figure (see

**FIGURE 5**  *Incomplete Figures.*

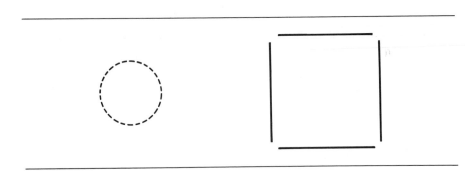

Fig. 6), the figure and the ground would tend to shift back and forth as one continued to fixate upon them. In the illustration, one might first see two faces opposite each other, then one's perception would shift to see a vase. The relationship between figure and ground can also be seen in the circle illusion (see Fig. 7).

## Principle of Isomorphism

To understand the principle of isomorphism as it relates to Gestalt psychology, we must refer to Wertheimer's first experiment with the Phi phenomenon. When two lines were presented in alternation, at a certain point, rather than seeing the lines alternating, one perceived actual movement—one line shifting back and forth. Since the perceptual field of movement was not the same as what happened physically, how were we to explain the phenomenon? The reader will recall (p. 239) that the eye movement and inference theories were ruled out. Consequently, the actual movement had to take place in the brain field. For the Gestalt psychologists, the isomorphic principle assumed a one-to-one relationship between what one actually perceived and what happened in the cortex of the brain. The movement thus took place *in the brain.* As an analogy, Woodworth[8] suggested the relationship between a map and the country it represented. Although the two were not the same, there was an identity between them. The perceptual field and the physiological brain field also showed this direct relationship.

Just how did this take place? To understand what was happening in the brain field, one had to assume that there were both cohesive and restraining forces. The cohesive forces were tendencies to excitation of nerve impulses on the cerebral cortex which attracted each other if there was nothing to interfere

---

[8]Robert S. Woodworth, *Contemporary Schools of Psychology,* 2nd ed. (New York: The Ronald Press Co., 1948).

**FIGURE 6**  *Reversible Figure.*

with them. Restraining forces, on the other hand, would prevent the cohesive forces. A neurological movement was prevented because there had been some other stimulation present.

In Gestalt psychology, the concept that the brain could be thought of as a dynamic field was opposed to what might be called a machine theory, stated earlier. In the latter, the nervous system was a set of isolated conductors. Neural impulses traveled from one point to another according to fixed pathways. In Gestalt theory, the perception could not be obtained by such a rigid arrangement. Instead, they presumed that patterns of shifting forces occurred.

Was there any experimental evidence to support the isomorphic principle? The evidence that had been presented was quite meager and indirect. However, we shall cite a few studies used by the Gestalt psychologists to support their assumption. Köhler and Held[9] observed the electro-encephalograms (EEG, brain waves) from the visual area of the brain. When a test object was moved across the subject's visual field, some changes in the encephalographic record occurred. However, one should realize that the EEG is a very gross index of

[9]Wolfgang Köhler and R. Held, "The Cortical Correlate of Pattern Vision," *Science,* Vol. 110 (1949), pp. 414–19.

**FIGURE 7** *The Circle Illusion.* The two circles in the center of each figure are the same size, although the center circle on the left appears smaller.

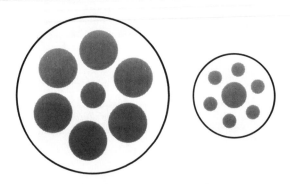

brain activity, and there were no direct signs that an outline occurred in terms of a cortical figure.

Köhler and Wallach[10] implied the possibility that prolonged fixation on certain figures caused a "satiation" phenomenon in the brain. If one fixated on black squares for as long as thirty-five seconds, the cortical areas so stimulated by the black squares presumably became satiated. Consequently, when one shifted the fixation to white squares, they tended to become distorted (smaller, for example) and also tended to shift. Similarly, when a curved line was fixated upon, and then one shifted one's glance to a straight line, the line would continue to look curved. Köhler and Fishback[11] found that illusions such as the Müller-Lyer (Fig. 8) might be made to disappear because of the same satiation effect. As the visual area of the cortex became satiated, the figures tended to "escape" by changing phenomenologically, as well as cortically.

The satiation phenomenon could be further understood if one assumed that parts of the cerebral cortex became polarized with direct currents as a result of the continued stimulation from the visual receptors. Consequently, increasing resistance occurred in these areas. When a new stimulation occurred in the cortex as one shifted to a new figure, the cortical currents tended to flow into the less satiated areas where there was lower resistance. The same explanation was given for the reversible figure (see Fig. 6). When the cortex became satiated

[10]Wolfgang Köhler and H. Wallach, "Figural After-Effects: An Investigation of Visual Processes," *Proceedings of the American Philosophical Society,* Vol. 88 (1944), pp. 269–357.

[11]Wolfgang Köhler and J. Fishback, "The Distortion of the Müller-Lyer Illusion in Repeated Trials, I. An Examination of Two Theories," *Journal of Experimental Psychology,* Vol. 40 (1950), pp. 267–91.

**FIGURE 8**    *The Müller-Lyer Illusion.* The two horizontal lines are equal in length, although the one on the right appears longer. According to Gestalt theory, one will naturally perceive this, even though one "knows" they are the same.

with continued fixation, the first figure escaped by changing into the second—for example, from seeing a vase to seeing two profiles.

***The Mind-Body Problem.*** Isomorphism, then, was the solution to the mind-body problem. It was a parallelism, but not the *psychophysical parallelism* of the structuralists, which had presumed a one-to-one relationship between the physical and the mental events. For the Gestalt psychologists, it became a *psycho-physiological parallelism* between the *phenomenological* (perceived or mental) field and the activity in the brain field. The picture created by the cohesive and restraining forces ran parallel to the mental. There was, of course, still a third field—that of the real physical world or geographical field. In many cases, as we have seen in the illusion of apparent movement, this did not necessarily correspond to the phenomenological.

This discrepancy was illustrated in a well-known quote from Koffka.[12]

> On a winter evening amidst a driving snowstorm a man on horseback arrived at an inn, happy to have reached shelter after hours of riding over the windswept plain on which the blanket of snow had covered all paths and landmarks. The landlord who came to the door viewed the stranger with surprise and asked him whence he came. The man pointed in the direction straight away from the inn, whereupon the landlord, in a tone of awe and wonder, said: "Do you know that you have ridden across the Lake of Constance?" At which the rider dropped stone dead at his feet.
>
> In what environment, then, did the behavior of the stranger take place? The Lake of Constance. Certainly, because it is the true proposition that he rode across it. And yet, this was not the whole truth, for the fact that there was a frozen lake and not ordinarily solid ground did not affect the behavior in the slightest. . . There is a second sense to the word environment according to which our horseman did not ride across the lake at all, but across an ordinarily

---

[12]Kurt Koffka, *Principles of Gestalt Psychology* (New York: Harcourt Brace Jovanovich, Inc., 1935), pp. 27–28, and (London: Routledge & Kegan Paul Ltd., 1935).

snowswept plain. His behavior was a riding-over-a-plain, but not a riding-over-a-lake.

## Learning

According to Gestalt theory, learning is a cognitive phenomenon. In the learning process, there is a perceptual reorganization of the field. After learning has occurred, one sees the situation in a new light.

### Insight

When first faced with a problem, the organism ponders several possible solutions. When learning occurs and a solution is found, the organism has gained *insight.* In the presolution period, an organism will set up a number of "hypotheses," or possibilities for solving the problem. In some ways, this stage resembles Thorndike's "trial and error" learning. However, once the solution has been reached, insight occurs and learning is sudden, rather than gradual. Typically, once the solution is learned, on further trials the organism will proceed immediately to the solution without any further random behavior.

In 1913 Köhler was appointed director of the anthropoid station at Tenerife in the Canary Islands. He was confined there because of World War I. However, from his studies with apes, in particular, came his famous book, *The Mentality of Apes,*[13] in which many of his studies were reported. In one experiment to illustrate insightful learning, Köhler used a dog in a simple detour problem. The dog was brought into a field enclosed by a wall that contained a length of fence. Food was placed directly before the dog on the other side of the fence where the food could be seen but not reached. The dog had to move away from the fence and explore the enclosure until it discovered a door, through which the dog could pass, in order to get out and retrieve the food on the other side (see Fig. 9). In the beginning there was considerable random behavior. Then, quite suddenly, the dog "saw" the opening and rather quickly ran through the door on the side and around to where the food was placed.

Perhaps Köhler's most important experiments involved chimpanzees. Usually, the chimp was confined in a barred cage. In one experiment a banana was placed outside the cage, but at a distance too great for the chimp to seize it directly with its hand. When a string was tied to one end of the banana and the other end of the string was placed on the ground beside the cage, the animal almost immediately took it and pulled in the banana. This so-called "single string" problem was not difficult to solve. But, if several strings were laid on the ground, only one of which was attached to the banana, the chimp would

---

[13]Wolfgang Köhler, *The Mentality of Apes* (New York: Harcourt, Brace and Co., 1925).

**FIGURE 9**  *Köhler's Detour Problem.*

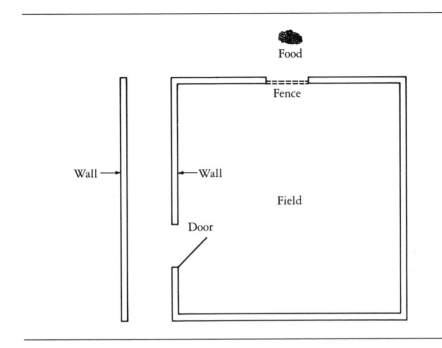

often pull the wrong strings. However, once the animal caught on to the problem (gained insight), on further trials it immediately selected the correct string.

As in the "single string" problem, the chimp quickly learned to reach a banana suspended from the ceiling by climbing on a box which enabled the chimp to reach it. But, when two boxes were required—one to be placed on top of the other in order to reach the banana—the problem became more difficult, and in most cases assistance was needed.

One of the most difficult problems solved by Köhler's most intelligent ape, named Sultan, was the jointed stick problem. Two bamboo sticks, neither of which was long enough to reach the banana, were presented to the chimp, but they could be joined end on end by fitting one into the other. Then the stick would be long enough to reach the banana. In the beginning, Sultan did a good deal of useless angling with the single sticks, but to no avail. Eventually, when by chance the chimp happened to join them together, it immediately was able to take the now-longer stick and pull in the fruit. In this case, the insight came later. What amazed Köhler was that on the following day, when the same problem was presented, the animal immediately found the solution which on the previous day had been so difficult to solve. In other words, Sultan had remembered.

All chimps were not as bright as Sultan. They failed to solve certain problems. For Köhler, the apes were not able to form the right Gestalt—that is, see the appropriate relationship.

Köhler considered insight to be a rather sudden mastery of a problem. It did not tend to be a gradual improvement with practice.

## Transposition

Other aspects of insight involved good retention and what the Gestalt psychologists called *transposition*, or "transfer," which involves learning a principle in one situation and applying it in another. What is carried over, however, is a "whole," or Gestalt, and not an identical element, as proposed by Thorndike.

One of Köhler's earliest studies on transposition involved chickens. It was rather simple and straightforward, but it brought the Gestalt principles into the field of learning. He presented to the hens two papers of different shades of gray on which grain was scattered. If they pecked at the grain on the darker of the two, they were permitted to swallow it, but if they pecked on the lighter shade, they were driven away. It took hundreds of trials, but the hens eventually learned the discrimination, to peck at grain only on the darker shade of paper. In the next step, Köhler presented his *original* dark gray paper along with an even darker gray, instead of the original lighter one. In the second series, as a rule the hens pecked again at the *darker* of the two and not on the one they had originally learned to peck. This indicated that they had reacted to the whole situation, and a Gestalt had been formed. The principle was pecking at the darker of the two and not the same one they had originally learned to peck on. They had not learned a specific elemental response but had learned a pattern. Köhler considered this learning of a relationship rather than a response to an isolated stimulus a simple form of *insight*. Insight meant seeing into a problem, rather than a blind trial-and-error fumbling.

The Gestalt interpretation of learning by insight was diametrically opposed to Thorndike's notion of trial-and-error learning, although certainly in some of Köhler's experiments, there seemed to be a good deal of what appeared to be trial and error before insight was attained.

In his book, *The Growth of the Mind*,[14] Koffka, like Köhler, tended to reject trial-and-error learning. He suggested that such apparatus as the puzzle boxes of Thorndike and the common mazes used by numerous animal psychologists forced the subjects to use trial and error because no other approach was possible. In more appropriate learning situations, insight should take the place of constant repetition as a basic principle of learning. The only advantage of practice once learning had occurred was that it made a problem easier to solve.

---

[14]Kurt Koffka, *The Growth of the Mind* (London: Kegan Paul, 1924).

## Productive Thinking

The Gestalt theory of learning led to wider applications of problem-solving in children and adults. In Wertheimer's last book, *Productive Thinking,*[15] he explored the principles of productive thinking from simple geometrical problems for young children to the study of how Einstein arrived at his theory of relativity.

The basic principle for productive thinking was to let the whole dominate its parts. In solving a problem, one should never lose sight of the problem as a whole, even though it might be necessary to attend to certain details. In the process, it might be necessary to change one's attack, such as to regroup or reorganize. Nevertheless, one should take no step blindly or haphazardly. The procedure was from above downwards, or from the whole to its parts.

Wertheimer distinguished three types of thinking—*a, b,* and *y*. Type *a* was the most productive. It involved the process of centering and recentering. In centering, one attained a detached view of the situation, viewing it objectively and as a whole. In recentering, there was a taking on of a new perspective, involving a new approach from which to view the problem and leading to an achievement of a solution.

Type *y* thinking was usually a blind trial-and-error approach. If a solution were achieved, it occurred quite by accident. This was definitely unproductive thinking which should be avoided. Type *b* was partly productive and partly nonproductive.

In one of the most quoted studies, Wertheimer worked with children teaching them how to find the area of a triangle by considering that it was divided up into little squares. The area could be found by multiplying the numbers of squares in a row by the number of rows. He then presented them with an oblique parallelogram and asked the children how its area could be found. Those who had gained insight saw that the middle portion of the parallelogram was like a rectangle and the ends could be taken off by a vertical cut as two triangles and fitted one onto the other to make a complete rectangle of the parallelogram.

Wertheimer had criticized education as being too dependent on endless drill and repetition. Too often it led to habits of sheer mechanized action instead of to a freer approach of looking at a problem in a more flexible and productive way.[16]

## Memory

Finally, the Gestalt psychologists had given some attention to the problems involved in memory, particularly as they related to perception. Traditionally, one theory of memory was that when we perceived an object and subsequently

---

[15]Max Wertheimer, *Productive Thinking* (New York: Harper and Bros., 1945).
[16]*Ibid.,* p. 112.

were able to recall it, the reason was that a "trace" had been left in the brain. As we forgot, this "trace" gradually died out. The Gestalt psychologists tended to reject such a decay-like theory, although they retained the idea of a "trace" in the brain. Their view was that memory was a dynamic process in which traces underwent progressive changes as time passed; and these changes were in accordance with the principles of organization that governed the original perceptions. We can cite the principle of Prägnanz as an example. The traces tended to be perceived as "good" Gestalts. Several studies were done which were intended to demonstrate how changes in the memory traces would follow some principle of organization. The first of these was done by Wulff,[17] who presented his subjects with simple geometric figures of irregular shapes. These were presented for five seconds initially. The subjects were then asked to draw the figures they had seen following time intervals of thirty seconds, twenty-four hours, and one week. In cases where the original figure was "weak" (very ambiguous), the subjects tended to sharpen and make it a better figure (good form). Gibson[18] and Bartlett[19] also found that when subjects were presented simple visual forms and later asked to recall them, distortions tended to occur, but in the direction of good form (see Fig. 10). In working with verbal materials, Allport and Postman[20] presented "rumors" to their subjects and later asked them to recall them. Again, considerable leveling occurred. Shortening and simplifying of the reports resulted, which the Gestalt psychologists felt supported their hypothesis.

---

## Evaluation

### Criticisms of Gestalt Psychology

Just as Gestalt psychology arose as a protest against systems that were mechanistic and analytical, and where learning was considered a trial and error affair, so too the Gestaltists received their counterattacks. The main objections to Gestalt psychology might be summarized as follows:

Gestalt psychology had been too dependent on theory, and lacked positive empirical evidence to support the theory. Marx and Cronan-Hillix[21] have

---

[17]F. Wulff, "Über die Veränderung von Verstellungen," *Psychologische Forschung*, Vol. 1 (1922), pp. 333–73.

[18]J. J. Gibson, "Reproduction of Visually Perceived Forms," *Journal of Experimental Psychology*, Vol. 12 (1929), pp. 1–39.

[19]F. C. Bartlett, *Remembering: An Experimental and Social Study* (London: Cambridge University Press, 1932).

[20]G. W. Allport and L. Postman, *The Psychology of Rumor* (New York: Henry Holt & Co., 1947).

[21]M. H. Marx and W. A. Cronan-Hillix, *Systems and Theories in Psychology* (New York: McGraw-Hill Book Co., 1987).

**FIGURE 10**    *Changes in Figures Within the Method of Serial Reproduction.* (From F. C. Bartlett, *Remembering: An Experimental and Social Study,* 1932. Reprinted by permission of Cambridge University Press.)

|                  |                  |                  |
| ---------------- | ---------------- | ---------------- |
| Original         | Reproduction 1   | Reproduction 2   |
| Reproduction 3   | Reproduction 8   | Reproduction 9   |
| Reproduction 10  | Reproduction 15  | Reproduction 18  |

pointed out that the entire system had a nebulous character about it. For example, the whole concept of insight or the "aha" experience was hard to define.

Although Gestalt psychologists had used experimentation in their studies, these experiments were poorly controlled and lacked any real predictive power. Too often introspection was depended upon as the prime method, one which was hard to replicate.

The phenomenological approach was subjective and dualistic. It presumed a distinction between the phenomenological field or "behavior environment" and the real world without ever explaining how such a difference could exist. This kind of dualism, of course, was offensive to the behaviorists. In connection with the objection mentioned above, much of Gestalt data failed to be presented in a quantified way. Wolman[22] pointed out that the Gestaltists' objection to the quantification of data which used statistical methods was premature.

The isomorphic principle of a map in the brain corresponding to what one experienced was a pure physiological assumption. It was a unique explanation, but any proof was entirely indirect.

## Contributions of Gestalt Psychology

In light of these criticisms, has Gestalt psychology made any positive contributions? Certainly, its studies on perception gave a "new look" to the older kind of analysis of experience. Today, the renewed interest in cognitive psychology reflects strong Gestalt influences.

The Gestalt experiments in insight demonstrated that learning was not merely a haphazard affair. They have presented us with a new way of attacking problems of learning and thinking.

Whether or not its opponents like to admit it, the Gestalt movement remains today as an influence in psychology. Until Köhler's death in 1967, one of the main founders was still alive to foster the doctrine. The American Psychological Association thought enough of him to grant the Distinguished Contribution Award in 1956 and to elect him president in 1958, a position which is primarily of an honorary nature.

In all probability, Gestalt psychology has passed its prime. All of the founders are gone. In experimental psychology, the emphasis on more rigorous controls has not helped achieve a greater popularization of the system. However, Gestalt psychology has made the more mechanistic and analytical systems take a second look at their own tenets. They are still inclined to incorporate many of the Gestalt findings into their own theories.

In appraising the current status of Gestalt psychology, Hilgard and Bower[23] suggest that a transformation from systematic Gestalt psychology has taken place, so that the good ideas have persisted but have become unrecognizable, from those of "orthodox" psychology. For example, the renewed interest in cognitive psychology, the rejection of piecemeal analyses, and a greater emphasis on organizational principles in psychology persist.

---

[22]B. B. Wolman, *Contemporary Theories and Systems in Psychology* (New York: Harper and Bros., 1960).

[23]E. R. Hilgard and G. H. Bower, *Theories of Learning*, 3rd ed. (New York: Appleton-Century-Crofts, 1968).

In all likelihood, the final appraisal has not been made. In 1926 Koffka wrote a letter to Helson which was published by Helson in 1967.[24] Koffka said:

> That our present explanations are wanting in ever so many ways is obvious. They may even be in many cases altogether wrong. But this does not in the least affect the general principle. I believe, you will agree to all this (not all but the argument): but I find quite often that people believe they have refuted the Gestalt principle when they think they have refuted a special explanation given by the Gestaltists.

## Suggested Further Readings

Ellis, W. D., *A Source Book of Gestalt Psychology*. New York: Harcourt, Brace and Co., 1938.

Hartman, G. W., *Gestalt Psychology*. New York: The Ronald Press Co., 1935.

Katz, D., *Gestalt Psychology*. New York: The Ronald Press Co., 1950. Three basic texts summarizing the principles of Gestalt psychology.

Köhler, Wolfgang, *The Mentality of Apes*. New York: Harcourt, Brace and Co., 1925. One of the great classics in Gestalt psychology in which Köhler described his studies of "insight" with apes.

Wertheimer, Max, *Productive Thinking*. New York: Harper and Bros., 1945. Wertheimer's most famous book in which he applied Gestalt principles to thinking and problem-solving.

---

[24]H. Helson, "Some Remarks on Gestalt Psychology by Kurt Koffka," *Journal of the History of the Behavioral Sciences*, Vol. 3 (1967), pp. 43–46.

# CHAPTER

# 15

# *Field Theory*

In this chapter we shall discuss two examples of what has been known to psychology as *field theory*. The two examples we have chosen are those of Kurt Lewin and Edward C. Tolman. The two theories are quite different, but both share the concept of a psychological field. There are other field theorists—for example, Wheeler[1] and Brunswick[2]—but space does not permit us to discuss them all. J. R. Kantor has often been considered a field theorist, as indeed he is; but because of his strong behavioristic leanings, we have already considered him in chapter 13 on later behaviorism.

The concept of a field in psychology bears some relation to the notion of fields of force as found in physics, but the analogy is only very slight. Field theories in psychology consider that an organism is affected by factors in the field which surrounds it. In the case of Lewin, the first of the field theorists we shall discuss, motivational forces in the field are the key issue. In the case of Tolman, cognitive factors are the main point of focus.

## Lewin's Field Theory

Kurt Lewin (1890–1947) was born in Mogilno, Germany. He received his Ph.D. in psychology at the University of Berlin in 1914. In the early years, he was associated with the Gestalt psychologists Wertheimer and Köhler.

---

[1]R. H. Wheeler, *The Science of Psychology,* 2nd ed. (New York: Crowell, 1940).
[2]E. Brunswick, "The Conceptual Focus of Some Psychological Systems," in M. H. Marx, ed., *Psychological Theory: Contemporary Readings* (New York: The Macmillan Co., 1951).

Woodworth[3] considers that his system was an outgrowth of the Gestalt movement. This opinion, however, is not universally shared. Lewin began his early studies on associations, which was a significant departure from the Gestalt ideas. At the time, Lewin did not think of associations as having any kind of force, but he thought of them merely as links or connections between events, much as the couplings between the cars of a train.

From the Gestaltists, Lewin borrowed the concept of a field. This was not the isomorphic brain field which they stressed, but an environmental field containing one or more persons. However, he did consider the person and how the person viewed the environment in a phenomenological way.

When Hitler came to power, Lewin left Germany and came to the United States. He was a professor at Cornell University from 1933–1935 and then was at the University of Iowa Child Welfare Station for ten years. In 1945 he was appointed professor and Director of the Research Center for Group Dynamics at the Massachusetts Institute of Technology until his untimely death the following year at the age of 56.

## Lewin's System

Lewin considered his to be a *topological* and *vectoral* psychology.[4, 5] He borrowed the terms "topology" and "vectors" from mathematics. Topology is a form of geometry in which the concepts of "inside," "outside," and "boundary" are used. Topology investigates spatial properties—figures which remain unchanged under continuous transformation. Topological properties represent parts of a certain area of space. Actually as we examine Lewin's system, we shall see that the analogy to topology is rather superficial, and one need know nothing about topology to understand the system.

However, topology alone was not sufficient to account for all of Lewin's ideas. He, therefore, needed a concept of force, so he borrowed the concept of "vector," also from mathematics, to describe the resolution of forces. A vector is usually represented by an arrow, the length referring to the degree of force and the direction allowing for the line of application.

### The Life Space

Lewin began his system with a description of the life space. This was the psychological field, the space in which the person moved. It constituted the totality of facts that determined the behavior of an individual at any one time.

---

[3]Robert S. Woodworth, *Contemporary Schools of Psychology,* 2nd ed. (New York: The Ronald Press Co., 1948).
[4]Kurt Lewin, *Principles of Topological Psychology* (New York: McGraw-Hill Book Co., 1936).
[5]Kurt Lewin, *A Dynamic Theory of Personality* (New York: McGraw-Hill Book Co., 1936).

$B = f L$. Behavior was a function of the life space. The purpose of psychology was to determine the behavior of an individual from all the psychological facts that existed in the life space at any moment.[6] The facts that existed outside the life space Lewin called the *foreign hull*.

The life space existed for the individual, and the individual existed within the life space. This was a psychological rather than physical field, although in some cases the two might be quite similar. A person's life space included the person and other people and objects as the person perceived them. It could also include ideas. Lewin considered the life space to be quasi-physical, quasi-social, or quasi-conceptual. In the latter two cases, social and intellectual events might be operating at any one time in determining a person's behavior.

Life space was more than a mere subjective event—that is, perceiving the world through introspection. There might be forces going on about which the person was unaware. Life space, then, was a psychological construct, one which was designed to account for all the events that influenced a person at the time of examination.

The life space might be divided into regions, which were divided by boundaries. These need not be considered as disruptive barriers. Each region might constitute a psychological fact. For Lewin, a fact was not merely an observable thing like a table. It could be a social or intellectual event or something simply inferred.

The notion of regions and boundaries in the life space can be understood from an example given by Lewin of a boy who wanted to become a physician. In Figure 11, *P* represented the boy as a person. At the other extreme was his goal of being a physician, *G*. Intermediary regions were *ce* entrance examination, *c* college, *m* medical school, *i* internship, *pr* establishing a practice. Each of these constituted a region in the life space at that moment when he considered becoming a physician.

The boundaries had various dimensions, such as *nearness-remoteness*. In this figure, establishing a practice and becoming a physician as the goal were *near*, while college was a more remote region. Another dimension was that of *firmness-weakness*. Passing an examination could be a difficult task before allowing the person to move into the next region, that of medical school. The number of regions in the life space was determined by the number of facts that existed at any particular time.

## The Person

The person always existed in the life space and was usually designated by the letter *P*. Like the life space it could be subdivided into interconnected and interdependent units, as indicated in Figure 12. The outer part represented the *perceptual-motor region*, that which had closest contact with the outside world. One perceived and reacted to it. There was an inner core called the *inner-personal*

---

[6]*Ibid.*

FIGURE 11 *Situation of a Boy Who Wants to be a Physician.* (From *Principles of Topological Psychology* by K. Lewin, p. 48. Copyright 1936 by McGraw-Hill Book Company. Used with permission of the publisher.)

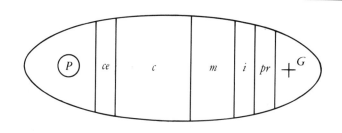

FIGURE 12 *Diagram of a Person, Showing the Inner-Personal and Motoric Regions.*

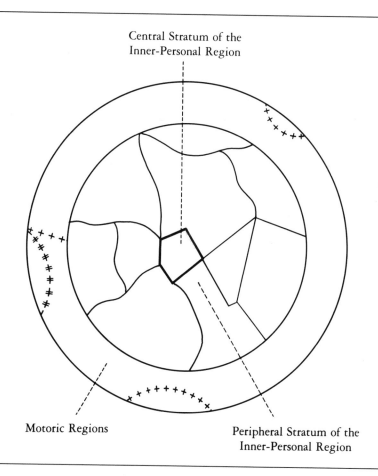

*region* (see the subdivisions). These internal cells could be thought of as traits or psychological characteristics. As one grew older, one became more differentiated—that is, one developed more separate modes of acting. This was represented by more inner cells. The newborn was rather undifferentiated and would have few inner-personal regions.

## Hodological Space

Topology, as Lewin borrowed it from mathematics, deals with directions, which he felt were a necessary construct in his system. If one moved from one region to another there had to be a pathway. Lewin invented a kind of geometry, deriving it from the Greek "hodos" meaning pathway. For him, the characteristics of a given path varied according to the situation, and the direction depended on the properties of the entire field.

Through locomotion, one might move from one region to another according to a given pathway, as seen in Figure 13. Locomotion through the psychological environment did not necessarily mean physical movement. For example, in joining a fraternity or sorority we might move from our present region into that of pledgeship and finally into full membership. A college teacher might move from the region of instructor through assistant and associate professor and finally to the region of full professor. One could consider anything which a person could perform as locomotion. The directions of the paths through which one moved would be determined by the strength of the boundaries between regions, and the ease with which one could pass through the regions and the dynamic forces which motivated one.

Figure 13 shows a path of locomotion from region *A* to region *G*. This could represent planning a trip where the regions *B*, *D*, and *E* represented

**FIGURE 13** *Locomotion in Life Space.*

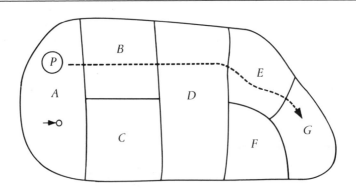

places one might wish to visit before achieving one's final destination at $G$. The regions of $C$ and $F$ were other possibilities which the person had chosen to ignore.

## Levels of Reality

Thus far we have considered only a two-dimensional life space. This was what Lewin called the level of reality. But there were levels of "irreality" in which imaginary locomotion might take place. In Figure 14, the first level $R$, one might be asked to join a fraternity/sorority and move directly into the appropriate region. The heavy line could represent a barrier, perhaps between the person and another fraternity/sorority to which the person was not invited. The second level was usually one of thinking or planning. The regions at the second level were more flexible. The third level, that of greatest "irreality," might be pure fantasy.

**FIGURE 14**   *Representation of Different Degrees of Reality.* R, more real level; I, more irreal level; P, person. In a level of greater reality the barriers are stronger and the person, P, is more clearly separated from the environment. (From *Principles of Topological Psychology* by K. Lewin, p. 200. Copyright 1936 by McGraw-Hill Book Company. Used with permission of the publisher.)

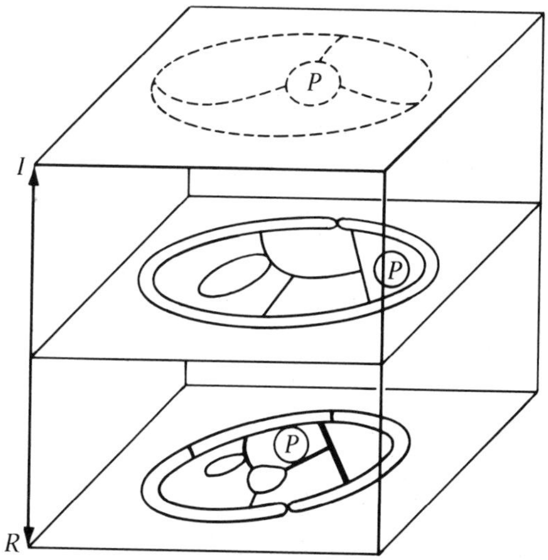

**FIGURE 15**  *Time Perspective in Planning.* (From R. G. Barker, T. Dembo, and K. Lewin, "Frustration and Regression: A Study of Young Children," *University of Iowa Studies in Child Welfare,* Vol. 18 (1941), No. 1, p. 210. Reproduced by permission of the publisher.)

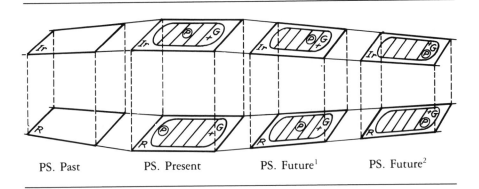

PS. Past          PS. Present          PS. Future[1]          PS. Future[2]

### The Time Dimension

So far, we have considered life space as those facts that influenced a person at a given moment. Lewin was much concerned with what affected a person in the present, but there were also thoughts of the future and hopes and expectations of things to come.[7] Figure 15 represents the present and the future. Notice the two levels of reality were also represented. The sequences of events started from left to right. The two levels of reality came closer as one extended to the future. There was less difference between reality and irreality as something planned was more nearly achieved. In the first stage, Present, the plan made the person nearer to the goal on the irreality dimension but in the final stage, Future, reality and irreality were the same. The goal was reached in thought and act.

### Motivation

Lewin departed drastically from the orthodox Gestalt psychology in his stress on motivation. Lewin's concept of motivation, which perhaps was the crux of his theory and the focus of most of its research, involved a number of constructs: energy, tension, need, valence, and force or vector. We shall consider each in order.

---

[7]Kurt Lewin, *Field Theory in Social Science;* D. Cartwright, ed. (New York: Harper and Bros., 1951).

## Energy

As in other theories, psychoanalysis for example, Lewin considered a person as a complex energy system, and like Freud, he felt the energy performed psychological work and was psychic rather than physical. Since Lewin's system was purely psychological, one that was nonreductionistic, he found no cause to resort to physiological processes as antecedent or causative factors.

## Tension

Simply stated, tension was a state of disequilibrium between a person and the environment. It arose when there was a lack of balance between the forces in his psychological environment.

One of the earliest examples to demonstrate tension and its reduction was found in an experiment by Zeigarnik[8] which has become a classic in the literature. She presumed that first, tension would be aroused when a subject was given a task to perform; and second, if the tension were not relieved as would ordinarily occur if the task were completed, the presence of tension would result in greater recall of the incompleted tasks. The achievement of a goal relieved the tension.

In Zeigarnik's experiment, she gave twenty-two tasks to one hundred and thirty-eight subjects. The tasks consisted of such things as modeling a figure from clay, laying out playing blocks in certain forms, or doing simple puzzles. The subjects were allowed to complete some of the tasks but were prevented from completing others. Zeigarnik's subjects later recalled many more of the incompleted tasks. The ratio of recalled unfinished tasks ($RU$) to recalled completed tasks ($RC$) was 1:9. The experiment has subsequently been repeated by others such as Alper[9] and Deutsch[10] and has become known as the *Zeigarnik effect*.

## Needs

Lewin's conception of needs fit into the general construct of the tension system. Needs gave rise to tension. Although Lewin preferred to keep his system on a purely psychological level, he did allow that such physiological conditions as hunger, thirst, and sex might arouse tension, but there were other purely psychological needs. The desire to do something, such as completing a task, could constitute a need. He did not bother to delineate the nature, source, or number of needs a person might have, but he did distinguish between needs and quasi-

---

[8]B. Zeigarnik, "Über das Behalten von erledigten und unerledigten Handlungen," *Psychologische Forschung*, Vol. 9 (1927), pp. 1–85.

[9]T. G. Alper, "Memory for Completed and Incompleted Tasks as a Function of Personality," *Journal of Personality*, Vol. 17 (1948), pp. 104–137.

[10]M. Deutsch, "Field Theory in Social Psychology," in G. Lindzey, ed., *Handbook of Social Psychology* (Cambridge, Mass.: Addison-Wesley, 1954), pp. 181–222.

needs. A need was the result of some inner state in the tension system of a person, and it was general. A quasi-need was a more specific intention, such as watching a particular TV show or eating at a special restaurant.

## Valence

Valence referred to the particular attractiveness or repulsion of an object in the life space. Those to which we were attracted had positive valences and were indicated by a + sign. The negative ones were indicated by a − sign. Some objects had no valence at all. A person would tend to move through his or her life space in the direction of positive valences. By contrast, those objects in a region in life space which the person moved away from had negative valences.

Often, our life space might contain several regions in which several valences existed at the same time. Then, a conflict arose. In adient-adient conflict two positive valences were presented. A child had to choose between going on a picnic or playing with friends. When faced with two negative valences, avoidance-avoidance conflict resulted. A child was offered a reward for a task the child did not wish to perform. (These examples are taken directly from Lewin.)[11]

Valences were coordinated with needs. If one were not hungry, food had no positive valence; but for a very thirsty person, a glass of beer might have a strong positive valence. In fact, Lewin considered valences in a kind of quantitative way. They could be weak, moderate, or strong.

In moving through the life space toward a region with a positive valence, one might encounter a barrier, that is, some object or event that obstructed the movement. In this instance, it was possible for the barrier to take on a negative valence. Suppose we wished to enter a fashionable restaurant in front of which stood a fancily dressed doorman. Because we did not have a reservation or were improperly dressed, we were not allowed to enter. The doorman became a barrier and took on a negative valence which drove us away.

According to Lewinian theory, as the distance between a person and an object is increased, the attractiveness of the valence is decreased. On the other hand, as a child came closer to a toy, its positive valence increased. Fajans[12] studied a group of children from ages one to six. She put toys of strong positive valences at distances from 5 to 100 centimeters away from the child. At greater distance, the valence tended to decrease as evidenced by the fact that there were fewer expressions of emotional outburst.

Another related Lewinian hypothesis with regard to valence was that an obstructed goal (introduced barrier) developed a stronger positive valence for the object. That is, the "grass on the other side of the river looks greener." Two

---

[11]Kurt Lewin, *A Dynamic Theory of Personality, op. cit.,* pp. 88–91.
[12]S. Fajans, "Erfolg, Ausdauer, Aktivität beim Säugling und Kleinkind," *Psychologische Forschung,* Vol. 17 (1933), pp. 268–305.

experiments were performed by Wright[13] to test the hypothesis. The subjects were waitresses in the Duke University student union. Desserts (cherry pie) which the waitresses were to get for themselves were placed in two parallel rows on serving tables. The two rows were 12 inches apart, and all slices of pie were uniformly cut. The procedure in selecting the desserts was repeated on 14 separate occasions. Results showed that the average number of choices for the remote desserts (second row) was 18 as opposed to 10 for the nearest or first row. The distance that the waitresses had to reach constituted the barrier. Thus, the waitresses tended to reach for the more remote desserts. But, when the rows were moved closer together, reducing the barrier, the averages were 16 for the more remote row and 12 for the nearer. However, when the desserts were merely a means to an end, as when the waitresses simply took the pieces of pie to set up tables, 97 per cent of them selected the desserts from the nearest row.

A second experiment used nursery school children as subjects. Two strings were suspended from a wall, and attached to the end of each string was a piece of stick candy. There was a slight tendency for the children to choose the less accessible one, which was hung higher up.

## Vectors or Forces

Force or vector constituted the push which directed a person toward a goal. The force might be directed toward or away from the object and was correlated with the object's valence. Force was not the same as tension for it was an aspect of the psychological environment. In Lewin's descriptive system it was designated by an arrow when related to the person $P$ as follows:

$$\longrightarrow \quad P$$

The vectors had three properties, (1) direction, as toward or away from an object, (2) strength, as correlated with the degree of attraction or repulsion of a valence, and (3) a point of contact.

Diagrammatically the direction in which the vector pointed was the direction of movement.

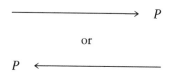

The longer the line, the greater the strength of the vector. In a conflict situation there were two opposing vectors.

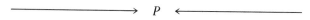

[13]H. F. Wright, "The Effect of Barriers on the Strength of Motivation," in R. G. Barker, J. S. Kounin, and H. F. Wright, eds., *Child Behavior and Development* (New York: McGraw-Hill Book Co., 1943), pp. 379–96.

## Conflict

Lewin designated three types of conflict: *approach-approach, avoidance-avoidance,* and *approach-avoidance* (see Fig. 16). In approach-approach conflict the person (P) is placed in a situation in which a choice must be made between two objects or conditions both of which have equal positive valences ( + ) and whose vectors are pushing the person in opposite directions. While dining at a restaurant, a person might have to choose either chicken or steak, both of which are equally desirable; or the person might be thinking, "Shall I wear the brown tweed or the blue blazer this morning?"

In avoidance-avoidance conflict, a choice must be made between two objects or situations, both of which have negative valences ( − ), or a person may be pushed in opposite directions by two equally unattractive or unpleasant conditions. For example, suppose a boy is invited to a birthday party given by a girl whom he dislikes; if he refuses to attend, his mother will spank him severely. Or suppose a college student were required to take one of two courses, the subject matter of which the student detests equally.

**FIGURE 16** *Lewin's Conception of the Three Types of Conflict.*

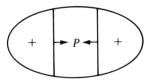

Approach-Approach Conflict

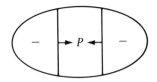

Avoidance-Avoidance Conflict

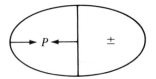

Approach-Avoidance Conflict

In approach-avoidance conflict the object or situation has both positive and negative valences at the same time, so the person is both attracted and repelled by it. One could be offered an attractive job, but its location is in the middle of nowhere. "Lobster is my favorite dish, but look on the menu; the price is $25.00 per serving!"

## Differentiation

One of the key aspects of Lewin's theory was that both the inner-personal regions of the person and the person's life space became more differentiated with age. The adult had many more inner tension systems as well as more possible life space regions. If a person regressed in his behavior, his personality became *dedifferentiated.* To test this aspect of the theory, Barker, Dembo, and Lewin[14] used the constructiveness of a child's play as their measure of differentiation or dedifferentiation. They first placed the children in a "free play" situation where they were presented with various toys—a doll and a teddy bear seated on a chair, a small truck and a trailer, a toy iron and an ironing board, and a toy telephone. The children were allowed to play, and the general characteristics of their play were rated as to age. Then the children were introduced to a much more elegant play situation with a large doll house that was lightly decorated and a toy lake filled with real water and toy boats. After playing in the new situation, a screen was lowered, and the children returned to their original play setting. They could still see through the screen but could not reach the more attractive toys. This constituted a situation of frustration in which a barrier had been introduced. Results indicated that the children regressed to earlier forms of play. They wandered around the room, sometimes ignoring the toys. The telephone which had been used for "play talking" was merely pounded on the floor in an infantile manner. Crayons used earlier to draw pictures were merely scribbled on paper. In the new setting the average play age had regressed 17.3 months. Accordingly, as a result of the frustration, the regression represented a dedifferentiation of the personality.

As we grow older, more inner cells develop and our personalities become more differentiated. The degree of differentiation is also a function of a person's basic intellectual functioning. Lewin has contrasted the normal and retarded child (see Fig. 17). First of all, it can be noted that the normal child has more cells, because he or she has developed more traits and behavioral characteristics. Second, it can be noted that the retarded child has fewer cells, and the boundaries are firmer and thicker. These heavier boundaries indicate that there is less communication between the systems. Typically, retarded children are more rigid in their behavior. They are less capable of transferring what they have learned from one situation to another.

---

[14]R. G. Barker, T. Dembo, and Kurt Lewin, "Frustration and Regression," in R. G. Barker, J. S. Kounin, and H. F. Wright, eds. *Child Behavior and Development, op. cit.,* pp. 441–58.

**FIGURE 17**   *Lewin's Conception of the Inner-Personal Regions of a Normal and Retarded Child.* The normal child (below) has more cells, and the boundaries are less rigid, indicating more traits and behavior, as well as greater flexibility. The thicker boundaries in the retarded child indicate less flexibility.

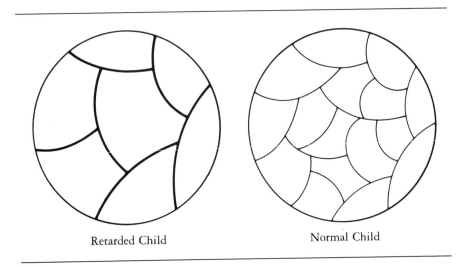

Retarded Child                    Normal Child

## Group Dynamics

In his later years, Lewin directed his attention to problems of social psychology. He developed the concept of group dynamics, which was an application to the group that was borrowed from the earlier psychology of the individual. Just as the person and the life space constituted the psychological field, the group and its environment formed the social field. One of the fundamental characteristics of the social field was the relative position of the members who constituted the group.[15] Group behavior became a function of the total situation. The group was characterized by the "dynamic interdependence" of its members. The actions of each member were a function of the actions of the other members. Topologically, a person's status depended on his or her region as it related to other regions (members of the group). The group was subject to cohesive and disruptive forces. Disruptive forces arose out of two strong barriers between members which hampered communication or out of a conflict between an individual's goals and those of the group. The group constituted a field of forces, and individuals were attracted or repelled depending on the kinds of valences existing in the group. When the relations between members were attractive,

[15]Kurt Lewin, *Field Theory and Social Science, op. cit.*

cohesive forces were operating, as when the group was in a position to satisfy the needs of its members.

The concept of group dynamics has led to several avenues of research. During World War II, Lewin[16] conducted a number of experiments that attempted to alter group decision-making. At the time, certain food products, such as meat, were rationed. Consequently, people were encouraged to buy more accessible products, such as brains, liver, kidneys, and heart and other animal organs not generally considered to be food items. He used two methods. The first was lecturing on the merits of the food, their nutritional values, how they could be tastily prepared, and so on. The second method involved group discussion. The same materials were presented in both cases. In the group discussion, there was participation by the members on the pros and cons of trying and eating and preparing such substances. In a follow-up study only 3 per cent of the lecture group took up the suggestions, while 32 per cent of the discussion group changed their food habits by trying the formerly unpopular products. Lewin concluded that in the discussion group more forces were made available for a change in behavior.

In another experiment, now famous in the literature, Lippitt and White[17] attempted to determine what effect "social climate" had on the behavior of members of various groups. In this study, groups of boys were matched, and the behavior of each group became a function of the kind of leadership involved. In the *democratic* group, the leader cooperated with the boys and encouraged group discussion and decision-making in the kinds of things they were to do. In the *authoritarian* group, the leader made all the decisions, gave orders, and so on. In the *laissez-faire* group, the leader remained completely passive, allowing the boys to do whatever they wanted. In the democratic group, the "social climate" was friendly. The boys were less aggressive and accomplished more of the tasks assigned. The authoritarian group was characterized by more aggression and the appearance of a "scapegoat" toward whom some of the aggression was directed. This particular boy finally had to leave the group. The laissez-faire group acted randomly and accomplished little. The experimenters concluded that the behavior of the group membership was determined by the "social climate" created by the leader.

## Mind-Body Problem

As such, Lewin was not concerned with the mind-body problem in the same manner as the earlier theorists were. In his system, the problem took on a much more sophisticated form. Nevertheless, the system was dualistic. Life space was both physical and mental. A clear distinction between the two was difficult to make. Further, Lewin delighted in using hypothetical, mentalistic constructs

---

[16]Kurt Lewin, "Forces Behind Food Habits and Methods of Change," *Bulletin of the National Research Council*, Vol. 108 (1943), pp. 35–65.

[17]R. Lippitt and R. K. White, "The 'Social Climate' of Children's Groups," in R. G. Barker, J. S. Kounin, and H. F. Wright, eds., *Child Behavior and Development, op. cit.*, pp. 485–508.

such as psychic energy, tension systems, valence, and vector. The vector was some kind of hidden force which somehow pushed a person towards a goal. Likewise, the tension states and needs were purely hypothetical. The solution seemed to be one of *psychophysical interaction,* all of which took place in a psychophysical life space.

## Evaluation

### Criticisms of Lewin

Lewin's system has been the subject of attack from various angles by different people. The most significant of these will be enumerated below.

The theory had many untestable hypothetical constructs. The concepts of energy systems, tensions, vectors, and so on were purely imaginative in so far as psychology was concerned, and to this day, they remain as purely hypothetical as when they were first formulated. Many of the constructs were never able to be put to the experimental test. The results of those that were are only by inference.

Lewin's representations told us nothing about behavior in an explanatory sense. They were merely descriptive portrayals of psychological situations. His representations were no more than mere pictorial analogies and illustrative metaphors.[18] They were pictures of what we already knew and added nothing new to our psychological knowledge.[19]

Lewin confused the objective world with his subjective impression of it. The life space might be physical in part, and at other times purely mental. Tolman[20] pointed out that the theory did not tell us how the objective world could produce changes in the life space. Lewin's theory fell into a trap of subjectivism from which only intuition could rescue it.[21] According to Allport,[22] the boundaries were sometimes actual physical barriers and sometimes "inner" mental barriers. In other words, Lewin confused the phenomenological with the outer physical events. The result was a hopeless muddle.[23]

Lewin misused his mathematical concepts. Terms like force, vector, valence, paths, and boundaries were removed from the context of physics, chem-

[18]C. B. Broyler, "Review of Lewin's *Principles of Topological Psychology,*" *Character and Personality,* Vol. 5 (1936–1937), pp. 257–58.

[19]I. D. London, "Psychologists' Misuse of the Auxiliary Concepts of Physics and Mathematics," *Psychological Review,* Vol. 51 (1944), pp. 266–91.

[20]Edward C. Tolman, "Kurt Lewin 1890–1947," *Psychological Review,* Vol. 55 (1948), pp. 1–4.

[21]C. S. Hall, and G. Lindzey, *Theories of Personality,* 3rd ed. (New York: John Wiley and Sons, 1978).

[22]G. H. Allport, *Theories of Perception and the Concept of Structure* (New York: John Wiley and Sons, 1955).

[23]*Ibid.*

istry, and mathematics and were misapplied to psychology.[24] London[25] further charged that Lewin borrowed certain terminology and gross conceptualization from the geometry of topology but had failed to apply it correctly. Actually, this criticism was a little harsh, for Lewin was not that sophisticated in understanding topology and only intended it as an analogy.

Lewin ignored the past history of the individual.[26] In his diagrams he presented the present situation. If one wished to explain present behavior, one must know about antecedent conditions. Lewin[27] denied this criticism, but the fact remains that if we depended only on his theoretical constructs, we would have merely a description of present activity. According to Hall and Lindzey,[28] the theory pretended to present a mathematical model from which predictions could be made, when in fact no predictions were possible. The system, in fact, was post-dictive rather than predictive.

## Contributions of Lewin

If nothing more, Lewin created an imaginative and ingenious theory that generated a tremendous amount of research. The studies of interrupted tasks (Zeigarnik effect), frustration and regression, and conflict all have remained as lasting contributions to psychological literature. They are frequently cited in texts of general psychology and personality. The question arose, however, about whether these researches could have been carried on outside the framework of Lewinian theory. In actuality, the findings did not demonstrate the validity of the constructs in any direct way. For example, the Zeigarnik studies were supposed to support the tension system hypothesis, but they neither proved nor disproved it. They stand as an interesting example of an ingenious research technique. It is said that Lewin got his idea from observing waiters in a Berlin restaurant who had a remarkable memory for the amount of each bill, until after it had been paid.[29]

Lewin did pioneering work in the field of social psychology, and his researches and those of his colleagues have helped establish it as a legitimate branch of psychology. The studies of "social climate" in boys' clubs stand as a classic experiment in the field. Likewise, the work on group dynamics made an impact that remains popular today. It opened new avenues of research in group behavior. These studies led further to practical applications in the modification of group attitudes outside the laboratory.

Lewin's psychology is not as popular today as it was a couple of decades ago. However, at the Massachusetts Institute of Technology, the Center for Group Dynamics still has ardent followers. In general, psychologists have been

[24]C. S. Hall and G. Lindzey, *op. cit.*, p. 251.
[25]D. London, *op. cit.*
[26]C. S. Hall and G. Lindzey, *op. cit.*, p. 251.
[27]Kurt Lewin, *Field Theory and Social Science, op. cit.*
[28]C. S. Hall and G. Lindzey, *op. cit.*
[29]G. W. Hartman, *Gestalt Psychology* (New York: The Ronald Press Co., 1935).

more willing to accept the research programs and experimental findings than the theoretical constructs. In conclusion, one should not forget the many fields of psychology that Lewin's studies have influenced, in particular, child psychology, psychology of personality, and social psychology.

## Tolman's Cognitive Field Theory

Edward Chace Tolman (1886–1959) started his career as an engineer, studying at the Massachusetts Institute of Technology. However, he changed to psychology and received his Ph.D. at Harvard in 1915. He taught at Northwestern University until 1918, and then spent the major portion of his career, except for two periods, at the University of California at Berkeley. During World War II he served in the Office of Strategic Services, and from 1950–1953 he left California because of the dispute involving the loyalty oath.

Many texts on theories and systems in psychology treat Tolman in chapters or sections devoted to behaviorism. In his early years, Tolman was much impressed by Watson's new behaviorism. He considered it a "relief" from the older schools which had stressed introspection. However, he soon departed from the typical stimulus-response kind of psychology and began to develop a different conception of learning. Still, Tolman considered himself a "purposive behaviorist." However, as he began to develop his ideas where greater emphasis was placed on cognition—how the organism "perceives" and "knows"—he departed from the traditional behavioristic position and leaned more towards a field theory approach. As we shall see, he borrowed a number of concepts from field theory, particularly from Lewin as well as from Gestalt psychology, so we can legitimately call him a field theorist. Further, Tolman introduced certain mentalistic concepts into his system which should automatically exclude him from the general group of rigid behaviorists who rejected all dualistic concepts.

Tolman never developed a very systematic theory, although MacCorquodale and Meehl[30] have attempted to systematize Tolman's position with a considerable degree of success. The interested student who wishes to delve further into his system might well consult their chapter in Estes' book, *Modern Learning Theory*.[31] Tolman's main statement of his position can be found in his most important book, *Purposive Behavior in Animals and Men*.[32]

Tolman's thinking was influenced by a number of theorists whom we have already considered; Watson is one example. Tolman was concerned with behavior, and spent a good deal of time in experimenting with the behavior of rats. He glorified that animal as the most useful organism for psychological research.

---

[30]K. MacCorquodale and P. E. Meehl, "Edward C. Tolman," in W. K. Estes, *et al.*, *Modern Learning Theory* (New York: Appleton-Century-Crofts, 1954).

[31]*Ibid.*, ch. 2.

[32]Edward C. Tolman, *Purposive Behavior in Animals and Men* (New York: D. Appleton-Century Co., 1932).

in's conception of valence.[36] It amounted to an acquired relationship between a motivating situation and an object. A child developed a relationship between its hunger and an ice cream cone.

2. **Equivalence beliefs.** Here, an organism reacted to a sub-goal (secondary reinforcement?) in the same way it would to the actual goal.

3. **Field expectancies.** These referred to the sign-gestalts of the earlier statement.

4. **Field cognition modes.** These were "higher order" modes of expectancy. They were dependent on previously learned field expectations. This amounted to a readiness to acquire new field expectancies in the areas of perception, memory, and inference.

5. **Drive discrimination.** Here, Tolman borrowed from Hull[37] and Leeper.[38] This involved the direction of the movement, such as whether an animal were hungry or thirsty involved the direction of its activity.

6. **Motor patterns.** Because his was basically not an *S-R* theory, Tolman needed some principle to account for his motor patterns, so he accepted Guthrie's account of conditioning by contiguity.

## Some Experimental Findings

Tolman's theory has generated a vast amount of research both by him and by his followers. The three experimental examples are presented primarily in support of his 1932 position, but do not contradict the later version.

1. Tinklepaugh,[39] using a monkey as the subject, placed food under one of two containers while the monkey was watching. After a period of delay, the monkey readily chose the correct container, which had a banana placed under it. Later, the experimenter placed a lettuce leaf (a less preferred food object) under the same container. When the monkey lifted the container and found the lettuce, the monkey rejected it. It was not what the animal *had expected.*

2. A more complicated experiment was set up by Honzik and Tolman[40] to demonstrate inferential expectancies and "insight." The best understanding

---

[36]E. R. Hilgard, *Theories of Learning,* 2nd ed. (New York: Appleton-Century-Crofts, 1956), p. 226.

[37]C. L. Hull, "Differential Habituation to Internal Stimuli in the Albino Rat," *Journal of Comparative Psychology,* Vol. 16 (1933), pp. 255–73.

[38]R. Leeper, "The Role of Motivation in Learning: A Study of the Phenomenon of Differential Motivational Control of the Utilization of Habits," *Journal of Genetic Psychology,* Vol. 46 (1935), pp. 3–40.

[39]O. H. Tinklepaugh, "An Experimental Study of Representative Factors in Monkeys," *Journal of Comparative Psychology,* Vol. 8 (1928), pp. 197–236.

[40]C. H. Honzik and Edward C. Tolman, "The Perception of Spatial Relations by the Rat, a Type of Response Not Easily Explained by Conditioning," *Journal of Comparative Psychology,* Vol. 22 (1936), pp. 287–318.

may be gained by referring to Figure 18. There were three paths, 1, 2, and 3, from the starting point to the goal box in this rather unique maze. These were labeled in order of length from the shortest to the longest. When path 1 was blocked, the rats chose path 2, which was shorter than path 3. When the rats gained familiarity with all three paths, a preference in order of 1, 2, and 3 was established, depending on which paths were blocked. The reader will observe that paths 1 and 2 also had a common segment leading to the final box. When the block in path 1 had been placed before the common segment (Block A in the diagram), the rats after backing up ran to path 2. Next the block was placed farther up (Block B), shutting off both paths 1 and 2. What the rats did after being blocked in path 1, rather than go to path 2 and be further frustrated, they ordinarily took path 3, the least preferred. The experiment intended to demonstrate

**FIGURE 18**   *Maze Used to Test Insight in Rats.* (From *Insight in Rats* by E. C. Tolman and C. H. Honzik, University of California Publications in Psychology, Vol. 4, p. 14. Published 1930 by The Regents of the University of California. Reprinted by permission of the University of California Press.)

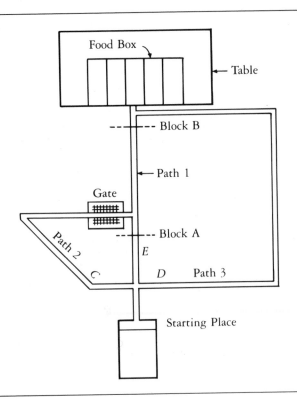

that the rats had learned a kind of "cognitive map" of the situation as a whole, and not just a series of blind habits. In other words, they gained a kind of "insight" into the situation.

3. In Tolman's sign-learning theory, the expectations that an organism established were important. This was in contrast to Hull and Skinner who stressed the major importance of reinforcement in the learning process. The question arose of whether or not learning could take place in the absence of reward of reinforcement. Tolman and his colleagues conducted extensive experiments on what has been called *latent learning,* that is, learning in the absence of some kind of reward. Tolman and Honzik's[41] classic experiment will serve as an illustration. They ran rats in a maze under three conditions: (1) no reward at all, (2) each trial rewarded with food, and (3) rats were first run for ten days without reward after which time food was introduced on the eleventh day. Figure 19 shows the results. The nonrewarded group showed little change, although a slight improvement could be noted. The constantly rewarded group gradually improved, as would be expected in a typical maze situation. Time and errors were gradually reduced on succeeding trials. The group that received food for the first time on the eleventh day suddenly showed a rapid improvement, finally matching that of the continuously rewarded group. In the early part of the experiment, this group did not seem to show much appreciable improvement. According to Tolman and Honzik, learning seemed to be taking place. The learning was, therefore, designated as *latent.* The reinforcement theorists found it difficult to explain these results. They claimed, however, (if one examined the graph carefully) that because of the nature of the apparatus (the rats could not retrace their steps because a series of doors was closed) some kind of reinforcement was operating. It should be noted in the graph that there was some decrease in errors in the nonrewarded groups. Possibly the reinforcement was simply being removed from the maze. The introduction of the food, according to the reinforcement theorists, simply added to the magnitude of the reinforcement, facilitating learning. On the other hand, Tolman's interpretation was that on nonrewarded trials the rats *were learning* some spatial relations. The introduction of the reward on the eleventh day simply led the rat to use its "cognitive map" and take the turns which led from one segment to the next. As a matter of fact, the late introduction of reward led to a better performance than that of the regularly rewarded group.

## Intervening Variables

Tolman was usually credited with introducing the concept of *intervening variables* into psychology. Of course, they had been used before, but were simply never

---

[41]Edward C. Tolman and C. H. Honzik, "Introduction and Removal of a Reward and Maze Performance in Rats," *University of California Publications in Psychology,* Vol. 4 (1930), pp. 257–75.

**FIGURE 19**    *Evidence for Latent Learning in the Maze.* (From *Introduction and Removal of Reward and Maze Performance by Rats* by E. C. Tolman and C. H. Honzik, University of California Publications in Psychology, Vol. 4, p. 17. Published 1930 by The Regents of the University of California. Reprinted by permission of the University of California Press.)

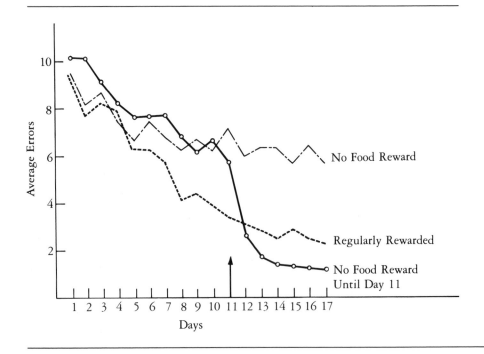

named as such. Whether or not the concept of an intervening variable was a good or bad thing in psychology was purely a theoretical issue which is still argued today. We noted in chapter 13 that Hull[42] borrowed the concept from Tolman and used intervening variables extensively in his system. On the other hand, Skinner[43] had dismissed them as adding nothing by way of explaining functional relationships. We already know that in a psychological experiment the antecedent conditions usually constitute the *independent variables* and the resulting behavior constitutes the *dependent variables*. In between these, Tolman introduced the intervening variables, which he felt were useful in the final explanation. Intervening variables were usually defined as *inferred or nonobserv-*

[42]C. L. Hull, *Principles of Behavior* (New York: Appleton-Century-Crofts, 1943).
[43]B. F. Skinner, *Science and Human Behavior* (New York: The Macmillan Co., 1953).

*able factors* which intervened between the independent and dependent variables. For Tolman, they constituted the determinants of behavior. The "cognitive map" referred to earlier was one such example.

Tolman[44] first set forth his concept of intervening variables in 1938. Although there was no basic difference in the fundamental issue, he later altered his list and introduced some new changes in his vocabulary.

We shall consider the later[45] (1951) model in which Tolman listed three kinds of intervening variables. At this point, the reader can see strong influences from Lewin. The three kinds of intervening variables were: (1) the *need system*, (2) the *belief value matrix,* and (3) the *behavior space.*

**1.** The *need* system referred to some kind of inferred state of drive which could be physiological or psychological.

**2.** The *belief value matrix* referred to inferred motives or a kind of preference for particular goal objects. As in Lewin's theory, one could consider the objects as having a kind of valence or strength.

**3.** The *behavior space* was the space in which locomotion took place toward the objects. It was very similar to Lewin's life space. Objects in the space might attract or repel the organism. Thus, an object was perceived as it was *expected* to be perceived.

In our discussion of Tolman, we have tried to point out the major aspects of his theory. It was primarily a theory of learning, and was one of the four which dominated the field of learning for many decades around the middle of this century. (The other three, by Guthrie, Hull, and Skinner, have already been discussed.) The theory was not so simple as this presentation might suggest, but to go into all of the ramifications and details is beyond the scope of this book.

To sum up, Tolman proposed a kind of behaviorism (and lots of historians of psychology considered him a behaviorist) that excluded consciousness from psychology as Watson had, but Tolman included purposivism and cognition not as mystical powers but as inferred states. Tolman called himself "a purposive behaviorist," but not a behaviorist like Watson or Skinner. To avoid any further muddling and hair splitting, it seemed better to discuss him under "Field Theory." In the strict sense, Tolman was a mentalist, but today his ideas are of particular interest because they were the forerunners of cognitive psychology, the subject of the next chapter.

---

[44]Edward C. Tolman, "The Determinants of Behavior at a Choice Point," *Psychological Review,* Vol. 45 (1938), pp. 1–41.

[45]Edward C. Tolman, *Collected Papers in Psychology* (Berkeley: University of California Press, 1951).

## *Evaluation*

### Criticisms of Tolman

The most persistent criticism has been that Tolman failed to present a logically integrated theory.[46] If our own presentation has seemed fragmented, it is because Tolman was fragmented in the formulation of his ideas. Too many questions were left unanswered, and too many variables unaccounted for.

While claiming to be a behaviorist, Tolman presented an undeniable dualism. He spoke of a rat's expectancies and "cognitive maps," which remained purely hypothetical constructs. Like Lewin, any testing of these hypotheses could only be inferential. Further, in his intervening variables, which he felt helped as explanatory principles, we found a subjectivism similar to Lewin and the Gestalt psychologists. From the point of view of a radical behaviorist like Skinner, the intervening variables added nothing by way of explanation and could just as easily be eliminated. For a basic explanation, Skinner suggested it would be better to go back to the independent variables.[47] Finally, Tolman failed to relate the overt behavior of the organism to the covert cognitive states.

Tolman admitted his dualism in the following statement although he felt he had somehow used operational terms. This, of course, is open to question.[48]

> Although I was sold on objectivism and behaviorism as *the* method in psychology, the only categorizing rubrics which I had at hand were mentalistic ones. So when I began to try to develop a behavioristic system of my own, what I really was doing was trying to rewrite a commonsense mentalistic psychology . . . in operational behavioristic terms.

The problems involved in purposivism and teleology had been introduced before on a number of occasions. There was no point in belaboring the issue. However, how could a system that claimed to be behavioristic maintain a teleological point of view? Perhaps it was possible, but most behaviorists who were usually determinists would fail to agree.

### Contributions of Tolman

Tolman's theories have exerted a strong influence in psychology over the past forty years. He introduced new and exciting methods and his research pointed to crucial issues. He has been highly regarded by students who were learning theorists, both past and present. The many varieties of the latent learning ex-

---

[46]M. H. Marx and W. A. Cronan-Hillix, *Systems and Theories in Psychology* (New York: McGraw-Hill Book Co., 1987).

[47]B. F. Skinner, *Science and Human Behavior, op. cit.*

[48]Edward C. Tolman, "Purposive Behavior," in S. Koch, ed., *Psychology, a Study of a Science*, vol. II, *General Systematic Formulations, Learning and Special Processes* (New York: McGraw-Hill Book Co., 1959), p. 94.

periment (see Hilgard[49] for more details) have made the reinforcement theorists think hard for adequate explanations. Some felt that he had pointed up a basic flaw in reinforcement theory which has not yet been resolved.

If Tolman did not introduce the rat into psychology, he certainly made it popular. For those more humanistically oriented, of course, this was no contribution at all; but animals can be subjected to much more adequate experimental controls than humans, and rats continue to maintain a prominent place in psychological experimentation.

Those who objected to the simple *S-R* reflex kind of psychology found Tolman's molar approach very appealing. Psychology, according to the wholistic approach, should be concerned with the behavior of the whole organism and not merely separate segments. There was considerable merit to the argument. To break behavior down into molecular units could result in a very artificial analysis. Kantor[50] suggested that we are dealing in psychology with the whole organism interacting with objects in its environment, and to treat specific molecular units leaves out a good deal of what psychology should be concerned with.

## Suggested Further Readings

Estes, W. K., *et al., Modern Learning Theory.* New York: Appleton-Century-Crofts, 1954, chs. 2 and 4. Two highly critical chapters on Tolman by MacCorquodale and Meehl and on Lewin by Estes. The learning aspects of these two field theories are carefully examined.

Hilgard, E. R., and Bower, G. H., *Theories of Learning,* 3rd ed. New York: Appleton-Century-Crofts, 1966, ch. 7. A highly readable chapter on Tolman's basic theory.

Leeper, R. W., *Lewin's Topological and Vector Psychology.* Eugene, Oregon: University of Oregon Press, 1943. A very readable and somewhat critical summary of Lewin's system. Much easier to understand than Lewin himself.

Lewin, Kurt, *A Dynamic Theory of Personality.* New York: McGraw-Hill Book Co., 1935. The best place to begin reading Lewin, but not easy going.

Tolman, Edward C., *Purposive Behavior in Animals and Men.* New York: Appleton-Century Co., 1932. Tolman's basic position and his most widely read book.

---

[49]E. R. Hilgard, *op. cit.,* ch. 6.
[50]J. R. Kantor, *Principles of Psychology,* 2 vols. (New York: Alfred A. Knopf, 1924–1926).

# CHAPTER

# 16

# *Cognitive Psychology*

Cognitive psychology has its roots in ancient philosophy and in the early movements in the psychology of the late nineteenth and early twentieth century. During the past three decades, beginning in the 1960s, there has been a rebirth of interest in the cognitive approach.

Many psychologists view the new cognitive psychology as a revolt against behaviorism. The cognitive psychologists of today, like those of the past, view behaviorism as too narrow an approach. Contemporary behaviorists consider psychology to be the study of objective, observable behavior that results directly from prior and present environmental conditions. The cognitive psychologists ask, What happens between the environmental stimuli and the resulting behavior? Certainly, there must be certain cognitions or mental processes that go on. Thus, as is so often the case, we have a counterrevolution at hand, in which the methods of investigations are, in fact, very behavioral but also in which theory depends on the postulation of an intervening mind or mental processes or whatever term one cares to apply to describe what intervenes.

Today, there is at least one great difference between those earlier psychologists—such as William James, Wilhelm Wundt, and Edward Titchener—and the modern cognitivists: Contemporary cognitive psychologists do not use the method of introspection—that is, looking into the contents of consciousness or mental life, nor do cognitive psychologists make use of the phenomenological method of the humanistic and existential psychologists (see chaps. 19 and 20). The phenomenological method is much like the "looking into" of the introspectionists.

## Definition and Subject Matter

Before considering briefly the antecedents of current cognitive psychology, let us examine how cognitive psychologists define and set forth the subject matter of their study. Some say, rather simply, that they study "how the mind works," and we already know what the behaviorists would say about that statement. As John Watson wrote in the early part of this century, a notion of mind or consciousness is nothing more than Monk's Lore or Old Wives' Tales.

Assuming that mind exists, one might ask further, "Where is the mind located?" Some cognitive psychologists might answer, "It doesn't matter; you don't have to put it any place." Others might say "in the brain." With the progress made by physiological psychologists—or more specifically, neuropsychologists—much is being learned about how the brain functions in the transmission of neural impulses and the encoding of neural information. Their findings are very agreeable to some cognitive psychologists, who feel that in the final analysis, when all the facts are in, the answer will be given in physiological terms, for the seat of the mind is in the brain.

Hayes[1] gives a good definition as follows:

> Cognitive psychology is a modern approach to the study of processes by which people come to understand the world—such processes as memory, learning, comprehending language, problem solving, and creativity. Cognitive psychology has been influenced by developments in language, computer science, and of course, earlier work in philosophy and psychology.

Certainly implied in this definition is the notion that cognitive psychology stresses the study of "higher mental processes." As Lichtenstein[2] has pointed out, one of the appealing aspects of cognitive psychology is the fact that it corresponds quite nicely to the commonsense psychology of the layperson. If one asks students to define psychology before they have had even an introductory course, they will usually say, "Psychology is the study of the mind." According to Neisser,[3] one of the early leading researchers in cognitive psychology, "Cognitive psychology refers to all the processes by which the sensory input is transformed, reduced, elaborated, stored, recovered, and used."

## Antecedents

The antecedents of modern cognitive psychology are to be found in the writings of many researchers already discussed in this book. The reader may wish to refer back to the discussions in earlier chapters.

---

[1]J. R. Hayes, *Cognitive Psychology: Thinking and Creating* (Homewood, Ill.: Dorsey Press, 1978), p. 1.

[2]P. E. Lichtenstein, "Theoretical Psychology: Where Is It Headed?" *Psychological Record,* Vol. 30 (1980), pp. 447–58.

[3]U. Neisser, *Cognitive Psychology* (New York: Appleton-Century-Crofts, 1967), p. 4.

## British Empiricism: Locke, Berkeley, and Hume

John Locke, in his *Essay Concerning Human Understanding*,[4] proposed a theory of knowledge in which he suggested an explanation of how we come to know the world. The word *cognition* means "knowing." Locke proposed that all knowledge came from experience and that the human mind could do only two things: it could receive experiences from the outside world, and it could reflect upon them. His notion of reflection was his attempt to explain higher mental processes, such as thinking and reasoning. In the fourth edition of his *Essay*, he explained that experiences came together, by association, to form complex ideas.

Shortly after Locke, George Berkeley[5] denied that the source of knowledge was the real world, but he believed that experiences did exist in the human minds of those who received them, and that they came from God. He also believed that minds did exist apart from the experiences they received.

David Hume,[6] about fifty years after Locke, believed that experiences were the stuff that knowledge was made of. Furthermore, he stressed various laws of association, which had only been touched on by Locke. For Hume, experiences could be associated by similarity (resemblance), contiguity (togetherness), or cause and effect, which he later reduced to mere contiguity (one thing follows another). For these theorists, and later for the British associationists, the principle of association was crucial in explaining how the mind worked. Thus, associations were used to explain complex thought processes. Today, some cognitive psychologists, but not all, also stress the importance of association.

## Nativism: Kant

Immanuel Kant[7] was much concerned with the operation of the mind. He believed in the existence of the mind but differed from the empiricists as to its nature and functions. For Kant, the mind worked in certain native, or inherent, ways and was not necessarily dependent on prior experiences or learning. Some implications of this position for contemporary cognitive psychology are to be found in the writings of Noam Chomsky,[8] a contemporary student of language, who has been strongly influenced by the cognitive movement. Chomsky has suggested that some of our knowledge of the grammar of language is innate, or inherited (see pp. 290–291). He believes, for example, that children's language skills develop far too rapidly to be accounted for entirely by experience and learning.

---

[4] J. Locke. *An Essay Concerning Human Understanding*, ed. A. C. Fraser (New York: Dover Press, 1959).

[5] G. Berkeley, *A Treatise Concerning the Principles of Human Knowledge*, in A. A. Luce and T. E. Jesop, eds., *The Works of George Berkeley*, Vol. II (London: Nelson, 1949).

[6] D. Hume, *A Treatise on Human Nature*, trans. J. Watson (New York: St. Martin's Press, 1929). (First published 1781.)

[7] Immanuel Kant, *Critique of Pure Reason*, F. M. Miller, trans. (London: Macmillan, 1881).

[8] N. Chomsky, *Language and Mind*, enlarged ed. (New York: Harcourt Brace Jovanovich, 1972).

## The Structuralists: Wundt and Titchener

The next step in the development of cognitive psychology occurs in the late nineteenth and early twentieth centuries, to the beginnings of experimental psychology (see chaps. 6 and 7). Wilhelm Wundt broke with philosophy to establish a new experimental science of psychology. Both he and his follower Titchener believed that conscious experience was the legitimate subject matter of psychology. In stressing the importance of experience, these men were following the empiricists. Two aspects of their psychology are significant for cognitive psychology:

1. They emphasized perception as the way we know, in part, the real world. Cognitive psychology considers perception a very important mental function.

2. They developed a method by which mental content should be studied. This method was introspection, an attempt to analyze the contents of the mind or consciousness.

Although cognitive psychologists today do not rely on introspection, they nevertheless would agree that some kind of methodology is necessary for studying cognition. Cognitive psychologists are not mere armchair philosophers who merely speculate regarding the nature of mental processes.

## Gestalt Psychology

As indicated in chapter 14, the great concern of Gestalt psychologists is the study of perception. They believe that perceptions should be studied as a whole and not divided into parts for analysis. In many cases, the way the mind works is native, or natural. Mental events are explained by the laws of perceptual organization. The significance for cognitive psychology is that perceptions are cognitions, or ways of knowing the world. Gestaltists emphasize closure, insight, and set, which are insignificant principles in explaining how the mind works.

## Early Cognitive Behaviorism

One of the first of the group of cognitive behaviorists was Edward Tolman (see chap. 15). Tolman called himself a "purposive behaviorist." In the 1930s, he introduced the idea of "cognitive maps," by which animals and humans were able to learn. Tolman was not an S-R (stimulus-response) psychologist like other behaviorists, such as Skinner, Guthrie, or Hull. For him, animals learned by signs or expectations or "what leads to what." When this process continued, a cognitive map was set up in the brain as a means of explaining the learning process. He relied on these processes, which intervened between the environment and behavior. Cognitive psychologists today are very much concerned with what goes on between the input (environment) and the output (resulting behavior). Tolman stressed behavior as the end result, but he also relied on the intervening cognitions that led to the behavior. Today, there is a group of psychologists who consider themselves cognitive behaviorists. They will be discussed in a later section in this chapter.

## World War II and the Beginnings of Contemporary Cognitive Psychology

Current interest in cognitive psychology began with human factors research during World War II. Human factors as a subject matter deals with the interaction of humans and machines, particularly with regard to improving human skills. This area of psychology emerged during the war when it became evident that the new technologies being developed required improvements in layout and design of instrumentation.

Nowhere was the problem of design layout more important than in the field of aviation. Broadbent[9] noted that certain aircraft instruments were monitored more carefully than others and, further, that too much information was displayed for pilots to be able to attend to all of it. Paying attention to so many gauges required substantial amounts of time.

The first implication of Broadbent's observation was that humans do not wait passively for stimuli to impinge upon them but rather seek out stimuli actively. Second, human information processing seemed similar to machine control mechanisms. Just as each machine mechanism responds to a particular type of informative, so likewise the human information processing system operates as a collection of such mechanisms. For a particular human being, the key problem becomes the allocation of attention necessary to direct the information processing of such mental events properly.

This, then, led psychologists to become interested in the computer. They realized that we can represent and organize knowledge, but with computers we can represent knowledge in a greater variety of ways. Thus, computers can simulate and mimic knowledge—that is, cognitive events.

## *Varieties of Cognitive Psychology*

Just as there is *no one* behavioristic, humanistic, or existential psychology today, there is *no one* cognitive psychology. These should be interpreted as movements within psychology today, in which a group of people share certain common ideas, but each person may differ in various ways from another. For example, both Guthrie and Skinner share certain beliefs, such as the denial of the mind or mental processes, and both relate objects in the environment to the responding organism. However, they differ in many of the specific tenets. Skinner stresses the importance of reinforcement; Guthrie does not. Likewise, cognitive

[9]D. E. Broadbent, "A Mechanical Model for Human Attention and Immediate Memory," *Psychological Review*, Vol. 64 (1954), p. 205.

psychologists stress cognitions and intervening mental processes, but will differ in many other respects. Leahey[10] has suggested what he calls "three paradigms for cognitive psychology":

1. **The "new" structuralism.** This movement, begun in Europe, has little to do with the structuralism of Wundt and Titchener. It stresses a structural approach to cognition—what its structures are and how they work. This group stresses the relationship of language to cognition. Two people are particularly prominent. One is Jean Piaget, the eminent developmental psychologist who studied the development of language and thought in children for many years. The second is Noam Chomsky, who has developed an elaborate theory of language in the light of its formal language structure.

2. **Man and machine.** The study of information processing and the computer. With the development of the computer after World War II, many analogies have been drawn between human cognition and the functions of the computer.

3. **The "new" mentalism.** Leahey's term for this group is not so clearly defined and has many broad meanings. Leahey states that this is a rather eclectic group. They could be cognitive psychologists who do not fit into the first two groups. What they have in common is that they do not stress principles of association considered important by some other cognitive psychologists.

Finally, although not included by Leahey, are the cognitive behaviorists, a group who stress the importance of behavior but, unlike radical behaviorists such as B. F. Skinner, do not object to using intervening cognitive principles as part of their explanations. Albert Bandura is a leader in this group.

---

## The First Paradigm: The "New" Structuralists

The general thrust of the "new" structuralists is to make explanations through reference to abstract structures, either logical or mathematical.

### Jean Piaget (1896–1980)

Piaget[11] was much concerned with epistemology, or the growth of knowledge. He attempted to plot the growth of knowledge in children and study it empirically. A Swiss psychologist originally trained as a zoologist, he started his work

---

[10]T. H. Leahey, *A History of Psychology,* 2nd ed. (Englewood Cliffs, N.J.: Prentice-Hall, 1987).

[11]J. Piaget, *The Construction of Reality in the Child,* trans. M. Cook (New York: Basic Books, 1954).

on the development of cognition while he was giving intelligence tests in the laboratory of Alfred Binet, who developed the first intelligence test. Piaget observed that children reasoned quite differently from adults, and that they differed in the way they perceived the world. He divided the growth of cognition into four phases or stages: (1) sensorimotor, (2) preoperational, (3) concrete operational, and (4) formal operational. A different type of intelligence operates in each stage. He believed that the intellect grew not only quantitatively but also qualitatively. For example, the five-year-old not only knows less than the ten-year-old, but also uses different thinking processes. There are different ways of knowing the world, and changes in the logical structure of children's minds occur as they grow:

1. **Sensorimotor stage.** Very early in life, the child does not have a concept of objects, but during the first two years, it begins to develop. The concepts of objects and space result from activity in adjusting to the world. Through these adjustments, the child accommodates itself to the world. It has to change so as to suit the environment. Piaget held that the child had many spaces—visual, buccal (mouth), auditory, and tactile. Just as intersensory coordination develops in reaching for an object, so sensorimotor coordination occurs in following a visual object with the eyes. Adaptation and organization are crucial to the development of cognition (intelligence). These he considered to be inherent capacities that are uniquely human. Of course, learning must also be involved. This first period lasts from birth to about two years. Although development is a continuous process, there are times when changes occur rapidly or more slowly.

2. **Preoperational stage.** This stage lasts from about two to seven years. In this period, logical thinking is relatively loosely organized. Children in this stage frequently contradict themselves but are not bothered by the contradiction. It follows that there are differences in understanding points of view which vary from child to child. Here Piaget emphasized the egocentric character of children's thinking. This is not the same as selfishness; it is self-centered thinking but not an attempt to take advantage of another child for purposes of self-advantage. Piaget observed egocentricism in watching children at play. Often children make remarks that are not directed at anyone. They come out as soliloquies, without any attention paid to the audience. Another observation that substantiates this assertion of egocentric thought is that when children argue they do not take into account their opponents' points of view.

   Another aspect of this period is that children make mistakes in judging the quantity of things. For example, they may believe that quantity changes with a change in shape, when actually the quantity remains the same. For example, if a child is shown two containers of juice, one that is tall and thin and another short and broad, the child will judge the tall, thin container as having more juice, when actually the quantity in both containers is the same. In this case, the child is considering only one characteristic of the object—the height. An older child will judge the quantity more accurately, so when a trade is made with another child it is fair and equal. The younger child might be taken advantage of in this respect.

3. **Concrete operational stage.** This stage runs from about ages seven to twelve. Here the child develops a set of rules, called groupings, which have special logical qualities. For example, A equals B in some characteristic such as length. If A is larger than B and B is larger than C, then it follows that A is larger than C.

There are relations among categories, which Piaget called classes. For example, a child understands at this stage that all oranges belong to the class of fruit and that all fruit belongs to the class of food. The reverse also holds. The class of food involves all fruits and other edible things.

Finally, the child in this stage can understand the specific attributes of objects, and that the same objects can belong to more than one class. For example, the child realizes that bananas can belong to the class of natural foods as well as to the class of sweet foods. Unlike the child in the preoperational period, the child in the concrete operational period is capable of developing concepts of conservation. The younger child believes that if you take a piece of clay and change its shape, the amount also changes, but the child in the concrete operational period understands that even if the shape is changed, the quantity remains the same. A child of five considers a ball and pancake unequal in quantity, but three years later the same child will understand that they are equal. The pancake is thinner but also wider.

Likewise, the child in this period can deal with relations. Some things are taller, thinner, shorter, or darker than others. The younger child has difficulty with this concept; the younger child has to deal in absolutes.

4. **Formal operational stage.** This period lasts from twelve years on to adulthood. The child in the previous period can think about facts, properties, and relationships, but these must involve real objects and events, such as buttons, candies, or containers. The child in the formal operational period can deal in the abstract by going beyond reality and thinking of things that *could* be.

First of all, Piaget believed that children in this stage can reason about hypothetical situations, which could involve algebraic statements or geometric theorems. They can reason about situations that are real or imagined.

Next, their thinking can involve a systematic search for a solution to a problem. In many problems, alternate solutions are possible. Suppose this child or adolescent is asked to describe how one would go from the child's home in one part of the city to Grandma's house in another. The possible solutions could involve riding in a car, taking a bicycle, walking, or taking the bus.

Finally, the child or adolescent can detect inconsistencies in beliefs. The child is told that God loves and looks after all little children, but if that is so, why is it that so many little children seem to have such a hard time? Is God not looking after them? These children can ponder this problem. In fact, Piaget believed that a concern with thinking is one of the main characteristics of this period.

## Noam Chomsky

Chomsky, who is primarily a linguist, first came to the attention of psychologists when he reviewed B. F. Skinner's book *Verbal Behavior* in the journal *Language*.[12] (For a discussion of Skinner's approach to verbal behavior, see pages 223–224.) In his review, Chomsky attacked Skinner's attempt to analyze verbal behavior in the light of Skinner's own behavioristic approach involving contingencies of reinforcement. In his long and caustic review, Chomsky stated that rather than providing the reader with a scientific analysis of language, Skinner had simply used his old terminology, previously used to describe the behavior of animals, particularly rats and pigeons, to an analysis of human speech. Chomsky basically attacked three aspects of Skinner's approach: (1) stimulus control, (2) reinforcing systems, and (3) response strength. Regarding stimulus control, Chomsky stated that what might be adequate for a rat or pigeon is totally inadequate for describing human speech in complex situations. Chomsky then went on to state that Skinner's analysis of human response strength was likewise inadequate. For example, suppose one stood in front of a painting and screamed at the top of one's voice "beautiful" many times. In this instance, the response strength would be very high, but would that necessarily indicate that the person thought the painting was really beautiful? Finally, Chomsky stated that Skinner dealt with reinforcement in an unscientific way when verbal behavior was under the control of private or unobservable reinforcements.

*Theory of Grammar.* Chomsky's main contribution to cognitive psychology has been in his analysis of grammar.[13] For him, grammar is a set of rules that has two functions: (1) to distinguish grammatical sentences from ungrammatical chains of words, and (2) to identify grammatical relations in various parts of a sentence. Grammar consists of sets of rules that generate proper sentences in much the same way as axioms in geometry are used to construct theorems.

Impressed with the logic of Chomsky's theory of grammar, cognitive psychologists set about to borrow what they could from Chomsky's analysis and apply it to psychological correlates. Perhaps there were relationships between the structure of grammar and the structure of mental processes.

Chomsky's analysis describes what he calls transformational grammar. This analysis is extremely complex, involving formal logic and mathematics. Basically, he feels that language is extremely creative; every sentence spoken is a new creative act. In criticizing Skinner, he states that Skinner's analysis can in no way account for the continuous creativity and flexibility of language. Be-

---

[12]N. Chomsky, "A Review of B. F. Skinner's *Verbal Behavior,*" *Language,* Vol. 35 (1959), pp. 26–58.

[13]N. Chomsky, *Language and Mind.*

cause the rules of grammar are logical and orderly, every person can create an endless list of sentences by repeatedly applying the rules of grammar.

Chomsky's approach is rational rather than empirical. His criticism of Skinner attacked, by extension, all empirical approaches to language. He considers language to be a unique human possession, and like René Descartes centuries before, he sets human beings completely apart from animals. Descartes believed that some knowledge was inherited. For Chomsky, competence in language rests on knowledge of the rules. Competence is different from performance, which is how a person actually uses the rules in speaking or writing. Competence is innate; growing children so readily acquire language that it is not possible to believe that all of it is learned. We are born with a general knowledge of what language is like. The fact that there are linguistic universals, characteristic aspects of language found in all languages, emphasizes his point. These universals reflect innate linguistic structures. He is simply arguing that all children are equipped with certain biological potentials that make it possible for any child to learn any language when exposed to it.

***Implications of Chomsky's Theory.*** To begin with, there is the concept of linguistic universals. If this notion is a valid one, there is the implication of a tremendous leap in our understanding of the basic skills of language and thought.

Next, the observation that children cannot acquire grammatical knowledge on their own leads to the notion of innate predispositions. This means that children are "grammatically programmed." It does not imply, however, that children are born with language as in Descartes' notion of the inheritance of "innate ideas." It merely means that each child inherits a "blueprint" that will be enhanced by the child's experience and exposure to the spoken language of others. This merely refers to the specific functions of our brains as well as our vocal apparatus.

## The Second Paradigm: Information Processing and the Computer

In the second paradigm for cognitive psychology, information processing and the computer stress an approach by which certain stimuli (input) are fed into the organism. The organism in turn processes the information somewhere inside and then uses it to construct the responses (output). Here the behavior is not the direct result of the stimuli but derives from the intervening mental processes. Modern neuropsychologists would like to think all this is done in the brain, but for our purposes in this section, the computer will serve as a useful analogy.

The idea of the human being as a machine goes back several centuries to Descartes, who proposed that animals were machines and that the human body worked basically in a mechanical way. A century later, Julian de la Mettrie proposed a similar idea in his materialism, as presented in his book *L'Homme Machine* (*Man, a Machine*).[14] For him, the seat of the mind was the brain, and it all worked in a very mechanical way.

With the development of the computer, psychologists had a new tool by which mental processes could be studied: information-processing models. Prior to the development of these models, behavioristic psychologists thought only of stimulus-response and did not worry about what went on in between.

The computer provided an additional way of interpreting mental processes. The first computer was developed in 1944 by Howard Atken. As the computer developed, information could be stored in what are called memory banks, and programs were developed to solve problems. In using a computer to solve problems, a person inserts the data (information) through an input, such as a teletypewriter. A program already developed has been stored in the computer's memory. Instructions are then given to the computer, which in turn solves the problem and presents results in the output.

To illustrate information processing, let us look at a classic experiment by Steinberg.[15] He wanted to discover how long it takes a person to perform a variety of mental processes. Steinberg devised a reaction-time apparatus that measured the time between the presentation of a stimulus and the organism's response, a process that usually takes place in milliseconds. The reaction time (RT) becomes longer when two or more similar stimuli are presented (choice RT). Steinberg's reaction-time experiments go back to the studies in Wundt's laboratory, where Wundt studied the reaction time of subjects to visual, auditory, and tactile stimuli.

In Steinberg's experiment, the subjects were given a list of items to memorize. The subjects were then shown a series of numbers. They had to indicate as quickly as possible whether a particular number appeared in the list or "memory set." Steinberg found that response times lengthened as the number of items in the memory set grew. He explained that the subjects had to make longer searches of their memories as the number of digits in the memory set increased. Each test item had to be compared with the memory for each item in the set, one after another.

An oversimplification of the information-processing model would look something like this:

Stimulus → memory → short-term → long-term → output
input        registry    storage      storage    behavior
                              subject to
                              rapid decay

---

[14] J. O. de la Mettrie, *L'Homme Machine* (*Man, a Machine*), trans. C. G. Bussey and M. W. Calkins (Chicago: Open Court, 1912).

[15] S. Steinberg, "Memory Scanning: Mental Processes Revealed by Reaction Time Experiments," *American Scientist*, Vol. 27 (1969), pp. 1–32.

Note that memory is broken into several subsystems, short-term memory (STM) and long-term memory (LTM). In the latter case, memory can be held for an indefinite period of time.

As Lachman, Lachman, and Butterfield put it, "The information-processing approach has . . . provided psychologists with a fundamentally new way of thinking about people . . . viewing the human being as an active seeker and user of information."[16]

In the same work,[17] these authors say that people must process information and that this fact legitimizes information-processing answers to questions about why people behave the way they do. For example, each time you walk to class you must process each familiar landmark anew. Drawing the appropriate information from your memory, you identify and respond to each landmark, one by one (like shifting gears in a car), until you reach your destination. Thus, information processing is forced upon us, and the only explanation of how we get to class or do anything else is other information processing, so the form of the question tells us the answer.

These authors would like to assert that information processing is real—something inside the organism that is observable neither to the person nor to the neuroscientist who is watching the person with whatever instruments are available. Rather, they can set up flow charts and thus be operational in keeping with an objective experimental psychology.

***The Computer.*** In 1967 Neisser introduced the idea of a parallel between the human being and the computer.[18] It seemed easy to think of people as information-processing objects that could receive inputs from the environment, which we interpret as perceptions, process them (something like thinking), then act upon to come out as output or behavior. It was then proposed further that psychological theories could be written as computer programs. So began the use of computer terminology in psychology. Terms like "coding," "search set," and "retrieval" became common.

Those who favor the analogy of the computer see it as a machine that receives input—that is, the information given it—then processes and stores that information, and finally uses it to produce the output, which may be the solution to a problem. Likewise, humans may act in the same way. We receive information through our senses, process it or store it in our minds or brains, and then use it to perform useful behavior. The notion of computer memory may be likened to human memory, in which information is stored for given periods of time.

There is an interesting analogy between human memory and the computer. Psychologists have differentiated between *short-term memory* and *long-term mem-*

---

[16]R. O. Lachman, J. L. Lachman, and E. C. Butterfield, *Cognitive Psychology and Information Processing: An Introduction* (Hillsdale, N.J.: Lawrence Earlbaum, 1979), p. 10.

[17]*Ibid.*

[18]U. Neisser, *op. cit.*

*ory,* which are quite different. An illustration of short-term memory is looking up a number in the telephone book, remembering it, and then dialing immediately. The capacity of short-term memory is about seven digits for the average person, for example, 397-1284. One remembers only long enough to dial the number. After this is completed, the memory almost immediately disappears. Long-term memory refers to the experiences from the past we can readily recall, even though they occurred many years ago. One may be able to recall the first day at school, a graduation, visiting a friend, or Thanksgiving dinner at Grandma's. So, in fact, we have two kinds of memory. Likewise, the computer has two memory systems and, in fact, the same terms are applied. In developing a program, the computer operator makes use of the short-term memory bank, which can be changed or erased. After the program is fully developed, it can be stored in the permanent memory of the computer, to be brought back when the program is needed to solve a new problem. Furthermore, the permanent memory of the computer can be used to store information indefinitely, as in keeping records, in much the same way a file is used for the storage of important information.

**The Stroop Effect.** In contrast to the memory span experiment cited above, which made use of simple memory functions, experiments on the "Stroop Effect"[19] depended on an easy but unusual set of circumstances. In one experiment by Kline, the subject was asked to report the color of a particular stimulus with disregard to its meaning. If the word "yellow" is fringed in *blue,* the subject will inevitably say "blue." Here we have the activation of two completely different color responses—one indicated by the color itself and the other by the *name* of the color. Even noncolor words with color connotations, such as carrot (yellow) and pea (green), produce significant slowing in the naming of conflicting color images. Once this has been repeated, the interference disappears.[20]

According to the cognitive psychologists, the conclusion to be drawn from these kinds of experiments is that there are numerous interacting activations in memory and these activations are unconscious. The subjects are unable to ignore such mental activity, even when they are told that associations are irrelevant. The Stroop Effect illustrates the way in which chains of associations interact in the memory traces quite apart from conscious activity.

## Artificial Intelligence (AI)

In cognitive research, the model is usually some verbal description of a mental event. It should have enough substance to allow for some research.

In artificial intelligence research, the model should take the form of some computer program that is capable of performing some task.

---

[19]J. R. Stroop, "Studies of Interference in Serial Verbal Learning," *Journal of Experimental Psychology,* Vol. 18 (1935), pp. 643–662.

[20]O. S. Kline, "Semantic Power Measures Through the Influence of Words with Color Meaning," *American Journal of Psychology,* Vol. 77 (1964), pp. 376–88.

***Evaluation of the Computer Model.*** There are those who have found the computer model to be the solution to most human intellectual problems—problem solving, memory, perception, even playing chess.

Putting aside for the moment the question of whether or not computers really engage in conscious mental activity, many of those who are most knowledgeable about computers are the most skeptical, just as they are of cognitive psychology in general. They acknowledge that we must not adopt an overly logical approach to human behavior at the expense of social and emotional factors. The computer has been a great invention and a boon to mankind. We do not mean to conclude that an overly logical approach to human behavior is always a fact of life. The computer model has its limitations, as do many other models in psychology.[21]

The idea of artificial intelligence developed along with the computer. Those who work with artificial intelligence look at the computer as a mind that has the potential of a human mind. Here, then, is an attempt to simulate human intelligence. An example is found in a study by Newell, Shaw, and Simon.[22] They observed how people go about solving a variety of logical and mathematical problems. They then attempted to write programs in which the computer solved problems in a similar way. From these programs, they abstracted the General Problem Solver, a program that could simulate the solution of a variety of problems.

Newell and Simon[23] have also developed the Logical Theorist, or LT, as an application of artificial intelligence. Discovering proofs in logic is similar to discovering proofs in geometry. One begins with a small set of axioms—statements assumed to be true without further proof. Theorems are then deduced from axioms. Proofs then follow, according to strict rules of inference. Two of the processes used by LT involve similarity testing and matching. The former finds theorems that have already been proven to work. Matching breaks the search for a solution into parts, testing each one at a time.

Many of those concerned with artificial intelligence, at least in psychology, like to think of the brain as their model. According to Pronko,[24] these people consider the brain to be a computer and the computer to act like a brain. However, there is still a great deal to be learned about the functions of the brain. The idea of the brain as a machine dates back to the eighteenth century French materialists (see pp. 167–168).

***Information Processing and Neurology.*** When cognitive psychologists refer to the information-processing approach, they usually refer to neurological events. These are not described specifically but in the abstract. The specific

---

[21]T. H. Leahey, *A History of Psychology: Main Currents in Psychological Thought,* 2nd ed. (Englewood Cliffs, N.J.: Prentice Hall, 1987).

[22]A. Newell, J. C. Shaw, and H. A. Simon, "Report on a General Problem Solving Program for the Computer," *Proceedings of the International Conference on Information Processing* (UNESCO, 1960), pp. 256–64.

[23]A. Newell and H. A. Simon, "The Logic Theory Machine," *Transactions on Information Theory,* Vol. 2 (1956), pp. 61–79.

[24]N. H. Pronko, *From AI to Zeitgeist* (New York: Greenwood Press, 1988), p. 1.

neurology involved has not yet been discovered. The presumption is that something is going on in the nervous system (brain), but neuroscience has not yet discovered just what it is. Presumably, different kinds of cognitive processes (memory, imaging, perception, problem solving, language, etc.) operate in different manners. However, neuroscience is advancing at a rapid rate, and more and more will be discovered in the decades to come.

## The Third Paradigm:
## The "New" Mentalism

The main characteristic of this aspect of cognitive psychology is the attempt to explain mental processes without resorting to principles of association. It has its basis in the Würzburg School of Psychology in Germany at the turn of the century. The Würzburg School was interested in studying the processes of thinking (see pp. 87–89). They gave subjects problems to solve and then asked them to describe what went on in their thought processes. The psychologists hoped to find what went on during thinking. They discovered, to their surprise, that thinking could occur in the absence of images. The school eventually became known as the school of "imageless thought." Their claim was that associations of ideas did not explain the thinking process. This interpretation was at variance with that of Wundt, who relied heavily on the principle of association to explain how elements in consciousness could hang together to form ideas (see p. 83). The eventual explanation by the Würzburg School was that the task itself developed a mental set that was a determining tendency. The mental set directed the thinking even before the problem was presented.

Schweller, Brewer, and Dahl[25] demonstrated that the way a subject paraphrased a sentence depended on the context in which it was given. For example, a father might say to his son, who has just asked for a new car, "I am not paid enough." This could be properly paraphrased as "I can't afford it." If the sentence is addressed to the boss, the man might say, "I want a raise." The paraphrase depended on the context within which the statement was presented, whether father-to-son or worker-to-boss. Brewer argues that what subjects store in their memories is not merely a string of words but the main idea described by the sentence. When an idea is recalled, it depends on the mental set of the speaker at the time. This discovery could have practical implications in court testimony. A witness might not report exactly what was seen in reporting an accident. The report could be influenced by the way the reporter felt, either positively or negatively, about the people involved.

---

[25]D. D. Schweller, W. F. Brewer, and D. Dahl, "Memory for Illocutionary Forces and Preillocutionary Effects of Certain Utterances," *Journal of Verbal Learning and Verbal Behavior,* Vol. 15 (1976), pp. 325–37.

A second line of evidence comes from the work of Bransford and Franks,[26] which showed how subjects would construct a unified representation from separately presented ideas. Their experiment was presented as evidence that people can form a sensible representation from completely different ideas. For example, given the words *ant, table, kitchen, jelly,* and *sweet,* the following sentence could be constructed: "The ants ate the sweet jelly which was on the table in the kitchen."

Another study showed that when subjects were given sentences that were vague when out of context, they had difficulty in remembering them. When the context was presented, recall improved markedly. First, subjects were given either an inappropriate context ("geyser") or the appropriate context ("hurricane"). Then they were given the sentence "The eye is comparatively calm." When the appropriate context had been given, recall was much better.

These studies were interpreted to mean that including a schema or a central idea, around which memory can be organized, improves recall. Bransford believes that associations are not necessary to explain memory and that cognitive psychology can explain memory better by using nonassociative principles, such as schema.

## What Is Cognitive Science?

There appears to be a new integration of those disciplines that study the nature of human knowledge. This new interdisciplinary field has become known as "cognitive science." It includes cognitive psychology, linguistics, philosophy, artificial intelligence, and the neurosciences.[27] Computer language has also been helpful. This approach provides a theoretical background for stating psychological hypotheses—partly because, in a way, computer programs provide a natural theoretical language for stating such hypotheses. Any theory that cannot be made specific enough to run on a computer becomes a faulty theory.

## Cognitive Behaviorism

Traditional behaviorism (see chap. 13) has characteristically studied the relationship between environmental events, and the responses an organism makes to them, without regard to what goes on in between. It makes no reference to cognitive events, such as memories, thoughts, or expectations. Today, some psychologists of the behavioristic persuasion feel that the traditional point of view does not tell the whole story. Such people as Bandura, Mahoney, and Michael believe that cognitive events are causally related to behavior.

According to Mahoney,[28] "From birth to death, only a small percentage of a person's behaviors are publicly observable. Our lives are predominantly com-

---

[26]J. D. Bransford and J. J. Franks, "The Abstraction of Linguistic Ideas," *Cognitive Psychology,* Vol. 2 (1971), pp. 331–50.

[27]B. J. Baars, *The Cognitive Revolution in Psychology* (New York: The Guilford Press, 1986).

[28]M. J. Mahoney, *Cognitive Behavior Modification* (Cambridge, Mass.: Ballinger, 1974), p. 1.

posed of private responses to private environments, ranging from monologues in the shower to senile reveries."

Although traditional behaviorism deals only with stimuli and responses, the cognitive behaviorists add intervening mental processes. These internal processes allow a person to interpret stimuli before making responses. Thus, the controlling factors lie not only in the environment but within the person as well. People will behave differently, according to their cognitive processes. Suppose that at a dinner party each guest was served a large piece of cherry pie with ice cream on top. One of the guests might eat the dessert with relish. Another might ponder the number of calories and play with the food without eating very much. A third might contemplate the possible dangers in eating butterfat and refined sugar.

In the traditional behavioristic position, Skinner holds that in the act of self-control a person simply arranges or rearranges the environment, because we all are under environmental control. The cognitive behaviorists believe that there are internal controls on behavior, so that not only the environment, but also the intermediary mental events, control us.

Traditional behaviorism looks for the reinforcements that maintain and strengthen behavior in the external environment. Things like praise, food, or money strengthen behavior when they are presented. Cognitive behaviorists, such as Bandura,[29, 30] emphasize self-reinforcement. If a person performs a task well, such as making a good shot in golf, the person has direct knowledge of having done well and does not need to be praised by some outside agency. Bandura has also stressed the importance of cognitive processes in observational learning, or modeling. One learns not only by doing but also by watching. In fact, Bandura believes that observational learning accounts for a vast amount of our acquired behavior. (For a more extensive discussion of Bandura's position, see pp. 230–234.)

Cognitive behaviorists have attempted to restore mental processes to the important position they held in earlier psychologies. In so doing, they believe they have presented a more complex and insightful view of human behavior.

---

## *Evaluation*

### Contributions of Cognitive Psychology

1. The proponents of cognitive psychology believe they have presented a "new look" into the nature of psychology. They have explored areas too often ignored by other psychologists—areas such as short-term and long-term

---

[29]A. Bandura, *Social Learning Theory* (Englewood Cliffs, N.J.: Prentice-Hall, 1977).

[30]A. Bandura, *Social Foundations of Thought and Action: A Social Cognitive Theory* (Englewood Cliffs, N.J.: Prentice-Hall, 1986).

memory, thinking, problem solving, and creativity. They have not been afraid to propose mental processes to explain behavior.

2. Cognitive psychologists have explored the nature and structure of language, which becomes an outward expression of internal mental activity. Language, they believe, is a uniquely human phenomenon and actually accounts for a great portion of human behavior. Chomsky and Piaget have provided novel approaches to the study of thought and language. They see mental processes as qualitatively different from other kinds of behavior.

3. Cognitive psychologists use modern technology, such as the computer, as a means of learning more about human thought and memory. This technology can be vastly helpful in understanding more about how the human mind works. This has proven to be an attractive alternative to behaviorism. The computer makes possible a sophisticated and precise theory as a model for understanding mental processes.[31]

4. Baars feels that the future of psychology will be based on information processing. The dominant theory will be mental processes based on cognitive psychology.[32] With the rapid advances in neuropsychology, there will be an integration of neurophysiology and psychological theory. Intelligence-based computer software will be increasingly used to perform psychological research.

## Criticisms of Cognitive Psychology

Just as cognitive psychologists have attacked behaviorism as being too narrow an approach, so also the behaviorists have responded. In 1977, Skinner wrote an article entitled "Why I Am Not a Cognitive Psychologist."[33] His points reflect the current status of criticism regarding cognitive psychology, and the behaviorists have been the principal critics of this movement:

1. Skinner's criticisms center around the use, by cognitive psychologists, of internal mental states or processes. Rather than dealing with behavior as a function of the environment, the cognitive psychologists invent internal surrogates, which become the subject matter of their study. When the causal conditions are not readily seen or known, they simply invent mental states as substitutes.

2. Skinner,[34] who was the most ardent opponent of cognitive psychology, made the following accusations. (He refers to cognitive science, a broader concept that includes cognitive psychology.)

---

[31]T. A. Leahey, *op. cit.*, p. 345.
[32]B. J. Baars, *op. cit.*
[33]B. F. Skinner, "Why I Am Not a Cognitive Psychologist," *Behaviorism*, Vol. 5 (1977), pp. 1–10.
[34]B. F. Skinner, "Cognitive Science and Behaviorism," *British Journal of Psychology*, Vol. 76 (1985), pp. 291–301.

He accuses cognitive science of simply speculating about internal processes, indicating that they have no appropriate means of observation.

He accuses cognitive science of emasculating the experimental analysis of behavior.

Likewise, he accuses cognitive scientists of reviving a theory that says feelings and states of mind determine behavior.

As with psychoanalysts, he accuses cognitive scientists of inventing explanatory systems, which are admired for their profundity which is properly inaccessibility.

Finally, he accuses cognitive scientists of relaxing standards of definition and logical thinking and releasing a flood of speculation inimical to science.

## Suggested Further Readings

Baars, B. J., *The Cognitive Revolution in Psychology*. New York: The Guilford Press, 1986. Traces the history of cognitive psychology and relates it to behaviorism.

Best, J. B., *Cognitive Psychology*. St. Paul: West Publishing Co., 1986. An excellent discussion of all aspects of cognitive psychology; very complete, with a very good introduction.

McCarthy, R. A., and Warrington, E. K. *Cognitive Neuropsychology: A Clinical Introduction*. San Diego: Academic Press, 1990. A good discussion of the neurological background of cognitive psychology. Reader will need knowledge of neurology. Not for beginners.

Cohen, J., *Cognitive Psychology,* 2nd ed. New York: Academic Press, 1983.

Kenney, R., *Cognitive Psychology,* 2nd ed. St. Paul: West Publishing Co., 1989.

Kenney, H., *Problem Solving*. New York: Open University Press, 1993.

Skinner, B. F., "Cognitive Science and Behaviorism." *British Journal of Psychology,* Vol. 76 (1985), pp. 291–301. A scathing critique of cognitive science from the standpoint of a behaviorist.

# CHAPTER

# 17

# *Psychoanalysis*

$W$hile some schools of psychology have died because they had nowhere to go and others have become enmeshed in the mainstream of psychology, this cannot be said for psychoanalysis. Today, it is very much alive. Psychoanalysis arose in a very different tradition from other schools. Other theories and systems had been developed by people who considered themselves academic psychologists. They maintained their association with universities, expounded their theories, and did experiments and other forms of observation to support the validity of their ideas. Such was not the case with psychoanalysis. It evolved in a medical and clinical tradition.

Throughout most of his adult life, Sigmund Freud (1856–1939), its founder, was a practicing physician. In his early years he was interested in neurology and did experiments, but these had little relevance, if any, to the development of his psychoanalytic theory. Only in a very general way did psychoanalysis deal with the typical topics psychologists considered important—sensation, perception, learning, and forgetting. Still, it did not ignore these matters completely. Freud's was a purely human psychology, a psychology of personality. As Woodworth[1] has suggested, it was really a school of psychiatry, since Freud's writings were often concerned with various forms of behavioral deviation.

We are not concerned here with psychoanalysis as a method of treating neurotic people. However, it will be necessary to make references to abnormal behavior at least in the early part of our discussion because, to Freud, the theory and practice went hand in hand. Our primary concern is with a theory of normal personality (or behavior, in the broadest sense). Perhaps more than any other system, psychoanalysis has spread its influences on other intellectual develop-

[1]Robert S. Woodworth, *Contemporary Schools of Psychology,* 2nd ed. (New York: The Ronald Press Co., 1948), ch. 6.

ments as diverse as art, drama, literature, sociology, and anthropology, as well as psychology even in its academic tradition. Although Freud was trained in medicine and neurology, in his early years he began to question the purely "somatic" interpretations of behavior disorders. He revolted against the German psychiatrists, such as Kraepelin, who had denied the possibility of any psychological influences as causative factors in mental disorders. In the evolution of his theories, Freud became very much of a psychologist, not only in his descriptions but also in his explanations.

## Antecedents

Certainly no other personality theory has had a stronger influence on the intellectual life of the twentieth century. The intelligent layperson who has not studied psychology in the traditional sense is acquainted with some aspects of Freud's theory. Many of Freud's major works are available in paperback editions, along with numerous commentaries, which can be purchased at most bookstores.

Although some of the most ardent disciples of the orthodox Freudian doctrines might be reluctant to admit it, Freud did not invent his system without earlier influences. Psychoanalysis, like all other systems, had its antecedents.

### Leibnitz

Perhaps we could go back even further to St. Thomas in the Middle Ages, but we shall start with the eighteenth century and Leibnitz's theory of the monads (see pp. 43–44). Remember that the monad was a point of force or energy. Monads constituted the elements of both physical and mental reality. They did not interact with each other, but each was endowed with its own predestination. Monads also had degrees of clarity or consciousness. There were all degrees of clearness, from the most conscious to the least clear or unconscious.

Two points from Leibnitz's theory had implications for psychoanalysis. The first was that of energy, for Freud was the first to create a dynamic psychology in which the concept of energy (although psychic) was to play an important part. Second, and more obvious was the division between consciousness and unconsciousness, and in particular the degrees of unconsciousness.

### Herbart

A century later, Herbart was to develop the notion of a threshold between consciousness and unconsciousness (see pp. 58–59). Ideas existed in both the conscious and unconscious. If an idea in the unconscious were compatible with one in the conscious, it could gain entrance. On the other hand, ideas might join forces in the unconscious and force their way into consciousness. If two ideas in consciousness were incompatible, one of them might be forced into the unconscious. This involved the concept of a conflict between consciousness and unconsciousness. Boring[2] has suggested that Leibnitz foreshadowed the notion of an unconscious, but it was Herbart who gave it full recognition. As we have pointed out earlier, Ernest Jones,[3] Freud's biographer, wrote that Freud was directly acquainted with the writings of Herbart.

## Schopenhauer and Nietzsche

Arthur Schopenhauer (1788–1860) also believed in the existence of the unconscious. He wrote of the opposition of the Will to repulsive ideas whose breakthrough into consciousness could cause insanity. This basic concept—repression—was adopted by Freud and became one of the cornerstones of psychoanalysis. In later Freudian theory, one of the functions of the ego was to keep in check ideas threatening to it and further to use its energy to force unpleasant ideas from consciousness into the unconscious. Furthermore, Freud shared Schopenhauer's rather pessimistic ideas of human nature. Finally, Schopenhauer anticipated Freud's notion of sublimation, an escape from the irrational instinctual forces through music or poetry or Platonic philosophy.

Friedrich Nietzsche (1844–1900) believed that humans were basically animals and that much of this basic animal nature has to remain in the unconscious, in order to meet the dictates of a civilized society. Nietzsche also stressed the aggressive nature of human beings. In Freud's later theory, human aggression is derived from the death instinct. Nietzsche also recognized the problems that occur when aggression is repressed. When these impulses cannot be vented, the result may take the form of perverted behavior. Sometimes Freud acknowledged that his ideas originated with Schopenhauer and Nietzsche, but at other times the influence of these philosophers is only implied.

## Darwin

Freud was born just three years before Darwin published the *Origin of Species*.[4] Darwin's theory (see pp. 117–119) influenced Freud in at least two ways. First, Darwin presented a kind of determinism in his evolutionary theory. There were reasons for natural selection. As we shall see later, Freud applied the deterministic principle wholeheartedly to the development of the normal human personality, as well as those instances where neurotic symptoms developed.

The second influence from Darwin was the belief that humans were akin to the animals. Freud not only looked on the human being as a part of nature but also as one who shared with lower forms many characteristics, particularly

---

[2]E. G. Boring, *A History of Experimental Psychology,* 2nd ed. (New York: Appleton-Century-Crofts, 1950).

[3]Ernest Jones, *The Life and Work of Sigmund Freud,* 3 vols. (New York: Basic Books, Inc., 1953–1957).

[4]Charles Darwin, *Origin of Species by Means of Natural Selection* (London: Collier, 1909).

instincts. Humans were not so governed by intellect as earlier writers had professed. They were, in many ways, irrational beasts.

## The Life of Sigmund Freud

There have been many accounts of Freud's life and works. One of the best of these is Ernest Jones' *Life and Work of Sigmund Freud,* 3 volumes.[5] In the following biographical sketch we shall deal primarily with the reports from Jones along with Freud's own *Autobiography.*[6] Because the development of Freud's theory was so intimately related to his life and the influences of people with whom he interacted, we shall devote more space to this section on Freud's life, particularly the early period, than we have done for other founders of psychological systems.

Sigmund Freud (1856–1939) lived a long and tremendously productive life. Although he aroused much controversy, even his most ardent enemies would find it hard to deny that he was one of the intellectual giants of our times. His influences remain. At the time of his birth on May 6, 1856, the Austro-Hungarian Empire was still intact and maintained a powerful political influence. He was born in the little town of Freiburg, Austria (now Pribor, Czechoslovakia). His father was a poor wool merchant who was not very successful. When Sigmund was four years old, the family moved to Vienna, where Freud remained until the year before his death. With the Nazi invasion in 1938, it became necessary for him to escape to England where he died the following year.

Freud showed his intellectual promise early, and this was recognized by his family. As one of eight children, his room was the only one illuminated by a lamp while the other rooms had candles. At the time, anti-Semitism was rampant in Vienna, and the only professions open to Jews were medicine and the law. Freud chose the former, not because of any compelling desire for medicine, but because it was an opening into the field of science and, in particular neurology, which was later to occupy his interest. He entered the University of Vienna in 1873, but it took him eight years before he finally received his degree. During this period he was influenced by a famous neurologist of the time, Ernest Brücke. Freud published a number of articles on anatomy and neurology and discovered the analgesic properties of cocaine, but failed to recognize its application for human anesthesia. He also dissected hundreds of testes of eels in order to determine their precise structure. This was his first study involving sex. Whether or not this investigation had any influence on the psychosexual theories he developed later is only a matter of conjecture.

[5]Ernest Jones, *op. cit.*
[6]Sigmund Freud, *Autobiography* (New York: W. W. Norton and Co., 1935).

Shortly before obtaining his medical degree, Freud had become acquainted with Joseph Breuer, an eminent and sophisticated physician of Vienna. This friendship was to last until 1895 with the publication by the two men of *Studies in Hysteria.*[7] This date is significant, because it marks the founding of psychoanalysis.

In 1889 Breuer had begun to treat a 21-year-old woman named Bertha Pappenheim. (The case was published in *Studies in Hysteria* under the pseudonym of Fräulein Anna O.) Two years later Freud learned about the case from Breuer, and the two of them discussed it at great length. Anna O. was a classical case of hysteria, a neurotic disorder quite common at the time. She suffered from a variety of symptoms—arm and leg paralysis, anesthesia, blurred vision, and confusion. Apparently, some of her symptoms had begun while she was caring for her dying father. When she first saw Breuer she could not recall many of the earlier traumatic experiences of her life. Anna began talking about her emotionally arousing experiences, after which she reported feeling better. During part of her treatment she had developed a phobia for drinking from a glass despite the fact that she was thirsty. When she recalled that, as a girl, she had seen a dog being allowed to drink from the water glass, which repulsed her, the phobia disappeared. Anna referred to these interviews with Breuer as the "talking cure" or "chimney sweeping."

During his association with Breuer, Freud went to Paris in 1885 to study with a famous French physician, Charcot. Charcot had been using hypnosis in the treatment of hysterical patients, attempting to suggest away the symptoms.

A particular incident is often recorded in a statement made by Charcot. With regard to the cause of a certain patient's difficulties, Charcot said, "But in this kind of case, it is always something genital—always, always, always."[8] Charcot later denied making the statement, but the statement and its denial are reported by Freud in *The History of the Psychoanalytic Movement.*[9] In any event, some scholars seem to feel that this statement first gave Freud the idea of a relationship between sex and neurotic disorders.

Freud stayed in Paris only five months, and returned to Vienna to resume his association with Breuer. Freud and Breuer resumed the use of hypnosis, but after a while Freud began to abandon it in favor of the "talking out" method. For one thing, some patients could not be hypnotized, and many more could not be brought into a deep enough hypnotic state where they could recall forgotten memories. Freud began to realize that these memories were not really forgotten but only *repressed,* since their recall was so disagreeable to the patient. Furthermore, Freud found that the transference of affection of the patient to the analyst was useful in unearthing hidden troubles. Finally, Freud and Breuer

[7]Joseph Breuer, and Sigmund Freud, *Studies in Hysteria* (London: Hogarth Press, 1955). (In *The Standard Edition,* Vol. 2.)
[8]E. G. Boring, *op. cit.,* p. 709.
[9]Sigmund Freud, *History of the Psychoanalytic Movement,* in A. A. Brill, ed., *The Basic Writings of Sigmund Freud* (New York: Random House, 1938), pp. 933–37.

parted company, and Freud continued to refine his free association method by having the patients lie down on his couch and tell him whatever came into their minds.

## The Founding and Early Development

If a date can be set for the founding of psychoanalysis it would be 1895, with the publication of *Studies in Hysteria.*[10] It was Freud's first full-scale attempt at a psychological explanation. Among the cases reported was that of Anna O.; but some of the germs of psychoanalysis were also there—the influence of early childhood, repression, and a discussion of Freud's therapeutic technique. The book caused little stir and received few reviews, mostly unfavorable. It sold only six hundred and twenty-six copies in the next thirteen years.

The following year, 1896, turned out to be a rather traumatic one for Freud. By this time he was becoming increasingly impressed with the significance of sex, not only in personality development but also in sexual traumas as being related to neurotic symptoms. He gave a paper before the Society of Psychiatry and Neurology in Vienna in which he reported that his patients had revealed in the process of their analysis that sexual seduction had occurred during childhood. The seducer was usually an older relative, often the father. His patients were usually reluctant to recall these facts. To say the least, according to Jones,[11] the paper received an "icy reception." Soon afterwards the "horrible truth" began to occur to Freud. His patients had not actually been seduced, but the statements were the product of their fantasies. Freud accepted his mistake, but became even more impressed with the importance of sex in the etiology of psychological disorders.

In 1897 Freud realized that if he were to continue to psychoanalyze his patients he must engage in his own self-analysis. Since he found it difficult to play the dual role of patient and analyst at the same time, most of his analysis was to come from his own dreams. Today, dreams are considered an important source of data in the therapeutic process. Much later, in 1942, Karen Horney, in her book *Self-Analysis,*[12] elaborated the possibility of a person being her or his own "patient" and "analyst," but there is little data available to suggest that such a technique can be successful.

Arising out of his self-analysis came one of Freud's most important books, *The Interpretation of Dreams.*[13] This turned out to be a major work not only because of the discussion of dream analysis but also because other major psy-

---

[10]Joseph Breuer, and Sigmund Freud, *op. cit.*
[11]Ernest Jones, *op. cit.*
[12]Karen Horney, *Self-Analysis* (New York: W. W. Norton and Co., 1942).
[13]Sigmund Freud, *The Interpretation of Dreams* (London: Hogarth Press, 1955). (In *The Standard Edition,* Vols. 4 and 5.)

choanalytic concepts were presented, among them the Oedipus complex. Freud was also realizing the great role that the unconscious played for the human personality. *The Interpretation of Dreams*[14] was published in 1900 and, like *Studies in Hysteria,* "fell flat off the press." That is, it received little attention.

However, Freud did not give up. In 1904 *The Psychopathology of Everyday Life*[15] was published, in which Freud further established his deterministic views. In slips of the tongue, forgetting, and losing objects, even accidents, there was unconscious motivation. In other words, these were not mere accidents or happenings of chance, but had actual underlying causes.

During the first decade of the twentieth century, psychoanalysis began to gain attention. At first, it attracted only a few adherents. In 1902 the Wednesday Evening Discussion Group was established, which was attended by Alfred Adler and Carl Jung (see next chapter). During these meetings various psychoanalytic concepts were discussed. By 1909 Freud's fame had crossed the Atlantic, and he was invited by G. Stanley Hall, a pioneering American psychologist and president of Clark University, to give lectures on psychoanalysis in celebration of the University's twentieth anniversary. Jung also went along. Freud never liked America, and attributed his bowel troubles to American food. According to Jones,[16] the difficulty had existed prior to Freud's visit. Freud commented that the only excuse for Columbus' great mistake was the discovery of tobacco, since Freud smoked about twenty cigars daily.

Jung later returned to America and wrote back to Freud that the American people were ready to accept the psychoanalytic doctrine except for the overemphasis on sex. Freud obviously did not take well to this remark, and the two of them eventually parted.

In 1910 the International Psychoanalysis Association was established with Jung as president, over the objection of Freud's Viennese colleagues, most of whom were Jewish while Jung was not. In 1911 the break came with Adler, and by 1914 Freud and Jung had spoken their last words to each other (see next chapter).

By 1933 Hitler had come to power, and most of the German psychoanalysts soon fled to America. In 1933 the Nazis made a bonfire of Freud's books in Berlin. According to Jones, Freud commented, "What progress we are making. In the Middle Ages they would have burnt me, nowadays they are content with burning my books."[17]

Freud had been encouraged earlier to leave Austria but he stubbornly resisted. By 1938 the Nazis had taken over Austria, and Freud's home was invaded by the Gestapo. Through the efforts of Ernest Jones, an Englishman, and William Bullitt, American ambassador to France, Freud was allowed to leave Vienna for London. In order to leave and receive an exit visa, Freud had

---

[14]*Ibid.*
[15]Sigmund Freud, *The Psychopathology of Everyday Life,* in A. A. Brill, ed. *The Basic Writings of Sigmund Freud* (New York: Random House, 1938), pp. 35–178.
[16]Ernest Jones, *op. cit.*
[17]*Ibid.,* Vol. 3, p. 182.

to sign a paper attesting to the respectful and considerate treatment he had received from the Gestapo.

Freud was well received in England. During the short period before his death he completed his last book, *Moses and Monotheism*.[18] The book was of little psychological significance. In it, Freud speculated that Moses was really not a Jew, but an Egyptian who carried a monotheistic religion into the promised land. Freud died on September 23, 1939.

## Freud's Systematic Position

Freud never wrote a systematic psychology as had many of the psychologists raised in a more academic tradition. His psychology must be gleaned from his many writings which are now available in *The Standard Edition of the Works of Sigmund Freud*, 24 volumes edited by J. Strachey.[19] Perhaps Freud's best statement of his own position is to be found in *Outline of Psychoanalysis*.[20] Calvin Hall, among others, has done an excellent job of organizing Freud's psychology in *Primer of Freudian Psychology*,[21] which explains Freud's fully developed theories in a most readable and concise manner. This book deals entirely with Freud's "normal" psychology. As a practicing analyst, Freud developed theories about neurotic and other forms of abnormal behavior; but these are beyond the scope of the present volume.

### The Conscious, Preconscious, and Unconscious

In his early writings, before he had developed the concept of ego, superego, and id, Freud had divided the mind basically into the conscious and the unconscious. The preconscious was actually part of the unconscious, that part nearest to the threshold of consciousness. In the process of the development of his ideas, Freud made some alterations but never abandoned this concept of the mind.

As in the "iceberg" analogy, the unconscious was by far the largest and most important part of the mind, but the least accessible. Here lay the determining forces of the personality. In the unconscious were repressed memories from earlier life, the source of psychic energy, and the instincts. Through the process of free-association and dream analysis the unconscious might be discovered. As Freud developed his concept of the id, he incorporated into it much of what he had said earlier about the unconscious.

---

[18]Sigmund Freud, *Moses and Monotheism* (New York: Alfred A. Knopf, 1939).
[19]Sigmund Freud, *The Standard Edition of the Complete Works of Sigmund Freud*, J. Strachey, ed. (London: Hogarth Press, 1955).
[20]Sigmund Freud, *An Outline of Psychoanalysis* (New York: W. W. Norton and Co., 1949).
[21]Calvin S. Hall, *A Primer of Freudian Psychology* (Cleveland: World Publishing Co., 1954).

The preconscious bridged the gap between the conscious and the unconscious. It contained memories and ideas which could usually be readily recalled. Being able to remember much of yesterday's events would mean that they had remained in the preconscious readily accessible to the conscious.

Consciousness, itself, consisted of only a small part of the mind, things which one was aware of at any given moment. However, it had direct contact with the world of reality (see Fig. 20).

## The Mental Apparatus

As Freud developed his system, the mental apparatus became one of his most important constructs. It consisted of three divisions: the *ego, superego,* and *id.* In the normal person these three systems should operate as a unified organi-

**FIGURE 20**    *A Hypothetical Drawing of Freud's Mental Apparatus.* Note the relationship between the id, ego, and superego and the three levels of consciousness—the unconscious, preconscious, and conscious. The superego and ego are partly conscious, preconscious, and unconscious, whereas the id is entirely unconscious.

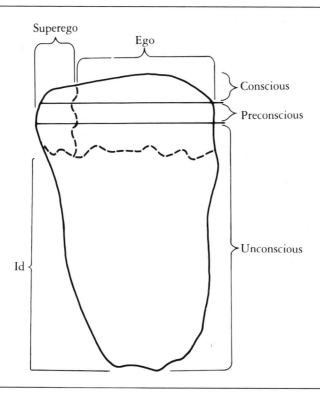

zation. If one system became more powerful the others would suffer (see Fig. 20).

The *id* was the most fundamental and basic aspect of the personality. It acted like a spoiled child, for it wanted immediate gratification of its desires. It represented the *pleasure principle.* In its most elementary form it operated like a reflex apparatus. The neonate was only an id. It sneezed, coughed, sucked, and eliminated. If life were completely satisfactory at this primitive level, there would be no need for further personality development. The id did not want frustration, but it must endure it. Consequently, there came into function a second aspect of the id called the *primary process,* which presented an image in the id of the object it desired. Since the id was completely subjective, the image of the object could not be distinguished from the real object. For example, if an infant were hungry but its mother were delayed in feeding, the primary process would manufacture an image of the bottle or nipple. It was through dreams, which were typically wish fulfilling, and hallucinations that we gained evidence of the existence of primary process. The id was the only system of the mental apparatus that was entirely unconscious.

In the id were also the instincts (see next section). They served as the source of psychic energy that controlled the personality. The id was also the receptacle of repressed memories. It was archaic and always infantile. Freud called it "a cauldron of emotions." It knew no right or wrong. It had to be held in check by the ego. If the ego relaxed its restraints, an impulsive act might occur. The id could not think, it could only desire.

As personality developed, the *ego* came into being, evolving out of the id. By siphoning off energy from the id, the ego was able to perform psychological activity. Eventually, the ego became the executive of the personality, controlling both the demands of the id and the superego. Just as the id represented the pleasure principle, the ego was the *reality principle.* It was partly conscious and partly unconscious.

One of the main functions of the ego was to find ways of satisfying the demands of the id. Often this had to be delayed until the appropriate time. In so doing, the ego had to use some of its energy to check the demanding forces of the id.

Another important function of the ego was the *secondary process.* This took over where the primary process of the id left off. The secondary process involved taking a plan of action, or solving a problem. If the id were hungry, the ego had to find the food. In finding ways of satisfying the id, the ego had to be realistic so as not to get the personality in trouble. The ego also perceived the outside world, remembered, and performed other kinds of psychological activity. It became the intermediary between the world of reality and the id.[22]

The *superego* developed out of the ego as the child took on the standards set by its parents. In early development, during the preschool years, the child had to learn right from wrong. It was rewarded for doing right and punished for

---

[22]Sigmund Freud, *The Ego and the Id* (London: Hogarth Press, 1947).

doing wrong. With the incorporation of this training, the superego was formed and could take on the functions by itself.

The superego had two sides or subsystems, the *conscience* and the *ego-ideal*. The conscience consisted of one's conception of what was wrong and what one should not do. The ego-ideal constituted what was right and proper. The superego was the *morality principle*. It might punish the ego for bad thoughts or deeds. Because the superego, like the id, was subjective, a wrong thought was the same as a wrong deed. Its means of punishment were to give the ego feelings of guilt or, in a physical sense, to cause an accident. It rewarded the ego for doing good deeds by giving it a feeling of pride or allowing an indulgence. If one never learned right from wrong, one would never develop a superego. A highly virtuous person had a strong superego, while a criminal had a weak one. When the superego and id were at odds with each other, the ego was caught in the middle. Again, it had to mediate between the two by either checking the id or the superego. Thus, a conflict often existed within the personality.

Other agents that helped in the development of the superego besides parents might be teachers and the demands and dictates of society in general.

## Psychic Energy and the Instincts

In a dynamic system as developed by Freud, the concept of energy was most important. Freud thought of his concept of psychic energy as being very real, just as were other forms of energy in nature. It was psychic energy which operated the three basic systems of the mental apparatus. It was by means of psychic energy that the personality could perform psychological work, such as problem-solving, perceiving, and remembering.[23]

Freud considered the mental apparatus as a series of energy systems. All energy originated in the *instincts* in the id, but somehow it was converted into psychic energy, the energy which controlled the personality. Just how this transformation took place from instinctive energy to psychic, Freud never made clear. Partly through maturation and partly through gaining psychic energy from the id, the ego came into being. The process whereby the ego gained its energy, Freud called *identification*. Identification meant taking on the qualities of a thing without the thing itself. By this process, the ego acquired its energy to do its psychological work. Part of its energy was used to satisfy the needs of the id. When psychic energy was thus invested in an object, the process was called *cathexis*. On the other hand, it was often necessary for the ego to hold in check the impulsive forces of the id, so a process of *anti-cathexis* took place. Other forces of the id, as found in repressed memories, also had to be kept in check, for their recollection might be too painful to the ego.

When the superego evolved, developing out of the ego, a similar process of identification took place. In this case, the identification arose out of the demands and censures, the rewards and punishments of one's parents and other

---

[23]Sigmund Freud, *The Instincts and Their Vicissitudes* in *Collected Papers*, Vol. IV (London: Hogarth Press, 1935).

agents of society. Before the superego came into being, a child was usually directly rewarded or punished by its parents. As the superego evolved it could take on these functions for itself. Thus, the superego could reward or punish the ego. It might cathect the ego by punishing it for an evil idea or act. The punishment took the form of feelings of guilt. When the ego was particularly good, it might be rewarded by the superego through feelings of pride. The superego might also anti-cathect the ego by checking one of its acts.

The balance of energy that a particular system had was related to the kind of a personality one happened to be. When the id had too much energy, the person would be very impulsive. A person of great moral fiber would have a strong superego. A well-adjusted person would have a strong ego with enough energy to check both the superego and id, and still have enough energy left over to do useful psychological work. However, if the ego had to invest too much of its energy in checking the superego and the id, the result would be a very restricted personality, for the ego was left with little energy to do anything else.

Sometimes the superego and id were at odds with each other, such as when the id wanted immediate satisfaction of its desires and the superego said, "no." Such conflicts always involved the ego, which was caught in the middle. The conflict was internal or within the mental apparatus and was called *intrapsychic*. This was in distinction to those conflicts involving the outer world. The latter kind of conflict would be identified as external frustration.

Each instinct had a *source,* an *aim,* an *object,* and an *impetus.* The aim was to eliminate the instinctive need, creating a reduction of the tension which had arisen earlier because of the instinctive need. In the case of the sex instinct, the final aim was the reduction of the bodily need. The source referred to the need itself. The object was that which could satisfy the instinct, such as food for hunger. The impetus involved the strength or force of the instinct.

In his later writings after 1920, Freud distinguished two classes of instincts—the *life* and *death,* Eros and Thanatos.[24] The life instincts operated for self-preservation, such as hunger and thirst. Freud included sex among the life instincts because it operated for the preservation of the species. The energy of the life instincts Freud identified as *libido.*

At the opposite pole was the death instinct, that which operated for destruction, either of oneself or of other people or objects. The ego, as the executive of the personality, was the agent of the life instincts. It operated to achieve their fulfillment. Although the death instinct was just as important and needed satisfaction as well, it had to operate in a more indirect or devious manner. Hate and aggression were expressions of the death instinct. Sometimes the two instincts could operate towards the same end. Eating, for example, preserved life but destroyed the material eaten.

Freud considered the instincts very much in a biological sense. The sources of the life instincts were in the physiological needs of the organism. Likewise as tissues decayed, we found the basis of the death instinct.

---

[24]Sigmund Freud, *Beyond the Pleasure Principle* (London: Hogarth Press, 1955). (In *The Standard Edition,* Vol. 18.)

## Displacement

Because of the demands of the superego and those of society, along with the possible inaccessibility of an instinctual object, the energy of a particular instinct might have to be directed in an alternate direction when it could not be directly satisfied. Consequently, a process called *displacement* resulted. Freud pointed out that our psychological development proceeded along the lines of a series of *energy displacements* and *object substitutions*. However, it was the energy that became displaced, not the object itself. For example, a failure of direct heterosexual satisfaction might result in reading "sexy" novels, looking at pornographic pictures, other forms of sexual outlets, or merely telling off-color stories. A person who chronically talked about sex was very likely not being directly satisfied. Frequently, compelling hobbies that used up a great deal of one's psychic energy might be the result of the displaced energies of some instinct. The more remote the displaced object was from the original instinctual object, the more energy must be exerted for the instinctual fulfillment.

In particular, the death instinct was subject to considerable displacement. Because the ego was the agent of the life instincts, we did not ordinarily kill others or ourselves. Thus, the death instinct had to gain its satisfaction in alternate ways. Frequently, athletic contests such as prize fighting or football might operate as substitute satisfactions. Milder expressions could be found in verbal sarcasms or caustic remarks.

When a displacement took the form of a higher cultural activity, the displacement was called a *sublimation*. Artistic, musical, or literary expressions might actually be displaced expressions of more basic desires. Freud mentioned Leonardo da Vinci's paintings of "The Madonna" as such an example. Some of Richard Wagner's most sensuous music could be interpreted as a displaced expression of a frustrated sexual life.

Displacement frequently occurred in dreams since the actual fulfillment of the unconscious desire of the dreamer would be too threatening to the ego. Consequently, the actual wish of the dream might take a displaced symbolic form. Many of Freud's dream symbols were expressions of unfulfilled sexual impulses. The adolescent who frequently dreamed of snakes (a symbol of the male genitalia) was expressing an unfulfilled sexual desire in the displaced dream.

## Anxiety

When the ego was threatened with danger, it experienced anxiety. Freud was rather vague in his definition of anxiety, but he considered it a painful emotional experience produced by the excitation of internal organs.[25]

*Reality anxiety* was nothing more than normal fear where the threats came from dangers in the outside world. In *neurotic anxiety* the threats came from the id. This was much more difficult to cope with since the id was entirely unconscious. The ego experienced this fear in a number of ways. Sometimes the

---

[25]Sigmund Freud, *The Problem of Anxiety* (New York: W. W. Norton and Co., 1936).

anxiety was "free floating." One felt anxious but did not know why. Phobias and panic reactions were other expressions of neurotic anxiety.

*Moral anxiety* came from the threats of the superego. The ego experienced this in feelings of guilt or shame. Freud pointed out that the very virtuous person with a strong superego was going to experience a great deal more moral anxiety or guilt than one who was less virtuous.

## Mechanisms of Defense

In order to cope with the anxiety which was painful, the ego had to develop some kinds of defensive reactions.[26] The most important of these defenses was *repression*. In repression, the ego mustered its energy, forcing the unpleasant thoughts down into the id. The unpleasant memory might remain there since it was charged with its own energy. A conflict resulted between the repressed idea wanting expression and the ego's repressing forces.

Freud placed great emphasis on the process of repression, which operated as an anti-cathexis of the ego. He distinguished between *primal repression* and *repression proper*. In the former, ideas or instinctive desires which had never been conscious were kept in the id. In the latter, the ideas had originally been conscious but were forced by repression into the unconscious id.

The significance of repression was that what we ordinarily considered to be forgotten was really only repressed. Many of our ideas and memories of past events were not really lost but were merely repressed. Some of these ideas or memories could be the source of psychological difficulties. Early in his career, Freud had used hypnosis to unearth repressed ideas. Later he depended on the process of "free association" or the talking out method mentioned earlier in this chapter.

Furthermore, it should be re-emphasized that Freud placed a great deal of significance on the importance of early childhood experiences as affecting personality development. Often these experiences were very traumatic and because of their unpleasant nature, they were repressed in the id, where they might remain for years, only to be transformed later into a neurotic symptom such as a phobia. The case of Fräulein Anna O., mentioned earlier, illustrates this point.

Often, repressed ideas might slip by the anti-cathetic forces of the ego and take the forms of slips of the tongue or pen, or losing things, or "forgetting" an unpleasant appointment. Freud mentioned that he often "forgot" to call on patients who had failed to pay his fees.

Sometimes, repressed experiences might be released in the form of dreams. During dreaming, the anti-cathexis of the ego was somewhat relaxed, so a repressed idea might gain expression in the dream. This usually had to take a disguised form for the ego's anti-cathexis was not completely eliminated. Through an analysis of the dream, the nature of the dream might be understood. The part of the dream as reported by the dreamer was identified as the

---

[26]Anna Freud, *The Ego and Mechanisms of Defense* (London: Hogarth Press, 1937).

*manifest content.* This was the disguise often expressed in symbolic form; but the underlying nature of the dream was the *latent content* which, when properly interpreted, could reveal the actual nature of the repression.

In *projection* the internal threat was externalized. It was easier for the ego to cope with an external threat than with one that was unconscious. Rather than accept the fact that one was at fault, which would be too threatening, one might blame the other person. Professors who thought that all of their students were stupid might actually be very incompetent themselves.

*Rationalization* was a special form of projection in which an excuse or alibi was set up that was socially acceptable. A student who failed a test might say that the test was ambiguous or unfair. Most students would agree. In reality, the student might have failed because of careless preparation or low intelligence.

As we developed psychologically, we cast off old modes of behavior and acquired new ones which were more appropriate to the developmental process. Sometimes, however, it was threatening to take the next step. One might prefer to stay where one was. In this sense we might say that one was *fixated.* A child might be fixated on its mother, never wanting to break the bonds. Freud wrote that a child might be tied to its mother's apron strings more out of fear than love. Freud called this fear *separation anxiety.* Some men might never marry because they were afraid of the responsibilities of taking on a wife and having a family. Since marriage was the culmination of psychosexual development, the man might be fixated at the latent period of his development (see p. 317). We often say that "some people never grow up." In this sense, they might be fixated at a childish or adolescent level.

In fixation, one went only so far in some part of one's psychological development. *Regression* was taking a step backwards. A child who had already been toilet trained might resume wetting its pants when a new baby brother was born. The new member of the family became a threat to the older child. A young bride might run home to her mother after the first fight with her husband. Security from danger was derived from resuming earlier ways of acting.

When the expression of some instinct or its derivative led to excessive anxiety, its opposite might be substituted. This defense was called *reaction formation.* It could often be identified by its exaggerated expression. People who appeared highly virtuous or self-righteous might have been *bon vivants* or reckless characters earlier in their lives. In a phobia, one might really want the object one feared. Those who constantly harped on the evils of alcohol might have been excessive drinkers and found that they could not properly handle the problems which resulted. Unconsciously, they might wish they could still drink like normal people. One who had given up cigarette smoking for fear of its danger to one's health might be the first to criticize others who maintained the habit.

## Psychosexual Development

Freud took a rather broad view of sex. For him, sexual pleasure was not limited to genital activity but could involve other parts of the body. The regions of the body that were sexually stimulating were called *erogenous zones*. They included the mouth, the anus, and the genital organs.[27]

***Oral Period.*** In a sense, sex began at birth, when the infant gained pleasure from sucking and taking in food. This early period was called *oral erotic*. Later, when teeth began to appear, pleasure was gained from biting. This was *oral sadistic*. The oral period extended from birth until the second year of life. Often, when the bottle was missing, the baby might suck its fist and later its thumb. This was referred to as a displacement (finding a substitute for the real object). The displaced object might not be as satisfying as the original one, but it might be better than nothing. In a sense, many of us are still fixated at the oral period or have regressed to it. We smoke cigarettes, chew gum, or bite on a pencil.

***Anal Period.*** About the middle of the second year, the source of sexual stimulation switched to the anus. In *anal expulsion,* pleasure was gained through elimination. As adults, anal expulsive people might be messy, disorderly, or wasteful. One might gain displaced anal satisfaction by verbally "dumping" on somebody. In *anal retention,* the pleasure was gained through holding on to the feces. As adults, these people might be collectors, possessive, or stingy. They did not wish to give away that which was satisfying.

***Phallic Period.*** About the third year of life the child got pleasure out of touching or manipulating his genital organs. The boy recognized his penis, and to touch it was fun. He also realized that he was different from his little sister. During the phallic period the *Oedipus complex* arose, which Freud considered to be one of his greatest discoveries. He first wrote about it in *The Interpretation of Dreams*.[28]

The Oedipus myth was best known from the play by Sophocles. The story revolved around Oedipus killing his father (unknowingly) and marrying his mother. Freud believed that in every boy there was a symbolic playing out of the age-old story. During this period, there appeared an increasing attachment to the mother and a growing hostility toward the father. Unconsciously, the boy wished to marry his mother. Along with the Oedipus complex arose the *castration anxiety,* the fear that his father would castrate him. In fact, it was this castration anxiety which helped resolve the complex, since the boy quite obviously did not wish to lose his penis. Normally, along with repression (the boy realized the impossibility of the whole thing) and maturation, the Oedipus complex was resolved. The resolution of the Oedipus complex ended the phallic period. Following this period, the boy changed his earlier strong identification with his mother and identified with his father and other male figures.

There was also the female counterpart of the Oedipus complex, in which the girl developed an intense attachment to her father and a jealousy for her mother, who became her rival for the father's affection. Unconsciously, she

---

[27]Sigmund Freud, *An Outline of Psychoanalysis, op. cit.*
[28]Sigmund Freud, *The Interpretation of Dreams, op. cit.*

would like to bear her father a child, and blamed her mother for denying her the penis. She preferred the father who had the organ she lacked. This was called *penis envy* and was the female counterpart of the castration anxiety in the male. With the resolution of the female Oedipus complex the phallic period ended for the girl, when she reidentified with her mother and other females.

Some people became fixated at the Oedipal period. They might never marry, maintaining their attachment to the parent of the opposite sex.

**Latency Period.** With the resolution of the Oedipus complex there began the latency period, which continued from about the age of five to eleven. Here, there was a general repression of sexual interests. Boys associated with boys, and girls associated with girls. There tended to be a kind of sex antagonism. A boy who played with girls was called a sissy, and the girl a tomboy. Boys continued to identify with male figures and girls with the females.

**Genital Period.** The oral, anal, and phallic periods combined are known as the *pre-genital period*. With the approach of puberty, there was a rearousal of sexual interest, but this time the attachments began to be for the opposite sex. In its early part, the expression of the genital period might take the form of a "crush" on a teacher of the opposite sex. There often followed a kind of "puppy love" and a kind of "horsing around" between the sexes. Finally, more mature sexual interests appeared, involving dating, which finally culminated in court-ship and marriage. The genital period continued throughout the years of ma-turity. However, it never completely replaced the earlier pre-genital period. Although some people might be excessively fixated at the pre-genital period, it was not abnormal to continue to gain sexual pleasure through oral and anal activity.

## Freud's Social Psychology

Perhaps Freud's first statement of his concern for social psychology was a psy-choanalytic interpretation of primitive humans and their religion set forth in 1913 in *Totem and Taboo*.[29] He suggested that sometime in antiquity there may have been the murder of a father by his sons. This kind of prehistoric family group was referred to as the "primal horde." This event, Freud speculated, resulted in the institutionalizing of their remorse. Consequently, certain taboos were set up, particularly against incest and murder. From this there gradually evolved civilized systems of morality and religion.

Freud later developed the concept of the mental apparatus consisting of the superego, ego and id referred to earlier.[30] Here his concern for social psychology involved the superego which developed not only out of parental rewards and

---

[29]Sigmund Freud, *Totem and Taboo*, in *The Standard Edition of the Complete Works of Sigmund Freud* Vol. 13 (London: Hogarth Press, 1955). (First published in 1913.)

[30]Sigmund Freud, *The Ego and the Id* (London: Hogarth Press, 1955). (In *The Standard Edition*, Vol. 19.)

punishments, but also out of the dictates of society to be found outside the family.

In *Group Psychology and the Analysis of the Ego*[31] Freud was influenced by Gustav Le Bon's study of crowd behavior.[32] The basis for group formation was to be found in the emotional ties developed between people. A typical group would have a chief or leader and, at least temporarily, the leader would become the common object of their emotional ties. This became a substitute for the ties between parents and children, which helped form the superego. Along the lines of forming a group, Freud found it useful to speak of a "herd instinct." Actually, he did not feel that this was necessarily innate like the life and death instincts. Furthermore, he again suggested that groups could be a carryover from the notion of the primal horde referred to earlier in *Totem and Taboo*. He suggested that characteristics of the primal horde were recreated in later groups. The group leader could take on something of the quality of the dreaded primal father, allowing the group to fulfill a strong need for an authority figure.

In *Civilization and Its Discontents*[33] Freud presented his analysis of civilization. The main theme of the work was the inevitable conflict between basic human instincts, which were innate and biological in nature, and the requirements of civilization. First of all there was the sex instinct or genital love; then its derivative, affection. Freud thought these were at odds with the intents of civilization. The conflict lay in civilization's restrictions on human sexual life.

Another problem lay in aggression, a derivative of the death instinct. In the interests of a civilized society, natural human aggressiveness had to be suppressed. Part of the process resulted in the incorporation of aggression into the superego which, as it developed, had the capacity to punish the ego. One form of punishment the superego could inflict on the ego was guilt. Such guilt was necessary for civilization in order to control aggression. On the other hand, just as the sexual impulse must be repressed by the demands of society, so too the aggressive impulse must be repressed. This repression inhibited basic human happiness or the fulfillment of the pleasure principle. Freud felt that this was the price we had to pay for civilization and its advances. When happiness is lost, feelings of guilt are strengthened. Although Freud was generally pessimistic about humankind, he did shed a ray of hope on the possibility that civilization might become less restrictive. Freud was perhaps a bit prophetic as we can observe from the change in attitudes towards sexual behavior which has come about in the past several decades. There has been a relaxation of our mores regarding sex and aggression. In developing a social psychology, Freud was pointing in a direction followed by some of the social analysts such as Erich Fromm and Karen Horney (see next chapter). These analysts objected to Freud's

---

[31]Sigmund Freud, *Group Psychology and the Analysis of the Ego* (London: Hogarth Press, 1955), (in *The Standard Edition*, Vol. 20). (First published in 1922.)

[32]Gustav Le Bon, *The Crowd: a Study of the Popular Mind* (London: T. Fisher, 1896).

[33]Sigmund Freud, *Civilization and Its Discontents* (in *The Standard Edition*, Vol. 21). (First published in 1930.)

earlier emphasis on the biological nature of human beings as the source of their basic strivings.

During and after Freud's time, there were many believers in God—Christian, Jewish, or whatever. Yet some had doubts about religious teachings, and Freud was one of them. Freud felt that religion was a crack in the construction of civilization.[34] Freud had no doubts. Putting it simply, he thought that religion was an illusion, nothing more than a tremendous attempt at wish-fulfillment. These ideas he set down in *The Future of an Illusion* (1921). According to Freud, religion is the result of our infantile feelings of helplessness and the consequent desire to be protected by an all-powerful God. Furthermore, religion can be dangerous in that it stunts the intellect, retarding its growth. By cashing out religion in favor of scientific research, we are able to allow our intellect to reach its full potential.

Of all his works, Freud considered *The Interpretation of Dreams* (1900) to be his best. Most psychologists of the time, such as Wundt, gave little importance to dreaming, considering it to be a nighttime confusion of the previous day's waking activity.

In the publishing business, the book could have been said at the time to have "fallen flat off the press," meaning that most people, including important scholars of the time, did not think it was worth much. One exception was Alfred Adler, a junior colleague of Freud's (see next chapter), who gave it a good review and helped draw public attention to it. It is not only important for dream interpretation but in it Freud set down many of his basic concepts.

Regarding dreams, Freud's basic premise was simple, although its basic ramifications became more complicated. His premise was that all dreams are wish-fulfilling. Dreams cannot be accepted at face value and consequently need to be interpreted. Dreams are the expressions of repressed wishes residing in the unconscious in an active manner. During sleep, the censorship of the ego is relaxed, allowing dreams to express themselves in disguised form.

Dreaming is a compromise that allows us to remain asleep while gaining partial satisfaction of the wishes that are obviously unacceptable to our waking consciousness. Thus, Freud maintained that dreams are disguised expressions of unconscious desires. He felt that "dreams were the keys to the unconscious" and that dreams could lead us "down the royal road to the unconscious."

Because dreams are disguises, one can make a distinction between what Freud called the *manifest content* and the *latent content* of a dream. The manifest content is the dream as reported upon waking. The *latent content* is the real meaning of the dream—the meaning behind the disguise—which in waking life is too dangerous or threatening to the dreamer, being unacceptable to the dreamer's consciousness.

Freud believed that there were two means of getting at the real meaning, or latent content, of a dream. The first method was to use *free association,* in which the person associated with some element of the dream whatever objects

---

[34]Sigmund Freud, *The Future of an Illusion,* in *The Standard Edition of the Complete Works of Sigmund Freud,* Vol. 21 (London: Hogarth Press, 1961). (First published in 1927.)

or concepts it brought to mind. This aided the analyst or whoever was interpreting the dream to find its real meaning. In the second instance, the disguise took on the form of a fixed symbol, which for most people had more or less the same meaning. Freud based his idea of fixed symbols on similarities among legends, myths, and general parlance. Many of the symbols were sexual in nature. For example, long, pointed objects (pens, pencils, and church steeples) represented the male genitalia whereas caves, houses, gardens, and open objects symbolized the female genitalia. Things going up and down, such as elevators, horseback riders, and pens in ink wells, represented sexual intercourse.

*The Interpretation of Dreams* gives us the first statement of Freud's Oedipus complex, discussed earlier.

Dreams were regressive and often infantile, going back to the dreamer's earlier years. This regression made it easier for the wish to get by the ego's censorship.

Freud also spoke of the "day's residue," which referred to some event of the previous day's activity that operated to set off the unconscious processes of the dream world, but Freud did not believe that dreams were merely recollections of previous days' events. The real meaning lay in the past repressed experiences. For Freud, sex began at birth, not at puberty.[35]

### The Mind-Body Problem

Actually, Freud was never concerned with the issue, as such. Nevertheless, his system was unquestionably dualistic. In his mental apparatus, we had a system that was partly real and physical, involving bodily functions since the instincts involved bodily needs. Still, we had an ego and superego which were very much mental. The superego became a self-contained mental unit which could reward and punish the ego as it chose. Since there was constant interaction among the three systems, Freud's main solution to the mind-body problem was *psychophysical interactionism.*

In other instances, Freud separated the mental process from the physical, so in some cases we found a *psychophysical parallelism.*

## *Evaluation*

### Contributions of Freud

1. Even the most ardent anti-Freudians must admit that Freud was one of the great intellectual figures of the twentieth century. He developed an entirely new kind of psychology, one that stressed a developmental approach to an

---

[35]S. Freud, *The Interpretation of Dreams,* in *The Standard Edition of the Complete Works of Sigmund Freud,* Vols. IV and V (London: Hogarth Press, 1955).

individual's personality. He recognized the significance of early childhood experiences as affecting later behavior. This fact has been objectively verified many times over.

**2.** He also recognized the significance of motivation. Other psychologies might not think in terms of instinct in the orthodox Freudian sense, but modern learning theory was very dependent on the concept of drive reduction (Hull) or deprivation (Skinner). Likewise, the concepts of reinforcement were relevant.

Hilgard and Bower[36] have pointed out a number of Freudian principles that have parallels in learning theories. For example, was not Freud's pleasure principle related to Thorndike's law of effect or Hull and Skinner's principle of reinforcement? Was not the reality principle very much involved in the process of learning and problem-solving?

**3.** Psychologists have also recognized the importance of anxiety. Experimental psychologists such as Miller,[37] Mowrer,[38] and Skinner[39] have related anxiety reduction to avoidance learning. Other theories of personality have also recognized the importance of anxiety as an antecedent for behavior disorders. Freud was the first to stress this important issue.

**4.** Many of the Freudian defenses have been subjected to experimental verification—displacement, repression, fixation, and regression can be demonstrated as real, objective phenomena. For a detailed report on the experimental verification of Freudian defenses see Lundin's *Personality: A Behavioral Analysis,* particularly chapter 14.[40]

**5.** Those sympathetic with psychoanalytic thinking would also point out that Freud recognized a part of man previously ignored by other psychologies— namely, the role of the unconscious. Freud was not afraid to tackle the problem of dreams as an expression of the unconscious, an area which most psychologists have avoided until recently.

**6.** Freud's strong stand on determinism would be considered by many as a major contribution. Although he did not state it as such, the implications were clear that he considered behavior to be lawful. The attitude that behavior being lawful must be determined and not merely the subject of caprice was shared with modern behaviorism.

---

[36]Ernest R. Hilgard and G. H. Bower, *Theories of Learning,* 3rd ed. (New York: Appleton-Century-Crofts, 1966), ch. 9.

[37]N. E. Miller, "Studies of Fear as an Acquired Drive, I. Fear as Motivation and Fear Reduction in the Learning of New Responses," *Journal of Experimental Psychology,* Vol. 38 (1948), pp. 89–101.

[38]O. H. Mowrer, "A Stimulus-Response Analysis of Anxiety and Its Role as a Reinforcing Agent," *Psychological Review,* Vol. 46 (1939), pp. 553–65.

[39]B. F. Skinner, *Science and Human Behavior* (New York: The Macmillan Co., 1953).

[40]Robert W. Lundin, *Personality: A Behavioral Analysis,* 2nd ed. (New York: The Macmillan Co., 1974).

7. Finally, Freud's influence on the broader cultural scene cannot be ignored. Besides his influence on psychology and psychiatry, such fields as visual art, drama, literature, and the cinema have reflected his ideas. Contemporary pictorial art often gives expression to Freudian symbolism. The school of surrealism is expressively Freudian in nature.

A number of the plays of Eugene O'Neill, as an example, show strong Freudian influences, in particular, *Mourning Becomes Elektra* and *Strange Interlude*. In the latter play, the dual roles of the conscious and unconscious are expressed in the actors' lines.

Just how much Freudian interpretation one wishes to give to certain artistic creations (including literary) is a matter of the particular interpreter's background in Freudian psychology. The fact that interpretations of the various art forms fall within a Freudian framework is an indication of a strongly felt influence.

### Criticisms of Freud

Just as Freud has been praised by his followers and sympathizers, he has also probably been more strongly attacked than most others. Despite these attacks, the Freudian system has retained its popularity. One of the reasons is that, as a theory, it is a rather romantic one as opposed to a rigid experimental and statistical analysis, which some people find rather dull.

Some of the most frequently stated criticisms can be elaborated as follows:

1. **Unreliability of the data.** Freud developed his theories from his own personal observations of people. Much of it came from his analysis of his own behavior. In the worst sense, this became merely anecdotal. Other sources were what his patients told him in their free-associations as they lay on his couch. It has been questioned, and somewhat unfairly, how one could develop a system of normal psychology from the verbal meanderings of rich, neurotic Viennese women. This, of course, was an overstatement. Finally, there were his dreams and those of his patients. Most of this data was impossible to verify. If one wished to establish a principle in psychology, it must be done through experimentation and controlled observation which, if properly reported, can be replicated by other psychologists. Much of what psychoanalysis reports as its data has to be taken on faith.

2. **Unverified theoretical constructs.** Because of the nature of some of Freud's theories and hypotheses, they could *never* be put to a test and had to always remain as theoretical constructs. Perhaps the best example of this was the mental apparatus. How can one ever prove the existence of a superego? There is nothing wrong with theorizing as such, but those theories which cannot be proven or refuted are bad theories. The same was true for the concept of psychic energy. One could measure other forms of energy, but this did not hold for psychic energy, for it was nothing more than an unproven hypothesis. We have already pointed out that the theory was dualistic. Freud posited a mind and accepted it as reality.

3. **Fictional concepts.** According to some, Freud depended too much on mythology. Perhaps the worst of these fictions was the Oedipus complex. To propose that the immature child had in his unconscious the innate idea of having sex relations with his parents approached the absurd. The same was true for castration anxiety. How could a little girl who had never seen a penis (and this was possible) envy it? Freud's concept of the Oedipus complex, which was supposed to be universal, implied that it was inherited. But where did it begin? Freud went back to ancient Greece, but then are we all related to the Greeks? The notion of the inheritance of ideas is not generally accepted in psychology today.

4. **Lack of quantification.** This criticism is related to the first. Skinner[41] criticized Freud for his failure to describe the nature of the act, not really giving it any dimensions. Freud talked about memories, ideas, and so forth. There were no units which could be measured. Such concepts as "libido" or "cathexis" remained as rather vague hypothetical entities.

5. **Intervening variables.** Skinner[42] also suggested that Freud looked into intervening variables for his explanation, and merely stopped there without going to the original causes. For example, in Freud's explanation, I might feel guilty because my superego punished me. The mental apparatus was, of course, an intervening variable. Would it not be better to say that I felt guilty because I had excessive conditioning in anxiety early in my childhood which was never extinguished? Of course, Freud did go back to the original events when he spoke of the influence of early childhood, but the invention of an intervening variable such as the mental apparatus added nothing to the final explanation.

There were a number of other criticisms which some would consider important, but others would disregard as insignificant. Some of these might include Freud's overemphasis on sex and early childhood sexual traumas, as well as the failure of the psychoanalytical technique itself.

We have purposely not gone into psychoanalysis as a method of treatment because this book does not deal with therapy as such. However, it might be pointed out, in conclusion, that psychoanalysis as a therapy has tended to decline in popularity during the past decades. Hilgard and Bower[43] have suggested that the reason may be the increase in popularity of such behavior therapies as Wolpe's desensitization method and other forms of behavior modification such as reinforcement therapy. These are based on modern learning theory. The methods work far quicker than the prolonged traditional free association, and the results have been reported in an objective and quantified manner. With the decline in popularity of psychoanalysis as therapy, it might

[41]B. F. Skinner, "Critique of Psychoanalytic Concepts and Theories," *Scientific Monthly,* Vol. 79 (1954), pp. 300–305.
[42]*Ibid.*
[43]Ernest R. Hilgard, and G. H. Bower, *op. cit.*

seem to follow that the whole theoretical system might lose some of its impetus. It should be pointed out, however, that orthodox psychoanalysis as a system is far from dead. Its influences are still dominant in psychiatry and clinical psychology. Many of Freud's basic concepts are still adhered to and accepted without question.

## Suggested Further Readings

Bakan, David, *Sigmund Freud and the Jewish Mystical Tradition*. Princeton, New Jersey: D. Van Nostrand and Co., 1958. Some new insights into Freud's life and heritage. Scholarly and well written.

Freud, Sigmund, *The Psychopathology of Everyday Life* in *The Standard Edition*, Vol. 6. London: Hogarth Press, 1953. Also available in paperback. A very good place to begin reading Freud. It's short and fun to read.

Freud, Sigmund, *The Basic Writings of Sigmund Freud*, trans. A. A. Brill. New York: Random House, 1938. Includes *The Interpretation of Dreams, Three Essays on a Theory of Sexuality*, and other important writings.

Hall, Calvin S., *A Primer of Freudian Psychology*. Cleveland, Ohio: World Publishing Co., 1954. Also available in paperback. A short book, but every page is full of important information on Freud's theory of normal personality. The organization is excellent, and the text is very readable.

Jones, Ernest, *The Life and Works of Sigmund Freud*, 3 vols. New York: Basic Books, 1953–1957. The most complete and authoritative biography of Freud. Along with the general biography, Freud's works are outlined. Also available in a condensed one-volume edition.

Salter, A., *The Case Against Psychoanalysis*. New York: Henry Holt Co., 1955. A scathing criticism of Freud and all he stood for. Some of the criticisms are reasonable, others quite unfair, but Salter would just as soon see the whole psychoanalytic movement buried six feet under.

Skinner, B. F., "A Critique of Psychoanalytic Concepts and Theories." *Scientific Monthly*, Vol. 79 (1954), pp. 300–305. Also available in Skinner, B. F., *Cumulative Record*, rev. ed. New York: Appleton-Century-Crofts, 1961. A more reasonable criticism of Freud's theories written from the standpoint of a behaviorist.

# CHAPTER

# 18

# *Heirs to Freud*

Freud had set the stage for a movement that was to have a strong impact on psychology and psychiatry today. Even now, there are many people in a variety of intellectual disciplines who follow the ideas set forth in Freud's writings very closely. However, there were also those whose ideas deviated enough from his thinking to cause a break with the original psychoanalytic movement.

The first of these was Alfred Adler. Adler had read *The Interpretation of Dreams*[1] and was much impressed with it. In 1902 Adler was invited to join the Wednesday Evening Discussion Group. His association with Freud was not a long one for in 1911 Adler walked out and founded his own movement, which he eventually identified as *Individual Psychology*.

The second major figure to break with Freud was Carl Jung. Freud liked Jung's ideas on word association and, as a result, both of them came to America in 1909 to lecture at Clark University. Even at that time, however, their friendship was starting to cool. Jung was elected as the first president of the International Psychoanalytic Association and Freud had hoped Jung would be his successor, but in 1914 the break was complete and Jung, like Adler, was to found his own movement, which he identified as *Analytical Psychology*.

Like Adler, Jung formulated a psychology which retained some of the Freudian ideas, rejected others, and evolved as a completely separate system. Jung accepted the concept of a dynamic psychology involving psychic energy, a division between consciousness and unconsciousness with greater importance being placed on the latter, and the concept of a mental apparatus (although much different from Freud's).

There were others not necessarily directly associated with Freud, but who had been either directly trained in psychoanalysis or at least well acquainted

---

[1] Sigmund Freud, *The Interpretation of Dreams* in *The Standard Edition*, Vols. 4 and 5 (London: Hogarth Press, 1953).

with it. Among these were Karen Horney, Erich Fromm, Harry Stack Sullivan, and Erik Erikson. Thus, this chapter will be concerned with the works of these six people—Adler, Jung, Horney, Fromm, Sullivan, and Erikson. The latter four have frequently been referred to as the *Social Analysts* because of their strong feelings that culture and society play an important role in personality development along with its deviations.

## Alfred Adler's Individual Psychology

Before going into a description of Adler's position, let us begin with some of the basic differences between the thinking of Freud and that of Adler.

Adler can be considered the first of the social analysts as he stressed the social nature of human beings. He considered people to be inherently social beings who were strongly influenced by the social forces in their environment. Freud, on the other hand, had stressed the primarily biological nature of human beings to a far greater degree.

Adler was much more of an ego psychologist. For him, consciousness was the most important aspect of the mind. In the psychoanalytic tradition, Adler did not completely dismiss the unconscious, but simply did not stress the strong unconscious determinants as Freud had. What was unconscious became conscious, said Adler, and when it became conscious it then became important in studying human nature. In retrospect, it would seem that Adler probably overstated his case for consciousness, as we shall see in his *fictional finalism* where he stressed motives which were unconscious. Nevertheless, for Adler, consciousness remained the focal point of the personality.

Although Adler, like Freud, allowed for the significance of early environmental events and past experiences (for example, order of birth), it was people's future goals that were important. Adler presented a predominantly teleological psychology in which aims toward the future determined present behavior. We have already encountered teleological viewpoints in the works of McDougall and Tolman (see chaps. 11 and 15). Freud remained the determinist—always stressing the past.

Adler felt that Freud had completely overemphasized the role of sex as a primary motivating force in personality. It must be recalled that in Freud's early writings (despite the mistakes of the seduction fantasies) he had stressed the libido energy as stemming from the sex drive as well as the significance of early sexual experiences in childhood. In Adler's early writings he placed more emphasis on aggression and striving for power, which later became tempered to become striving for superiority and finally, social interest.

Adler placed greater emphasis on human individuality, as implied in the title of his system. Each person was a unique individual who had a unique style of life with different goals. Adler considered the personality as a whole, as a unique system which was not divided into individual sub-systems, but which tended to be the same for everyone. This does not mean that Freud considered everyone to be alike, but for him we all had the same kind of mental apparatus and shared a commonness of instincts. The difference was simply that Adler placed greater stress on a person's individuality.

## The Life of Alfred Adler (1870–1937)

In 1870, Vienna was one of the great cultural centers of Europe. It was noted for its art, music, and science. Alfred was the second of six children. His father, Leopold, was a wealthy grain merchant. As a small child, Alfred was very frail; he suffered from rickets. He remembered his doctor saying, "Your boy is lost."[2] He later recalled that he considered this man to be a "bad doctor." At the age of five, Adler was determined to be a doctor, and a "good doctor."[3]

As if his delicate physique were not enough of a problem, he was run over twice in his early childhood. His weakness caused his parents to pamper him. In school he was clumsy and participated little in games and sports. As an adult, he recalled that his childhood had been an unhappy one. He resented his older brother who was a model child and his mother's favorite. Consequently, Alfred attached his affections to his father.[4]

True to his early ambition, he attended the University of Vienna and received his medical degree in 1895. He began his medical practice specializing in ophthalmology (diseases of the eye), but later changed to general medical practice, and finally to psychiatry.

In 1902 he began his first association with Freud and became president of the Vienna Psychoanalytic Association.[5] In 1907 he published an important paper on organ inferiority and its compensations,[6] which was really the beginning of his new approach to psychology. At the time it seemed to fit quite well with Freud's views since Freud had talked about compensation for sexual difficulties. However, Adler's views began to differ too much from Freud's and the orthodox psychoanalysts of the Vienna group. For one thing, Adler objected to Freud's strong sexual implications. Finally in 1911, Adler and a group of his followers withdrew from the Wednesday Evening Discussion Group and founded the Society for Free Psychoanalytic Research. This eventually led to the name of *individual psychology*. In time, Adler became more and more interested in child psychology and participated actively in child guidance clinics and the public schools.

---

[2]Hertha Orgler, *Alfred Adler: The Man and His Works* (New York: Liveright Publishing Co., 1963).
[3]*Ibid.*
[4]*Ibid.*
[5]Ernest Jones, *The Life and Work of Sigmund Freud*, Vol. II (New York: Basic Books, Inc., 1953).
[6]Alfred Adler, *Study of Organ Inferiority and Its Psychical Compensations* (New York: Nervous and Mental Disease Publishing Co., 1917).

Adler visited the United States several times. To avoid Nazi persecution (since he also was a Jew), he came to this country in 1934 to live permanently. He lectured widely in this country and abroad. He died of a heart attack while on a lecture tour in Aberdeen, Scotland, in 1937.

## Adler's Psychology

### Inferiority and Compensation

One of his earliest papers (1907) was *The Study of Organ Inferiority and Its Psychical Compensations.*[7] In it, Adler pointed out that often a person with an organ inferiority, such as poor vision, would make up for it by developing sharpened hearing. However, the attitude one adopted toward one's defects was particularly important. One might compensate by making very desirable adjustments, or one might end up by adopting evasive devices. Adler further developed his concept of inferiority, and by 1910 he realized that inferiority feelings could be quite universal, developing out of the general feeling we had of being helpless as infants. In extreme cases these feelings might take the form of timidity, insecurity, shyness, or even cowardliness. Undesirable compensations might be exhibited by defiance or in ideas of grandeur. Inferiority feelings might take the form of being slighted, with the expectation of triumph and redemption, as the Cinderella myth exemplified.[8]

However, sometimes the inferiority feelings could result in more desirable activities. In Adler's own case, his frailty and unhappiness as a child led to his compensation in becoming an eminent physician who was world renowned.

Adler also mentioned cases of compensation or overcompensation among historical persons. In the latter case, the inferiority was directly overcome. Demosthenes, the stutterer, became an outstanding orator. Klara Schumann, the wife of the famous German romantic composer, Robert Schumann, suffered from poor hearing as a child; yet she became an eminent concert pianist. Inferiority feelings could operate to drive one towards greater accomplishments and individual improvement.

Closely related to the concept of inferiority and compensations was Adler's concept of the *masculine protest.*[9] This was a striving to be strong and powerful as a compensation for feeling unmanly and inferior. At this time, in 1910, Freud and Adler were still associated, so the masculine protest seemed to have some sexual overtones. To be masculine was to be superior and to be feminine was to be inferior. In Adler's later writings, the *striving for superiority* replaced

---

[7]*Ibid.*
[8]H. L. Ansbacher and R. Ansbacher, eds., *The Individual Psychology of Alfred Adler* (New York: Basic Books, Inc., 1956), ch. 1.
[9]*Ibid.*, ch. 2.

the masculine protest, and the latter concept became more restrictive. It later referred to the protest that women expressed for having to play the feminine role. Women, being weaker than men, were thus inclined toward inferiority. Some might compensate by becoming doctors, lawyers, or business executives—roles usually played by men. Often they either did not marry or they did not want to have any children. This more restricted concept of the masculine protest in women had its counterpart in the Freudian concept of penis envy. Throughout history, women have strived for greater equality. They attained the right to vote, to drink in bars, to smoke cigarettes, and to wear pants. Today, the feminist movement is a current expression of the masculine protest.

## Dynamic Strivings and Superiority

Like Freud's, Adler's was a dynamic psychology that presumed basic motivating forces within the personality. Adler had antedated Freud by presuming an aggressive drive in 1908. This was expressed first in the masculine protest. Adler mentioned the expression of the aggression drive in children in their crying tantrums, fighting, and biting. In adults it gained expression in the behavior of criminals and revolutionary heroes.[10]

Soon thereafter, Adler modified his aggressive drive and called it a *striving for superiority*. This notion continued to remain a basic tenet of his system. It became a drive from inferiority to superiority—from "below" to "above." The "above" meant power and self-esteem. Later, he tempered the notion of superiority to be a striving for perfection and completion. The striving was normal and inborn. As opposed to Freud, Adler took a very optimistic view of people. The striving for superiority continued throughout life, involving accomplishment and fulfillment.[11] Adler believed each of us could achieve our strivings for superiority in many different ways. One might gain success by being an artist, another by being superior in one's occupation. Less desirable ways might be by being a tyrant in the home or by bossing one's underlings.

## Social Interest

The culmination of Adler's theory of superiority was to be found in his theory of *social interest*.[12] Human beings had three basic social ties: occupation, society, and love. Social interest was the inherent potential through which a person could be responsive to a social situation. It became an integral part of one's own personal striving for superiority. It was an innate disposition, but had to be developed with the help of society. In the finest sense, one with social interest became "other directed," concerned for the betterment of society and one's fel-

---

[10]*Ibid.*, p. 34.

[11]Alfred Adler, *Practice and Theory of Individual Psychology* (Totowa, N.J.: Littlefield, Adams, 1920).

[12]Alfred Adler, *Social Interest* (New York: Putnam, 1939).

low human beings. The child's first expression of social interest involved its mother. In opposition to Freud, Adler felt that a child's expressions of affection were directed toward others rather than toward itself.

Some people never developed social interest. These were the failures, neurotics, drunkards, criminals, prostitutes, and perverts. Their goal was only one of personal superiority. Greater social interest generally resulted in more successful adaptation to life.

## Fictional Finalism

In 1911, a German philosopher, Hans Vaihinger, published a book entitled *The Philosophy of "As If."*[13] This impressed Adler and influenced his thinking about the direction of human strivings. According to Vaihinger, human beings lived by fictions which had no counterpart in reality: "You will get your reward in Heaven" or "All men are created equal." Accordingly, these fictions enabled us to deal with reality better than we otherwise could. Fictions were never reduced to objective reality but always remained purely subjective. If we combined the notion of the fictions with that of a final goal we found our lives guided by fictional goals. The future was always subjective since we never knew exactly what was in store for us. In Adler's exposition of fictional finalism we had an excellent expression of his teleology—that our future strivings determined our present actions. For example, my future strivings to bring this book into print determine my present behavior as I write these words.

Our goals might be conscious or unconscious, but there was a final end toward which we strove. The fictional goal could not be reduced to objective determinism. It was possible for objective facts, such as our environment or organ inferiority, to be utilized in the process of forming the final goal, but it still remained a fiction, a result of our own creation.

The fictional nature of the goal implied its unconscious character. The goal was within, but was not understood by, the individual. It was the true nature of this goal that constituted the basic character of the unconscious.[14]

## Degrees of Activity and Personality Types

According to Adler the three primary factors of human behavior were: (1) striving for superiority, (2) social interest, and (3) degrees of activity. Except in the development of a personality typology, degree of activity was the least important of these three. The description of degree of activity was not given in any quantitative sense. However, Adler cited some examples. The child who ran away from home or started a fight in the street had a higher degree of activity than the one who simply sat at home and read a book.

If we combined high and low degrees of activity with high and low social interest we got a typology as follows:

---

[13]H. Vaihinger, *The Philosophy of "As If"* (New York: Harcourt Brace and Co., 1925).
[14]H. L. Ansbacher, and R. Ansbacher, *op. cit.*, p. 89.

|              | **High Social Interest** | **Low Social Interest** |
| ------------ | ------------------------ | ----------------------- |
| High Activity | Socially useful person  | Ruling person           |
| Low Activity |                          | Getting person          |
|              |                          | Avoiding person         |

The nature of the socially useful person need not be elaborated. This was the most desirable personality type. It was impossible to have low activity and high social interest. The ruling type might be sadists, tyrants, or delinquents. The getting type accepted everything and gave nothing in return. The avoiding person became a recluse.

## The Style of Life

Throughout his writings Adler described the style of life in many different ways: (1) one's individuality, (2) methods of facing problems, (3) individual forms of creative activity, (4) compensations for inferiorities, (5) ways of achieving the fictional goal, and (6) specific goals and ways of achieving them.[15]

The style of life began to develop in early childhood. By the age of five, one's attitudes toward one's environment were pretty well formulated, and one would continue to proceed in more or less the same direction. Here Adler agreed with Freud in stressing the significance of early childhood. Adler suggested that one way of discovering one's style of life was to look into the earliest childhood memories. He questioned a number of successful doctors about their earliest memories. The general reply was that they wanted to be doctors.

Adler distinguished three faulty styles of life: (1) the inferior, (2) the pampered, and (3) the neglected. The inferior arose out of some inferiority. These people failed to make adequate compensations. They might take the route of escape or avoidance or become socially useless persons.

The pampered or spoiled style lacked social interest. These people might become despots and expect everyone around them to conform to their selfish demands. They became self-centered, and could be potentially dangerous to society.

The neglected was much like the spoiled except that the neglected *wished* to be pampered.

The following case[16] illustrates the inferior style of life with inadequate compensations and a lack of social interest.

> Harry was born into an extremely modest background. He never went to college like many of his friends had, but instead, became a mortician. When World

---

[15]*Ibid.*, p. 174.
[16]R. W. Lundin, *Alfred Adler's Basic Concepts and Implications* (Muncie, IN: Accelerated Development Publishers, 1989).

War II came along, he was classified as 4F because of a heart condition. He found employment at a funeral home that catered to the well-to-do. Here he came in contact with many wealthy people. Eventually, he met a very rich widow without children. She was at least twice his age. He became her companion, escorting her to the opera, symphony, and other cultural events which she enjoyed. He gave up his job and became her constant companion. They spent winters at Palm Beach, Florida, and summers at Bar Harbor, Maine. Through her he met many socially prominent people. As she became more elderly, she needed more help to get around. When she became an invalid, he prayed she would die.

Since she had no living relatives, he persuaded her to leave her fortune to him. Eventually, she passed on, but, ironically, he developed cancer and died six months later so he was never able to enjoy the money he had waited so long to inherit.

## Safeguarding Devices

Rather than adopting the Freudian concept of *mechanisms of defense* for protection of the ego from threats and anxiety, Adler developed what he called *safeguarding devices* for bolstering of self-esteem. Although the terms are different, some of Adler's devices closely resemble some of Freud's defense mechanisms.

*Excuses* is an Adlerian device that in some ways is similar to the Freudian notion of *rationalization* (see p. 315). One example is the "yes, but" device. A person who does not like to travel might say, "Yes I would like to take the trip to the mountains, but I think the traffic would be too dangerous over that holiday weekend." The "if only" excuse manifests itself in statements such as "If only I had had a college education, I would not have missed out on the promotion."

*Aggression* was given as a primary driving force in Adler's early writings, but when he decided that basic human strivings were based on a desire for superiority, he made aggression a safeguarding device.

In *depreciation* of another individual, the depreciator undervalues or makes light of the other person. In the workplace, for example, depreciation might take the form of belittling another person or overvaluing one's own potential or ability: "I never would have made such a stupid mistake in following a simple map showing the way to highway 66."

*Oversolicitousness* results from presumptions that other people are incapable of caring for themselves, as in "Dudley, you can't possibly do that by yourself—let me help you" or "Let me carry the suitcase—you'll never make it to the cab stand."

*Distance* is really a means of escape in which a psychological barrier is set up between oneself and the problem. In *moving backward,* one protects one's self-esteem by reverting to an earlier stage in his or her development. This is similar to Freud's concept of *regression* (see p. 315). A woman says to her husband, "You're impossible. I'm going home to Mama." In *standing still,* which is similar to Freud's *fixation* (see p. 315), one avoids the dangers of taking the "next step forward." Adler likened it to standing in a witch's circle that has been drawn around one. Standing still prevents a person from drawing closer to the realities of life. If one does nothing, the problem sometimes solves itself.

In *hesitation,* one secures *distance.* Often this takes the form of wasting time, leaving work unfinished, or not being able to make up one's mind.

*Exclusive tendencies* was a later Adlerian concept that amounted to setting up a "psychological wall" against the demands of society, typically in a social community. This device constitutes a withdrawal from social contacts. In short, the individual or group becomes inaccessible to the behavior of others. On the individual level are people who are difficult to communicate with. On the group level are exclusive groups ("exclusive country clubs") that discriminate against others for special reasons.

## Evaluation

### Contributions of Adler

Adler's psychology was well received from the beginning, particularly by those who were repelled by many of Freud's concepts, especially his pan-sexuality. For example, Adler took a more realistic attitude toward Freud's Oedipus complex. If it existed at all, he said, it was merely the result of excessive childhood pampering.

Adler was also much more optimistic about the nature of humankind. His psychology reflected his own personality, which was cheerful, social, and kindly. In stressing human social nature, he was expressing a realistic attitude toward the significance of society and, more specifically, the environmental influences that molded our behavior. This was to be accepted warmly by many later social analysts, social psychologists, and other social scientists.

Adler's was very much of a "commonsense" psychology in that it could be readily understood and applied. Most of his concepts could be easily grasped. He wrote for the professional person, but many of his books were directed to lay readers as well.

His concept of compensation has been widely accepted. It can be operationally defined and put to the experimental test.[17] His concept of inferiority feelings has become an integral part of personality psychology. In suggesting the universality of inferiority feelings Adler overemphasized the fact, but there is no doubt that it is a household word and a concept that is widely used in clinical psychology.

### Criticisms of Adler

Most of the criticisms levied against Freud are equally applicable to Adler: unreliability of the data, untestable hypotheses, dualism, and fictions. Perhaps one of his least successful concepts was the notion that we were directed by

---

[17]Robert W. Lundin, *Personality: A Behavioral Analysis,* 2nd ed. (New York: The Macmillan Co., 1974), ch. 13.

unconscious fictional goals. The use of fictions was unsubstantial, but to suggest that our fictions could not even be identified made the whole concept invalid.

Likewise, the notion of the creative self will always remain at the theoretical level. It was nothing more than a regression to the medieval concept of a soul, disguised in modern terms. It added nothing as an explanatory principle.

Although Adler's psychology still has its adherents and their ideas are expressed in their own journal, *The American Journal of Individual Psychology,* it never achieved the fame and popularity of Freud's system. Some have considered it rather simple-minded and shallow.

Adler's teleology is certainly incompatible with those who maintain a deterministic view. The rejection of determinism seems to be out of keeping with current thinking in objective psychology. It is a pleasant thought to believe that one can be master of one's fate, but is this really true?

A final criticism of Adler was that his theory was incomplete and often contradictory. He seemed to deny determinism in favor of teleology, and yet he was very much a determinist in emphasizing early childhood influences that set forth the style of life, the order of birth, and conditions in society. Adler accepted social interest as an innate disposition, but it remained up to the environmental influences to actualize it. Was this not deterministic?

## The Analytical Psychology of Carl Jung

Carl Gustav Jung was the second of Freud's early associates to make the break and found his own system. The break followed shortly after Adler's departure.

Like Adler, Jung formulated a psychology which retained some of the Freudian ideas, rejected others, and evolved as a completely separate system. Jung accepted the concept of a dynamic psychology involving psychic energy, a division between consciousness and unconsciousness with greater importance being placed on the latter, and the concept of a mental apparatus (although much different from Freud's).

### Basic Differences Between Freud and Jung

As we did with Adler, it might be useful to point out some of the basic differences between Jung and Freud which the reader may keep in mind while following the exposition of Jung's psychology in the next sections.

Freud was a thoroughgoing determinist, with the emphasis on the past as the causative factor in present behavior. Adler proposed the opposite view in his teleology which stressed the importance of future goals affecting the present. Jung took both a deterministic and a teleological position. He felt that humans lived by future aims as well as by past causes.

Although both Jung and Freud stressed the unconscious, Jung considered the significant part of the unconscious to be archaic and racial; it had a universal nature.[18] Freud had touched on the notion of a racial unconscious in his concept of the Oedipus complex, but it remained for Jung to give the concept many further implications.

Both Jung and Freud accepted psychic energy, which developed from some biological bases, but Jung, like Adler, opposed Freud's sexual implications. For Jung, the origin of the psychic energy was not rooted in specific instincts, but arose from various bodily processes forming a basic life urge. Many have compared it to Bergson's *élan vital*—a drive to live.

## The Life of Carl Jung (1875–1961)

Jung was born in a small village in Switzerland on the shores of the Lake of Constance. His father was a minister in the Swiss Reformed Church. The early religious influences were to play a strong part in Jung's later psychology.[19] He studied medicine at the University of Basle, receiving his degree in 1900. He was then appointed to the psychiatric clinic at the University of Zurich, where he remained until 1909.

After reading *The Interpretation of Dreams*,[20] Jung was much impressed with Freud, as Adler had been. By 1906 Freud and Jung had begun corresponding, and the following year he met Freud in Vienna and participated in the Wednesday Evening Discussion Group. During the next few years they developed a strong friendship which was to last only a short time, with the final and complete break coming in 1914.[21]

In 1911, over the protests of Freud's Viennese colleagues, Jung was made president of the International Psychoanalytic Association. By 1912, his relationship with Freud had become extremely cool. Freud was placing great emphasis on the sexual nature of early traumatic childhood experiences, as well as on the sex drive, as the basis for much psychic energy. This became totally unacceptable to Jung, who considered the libido's energy as originating in life and growth processes. In 1912 Freud and Jung terminated their personal correspondence, and by 1914 Jung resigned from the International Psychoanalytic Association. He founded his own school, and called it *analytical psychology*.

The rest of Jung's life is of no great concern to us. He continued to work and to hold university positions mainly in Switzerland. During the 1920s, he made a number of field expeditions. In 1921, he went to North Africa. He also visited the United States to study the Pueblo Indians in Arizona and New Mexico. In 1926, he returned to Africa and to Kenya to study the natives. His studies in medieval alchemy and oriental religions led to further developments

[18]Carl G. Jung, "The Psychology of the Unconscious," in *Two Essays on Analytical Psychology* (New York: Pantheon Press, Number XX in Bollingen Series, 1953–1963).
[19]Carl G. Jung, *The Psychology of Religion* (New Haven: Yale University Press, 1938).
[20]Sigmund Freud, *The Interpretation of Dreams, op. cit.*
[21]Ernest Jones, *op. cit.*

of his theory. In 1948, the C. G. Jung Institute was founded in Zurich to foster his theory and therapeutic techniques. Jung lived a long and productive life, continuing to write and advance new theories.

## Jung's Psychology

### Consciousness and Unconsciousness

Like Freud, Jung made a division between consciousness and unconsciousness. However, for Jung the unconscious seemed to be even more important, as he deemphasized the role of consciousness in favor of that of the unconscious even more than Freud did.[22]

The unconscious was divided into two parts—the personal unconscious and the collective unconscious. The *personal unconscious* was nearest to the conscious and contained the repressed and forgotten memories from earlier life. For each of us it was different and unique, depending on the kinds of past experiences we had had. In the personal unconscious resided the "complexes" which constituted a kind of nucleus of emotionally charged energy that could also attract related charged ideas to it. One could speak of an inferiority complex, a mother complex or a power complex. Through Jung's method of word association, these complexes could become unearthed by means of what Jung called "complex indicators." These indicators might include an unusual word or response, repetition of the given word, slow reaction time, or no response at all to a crucial word. Galton and Wundt had worked with word associations earlier, but it was Jung who developed the technique that was most useful to later clinical psychology.

### The Collective Unconscious

The idea of the collective unconscious was by far the most important. It was transpersonal in that it was shared by all human beings. It contained not only their human ancestral past but also their prehuman nature. It consisted of inherited memory traces and had evolved over countless generations, resulting from our ancestors' previous experiences. These memory traces were resident in the brain, and its collective nature could be attested to by the similarity in brain structure that all humans shared.

The racial memories were not inherited ideas as such, in the sense that Descartes had thought. They were merely brain traces—predispositions to act to the outside world in a selective way. For example, we were predisposed to love mother, to fear snakes and the dark, and to know God. These were easily actualized, since countless previous generations had had the same experiences.

---

[22]Carl G. Jung, *The Psychology of the Unconscious, op. cit.*

The collective unconscious was the foundation of the entire personality structure. Jung wrote that in the collective unconscious were found the wisdom and experience of uncounted centuries.

## The Archetypes

Archetypes constituted "primordial images" or the "universal thought forms." When our ancestors experienced the same events over and over again, an archetype might finally be formed. For example, there was the archetype of the mother—her nature, what she did and represented. Other archetypes included: the hero, Savior King, the devil, magic, God, the wise old man, and the Earth Mother.

Some archetypes became so important in our evolution that they formed their own systems within the personality structure. Some of the more important ones included: the *persona, shadow, anima-animus,* and the *self.*

1. The *persona* actually arose out of the unconscious to take the form of a "mask" and become our public personality. It was that rather superficial part of our personality which we showed to the outside world. It was our expression of social convention. Sometimes it was the personality that we "turned on" to impress others. Through countless ages, human beings had worn masks, psychologically speaking, so the archetype of the persona had evolved.

2. The *anima* was the femininity in man and the *animus* was the masculinity in woman. In this sense we were all bisexual—containing both the masculine and feminine. The anima-animus existed in all of us. Through the amina-aminus we were able to understand the opposite sex. As a male, I possess an amina which enables me to understand my wife and other females better. The amina had two sides; it was the pure and good, the noble goddess. On the other hand, it might be the prostitute, the seductress, the *femme fatale* or the Lorelei.[23]

3. The *shadow* represented the darker side of our nature. It contained the instincts that had been carried over from lower forms. Part of it was our past animal nature. The shadow also contained the archetypes of original sin, the devil, and the enemy.

4. The *self* was perhaps the most important system of the personality. It represented our striving for unity and wholeness. It was symbolized by the mandala or magic circle. In the mature person, the self became the focal point of the personality. In early development it was entirely unconscious, but if one developed into a psychologically mature being, the self emerged from the unconscious to be partly conscious and partly unconscious—the center of the entire personality structure. The self gave our personality equilibrium and stability.

---

[23]F. Fordham, *An Introduction to Jung's Psychology* (London: Penguin, 1953).

Religious experiences were a good example of how the self might be fulfilled. Jung said he discovered the self in his studies of oriental religions. The self could achieve realization in symbolic form.[24] Jung placed great emphasis on the role of symbols as expressions of the archetypical strivings for expression. In this sense, the symbols had two sides—one, the representation of the past, and the other, the striving for future expression. Some symbols of the self included: a pearl, a diamond, a circle or wheel, the chalice, the rose window, or any other object that had a central point.

Jung discussed many other universal archetypes, such as the "wise old man," the "earth mother" from Norse mythology, the child, the hero, the devil, and so on.

## Attitudes and Psychological Functions

The personality could be oriented in one of two directions—toward the outside world, as in *extraversion,* or inwardly, as in *introversion.* This was the beginning of Jung's typology—the notion that people could be divided into two sorts, introverts and extraverts.

There were also the psychological functions: *thinking, feeling, sensing,* and *intuiting.* Thinking and feeling were the rational functions, while sensing and intuiting were irrational. Usually, one of these functions would be the superior function, since it predominated in our actions. Its opposite would be the inferior function. For example, if one's superior function were that of sensing, its opposite, intuiting, would be the inferior. In the sensory function we lived for the satisfaction of our senses, and this became the direction of our activity. Intuiting acted on "hunches" or impulses. In intuiting, one acted in a certain way but could not tell why. The thinking function was oriented toward the intellectual activities and problem-solving. Feelings referred to activity which involved making value judgments.

By multiplying the two attitudes (introversion and extraversion) by the four functions (sensing, intuiting, thinking, and feeling) we come out with eight personality types.

*Extraverted-sensing* people live by their senses. These people enjoy the sights, sounds, and smells of nature. They enjoy beauty, are fun loving, like to be with people and go to parties, and like to eat and drink. They may be hard-headed business people and can be crude at times.

*Introverted-sensing* individuals are more likely to be artists, performing music or creating visual art objects. They appear to be calm and controlled but at times can be boring.

*Extraverted-thinking* people may be research scientists. They tend to reject the feeling function and to stress objective reality. They abide by their own conceptions of reality and expect the same from others.

---

[24]Carl G. Jung, *Psyche and Symbol* (Garden City, N.Y.: Doubleday and Co., 1958).

*Introverted-thinking* individuals are the problem-solvers. They, too, can be scientists, but they are more likely to confine themselves to their own laboratories, working alone. They may be accountants, and they enjoy working by themselves without the distraction of others.

*Extraverted-feeling* people live with their emotions. They like to make value judgments. They can be changeable and moody, but they also can form strong attachments to others. They like to follow fads and fashions. Jung found this type to be more common among females.

*Introverted-feeling* people are likely to keep their feelings hidden. They are often silent and unapproachable. They give the impression of inner harmony but occasionally are capable of outward "blowups." The expression "still waters run deep" applies to them.

*Extraverted-intuiting* individuals jump from one situation to another. They are often flightly, always looking for new worlds to conquer. Because they are deficient in the thinking function, they do not pursue their goals for long. They may jump from one job to another and fritter their lives away.

*Introverted-intuiting* individuals are the dreamers and visionaries. They can also be cranks. People often consider them enigmas. They are often out of touch with reality and conventional situations. On occasion, they may have brilliant intuitions, of which others may take advantage.

## Psychic Energy

Like Freud, Jung believed that the entire personality structure was charged with psychic energy. The complexes in the personal unconscious as well as the archetypes in the collective unconscious were charged with forces that desired to gain expression. The energy which controlled the personality originated from the biological life processes.

Borrowing from physics, Jung formulated the two principles of *equivalence* and *entropy*. By these principles the energy might be invested and distributed throughout the systems of the personality. The principle of equivalence (first law of thermodynamics or conservation of energy) stated that energy may be transformed but not lost. Psychologically speaking, as a child, much psychic energy was transformed to one's parents. But, as one grew older and had a family, the family took up more of one's energy, leaving less for one's parents. The *psychic value* (amount of energy) had changed.

In the principle of entropy (the second law of thermodynamics), when two bodies were placed together the energy from the higher charge would flow to the one of the lower charge until they were equal. (Water tends to seek its own level.) Applied to the personality structure, there was a tendency toward a balance of energy charges among the various systems.

## Principle of Synchronicity

Freud was a strong determinist, believing that the events of today are caused by events in our earlier lives. On the other hand, Adler tended to be very teleological, believing that future goals affect our current behavior. Jung was both a determinist and a teleologist. He also espoused a third principle—

*synchronicity.* This principle holds that events occurring together in time and appearing to be related may neither cause nor be caused by each other. This implies that there may be another order in the universe besides the one being caused by events of a prior nature—in other words, an order appearing to have causes but not subject to the law of causality. This appears in Jung's belief in parapsychology (extrasensory perception, mental telepathy, clairvoyance, etc.). Jung applied this principle as an explanation for his archetypes, discussed earlier.

### Self-Actualization and Development

The goal of personality development was the actualization or fulfillment of self. This not only involved the differentiation of the various systems within the structure (individuation) but also a binding together in harmony of all parts (transcendent function). The self attained the center of the personality, achieving a unity. Each system should be allowed to achieve its most complete fulfillment. No one system should overshadow or dominate another.

In the early stages of our development we were rather biologically oriented. The infant was concerned with the fulfillment of its bodily needs. In our youth and early adult years we provided for our own needs and the needs of our family; we married and had children. These all involved vital bodily processes. Jung did not ignore sex, for it was obviously significant for courtship and marriage and the begetting of offspring. In our late thirties and early forties a process of transvaluation ideally took place. One became less of a biological organism and was more culturally oriented. One was transformed from a biological to a spiritual person. This was a most significant event.

This transformation had to take place to achieve the actualization of the self. In Jung's discussion of therapy[25] he pointed out that some people never went beyond the biological stage of their development. In a sense they became fixated, satisfying their needs and leading a hum-drum existence. One of the ways to achieve selfhood and become a spiritual person was through religion, but this was not the only way. There were other forms of self-expression— through achievement in the arts, sciences, or one's work.

## *Evaluation*

### Contributions of Jung

Jung's position is difficult to evaluate. He has been strongly criticized and highly praised (particularly by philosophers). There is no doubt that he was a provocative and imaginative thinker. Like Freud, his influences have reached beyond psychology and psychiatry into history, art, literature, and music. Great

[25]F. Fordham, *op. cit.*

thinkers, such as the historian Arnold Toynbee and the writer Philip Wylie, have acknowledged his influence.[26] Robert Donnington has analyzed Wagner's "Ring Cycle" in terms of Jungian symbols both in the musical motives and the mythology on which the cycle of four consecutive operas was based.[27]

Jung's word association technique has been subjected to much investigation since he first proposed it, and it has been a useful technique in discovering emotional difficulties, as well as in the detection of lies.

His concept of self-actualization has been incorporated into the writings of a number of other personality theorists such as Maslow,[28] Allport,[29] and Murphy.[30] Apparently, these writers also found self-actualization a useful explanatory principle.

Cattell[31] and Eysenck[32] have done numerous statistical studies to demonstrate the validity of Jung's principle of introversion-extraversion. The Myers-Briggs Type indicator[33] was developed as a test to determine in which of the basic types the test taker belonged.

## Criticisms of Jung

All the difficulties levied against Freud's system applied to Jung's as well. Most of the theories were untestable and the data were not subject to the usual methods of scientific quantification.

There were further difficulties. Although Jung had suggested that the inheritance of a racial unconscious could be reduced to biological terms, there was still the belief that ideas which were experienced by our primitive ancestors could be passed on to us today. This was simply a restatement of the Lamarckian hypothesis of the inheritance of acquired characteristics, which is generally unacceptable in biology today.

Unlike Freud, Jung was not a clear writer. His writings were unsystematic, vague, and often contradictory. In his later writings he was no longer the psychologist, but a mystic and metaphysician. Even those who were well versed in Jung's early theories have found his later writings often incomprehensible. Yet he is still widely read and considered a great intellect. In the kindest sense, perhaps, we should consider him a mystic-philosopher rather than strictly a psychologist.[34]

---

[26]C. S. Hall, and G. Lindzey, *Theories of Personality,* 3rd ed. (New York: John Wiley, 1978).

[27]R. Donnington, *Wagner's "Ring" and Its Symbols: The Music and the Myth* (London: Farrar and Farrar, 1963).

[28]A. H. Maslow, *Motivation and Personality* (New York: Harper and Bros., 1954).

[29]Gordon Allport, *Personality: A Psychological Interpretation* (New York: Henry Holt and Co., 1937).

[30]G. Murphy, *Personality: A Biosocial Approach to Origins and Structures* (New York: Harper and Bros., 1947).

[31]R. B. Cattell, *Description and Measurement of Personality* (New York: World Book Co., 1946).

[32]H. J. Eysenck, *Dimensions of Personality* (London: Routledge and Kegan Paul, 1947).

[33]E. B. Myers, *The Myers-Briggs Type Indicator* (Princeton, N.J.: Educational Testing Service, 1962).

[34]Carl G. Jung, *Collected Works,* C. H. Read, M. Fordham, and C. Adler, eds., 18 vols. (New York: Pantheon Press, Number XX in Bollingen Series, 1953–1963).

## Karen Horney (1885–1952)

Like many of the other social analysts, Horney was born abroad and later moved to America. She was born in Hamburg, Germany on September 18, 1885. Her medical training was at the University of Berlin where she was first introduced to psychoanalytic theory. She received her medical degree in 1913 and started her career as an orthodox Freudian, having been psychoanalyzed by Karl Abraham and Hans Sachs, two of the most eminent Freudian analysts of the time. For many years Horney followed the Freudian tradition. In 1932 she came to the United States where she was to develop her new theories. After her arrival in this country, she was associated with the Chicago Psychoanalytic Institute and later with the New York Psychoanalytic Institute.

## Horney's Psychology

In her most important writings Horney did not present any systematic psychology. All we can do is piece together some of her more important ideas. Most of her writings were directed toward a theory of neurosis, which is not our basic concern here. Nevertheless, she did present a new approach to psychology, still keeping some flavor of psychoanalytic thinking.

### Basic Anxiety

One of her most important concepts was that of the *basic anxiety*. It was not inherited, but was the product of our culture and upbringing.[35] Basic anxiety was the feeling of being helpless in a hostile world. The feeling of helplessness could be a primary condition for later personality difficulties. Out of this anxiety arose a basic drive for *safety* or *security*. To be secure meant to be free of anxiety. Although anxiety tended to be quite universal in the western world, it was not inherited.

To quote Horney,[36] basic anxiety was:

> . . . the feeling a child has of being isolated and helpless in a potentially hostile world. A wide range of adverse factors in the environment can produce this insecurity in a child: direct or indirect domination, indifference, erratic behavior, lack of respect for the child's individual needs, lack of real guidance, disparaging attitudes, too much admiration or the absence of it, lack of reliable warmth, having to take sides in parental disagreements, too much or too little responsibility, overprotection, isolation from other children, injustice, discrimination, unkept promises, hostile atmosphere and so on and so on.

---

[35]Karen Horney, *The Neurotic Personality of Our Time* (New York: W. W. Norton and Co., 1937).
[36]Karen Horney, *Our Inner Conflicts* (New York: W. W. Norton and Co., 1945), p. 41.

The need for security became a driving, motivating force. Frequently, when a child strove for security and was rebuffed, greater anxiety arose and the *vicious circle* developed. The harder the child strove, the more anxiety was generated. When further security was not achieved, more anxiety occurred and the vicious circle continued over and over again.

## Neurotic Needs

As a result of various failures to solve the problems of life, certain needs were developed.[37] Horney called these "neurotic," because they did not result in rational solutions. However, one should realize that these needs were not limited to neurotic people. We may all express them to a greater or lesser degree.

**1.** Neurotic need for affection and approval (to be adored and admired).

**2.** Neurotic need for a partner (to give in and be protected).

**3.** Neurotic need to restrict one's life (excessive modesty and isolation).

**4.** Neurotic need for power (to despise weakness and glorify strength).

**5.** Neurotic need to exploit others (to win, to take advantage of others).

**6.** Neurotic need for prestige (to receive public recognition).

**7.** Neurotic need for personal admiration (to be flattered and complimented).

**8.** Neurotic need for ambition and personal achievement (to be rich and famous, regardless of the consequences).

**9.** Neurotic need for self-sufficiency and independence (to set one's self apart from others).

**10.** Neurotic need for perfection (to be infallible and sensitive to criticism).

The following case is reported by Karen Horney in her book *Self Analysis*.[38]

> Clara was an unwanted child. Several attempts at abortion on the part of her mother had failed. Her father was a country doctor so he was seldom at home. In a tangible way she was treated like her brother: just as many gifts, similar private schools, and music lessons. In less tangible ways, she received less tenderness, less interest in her school work, less concern when she was ill and in many little ways she was ignored. On the other hand, there was a strong feeling of affection between her brother and mother. Clara tried to get close to her father but to no avail. As a result Clara never developed any sense of self-confidence. Gradually, Horney reports, she developed certain neurotic trends. She became excessively modest, always putting herself in second place, she thought less of herself, became dependent and lost the capacity to take life into

---

[37]Karen Horney, *Self-Analysis* (New York: W. W. Norton and Co., 1942).
[38]*Ibid.*

her own hands. Furthermore, she developed the neurotic need for a partner or a friend or a lover. Then, she developed the neurotic need to excel, to triumph over others.

Finally, Clara entered psychoanalysis at the age of 30 because of paralyzing fatigue which made it impossible for her to work.

## Inner Conflicts

In her book *Our Inner Conflicts* Horney divided these needs into three categories, which related to three striving forces to move (1) toward people, (2) against people, and (3) away from people.

Moving toward, away from, or against people all represented a basic orientation. These could quite obviously come into conflict with each other. The normal person resolved the conflict by integrating the three orientations. Further, the conflicts might be avoided or resolved if a child were raised in a home where there was love and respect, where the child was made to feel wanted and secure, and where there was trust.

If one took a particular orientation to the exclusion of others, three types of personality might develop.

1. **The compliant type.** (moving toward). Compliant people overvalued affection and approval and became overly dependent.

2. **The hostile type.** (moving against). Hostile individuals might become aggressive, suspicious, and anti-social. Like themselves, they believed everyone else to be hostile.

3. **The detached type.** (away from). Detached people might be withdrawn, egocentric, and aloof.

## The Idealized Image

One way to resolve the conflict might be to create an idealized image of oneself, one that was somewhat (but not entirely) fictitious and illusory. In this case, there would be a big discrepancy between the image and the real self. It would be unrealistic and exaggerated. Through self-deception, one created a self-image of what one believed or felt one ought to be. The image might be one of a saint, a mastermind, or a Casanova. It was an expression of the fact that one could not tolerate one's true self.[39]

## Evaluation of Horney

Horney's main contribution was her emphasis on the effect social conditions had on the developing personality. She stressed that our personality was both a reflection of the culture in which we lived, and of our personal family relationships; and she verified this in a clinical way. A child was the product of both

---

[39]Karen Horney, *Neurosis and Human Growth* (New York: W. W. Norton and Co., 1950).

environment and heredity. Horney stressed the environment, but did not deny hereditary potentials. She simply dismissed much of the untestable, inherent forces on people, so important for the more orthodox psychoanalytic system.

Compared to Freud's, her model of personality was very incomplete. She was primarily concerned with a theory of neurosis from which one might try to extract a theory of normal personality. The same criticism could also be levied against Freud, but he presented a much more detailed and systematic position so one could erect a theory of normal behavior.

As Wolman[40] points out, Horney

> paved a new road to psychoanalysis, but it has not turned out to be one well traveled. The system is too incomplete. Too many questions are left unanswered.

Compared to the prolific contributions of Freud, Adler, and Jung (whether one agreed with them or not), Horney was a much less important figure in history of the psychoanalytic movement.

At the risk of being repetitious, the criticisms levied earlier against Freud and others can apply to Horney as well.

## Erich Fromm (1900–1980)

Fromm, even more than Horney, departed from the Freudian framework. Like her, he never developed any carefully worked out system. In the typical social analytical trend, he was concerned with social influences, in particular, the relationship of human beings to society. Furthermore, the relationship between humans and their society was a constantly changing one—not so static as Freud had implied.

Fromm was born in Frankfurt, Germany on March 23, 1900. He received his Ph.D. at the University of Heidelberg in 1922. He studied at Munich and at the Psychoanalytic Institute in Berlin. In 1934 he came to America and taught at the National Institute for Social Research in New York until 1939. He was guest lecturer at Columbia University from 1940 to 1941 and served on the faculty of Bennington College from 1941 to 1950. His other academic appointments included the National University of Mexico and Michigan State University.

### Escape from Freedom

In his first book, *Escape from Freedom*,[41] Fromm acknowledged human beings' biological past, but accepted them as social animals. The basic theme was human loneliness. As people developed, they gained greater independence, but in

[40]B. B. Wolman, *op. cit.*, p. 355.
[41]Erich Fromm, *Escape from Freedom* (New York: Farrar and Rinehart, 1941).

so doing, became more isolated and lonely. Freedom, then, became a condition from which to escape.

According to Fromm, human beings started out in cosmic unity with each other and with the universe about them. At this point, the feeling of complete identity kept them from being lonely, but it bound them to nature. Primitive humans used both myths and religion to bind them to their clans, which told them how to act and gave them security. By the Middle Ages, humans had cast off some of their earlier subservience to the primitive clan and nature but had social solidarity. Their political, social, and economic life was bound to the Church. The Church gave them security and offered them God's love.

In the late Middle Ages, the structure of society began to change. A new merchant class arose, based on individual enterprise, and a growing individualism began to appear. The old static society began to vanish, and social status became more mobile. With the Reformation, some of the identification with God was lost. Again, people gained greater freedom. Today, people have gained independence, but they are alone and insecure. Modern industrial society lacks any frame of reference, and people have attempted to escape from their intolerable helplessness and loneliness. The development of totalitarian states has arisen against this loneliness.

There were two solutions. One was to join with others in a spirit of love and social work. The second was to submit to authority and conform to society. The ideal solution was to develop a society in which there was equality for all, where each person had the opportunity to become purely human, where people related to others in a loving way, and where they could become rooted in a human kinship.

## Methods of Escape

Too often, today, people have chosen undesirable methods of escape. These have some relevance to Freud's ego defenses.

In *masochism,* a person gave up independence, developed a strong desire for affection and became helplessly dependent. In *sadism,* there was a tendency to rule and exploit others. A need for power developed to the degree that others suffered. In *destruction,* one escaped from helplessness by destroying the outside world. Finally, in *automation conformity,* one behaved exactly as others expected one to behave. This could take the form of neurotic submission. By refusing to face differences and wishing only to conform, one could be relieved of one's sense of helplessness. This involved giving up anything that was original and independent. It became a blind acceptance of the social order—a willingness to obey without question.

## Personality

To Fromm, personality was the totality of inherited and acquired characteristics. He distinguished *temperament* from *character.*[42] *Temperament* referred to that

---

[42]Erich Fromm, *Man for Himself* (New York: Rinehart, 1947).

which was inherited, constitutional, and unchangeable. *Character* was developed through social influences. There was the "individual character" which developed from specific influences in one's environment and which constituted one's individuality. The "social character" accounted for those reactions one shared with other members of one's society.

## Types

Personality types arose out of people's attempts to assimilate their own characters with society as well as to relate themselves to that society. These could be distinguished as assimilation and socialization.

*Receptive characters* demanded that all they had must come from the outside world that they accepted. For them, love meant being loved. Receptive characters became very anxious when their sources of supply were cut off.

For the *hoarding character,* the outside world became a threat. Security was assured when one could save and keep. These people tended to be selfish, pedantic, and orderly.

*Exploitative characters* satisfied their desires by force and cunning. They were aggressive towards others. They would take or steal whatever they could.

*Marketing characters* considered themselves commodities that could be bought and sold like bales of hay. Success meant that one was valuable to others. The unsuccessful was useless. Marketing characters evaluated themselves on the basis of "how well they could sell themselves to others."

Fromm distinguished a fifth, and more desirable, type—the *productive character.* Productive people could gain genuine love, care, and responsibility. For them love meant love of the human race. Being productive meant the realization of their useful potentialities. They expressed a devotion to the welfare and well-being of their fellow humans.

## The Basic Needs

In the beginning, human beings were tied to nature and shared many biological needs with animals.[43] As society developed, people developed other needs, which arose out of their relationship with society. Fromm distinguished five needs. (1) *Relatedness* stemmed from one being torn apart from one's cosmic union. People had to create relationships with their fellow humans. One way of relating was through productive love, which involved mutual respect and understanding. (2) *Transcendence* was expressed in a desire to rise above one's animal nature. People had become rational animals who could think and create. (3) In *rootedness,* one wanted to be a part of the world in which one lived. One wanted to belong. (4) The need for *identity* implied people's desire to be unique individuals. People wished to distinguish themselves from others, achieving a feeling of personal identity. Of course, one might achieve this identity with a group, a club, or one's country. (5) The need for *orientation* meant finding a

---

[43]Erich Fromm, *Sane Society* (New York: Rinehart, 1955).

frame of reference. One desired a consistent way of understanding the world. These all tended to be human needs embedded in human nature.

Fromm felt that capitalism and communism failed as economic systems in fulfilling basic human needs. However, it was possible to form a society in which people would relate to each other by means of productive love. In this society, there would be neither loneliness nor despair. Such an idealistic society Fromm called a humanistic communitarian socialism—one in which there would be equality for all, where every individual would gain a full sense of self and the will to relate to others lovingly, and one which would be rooted in friendship and solidarity.[44]

### Evaluation of Fromm

Fromm presented an optimistic and loving approach to human nature. He used history as his laboratory and yet, as Wolman points out, he distorted history.[45]

> For example, his story of man's alleged loneliness and group formation does not correspond to any data, his picture of medieval life is highly idealized, he has omitted all the physical and mental hardships produced by despots, fanaticism . . . plagues, wars and other disasters. The era of the Renaissance and Reformation is painted black in disregard for the positive and productive aspects of the times. Fromm's story of freedom and escape is an interesting one but . . . it does not correspond to any historical data.

Fromm's theory was highly idealistic and, as such, also unrealistic. He lacked data from historical sources and other reasonable sources as well. The realization of the kind of society he proposed will remain a purely imaginative one, at least in the foreseeable future. Perhaps, we should not call him a psychologist at all, but rather a historical and ethical philosopher.

## Harry Stack Sullivan (1892–1949)

Of all the analysts described in this and the preceding chapter, Sullivan was the only one born and trained in America. Because of earlier psychoanalytic influences on him, it would probably be incorrect to say that his theory was truly American. His theory showed greater influences from nonpsychoanalytic sources, and he deviated the furthest from the Freudian position. Yet, there were enough elements from psychoanalytical thinking to allow him to be considered in a chapter with other analysts. Like Freud's, his was a dynamic psy-

---

[44]*Ibid.*, p. 362.
[45]B. B. Wolman, *op. cit.*, p. 367.

chology, placing great stress on needs, tensions, and anxiety. Also, like Freud, he placed great stress on the significance of distinct periods in personality development. Sullivan's was thus a truly developmental theory.

Sullivan was born on a farm in New York State on February 2, 1892. He studied medicine at the Chicago College of Medicine and Surgery, receiving his degree in 1917. He served on the staff of a number of hospitals and medical schools—St. Elizabeth's in Washington, D.C. and The University of Maryland. He served as president of the William Alanson White Foundation from 1933 to 1943. Until his death in 1949, he was director of the Washington School of Psychiatry.

During his life Sullivan had only one book published, *Conceptions of Modern Psychiatry*.[46] Other books have been published posthumously. They consisted of edited series of lectures which he had given from time to time. However, when combined, they did help to develop an integrated theory of personality.

Sullivan's theory has been considered an *interpersonal one,* since it was based on human relationships. The concept of personality, as such, was only a hypothetical entity for no personality existed outside interpersonal relationships. Human beings could not be studied outside the interpersonal field in which they lived.

## Dynamisms

In the interpersonal relationship, the smallest unit of study was called a *dynamism.* It was an energy transference, which meant any unit of behavior, either an overt act or a private mental experience. Dynamisms usually became habitual ways of acting involving some part of the body—the mouth, anus, hands, arms, legs, and so forth. One could identify numerous dynamisms: the fear dynamism, lust dynamism, intimate dynamism, malevolent dynamism, and so forth.

## The Self System

The self system was one kind of dynamism, and a very important one for the personality structure. It operated as a security measure to protect the individual from anxiety. (Anxiety played an important role in Sullivan's system.) In the child there was the "good-me," the "bad-me," and occasionally the "not-me" dynamism. The "good-me" evolved out of the child's security, while the "bad-me" would forbid a certain activity because it had been punished. In Sullivan's system the concept of the self system had some corollary with Freud's concept of the superego. The self system was developed because we all experienced anxiety. It often began with the infant's relationship with its mother in the feeding operation.

---

[46]Harry S. Sullivan, *Conceptions of Modern Psychiatry* (Washington, D.C.: W. A. White Foundation, 1947).

## Personifications

Personifications (which were also dynamisms) constituted images one had of oneself or of another person. They could be a complex of feelings, attitudes, or conceptions that arose out of interpersonal relations. A child might have a personification of the "good mother," "bad mother," or "overprotective mother." Personifications were also related to the self system, when they operated to relieve anxiety and satisfy needs. One had personifications of oneself as well as of others. They might often be inconsistent and might interfere with more objective evaluations of one's relationships with others.

## Stereotypes

Stereotypes were personifications that one tended to share with others. They were not necessarily correct, but tended to perpetuate themselves. They were not unlike the general notion of stereotypes. Such stereotypes as the tough businessperson, absent-minded professor, temperamental artist, or mad Russian were common.

## Types of Experience

Experience came to us in three modes—*prototaxic, parataxic,* and *syntaxic.*[47] The *prototaxic* was the earliest. It was a flowing of sensations, feelings, and images without any necessary connection between them. Hall and Lindzey[48] have compared the prototaxic experience to William James' concept of the "stream of consciousness." However, this type of experience was necessary in order for the later ones to develop. In *parataxic* experiences, we began to develop relationships. Although these might not be logical, they could be compared to simple conditioning. Rewards and reinforcements followed certain responses. Often parataxic experiences involved inferences such as the idea that day followed night, or good behavior would be rewarded and bad behavior punished. Superstitions were one kind of parataxic experience. Even though they might be incorrect, relationships were implied. Breaking a mirror would be followed by bad luck. On the other hand, what we referred to as cause-and-effect relationships were parataxic experiences. The most highly developed experiences were the *syntaxic.* Syntaxic experiences took symbolic form in the use of words and numbers. They were by far the most complex and served as the basis for much of our intellectual activity.

[47]Harry S. Sullivan, *The Interpersonal Theory of Psychiatry* (New York: W. W. Norton and Co., 1953).
[48]C. S. Hall, and G. Lindzey, *Theories of Personality,* 3rd ed. (New York: John Wiley and Sons, 1978).

## Tensions, Needs, and Anxiety

In Sullivan's treatment of personality, his discussion of the dynamic nature of human beings reflected earlier psychoanalytic influences. Sullivan thought of the personality as a tension system. Tensions arose and had to be relieved. Although he did not directly speak of psychic energy, in the interpretation of this writer, the concept was implicit. There were two basic sources of tension: needs and anxiety. Needs typically arose out of biological functions, such as hunger, thirst, or sex. When they were relieved, the person experienced a feeling of satisfaction.[49] Although Sullivan did not directly state it, there were certainly implications of Freud's pleasure principle. Complete satisfaction or the relief of tension resulted in a feeling of euphoria.

The second source of tension was found in anxiety. Anxiety arose out of real or imagined threats. The most extreme form of tension as expressed in anxiety was terror. So, terror became the ultimate form of tension, while euphoria became the ultimate relaxation. Each represented an opposite pole. Anxiety was a state to be avoided for it interfered with the efficient operation of the need-satisfaction sequence, disturbed interpersonal relationships, and confused thinking. The degree of anxiety generally varied with the intensity of the threat. Anxiety was often transmitted from mother to child as a failure in the nursing process. The reduction of anxiety gave rise to a feeling of security.

When a person performed some sort of work, energy was *transformed*. Work could be of a physical kind, as in muscular activity, or it could be mental, as in thinking or perceiving. The concept of energy transformation was not so completely elaborated as in Freud's system, but the same implications were certainly there.

## Personality Development

With the exception of Freud, Sullivan presented a more detailed and elaborate description of the stages of human growth than any of the other analytical psychologists. For Freud, the development was psychosexual. For Sullivan, development was in the direction of gaining greater personal relationships. Basically, he discussed seven stages: (1) infancy, (2) childhood, (3) juvenile period, (4) preadolescence, (5) early adolescence, (6) late adolescence, and (7) adulthood.

*Infancy* started at birth and developed to the stage where early language began—at about eighteen months. In its early phase it was much involved with the mouth. Furthermore, nursing was the beginning of the infant's first interpersonal relationship. There was the dynamism of the "good nipple," where nursing was satisfactory, the "wrong nipple," where there was no milk; and the "bad nipple," where mother was anxious in the feeding process.

---

[49]Harry S. Sullivan, *op. cit.*

In infancy, the first expressions of the self system developed. When the infant's behavior was accepted and praised, the "good me" self emerged. Anxiety gave rise to the "bad me" self, while experience of extreme shock might be unconsciously experienced in the "not me" self.

*Childhood* began with the acquisition of language and continued during the preschool years. Syntaxic experience evolved. Interpersonal relationships spread to those outside the immediate family, to the early playmates. The child learned a "capacity for living with compeers." During childhood one acquired many dynamisms. One learned to eat, was toilet trained, and acquired other habits of behavior considered by society to be correct and proper. One also learned that one's desires were not always immediately satisfied; they had to be *sublimated*—that is, directed in ways which would give substitute satisfactions. Children typically engaged in *dramatizations* or playing "as if." Little girls had their tea parties or dressed up in mother's clothes, while little boys rode on toy engines or played with fake guns.

The dynamism of *malevolent transformation* appeared during the childhood years. Sullivan expressed this as a feeling that one lived among enemies—a concept not unlike Horney's "basic anxiety." It often arose out of the child's first rebuffs from its parents and others.

The *juvenile period* corresponded to the grade-school years, from about six to eleven. Interpersonal relations were broadened as one played and worked with other children. Competition, cooperation, and compromise developed.[50] In this period one had to learn to subordinate oneself to authority figures such as teachers and parents. New stereotypes were formed, such as the old-maid school marm or cops as the "good guys."

*Preadolescence* was a short period from about eleven to thirteen. In it, there was an intensity of relations with members of the same sex. An *intimate* dynamism was formed, as expressed in the need for a pal or best friend. According to Sullivan, the period marked the beginnings of "genuine human relations." A sense of equality with one's peer group developed in which there had to exist a feeling of mutual respect.

*Early adolescence* was marked by an interest in heterosexual activity. Out of the biological changes which were beginning to take place, the *erotic dynamism* appeared. The genital zones came into focus. The *intimacy dynamism* had already been formed in the preadolescent period. There had to be a separation of these two dynamisms or homosexual relationships might arise. The early adolescent period continued until more stable heterosexual relations were made. The period continued through the middle high school years.

*Late adolescence* constituted the later high school and early college years. During this period, a person should develop full and mature interpersonal relationships.[51] One learned the necessities for full responsibilities and citizenship in an organized society. Mature heterosexual relationships evolved. Effective

---

[50]Harry S. Sullivan, *Conceptions of Modern Psychiatry, op. cit.*
[51]Harry S. Sullivan, *The Interpersonal Theory of Psychiatry, op. cit.*

sublimations were developed, and stronger security measures operated as protections against anxiety.

In *adulthood*, one became completely heterosexual and completely stabilized. Society had transformed one into a completely social being.

### Evaluation of Sullivan

Interpersonal relationships constituted the basic principle in Sullivan's theory. Because we were human, it was impossible not to interact with other people. What we were was the result of the interpersonal contacts we had made earlier in our lives.

Second in importance was Sullivan's concept of tension. It was defined in a rather nebulous way, but the reduction of tension became a primary motivating force in life. Through the development of dynamisms, a person learned to reduce these tensions. Although each was stated in slightly different ways, the concepts of societal influences and anxiety seemed to tie these three systems of Horney, Fromm, and Sullivan together. All three stressed society's influences; although, for Sullivan, the influences were much more personal and direct. In addition, for all three the world was a very anxious place in which to live. (In Fromm's system we had to equate loneliness with anxiety.)

Unlike Horney and Fromm, Sullivan had constructed a fuller and more systematic theory of personality and, consequently, achieved wider acceptance in psychiatric and psychological circles. Although Sullivan's system had many hypothetical constructs (energy transformation, tension, the self system, etc.), he employed a much more objective language in describing his theory. One had the impression that he was dealing with concepts, some of which could be objectively tested. His data, although entirely clinical, seemed closely related to his observations of real people interacting with each other. At least some of his concepts involved observable behavior and he indulged less in fictions than did other analysts.

## *Erik Erikson (1902–1994)*

Today, the most influential variant of Freudian theory appears to be the developmental approach of Erik Erikson. Unlike Adler, Jung, Horney, Fromm, or Sullivan, Erikson remains faithful to Freud's tripartite structure of personality—the ego, superego, and id—but places greater stress on the importance of the ego. Thus, Erikson is identified as an ego psychologist. Also, he holds true to Freud's emphasis on psychosexual development and the importance of infantile sexuality.

Erikson was born of Danish parents in Frankfurt, Germany, of a Protestant father and Jewish mother. With the rise of Hitler in the 1930s, he came to the United States and became a naturalized citizen in 1936. His important books include *Childhood and Society*[52] (2nd ed. 1963), *Identity: Youth and Crisis*[53] (1968), and *Gandhi's Truth*[54] (1968), a study of psychohistory for which he received the Pulitzer Prize and National Book Award. Later, *Toys and Reason*[55] (1977) appeared.

## Ego Psychology

Erikson accepts the basic Freudian psychological processes of ego functioning in the psychological processes of perceiving, remembering, problem solving, and defensive activity. In placing greater emphasis on the ego, he goes beyond Freud in stressing many other characteristics of the ego, including *mastery* and *identity*. The concept of identity, or its failure (identity confusion or identity crisis), is one of the cornerstones of Erikson's theory. It involves the inner, but conscious, sense of uniqueness or individuality; a feeling of inner wholeness and synthesis; a feeling of continuity with the past and present; and a feeling of solidarity in ideas and values with a group from which a person receives support.

A sense of identity begins very early in life as an infant identifies with its mother. It continues to develop, achieving its fullest expression in adolescence. It is not uncommon for a person at that time of life to develop an identity crisis, which is expressed as a feeling of confusion or a lack of understanding of where his or her life is directed. It can be expressed in apathy, moodiness, absorption in fantasy, or a feeling of floundering or wandering aimlessly. Erikson feels that the identity crisis is the most important problem confronting contemporary psychology. For a proper sense of identity to occur, a person needs the support of significant others—members of the family, relatives, close friends, and so on.

Society plays an important role in ego development. To affirm the significance of social development, Erikson studied the Sioux Indians of South Dakota and the Yurok salmon fishermen of Northern California. He observed the Sioux to be trusting and generous, whereas the Yurok were miserly and suspicious. For Erikson, the role of society in molding the developing personality is far more important than it was for Freud.

## Stages of Development

One of Erikson's most significant contributions to neo-Freudian theory is his description of the eight stages of human development. He accepts the Freudian oral, anal, phallic, latent, and genital periods and adds three more—early adulthood, middle adulthood, and maturity (old age). Each stage has its own

---

[52]E. Erikson, *Childhood and Society*, 2nd ed. (New York: W. W. Norton, 1963).
[53]E. Erikson, *Identity: Youth and Crisis* (New York: W. W. Norton, 1968).
[54]E. Erikson, *Gandhi's Truth: On the Origins of Militant Nonviolence* (New York: W. W. Norton, 1969).
[55]E. Erikson, *Toys and Reason* (New York: W. W. Norton, 1977).

developmental characteristics and a typical crisis involving a turning point; each crisis is brought about by increasing physical maturity, along with greater demands placed upon the person by parents, society, or both. The crisis inherent in each stage should be resolved by the ego during that period. All stages can be interpreted as being both psychosexual and psychosocial. Finally, when each stage is brought to a successful conclusion, a particular virtue is achieved:

1. **Infancy: The oral-sensory stage.** (corresponding to Freud's oral stage). This stage centers around the nursing process and involves a person's first interaction with another person (usually the mother). The basic crisis is *trust versus mistrust*. If the nursing is satisfactory, involving relief of hunger and the giving of affection, a sense of *trust* is established as the infant's first significant social contact is achieved. If hunger is too commonly ignored or if the mother is overly anxious, a sense of impending danger results, in the form of *mistrust*. Because no parent is going to be completely successful, there will always be some mixture of trust and mistrust, but if all goes reasonably well, the virtue of *hope* will result.

2. **Muscular-anal stage.** As in the Freudian system, the emphasis during this period is on the process of toilet training; the child learns to retain or eliminate the basic wastes from its body. As it succeeds in eliminating appropriately, a sense of self-sufficiency is established. But if the training is overly strict or erratic, failures will occur. Here the crisis is *autonomy versus shame or doubt*. Failure in the training process will result in accidents and punitive measures. With success, the child becomes autonomous and able to act on its own. Failures and punishments result in shame. The basic virtue in this stage is *will*.

3. **Locomotor-genital stage.** (corresponding to the Freudian phallic stage). This stage is characterized by locomotion—walking and running—which operate to further the ego's basic function of mastery. During this stage, the child learns to distinguish between the two sexes. Here the crisis is *initiative versus guilt*. With increasing locomotion, new accomplishments are possible, giving rise to initiative, followed by approval for accomplishments. Also, during this stage the Oedipus complex arises and, ideally, is appropriately resolved. The illicit wishes of the complex (desire for intercourse with the parent of the opposite sex) may result in guilt. As guilt is overcome and initiative is strengthened by repressing sexuality, the basic virtue of *purpose* will follow.

4. **Latency stage.** As with Freud, Erikson finds this stage characterized by repressed sexuality. This is the stage of the grade-school years. The child learns to work to master school studies. Here the crisis is *industry versus inferiority*. Success in work leads to a sense of industry, while failures in school or other accomplishments and relations with friends lead to inferiority. Through success in one's accomplishments, the virtue of *competence* results.

**TABLE 2**

## Principles of Freud and His Heirs

| Theorist | Personality structure | Instincts, drives, urges | Guiding principles | Developmental stages | Special features |
|---|---|---|---|---|---|
| Freud | Conscious/unconscious; ego, id, superego | Life instinct (including sex); death instinct | Pleasure principle; primary process; secondary process | Infantile, oral, anal, phallic, latent, genital | Unconscious conflict; anxiety and ego defenses |
| Jung | Consciousness; personal unconscious, collective unconscious | Psychic energy; instincts; archetypes | Entropy, equivalence, synchronicity | Not spelled out | Introversion-extraversion. Personality types: thinking, feeling, sensing, intuiting |
| Adler | Creative self; primarily consciousness | Striving for superiority; social interest | Compensation for inferiority; fictional finalism; style of life | Not clearly specified | Birth order; importance of early memories |
| Horney | Basically Freudian in nature | Need for security; rejection of Freudian instincts | Basic anxiety resulting from helplessness; safety devices resulting from defenses | Not emphasized | Analysis of cultural sources of conflict |

| | | | | |
|---|---|---|---|---|
| Fromm | Conscious/unconscious | Basic needs: relatedness, rootedness, identity, transcendence, frame of reference | Methods of escape from freedom; forces for growth if permitted by society | Not spelled out | Analysis of an ideal society |
| Sullivan | Dynamism rather than specific structure | Tension; needs; anxiety; loneliness | Cognitive development; prototaxic, parataxic, syntaxic experiences | Infancy, childhood, juvenile, preadolescence, early adolescence, late adolescence, adulthood | Defective parental relationships |
| Erikson | Basically Freudian; more emphasis on ego | Same as Freud | Crisis in each stage, ex. identity crisis | Eight stages of development, from infancy to maturity | Reaffirmation of rational processes in people |

5. **Adolescence.** (corresponding to Freud's genital period). This period begins with puberty and is characterized by the resurgence of sexual impulses. An interest in the opposite sex begins to predominate. For Erikson, this is one of the most important periods of development. Here the crisis is *identity versus identity crisis,* and the task is to develop a sense of identity. This is the period in which in-groups, or "cliques," are formed, in part to fulfill one's need to identify, and identity is achieved by establishing a proper sex role. The confusion of floundering in the identity crisis may result in quitting school or attempting to belong to variant groups involved with delinquency, drugs, or alcohol. When and if the identity crisis is re-solved, the virtue of *fidelity* results—the ability to sustain loyalties, freely pledged.

6. **Young adulthood.** This is the period after the school years, which involves getting a job to sustain one's livelihood and seeking a partner in marriage. The crisis is *intimacy versus isolation.* If one is successful in finding a mate, an intimate contact with the opposite sex is achieved. This is necessary for successful marriage and lasting friendships. Isolation results in too much concern for one's own selfish needs. Success in going through this stage results in the virtue of *love.*

7. **Adulthood.** This is the longest stage, running from the middle twenties until about age sixty-five. During this stage, one establishes a career and propagates children, who should be cared for. The basic crisis is *generativity versus stagnation.* Generativity involves procreation and caring for one's off-spring until they are able to strike out for themselves. It also involves productivity in many of life's endeavors, work, creativity, and recreation. Frequently, during the adult years a person becomes bogged down. A fail-ure to care for others or a selfish concern for one's indulgences will result in *stagnation.* Success in this stage results in the virtue of *care*—a concern for what a person has created, both biologically and materially.

8. **Maturity.** If one has gone through the preceding stages successfully, a feel-ing of accomplishment for the life one has led should result. The crisis in this stage is *integrity versus despair.* The satisfaction of a life well led results in integrity, whereas a fear of death coming before the person has reached his goals will result in despair. Too many senior citizens, either by their own foolishness or environmental disasters, encounter despair. If integrity can overcome despair, which Erikson believes is usually the case, the virtue of *wisdom* will result. Wisdom is a detached concern for life itself in the face of death. If the mature generations can manifest their integrity, their children will neither fear life nor subconsciously seek death.

## Evaluation of Erikson

According to those sympathetic to Erikson's ideas, he has broadened and brought new insights to the psychoanalytic theory. His stress on the place of environment and society in molding individual personalities finds its validity in current sociology and social psychology. They feel that he has kept the best aspects of Freudian theory and found more appropriate reinterpretations for its failures.

Those who oppose Erikson do so on much the same grounds as they oppose more orthodox Freudian theory. There is still a strong emphasis on infantile sexuality, the Oedipus complex, and what opponents call "fictional concepts." Furthermore, like his predecessors, Erikson's ideas are still highly theoretical and unverified. Many, finding little data to support the universality of the "eight stages of man," question his theories.

## Principles of Freud and His Heirs

A comparison of the various principles of Freud and his heirs is presented in Table 2 (see pp. 356–357). It is intended to clarify the similarities and differences of the theories of Freud, of those who broke away from his psychoanalytic group (Adler, Jung), and of those who followed in the psychodynamic tradition. Many of them were psychoanalyzed (Horney, Fromm, Erikson) and then digressed, forming their own theories.

Comparisons to be drawn fall under the various headings *Personality structure, Guiding principles, Developmental stages,* and so on. It is hoped that this table will enable the reader to make useful comparisons.

### Suggested Further Readings

*Adler and Jung*

Adler, Alfred, *The Practice and Theory of Individual Psychology.* New York: Harcourt, Brace and Co., 1927.

Adler, Alfred, *Social Interest.* New York: Putnam, 1939. Two good books to begin with in reading Adler.

Ansbacher, H. L., and Ansbacher, R., eds., *The Individual Psychology of Alfred Adler.* New York: Basic Books, 1956. A large book filled with Adler's original writings. Particularly helpful are the extensive commentaries by the editors.

Corsini, R., ed., *Current Personality Theories.* Itasca, Illinois: Peacock Publishing Co., 1977, chs. 2 and 3. A very good introduction to the systems of both Adler and Jung.

Fordham, F., *An Introduction to Jung's Psychology.* London: Penguin Books, 1953. The best available summary of Jung's psychology. The book bears Jung's stamp of approval. However, it is devoted primarily to Jung's early works.

Hall, C. S., and Lindzey, G., *Theories of Personality,* 3rd ed. New York: John Wiley and Sons, 1978, chs. 3 and 4. The discussion of Jung is well-organized and highly informative. Adler is "short-changed."

Hall, C. S., and Norby, V. J., *A Primer of Jungian Psychology*. New York: New American Library, 1973. On the same order as Hall's Freudian primer. The basic principles are outlined in a readable manner.

Jacobi, J., *The Psychology of C. G. Jung*. New Haven: Yale University Press, 1951. A close second to the Fordham book, but pitched at a higher level.

Lundin, Robert W., *Alfred Adler's Basic Concepts and Implications*. Muncie, Indiana: Accelerated Development Publishers, 1989.

Orgler, H., *Alfred Adler: The Man and His Work*. New York: Liveright Publishing Co., 1963.

Way, L., *Adler's Place in Psychology*. New York: Collier Books, 1962. Two good summaries of Adler's psychology.

## Horney, Fromm and Sullivan

Brown, J. A. C., *Freud and the Post-Freudians*. New York: Penguin Books, 1961. Special chapters devoted to Fromm, Horney, and Sullivan.

Fromm, Erich, *Escape from Freedom*. New York: Rinehart, 1941. A good place to begin, with one of Fromm's most popular books.

Hall, C. S., and Lindzey, G., *Theories of Personality*, rev. ed. New York: John Wiley and Sons, 1970, ch. 4. The chapter deals briefly with these three social analysts—Horney, Fromm, and Sullivan. The discussion of Sullivan is good.

Horney, Karen, *Collected Works*, 2 vols. New York: W. W. Norton and Co., 1953. As indicated, Horney, as compared with others in the psychoanalytic movement, was not a prolific writer. However, all her books are very readable.

Munroe, R., *Schools of Psychoanalytic Thought*. New York: Henry Holt and Co., 1955. The social analysts, along with Freud, Jung, and Adler, are given very comprehensive treatment.

## Erikson

Erikson, Erik, *Childhood and Society*, 2nd ed. New York: W. W. Norton, 1963. This early book presents most of his theoretical concepts. It also describes Erikson's studies with the Sioux and Yurok Indians. Very comprehensive and readable.

Erikson, Erik, *Gandhi's Truth*. New York: W. W. Norton, 1969. His prize-winning psychohistory of one of the most famous men of the twentieth century.

Erikson, Erik, *Identity, Youth and Crisis*. New York: W. W. Norton, 1968. An expansion of his earlier ideas, in particular the identity crisis. This work is written in a more formal and academic manner.

# CHAPTER

# 19

# *Humanistic Psychology*

In 1954 Abraham Maslow[1] conceived the idea of a humanistic psychology. He felt that other current approaches to psychology were neglecting the "healthy human being's functioning," "modes of living" and "goals in life." Thus, he suggested humanistic psychology as a *third force,* the other two being *psychoanalysis* and *behaviorism.* Since the 1950s, opponents of these latter two movements have begun to make themselves heard. Those sympathetic to a humanistic movement have felt that behaviorism, particularly as represented by B. F. Skinner, is too cold, too narrow and lacking in any real understanding of the human being. The behaviorist has reduced the human being "to a large white rat or a slower computer."[2] Thus, behaviorism does not face up to the highly subjective qualities and capacities of humans that distinguish them from laboratory animals such as rats, pigeons or monkeys.

Likewise, humanistic psychology has criticized psychoanalysis for studying only disturbed individuals. By using abnormal people as one's focus of study, Maslow[3] asks, how can the psychoanalysts learn about the positive side of humans? One of Maslow's quotes often stated on the issue is as follows:[4]

> The study of crippled, stunted, immature and unhealthy specimens can yield only a cripple psychology and cripple philosophy.

Some evidence for the growing movement of humanistic psychology is worth noting. In 1961, the *Journal of Humanistic Psychology* was founded. In 1962 the *American Association of Humanistic Psychology* was established. Then, in

---

[1]A. Maslow, *Toward a Psychology of Being* (Princeton, N.J.: D. Van Nostrand, 1962).
[2]J. Bugental, *Challenges of a Humanistic Psychology* (New York: McGraw-Hill Book Co., 1967), p. vii.
[3]A. Maslow, *Motivation and Personality* (New York: Harper and Row, 1954), p. 234.
[4]*Ibid.*

1971, a Division of Humanistic Psychology of the American Psychological Association was voted in.

## Antecedents

Although humanistic psychology began to gain momentum, particularly in the writings of Abraham Maslow and Carl Rogers, the ground had already been prepared.

### Early Humanism

The concept of humanism existed during the Renaissance and even before, in the form of concern for the lives of those who were less fortunate. This was an integral part of Christianity through the centuries. Humanism was not only a matter of altruism and charity, but it evolved as a matter of concern for human *individualism*.[5] This was a concern for the unique individual who had become enlightened. The humanities, as they are called today, relied on a knowledge and preservation of ancient Greek and Latin writings, of art and philosophy. They became a means whereby the privileged classes could work toward a noble and honorable end.

### William James

According to Rollo May[6] every book that James ever wrote gave evidence that he (James) was a human being. His writings reflected his concern for life's problems. In fact, every problem for James, sooner or later, became a question of how he could ameliorate the human condition. His whole theory of pragmatism reflected his passionate concern for human need.

Perhaps a more direct influence from James comes from his chapter on the *Self* in his *Principles of Psychology*,[7] published in 1890 (see pp. 108–109). Certainly, other *self* theorists of today have been influenced either directly or indirectly by James' ideas. He divided the self into a hierarchy beginning with (1) the material self, (2) the social self or selves, (3) the spiritual self, and finally, (4) the Pure Ego. This latter concept is the most relevant one for the self theorists of today. The material self consisted of one's body, friends and possessions; the social self related to one's interactions with other people; the spiritual self contained one's psychological functions and potentialities. The Pure-ego was a more difficult concept and gave James some difficulties in interpretation. It

[5] D. N. Robinson, *An Intellectual History of Psychology* (New York: Macmillan Publishing Co., 1976), p. 166.
[6] R. May, "William James' Humanism and the Problem of Will," in *William James: Unfinished Business* (Washington, D.C.: The American Psychological Association, 1969), pp. 74–75.
[7] W. James, *Principles of Psychology* (New York: Henry Holt, 1890), ch. X.

became the "I" or self as *knower* (see pp. 108–109) while the others were the self as "me" or the self as *known*. This became something that resided above the others, possibly a kind of knowing "soul."

## Other Self Theories

Since the concept of the self has become an integral part of many humanistic psychologies, particularly that of Carl Rogers, the leading humanist today (see below), a few other self theories bear mentioning.

George Herbert Mead, in his book *Mind, Self and Society,*[8] set forth the notion of self as an object of awareness rather than a series of processes or functions. At birth a person had no self. As self consciousness emerged one would become aware of other objects outside oneself. One would learn to think, and would have attitudes and feelings about oneself. Society also played an integral role in the development of the self. Like James, Mead believed that one could develop different selves as one encountered different social groups and agencies.

As rather immediate forerunners of a humanistic psychology, Snygg and Coombs[9] made reference to a phenomenal self somewhat like the Gestalt concept of the phenomenological field (see p. 240). This consisted of all of the experiences a person might be aware of at a given time. This kind of awareness determined how a person was going to act at a given moment.

## Existential Psychology

Existential psychology (to be discussed in the following chapter) as well as existential philosophy have exerted strong influences on the humanistic movement. Because of a number of similarities to be discussed later, some psychologists find the two movements hard to separate. The existential movement has also been referred to as the "third force" discussed at the beginning of this chapter.

---

# Some Basic Tenets of Humanistic Psychology

As mentioned earlier, humanistic psychology is a movement rather than a tightly knit system of a single person or group of people banded together. All humanistic psychologists do not think exactly alike, but they do have certain ties that bind them together.

Actually, the roots of humanistic psychology go back to the publication of Rogers' first book, *Counseling and Psychotherapy: Newer Concepts in Practice*

---

[8]G. H. Mead, *Mind, Self and Society* (Chicago: University of Chicago Press, 1934).
[9]D. Snygg and A. W. Coombs, *Individual Behavior* (New York: Harper and Row, 1949).

(1942),[10] in which he introduced the non-directive approach to therapy in which the therapist does not give advice but merely reflects the feelings expressed by the client. This work was followed by Rogers' *Client Centered Therapy: Its Current Practices, Interpretation and Theory* in 1951.[11]

In 1967 the *American Association for Humanistic Psychology* published a four-part statement on the themes of humanistic psychology. This statement was presented by Buhler and Allen in 1972:

1. Humanistic psychology focuses on centering attention on the experiencing individual. Thus, experiencing is the primary phenomenon. Other events, theoretical explanations, and behavior are secondary to the experience and the meaning of the individual.

2. The emphasis is on distinctive human qualities such as choice, creativity, evaluation, and self regard (realization) as opposed to considering people in reductionistic or mechanistic terms.

3. The emphasis is on meaningfulness in the selection of problems to study. Research procedures are opposed to a primary objectivity as the significant experience.

4. An ultimate concern with valuing human dignity and an interest in the development of the potential inherent in every person.[12]

Charlotte Buhler,[13] one of the leading humanistic psychologists today, has set down what she considers to be some of the basic concepts of humanistic psychology. According to Buhler, humanistic psychology stresses some of the following:

1. The person as a *whole* is the main subject of humanistic psychology. This, of course, is not new to psychological theorizing. Existential psychology also considers the person as a unity. However, the direction of the humanist is towards the emphasis of *understanding* rather than *explaining*. According to Maslow, each person must be approached as a unique individual. The same point is made by the existential psychologists. Furthermore, did not Adler foster what he called an *individual psychology?* (p. 326)

2. Humanistic psychology is concerned with the knowledge of a person's entire life history. This notion is typically applied in taking the history of a person in both psychiatry and clinical psychology. The student of abnormal

---

[10]C. R. Rogers, *Counseling and Psychotherapy: Newer Concepts in Practice* (Boston: Houghton Mifflin Co., 1942).

[11]C. R. Rogers, *Client Centered Therapy: Its Current Practices, Interpretation and Theory* (Boston: Houghton Mifflin Co., 1951).

[12]C. Buhler and M. Allen, *Introduction to Humanistic Psychology* (Monterey, Cal.: Brooks/Cole, 1972).

[13]C. Buhler, "Basic Theoretical Concepts in Humanistic Psychology," *American Psychologist,* Vol. 26 (1971), pp. 378–386.

psychology depends to a great extent on the "case history method" as a means of understanding a person's problems. Buhler, however, claims that so-called life cycle studies are still scarce.

3. Human existence and intention are also of great importance. Here, Buhler admits sharing the same idea with existential psychologists. Perhaps, humanistic psychology places more attention on *intention*. By this is meant a person's experiencing his or her own identity.

4. Life goals are of equal importance. Here, humanistic psychology is not concerned with purely biological satisfaction of needs or the fulfillment of Freudian instincts, but self-realization or self-actualization as the goal(s) of life. Such concepts were first introduced by Jung, and have become important aspects of Maslow's and Rogers' personality theories (see below). Fulfillment of the goal of self-realization is another term frequently used. Furthermore, various humanistic psychologists stress basic life conflicts. Buhler stresses the importance of the integrative process as a resolution. Jung had earlier stressed this concept in the transcendent function.

5. Man's creativity has a primary place in humanistic psychology. Creativity becomes a universal human function that leads to all forms of self-expression. It is also related to the general goal-seeking of a person. Adler had stressed the idea of a creative self, and Fromm had talked about creativity in terms of productivity.

6. Humanistic psychology is frequently applied to psychotherapy. The aim of therapy is self-understanding. Also, the therapeutic process should lead to a greater understanding of others.

It should be clear from this brief summary that nothing new or unique is presented in humanistic psychology. It has borrowed heavily from existential psychology and a variety of psychoanalytic theories mentioned in previous chapters. If it has served any function as a movement, that function has been to integrate or gather together several concepts already prevalent in various psychological theories. Like existential psychology, it has developed as a revolt against those psychologies that deal with bits and pieces of behavior and ignore the human being as a whole. One can hardly follow existential ideas without being a humanist. However, the reverse is not necessarily true. But, in both cases, the emphasis is on the unique human being.

## The Self (or Person-Centered) Theory of Carl Rogers

Of the humanistic psychologists who abound today in psychology, perhaps the most eminent is Carl Rogers. We have, therefore, singled out his theories for more detailed discussion because he is the major representative of the movement.

Out of a system of psychotherapy called *Client Centered,* Rogers has developed a theory which has been most commonly called a *self theory.* More recently, Rogers[14] has been called a *person-centered theorist.*

Carl Rogers (1902–1988) was born in Oak Park, Illinois on January 8, 1902. As he points out,[15] both hard work and a commitment to Protestant Christianity were equally stressed in his youth. Certainly, the latter is particularly implicit in his theory. He graduated from the University of Wisconsin in 1924, then attended Union Theological Seminary in New York City. Rogers transferred from the Seminary to Teacher's College, Columbia University where he received his Ph.D. in 1931. He has taught at Ohio State University, the Universities of Chicago and Wisconsin and has been a Fellow at the Western Behavioral Science Institute in California.

Like the theories of Freud, Jung, Adler, Horney and others mentioned in previous chapters, Rogers' theories have evolved out of his experiences as a psychotherapist. His method of therapy was first set forth in his books *Counseling and Psychotherapy* (1942)[16] and *Client Centered Therapy*[17] (1951). Rogers has conceived the therapeutic process as one in which the individual (designated as client rather than patient) interacts with the therapist in such a way that the former becomes increasingly aware of his or her own feelings and experiences. It is a non-directive approach in that the therapist never gives advice but merely reflects the feelings of the client as they are expressed. The relationship becomes warm and friendly, and the therapist may never make any critical or punishing statements.

Rogers' theory was first stated in *Client Centered Therapy,*[18] then in S. Koch, *Psychology: The Study of a Science,* volume III,[19] and in Rogers' *On Becoming a Person.*[20] The most recent statement is in a chapter by Holdstock and Rogers in R. Corsini's *Contemporary Theories of Personality.*[21]

## The Organism and the Self

Rogers' concept of the organism is interpreted a bit differently from the ordinary use of the term in psychology, which usually refers to a biological being who responds to certain stimuli in its environment. For Rogers, the notion of

---

[14]T. L. Holdstock and C. R. Rogers, "Person Centered Theory," in R. Corsini, ed., *Current Personality Theories* (Itasca, Ill.: F. E. Peacock Publishers, Inc., 1977).

[15]C. R. Rogers, "A Theory of Therapy, Personality and Interpersonal Relationships as Developed in the Client Centered Framework," in S. Koch, ed., *Psychology: the Study of a Science,* Vol. 3 (New York: McGraw-Hill Book Co., 1959).

[16]C. R. Rogers, *Counseling and Psychotherapy: Newer Concepts in Practice* (Boston: Houghton Mifflin Co., 1942).

[17]C. R. Rogers, *Client Centered Therapy: Its Current Practice, Implications and Theory* (Boston: Houghton Mifflin Co., 1951).

[18]*Ibid.*

[19]C. R. Rogers, (1959), *op. cit.*

[20]C. R. Rogers, *On Becoming a Person* (Boston: Houghton Mifflin Co., 1961).

[21]T. L. Holdstock and C. R. Rogers, *op. cit.*

an organism has reference to a totality of experiences going on in the whole individual at a particular time. These experiences constitute the phenomenal field. They are inner experiences and can never be really known by another person. This becomes one's subjective reality. Although these experiences are within, the sources may come from both inside and outside the person.

Out of this totality of experiences, the self emerges. Rogers defines the self or self-concept as follows:[22]

> the organized, consistent, conceptual gestalt composed of perceptions charac-
> teristic of the "I" or "me" and the perceptions of the relationships of the "I" or
> "me" to others and the various aspects of life together with the values attached
> to these perceptions.

What is the relationship between the organism and the self? The self emerges out of the organism. In a normal, well adjusted person, those experiences that constitute the self should be in line with the experiences of the organism. However, the concept of incongruence between the two is critical to the theory. If the two do not match, threat and anxiety will result. One behaves defensively. Another possibility for incongruence is between the organism (phenomenal field) and objective reality.

In the world of experience, not everything is conscious. In the unconscious aspects of experience, there is a tendency to value experiences as positive or negative. An infant values food in a positive way when it is hungry. Experiences such as pain and discomfort are valued in a negative way. In the *organismic valuing process* these unconscious valuing experiences constitute an addition to all of our conscious experiences. These values are the forerunners of self-actualization (see following section). Rogers trusts these experiences more than the experiences that result in conscious judgments. "It is fallible, I am sure, but I believe it to be less fallible than my own conscious mind."[23]

## Self-Actualization

Self-actualization is a concept that is shared by most humanistic psychologists. According to Rogers, each person has an inherent tendency to actualize his or her unique potential.[24] This involves the development of one's capacities in ways that serve to maintain and enhance the organism. Self-actualization is a growth force that is part of the human genetic makeup. Like Maslow, Rogers feels this goes beyond basic biological potentials. It involves psychological growth, a moving forward, and also becomes an important part of Rogers' system of psychotherapy. Among other things, the person who goes into therapy has been stunted in the self-actualizing process.

---

[22]C. R. Rogers, (1959), *op. cit.,* p. 200.
[23]*Ibid.,* p. 23.
[24]T. L. Holdstock and C. R. Rogers, *op. cit.,* p. 132.

In the process of human growth, self-actualization goes from simple to complex. Part of this growth involves creativity. First of all, the self has to be created. Then, the urges for further creativity in artistic forms, inventions, writing, innovative solutions in business, politics and social agencies follow. The more experiences a person has, the better the self can be actualized, allowing greater creativity.

Somewhat similar to the psychoanalytic systems, self-actualization is a dynamic force. One should never stop, but should keep moving forward. However, unlike Freud who took a very deterministic view of humans, Rogers feels that self-fulfillment is not merely the result of things that have happened in the past. Human beings are not robots as the behaviorists would have us believe. They have freedom to continue the self-actualizing process. There is always the possibility of an undetermined subjective choice.

Further, Rogers states, "Each person is born with an inherent bodily wisdom which enables differentiation between experiences that actualize and those that do not actualize potential."[25]

Related to the self-actualization process are the needs for *positive regard* and *positive self-regard.* These develop in childhood as the self-concept is formed and are strongly related to the affection and approval given by important people, such as parents, who are referred to as *significant others.* We need to be loved and touched.

Rogers makes a distinction between *conditioned* and *unconditioned regard.* In *unconditional positive regard,* the acceptance is total. This is partly hypothetical, because parents and significant others are more likely to respond to the child with *conditional positive regard.* Here the parents provide love, affection, and approval only if the child's self-concept is in keeping with what they desire. The child may run some risk of being rejected if his or her actions differ from what is expected by the significant others. Usually the need for positive regard is so great that the child chooses to follow the expectations of others. Thus, the child will introject (borrowed from Freud)—incorporate the standards of significant others into his or her own self-concept.

The final development in what Rogers calls the *fully functioning person* is to experience and have *unconditional positive self-regard*—an ideal condition of total self-acceptance. This is theoretically possible and results from receiving unconditioned positive regard. Because this is not likely to occur in reality, *conditioned positive self-regard* usually will result. Self-acceptance will occur if one takes on the introjected standards of the significant others.

When one introjects the standards of others, a *condition of worth* results, which is a basis for *conditional positive self-regard.* In unconditioned positive self-regard, the condition of worth would be absent, because such a standard would be restrictive; the self-concept would be congruent with the totality of experiences. Such an openness to experience would not be hindered by the "shoulds"

---

[25]*Ibid.*

and "oughts" imposed by society. More likely, a condition of worth will be present, because conditioned positive self-regard is the usual case.

## Variance Between Organism and Self

As a person grows older, there may develop a rift between what is actually experienced (the organism) and the self. This means that experiences are perceived which are at variance with the self-concept. Thus, certain experiences may be selectively distorted or denied. Those experiences that accord with the self-concept are symbolized accurately into one's awareness. When the rift between the organism and the self becomes too great, anxiety and threat result. One defense against this is *denial*. Thus, the self-concept becomes distorted. This in turn will influence a person's relations with other people and lead to further maladjustment. If this variance becomes too great, defensive systems such as denial will be inadequate. The self-concept may be overwhelmed and break down. The result is a disorganization of behavior. Under these conditions psychotherapy will be in order.

## The Fully Functioning Person

The fully functioning person is characterized by an absence of unfortunate defenses (denial, repression, etc.). This person, therefore, expresses an unconditional positive self-regard. His or her self concept remains congruent with the totality of experience. There is an absence of anxiety and no need for defenses, so experiences can enter awareness with accuracy. The valuing process is relatively free from the "shoulds" and "oughts" of others. Poor choices are quickly corrected. One accepts mistakes openly so that self-actualization tendencies can operate for one's particular innate potential. Creative people do not hide behind only that which is socially acceptable. They trust their inner experiences and live in accord with their inner values, thus enabling themselves to exhibit behavior that is unique and personally acceptable. They accept and like others and are able to form successful interpersonal relationships. They live in the present (rather than the past), responding freely to their experiences, and regard happiness as a changing entity. For them, life is a process, not a static situation.

## Evidence

In other chapters in this book we have cited, within the context of a system or theory, evidence which may serve to support or refute it. Since humanistic psychology (and Rogers' theory in particular) does not lend itself to laboratory research, objective experimentation is impossible. However, those who support Rogers' position point out that evidence is not lacking, and certain studies may directly or indirectly support the theory. Two lines of support may be singled out, the *Q-Sort* method and *Content Analysis* of therapeutic interviews.

## Q-Sort

The goal of the Q-Sort method is to discover the ideas people have about themselves. The basic procedure is to give a person a packet of cards each of which contains a different statement, and then have the person sort the cards on a continuum from the statement that best describes the person to the statement that least describes him or her. One can sort in terms of how one actually perceives one's self (self-sort) or how one would like to be (ideal-sort). One study by Butler and Haugh[26] will serve as an illustration. Their subjects were people in counseling matched with a control group. In the counseling group, the correlation between the self-sort and the ideal-sort was zero; but in the control group the correlation between the two sorts was .58, indicating some degree of relationship. Following counseling (average 31 sessions per client), this group was asked to sort again. The results indicated a correlation of .34, a significant improvement over zero.

## Content Analysis

This method involves forming categories of statements made by clients in therapy and analyzing changes in the kinds of statements made as therapy progresses. One study by Seeman[27] will illustrate the method. The analysis consisted of 16 interviews involving 10 clients at various stages of therapy. The verbal statements of these clients were classified into four categories: (1) expressions of problems or symptoms, (2) acceptance of therapists' responses, (3) understanding or insight and (4) discussion of plans for the future. Seeman found that as therapy progressed, there were fewer statements of troubles and problems. Signs of acceptance rose in the beginning and then declined. In later interviews, clients showed greater understanding of their difficulties and gave more statements expressing plans for the future. This study is considered, according to those sympathetic with Rogers' theory, as giving validity to his basic concept of growth.

## Therapy

Along with his theory, Rogers developed a method of nondirective or client-centered therapy.[28] To Rogers, part of the therapeutic process must involve therapeutic insight—the insight that enables a person to do something positive about his or her problems. Rogers believed that one has to understand the role one is playing in life and recognize repressed impulses within the self.

---

[26]I. M. Butler and G. V. Haugh, "Change in the Relationship of the Self-Concept and Ideal Concepts Consequent upon Client Centered Counseling," in C. R. Rogers and R. D. Dymond, *Psychotherapy and Personality Change* (Chicago: University of Chicago Press, 1954), pp. 51–76.

[27]J. Seeman, "A Study of the Process of Non-Directive Therapy," *Journal of Consulting Psychology*, Vol. 13 (1949), pp. 157–168.

[28]C. R. Rogers, *Counseling and Psychotherapy* (Boston: Houghton Mifflin, 1942).

Rogers cites the case of Cora, an adolescent girl who was brought to the psychological clinic and the children's court, because of ungovernable behavior at home. Her mother was an invalid so the stepfather had to assume responsibility for the care of Cora. As tensions in the home heightened, Cora was eventually placed in a foster home. Through the therapeutic process, Cora gained insight into her problems. First of all, she realized that her stepfather had sexual interests in her and that he had become jealous of her. Gradually, she began to realize that she had been encouraging his sexual interest, and she had adopted various ways to continue his role as the older "boyfriend." With this insight into her own behavior, she became capable of acquiring a more adult role and her highly aggressive behavior was no longer necessary as a substitute for her conflicts.

## The Humanistic Psychology of Abraham Maslow (1908–1970)

Maslow was born in Brooklyn, New York, and took all of his academic degrees at the University of Wisconsin. His academic career was spent primarily at Brooklyn College and Brandeis University. His best known books include *Motivation and Personality* (1970),[29] *Toward a Psychology of Being* (1968),[30] and *The Further Reaches of Human Nature* (1971).[31]

Maslow shares Rogers' positive and optimistic view of human nature. He believes people have an inherent capacity for kindness, love, and generosity. However, these have to be nurtured by the environment and society. In the wrong society or culture, these tendencies could be drowned and squelched. A pathological environment would inhibit these positive growth potentials and could lead to excessive aggression and self-defeat.

### Theory of Motivation

Maslow is probably best known for his theory of needs. He uses the term *instinctoid* to refer to these motives because they are all seeded in basic human nature but must be properly cultivated by the environment. He distinguishes between *deficiency needs and growth needs.* The deficiency needs (deficit or D motives) refer to lacks that must be fulfilled through appropriate external objects or people. The growth needs (being motives or B motives) are more independent of the environment and refer to the need to fulfill certain inherent capacities and potentialities:

---

[29] A. H. Maslow, *Motivation and Personality,* 2nd. ed. (New York: Harper and Bros., 1970).
[30] A. H. Maslow, *Toward a Psychology of Being,* 2nd. ed. (New York: Van Nostrand, 1968).
[31] A. H. Maslow, *The Further Reaches of Human Nature* (New York: Viking Press, 1971).

> Growth is, *in itself,* a rewarding and exciting process . . . the fulfilling of yearn-
> ings and ambitions . . . the acquisition of admired skills . . . the steady in-
> crease of understanding about people: the development of certain creativeness
> in whatever field, or most important, simply the ambition to be a good human
> being.[32]

Deficiency needs operate for self-preservation, whereas growth needs refer to a
healthier and a higher level of functioning.

Maslow describes this theory in terms of a hierarchy (see Fig. 21). At the
bottom of the hierarchy are the *physiological needs,* which include hunger, thirst,
sex, air to breathe, sleep, and elimination of body wastes. In Maslow's example,
a starving person would care little for the higher virtues of creativity or self-
fulfillment. The principal desire would be to obtain food.

Next on the hierarchy are the *safety* needs. In our reasonably prosperous
society the physiological needs are readily satisfied. On those occasions when
they are not fulfilled by the person, society will usually intervene to help, as
in the case of welfare. The safety needs include finding an environment that is
organized and stable and free from stress and anxiety. A growing child seeks
reassurance from its parents when threatened by a hostile animal or exposed to
loud noises or bright lights. As adults we buy insurance as protection against
accidents, illness, destruction of property, or liability. Also included in the
safety needs is the desire for privacy as a protection against the intrusion of
unwanted visitors. "In a choice between giving up safety or giving up growth,
safety will ordinarily win out."[33]

As the physiological and safety needs become more or less satisfied, the
belonging and love needs become preeminent. These also belong to the class of
deficiency needs. We yearn for love and affection from our families, to have
friends, and to belong to groups, in order to avoid loneliness. At this level of
the hierarchy, there is also the need for a partner—a wife or husband—and to
have children. The fulfillment of these needs is necessary before the growth
needs can be considered.

At the next level of the hierarchy, the *esteem* needs come into operation;
these correspond to Alfred Adler's striving for superiority and Erik Erikson's
need for mastery. This group also includes the need for respect and self-
confidence. These needs come into operation only when the needs in the lower
hierarchies are at least partially fulfilled. They can be satisfied through significant achievements in various endeavors of life, such as in being superior in a
sport, making money, creating a piece of art, being an expert at cards, winning
a case in court, or competence in one's vocation.

After esteem needs, Maslow places the cognitive needs: the needs to know,
to understand, to be curious, and to explore.

Next come the aesthetic needs (not necessarily universal): the needs for
symmetry, order, and beauty (aesthetically pleasing experiences).

---

[32]A. H. Maslow (1968), op. cit., p. 29.
[33]*Ibid.,* p. 49.

**FIGURE 21**   *Abraham Maslow's Hierarchy of Needs.*

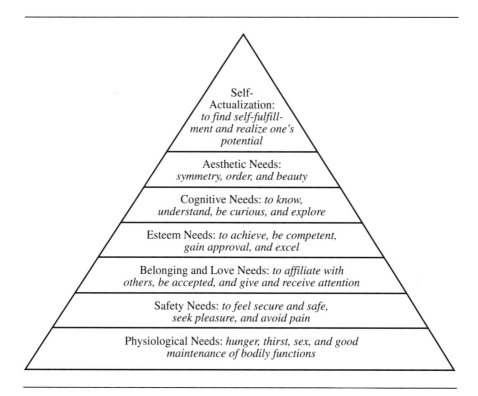

At the top of the hierarchy is the need for *self-actualization*. Maslow, like Rogers, stresses the significance of this need as an ultimate striving. This is a fulfillment of one's inner potential. "What a man *can* be, he must be."[34] The way self-actualization is achieved is very much an individual matter. For a musician, it could be making music; for an architect, the designing of an important building; for an industrialist, running a successful operation. Like Rogers, Maslow considers this a growth need, but unlike Rogers, he feels that it cannot be fulfilled until those on the lower levels on the hierarchy are fulfilled. As human beings, we share with the lower animals the more basic needs (physiological, safety) but the higher needs (esteem, self-actualization) are strictly human.

Maslow allows that only a small percentage (perhaps 10 percent) of people really become self-actualized, or "fully human." In order to study the process better, Maslow has selected a small group of people, both living and dead,

---

[34]A. H. Maslow (1970), op. cit., p. 176.

whom he considers to be truly self-actualized, in order to discover what particular characteristics they have in common.[35] His list includes Thomas Jefferson, Abraham Lincoln, Albert Einstein, Eleanor Roosevelt, William James, and Albert Schweitzer. Their characteristics include some of the following:

1. They have a greater-than-average perception of reality. They are free from prejudice and other factors that distort reality, and their judgments of people and events are more accurate.

2. They have a greater knowledge of themselves. They fully understand their own motives, emotions, capacities, and shortcomings.

3. They have a greater concern for external problems. Frequently, they have a particular mission to accomplish. They are very much concerned with ethical and philosophical issues.

4. They have a greater need for privacy and autonomy. They maintain a healthy detachment, so they are less dependent on other people in their environment. They rely on their own feelings and values and have less of a tendency than other people to seek personal rewards and physical possessions.

5. They have more frequent peak experiences. The peak experience is difficult to define, but it can be described as a feeling of complete perfection or ecstasy. It can be experienced in love, appreciation of a great work of art, profound insight, scientific discovery, or creativity.

6. They have greater social interest and concern for positive human relations. They have a genuine concern for helping others. However, their concern is detached rather than possessive.

Other characteristics of these self-actualized individuals include a careful distinction between good and evil, a democratic attitude toward all classes of people (racial or ethnic groups), a sense of humor that is genuine and not based on feelings of superiority or jokes that degrade other people, and finally, greater creativity. This creativity is not limited to "artistic" endeavors; it can also apply to a cook who makes gastronomical delights, a medical practitioner who develops new techniques, or the industrialist who develops new marketing procedures. Their new ways of doing things can benefit other people.

Maslow makes clear that self-actualization is not an all-or-nothing process but rather is a matter of degree. "There are no perfect human beings."[36] Even a self-actualized person is subject to human frailty in biases, inconsistencies, emotional outrage, or foolishness, but he or she more frequently engages in the kinds of attitudes and behavior described above, which typify the self-actualized individual.

---

[35]*Ibid.*
[36]*Ibid.*

## The Future of Humanistic Psychology

The behaviorists might hope that humanistic psychology would crawl into the nearest corner and die; but this does not appear to be the case for the near future. On pages 361–362, evidence was presented which indicates that the humanistic movement is growing. In the following quotation from Rogers in an article in the *American Psychologist,* he presents a rather optimistic view.[37]

> In all candor, I must say that I believe that the humanistic view will in the long run take precedence. I believe that we are, as a people, beginning to refuse to allow technology to dominate our lives. Our culture, increasingly based on the conquest of nature and the control of man, is on the decline. Emerging through the ruins is a new person, highly aware, self-directing, an explorer of inner, perhaps more than outer space, scornful of the conformity of institutions and the dogma of authority.

## *Evaluation*

### Criticisms of Humanistic Psychology

1. The behaviorists have been the severest critics of humanistic psychology. A phenomenal view, they feel, is purely subjective and dualistic. Thus, the theories lack any empirical validity. Scientific method is abandoned in favor of introspection. On several occasions Rogers and Skinner engaged in public dialogues or debates. The general conclusion reached was that the two men were at opposite poles and would never agree.

2. Introspective self-reports are notoriously unreliable. It is no more than an assumption to consider that what one says is really what one feels. Probing into a hypothetical innerself is nothing more than dealing in fictions.

3. Humanistic psychology has been considered, by some, to be a kind of religion. These concepts must simply be taken on faith so that any kind of notion that psychology should be considered a branch of natural science is abandoned. The humanistic approach has regressed psychology back to the Middle Ages and the Church Fathers. It is undoing all the efforts of the more objective and experimentally minded psychologists to help achieve the goal of psychology as an objective study of behavior.

[37]C. R. Rogers, "In Retrospect: Forty-six Years," *American Psychologist,* Vol. 29 (1974), pp. 115–123.

## Contributions of Humanistic Psychology

**1.** Humanistic psychologists believe that the humanistic movement has brought psychology back to the study of people as human beings. The person to be studied is one who experiences, feels, knows and loves. The stress is on the person as a vital, living being and not merely as a mechanical creature to be manipulated and controlled by external events.

**2.** Humanistic psychology is a positive and optimistic theory. It puts forward the notion that human beings are basically good, and that they have tremendous possibilities for self-fulfillment. The goal of self-actualization lends great promise for the future of humankind. It implies that we are all capable of achieving the ends that our Creator intended. We are the masters of our own fate and not merely the products of environmental control. Of course, those who oppose the entire concept of self-actualization believe that the concept lacks any empirical validity and will always remain merely a hypothetical construct.

**3.** One of the great contributions of humanistic psychology has been in the field of psychotherapy. In particular, Rogerian therapists believe, on the basis of empirical research including taped interviews, that the psychotherapist can provide a climate that is conducive to self-directed personal growth.

**4.** Rogers' approach emphasizes the democratic principles of the United States. We are advised to treat each other as equals. The emphasis on a person-centered psychology of self-direction is in keeping with the principles of democracy.

## Suggested Further Readings

Buhler, C., and Allen, M., *Introduction to Humanistic Psychology.* Monterey, Cal.: Brooks/Cole, 1972. A brief introduction to the general principles shared by many humanistic psychologists. It contains discussions of what such humanistic psychologists as Buhler, Maslow and Rogers have in common. The principles are also related to culture and psychotherapy.

De Carbalbo, J. R., *The Foundations of Humanistic Psychology.* Greenwood, S.C.: Praeger, 1991.

Holdstock, T., and Rogers, C. R., "Person Centered Theory," in Corsini, R., ed., *Contemporary Personality Theories,* Itasca, Ill.: F. E. Peacock Publishers, Inc., 1977. The most recent summary of Rogers' theory. Within the chapter, the theory is presented, assessed and applied with validating evidence.

Maslow, A. H., *Motivation and Personality,* 2nd ed. New York: Harper and Bros., 1970. Probably Maslow's best-known book. It describes in detail his unique theory of motivation, which has been widely quoted in many books in psychology.

Rogers, C. R., *Client-Centered Therapy*. Boston: Houghton Mifflin, 1951. An elaboration of the ideas and methods of psychotherapy presented earlier in Rogers' *Counseling and Psychotherapy* (1942). This is probably one of Rogers' most important books in which his theories of therapy and personality are described and related. Most of the book is devoted to his technique of therapy, but there are also references to his general theory as it was evolving at that time.

Rogers, C. R., *On Becoming a Person*. Boston: Houghton Mifflin, 1961. Rogers' theory is presented in a more informal manner than in some of his other works. The book is chatty with lots of examples.

# CHAPTER

# 20

# *Existential Psychology*

Like humanistic psychology, existential psychology is not an organized system. Rather, both psychologies can be considered as movements. In fact, they are very much interrelated, and both have been considered as a "third force" in psychology today. In this chapter we shall consider some of the basic characteristics of existential psychology and then draw some comparisons between it and humanistic psychology.

Existential psychology first developed in Europe and has gradually spread to America. Its background is heavily steeped in European existential philosophy. As a movement in psychology, it developed as a revolt against behaviorism in particular, which had stressed laboratory investigations using primarily subhuman species. According to the existential psychologists and those who were sympathetic to the movement, behaviorism and all that related to it had "dehumanized" the individual, leaving nothing more than a machine made up of chains of conditioned and unconditioned reflexes. Existentialism, then, is a revolt against those psychologies that have failed to consider our basic nature, which is *human*. Although existential psychology is expressed in the writings of individuals with rather diverse opinions, it would be unfair to conclude this book without at least giving the reader some flavor of what existential psychologists are talking about today. As a current movement, it seems to be gaining adherents, and for the moment, at least, it is part of the contemporary scene.

According to existential psychologists, psychology has tried too hard and has gone too far in its attempts to be scientific. They believe it is time for us to take a new and fresh look at the nature of human beings.

## Philosophical Background

The beginnings of existential philosophy go back to the nineteenth-century Danish philosopher Sören Kierkegaard. Later, as a European philosophical movement, existentialism gained momentum between World Wars I and II in the philosophies of Martin Heidegger and Karl Jaspers in Germany, and Gabriel Marcel, Jean-Paul Sartre, Maurice Merleau-Ponty, and others, in France.

Existential philosophy has as many facets as the ideas of its various proponents. As a philosophy, it is highly complex and technical with a varied and often difficult language. Even trained philosophers have found it hard to understand. The one concept that holds it together as a movement is that of *existence*. It directs its attention not to the *essence* of things, but to their existence and, in particular, to human existence. Regarding essence, the reader will recall John Locke's concern with the nature of objects in the real world and their qualities. Traditionally, philosophy has been concerned with essence, "that which makes things as they are." The existentialists, on the other hand, deny that essence is primary. Existence is the only concrete thing, the rest is mere abstraction.[1]

Before considering existential psychology, let us consider a few basic ideas of some of the more prominent existential philosophers. What we shall present is at best fragmentary and oversimplified, but it may give the reader some idea of the kind of issues that existential philosophers talk about.

## Sören Kierkegaard (1813–1855)

Kierkegaard was a religious philosopher who was an existentialist in that he saw human beings as having a continuing desire for eternity with God, while at the same time realizing that their own existence was only temporal. Humans were continually occupied with the trivialities of their own existence, but desired the infinite. A conflict, therefore, arose between their desire for eternity and their recognition of their own temporal and finite existence. As a result, there was anxiety, torment, and dread.

## Martin Heidegger (1889–1976)

For Heidegger, human existence was closely tied up with the world (being-in-the-world) and with other human matters. Of all animals, humans alone had consciousness of their own existence. Like Kierkegaard, Heidegger considered human beings in conflict. Humans existed in a temporal world of strange peoples and threats. Furthermore, they contemplated the thought of inescapable death, which resulted in the experience of anguish and dread. They tried to overcome this dread by acting in a conventional way. This Heidegger considered to be "unauthentic." Therefore, humans had to accept the fact that death

---

[1]H. Misiak and V. S. Sexton, *History of Psychology, An Overview* (New York: Grune and Stratton, 1966), p. 435.

was inevitable and nothingness followed. Then, they could be true to themselves and have an authentic existence.[2] Human existence was neither of their own making nor of their own choice. It was thrust upon them and would continue to be theirs until death.

## Jean-Paul Sartre (1905–1980)

It is probably through his plays and novels that Sartre has become one of the most well-known existential philosophers. The best explanation of his position is in his book *L'Être et le néant*[3] (*Being and Nothingness*). For Sartre, the central question is the meaning of human existence. His answer is that human beings and their existence in the world have no meaning. There is no reason why the world and people should exist at all. God cannot be the reason, since there is no God. For Sartre, consciousness is the main reality, and yet it is incomprehensible with regard to its origin and continuity.[4] In the typical existential vein, people do have freedom and choice. They are constantly plagued with making decisions. If they try to escape this freedom, they are left only with anxiety and despair.

Our discussion of these different existential philosophers is only meant to give the reader a feeling for their involvements. As a movement, we may say that existential philosophy is concerned with human beings and the unique problems of human existence. The concern is with humans in an existing world including other humans We share common conflicts, dreads, and anxieties. We are aware of our own existence and what will happen when we reach nonexistence. As such, existential philosophy is not materialistic, or pragmatic, or rationalistic. It focuses on the human side of human beings on the personal subjective experience.

## Definition of Existential Psychology

Existential psychology presents a new approach and attitude toward psychology. As already indicated, it has arisen out of existential philosophy. Its aim is to understand human beings in their total existential reality, especially in their subjective relationships to themselves, to their fellow humans, and to the world. It employs all methods of understanding, but considers the phenomenological approach to be the one most appropriate for the study of human existence.

---

[2]*Ibid.*, p. 437.
[3]Jean-Paul Sartre, *L'Être et le néant* (Paris: Éditions Gallimard, 1943).
[4]*Ibid.*

## Some Basic Tenets
## of Existential Psychology

In dealing with existential psychology, it is hard to know where the philosophical aspects begin and end. They are all very much intertwined, for this can truly be called a philosophical psychology.

Existential psychology began in Europe, and has gradually gained more popularity in America. As American psychology has become more behavioristic and ruggedly experimental, those who have opposed such a point of view have suggested that we take a "new look" at the nature of human beings. They believe that psychology today has failed to contribute to the understanding of human beings in the totality of their human nature.

Existential psychology is no clear-cut system. It has gained adherents who have a wide range of diverse views. As a movement, it is continually evolving. Before considering some of the statements of specific individuals, we shall try to set down some of the basic ideas that existential psychologists share.[5]

**1.** Existential psychology deals with human beings as individuals—ones who exist as beings-in-the-world.

**2.** Each of us has a unique inner life with various perceptions and different evaluations of the world outside. Not only is our inner life unique, but we as existing organisms are unique from all other species. We cannot be placed on the top of the phyletic scale of the animal kingdom. We are special creatures with endowments unlike those of other animals.

**3.** The aim of existential psychology is the understanding of human beings in their total existential reality. It deals with the problems peculiar to each individual person rather than with delving into gross generalizations which are shared by all people.

**4.** Existential psychology is concerned with human consciousness, feelings, moods, and personal experiences as they relate to our existence in the world of other people. However, it has an ultimate aim of understanding human nature in its entirety.

**5.** There are certain persistent themes, borrowed from existential philosophy, which seem to concern many of the existential thinkers. These include: human person-to-person relationships, human values, the meaning of life, suffering, anxiety, and death.

**6.** From the above, it should be obvious that the deepest concerns of the existentialists in psychology are in the areas of personality, psychotherapy, and counseling.

---

[5]H. Misiak and V. S. Sexton, *op. cit.,* pp. 442–43.

**7.** Human beings have the freedom to choose. As such, they are responsible for their own existence. They need not be under the control of their environment, but they alone decide what they will or will not do. Thus, any kind of external determinism is completely rejected.

## Methodology

Like humanistic psychology, existential psychology is not experimental. Its method of analysis is phenomenological. This involves describing experiences, the nature of consciousness and subjective reality. The phenomenological method should describe all that is experienced, imagined or felt. One must grasp the essence of what appears in consciousness.

The phenomenological technique distinguishes three aspects: (1) *intuiting,* (2) *analyzing* and (3) *describing.* In *intuiting* one must concentrate intensely on the phenomenon of one's consciousness. *Analyzing* involves a focusing on various aspects of consciousness and their relationship to each other. *Describing* involves giving an account in a language that can be understood by others. The usual procedure is for the investigator to make an analysis of a subject's verbal reports.

Existential psychology is opposed to the more traditional experimentation in psychology where controls are specified and independent variables are manipulated by the experimenter. For the existentialists, this is a kind of push and pull technique in which the organism experimented upon is treated like a robot.

A proper understanding of human beings is to be found in the phenomenological analysis described above. Since humans are free to choose their own existence, the notions of prediction and control used in traditional experimental psychology are impossible.

## Ludwig Binswanger (1881–1966)

Binswanger was one of the most important exponents of existential psychology. Although he was European (Swiss), his writings are equally well known in this country. Like Freud, he was trained in medicine and, like other existential psychologists, he applied existential ideas to psychotherapy. The interested reader may refer to his three chapters which appear in Rollo May's edited book *Existence,*[6] and to his own work, *Being-in-the-World, Selected Papers by Ludwig Binswanger.*[7]

Typical of existential psychologists, Binswanger rejected positivism, determinism, and materialism. By rejecting determinism or what some might call cause-effect relationships, Binswanger felt that humans were the products of

---

[6]Rollo May, ed., *Existence: A New Dimension in Psychology, and Psychiatry* (New York: Basic Books, Inc., 1958).

[7]L. Binswanger, *Being-in-the-World, Selected Papers by Ludwig Binswanger* (New York: Basic Books, 1963).

neither heredity (genetic factors) nor environmental influences (particularly early ones). Therefore, they were left with a complete freedom of choice, in other words "free will." Consequently, they were completely responsible for their own existence. Humans alone could decide what they would or would not do. This does not mean that given freedom of choice, they would necessarily act to their own best ends. If this were so, then there would be no misery, dread, or neurotic ailments. It was a matter of whether or not they could live an authentic or unauthentic life.

Being-in-the-world (*Daesin*) is the most fundamental concept of all existential psychology. *Daesin* is literally translated "to be there." As human beings, we have no existence apart from the world, and the world does not exist apart from people. There is no gap separating human beings and objects in the world. Thus, a oneness exists between people and the world of things.

Being-in-the-world was the whole of human existence. Human beings did not live apart from the world or exist in a world apart from them. It was possible for them to go beyond the world, often in a transcendent way. In particular, this meant that they could realize the full possibilities of their being. When humans let others dominate them or yielded to environmental influences, their existence became unauthentic.

Humans also developed *world designs,* which were their own modes of being-in-the-world. Binswanger gave us many examples of patients of his who had inadequate world designs. A businessman who became inactive and dull had developed a world design based on pressure, aggression, and fear. His design resulted from pushing and from being pushed.

There were many modes of being-in-the-world. A *singular* mode was one in which a person lived only to himself or herself (perhaps a kind of "loner"). There was also a *dual* mode which was achieved by two people in love: "you" and "I" became "we." This was considered a very authentic way of being human. A *plural* mode involved being in a world of people interacting. This included competition, struggle and strife. A mode of *anonymity* referred to a person who got lost in a crowd.

Being-in-the-world also consisted of a threefold reality. First of all there was the *physical,* consisting of one's surroundings. Secondly, there was the *human environment;* and finally, there was the *person.* But there was more than just being. Humans also desired to go beyond-the-world. Binswanger did not mean another world like the hereafter, but rather that humans thought in terms of the future possibilities of their being. Thus, Binswanger spoke in the words of the earlier existential philosophers of the authentic and unauthentic existence. The authentic existence involved the actualizing of future possibilities. The unauthentic existence involved a restriction of one's possibilities or a domination by one's environment. As always, humans had the freedom to choose which kind of existence they desired.

Although Binswanger rejected hereditary and environmental explanations for a person's particular existence, he did allow that an infant's mode of existence was going to be different from a child's or an adult's. The concept of *becoming* was what was important to human development. This meant becoming something more than what one was at the moment. Existence changed, so there was always the possibility of becoming something new or better. A person who refused to *become* remained static (fixated?). People who developed neurotic or psychotic ailments had refused to grow or *become*. This process of becoming, or growth, was shared by a number of existential psychologists (see below).

### Medard Boss (1903–    )

Like his colleague, Ludwig Binswanger, Boss was born in Switzerland and received a degree in medicine. He has taken a strong existential position regarding both psychology and psychotherapy. Some of his important books have been translated into English. These include *Psychoanalysis* and *Daesinanalysis* (1963)[8] and *Existential Foundations of Medicine and Psychology* (1977).[9] Much of what has been said of Binswanger also applies to Boss's psychology. Boss does not speak of modes of existence, of being-in-the-world, but rather describes several characteristics inherent in every human existence, which he calls *essentials*.

1. **Spatiality.** Spatiality refers to openness or closeness to other people and should not be confused with physical space. A person could be psychologically much closer to a friend 3000 miles away than to a neighbor next door.

2. **Temporality.** This, again, is not time as measured by a clock or reported on a calendar but rather having time or not having time to do something. One could say, "I have only a minute" or "I have all the time in the world."

3. **Bodyhood.** This is not limited to the physical human body but also extends to our relations with the world. A person could point a finger at another person, and this pointing could go way beyond the object to extend to all human relations.

4. **Sharing.** Human existence involves sharing the world with other people.

5. **Mood (or attunement).** The ways in which we perceive the world depend on our moods at that moment. A happy person is attuned to friends. Despair, on the other hand, changes a bright outlook into one of darkness.

Like most existential psychologists, Boss rejects causality in favor of freedom. A human being is free to choose an authentic or an inauthentic life. To choose properly, one must be aware of one's own potentialities. If this is so, we may ask, why is there so much anguish and despair in the world? Is it true that one can transcend an immediate miserable existence, as Viktor Frankl did in describing his existence in a concentration camp during World War II? The answer is that we can never transcend our own guilt, because guilt is a funda-

---

[8]M. Boss, *Psychoanalysis and Daseinanalysis* (New York: Basic Books, 1963).
[9]M. Boss, *Existential Foundations of Medicine and Psychology* (New York: Aronson, 1977).

mental aspect of being-in-the-world. Furthermore, no human person can avoid dread, because anxiety is a part of life.

True to the existential tradition, Boss stresses *becoming*. Existence is constantly a process of becoming something new. When we can fulfill our potentialities, we have fulfilled the possibilities of being-in-the-world. Because we have freedom, we are capable of changing and growing. Some people stagnate and refuse to grow, but they can change the direction of their lives toward greater fulfillment of their potentialities.

Because humans are existential beings, they are also concerned with their own mortality. Death is inevitable, and a realization of the termination of existence has been a concern for both existential psychologists and philosophers.

***Daesinanalysis of Dreams.*** For Boss, a dream is another mode of being-in-the-world. First of all, dreams may duplicate the same modes of existence of waking life. In other instances, the dream may give rise to a new understanding of the *Daesin* of waking life. These can be aspects of one's being that one is not aware of in waking life. Boss rejects the symbolic analysis of dreams used by many of the psychoanalysts, such as Freud and Jung. He believes that a dream may have more than one meaning. This can be understood by questioning the dreamer. Dreams, however, are not disguises but give other expressions of modes of being. A person undergoing psychotherapy should move from an inauthentic existence to a more authentic one. This change can be discovered by the therapist as the therapeutic process proceeds. In his analysis of 823 dreams of a person in therapy, Boss noted that changes in the content of the dreams paralleled improvements in the patient's waking existence.

## Rollo May (1909–1994)

The existential psychology movement began in Europe, and many of its important representatives live there (Van Kaam, Binswanger, and Boss). May, the chief exponent of existential psychology in the United States, was born in Ada, Ohio, and received his Ph.D. from Columbia. Like his European colleagues, he engaged in the practice of psychotherapy. His important books included an edited book, *Existential Psychology* (1969),[10] *Love and Will* (1969),[11] and *Man's Search for Himself* (1953).[12]

Like other existential psychologists, he stressed the human need for being-in-the-world (*Daesin*). Because human beings are inseparable from their environment, a simultaneous relationship exists, involving three modes: (1) the physical and physiological, (2) the social environment of other people, and (3) human beings' relationship to their inner nature. The fulfillment of being-in-

[10]Rollo May, ed., *Existential Psychology,* 2nd ed. (New York: Random House, 1969).
[11]Rollo May, *Love and Will* (New York: W. W. Norton, 1969).
[12]Rollo May, *Man's Search for Himself* (New York: W. W. Norton, 1953).

the-world requires effort and an unflagging responsibility to choose one's own freedom and be accountable for one's acts.

Human beings realize the prospect of nonbeing, which evokes anxiety. Further, their inability to fulfill all of their potentialities results in guilt. Both of these emotions are normal for most people and lead to trouble only when they get out of control. Despite his emphasis on anxiety and guilt, May was more optimistic about people than some other existential psychologists. On the more positive side, May placed great emphasis on the human capacity to *will*. This involves an active desire to choose the best of all possibilities, and to plan for the future and actualize one's potentials. *Love* is also an essential part of human nature. It has four components: *sex, eros* (striving to unite oneself with significant others), *philia* (a concern for the welfare of others) and *agapé* (love for all humanity, involving the three modes of being).

For May, the importance of existential psychology was that it established the principles that enable us to define the characteristics that distinguish people from animals—that is, to define the essence of what it means to be a human being.

## Viktor Frankl and the Search for Meaning

Viktor Frankl, a former student of Freud and a member of the Jewish faith, spent the years 1942–1945 in Nazi concentration camps, including Auschwitz, along with the rest of his family. All except Frankl were subsequently killed.

Amid the horrors of the camps, Frankl observed that prisoners who were able to survive found some meaning in their suffering. That meaning was in their spiritual lives.

Besides the physical and psychological sides of their lives, there was a third dimension, the *spiritual side*. This spiritual dimension gave both men and women the foundation for their freedom and responsibility and dignity, which in turn gave meaning to their troubled existence and allowed them to confront and deal with their suffering.

In Frankl's view, this meaning was a moral duty. Without the spiritual life, attained through the discovery of meaning, we are unable to accept responsibility and rise above whatever obstacles confront us:

> Ultimately man should not ask what the meaning of life is, but rather he must recognize that it is *he* who is asked. In a word, each man is questioned by life, and he can only respond by being responsible. [13]

## The Existential Neurosis

Binswanger, Boss, and May are all concerned with psychotherapy, the treatment of human psychological ills. As a result of existential theorizing, some psychologists believe they can identify a new kind of neurotic disorder called the

---

[13]V. Frankl, *Man's Search for Meaning* (Boston: Beacon Press, 1962), p. 101.

existential neurosis. So far, this has not been included in the classification system of the American Psychiatric Association (DSMIII—R). It was first described by Maddi in 1967.[14] According to Maddi, the neurosis is characterized by depersonalization (a loss of self-identity) and apathy. On the cognitive side, a person expresses a chronic inability to believe in the truth of anything. He lacks interest in the things he is supposed to be doing. On the affective side, the individual is bored with life. This boredom is accompanied by occasional feelings of mild depression. However, the depression becomes less evident as the disorder continues. In general, the existential neurotic no longer finds any meaning in life. The neurosis results from increased stress in living at a time of social change in an industrialized and mechanized world where people have lost their individuality.

# Existential and Humanistic Psychology: Similarities and Differences

Although we have dealt separately with these two movements in psychology, they are so interrelated that some authors simply use the term *existential/ humanistic psychology*. First of all, what do they have in common?

## Similarities

1. As opposed to the objective psychology of behaviorism, both existential and humanistic psychology are subjective. They speak of human inner being, experiences, images, and feelings.

2. Their methodologies are phenomenal in their analyses of these inner experiences.

3. They both stress human uniqueness and individuality. Each person is different and has the right to approach the world in his or her own way.

4. Far from being deterministic like behaviorism and psychoanalysis, they believe in a free will and in the freedom of each person to choose his own life style. This kind of freedom is strictly human, and so the human being is not just another animal under the control of inherited traits and the external environment. This freedom brings with it a responsibility to order one's own life in a creative way.

5. Since both are concerned with psychotherapy, they are also concerned with abnormal behavior. Personality disturbances arise out of a variance in the

---

[14]S. Maddi, "The Existential Neurosis," *Journal of Abnormal Psychology*, Vol. 72 (1967), pp. 311–325.

perception of many things. Such distortions in perception disrupt human psychological growth.

## Differences

1. The humanistic psychologists place greater stress on human needs—particularly on the striving for self-actualization. The existential psychologists, true to their philosophical background, think more in terms of being-in-the-world, a strictly human condition.

2. Humanistic psychology stresses the potential for good in all of us. This position is very optimistic with regard to our basic nature, our future, and our potentialities. Existential psychology tends to be more pessimistic. There is greater stress placed on fear, anguish, and sorrow, which are a natural part of human existence. Hope does not necessarily spring eternal. Here existential psychology shares some ground with Freud who was generally pessimistic about humanity. Although both stress freedom, existential psychology, particularly as expressed in Frankl's book *Man's Search for Meaning,*[15] indicates that freedom may often lead to suffering as well as joy.

3. Existential psychology places more stress on present existence, or being-in-the-world. The modes of existence are well described in Binswanger's modes of being (see pp. 382–384).

4. Another difference between the two movements lies in the interpretation of motivation. Humanistic psychology has stressed the process of *self-actualization* or self-fulfillment (see pp. 367–369). Existential psychology has tended to stress the pursuit of *spiritual meaning* in our lives. This pursuit is well described by Frankl.[16] Without denying biological needs, Frankl has stressed the spirit that gives us our freedom, responsibility, and dignity, making us responsible for our own lives. It is the mission of human beings to find some reason for their troubled, finite, and complicated existence.

---

## *Evaluation*

### Criticisms of Existential Psychology

Criticisms that can be levied against humanistic psychology (see chapter 19) can apply equally well, for the most part, to existential psychology.

---

[15]V. E. Frankl, *Man's Search for Meaning* (Boston: Beacon Press, 1962).
[16]*Ibid.*

1. As with humanistic psychology, the strongest reactions against existential psychology have come from the behaviorists and the experimental psychologists. They point out that its subjectivism, dualism, and lack of objective referents for its terms amount to a complete reversion to medieval psychology; and that its introspection is similar to that of St. Augustine. Existentialists talk about exploring the human inner life and finding the "nature of mankind," but give us no specific guidelines about how to do so. With existentialism, psychology has gone the full cycle—from the complete subjectivism of the Middle Ages, through objective experimental psychology, and back to subjectivism. In the late 19th century Wundt proposed a subjective introspective approach; but one must look at Wundt in the light of the psychology of his time. He intended to be experimental and to develop a science of psychology by breaking the bonds with philosophy. Existential psychology has intentionally brought us right back into the arms of philosophical speculations. The lack of an objective methodology and of principles that can be operationally defined can hardly be considered as any advancement in achieving psychological knowledge. It is rather a return to philosophical and theological conjectures.

2. Existential psychology may also be criticized for its vague suppositions and obscure language. Any referents to real events in a world of space and time are sparse. One is left with a vague terminology, which is little more than mere verbiage. If this discussion of existential psychology has seemed obscure to the reader, it is because existential psychology has failed to formulate any specific principles which are other than vague. Its attempts to describe "inner states" or the "nature" of mankind are completely nebulous. It is no wonder that objectively minded psychologists are distressed with the fact that many respectable psychologists, such as those mentioned in this chapter, are willing to take the movement seriously.

## Contributions of Existential Psychology

1. Existential psychologists feel that the concepts of their discipline offer a new challenge for the enrichment of psychology. For too long psychologists have been concerned with minute analysis of separate events and have neglected the basic aspects of the whole human being and human nature. Existential psychology is concerned with the human animal and how it relates to those around it. So much laboratory research goes on year after year without ever relating to the real problems of life. A person may spend a whole career studying schedules of reinforcement which, after it is all over, can be printed in countless journal articles to be filed away on library shelves never to be looked at again.

2. According to Salvatore Maddi, existential psychology has a bright future. It employs the interactions between the person and situational variables.

3. Existential psychology stresses cognitive processes, consciousness, and decision making. It emphasizes the dialectic between possibility and fact. It emphasizes decision making, planning, symbolism, imagination, and judgment. It stresses the subjective experience too long ignored by the experimental, objective psychologists.

4. Being-in-the-world offers a valid and new way of conceptualizing the human person.

5. The existentialist's emphasis on our repressed fear of death has opened up a new field of psychological thinking and experimentation. Courses on "death and dying" are now being offered by many college psychology departments.

In many ways this chapter is a logical successor to the previous ones on humanistic psychology and the social analysts Horney, Fromm and Sullivan. All were deeply concerned with the problems of real people. Fromm and Horney were very much interested in the human person and how that person related to society, while Sullivan stressed interpersonal relations.

As one of the newer movements in psychology, the fate of existential psychology remains to be seen. In conclusion, one might note that the first symposium on existential psychology took place at the annual convention of the American Psychological Association in 1959. The book *Existential Psychology,* cited earlier, reported the contributions of the members of that symposium and was printed in 1961.[17] Since that time other papers on existential psychology have been presented at various meetings of psychologists.

## Suggested Further Readings

Hall, C. S., and Lindzey, G., *Theories of Personality,* 3rd ed. New York: John Wiley and Sons, 1978. In their revision, these authors have devoted an entire chapter to existential psychology. Much of their discussion would be a good supplement to what is to be found in this chapter.

May, R., ed., *Existence: A New Dimension in Psychology and Psychiatry.* New York: Basic Books, 1958. A variety of papers by different theorists who favor an existential psychology.

Misiak, H., and Sexton, V. S., *History of Psychology: An Overview.* New York: Grune and Stratton, 1966. The last chapter is devoted to existentialism and psychology. Particularly good for the discussions of philosophic background.

van Kaam, A., *Existential Foundations of Psychology.* Pittsburgh, Pa.: Duquesne University Press, 1966. If one had to pick a basic book written by an existential psychologist, this is as good a place as any to begin.

---

[17]Rollo May, ed., *Existential Psychology* (New York: Random House, 1961).

# 21

# *Psychology Yesterday, Today, and Tomorrow*

We have examined the past and the present in the development of psychology; so the question arises, where are we going from here? We can make some fairly accurate guesses for the immediate future since we are aware of the current trends. But our guesses will have to be more speculative about the distant future.

The theory that history repeats itself would appear to be true when applied to psychology. Two cycles have emerged in the evolution of psychology from ancient Greece. Although they are not completely unrelated, let us consider them separately for the moment. The first cycle we could identify as objective-naturalistic, and the second cycle as subjective-dualistic.

## *Objective-Naturalistic Cycle*

On the objective side we observed how psychology started with a naturalistic explanation of psychological events, particularly in the writings of the ancient Greeks of the Hellenic period and more especially in the writings of Aristotle. Subsequently, we followed the body route through the natural sciences—biology and physics in particular. Then, in the second decade of the 20th century, we saw how John Watson took up the objective attitude again, and how, in the ensuing decades, psychology resumed the attitude of a natural science. Others followed Watson with different theories, but all of their efforts were directed toward making psychology the study of real, observable events, and nothing else. The behavioristic movement, despite its schisms, has continued to gain strength, primarily through the methodology of experimentation. The objective attitude is expressed through rigorous research even though many who engage in such activities might not identify themselves with a particular systematic viewpoint. Today, the rather rigid objectivists continue to move forward, and the future looks bright for the development of new principles of behavior, regardless of what species of animals these experimenters use as their subjects. There is no indication that this cycle will come to an end in the near future.

## Subjective-Dualistic Cycle

The second cycle, which we may regard as subjective, began with the early Christian writings, particularly those of St. Augustine. It continued through the Church Fathers and eventually followed through the lines of philosophy (the mind route). Although some empiricists, such as John Locke, felt they were dealing with a real world, what they were studying were inner experiences, and consequently their approach remained basically subjective. When Wundt broke with philosophy in the late 19th century to establish psychology as a separate discipline, he attempted to take a scientific approach, but again his method of introspection was completely subjective. Later structuralists and the Gestalt movement continued to maintain basically a subjective, dualistic tradition. Other schools followed, such as functionalism, later associationism, and hormic psychology, to name only a few. They tried to take a more objective attitude, but they never succeeded in breaking from the dualistic tradition. More recently, as a reaction against the growing strength of the behavioristic movement, the movements of existential and humanistic psychology have developed. These are growing in popularity, and their adherents are not reluctant to admit that they want to study the "inner person"—feelings, desires, and experiences. So, the "inner person" concept, so vital during the Middle Ages, has become revitalized. This cycle also gives no indication that it has completed its course. Schultz[1] has suggested, with a question mark, that the future of psychology may lie in the humanistic movement. Likewise, cognitive psychology is becoming increasingly popular with its analogies to neuroscience and the computer (see p. 22).

## Psychology Today

In a sense, viewing these two cycles in psychology brings us back to where we started. By this we mean that history has repeated itself. Much knowledge has accumulated in the meantime, and in understanding and identifying psycho-

---

[1]Duane Schultz, *A History of Modern Psychology,* 2nd ed. (New York: Academic Press, 1975).

logical events we are more knowledgeable than we were in ancient Greece or during the Middle Ages.

Today, psychology is as fragmented as it was during the early years of structuralism, Act psychology, functionalism, and behaviorism. The differences are that more people are involved in the field, and that there are more ideas and complex theories available.

As an example of the fragmentation and diversification of psychology, one need only look at a directory of the American Psychological Association. Founded in 1892 by a mere handful of psychologists, the organization has grown to include some 50,000 members working in areas ranging from physiological research to personality theory to counseling.

Over the years, the association has attempted to deal with this diversity by breaking into smaller groups devoted to various theoretical schools, methodologies, special interests, and applications. Some divisions reflect subject areas, such as general, social, and developmental psychology, as well as personality theory and physiological studies. Other groups focus on particular applications of psychology in industry, consumer research, and military organizations. Then too, other groups break into methodological camps, with experimental psychologists belonging to one division, and testing advocates and counseling professionals belonging to their own. Behaviorists, humanistic psychologists, and psychoanalysts can also claim separate groups, as can psychologists working in special interests such as religious studies and gay and lesbian concerns.

## Current Movements

***Psychoanalysis and Related Theories.*** Today, introductory texts do not devote as much space to orthodox Freudian psychology as they did twenty years ago. Freud's approach to psychology, however, is far from dead. The chapters on motivation, abnormal behavior, personality, and therapy have strong psychoanalytic implications. Also, the Neo-Freudians such as Alfred Adler, Carl Jung, Karen Horney, Harry Stack Sullivan, Erich Fromm, and Erik Erikson are represented in nearly all personality and abnormal psychology texts. Thus, the psychodynamic theorists still constitute an important force in psychology today.

***Humanistic and Existential Psychology.*** The humanistic and existential movements have reacted against the objectivism of behaviorism by proposing an analysis of the inner person, based on the method of phenomenology. Here we have a resurgence of a subjectivism that began in the early 1960s, as part of the reaction against the Vietnam War. Some students and psychologists disliked the mechanistic, behavioristic approach in favor of a person-centered psychology, with its emphasis on human values and freedom.

With the deaths of Abraham Maslow in 1970 and Carl Rogers in 1988, this author believes that the heyday of humanistic psychology came to an end. There was a time when some psychologists thought that humanistic psychology would become the dominant movement. They felt that behaviorism had no place to go, and that the exploration of the human inner self would take precedence. It seems that existentialism is also on the wane—at least in psychology.

**Behaviorism.** Many articles in theoretical psychology claim that behaviorism is alive and well. Certainly, behaviorists would like to think so. During its long career, this movement has spawned a methodology, established many principles, and made several contributions to other fields, such as psychopharmacology and behavior therapy. Furthermore, much experimental psychology is based on behavioral tenets. Even when the experimentalists do not follow every aspect of Skinner's behavioral framework, they are not always incompatible. The number of journals devoted to behaviorism's theory and methodology alone prove the movement is still a potent force. *Behaviorism, The Journal of the Experimental Analysis of Behavior,* and *The Journal of Applied Behavior Analysis* are notable examples. *The Psychological Record,* founded by J. R. Kantor, also frequently publishes behavioristic-oriented articles. Furthermore, the behaviorists have their own division of the American Psychological Association (Division 25) and their own society, The Association for Behavior Analysis, with its own journal, the *Behavior Analyst.* Recently, an entire issue of the *American Psychologist* was devoted to the work of B. F. Skinner.[2]

From the 1930s to the 1950s, many psychologists believed behaviorism would simply take over psychology. There are phenomena, however, that behaviorism has difficulty explaining, and so humanists and cognitive psychologists began to enter the picture.

**Cognitive Psychology.** During the past two decades a new cognitive psychology has emerged. Its studies on information processing have become a welcome addition to our understanding of how mental processes work. Using sophisticated computer techniques, cognitive psychologists have provided a greater understanding of thinking, problem-solving, and memory abilities, particularly in humans. Like the behaviorists, the cognitive psychologists are interested in using experimental methodology to find answers to their questions. But here the similarity ends.

With continued advances in computer science, cognitive psychology is entering many areas of the field, including social, developmental, and even therapy. The idea of "conscious mental processes" has returned to psychology along with the word "mind." Some call it a revolution; others merely see it as a revolt against behaviorism and psychoanalysis. But whether the behaviorists like it or not, cognitive psychology has taken hold. Skinner[3] noted that the use of the word "cognitive" had become fashionable. What also has happened is that psychologists who have been studying human memory, thinking, and perception for years are now beginning to call themselves "cognitive psychologists."

[2]*American Psychologist,* "Reflections on B. F. Skinner and Psychology," Vol. 47 (1992), No. 11.
[3]B. F. Skinner, *A matter of consequences* (New York: Alfred A. Knopf, 1983).

For one thing, the cognitive psychologists have dared to tackle areas of subtle behavior that the behaviorists have ignored, such as imaging, memorizing, judging, creating, and thinking.

***Physiological Psychology.*** Like the behaviorists, the physiological psychologists contend that psychology is a *science.* Such theorists as D. O. Hebb[4] and K. H. Pribram contend that psychology is a *biological science.* This includes social and clinical psychology because the human being is a *social animal.* The physiological psychologists are particularly concerned with how the brain works, although they would not ignore a study of biological processes involved in sensation and motivation. Their concern is with the mind and the brain, because, for them, the mind *is* the brain, and thought, as a primary psychological function, is the integrative activity of the brain. Furthermore, they contend that consciousness is produced by the brain.

"I don't know, in general, that the objective-biological-physiological is always clarifying, but I do know we have nowhere else to look for ideas about the mechanics of thought," asserts D. O. Hebb.[5] Furthermore, Hebb contends that if psychology is to be a science, it must be self-limiting in its procedures. To mix it up with other ways of knowing human behavior, as suggested by the poets and the artists, is a detriment to psychology's central concern—the mind (brain).

Space does not permit a review of recent findings in the physiology of the brain, but research in physiological psychology continues to be of great importance. In the following paragraphs, a few samples of applications of neuropsychology to the study of drugs (including alcohol), stress, abnormal psychology, and obesity are presented.[6]

Addiction has been basically defined as a physiological dependence on some substance, typically drugs or other chemical substances. When some drugs are taken with regularity and then suddenly withdrawn, symptoms of withdrawal distress may occur, indicating that the body's neurochemistry has changed to accommodate the drug. Painful symptoms (shaking, shivering, cramps, nausea, etc.) may follow. Many researchers are attempting to discover the mechanisms through which brain cells are altered by the exposure to an addicting substance, rendering people dependent on the drug.

According to current physiological psychology, severe behavioral disturbances such as schizophrenia or the manic-depressive disorder are, in fact, neurological disorders. However, no hard evidence as yet exists. Most environmentalists strongly oppose such ideas.

On the other hand, physiological psychologists are finding many behavior disorders in which there is tangible evidence of brain abnormality. Senile de-

---

[4]D. O. Hebb, "What Psychology Is About," *American Psychologist,* Vol. 29 (1974), pp. 71–79.
[5]*Ibid.,* p. 76.
[6]W. C. Watson, *Physiological Psychology: An Introduction* (Boston: Houghton Mifflin, 1981).

mentia, for example, is often accompanied by the loss of neurones, while an abnormal firing of neurones appears to occur in epilepsy.

Physiological psychologists have also made progress in determining the physiological interactions of stress. Selye[7] has carefully analyzed the physiological processes that occur under conditions of prolonged stress in lower animals. These reactions have been called the general adaptation syndrome. In humans, individuals respond differently to stress. Some people are very susceptible, others can tolerate a great deal. So far, the reasons for these individual differences are not known. However, Selye has shown that interactions clearly exist between environmental stress and performance of the central and autonomic nervous systems.

Approximately 30 percent of Americans are obese. That is, their weight exceeds 20 percent of their ideal body weight. The reasons for obesity are complex. Physiological psychologists have identified four conditions relevant to overeating: (1) visceral sensations reported as hunger pangs, (2) the sight and smell of tasty food, (3) a satiety mechanism, which involves a chemical in the intestines that curbs appetite, and (4) stress. All of these involve in one way or another the physiology of the organism whether in activity of the sense organs, the viscera, the autonomic nervous system, or the brain.

*Sociobiology.* Sociobiology studies the biological basis of human social behavior and represents a possible application of neo-Darwinism. The basic idea behind sociobiology is that behavioral traits, like morphological traits, are shaped by natural selection. Because aggression, communal living, cooperation, and other forms of social activity help determine whether a person succeeds or fails in growing up and begetting offspring, it seems that evolution has helped shape social behavior in both animals and humans and under different environmental circumstances. This thesis, set forth by E. O. Wilson in his book *Sociobiology: The New Synthesis* (1975),[8] set up a controversy among students of both animal and human behavior.

Despite the growing influences of biology and neurophysiology on psychology, it does not seem likely that psychology will soon vanish by absorption into the other sciences or into humanism, as some psychologists (such as Churchland) would have us believe. In light of the current status of behaviorism and the growth of cognitive psychology, such an absorption, if it occurs at all, seems far in the future.

*The Schism.* For the past several decades, more and more students have chosen to receive their graduate degrees in the health care areas of psychology (clinical, counseling, and other related professions). Their directions are professional rather than academic-research oriented. This emphasis became reflected in the membership of the American Psychological Association (APA).

---

[7] H. Selye, *The Stress of Life* (New York: McGraw Hill, 1976).
[8] E. O. Wilson, *Sociobiology: The New Synthesis* (Cambridge, Mass.: Harvard University Press, 1975).

Therefore, in 1988, an attempt was made at a reorganization of the association. A vote of the entire membership was taken, but the plan for reorganization was defeated by 57 percent to 43 percent. This split corresponds in part to the proportion of membership (professional to academic-research) of the organization. There was a strong feeling on the part of both groups that the APA was moving from a scholarly learned society to a professional one, and the professionals were becoming dominant.

As a result of the defeat of the reorganization plan, a group of distinguished, scientific psychologists formed the American Psychological Society (APS) to "promote, protect, and advance the interests of scientifically-oriented psychology in research, application, and the improvement of human welfare." The Society offered a science-of-psychology alternative. The publication of their newsletter, *The Observer,* began in 1989. The first annual meeting of the APS was held in June, 1989, in Arlington, Virginia. By the end of 1989 the membership of APS had reached 5,000.

What will happen to the membership of the APA? Probably, it will decline as some members join the APS. Although some psychologists will belong to both groups, the American Psychological Society does not anticipate having as many members as the APA.

## Psychology Tomorrow

What is the future of psychology? With the formation of the APS, psychology will go in at least two different directions. The practitioners/professionals will stress the application of psychology to therapy and diagnosis through testing. They will work with, and sometimes compete with, psychiatry. Their aim will be to help people.

The advancement of psychology as an intellectual discipline, however, will have to come from the scientists.

Psychology exists as a unique field of study. Because of the variety of viewpoints as outlined in this book, disagreements will arise over basic facts and methods. It tends to lack a common ground. This makes it different from geology, physics, biology, and chemistry. The people in these fields can more easily share their ideas within their own disciplines. For example, consider the approaches of contemporary behaviorism and existential psychology. Among their differences, the behaviorists think of psychology as a natural science using objective methods of observation, while the existentialists prefer a more subjective approach.

Having seen where the professionals/practitioners are going, what about the scientists?

1. **Behaviorism.** By the 1930s, behaviorism seemed to be solidly entrenched in American psychology. Behaviorism still has many disciples and will continue to be a force in psychology.

2. **Cognitive psychology.** The aim of cognitive psychologists is to find mental processes whereby we can explain behavior. Like those of the behaviorists, their data are behavioral rather than phenomenological. Their idea of what psychology is all about conforms rather closely to what the average layperson thinks about psychology. The cognitivists liken the brain to a computer. In the future, the information-processing model will continue to be an important force. It will also serve as a link between philosophy and psychobiology.

3. **Ecological psychology.** This part of psychology considers that the behavior of the organism is inseparable from its context. The context includes interpersonal, social, and physical aspects.

4. **Biopsychology.** With increasing knowledge of the brain, there is hope on the part of some psychologists that the brain holds the answer to the future of psychology. Such a reductionist attitude has had a long history in psychology. We can go back to the 1920s and 1930s and the work of Karl Lashley, who sought to explain how the brain worked.

   It would appear that the cognitive and physiological psychologists, and even some behaviorists, would like to find future answers in the brain and nervous system. However, a warning from Gregory[9]; must be attended:

   > When we consider neural functions we find ourselves beset with far greater difficulties than in the study of neural structures. This is because, except for its most obvious roles, we do not really know what the function of the nervous system actually is . . . With man-made information-processing machines, we know what the mechanism is and the nature of the operations performed because we construct the machine in a particular way and for a particular purpose. With the nervous system, we did not construct the mechanism, and we have not been able so far, to define some of the operations.

5. **Psychoanalysis and its variations.** Although some behaviorists and experimentally minded psychologists, as well as the neuroscience group, would like to see psychoanalysis and its variations wiped out, the fact remains that the various forms of psychoanalytic thinking are still alive. When the schism hit (see pp. 396–397), the experimentalists felt that the clinicians were taking over control of the American Psychological Association. Many clinical psychologists continue to be very psychoanalytically and humanistically minded. Nobody knows how long this will continue to be the case, but at present such psychologists are still very much in evidence.

When Wundt broke with philosophy in the 1870s, a new intellectual discipline was founded. As the saying goes, "Psychology has had a long past but a short history." That history is only a little over one hundred years. In the centuries to come, perhaps psychology will be only a "flash" in man's intellec-

---

[9]R. L. Gregory, ed., *The Oxford Companion to the Mind* (Oxford: Oxford University Press, 1987), p. 542.

tual development and will be absorbed by those disciplines from which it came: philosophy, physics, and biology. Certainly, the growth of interdisciplinary approaches is a basis for this possibility. There is physiological psychology, animal psychology (related to biology), psychopharmacology (the study of the action of drugs on behavior), and philosophical psychology. In fact, there seems to be a psychology of just about everything: politics, economics, history, art, music, literature, and religion.

So here ends our story. Psychology has come of age. It is a thriving discipline that attracts undergraduate and graduate students alike. We can be confident that the best is yet to come.

# Glossary

**Act psychology.** Early system of psychology that emphasized the acts of the mind (ideating, judging, feeling), rather than the contents of consciousness. (Brentano)

**Adaptive act.** The basic unit for Carr's functional psychology. It consists of (1) the motivating stimulus, (2) a sensory stimulus, and (3) the responses that allowed a situation to satisfy the motivating stimulus.

**Analytic psychology.** Name given by Carl Jung to his version of psychoanalysis.

**Anima-animus.** Jungian archetype in the collective unconscious of the female/male characteristics.

**Anthropomorphism.** Attributing strictly human characteristics such as reason, intelligence, or will to plants or animals.

**Anthroponomy.** Walter Hunter's attempt to give a new name to psychology. "Psychology" was inappropriate, he argued, because "psyche" meant soul.

**Anxiety.** An emotion arising from threats and fear, which has been interpreted in various ways by different theories and systems.

**Apperceptive mass.** The sum of all the components of the mind at any given time. (Herbart, Wundt)

**Archetype.** The innate capacity in the collective unconscious to perceive certain images and emotions set down in a universal way during early experiences of our ancestors. (Jung)

**Artificial intelligence.** Computer programs that enable computers to exhibit general intelligence.

**Associationism.** The theory that behaviors, experiences, or ideas are linked together either through contiguity in space and time or similarity.

**Basic anxiety.** The feeling a child has of being helpless in a potentially hostile world. (Horney)

**Basic needs.** Universal human needs such as rootedness, relatedness, transcendence, identity, and orientation. (Fromm)

**Behavior equipment.** A single organism-stimulus object interaction. (Kantor)

**Behavior modification** (also Behavior therapy). Application of principles of respondent and operant conditioning to real-life situations in an attempt to eliminate undesirable behavior or establish more desirable behavior.

**Behaviorism.** School of psychology that excludes concepts of mind, spirit, and consciousness from the study of psychology and limits the subject matter to behavior.

**Being-in-the-world (Daesin).** Philosophical and psychological concept that there is no existence apart from being. The world does not exist apart from people. Daesin means literally "to be there." (Existential philosophy and psychology)

**Birth trauma.** The emotional experience of the infant, ending its prenatal life.

**Broca's area.** Area in the central cerebral hemisphere of the brain, discovered by Broca, that controls speech.

**Cathexis.** An investment of psychic energy in an image or object. (Freud)

**Closure.** A principle in Gestalt psychology that holds that a person will tend to "fill in the gaps" to make a partial perception a more meaningful whole.

**Cognitive map.** Internal (brain) representation of special behavioral pathways or layouts. (Tolman, cognitive psychology)

**Cognitive Psychology.** The study of the processes whereby people come to understand the world, in particular, memory, learning, perceiving, language, problem solving, and creativity.

**Collective unconscious.** The transpersonal aspect of the unconscious mind where archetypes exist. (Jung)

**Compensation.** The tendency of an organism or a behavioral characterization to make up for a deficiency by increasing its function or by substituting the function of another organ or behavior. (Adler)

**Complex.** An emotionally charged group of associations that are organized in the personal unconscious. (Jung)

**Computer.** A device, usually electronic, that carries out a series of operations under the control of a stored program.

**Conative.** Having to do with motivation or purpose.

**Conditional positive regard.** Liking and accepting another person only if that individual's feelings and self-concept meet one's own standards. (Humanistic psychology)

**Conditioned response. (CR).** A response to a conditioned stimulus that can be acquired during conditioning. (Pavlov)

**Conditioned stimulus.** A previously neutral stimulus that acquired positive or negative properties through association with an unconditioned stimulus.

**Conflict.** The simultaneous occurrence of two or more contradictory tendencies.

**Consciousness.** Awareness of one's own mental activity, such as thinking, perceiving, remembering; awareness of events coming from outside world or internal processes.

**Constancy hypothesis.** A one-to-one relationship that exists between an experience in the mind and an event in the physical world.

**Construct.** A concept that expresses a relationship between objects and events.

**Context theory of meaning.** The view that the meaning of anything results from the context in which it occurs. (Titchener)

**Contiguity.** Nearness or togetherness in space and time.

**Creative synthesis.** The proposition that new ideas emerge from the combination of older ones. (Wundt)

**Critical period.** A period in which a particular behavior can occur or be acquired.

**Dedifferentiation of the personality.** The tendency of an individual to regress to an earlier stage of development in cases of conflict or frustration. (Lewin)

**Defense mechanism.** A process employed by the ego to protect itself from anxiety. (Freud)

**Delayed conditioning.** The process of presenting the conditioned stimulus constantly for eight seconds or more, then presenting the unconditioned stimulus. (Pavlov)

**Dependent variable.** The variable in an experiment that is a function of the independent variables. In psychology, some aspect of the subject's response.

**Determinism.** The theory that any event is completely explained and controlled by present and prior events. This implies that perfect prediction of behavior is possible if all relevant and antecedent conditions are known and controlled.

**Difference limen (DL).** The minimal difference that can be detected between two stimuli.

**Differentiation.** The shaping of a discrete response out of its original variability by a series of successive approximations and selective reinforcement. (Skinner)

**Differentiation of the personality.** As a person develops, more and more traits or cells are acquired in the personality structure to constitute more and more parts. (Lewin)

**Discrimination.** The process of differentiating between similar stimuli.

**Displacement.** The redirection of the energy of a particular drive (instinct) to an object other than the one naturally intended. An energy transformation. (Freud)

**Double aspectism.** A psychophysical solution to the mind-body problem in which the mind and body are considered two different aspects or ways of considering the same event.

**Dramatization.** Children playing as if they were grown ups. (Sullivan)

**Drive.** A physiological need or reaction to deprivation.

**Drive reduction.** The concept that behavior is best explained by the reduction of tension, which is associated with needs. (Hull)

**Dualism.** A view that considers human beings to consist of mental and physical elements.

**Dynamic psychology.** Any psychology that stresses the concept of drive or motivation. (Woodworth)

**Dynamism.** The smallest unit in the study of personality. An energy transformation, which can be an overt act or a mental experience. (Sullivan)

**Effect, Law of.** A principle that considers a response to be stamped in or learned when it has led to satisfying consequences or rewards. (Thorndike)

**Effect, spread of.** The rewarding, and thus strengthening, of incidental responses that are related to the stimulus only by contiguity.

**Ego.** The conscious or partly conscious part of the mental apparatus. (Freud, Jung, Erikson)

**Ego psychology.** A neo-psychoanalytic theory that places more emphasis on the ego and its functions than did Freud. (Erikson)

**Empiricism.** (1) A school of philosophy that believes all knowledge comes from experience. (2) A method that emphasizes investigation by direct observation and experimentation.

**Equipotentiality.** A concept that supposes each part of the brain is just as important as any other. (Lashley)

**Esse est percipi.** Being is perceiving. (Berkeley)

**Ethology.** The study of the behavior of animals in their natural habitats.

**Existential psychology.** A psychological movement, which evolved from existential philosophy, that stresses the modes of existence and being-in-the-world.

**Existentialism.** A philosophical movement that is involved with the analysis of existence.

**Experimental neurosis.** A condition that occurs in respondent (Pavlovian) conditioning when an organism is required to respond beyond its discriminative capacity. It leads to a breakdown in previously learned behavior.

**Extinction.** In operant or respondent conditioning, the withholding of the conditioned stimulus or reinforcing stimulus until the response finally dies out.

**Extraversion.** A personality trait in which the individual tends to turn toward the outside world and people.

**Fictional finalism.** A concept that considers people to live by fictional goals of which they are not aware. (Adler)

**Fictions.** Unrealistic life goals, which significantly influence behavior.

**Field theory.** Any system or theory that concerns itself with vectors or forces among the elements in the field. (Lewin)

**Fixation.** In psychological development the persistence of a part of the personality or behavior. A Freudian defense against separation anxiety.

**Foreign hull.** Factors or events outside the life space of an individual. (Lewin)

**Free association.** A technique in which an unrestrained sequence of ideas and thoughts is elicited by having the person respond without instruction.

**Functionalism.** A school of psychology, which arose partly as a protest to structuralism, that emphasizes the importance of activities or psychological functions. These functions typically take the form of adjustments to the environment.

**Generalization.** A process whereby a conditioned response is made to a variety of similar stimuli.

**Genital phase.** The last stage of psychosexual development, in which the person responds to members of the opposite sex.

**Gestalt psychology.** A psychological system founded in Germany around 1912 that stresses the concepts of wholes or form or configurations.

**Group mind.** A combination of individual minds that is used to account for the activities of crowds, audiences, mobs and other aggregates of people. (Wundt, McDougall)

**Hedonism.** The position in philosophy that behavior is designed to elicit pleasure.

**Hellenic period.** In Greek history, a period that dates from Thales (600 B.C.) to the death of Aristotle in 322 B.C.

**Hellenistic period.** In Greek history, a period that dates from the death of Aristotle (322 B.C.) to the closing of the schools at Athens in 539 A.D. by the emperor Justinian.

**Heuristic function.** Aspect of a psychological system or theory that stresses experimentation, research, and discovery.

**Hodological space.** A pathway of movement from one region to another or in the life space to an individual. (Lewin)

**Humoral psychology.** A theory proposed by Hippocrates and Galen that personality is a function of bodily fluids such as yellow and black bile, phlegm, and blood.

**Hypothesis.** (1) A prediction expressing the relationship between variables. (2) A tentative explanation.

**Id.** That portion of Freud's mental apparatus that is entirely unconscious, and is the seat of the instincts and repressed memories.

**Idealized image.** A fictitious and illusory self-image, i.e. belief that one is a saint, genius or Casanova. (Horney)

**Identification.** Taking on the characteristics of an object or person, somewhat similar to Bandura's notion of modeling.

**Identity crisis.** A lack of personal direction, frequently experienced by adolescents. (Erikson)

**Imageless thought.** Mental processes that elude introspection. (Kulpe)

**Immediate experience.** The contents of consciousness. That aspect of experience that is studied by psychology. (Wundt)

**Independent variable.** The factor that is manipulated in a psychological experiment so that its influence on the dependent variable can be observed.

**Individual psychology.** The name Adler gave to his theory of personality.

**Inferiority complex.** A feeling of being less than, not as good as others. Feeling small or helpless. (Adler)

**Information processing.** The reception, coding, manipulation, storage (in memory), and retrieval of information by an organism.

**Insight.** A perceptual reorganization of the field in Gestalt psychology. Sudden learning as opposed to the trial-and-error learning of Thorndike.

**Instinct.** (1) A pattern of unlearned behavior. (2) In Freudian psychology, the life and death drives.

**Interactionism.** A doctrine that mind and body interact.

**Interbehaviorism.** Psychological system developed by J. R. Kantor in which psychology is defined as the interaction of organisms and stimulus objects.

**Intervening variable.** An inferred factor that intervenes between an independent and dependent variable.

**Introjection.** A defense mechanism, whereby a person absorbs aspects of the outside world and incorporates them into his or her psyche.

**Introspection.** Examination and analysis of one's own conscious experience. (structuralism)

**Introversion.** A process in which a person turns predominantly inward, toward the inner world of subjective reality.

**Irradiation.** Pavlovian physiological counterpart in the brain of the concept of generalization. In conditioning, a spreading out of nerve impulses throughout the brain.

**Isomorphism.** The parallel between the perception or mental event and the corresponding brain field. Psycho-physiological parallelism.

**Latent learning.** Learning that occurs but is not apparent in performance (Tolman)

**Libido.** The psychic energy of the life instincts; also refers to the energy of the sex instinct. (Freud)

**Life space.** (B = fls) Behavior is a function of the life space; the sum total of factors in the field, which affect a person's behavior. (Lewin)

**Lloyd Morgan's Canon.** A principle, derived from the law of parsimony or Occam's razor, which states that an act should not be explained by a higher psychological function if it can be interpreted by a lower one.

**Logical positivism.** A position maintained to rid philosophy of metaphysics.

**Malevolent transformation.** Childhood personification that one is living among enemies. (Sullivan)

**Mandala.** A Sanskrit word used in Jungian psychology to describe an image representing the archetype of the self. A symbol of the center of the personality. (Jung)

**Masculine protest.** (1) An aggressive drive. (2) A desire or protest of women against their lower status, which can also occur in men. (Adler)

**Mass action.** A concept that suggests learning depends on the brain as a whole rather than specific neural connections. (Ashley)

**Mechanism.** How a particular behavior occurs as opposed to drive, which is the cause of behavior. Mechanism can become drive when the behavior itself takes on its own driving force. (Woodworth)

**Mechanism of escape.** An undesirable method for resolving threatening feelings of isolation and loneliness; includes automation conformity, destructiveness, and authoritarianism. (Fromm)

**Media of contact.** The properties that allow the organism and stimulus object(s) to interact, such as light or sound. (Kantor)

**Mediate experience.** That aspect of experience studied by other scientists. Physicists study light waves and sound waves, for example. (Wundt)

**Mental chemistry.** The fusion of mental elements so that an experience is not merely an addition of its separate components. (J. S. Mill)

**Mental mechanics.** A doctrine, proposed by James Mill, that accepts the notion that a complex idea is no more than a combination of simple ones.

**Mentalism.** Any view in psychology that embraces concepts such as mind, soul, spirit, and consciousness, which typically refer to unobservable events.

**Mind.** (1) Spirit or soul. (2) Unobservable aspects of behavior. (3) Consciousness. (4) In cognitive psychology, what intervenes between input and output.

**Mind-body problem.** The problem of the relationship between the mind (mental) and body (physical), presuming that both exist.

**Modeling.** Learning by observing the behavior of others. Imitation. (Bandura)

**Molar.** Considering a certain unit of psychology as a whole. The study of behavior of the entire organism rather than its separate aspects.

**Molecular.** Breaking down a unit of psychology into its separate parts or components. The opposite of molar.

**Monad.** The element of all being. (Leibnitz)

**Monism.** The idea that ultimate reality is of one sort. In psychology, the belief that the mind and body are inseparable. Singularism as opposed to dualism.

**Nativism.** An approach that considers certain aspects of behavior as inherent, unlearned, or inborn. In modern psychology, an approach that emphasizes heredity.

**Naturalistic observation.** The study of things in their natural states without the use of experimentation or other devices.

**Need reduction theory.** The position that the reduction of needs is necessary in order for learning to take place.

**Negative reinforcement.** A behavior that is strengthened by the removal of an aversive stimulus.

**Nonsense syllable.** Three-letter combinations that usually consist of a consonant, vowel, and consonant (CVC), but does not constitute any three-letter word in a given language.

**Objectivism.** An approach that suggests whatever can be observed by one or more of the senses can be measured directly and precisely.

**Oedipus complex.** Intense desire of a boy for his mother arising during the phallic period of personality development. In females the desire for father. (Freud, psychoanalysis)

**Operant conditioning.** Learning in which a response is modified by its consequences. The consequences are usually called reinforcement.

**Operationism.** A movement to clarify the language of science. An operational definition is one in which the meaning of a term is set by a series of operations.

**Oral stage.** The first period in Freud's (psychoanalytic) stages of development, marked by a primary interest in oral activity.

**Paradigm.** A more or less inclusive framework of concepts within which some scientific framework is carried out.

**Parallelism.** A belief that a mental event has a parallel physical event.

**Peak experience.** A mystical, transcendent, episodic experience that represents the highest form of human functioning. (Maslow)

**Penis envy.** The more or less repressed desire of a female to possess a penis, the female form of castration anxiety in the male. (Freud)

**Person-centered theory.** Carl Roger's theory of psychology, which sees therapy as nondirective or client-centered process.

**Persona.** A false mask of self. One's public personality. (Jung)

**Personality.** (1) In layman's terms, the way one appears to others. The persona. (2) Behaviorism's sum total of a person's behavior. (3) The Freudian mental apparatus.

**Personification.** The image a person has of himself or herself. A mental dynamism. (Sullivan)

**Phenomenological field.** The field of perception as it appears to the individual. It may not completely correspond to the absolute physical or geographical field. (Gestalt)

**Phi phenomenon.** The illusion of movement.

**Phrenology.** A pseudo-psychology that is based on the belief that there is a relationship between personality traits and bumps on the skull.

**Pleasure principle.** The principle of the id to seek pleasure and avoid pain. (Freud)

**Positive reinforcement.** The strengthening of behavior by its consequences.

**Postulate.** (1) A basic accepted assumption. (2) A theoretical proposition that is subject to testing.

**Preconscious.** (also fore conscious) An area of the mental apparatus that can be brought readily to consciousness, which resides between the conscious and the unconscious. (Freud)

**Primary process.** (also identity of perception) Capacity of the id to make an image of the object it desires. The image can not be distinguished from the real object. (Freud)

**Primary qualities.** Qualities of experience that actually exist in the object. (Locke)

**Programmed learning.** Learning new material (usually verbal) by proceeding through small steps, each reinforced by getting the correct answer. (Skinner)

**Projection.** Unconsciously attributing one's own threatening impulses, emotions, or beliefs to other persons or things.

**Prototaxic experience.** Raw, unrelated sensory experience. The first experience of an infant. (Sullivan)

**Psyche.** Mind or soul.

**Psychophysics.** The scientific study of the relationship between stimuli and sensations.

**Punishment.** An aversive stimulus designed to reduce the occurrence of a response. (Skinner)

**Q-sort.** A group of cards with words or sentences to be sorted according to some preplanned distribution and then mathematically correlated to determine degrees of correspondence. (Humanistic psychology)

**Reaction formation.** A defense mechanism in which one substitutes the opposite instinct, emotion, or activity as a protection against anxiety. (Freud)

**Reaction time.** The time that elapses between the onset of a stimulus to the response to it (usually measured in milliseconds).

**Reactional biography.** The history of interactions an organism has had with various stimulus objects. (Kantor)

**Reality testing.** Checking out hypotheses by relating them to people and events.

**Reciprocal determinism.** The mutual interrelationship of behavior, internal factors (thoughts, beliefs, etc.), and environmental influences. (Bandura)

**Reductionism.** The concept of reducing data to simpler components.

**Reflexology.** A theory of Pavlovian psychology that proposes that human beings are made up of countless reflexes and conditioned reflexes.

**Regression.** A defense mechanism in which one reverts to behavior characteristic of an earlier stage in one's development.

**Reinforcement.** Strengthening of behavior by the presentation of some consequence (positive) or removal of some aversive stimulus (negative). (Skinner)

**Repression.** A defense mechanism in which one blocks from consciousness certain unpleasant impulses or memories.

**Respondent behavior.** Behavior that consists of conditioned and unconditioned reflexes. (Pavlovian)

**Salivary conditioning.** The process whereby the salivary response becomes capable of being elicited by other stimuli.

**Schedules of reinforcement.** Delivery of reinforcement intermittently rather than following every response—for example, on the basis of time (fixed interval, variable interval) or according to a given ratio (fixed or variable) of unreinforced to reinforced responses.

**Secondary process.** An ability of the ego to solve problems, to find objects that will satisfy the instincts. (Freud)

**Secondary qualities.** Qualities of experience that exist in the mind of the experiencing individual. (Locke)

**Secondary reinforcement.** Stimuli associated with primary reinforcers (food, water, etc.) that take on the function to reinforce in their own right, such as money, prizes, and approval.

**Self.** (1) A Jungian archetype of order that involves centering and integration. (2) A concept used by William James to identify different aspects of the personality. (3) A concept used in humanistic psychology to separate the real person from other surrounding experiences.

**Self-actualization.** An inherent tendency to actualize one's potentialities in ways that will enhance the individual. (Jung, Humanistic psychology)

**Self-regard.** Develops in childhood as the self-concept is formed, strongly related to affection and approval given to the person by important people in one's life. (Humanistic psychology)

**Self-reinforcement.** Feeling of satisfaction or pride one has for a job well done. (Bandura)

**Sentiment.** A combination of instincts. (McDougall)

**Separation anxiety.** Anxiety brought on by separation from a loved one.

**Shadow.** Archetype containing the instincts and other aspects of the darker side of the personality. (Jung)

**Shaping.** A technique for producing a desired response through a series of successive approximations to the final desired response.

**Sign learning.** Learning by following a series of signals (or signs) that act as cues leading from "what to what." (Tolman)

**Sign-significate or sign-gestalt.** In learning, the organism moves through a path guided by various stimuli that act as signs or meanings. (Tolman)

**Significant others.** Other people in one's personal relationship: parents, friends, relations who participate in the development of a positive self-regard. (Rogers)

**Social interest.** A genuine concern for others; a desire to better the group or society. (Adler)

**S-O-R (stimulus-organism-response).** The notion that the response is a function both of the stimulus and of what goes on within the organism. (Woodworth)

**Soul.** (1) The spiritual or nonmaterial side of mankind. (2) Spirit in the Christian sense.

**Spontaneous recovery.** After a lapse of time following the extinction of response, there may be a return of the response indicating the response was not completely extinguished in the first place. Occurs in both respondent and operant behaviors.

**Stereotype.** A generalized personification one has of others. (Sullivan)

**Stimulus evolution.** The process of stimulus function development of objects in psychological interactions. (Kantor)

**Stimulus generalization.** Response to stimuli similar in characteristics to the original conditioning stimulus.

**Stream of consciousness** (thought). Subjective experience, which is continuous, constantly changing, personal, and selective. (James)

**Structuralism.** A school of psychology founded by Titchener that considered psychology to be the study of conscious experience.

**Style of life.** The way one goes about living and solving life's problems, overcoming inferiorities, and achieving life's goals. (Adler)

**Subjective idealism.** A notion of Berkeley that all we know are our experiences, that there is no proof of a real world.

**Subjective monism.** The belief that all that exist are experiences. (Hume)

**Subjectivism.** The belief that private or inner experiences are not directly observable. The opposite of objectivism.

**Superego.** A part of Freud's mental apparatus that develops out of the ego and involves the incorporation of one's social standards. Consists of both the conscience and the ego ideal.

**Superiority complex.** A compensation for real feelings of inferiority in which the person acts self-centered. (Adler)

**Superiority strivings.** The striving from down to up self-esteem or perfection. (Adler)

**Syntaxic experience.** Experiences that can take on symbolic form as in language and speech.

**System, psychological.** A coherent and inclusive organization and interpretation of the facts and special theories of psychology.

**Tabula rasa.** (Latin) Blank slate referring to John Locke's concept that the newborn's mind lacks any experience.

**Teleology.** Purposivism. An organism's behavior is best explained in terms of orientations towards future goals.

**Theory.** A generalized principle or formula proposed for the purpose of explaining a given group of facts.

**Third force.** Humanistic psychology—third approach to psychology, introduced by Maslow. The other two forces are behaviorism and psychoanalysis.

**Topological psychology.** The system of Lewin based superficially on the mathematics of space.

**Transfer, theory of.** Responses learned in one situation can affect response in other situation, can be either positive or negative. The positive facilities the other behavior and the negative interferes with. (Thorndike)

**Transposition.** A transfer of a principle or Gestalt from one learning situation to another.

**Tri-dimensional theory of feelings.** Every feeling can be located somewhere on a hypothetical three dimensional space. Calm–excitement, strain–relaxation, pleasure–displeasure. (Wundt)

**Trial-and-error learning.** Learning occurs when a series of accidental trials are successful, others, the unsuccessful will drop out. (Thorndike)

**Unconditioned response (reflex).** A response that naturally occurs when certain natural stimuli are presented.

**Unconditioned stimulus.** Stimulus that naturally elicits a response, such as pupil contraction to light.

**Unconscious.** That part of the mental apparatus of which one is unaware.

**Valence.** The particular attractiveness or repulsion of an object for a person. (Lewin)

**Vector.** Force that pushes a person toward or away from an object. Correlates with valence. (Lewin)

**Vibratiuncles.** Minute vibrations in the brain that originate in the outside world. (Hartley)

**Vicarious reinforcement.** Being reinforced by observing others being reinforced. "Your happiness is my happiness."

**Völkerpsychologie (folk psychology).** The psychology of myths, legends, customs, and language. (Wundt)

**Weber's law.** A principle that considers a just noticeable difference in a sensation to bear a constant relationship to the magnitude of a physical stimulus.

**Zeigarnik effect.** A concept that states people remember tasks they do not complete better than they remember tasks they have completed. (Lewin)

**Zeitgeist (spirit of the times).** Cultural, social, or artistic values found in a society at a particular point in time.

# References

Adler, A. *Study of Organic Inferiority and Its Psychical Compensation.* New York: Nervous and Mental Disease Publishing Co., 1917.
___. *Practice and Theory of Individual Psychology.* Tutua, New Jersey: Littlefield, Adams, 1920.
___. *Social Interest.* New York: Putnam, 1939.
Allport, F. H. *Theories of Perception and the Concept of Structure.* New York: John Wiley and Sons, 1955.
Allport, G. W. *Personality: A Psychological Interpretation.* New York: Henry Holt and Co., 1937.
Allport, G. W. and Postman, L. *The Psychology of Rumor.* New York: Henry Holt and Co., 1947.
Alper, T. G. "Memory for Completed and Incompleted Tasks as a Function of Personality." *Journal of Personality,* Vol. 17 (1948), pp. 104–37.
American Psychological Association. *William James: Unfinished Business.* Washington, D.C.: American Psychological Association, 1969.
*American Psychologist.* "Reflections on B. F. Skinner and Psychology." Vol. 47 (1992), No. 11 (entire issue).
Anastasi, A. *Psychological Testing,* 3rd ed. New York: Macmillan Publishing Co., 1968.
Angell, J. R. "The Relation of Structural and Functional Psychology to Philosophy." *Philosophical Review,* Vol. 12 (1903), pp. 243–71.
___. *Psychology: An Introductory Study of the Structure and Function of Human Consciousness.* New York: Henry Holt and Co., 1904.
___. "The Province of Functional Psychology." *Psychological Review,* Vol. 14 (1907), pp. 61–91.
Ansbacher, H. and Ansbacher, R., eds. *The Individual Psychology of Alfred Adler.* New York: Basic Books, 1956.
Aquinas, St. Thomas. *Summa Theologica,* Vols. I and II, A. C. Pegis, ed. New York: Random House, 1944–1945.
Aristotle. *De Anima.* A. J. Smith and W. D. Ross, eds. Oxford: Clarendon Press, 1940.
Arnold, W. J. "Simple Reaction Chains and Their Integration, I. Homogeneous Chaining with Terminal Reinforcement." *Journal of Comparative and Physiological Psychology,* Vol. 40 (1947), pp. 349–63.
Augustine, St. *Confessions,* Trans. W. Watts. London: Heinemann, 1912.
Azrin, N. H. and Holz, W. C. "Punishment," in *Operant Behavior: Areas of Research and Application,* W. Henig, ed. New York: Appleton-Century-Crofts, 1966.
Baars, B. J. *The Cognitive Revolution in Psychology.* New York: Guilford Press, 1986.
Baer, D. M. "Laboratory Control of Thumbsucking by the Withdrawal of Reinforcement." *Journal of the Experimental Analysis of Behavior,* Vol. 5 (1962), pp. 525–26.
Bain, A. *The Senses and the Intellect.* London: Parker, 1855.
___. *The Emotions and the Will.* London: Parker, 1859.
Bandura, A. *Principles of Behavior Modification.* New York: Holt, Rinehart and Winston, 1969.
___. *Social Learning Theory.* Englewood Cliffs, New Jersey: Prentice Hall, 1977.
___. *Social Foundations of Thought and Action: A Social Cognitive Theory.* Englewood Cliffs, New Jersey: Prentice-Hall, 1986.

Bandura, A. and R. H. Walters. *Adolescent Aggression.* New York: Ronald Press, 1959.

——. *Social Learning and Personality.* New York: Holt, Rinehart and Winston, 1963.

Barclay, J. R. "The Role of Comprehension in Remembering Sentences." *Cognitive Psychology,* Vol. 4 (1973), pp. 229–54.

Barker, R. G., Dembo, T. and Lewin, K. *Frustration and Regression in Child Behavior and Development,* R. G. Barker, J. S. Kounin and H. F. Wright, eds. New York: McGraw-Hill Book Co., 1943.

Bartlett, F. C. *Remembering: Experimental and Social Study.* London: Cambridge University Press, 1932.

Bekhterev, V. M. *Human Reflexology,* trans. W. H. Gantt. London: International Universities Press, 1922.

Berkeley, G. "An Essay Towards a New Theory of Vision," in *The Works of George Berkeley,* A. A. Luce and T. E. Jessop, eds., Vol. I. London: Nelson, 1948.

——. "A Treatise Concerning the Principles of Human Knowledge," in *The Works of George Berkeley,* A. A. Luce and T. E. Jessop, eds., Vol. II. London: Nelson, 1948.

Binswanger, L. *Being-in-the-World: Selected Papers of Ludwig Binswanger.* New York: Basic Books, 1963.

Bischof, L. *Integrating Personality Theories,* 2nd ed. New York: Harper and Bros., 1970.

Boring, E. G. "Edward Bradford Titchener, 1887–1927." *American Journal of Psychology,* Vol. 38 (1927), pp. 489–506.

——. *The Physical Dimensions of Consciousness.* New York: The Century Co., 1933.

——. *A History of Experimental Psychology,* rev. ed. New York: Appleton-Century-Crofts, 1950.

——. "A History of Introspection." *Psychological Bulletin,* Vol. 50 (1953), pp. 169–87.

Boss, M. *Psychoanalysis and Daseinanalysis.* New York: Basic Books, 1963.

——. *Existential Foundations of Medicine and Psychology.* New York: Aronson, 1977.

Bransford, J. D. and Franks, J. J. "The Abstraction of Linguistic Ideas," *Cognitive Psychology,* Vol. 2 (1971), pp. 331–50.

Brennan, R. E. *Thomistic Psychology.* New York: The Macmillan Co., 1941.

Brentano, F. *Psychologie vom empirischen Standpunkt,* O. Kraus, ed., 2 vols. Leipzig: Mainer, 1924–1925.

Breuer, J. and Freud, S. *Studies in Hysteria* in *Standard Edition of the Complete Works of Sigmund Freud,* J. Strachey, ed., Vol. II. London: Hogarth Press, 1955.

Broadbent, D. E. "A Mechanical Model for Human Attention and Immediate Memory." *Psychological Review,* Vol. 64 (1954), p. 205.

Brown, T. *Lectures on the Philosophy of the Human Mind.* Edinburgh: Tait, 1820.

Broyler, C. B. "Review of Lewin's *Principles of Topological Psychology.*" *Character and Personality,* Vol. 5 (1936–37), pp. 257–58.

Brunswik, E. "The Conceptual Focus of Some Psychological Systems," in *Psychological Theory: Contemporary Readings,* M. H. Marx, ed. New York: The Macmillan Co., 1951.

Bugental, J. *Challenges of a Humanistic Psychology.* New York: McGraw-Hill Book Co., 1967.

Buhler, C. "Basic Theoretical Concepts in Humanistic Psychology," in *American Psychologist,* Vol. 26 (1971), pp. 378–386.

Buhler, C. and Allen, M. *Introduction to Humanistic Psychology.* Monterey, California: Brooks/Cole, 1972.

Butler, I. M. and Haugh, G. V. "Changes in the Relationship of the Self-Concept and Ideal Concepts Consequent on Client Centered Counseling," in Rogers, C. R. and Dymond, R. D. *Psychotherapy and Personality Change.* Chicago: Univesity of Chicago Press, 1954.

Carr, H. A. *Psychology: A Study of Mental Activity.* New York: Longmans, Green, 1925.

Cattell, R. B. *Description and Measurement of Personality.* New York: World Book Co., 1946.

Chomsky, N. "A Review of B. F. Skinner's *Verbal Behavior.*" *Language,* Vol. 35 (1959), pp. 26–58.

___. *Language and Mind,* enlarged edition. New York: Harcourt, Brace and Jovanovich, 1972.

Cohen, J. *Cognitive Psychology,* 2nd ed. New York: Academic Press, 1983.

College Entrance Examination Board. *A Description of the College Board Scholastic Aptitude Test.* New York: CEEB, 1967.

Comte, A. *The Positive Philosophy,* trans. H. Martineau. London: G. Bell, 1896.

Corsini, R., ed. *Current Personality Theories.* Itasca, Illinois: F. E. Peacock Publishers, Inc., 1977.

Darwin, C. *The Descent of Man.* New York: D. Appleton Century Co., 1871.

___. *The Expression of Emotions in Man and Animals.* London: Murray, 1873.

___. *Origin of Species by Means of Natural Selection,* 6th ed. New York: D. Appleton Century Co., 1897.

De Carbalbo, R. D. *The Foundations of Humanistic Psychology.* Praeger, 1991.

Descartes, R. *The Passions of the Soul,* trans. G. T. B. Ross, in *The Philosophical Works of Descartes,* Vol. I. Cambridge: Cambridge University Press, 1931.

Deutsch, M. "Field Theory in Social Psychology," in *Handbook of Social Psychology,* G. Lindzey, ed. Cambridge, Mass.: Addison-Wesley, 1954.

Dewey, J. "The Reflex Arc Concept in Psychology." *Psychological Review,* Vol. 3 (1896), pp. 357–70.

Donnington, R. *Wagner's "Ring" and Its Symbols, The Music and the Myth.* London: Farrar and Farrar, 1963.

Ebbinghaus, H. *On Memory,* trans. H. A. Ruger and C. Bussenus. New York: Teachers College, Columbia University Press, 1913.

Erikson, E. *Childhood and Society.* 2nd ed. New York: W. W. Norton, 1963.

___. *Identity: Youth and Crisis.* New York: W. W. Norton, 1968.

___. *Gandhi's Truth: On the Origins of Militant Nonviolence.* New York: W. W. Norton, 1969.

___. *Toys and Reason.* New York: W. W. Norton, 1977.

Estes, W. K. "An Experimental Study of Punishment." *Psychological Monographs,* Vol. 57 (1944), No. 263, pp. iii–40.

___. "Toward a Statistical Theory of Learning." *Psychological Review,* Vol. 57 (1950), pp. 94–107.

Estes, W. K. and Skinner, B. F. "Some Quantitative Properties of Anxiety." *Journal of Experimental Psychology,* Vol. 19 (1941), pp. 390–400.

Estes, W. K., *et al. Modern Learning Theory.* New York: Appleton-Century-Crofts, 1954.

Eysenck, H. J. *Dimensions of Personality.* London: Routledge and Kegan, Paul, 1942.

Fajans, S. "Erfolg, Ausdauer, Aktivität beim Säugling und Kleinkind." *Psychologische Forschung,* Vol. 17 (1933), pp. 280–305.

Fechner, G. *Elemente der Psychophysik,* 2 vols. Leipzig: Breitkopf and Hartel, 1860.

Ferster, C. B. and Skinner, B. F. *Schedules of Reinforcement.* New York: Appleton-Century-Crofts, 1957.

Fordham, F. *An Introduction to Jung's Psychology.* London: Penguin, 1953.

Frankl, V. E. *Man's Search for Meaning.* Boston: Beacon Press, 1962, p. 101.

Freud, A. *The Ego and the Mechanisms of Defense.* London: Hogarth Press, 1937.

Freud, S. *Autobiography.* New York: W. W. Norton and Co., 1935.

___. *The Instincts and Their Vicissitudes,* in *Collected Papers,* Vol. IV. London: Hogarth Press, 1935.

___. *The Problem of Anxiety.* New York: W. W. Norton and Co., 1936.

___. *History of the Psychoanalytic Movement* in *The Basic Writings of Sigmund Freud,* A. A. Brill, ed. New York: Random House, 1938.

——. *The Psychopathology of Everyday Life* in *The Basic Writings of Sigmund Freud,* A. A. Brill, ed. New York: Random House, 1938.

——. *Moses and Monotheism.* New York: Alfred A. Knopf, 1939.

——. *The Ego and the Id.* London: Hogarth Press, 1947.

——. *An Outline of Psychoanalysis.* New York: W. W. Norton and Co., 1949.

——. *Civilization and Its Discontents* in *Standard Edition of the Complete Works of Sigmund Freud,* J. Strachey, ed., Vol. 21. London: Hogarth Press, 1953 (first published in 1930).

——. *The Future of an Illusion* in *Standard Edition of the Complete Works of Sigmund Freud,* J. Strachey, ed., Vol. 21. London: Hogarth Press, 1953.

——. *Group Psychology and the Analysis of the Ego* in *Standard Edition of the Complete Works of Sigmund Freud,* J. Strachey, ed., Vol. 20. London: Hogarth Press, 1953 (first published in 1922).

——. *Totem and Taboo* in *The Standard Edition of the Complete Works of Sigmund Freud,* J. Strachey, ed., Vol. 13. London: Hogarth Press, 1953 (first published in 1913).

——. *Beyond the Pleasure Principle* in *The Standard Edition of the Complete Works of Sigmund Freud,* J. Strachey, ed., Vol. XVIII. London: Hogarth Press, 1955.

——. *The Interpretation of Dreams* in *The Standard Edition of the Complete Works of Sigmund Freud,* J. Strachey, ed., Vols. IV and V. London: Hogarth Press, 1955.

——. *The Standard Edition of the Complete Works of Sigmund Freud.* J. Strachey, ed. London: Hogarth Press, 1955.

Fromm, E. *Escape from Freedom.* New York: Farrar and Rinehart, 1941.

——. *Man for Himself.* New York: Rinehart, 1947.

——. *Sane Society.* New York: Rinehart, 1947.

Fuller, B. A. G. *A History of Philosophy.* New York: Henry Holt and Co., 1938.

Galton, F. *Hereditary Genius.* London: The Macmillan Co., 1869.

——. "Psychometric Experiment." *Brain,* Vol. 2 (1879), pp. 49–62.

Geis, G. W., Stebbins, W. C. and Lundin, R. W. *The Study of Behavior,* Vol. I, *Reflex and Operant Conditioning.* New York: Appleton-Century-Crofts, 1965.

Gibson, J. "Reproduction of Visually Perceived Forms." *Journal of Experimental Psychology,* Vol. II (1929), p. 1039.

Goldstein, K. *The Organism: A Holistic Approach to Biology Derived from Psychological Data on Man.* New York: American Book Co., 1939.

Gregory, R. L., ed. *The Oxford Companion to the Mind.* Oxford: Oxford University Press, 1987.

Guthrie, E. R. *The Psychology of Learning.* New York: Harper and Bros., 1935.

——. *The Psychology of Human Conflict.* New York: Harper and Bros., 1938.

——. "Conditioning: A Theory of Learning in Terms of Stimulus, Response and Association," in *The Psychology of Learning.* National Society for Studies in Education, 41st Yearbook, 1942.

——. *Association by Contiguity* in *Psychology: A Study of a Science,* Vol. II, *General Systematic Formulations,* S. Koch, ed. New York: McGraw-Hill Book Co., 1959.

Guthrie, E. R. and Edwards, A. L. *Psychology: A First Course in Human Behavior.* New York: Harper and Bros., 1949.

Guthrie, E. R. and Horton, C. P. *Cats in a Puzzle Box.* New York: Henry Holt and Co., 1946.

Hall, C. S. *A Primer of Freudian Psychology.* Cleveland, Ohio: World Publishing Co., 1954.

Hall, C. S. and Lindzey, G. *Theories of Personality,* 3rd ed. New York: John Wiley and Sons, 1978.

Hartley, D. *Observations on Man, His Frame, His Duty and His Expectations,* 4th ed. London: Johnson, 1801.

Hartman, G. W. *Gestalt Psychology.* New York: The Ronald Press Co., 1936.

Hayes, J. R. *Cognitive Psychology: Thinking and Creating.* Homewood, Illinois: Dorsey Press, 1980.

Hebb, D. O. "What Psychology Is About." *American Psychologist,* Vol. 29 (1974), pp. 71–79.

Heidbreder, E. *Seven Psychologies.* New York: Appleton Century Co., 1933.

Helmholtz, H. L. von. *On the Sensations of Tone,* trans. A. J. Ellis. New York: Dover, 1954.

Helson, H. "Some Remarks on Gestalt Psychology by Kurt Koffka." *Journal of the History of the Behavioral Sciences,* Vol. 3 (1967), pp. 43–46.

Henle, M. "Some Problems of Eclecticism." *Psychological Review,* Vol. 64 (1957), pp. 296–305.

Hilgard, E. R. *Theories of Learning,* 2nd ed. New York: Appleton-Century-Crofts, 1956.

___. *Psychology in America: A Historical Survey.* Washington, D.C.: American Psychological Association, 1987.

Hilgard, E. R. and Bower, G. H. *Theories of Learning,* 3rd ed. New York: Appleton-Century-Crofts, 1966.

Hobbes, T. *Human Nature or Fundamental Elements of Policy.* London: Fra Boman of Oxon, 1651.

___. *Leviathan.* Reprint. (First published in 1651.) Cambridge: University Press, 1904.

Holdstock, T. L. and Rogers, C. R. *Person Centered Theory in Current Personality Theories,* R. Corsini, ed. Itasca, Illinois: F. E. Peacock Publishers, Inc., 1977.

Holland, J. G. and Skinner, B. F. *The Analysis of Behavior, A Program for Self-Instruction.* New York: McGraw-Hill Book Co., 1961.

Holt, E. B. *The Freudian Wish and Its Place in Ethics.* New York: Macmillan, 1914.

Honzik, C. H. and Tolman, E. C. "The Perception of Spatial Relations by the Rat, a Type of Response Not Easily Explained by Conditioning." *Journal of Comparative Psychology,* Vol. 22 (1936), pp. 287–318.

Horney, K. *The Neurotic Personality of Our Time.* New York: W. W. Norton and Co., 1937.

___. *New Ways in Psychoanalysis.* New York: W. W. Norton and Co., 1939.

___. *Self-Analysis.* New York: W. W. Norton and Co., 1942.

___. *Our Inner Conflicts.* New York: W. W. Norton and Co., 1945.

___. *Neurosis and Human Growth.* New York: W. W. Norton and Co., 1950.

Hull, C. L. *Aptitude Testing.* Yonkers-on-Hudson, New York: World Book Co., 1928.

___. "Differential Habituation to Internal Stimuli in the Albino Rat." *Journal of Comparative Psychology,* Vol. 16 (1933), pp. 255–73.

___. *Hypnosis and Suggestibility: An Experimental Approach.* New York: D. Appleton Century Co., 1933.

___. "The Concept of Habit Family Hierarchy in Maze Learning." *Psychological Review,* Vol. 41 (1934), pp. 33–54.

___. "The Rat's Speed of Locomotion Gradient in the Approach to Food." *Journal of Comparative Psychology,* Vol. 17 (1934), pp. 398–422.

___. *Mathematico-Deductive Theory of Rote Learning.* New Haven: Yale University Press, 1940.

___. *Principles of Behavior.* New York: Appleton-Century-Crofts, 1943.

___. *Essentials of Behavior.* New Haven: Yale University Press, 1951.

___. *A Behavior System: An Introduction to Behavior Theory Concerning the Individual Organism.* New Haven: Yale University Press, 1952.

Hume, D. *A Treatise on Human Nature,* E. A. Selby-Briggs, ed. Oxford: Clarendon Press, 1896.

Issacs, W., Thomas, J. and Goldiamond, I. "Shaping Vocal Responses in Mute Catatonic Schizophrenics." *Journal of Speech and Hearing Disorders,* Vol. 25 (1960), pp. 8–12.

Jacobson, E. "The Electrophysiology of Mental Activities." *American Journal of Psychology,* Vol. 44 (1932), pp. 677–94.

James, W. *Principles of Psychology,* 2 vols. New York: Henry Holt and Co., 1890.

——. *Psychology: Briefer Course.* New York: Henry Holt and Co., 1892.

——. Talks to Teachers on Psychology: and to Students on some of Life's Ideals. New York: Henry Holt and Co., 1899.

——. *Varieties of Religious Experience.* New York: Longmans, Green, 1902.

——. *Pragmatism: A New Name for Old Ways of Thinking.* New York: Longmans, Green, 1909.

Jones, E. *The Life and Works of Sigmund Freud,* 3 vols. New York: Basic Books, 1953–1957.

Jung, C. G. *Studies in Word Association.* London: Heinemann, 1918.

——. *The Psychology of Religion.* New Haven: Yale University Press, 1938.

——. *The Psychology of the Unconscious* in *Two Essays on Analytical Psychology.* New York: Pantheon Books, Inc., 1953.

——. *Collected Works,* C. H. Reed, M. Fordham and C. Adler, eds., 18 vols. New York: Pantheon Press (Number XX in Bollingen Series), 1953–1963.

——. *Psyche and Symbol.* Garden City, New York: Doubleday and Co., 1958.

Kant, I. *Anthropology* in *Immanuel Kant's Works,* E. Cassirer, ed., Vol. VIII. Berlin: B. Cassirer, 1922.

——. *The Critique of Pure Reason.* New York: The Macmillan Co., 1929.

Kantor, J. R. *Principles of Psychology,* 2 vols. New York: Alfred A. Knopf, 1924–1926. Reprinted, Granville, Ohio: The Principia Press.

——. *An Outline of Social Psychology.* Chicago: Follett Publishing Co., 1929.

——. *A Survey of the Science of Psychology.* Bloomington, Indiana: The Principia Press, 1933.

——. "The Aim and Progress of Psychology." *American Scientist,* Vol. 34 (1946), pp. 251–63.

——. *Problems in Physiological Psychology.* Bloomington, Indiana: The Principia Press, 1947.

——. *Interbehavioral Psychology.* Chicago: The Principia Press, 1958.

——. *The Scientific Evolution of Psychology,* 2 vols. Chicago: The Principia Press, 1963–1969.

——. "An Analysis of the Experimental Analysis of Behavior." *Journal of the Experimental Analysis of Behavior,* Vol. 13 (1970), pp, 101–108.

——. *Psychological Linguistics.* Chicago: The Principia Press, 1977.

——. *Cultural Psychology.* Chicago: Principia Press, 1982.

——. *The Aim and Progress of Psychology.* Chicago: The Principia Press, 1983.

Keller, F. S. and Schoenfeld, W. N. *Principles of Psychology.* New York: Appleton-Century-Crofts, 1950.

Kenney, R. *Cognitive Psychology,* 2nd ed. St. Paul: West Publishing Co., 1989.

Klein, D. B. *A History of Scientific Psychology.* New York: Basic Books, 1970.

Kline, O. S. "Semantic Power Measures Through the Influence of Words with Color Meaning." *American Journal of Psychology,* Vol. 77 (1964), pp. 376–88.

Koch, S., ed. *Psychology: A Study of a Science,* Vol. II, *General Systematic Formulations.* New York: McGraw-Hill Book Co., 1959.

Koch, S. and Leary, David L., eds. *A Century of Psychology as Science.* New York: McGraw Hill Book Co., 1985.

Koffka, K. *The Growth of the Mind.* London: Kegan, Paul, 1924.

——. *Principles of Gestalt Psychology.* New York: Harcourt, Brace and Co., 1935.

Köhler, W. *The Mentality of Apes.* New York: Harcourt, Brace and Co., 1925.

——. *Gestalt Psychology.* New York: Liveright Publishing Co., 1929.

——. *Gestalt Psychology: An Introduction to the New Concepts in Modern Psychology.* New York: Liveright Publishing Co., 1947.

Köhler, W. and Fishback, J. "The Distortion of the Müller-Lyer Illusion in Repeated Trials,

I. An Examination of Two Theories." *Journal of Experimental Psychology,* Vol. 40 (1950), pp. 267–91.

Köhler, W. and Held, R. "The Cortical Correlates of Pattern Vison." *Science,* Vol. 110 (1949), pp. 414–19.

Köhler, W. and Wallach, H. "Figural After-Effects: An Investigation of Visual Processes." *Proceedings of the American Philosophical Society,* Vol. 88 (1944), pp. 269–357.

Kounin, J. S. and Wright, H. F., eds. *Child Behavior and Development.* New York: McGraw-Hill Book Co., (1943), pp. 379–96.

Külpe, O. *Grundriss der Psychologie.* Leipzig: Engelmann, 1893.

Lachman, R. O., Lachman, J. L. and Butterfield, E. C. *Cognitive Psychology and Information Processing: An Introduction.* Hillsdale, New Jersey: Lawrence Earlbaum, 1979, p. 10.

La Mettrie, J. O. de. *Man, A Machine,* trans. C. G. Bussey and M. W. Calkins, Chicago: Open Court, 1912.

Lashley, K. "The Behavioristic Interpretation of Consciousness." *Psychological Review,* Vol. 30 (1923), pp. 329–52.

———. *Brain Mechanisms and Intelligence.* Chicago: University of Chicago Press, 1929.

Lashley, K. S., Chow, K. L. and Semmes, J. "An Examination of the Electrical Field Theory of Cerebral Integration." *Psychological Review,* Vol. 58 (1951), pp. 123–36.

Leahey, T. H. *A History of Psychology: Main Currents in Psychological Thought,* 2nd ed. Englewood Cliffs, New Jersey: Prentice Hall, 1987.

LeBon, G. *The Crowd: A Study of the Popular Mind.* London: J. Fisher, 1896.

Leeper, R. W. "The Role of Motivation in Learning: A Study of the Phenomenon of Differential Motivational Control of the Utilization of Habits." *Journal of Genetic Psychology,* Vol. 46 (1935), pp. 3–40.

———. *Lewin's Topological and Vectoral Psychology.* Eugene, Oregon: University of Oregon Press, 1943.

Lewin, K. *A Dynamic Theory of Personality.* New York: McGraw-Hill Book Co., 1935.

———. *Principles of Topological Psychology.* New York: McGraw-Hill Book Co., 1936.

———. "Forces Behind Food Habits and Methods of Change." *Bulletin of the National Research Council,* Vol. 108 (1943), pp. 35–65.

———. *Field Theory in Social Science,* D. Cartwright, ed. New York: Harper and Bros., 1951.

Lichtenstein, P. E. "Psychological Systems: Their Nature and Function." *Psychological Record,* Vol. 17 (1967), pp. 221–40.

———. "Skinner's Radical Environmentalism" *Denison Journal of Biological Sciences,* Vol. 9 (1972).

———. "Theoretical Psychology: Where Is It Headed?" *Psychological Record,* Vol. 30 (1980), pp. 447–58.

Lippitt, R. and White, R. K. "The 'Social Climate' of Children's Groups" in *Child Behavior and Development,* R. G. Barker, J. S. Kounin and H. F. Wright, eds. New York: McGraw-Hill Book Co., 1943.

Locke, J. *An Essay Concerning Human Understanding,* A. C. Fraser, ed. New York: Dover Press, 1959.

London, I. D. "Psychologists' Misuse of the Auxiliary Concepts of Physics and Mathematics." *Psychological Review,* vol. 51 (1944), pp. 266–91.

Lorenz, K. "The Comparative Method in Studying Innate Behavior." *Symposia for the Study of Experimental Biology,* Vol. 4, pp. 221–68.

Lundin, R. W. *Principles of Psychopathology.* Columbus, Ohio: Charles E. Merrill Books, 1965.

———. *Personality: A Behavioral Analysis,* 2nd ed. New York: The Macmillan Co., 1974.

———. *Alfred Adler's Basic Concepts and Implications.* Muncie, Indiana: Accelerated Development Publishers, 1989.

MacCorquodale, K. and Meehl, P. E. "Edward C. Tolman," in Estes, W. K. *et al., Modern Learning Theory.* New York: Appleton-Century-Crofts, 1954.

McCarthy, R. A. and Warrington, E. K. *Cognitive Neuropsychology.* San Diego: Academic Press, 1990.

McDougall, W. "A Contribution Towards an Improvement in Psychological Method, II." *Mind,* Vol. 7 (1898), pp. 159–78.

——. "On the Seat of Psychological Processes." *Brain,* Vol. 24 (1901), pp. 577–630.

——. *Physiological Psychology.* London: J. M. Dent, 1905.

——. *And Introduction to Social Psychology.* London: Methuen and Co., 1908.

——. *Body and Mind: A History and Defense of Animism.* London: Methuen and Co., 1911.

——. *An Introduction to Social Psychology,* 5th ed. London: Methuen and Co., 1912.

——. *The Group Mind.* New York: Putnam, 1920.

——. "Fundamentals of Psychology." *Psycho,* Vol. 5 (1924), pp. 13–32.

——. *An Outline of Abnormal Psychology.* New York: Charles Scribner's Sons, 1926.

——. *The Energies of Men, A Study of the Fundamental Dynamics of Psychology.* London: Methuen and Co., 1932.

——. "The Psychological Experiment." *Character and Personality,* Vol. 1 (1932–33), pp. 195–213.

——. "Fourth Report on a Lamarckian Experiment, Pts. I–IV." *British Journal of Psychology,* Vol. 28 (1938), pp. 231–45.

McGeoch, J. A. "The Formal Criteria of a Systematic Psychology." *Psycholgical Review,* Vol. 40 (1933), pp. 1–11.

——. *The Psychology of Human Learning.* New York: Longmans, Green, 1942.

Maddi, S. "The Existential Neurosis." *Journal of Abnormal Psychology,* Vol. 72 (1967), pp. 311–25.

Mahan, H. C. *The Interactional Psychology of J. R. Kantor.* San Marcos, California: Project Socrates Press, 1968.

Mahoney, M. J. *Cognitive Behavior Modification.* Cambridge, Massachusetts: Ballinger, 1974.

Marx, M. H. and Cronan-Hillix, W. A. *Systems and Theories in Psychology.* New York: McGraw-Hill Book Co., 1987.

Maslow, A. *Motivation and Personality.* New York: Harper and Bros., 1954.

——. "Drives and Growth." *Merrill-Palmer Quarterly,* Vol. 3 (1966), pp. 36–47.

——. *Toward a Psychology of Being,* 2nd ed. Princeton, New Jersey: Princeton University Press, 1968.

——. *The Further Reaches of Human Nature.* New York: Viking Press, 1971.

Max, L. W. "Action-Current Responses in the Deaf During Awakening, Kinesthetic Imagery and Abstract Thinking." *Journal of Comparative Psychology,* Vol. 24 (1937), pp. 301–44.

May, R. *Man's Search for Himself.* New York: W. W. Norton, 1953.

——. *Existence: A New Dimension in Psychology and Psychiatry.* New York: Basic Books, Inc., 1963.

——. *Existential Psychology,* 2nd ed. New York: Random House, 1969.

——. *Love and Will.* New York: W. W. Norton, 1969.

——. "William James' Humanism and the Problem of Will," in *William James, Unfinished Business.* Washington, D.C.: American Psychological Association, 1969.

Mead, G. H. *Mind, Self and Society.* Chicago: University of Chicago Press, 1934.

Melton, A. W., "Learning" in *Annual Review of Psychology,* Vol. I, C. P. Stone, ed. Stanford, Calif.: Annual Reviews, 1950, pp. 9–30.

Mill, J. *Analysis of the Phenomenon of the Human Mind.* London: Longmans and Dyer, 1829.

Miller, G. A. *Psychology: The Science of Mental Life.* New York: Harper and Bros., 1962.

Miller, N. E. "Studies of Fear as an Acquired Drive." in *Journal of Experimental Psychology.* Vol. 38, (1948), pp. 89–101.

Misiak, H. and Sexton, V. S. *History of Psychology.* New York: Grune and Stratton, 1966.

Morgan, C. L. *Introduction to Comparative Psychology.* London: W. Scott, 1891, rev. ed., 1899.

Mowrer, O. H. "A Stimulus-Response Analysis of Anxiety and Its Role as a Reinforcing Agent." *Psychological Review,* Vol. 46 (1939), pp. 553–65.

Müller, J. *Elements of Physiology,* trans. W. Baly, 2 vols., 2nd ed. London: Taylor *Theory,* W. K. Estes, ed. New York: Appleton-Century-Crofts, 1954.

Müller, J. *Elements of Physiology,* trans. W. Baly, 2 vols., 2nd ed. London: Taylor and Walton, 1839–1842.

Murchison, C., ed. *Psychologies of 1925.* Worcester, Massachusetts: Clark University Press, 1928.

——. *Psychologies of 1930.* Worcester, Massachusetts: Clark University Press, 1930.

Murphy, G. *Personality: A Biosocial Approach to Origins and Structures.* New York: Harper and Bros., 1947.

——. *An Historical Introduction to Modern Psychology,* rev. ed. New York: Harcourt, Brace and Co., 1949.

Myers, E. B. *The Myers-Briggs Type Indicator.* Princeton, New Jersey: Educational Testing Service, 1962.

Neisser, U. *Cognitive Psychology.* New York: Appleton-Century-Crofts, 1967.

Newell, A. and Simon, H. A. The Logic Theory Machine. *Transactions on Information Theory,* Vol. 2 (1956), pp. 61–79.

Newell, A., Shaw, J. C. and Simon, H. A. Report on a General Problem Solving Program for the Computer. *Proceedings of the International Conference in Information Processing* (UNESCO, 1960), pp. 256–64.

Orgler, H. *Alfred Adler: The Man and His Works.* New York: Liveright Publishing Co., 1963.

Pavlov, I. P. *Conditioned Reflexes.* London: Oxford University Press, 1927.

——. *Lectures on Conditioned Reflexes,* trans. W. H. Gantt. New York: International Press, 1928.

Peters, R. S. *Brett's History of Psychology,* abridged one-volume edition. London: George Allen and Unwin, Ltd., 1953.

Piaget, J. *The Construction of Reality in the Child,* trans. M. Cook. New York: Basic Books, 1954.

Pronko, N. H. *Panorama of Psychology.* Belmont, California: Brooks/Cole, 1969.

——. *Psychology from the Standpoint of an Interbehaviorist.* Monterey, California: Brooks/Cole Publishing Co., 1980.

——. *From AI to Zeitgeist.* New York: Greenwood Press, 1988.

Reid, T. *Essays on the Intellectual Powers of Man.* W. Hamilton, ed. Edinburgh: Malcachian Stewart, 1949.

Roback, A. A. *History of American Psychology.* New York: Library Publishers, 1952.

Robinson, D. N. *An Intellectual History of Psychology,* 2nd ed. New York: Macmillan Publishing Co., 1981.

Rogers, C. R. *Counseling and Psychotherapy: Newer Concepts in Practice.* Boston: Houghton Mifflin Co., 1942.

——. *Client Centered Therapy: Its Current Practices, Interpretation and Theory.* Boston: Houghton Mifflin Co., 1951.

——. "A Theory of Therapy, Personality and Interpersonal Relationships as Developed in the Client Centered Framework," in S. Koch, *Psychology: A Study of Behavior,* Vol. 3. New York: McGraw-Hill Book Co., 1959.

——. *On Becoming a Person.* Boston: Houghton Mifflin Co., 1961.

___. "In Retrospect: Forty-six Years," *American Psychologist,* Vol. 29 (1974), pp. 115–123.

Romanes, G. J. *Animal Intelligence.* London: Kegan, Paul, 1886.

Sahakian, W. *History and Systems of Psychology.* New York: Halsted Press, a division of John Wiley and Sons, 1975.

Sartre, J. P. *L'Être et le néant.* Paris Éditions Gallimard, 1943.

Schultz, D. *A History of Modern Psychology.* New York: Academic Press, 1969.

Schultz, D. P. and Schultz, S. E. *A History of Modern Psychology,* 4th ed. New York: Harcourt, Brace and Jovanovitch, 1987.

Schweller, D. D., Brewer, W. F. and Dahl, D. "Memory for Illocutionary Forces and Pre-illocutionary Effects of Certain Utterances." *Journal of Verbal Learning and Verbal Behavior,* Vol. 15 (1976), pp. 325–37.

Seashore, C. E. *Seashore Measures of Musical Talents.* New York: The Psychological Corp., 1939, rev. ed., 1960.

Seeman, J. "A Study of the Process of Nondirective Therapy." *Journal of Consulting Psychology,* Vol. 13 (1949), pp. 157–68.

Seyle, H. *The Stress of Life.* New York: McGraw-Hill, 1976.

Sherman, M. "The Differentiation of Emotional Responses in Infants." *Journal of Comparative Psychology,* Vol. 7 (1927), pp. 264–84.

Skinner, B. F. *The Behavior of Organisms.* New York: D. Appleton Century Co., 1938.

___. *Walden Two.* New York: The Macmillan Co., 1948.

___. "Are Theories of Learning Necessary?" *Psychological Review,* Vol. 57 (1950), pp. 193–216.

___. *Science and Human Behavior.* New York: The Macmillan Co., 1953.

___. "Critique of Psychoanalytic Concepts and Theories." *Scientific Monthly,* Vol. 79 (1954), pp. 300–305.

___. *Verbal Behavior.* New York: Appleton-Century-Crofts, 1957.

___. *The Technology of Teaching.* New York: Appleton-Century-Crofts, 1968.

___. *Beyond Freedom and Dignity.* New York: Alfred A. Knopf, 1971.

___. *Particulars of My Life.* New York: Alfred A. Knopf, 1976.

___. "Why I Am Not a Cognitive Psychologist," *Behaviorism,* Vol. 5 (1977), pp. 1–10.

___. *The Shaping of a Behaviorist.* New York: Alfred A. Knopf, 1978.

___. *A Matter of Consequences.* New York: Alfred A. Knopf, 1983.

___. "Cognitive Science and Behaviorism." *British Journal of Psychology,* Vol. 76 (1985), pp. 291–301.

Smith, S. and Guthrie, E. R. *General Psychology in Terms of Behavior.* New York: Century Publishing Co., 1921.

Snygg, D. and Coombs, A. W. *Individual Behavior.* New York: Harper and Row, 1949.

Spence, K. W. "Clark Leonard Hull (1884–1952)." *American Journal of Psychology,* Vol. 65 (1952), pp. 639–46.

___. *Behavior Theory and Conditioning.* New Haven: Yale University Press, 1956.

Spencer, H. *Principles of Psychology,* 2nd ed. London: Williams and Norgate, 1870–1872.

Spiegelberg, H. *The Phenomenological Movement: A Theoretical Introduction.* Haag: Nynof, 1960.

Spranger, E. *Types of Men.* Halle: Max Neimeyer, 1928.

Steinberg, S. "Memory Scanning: Mental processes revealed by reaction time experiments." *American Scientist.* Vol. 27 (1969), pp. 1–32.

Stevens, S. S. "The Attributes of Tone." *Proceedings of the National Academy of Science.* Vol. 20 (1934), pp. 457–59.

Stroop, J. R. "Studies of Interference in Serial Verbal Learning." *Journal of Experimental Psychology,* Vol. 18 (1935), pp. 643–662.

Stumpf, C. *Tonpsychologie.* 2 Vols. Leipzig: S. Hirzel, 1883–1890.

Sullivan, H. S. *Conceptions of Modern Psychiatry*. Washington, D.C.: W. A. White Foundation, 1947.
——. *The Interpersonal Theory of Psychiatry*. New York: W. W. Norton and Co., 1953.
Terman, L. M. and Merrill, M. *Stanford-Binet Manual for the Third Revision*. Boston: Houghton Mifflin, 1960.
Thorndike, E. L. "Animal Intelligence: An Experimental Study of the Associative Process in Animals." *Psychological Review, Monographs,* No. 8 (1898).
——. *Animal Intelligence*, rev. ed. New York: The Macmillan Co., 1911.
——. *Education: A First Book*. New York: Macmillan, 1912.
——. *The Psychology of Learning*. New York: Teachers College. Columbia University Press, 1913.
——. *The Psychology of Arithmetic*. New York: Macmillan, 1922.
——. *Educational Psychology*, 3 vols. New York: Greenwood Press, reprint of 1913–1914 edition.
——. "Rewards and Punishment in Animal Learning." *Comparative Psychology Monographs,* Vol. 8 (1932), No. 39.
——. *Selected Writings from a Connectionist's Psychology*. New York: Apple-Century-Crofts, 1949.
Thorndike, E. L. and Woodworth, R. S. "The Influence of Improvement in One Mental Function upon the Efficiency of Other Functions." *Psychological Review,* Vol. 8 (1901), pp. 247–61.
Thorndike, R. L., Hagen, L. P. and Salter, J. L. *Manual for the Stanford-Binet Intelligence Test,* 4th ed. New York: Riverside Publishing Co., 1986.
——. *The Study of Instinct*. New York: Oxford University Press. 1951.
Tinbergen, N. *Social Behavior in Animals*. New York: John Wiley and Sons, 1953.
Tinklepaugh, O. H. "An Experimental Study of Representative Factors in Monkeys." *Journal of Comparative Psychology,* Vol. 8 (1928), pp. 197–236.
Titchener, E. B. *An Outline of Psychology*. New York: The Macmillan Co., 1896.
——. "The Postulates of a Structural Psychology." *Psychological Review,* Vol. 7 (1898), pp. 449–65.
——. *Primer of Psychology*. New York: The Macmillan Co., 1898.
——. "Structual and Functional Psychology." *Psychological Review,* Vol. 8 (1899), pp. 290–99.
——. *Experimental Psychology: A Manual of Laboratory Practice,* 4 vols. New York: The Macmillan Co., 1901–1905.
——. *Lectures on the Experimental Psychology of Feeling and Attention*. New York: The Macmillan Co., 1908.
——. *Lectures on the Experimental Psychology of Thought Processes*. New York: The Macmillan Co., 1909.
——. *Textbook of Psychology*. New York: The Macmillan Co., 1910.
——. "Brentano and Wundt, Empirical Experimental Psychology" (1920), in L. McAlister, *The Philosophy of Brentano*. Atlantic Heights, New Jersey: Humanities Press, 1971.
Tolman, E. C. *Purposive Behavior in Animals and Men*. New York: Century Co., 1932.
——. "The Determinants of Behavior at a Choice Point." *Psychological Review,* Vol. 45 (1938), pp. 1–41.
——. "Kurt Lewin, 1890–1947." *Psychological Review,* Vol. 55 (1948), pp. 1–4.
——. "There Is More Than One Kind of Learning." *Psychological Review.* Vol. 30 (1949), pp. 144–45.
——. *Collected Papers in Psychology*. Berkeley: University of California Press, 1951.
——. *Purposive Behavior in Psychology: A Study of a Science*. Vol. II, *General Systematic Formulation,* S. Koch, ed. New York: McGraw-Hill Book Co., 1959.

Tolman, E. C. and Honzik, C. H. "Introduction and Removal of a Reward and Maze Performance in Rats." *University of California Publications in Psychology,* Vol. 4 (1930), pp. 257–75.

Underwood, B. J. *Experimental Psychology.* New York: Appleton-Century-Crofts, 1949.

Vaihinger, H. *The Philosophy of "As If."* New York: Harcourt, Brace and Co., 1925.

Valentine, W. L. and Wiggins, D. D. *Experimental Foundations of General Psychology.* New York: Rinehart and Co., 1941.

___. *The Study of Instinct.* New York: Oxford University Press, 1951.

Voeks, V. W. "Acquisition of S-R Connections: A Test of Hull's and Guthrie's Theories." *Journal of Experimental Psychology,* Vol. 47 (1954), pp. 437–47.

___. "Formulation and Clarification of a Theory of Learning." *Journal of Psychology,* Vol. 30 (1950), pp. 341–63.

Wagman, M. *Cognitive Psychology and Artificial Intelligence.* Greenwood, S.C.: Praeger, 1992.

Watson, J. B. "Kinesthetic and Organic Sensations: Their Role in the Reactions of the White Rat to the Maze." *Psychological Monographs,* No. 33 (1907).

___. "Psychology as the Behaviorist Views It." *Psychological Review,* Vol. 20 (1913), pp. 158–77.

___. *Behavior: An Introduction to Comparative Psychology.* New York: Henry Holt and Co., 1914.

___. *Psychology from the Standpoint of a Behaviorist.* Philadelphia: J. B. Lippincott, 1919.

___. *Psychological Care of Infant and Child.* New York: W. W. Norton and Co., 1928.

___. *The Ways of Behaviorism.* New York: Harper and Bros., 1928.

___. *Behaviorism.* New York: W. W. Norton and Co., 1925, rev. ed., 1930.

Watson, J. B. and McDougall, W. *The Battle of Behaviorism.* New York: W. W. Norton and Co., 1929.

Watson, R. I. *The Great Psychologists,* 4th ed. Philadelphia: J. B. Lippincott, 1978.

___. *The Great Psychologists from Aristotle to Freud.* Philadelphia: J. B. Lippincott, 1963.

Watson, W. C. *Physiological Psychology: An Introduction.* Boston: Houghton Mifflin, 1981.

Weber, A. *History of Philosophy,* trans. P. Thilly. New York: Charles Scribner's Sons, 1928.

Wechsler, D. *Wechsler Adult Intelligence Scale, Revised.* New York: The Psychological Corp., 1981.

Weiss, A. P. A *Theoretical Basis of Human Behavior,* Columbus, Ohio: Adams, 1925.

Wertheimer, Max. "Experimentelle Studien über das Sehen von Bewegung." *Zeitschrift für Psychologie,* Vol. 61 (1912), pp. 161–265.

___. "Unterschungen zur Lehre von der Gestalt, II." *Psychologische Forschung,* Vol. 4 (1923), 301–50.

___. *Productive Thinking.* New York: Harper and Bros., 1945.

Wertheimer, Michael. A *Brief History of Psychology.* New York: Holt, Rinehart and Winston, 1970.

___. *Fundamental Issues in Psychology.* New York: Holt, Rinehart and Winston, 1972.

___. *Introduction to Psychology.* New York: Harper and Row, 1975.

Wheeler, R. H. *The Science of Psychology,* 2nd ed. New York: Crowell, 1940.

Wilson, E. O. *Sociobiology: the New Synthesis.* Cambridge, Massachusetts: Harvard University Press, 1975.

Wolman, B. B. *Contemporary Theories and Systems in Psychology.* New York: Harper and Bros., 1960.

Woodworth, R. S. *Dynamic Psychology.* New York: Columbia University Press, 1918.

___. *Psychology.* New York: Henry Holt and Co., 1921.

___. *Experimental Psychology.* New York: Henry Holt and Co., 1939.

___. *Contemporary Schools of Psychology,* rev. ed. New York: The Ronald Press Co., 1948.

___. *Dynamics of Behavior.* New York: Holt, Rinehart and Winston, 1958.

Woodworth, R. S. and Schlosberg, H. *Experimental Psychology,* 2nd ed. New York: Henry Holt and Co., 1954.

Wright, H. F. "The Effect of Barriers on the Strength of Motivation" in *Child Behavior and Development,* R. G. Barker, J. S. Kounin and H. F. Wright, eds. New York: McGraw-Hill Book Co., 1943.

Wulff, F. "Über die Veränderung von Verstellungen." *Psychologische Forschung,* Vol. 1 (1922), pp. 333–73.

Wundt, W. *Beiträge zur Theorie der Sinneswahrnehmung.* Leipzig: Winter, 1862.

——. *Grundriss der Psychologie,* 1st ed. Leipzig: Engelmann, 1896.

——. *Outline of Psychology,* trans. C. Judd. Leipzig: Engelmann, 1897.

——. *Grundzüge der Physiologischen Psychologie,* 5th ed., 3 vols. Leipzig: Engelmann, 1902–1903.

——. *Principles of Physiological Psychology.* New York: The Macmillan Co., 1904.

——. *Völkerpsychologie,* 10 vols. Leipzig: Engelmann, 1900–1909.

Yamoshevski, M. B. "I. M. Sechenov: The Founder of Objective Psychology" in *Historical Roots of Contemporary Psychology,* B. B. Wolman, ed. New York: Harper and Row, 1968.

Zeigarnik, B. "Über das Behalten von erledigten and unerledigten Handlungen." *Psychologische Forschung,* Vol. 9 (1927), pp. 1–85.

# A Selected List of Primary Sources

Adler, Alfred. *Social interest.* New York: Putnam, 1938.

Aquinas, St. Thomas. *Summa Theologica.* vols. I & II, Edited by A. C. Pegis. New York: Random House, 1944.

Aristotle. *The works of Aristotle.* Edited by A. J. Smith and W. D. Ross. Oxford: Clarendon Press, 1952.

Augustine, St. *The City of God.* Translated by C. E. McCracken. London: Heinemann, 1957.

Bandura, Albert. *Social Learning Foundations of Thought and Action: A Social Cognitive Theory.* New York: Prentice Hall, 1986.

Berkeley, George. "A Treatise Concerning The Principles of Human Knowledge," in *The Works of George Berkeley.* vol. II, London: Nelson, 1948.

___. "An Essay Towards a New Theory of Vision" in *The Works of George Berkeley,* vol. I. Edited by A. A. Lucas and T. E. Jessup., London: Nelson, 1948.

Binswanger, Ludwig. *Being-in-the-world: Selected papers of Louis Binswanger.* New York: Basic Books, 1963.

Brentano, Franz. *Psychologen von empirischen Standpunkt.* 2 vols. Edited by O. Krauss. Leipzig: Mainer, 1924.

Brewer, Joseph and Freud, Sigmund. "Studies in Hysteria" in *Standard Edition of the Complete Works of Sigmund Freud,* London: Hogarth Press, vol. II, 1953.

Brown, Thomas. *Lectures on the Philosophy of the Human Mind.* Edinburgh: Taft, 1820.

Carr, Harvey A. *Psychology: A Study of Mental Activity.* New York: Longmans, Green, 1925.

Darwin, Charles. *Origin of Species by Means of Natural Selection.* 6th edition. New York: Appleton Century Co., 1896.

Descartes, René. "The Passions of the Soul" in C. T. B. Ross, *The Philosophical Works of Descartes,* vol. I, Cambridge: Cambridge University Press, 1931.

Ebbinghaus, Herman. *On Memory.* Translated by H. A. Ruger and C. Bessinger. New York: Columbia University Press, 1913.

Erikson, Erik. *Identity, Youth and Crisis.* New York: W. W. Norton and Co., 1968.

Fechner, Gustav. *Elemente der Psychophysik,* 2 vols., Leipzig: Brectkopf and Hartel, 1860.

Freud, Sigmund. *The Standard Edition of the Complete Works of Sigmund Freud.* Edited by J. Streachey, London: Hogarth Press, 1953.

Fromm, Erich. *Escape from Freedom.* New York: Farrar and Rinehart, 1941.

Galton, Francis. *Hereditary Genius.* London: The Macmillan Co., 1869.

Guthrie, Edwin. *The Psychology of Learning.* New York: Harper and Row, 1935.

Guthrie, Edwin and Horton, C. P. *Cats in a Puzzle Box.* New York: Henry Holt and Co., 1946.

Hartley, David. *Observations on Man, His Frame, His Duty and His Expectations.* 4th edition, London: Johnson, 1801.

Helmholtz, Herman L. von. *On the Sensations of Tone.* Translated by A. J. Ellis, New York: Dover, 1954.

Hobbes, Thomas. *Human Nature or Fundamental Elements of Policy.* Cambridge, England: Cambridge University Press, 1839.

Horney, Karen. *New Ways in Psychoanalysis.* New York: W. W. Norton and Co., 1939.

___. *Our Inner Conflicts.* New York: W. W. Norton and Co., 1950.

Hull, Clark L. *A Behavior System: An Introduction to Behavior Theory Concerning the Individual Organism*. New Haven: Yale University Press, 1952.

Hume, David. *A Treatise on Human Nature*. Edited by E. A. Selby-Briggs. Oxford: Clarendon Press, 1896.

James, William. *Principles of Psychology*. 2 vols., New York: Henry Holt and Co., 1890.

Jung, Carl. *Collected Works*. Edited by C. H. Reid, M. Fordham, and C. Adler. New York: Pantheon Press, 1953.

Kant, Immanuel. *The Critique of Pure Reason*. New York: The Macmillan Co., 1929.

Kantor, Jacob R. *Principles of Psychology*. 2 vols., New York: Alfred A. Knopf. Reprinted by Principia Press, Chicago, 1924.

——. *Interbehavioral Psychology*. Chicago: Principia Press, 1958.

Koffka, Kurt. *The Growth of the Mind*. London: Kegan, Paul, 1924.

Köhler, Wolfgana. *The Mentality of Apes*. New York: Harcourt, Brace and Co., 1925.

La Mettrie, Julian O. de. *Man, A Machine*. Translated by G. C. Bussey and M. W. Calkins. Chicago: Open Court Press, 1912.

Lashley, Karl. *Brain Mechanisms and Intelligence*. Chicago: University of Chicago Press, 1929.

Leibnitz, Gotfried. *The Philosophical Works of Leibnitz*. Translated by G. W. Duncan. New Haven: Tuttle, Morehouse and Taylor, 1968.

Lewin, Kurt. *Principles of Topological Psychology*. New York: McGraw Hill Book Co., 1936.

Locke, John. *An Essay Concerning Human Understanding*. New York: Dover Press, 1959.

McDougall, William. *An Introduction to Social Psychology*. Boston: Luce, 1908.

Maslow, Abraham. *Motivation and Personality*. New York: Harper and Row, 1954.

May, Rollo. *Toward a Psychology of Being*. 2nd. edition. Princeton: Princeton University Press, 1968.

Mill, James. *Analysis of the Phenomenon of the Human Mind*. London: Longmans and Dyer, 1829.

Mill, John Stuart. *A Review of Logic*. London: Longmans, 1843.

Morgan, Conway Lloyd. *An Introduction to Comparative Psychology*. London: W. Scott, 1891.

Müller, Johannes. *Elements of Physiology*. Translated by W. Baly. London: Taylor and Watson, 1842.

Pavlov, Ivan P. *Lectures on Conditioned Reflexes*. Translated by W. H. Gantt. New York: International Press, 1928.

Reid, Thomas. *The Intellectual Powers of Man*. Edited by W. Hamilton. Edinburgh: Malcolm Stewart, 1949.

Rogers, Carl R. *On Becoming a Person*. Boston: Houghton Mifflin Co., 1961.

Romanes, George. *Animal Intelligence*. London: Kegan, Paul, 1886.

Skinner, B. F. *The Behavior of Organisms*. New York: D. Appleton Century, 1938.

——. *Science and Human Behavior*. New York: The Macmillan Co., 1953.

Sullivan, Harry Stack. *The Interpersonal Theory of Psychiatry*. New York: W. W. Norton and Co., 1953.

Thorndike, Edward L. *Animal Intelligence*. Revised edition. New York: The Macmillan Co., 1911.

Titchener, Edward B. *An Outline of Psychology*. New York: The Macmillan Co., 1896.

Tolman, Edward C. *Purposive Behavior in Animals and Man*. New York: Century Co., 1932.

Watson, John B. *Psychology from the Standpoint of a Behaviorist*. Philadelphia: J. B. Lippincott, 1919.

——. *Behaviorism*. New York: W. W. Norton and Co., 1925.

Wertheimer, Max. *Productive Thinking*. New York: Harper and Row, 1945.

Woodworth, Robert S. *Dynamics of Behavior*. New York: Holt, Rinehart, and Winston, 1958.

Wundt, Wilhelm. *Outline of Psychology*. Translated by C. Judd. Leipzig: Engelmann, 1897.

# Index